*Prevention and Treatment of* MENTAL RETARDATION

# Prevention and Treatment
## *of* MENTAL
## RETARDATION

**IRVING PHILIPS,** *editor*

*with the assistance of* **MARY ANN ESSER**

**BASIC BOOKS INC., PUBLISHERS**
*NEW YORK / LONDON*

830314

# Preface

After a long period of apathy and neglect, the mentally retarded are becoming a concern for all professional groups in the health and social sciences. Historically, the retarded generally were considered to be different and in need solely of institutional care. There were few services available to them, and they usually were isolated in their communities or institutionalized far from their homes in overcrowded, poorly budgeted, and insufficiently staffed hospitals or schools. Little was expected of them by society, and consequently they accomplished little.

Shortly after World War II, the citizenry of this country was aroused by the general neglect and poor care of both the mentally ill and the mentally retarded. In our more affluent society, there now was time to be attentive to the needs of the handicapped. There was increasing realization that our institutions were poorly supported. In the early 1950's, the number of parent groups interested in the mentally retarded increased markedly, and these groups exerted pressure for change and for redress of the many grievances that were apparent in all states. The pendulum, too long stationary, was beginning to move. This movement reached a high point with the interest of the late President John F. Kennedy, who called for the passage of legislation to develop better care and facilities for the mentally retarded.

> The care and treatment of mental retardation and research into its causes and cure have . . . been too long neglected. Mental retardation ranks as a major national health, social and economic problem. It strikes our most precious asset—our children. . . . The American people, acting through their government where necessary, have an obligation to prevent mental retardation whenever possible and to ameliorate it when it is present (Kennedy, Message to Congress, 1963, pp. 7–9).

This once neglected public health problem now was publicized as an area requiring close scrutiny. Attention was directed toward the development of better and more coordinated services to help the retarded lead more successful and productive lives—in their own communities if possible. National panels and statewide study groups were organized to develop better and more fruitful programs. The departments of health, education, and welfare of many states re-examined their own participation in the field of mental retardation. Federal legislation furnished funds to implement programs for the retarded. Professionals who had neglected this area for many years began to vie for control of funds and the development of programs. Thus, the retarded became a "popular" subject of professional concern.

The prevention and amelioration of mental retardation are concerns of a wide variety of specialties. Only many professional disciplines working together can meet the needs of the growing child and insure his best physical growth, personality development, intellectual achievement, recreation, vocational training and placement, protection of his rights to achieve according to his ability, and provision for help to compensate for his deficiencies. The needs of the retarded child differ little from those of his more favored peers.

The myths of our culture are so pervasive that they interfere with our perception of the retarded person as an individual with a limiting condition; we tend to cloak him with a diagnostic label that prevents our seeing him as a learning, developing person in a particular setting, with his own special skills as well as limitations. This book discusses the many issues and problems that confront professional groups working with the retarded in the preventive, diagnostic, treatment, and rehabilitation aspects of care.

As this book makes clear, mental retardation is not the province of any one discipline. The contributions of many build toward a common goal of satisfying and fruitful living for the retarded. This volume deals primarily with clinical issues and is directed toward the clinician. It discusses the various contributions of specialists dealing with those aspects of clinical care necessary to develop the best programming for the handicapped individual. The major achievements that occur in any clinical endeavor will result from prevention. Programming is prevention. If we can prevent retardation (primary and secondary prevention) or ameliorate the disability once it is established (tertiary prevention), the beneficial effects on the community and the individual will be great. We will provide for the greater productivity of our youth, and we will save tax dollars in the long run. The program for care of the mentally retarded child should begin before he is born and continue throughout his life. Problems are evident in all age periods, from birth to adulthood, and program development to deal with these problems is mandatory.

Consequently, in developing programs for the retarded we must emphasize programs that will not segregate the retarded from the main stream of community life, and we must include all mentally retarded individuals in our planning. Needless to say, the historical neglect of the retarded demands correction. It is necessary to educate society, to reduce prejudice and misinformation concerning retarded people. The retarded population must be integrated into the community. However, the efforts of many state commissions and departments, although laudable in their intent, tend to move the retarded into still greater isolation by recommending and developing programs specifically related only to the retarded population. This serves to emphasize the differences between the retarded and their more favored peers, thereby enhancing still further their isolation. This not only maintains but exaggerates the fiction that few if any similarities exist between the child with intellectual defect and the child with normal intelligence. Esquirol, in the early nineteenth century, remarked that "mental retardation is a condition not a disease." Retardation is first noted primarily in childhood and is only one of many childhood conditions. Unfortunately, the great clamor is for help for the retarded as a preferential group distinguishable from other children.

As programs develop, there will be special services for people who are retarded, but little provision for the many other needed services for children. Federal legislation has provided for the separate development of mental retardation and mental health centers. In some cities, counties, and states, these facilities will exist as separate entities. Duplication of personnel, facilities, programs, funds, training, and research will thereby develop needlessly in an area in which funds and skilled manpower are in short supply. The best service would be secured, not by such competition, but by integrated, coordinated planning to meet the broad medical and paramedical needs of all of our citizens.

With the development of separate programs for special groups, the specific condition of a child will determine what sort of services he will receive. For example, if he "passes" the implicit "means test" of intellectual deficiency, a wide gamut of services will be available to him. If his intelligence quotient is normal, however, his opportunities for help will be more limited, and he will have to compete for the few available services, probably being placed on one of the long waiting lists to secure vital health needs. What a child is labeled will determine what help he gets.

If, instead, we develop programs providing for the services needed by all children, in the long run we will develop the best services for the retarded, who need these basic services with the addition of some specialized services. Programs should provide for all areas of concern, without isolation of particular diagnostic groups. Better and more comprehensive programs for our total population of children, regardless of their condition or of the severity of their disorder, should be the aim of every program. Plans to meet such needs as children's hospitals, children's centers, school programs, and recreational and rehabilitation facilities would be consistent with sound medical care for both normal children and children with various handicaps, including mental retardation. The needs of the child, his family, and his neighborhood must be considered if we are best to provide and secure the benefits of good health to all children so that they may develop their fullest capabilities within their innate potential.

In planning programs, another consideration deserves attention. The retarded form a diverse group. Eighty-five per cent of them are only mildly retarded; most of these come from urban and rural pockets of poverty and socio-cultural deprivation. Unfortunately, the programs already developed and those being designed will reach primarily the remaining 15 per cent of the retarded who are moderately and severely retarded. The greatest pressure for care traditionally has been directed toward the severely retarded who need primarily medical and rehabilitation care throughout their lives. This group poses major problems to its families. As a result of the quite justified demands of these families, they tend to obtain services for this segment of the retarded population, with a consequent neglect of the needs of the mildly retarded. Medical research may result someday in the prevention of many of the conditions that afflict the smaller group. The 85 per cent of mildly retarded often are neglected. There are few if any voices to speak for their needs. They often are doubly segregated because of their socio-cultural situation and their intellectual condition. No child should be without adequate care, but we must consider all groups and not overlook major areas of concern. The 85 per cent present a serious problem to society and may comprise a significant number of school drop-outs, chronic unemployables, and social outcasts. Early and intensive efforts to help them may bring great rewards to this group and to society.

This book is concerned with the many clinical issues inherent in our present body of knowledge about prevention, treatment, and rehabilitation of mental retardation. It is hoped that these chapters will stimulate new and better programs as well as influence presently operating ones to provide the help that the individual retarded person needs if he is to develop his intellectual and social potential and become a member of the community with a feeling of self-worth, dignity, and productivity.

Many of these chapters were presented at a symposium sponsored by the Department of Psychiatry at the University of California School of Medicine, San Francisco, in November 1964. The interest in the field of mental retardation shown by Alexander Simon, M.D., Chairman of the Department of Psychiatry, stimulated the preparation of the symposium, which was presented under his direction and guidance, and with the help of Klaus Berblinger, M.D., Leon J. Epstein, M.D., Shirley Jahnson, Ph.D., and me. More than 500 people representing many professional disciplines registered for the symposium, and the enthusiastic response encouraged the development of this book. In addition to papers presented at the symposium, others have been added, so that the authors included in the volume represent the fields of psychiatry, pediatrics, public health, pathology, neurology, biological chemistry, genetics, sociology, social welfare, education, vocational rehabilitation, psychology, community organization, and law. The diversity necessary in the care of the retarded is the diversity of life itself. Consequently, some omissions are unavoidable. Although each chapter attempts to deal thoroughly with its subject, it is hoped that the reader will see each chapter as presenting only one facet of the continuum of care that can be provided in an integrated and collaborative program for the mentally retarded.

IRVING PHILIPS

*San Francisco*
*January 1966*

# Acknowledgments

Funds were made available for the presentation of the original symposium held at the University of California School of Medicine in San Francisco by the National Institute of Mental Health. It is a pleasure for me to acknowledge the many individuals, in the past and in the present, who have stimulated this book:

The late Henry Poncher, M.D., and Julius Richmond, M.D., inspiring teachers in medical school, who first brought to my attention the adaptive interaction of the physical, social, and psychologic elements in disease; my colleagues on the Children's Service of Langley Porter Neuropsychiatric Institute, who have helped me learn whatever skill I have in my profession; and, especially, the Director of the Children's Service, Stanislaus A. Szurek, M.D., whose guidance, integrity, and continued intellectual stimulation of new thoughts and ideas always have been a source of great pleasure; Mary Ann Esser, M.S., whose editorial assistance made this volume possible; Adele Srem, Sharon Brue, Gayle Hanes, and, especially, Pamela Cole, whose secretarial assistance and patience were of inestimable value. Finally, my wife, whose contributions are too numerous to recount.

# The Authors

NANCY BAYLEY, Ph.D., Research Psychologist, Institute for Human Development, University of California, Berkeley, California.

MICHAEL BEGAB, M.A., Social Science Advisor, Mental Retardation Program, National Institute of Child Health and Human Development, Bethesda, Maryland.

IRVING BERLIN, M.D., Professor of Psychiatry, Head, Division of Child Psychiatry, University of Washington, Seattle, Washington.

ELIZABETH M. BOGGS, Ph.D., Chairman, Research Committee, National Association for Retarded Children, Upper Montclair, New Jersey.

GEORGE BRABNER, Ed.D., Associate Professor of Education, Graduate School of Education, Yeshiva University, New York, New York.

DONALD M. BRAMWELL, M.D., Director of the New Hampshire State Department of Mental Hygiene, Concord, New Hampshire.

HAROLD D. CHOPE, M.D., Dr. P.H., Director, San Mateo County Department of Public Health and Welfare, San Mateo, California.

PETER COHEN, M.D., Associate Professor of Pediatrics, University of California School of Medicine, San Francisco, California.

PAUL F. CRANEFIELD, M.D., Ph.D., Senior Research Fellow, Department of Psychiatry, Albert Einstein College of Medicine, New York, New York.

ROBERT W. DAY, M.D., Chief, Bureau of Maternal and Child Health, Department of Public Health, State of California.

EDGAR A. DOLL, Ph.D., Consulting Psychologist, Bellingham, Washington Public Schools.

ARTHUR L. DREW, M.D., Professor of Neurology, Indiana University Medical Center, Indianapolis, Indiana.

MICHAEL M. GALAZAN, Director, Jewish Vocational Service, Milwaukee, Wisconsin.

STERLING D. GARRARD, M.D., Professor of Pediatrics, State University of New York, Upstate Medical Center, Syracuse, New York.

HERBERT GOLDSTEIN, Ed.D., Chairman, Department of Special Education, Graduate School of Education, Yeshiva University, New York, New York.

ELIAS KATZ, Ph.D., Director, Independent Living Rehabilitation Program (a project of San Francisco Aid Retarded Children); Psychologist, Cerebral Palsy Program, University of California Medical Center, San Francisco; Lecturer in Education, University of California, Berkeley, California.

RICHARD A. KOCH, M.D., F.A.A.P., Associate Professor of Pediatrics, University of Southern California School of Medicine; Director, Child Development Clinic, Children's Hospital, Los Angeles, California.

NATHAN MALAMUD, M.D., Clinical Professor of Psychiatry and Neuropathology, University of California School of Medicine, San Francisco, California.

STEWART E. PERRY, Ph.D., Lecturer in Sociology, School of Nursing, University of California Medical Center, San Francisco, California; Lecturer, Department of Sociology, University of California, Berkeley, California.

IRVING PHILIPS, M.D., Associate Clinical Professor of Psychiatry, University of California School of Medicine; Supervising Psychiatrist, Langley Porter Neuropsychiatric Institute, San Francisco, California.

JULIUS B. RICHMOND, M.D., Dean, Professor and Chairman, Department of Pediatrics, State University of New York, Upstate Medical Center, Syracuse, New York.

DONALD STEDMAN, Ph.D., Assistant Professor of Medical Psychology and Child Psychiatry, School of Medicine, Duke University, Durham, North Carolina.

STANISLAUS A. SZUREK, M.D., Professor of Psychiatry, University of California School of Medicine; Director, Children's Service, Langley Porter Neuropsychiatric Institute, San Francisco, California.

GEORGE TARJAN, M.D., Professor of Psychiatry, University of California School of Medicine, Los Angeles, California.

HARRY A. WAISMAN, M.D., Ph.D., Professor of Pediatrics and Director, Joseph P. Kennedy, Jr., Laboratory, School of Medicine, University of Wisconsin, Madison, Wisconsin.

# Contents

# PART I

## Diagnosis of
## Mental Retardation

# 1

# Historical Perspectives

## PAUL F. CRANEFIELD

It seems reasonable to assume that mental deficiency is as old as the human race. Nothing we know about the nature and cause of feeblemindedness contradicts this assumption. Yet it is extraordinarily difficult to find evidence for the existence of mental deficiency even in historical times. The medical writers of ancient Greece and Rome rarely mention it even though they describe a wide variety of neurologic and emotional disorders. There is no unequivocal reference to it in the Bible (in which the "fool" is the man who is not wise, the man who neglects his religious duties). This same apparent neglect of the subject persists throughout the Middle Ages. From the beginning of the historical period until nearly the sixteenth century, there is no substantial or systematic discussion of mental deficiency in the medical literature. To be sure, there are references to idiots in a few literary works, in occasional legal documents, and in occasional religious discussions. But, over all, the neglect of the subject is striking. The problems that this poses are many, and the explanation cannot be a simple one. Nevertheless, the one conclusion that seems to be rather safe is that whoever coped with the problems of mental deficiency, it was not the physician.

## PARACELSUS (1493–1541)

The first "medical" treatise devoted solely to mental deficiency was written by the curious and puzzling "Faustian" figure of the sixteenth century, Paracelsus. This work, *De Generatione Stultorum* ("On the Begetting of Fools"), was written about 1530. It remains an imposing and impressive document today, not because of its scientific insight, but because of its religious and humanitarian qualities. In it, Paracelsus asked, How can God

3

permit fools to be born, fools who cannot even grasp the nature of the sacrifice God made for them? And how is it that man, the noblest of creatures, is subject to giving birth to fools when the lesser creatures, the animals, do not do so? This and much else Paracelsus attributed to the fall of Adam. Since the fall of Adam, man is not, and has not been, created in the image of God. Thus fools are born, and cripples, and thieves and murderers too. And thus it is that man cannot know that he will not beget a fool. Paracelsus is one of the first writers to face the genetic problem, by asking how it is that wise men may beget fools and that fools may beget wise men. The answer he gave (apart from the fall of Adam) is found nowhere before him, nor is it repeated by later authors. Paracelsus envisioned a vast workshop in which artisans called "vulcani" "carve" men from the "wood" that is given them in the form of the conceptus. For, as Paracelsus said, the father and mother provide only the "raw material" of the child, analogous to the wood that a carver has when he begins to make a statue. Just as a bad carpenter will spoil a good piece of wood, so a bad vulcanus will produce a fool or a cripple. Paracelsus further noted that an inept vulcanus probably will damage both mind and body by his ineptness, so that fools frequently are physically deformed.

Paracelsus went far beyond these quasi-medical theories when he discussed the true nature of the fool. The fool has an unspoiled soul, an "inner man." All men have an inner man, but most use their cunning to turn away from the mandates of the soul and toward worldly things. Fools, however, lack the worldly cunning to turn away from their inner man. They also lack the ability to express what lies within them; but on occasion they can speak, and when they do they speak wisdom and truth. More than that, the fools are our brothers, since Christ died for all, not just for the wise. Before God, said Paracelsus, "all of us in our wisdom are like the fool." And when the fool comes to die, all that is weak and deformed in him moves away, and there is silence, and the fool is alone with God, assured of salvation.

The complexities of *De Generatione Stultorum* remind us more of a homily than they do of a medical treatise. Yet there is no doubt that it is the work of a man deeply familiar with the problem of mental deficiency and familiar with it through clinical experience. Paracelsus was a Swiss and the first medical writer to give a clear description of cretinism (Cranefield and Federn, 1963). More than that, he noted that cretinism is found in close association with endemic goiter and that both conditions are found with special frequency in areas where the water is in some way peculiar. It is worth noting that, in spite of its distinctive features, cretinism was not described in any medical treatise until the time of Paracelsus. It surely existed before Paracelsus and probably long before. That it was not described is further proof of the neglect of mental deficiency by the earlier medical writers.

## FELIX PLATTER (1536–1614)

The Swiss physician Felix Platter (Plater, Platerus) deserves attention for two reasons. He provided an excellent description of cretinism in 1602, a description that was not equaled for 150 years to come:

> . . . in the Valais . . . it is usual that many infants suffer from [innate folly] . . . the head is often misshapen; the tongue is huge and swollen; they are dumb; the throat is often goitrous. Thus they present an ugly sight; and sitting in the streets, and looking into the sun, and putting little sticks in between their fingers, twisting their bodies in various ways, with their mouth agape, they provoke passerbys to laughter and astonishment (Platter, 1602–1608, pp. 95–96).

Platter also gave a brief description of mental deficiency in general that is particularly interesting for the following sentence:

> In infants this dullness of the intelligence soon becomes evident, when they are educated, and forced to learn some things, and especially at the time when they are taught to read, since only by long and much exertion can they recognize the letters of the alphabet, put syllables together, and form complete words from them (Platter, 1614, p. 1).

This passage appeared in 1614 and assuredly shows that the notion that the "high-grade" defective, whose defect is revealed only when he goes to school, is not a new one. Nor can we assert that the moron is a modern "invention," created by universal education.

## THOMAS WILLIS (1621–1675)

The most remarkable discussion of mental deficiency in the seventeenth century (or the eighteenth century, for that matter) is that given by Thomas Willis in a chapter entitled "Of Stupidity or Foolishness," which appeared in 1672. In this chapter,[1] Willis discussed many of the problems that still are familiar to us. Like Paracelsus, he touched on the genetic problem, remarking that there are families in which "reckoning many descents backward, there is scarce one witty or wise man found." On the other hand, "wise men, and highly ingenious do beget fools and Changelings, or heavy witted." This he attributed to a series of causes that have a very modern sound: parents who are intemperate, or too old, or too young, or who have epilepsy, or are too much given to study, are prone to produce mentally defective children. Willis did not note whether he based his opinion on a retrospective or a prospective study.

[1] The chapter in question has been reprinted in English in Paul F. Cranefield (1961).

Willis also provided a classification of mental deficiency that is truly remarkable:

> Some being wholly fools in the learning of letters, or the liberal Sciences, are yet able enough for *Mechanical* arts. Others, of either of these incapable, yet easily comprehend *Agriculture,* or *Husbandry* and Country business. Others, unfit almost for all affairs, are only able to learn what belongs to eating or the common means of living: Others merely *Dolts* or drivling [sic] Fools, scarce understand anything at all, or do anything knowingly (Cranefield, 1961, p. 301).

Willis also touched on the treatment of mental deficiency. He remarked that drug therapy, and medical therapy in general, was most unsatisfactory. But, he said, there is a treatment that may help: the combined efforts of the physician and a teacher may result in improvement. Careful attention to the physical welfare of the patient should be combined with the efforts of a teacher guided by the principle that the "same things are to be inculcated again and again to them." Moreover, Willis warned that a trial period of this intensive medical and educational therapy should be used. If there is no improvement, further efforts will be in vain, but if there is improvement, a long course of treatment is indicated.

We cannot leave Willis without two further comments. First, there does not seem to have been anyone in the following hundred years or more who paid any particular attention to what he said. At any rate, he is seldom quoted and his recommendations and opinions do not seem to have been followed. Second, in the same treatise we have been discussing, Willis advanced the first clear distinction between schizophrenia and mental deficiency known in the medical literature:[2]

> There is commonly wont to be a distinction between *Stupidity* and *Foolishness,* for those affected with this latter, apprehend simple things well enough, dextrously and swiftly [Lucid schizophrenic conditions show no disorder of consciousness, if the latter is conceived as implying a loss of sensory contact with the environment—Bleuler] and retain them firm in their memory [memory as such does not suffer in this disorder—Bleuler], but by reason of a defect of judgment, they compose or divide their notions evilly, and very badly infer one thing from another [the associations lose their connections—Bleuler]; moreover, by their folly, and acting awkwardly and ridiculously, they move laughter in the bystanders. On the contrary, those who are *Stupid,* by reason of the defect of the Imagination and Memory, as well as of the Judgment, do neither apprehend well nor quickly, nor argue well; besides they behave themselves not as the others by

[2] The phrases from Bleuler that are inserted in the passage from Willis are from Paul Eugen Bleuler, *Dementia praecox oder die Gruppe der Schizophrenien* (Leipzig and Vienna: Deuticke, 1911). I have quoted them in the translation given by David Rapaport (1951, pp. 636, 626, and 583, respectively).

toying and gesticulation, but sottishly, foolishly, or like a dull Ass, so that the *simplicity* of these is the more miserable (Cranefield, 1961, pp. 300–301).

I should like to emphasize the significance of Willis' specific reference to the thought disorder, on which I rest my claim that he saw schizophrenics and saw that they were different from mental defectives. Like the rest of Willis' chapter, this observation remained without influence in later years, although it may have influenced John Locke in his formulation of a well-known passage on idiocy.[3]

## THE DISCOVERY OF CRETINISM

One of the important steps in understanding any disease is its identification. This may be a truism, but its importance is great in the area of mental deficiency where the great majority of patients still have no meaningful diagnostic label attached to them. It is clear, for example, that the testing of a new therapy can hardly be rational if the therapy is used on a mixture of different entities, some of which yield to it and others of which do not. This is particularly true when the therapy is tested on groups in whom the various diseases appear in (necessarily) unknown proportions.

The first important form of mental deficiency to be identified was cretinism, and the history of its discovery is long and confused.[4] As Professor F. Merke of Basel has pointed out, it is mentioned by Jacques de Vitry in *Historia Orientalis et Occidentalis,* which was written in 1220. Merke also has found abundant other evidence for the existence of cretinism in the Middle Ages.[5] But the first unequivocal description of cretins in medical literature was that given by Paracelsus mentioned above. Another important early description of cretins was that of Felix Platter which I have already quoted. In spite of these contributions, there is nothing to suggest that knowledge of the existence of cretinism entered into the medical literature until as late as the end of the eighteenth century. In the period from Platter until about 1790, it is possible to find many references to cretins in works of travel. Persons who visited the Alps, physicians and nonphysicians alike, frequently saw the deformed victims of cretinism and mentioned them as a curiosity when writing the memoirs of their trips.

[3] Hansruedi Isler (1965). Dr. Isler's book, the first full study of Willis, is scheduled to appear in English translation in an edition published by The Hafner Publishing Company, New York.

[4] Cranefield (1962a,b,c). References to earlier and to modern studies of the history of goiter and cretinism will be found in the first paper cited in this note.

[5] Professor Merke has in preparation a book summarizing his detailed and important studies on the early history of goiter and cretinism. This book is scheduled for publication by Karger (Basel).

It is not clear why more attention was not drawn to cretinism, but once again we seem to have an example of the general neglect of mental deficiency by the medical profession. When interest finally was aroused, it was because persons interested in entirely different problems seized on cretins as examples. For example, persons interested in the skull and its abnormalities became interested in cretins because they had abnormal skulls; persons interested in the then new concept of race became interested in cretins as a possible race of mankind; persons interested in social medicine became interested in cretins as an example of a deprived and oppressed group. And eventually, of course, people became interested in cretins and cretinism as such. The cretin remained an object of active interest throughout the entire nineteenth century, and by the middle of that century an enormous literature on the etiology of cretinism had accumulated. Nearly every theory that has ever been advanced about the cause of mental deficiency was advanced as a cause of cretinism. Diet, heredity, inbreeding, environmental deprivation, and so forth were asserted to cause cretinism. In the latter part of the nineteenth century, Sir William Gull described adult myxedema; not long after that the technically difficult operation of total thyroidectomy was perfected. When thyroidectomized patients became myxedematous and mentally sluggish, the connection between the thyroid and cretinism finally became clear. All of the theories previously advanced with such confidence fell apart when the truth became known. The situation reminds us of the recent profound re-evaluation of mongolism and reminds us that the future may hold similar re-evaluations in store.

## "Nihil est in intellectu . . ."

The notion that all ideas and all knowledge originate external to man and that his mind is simply a warehouse of information conveyed inward by the senses—*"Nihil est in intellectu quod non prius fuerit in sensu"*—is very old. In relatively modern times it was emphasized by Pierre Gassendi (1592–1655), on whose work Willis apparently based much of his psychology. In the treatise discussed above Willis says

> . . . from this manifold way of sension, proceeds the Knowledge of all things, according to that of the Philosopher, *All knowledge is made by the Sense.* . . . So the sense brings in the Imagination; this the memory or the Appetite . . . (Cranefield, 1961, p. 309).

The idea was popularized by John Locke (1632–1704) through his famous image of the mind as a *tabula rasa,* but it remained for Étienne de Condillac (1715–1780) to base on it a complete philosophic system known variously as sensualism, sensationalism, or ideology.

At the end of the eighteenth century, a "wild boy," the so-called savage of Aveyron, was found wandering the woods in France. Such "wild boys" are mental defectives who have wandered from home and have been found again after a few days, naked and capable only of uttering guttural animal-like sounds. But at the time of the discovery of the savage of Aveyron, there were many who thought that such creatures had been lost in infancy and reared by animals. Were this the case, they would be expected to lack normal intelligence since they had been deprived of the appropriate sensory input needed to create an intellect. Their existence could thus be held to support Condillac's theory. It occurred to a young French physician, Jean M. G. Itard (1774–1838), that a still better proof of the validity of Condillac's theory could be obtained by showing that if the savage of Aveyron were exposed to the right kind of sensory input his intelligence would develop.

Itard, therefore, with the consent and support of the government of France, took the savage of Aveyron under his care and embarked on a long program of education. His goal was, of course, to supply the "experience" that the boy had missed and to provide him with sensory- and motor-training. In doing this he actually became involved in motivating the boy, and his whole program became an intensive course of special education and "psychotherapy." That this is so can be judged from the detailed reports that he made to the French government.[6] The savage of Aveyron was, in fact, a rather seriously retarded boy, and Itard eventually confessed defeat, since, among other things, the boy never learned to speak. Most assuredly he did not develop that degree of intelligence that would have proved that Condillac was right. The "defeat" of Itard was, in fact, a victory in disguise, if looked at correctly. It had been shown to the world (for the work of Itard was very famous) that a rather seriously retarded boy could be enormously improved and could be brought to a very much higher level of function than anyone would have supposed.

One of the great pioneers in the education of the retarded, Edouard Seguin (1812–1880), based his entire program on the work of Itard. Seguin's sensory- and motor-training (Seguin, 1866), as well as his optimism with respect to the curability of idiots, became one of the great driving forces behind the establishment of special schools for the mentally defective in the first half of the nineteenth century (Kraft, 1961). It is interesting to note that the methods of Seguin were introduced into the special education of the mentally defective in Italy by Maria Montessori and later applied by her to the education of normal children. The Montessori kindergarten is very close in its inspiration to the techniques developed by Itard to treat the savage of Aveyron.

If we had to give the nineteenth century a label so far as our subject is

---

[6] Jean M. G. Itard (1932). The preface to this translation by G. and M. Humphrey contains a discussion of the background of Itard's work.

concerned, it would perhaps best be called the century of special education. Seguin had many followers, and there were many entirely independent efforts to educate the retarded. Notable among the other workers in this area were Jacob Guggenbühl [7] (1816–1863) and Samuel Gridley Howe (1801–1876), the Boston reformer who treated Laura Bridgeman and trained the teacher of Helen Keller. Schools for the mentally defective were founded throughout the Western world, and they often were well financed and staffed by devoted and able teachers. What is more, they were successful beyond any doubt. Within the framework of their time, they were at least as successful as our present-day special schools. It is not possible to discuss them at greater length in the brief space of this article, but it is well to note that they were doomed by a development that is discussed below—the eventual triumph of the theory of degeneration and of the pseudo-scientific eugenics movement of the late nineteenth and early twentieth centuries.

## MEDICAL ADVANCES IN THE NINETEENTH CENTURY

Important advances were made in the sphere of purely organic medicine in the nineteenth century. We have noted that the nature, cause, and treatment of endemic cretinism had become substantially understood by about 1895. But the great Paris clinics of Charcot and the general advance of clinical neurology throughout the century defined many new disease entities that have mental deficiency associated with them. We may mention the discovery of tuberous sclerosis by D. M. Bourneville (1840–1909), the description of the cerebral component of Tay-Sachs disease by Bernard Sachs (1858–1944), and the classic studies of cerebral palsy by Sigmund Freud (1856–1939). One of the most curious stories is attached to the identification of mongolism. It is hard to understand how this distinctive condition could have remained unnoticed until 1866, only to be independently described twice in one year, but that is what happened. Both J. Langdon H. Down (1828–1896) and Edouard Seguin described the condition, obviously entirely unaware of each other's work. It is annoying to find that the term "Down's syndrome" is gaining favor, since Seguin gave an excellent and concise description[8] (unfortunately naming the disease "furfuraceous cretinism"), while Langdon Down's description was not only less accurate, but was presented in the framework of an absurd theory (Down, 1866a, b).

[7] For a study of Guggenbühl, see Kanner (1964).
[8] Seguin's description of furfuraceous cretinism: . . . furfuraceous cretinism, with its milk-white, rosy, and peeling skin; with its shortcomings of all the integuments, which give an unfinished aspect to the truncated fingers and nose; with its cracked lips and tongue; with its red, ectropic conjunctiva, coming out to supply the curtailed skin at the margin of the lids (1866, p. 44).

The trend toward the identification of specific entities has continued since the end of the nineteenth century and has achieved notable triumphs in the field of the inborn errors of metabolism. It need only be remarked that each new isolation of a specific entity holds great promise, since, as I said earlier, we cannot hope to understand, prevent, or treat an entity until it is identified. The clearest recent example of this is phenylketonuria. On the other hand, specific entities (with the exception of mongolism) occur rarely, and the fact that many such entities have been discovered is no proof that even a moderate fraction of the cases of mental deficiency is organic in any simple sense, or in any sense at all.

## CATASTROPHE

Our survey of the history of mental deficiency must end on a note of confusion and chaos. In 1857, the brilliant French psychiatrist Benedict Morel (1809–1873) published a book that was destined to have the gravest consequences (Morel, 1857). Yet it was an intelligent book and Morel's motives were good. In studying the victims of insanity and mental deficiency, Morel reached the conclusion that there was a large group of allied disorders that were hereditary and that tended to become more serious with each succeeding generation. He lumped these diseases under the heading of degeneration, which he defined as follows:[9] "Degenerations are deviations from the normal human type, which are transmissible by heredity and which deteriorate progressively toward extinction." The progression might, for example, be from nervousness in one generation to neurosis in the next, then to psychosis and, finally, in the fourth generation, to idiocy. The fourth generation would be the last, since it would tend to be sterile. Among the possible causes of degeneration (some of which might also be its symptoms) were alcoholism, intrauterine damage, the social milieu, and various physical illnesses, such as tuberculosis. Morel long preceded the discoveries of modern genetics, and he did not regard the hereditary progression of degeneration as inevitable. Indeed, he was much concerned that all factors that contribute to degeneration be eliminated, where possible. Thus, he favored better housing, better food, better working conditions, and similar methods of promoting "regeneration." It should be noted that Morel based his conclusions on careful studies of individual patients and their families and that he undoubtedly saw many families in which a combination of poverty and physical illness did in fact lead to deterioration. It is well to remember the ludicrous weakness of pedigree studies: to this day the commonest so-called familial disease is tuberculosis. There was more excuse for Morel than for some of his successors.

[9] This translation is taken from E. H. Ackerknecht (1959, p. 48), which also contains an excellent brief description of the rise and fall of the idea of degeneration.

He had many successors, and it did not take long for some of them to tout degeneration as a natural process corresponding to evolution in reverse (Darwin's first publications followed Morel's by only two years). Richard L. Dugdale (1841–1883), in an often misinterpreted study of the "Jukes" family, actually resembled Morel in advocating a reform of social conditions.[10] But Dugdale popularized the idea of "familial" social inefficiency and set the stage for one of the greatest disasters in the history of mental deficiency, the coalescence of the infant science of clinical psychology with the infant science of Mendelian genetics. This coalescence was symbolized in the popular mind by Henry Goddard's famous study of the "Kallikak" family (Goddard, 1914). Goddard claimed to have shown unequivocally that feeblemindedness had been transmitted by heredity for generations in a family descended from Martin Kallikak and a "nameless feebleminded girl" by whom he had an illegitimate child. To make matters even more alarming, Goddard also claimed to have shown that Martin Kallikak had founded another family through marriage with a woman of "good stock" and that that family was distinguished by large numbers of eminent and able members.[11]

Goddard's book was but one of many that asserted that feeblemindedness and many other socially undesirable traits were hereditary. In the period from 1900 to 1910, the "eugenics" movement began to flourish (Haller, 1963). Able and intelligent men seriously believed that enough had been learned about human genetics to permit a rational program of eugenics that would lead to an improvement of the human race. Since essentially nothing was known about human genetics in 1910, this may seem incredible. It is clear in retrospect that many of the advocates of eugenics were motivated by quite different reasons from those that appeared on the surface. Consciously or unwittingly, they were attracted to a simplistic solution to the problems of society. In a nutshell, if the "problem" members of society would stop having children, the problems of society would soon go away. This is an elegant solution, and it frees its proponents from any sense of responsibility for social conditions. One need not feel guilty about slums if one knows that the children in them should never have been born. And one need not worry about the effects of slums on children if one knows that the children are genetically inferior, since it was genetic inferiority that led their parents to live in slums in the first place. All one need do is to advocate continence on the part of the socially inferior, and, that failing, one can agitate for compulsory sterilization.

[10] Dugdale (1910). The first appearance of Dugdale's work was in 1875. The fourth edition cited here was a reprint that was made to meet a demand for the book at a time when interest in eugenics was at a high point. Apparently his work was better remembered than was he himself, since the reprint has his first name wrong on the title page (giving Robert instead of Richard).

[11] For a magnificently sarcastic attack on Goddard's methods, see Abraham Myerson (1925, pp. 77–80).

We need not wonder where such thinking might lead, since we know what two of its consequences were. One was the "purification" of the racial stock in Germany; a purification that began with the murder of mental defectives and schizophrenics and was intended to end with the extermination of all of the population of Europe, apart from certain "Germanic" national groups. A second, and earlier, consequence was the virtual destruction of the special schools. It became obvious that the one great goal set before those charged with the care of the mentally defective was to prevent the birth of more mental defectives. Mental defectives were to be either sterilized or kept in institutions. In no circumstances were they to be trained or educated with a view to their return to society, for if they returned to society they might have children. Seldom in the history of medicine have so many intelligent and well-meaning men embarked on so vicious and brutal a program with so little scientific foundation for their actions.

Naïve population genetics and naïve eugenics are assuming a new popularity today. The neo-eugenicists presumably have made up their minds; but others would do well, not only to heed the experience of the past, but also to take care to learn just what is known as scientific fact in human genetics and what is "statistical inference" from ill-conceived or ill-controlled population—and pedigree-studies. As an easy way out, eugenics remains a great threat both to the humane treatment of mental defectives and to the painstaking sociologic, psychologic, psychiatric, clinical, and laboratory studies that alone can further our understanding of mental deficiency.

## REFERENCES

ERWIN H. ACKERKNECHT, *A Short History of Psychiatry* (New York: Hafner Publishing Company, 1959).

PAUL F. CRANEFIELD, "A Seventeenth Century View of Mental Deficiency and Schizophrenia: Thomas Willis on 'Stupidity or Foolishness,'" *Bulletin of the History of Medicine*, XXXV (1961), 291–316.

PAUL F. CRANEFIELD, "L'origine probable de l'introduction du mot 'Crétin' dans la langue écrite. Un manuscrit de 1750 par le Comte de Maugiron," *Gesnerus*, XIX (1962a), 89–92.

PAUL F. CRANEFIELD, "The Conquest of Cretinism: A Fable," *Journal of the Albert Einstein Medical Center*, X (1962b), 138–140.

PAUL F. CRANEFIELD, "The Discovery of Cretinism," *Bulletin of the History of Medicine*, XXXVI (1962c), 489–511.

PAUL F. CRANEFIELD and WALTER FEDERN, "Paracelsus on Goiter and Cretinism: A Translation and Discussion of 'De Struma, vulgo der kropf,'" *Bulletin of the History of Medicine*, XXXVII (1963), 463–471.

J. LANGDON H. DOWN, "Marriages of Consanguinity in Relation to Degeneration of Race," *London Hospital Clinical Lecture Reports,* III (1866a), 224–236.

J. LANGDON H. DOWN, "Observations on the Ethnic Classification of Idiots," *London Hospital Clinical Lecture Reports,* III (1866b), 259–262.

ROBERT [RICHARD] L. DUGDALE, *The Jukes. A Study in Crime, Pauperism, Disease and Heredity* (New York: Putnam, 1910).

HENRY H. GODDARD, *The Kallikak Family. A Study in the Heredity of Feeble-Mindedness* (New York: Macmillan, 1914).

MARK H. HALLER, *Eugenics: Hereditarian Attitudes in American Thought* (New Brunswick, New Jersey: Rutgers University Press, 1963).

HANSRUEDI ISLER, *Thomas Willis* (Stuttgart: Enke, 1965).

JEAN MARC-GASPARD ITARD, *The Wild Boy of Aveyron,* George and Muriel Humphrey (Trans.) (New York: Century Co., 1932).

LEO KANNER, *A History of the Care and Study of the Mentally Retarded* (Springfield, Illinois: Charles C Thomas, 1964).

IVOR KRAFT, "Edouard Seguin and 19th Century Moral Treatment of Idiots," *Bulletin of the History of Medicine,* XXXV (1961), 393–418.

ABRAHAM MYERSON, *The Inheritance of Mental Diseases* (Baltimore, Maryland: Williams and Wilkins, 1925).

BENEDICT A. MOREL, *Traité des dégénérescences physiques, intellectuelles et morales de l'espèce humaine* (Paris: Baillière, 1857).

PARACELSUS, *Philosophia de divinis operibis et secretis naturae. Volumen primum. (4) De generatione stultorum,* in Karl Sudhoff (Ed.), *Theophrast von Hohenheim gen. Paracelsus, Sämtliche Werke* (Munich and Berlin: Oldenbourg, 1931), Vol. XIV, pp. 82 ff.

FELIX PLATTER, *Observationum in hominis affectibus . . . libri tres* (Basel: Konig, 1614).

FELIX PLATTER, *Praxeos, seu de cognoscendis, praedicendis, praecavendis curandisque affectibus homini incommodantibus tractatus . . .* (Basel: Conrad Waldkirch, 1602–1608), Vol. I, pp. 95–96.

DAVID RAPAPORT, *Organization and Pathology of Thought* (New York: Columbia University Press, 1951).

EDWARD SEGUIN, *Idiocy: and Its Treatment by the Physiological Method* (New York: William Wood, 1866).

This chapter is based upon research supported by a grant from the National Institutes of Health (HD 01198–02).

# 2

# Some Current Concepts
# of Mental Retardation:
# Implications for Diagnosis

## JULIUS B. RICHMOND
## STERLING D. GARRARD

We are witnessing a resurgence of interest in the field of mental retardation. I use the word resurgence because this is not a new interest for physicians. In the early history of the field such physicians as Samuel Gridley Howe, Edouard Seguin, and Jean M. G. Itard were in the forefront of efforts to care for retarded persons in our population. It was through their efforts that many of the schools for the retarded were developed. Many of these physicians had a hopeful outlook for the prevention and management of this disorder; for example, in 1848, Howe, chairman of a commission for the Commonwealth of Massachusetts, wrote:

> . . . no idiot need be confined or restrained by force; that the young can be trained to industry, order, and self-respect; that they can be redeemed from odious and filthy habits, and there is not one of any age, who may not be made more of a man and less of a brute by patience and kindness directed by energy and skill (Kanner, 1964, pp. 41–42).

The medical profession has resumed its interest and, perhaps, some of the feelings of hope that were expressed by these medical pioneers in the field.

Unfortunately, in the early decades of this century, interest dwindled and programs, with some notable exceptions, remained static. This is the

15

period called "the great lull" by Leo Kanner (1964). The historical development of this field offers perhaps some explanation for this decline in interest and efforts by the medical profession and others. The challenges of the acute infectious diseases and the metabolic and nutritional disorders were great. Efforts directed at the control of these problems through research and the application of its findings have been highly productive, and the effects are reflected in a considerable reduction in infant mortality and morbidity as well as better health for children at all ages. It may well be that our very success in these areas, although the job is not completely done, brings us to a renewed concern with the problems of the mentally retarded. This is an area no less challenging and probably infinitely more complex. At the same time as the freeing of time and energy on the part of clinicians and investigators for a re-examination of this field, there has been a vigorous effort by parents and other lay groups to direct attention to this problem. Along with this has come the willingness of public officials, such as the late President Kennedy and his family, to acknowledge family problems associated with mental retardation and to bring it more pointedly into public and professional focus. The report of the President's Panel on Mental Retardation (1962) and the effort of the American Medical Association through its Council on Mental Health and Committee on Maternal and Child Care and the report of its National Conference on Retardation (*Mental Retardation Handbook,* 1965), are additional efforts to stimulate interest and competence in this area.

The prevalence of mental retardation in our population suggests that we should attend to this problem with diligence. Mental retardation is the most widespread of all childhood disorders. It is estimated that approximately 5,000,000 individuals diagnosed at some time in their lives as retarded are present in our population. Another way of indicating the prevalence is to note that approximately 126,000 children born each year will at some time be diagnosed as mentally retarded. The problem of accurate determination of the numbers of mentally retarded persons in our population is exaggerated because this disorder can be defined only in terms of functional characteristics and not as a specific diagnostic entity. Thus, we may note that in practically all studies of the prevalence of mental retardation, more individuals are found in the school years than during the preschool or post-school years. This probably reflects a difference in detection, since school provides a test of the functional characteristics of the individual when faced with formal learning tasks. This suggests, however, that we have considerable work before us in early detection of mentally retarded children if we are to undertake more effective efforts at management prior to the school years.

In his daily clinical work, the physician is faced with a complex integrative process as he gathers data about his patients historically, through physical examination, and through laboratory data. This leads him to arrive at judgments concerning the functional capacity of the patient. The clinician's task in this process is one of integrating his knowledge of biology with his knowledge of the social, psychologic, and physical environment of the patient. This is a dynamic process, ever changing and with continuing interaction among the various factors contributing to the homeostatic capacity of the organism (Richmond and Lustman, 1954), to use Walter B. Cannon's concept (Figure 2–1). In dealing with the problems of the re-

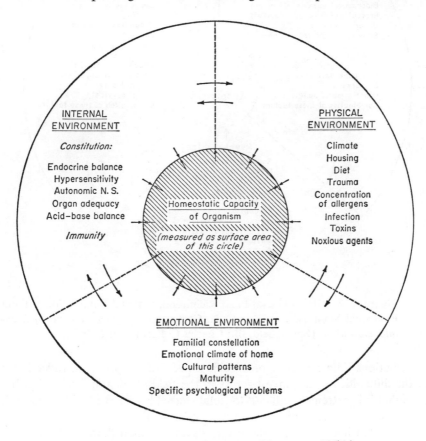

**Figure 2–1.** (After Richmond and Lustman, 1954.)

tarded child, the clinician is faced with a similarly complex task of integrating a wide variety of information into some judgments concerning causation and planning for management. We have, therefore, adapted this conceptual scheme (Garrard and Richmond, 1965) for a consideration of the issues in the field of mental retardation (Figure 2–2).

It is good to emphasize that the clinician does not enjoy the luxury of the research worker who may attempt to isolate any one of these factors for more intensive inquiry. The research worker may make his most effective

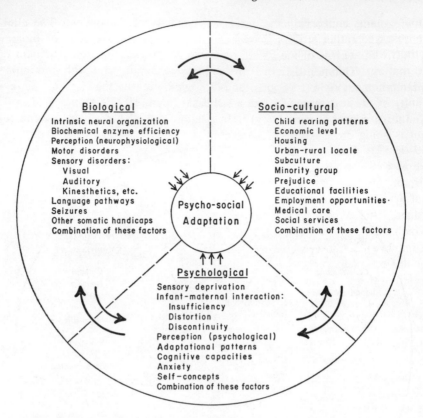

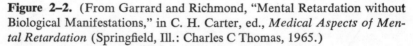

**Figure 2–2.** (From Garrard and Richmond, "Mental Retardation without Biological Manifestations," in C. H. Carter, ed., *Medical Aspects of Mental Retardation* (Springfield, Ill.: Charles C Thomas, 1965.)

contributions if he can focus on specific aspects of the problem. Indeed, one of the difficulties facing investigators in the field of mental retardation has been that it is extremely difficult to isolate variables for study while controlling all others. The clinician, however, cannot disregard the various data that come to him. Thus, in those rare cases in which there seems to be a specific genetic defect, such as in phenylketonuria or galactosemia, the physician cannot focus on the biochemical problem exclusively. The social milieu in which the child is reared may have extremely important implications for his development. Although we are grateful to individual investigators who have identified the basis of such metabolic defects, they have not by any means completely resolved problems of management. The nature–nurture controversy is a sterile one for the clinician, for regardless of any basic biologic issues, the psychologic, social, and physical environments have much to do with the outcome.

In studies of the development of individual differences in neural organization, even at such a primitive level as the autonomic nervous system, we have observed rather striking differences in newborn infants in patterns of reactivity and are investigating the fate of these differences as the infant and child mature (Richmond, 1964; Lipton and Steinschneider, 1964; Garrard and Richmond, 1963a). Of great interest currently is the development of the intrinsic neural organization of the infant. We know from the work of J. LeRoy Conel that the arborization of dendrites in the cortex of the infant is going on at a rapid rate during the early months of life (Conel, 1939–1959). This is the period in which considerable myelination is taking place as well. From studies in which infants have been raised in depriving environments (that is, receiving very little stimulation) we know that functional organization of the nervous system does not take place (Patton and Gardner, 1963; World Health Organization, 1962). Thus, the social matrix in which the infant is developing has much to do with the direction of neural organization (Provence and Lipton, 1962). For investigators, the challenge of the next decade will be to determine how experience in early life is reflected in the organization of the central nervous system. Among the problems being studied in our laboratory are the progress of learning in infants and in young children, including how children learn to learn, what kinds of stimulation in the environment determine the motivational capacity of youngsters for learning, the development of curiosity, the capacity to deal with abstractions, the ability to fantasize, and many other issues related to the emergence of mental activity (Caldwell and Hersher, 1964; Caldwell and Richmond, 1964).

It is in connection with these biologic considerations that some of the rather considerable advances in this field have taken place. We have become aware of discrete inborn errors of metabolism, such as phenylketonuria and galactosemia, as specific genetic factors. We may anticipate—and, indeed, we are noting already—the detection of many other specific inborn errors of metabolism that have an effect on cerebral function. The number of children so involved is not large, but, nonetheless, they constitute a significant group.

In the area of neurochemistry, we may anticipate much more information concerning the biochemical organization of the cortex. We may come to know much more about the molecular basis of how memories are acquired, stored, retrieved, and ultimately utilized. In the field of neurophysiology, advances are being made in earlier detection of sensory disorders, seizures, and communication difficulties, all of which have a significant bearing on the ultimate development of the child. In many instances, the mentally retarded child has multiple biologic problems. The physician is the professional person who is qualified to evaluate and to suggest corrective measures in relation to these problems. This responsibility cannot be delegated to other professional groups who have not had the background in biology that medical education provides.

Socio-cultural factors may be associated with mental retardation. Particularly with respect to mild retardation, we know that families living in very poor economic circumstances have, to a greater extent than other population groups, children who manifest mild degrees of mental retardation and often lack motivation in dealing with school tasks. Certainly, in relationship to the reproductive process, we know that families living under conditions of poverty are at considerably greater risk in terms of the incidence of prematurity, infant mortality, and complications that may result in handicapping conditions, particularly of the central nervous system. Although this is a social problem predominantly, the physician can be extremely influential in the development of efforts to provide adequate medical care and social services for families living in these circumstances. If we are to make any major impact in the field of prevention, it will be essential that some broad community effort be directed at this problem. Medical care is one factor in these efforts; and physicians, individually and in organized groups, have some responsibility for developing more adequate approaches to provide continuing medical care, starting with the prenatal period.

Many factors that bear upon intellectual development are related to the individual psychologic developmental background of the person. Although we have considerable information about the effect of insufficient, distorted, or discontinuous parent–infant interaction, we know little about the basis for this effect; that is, we know little of how it is mediated in the central nervous system. We know all too little about the development of motivation; some investigators have the feeling that it has its roots very early in life, perhaps within the first year. Certainly, the development of perceptual and cognitive capacities is influenced by the kinds of stimulation that the child has been receiving (Deutsch, 1964; Garrard and Richmond, 1963b). We know that personality development influences capacity for learning. At times, potentially normally functioning children may appear to be retarded because of emotional problems; indeed, this type of problem may occupy most of the time of the child psychiatrist who is dealing with middle class families. In recent years, because of the tremendous pressures for academic achievement, this has become particularly true.

For the physician, the major objective is the provision of help for the family that has experienced adversity. Although the physician's role in the management of this problem is similar to that of his role in the management of many chronic handicapping disorders, it does have certain unique aspects. We can regard the family as facing the challenge of a series of adaptations rather than making a single adaptation. Thus, there are predictable periods of crisis in the family with retardation.

The period surrounding the initial identification of the problem of retardation is certainly a family crisis. Generally, there is a period of disorganization and disbelief with which the physician deals; over time, better integrated plans and efforts can emerge if the family has the capacity to master adversity. Indeed, in contrast to the psychiatrist, the general physician or pediatrician commonly deals with families who master adversity very well; the psychiatrist tends to have his attention directed largely to those families that have broken down in the process of attempting to deal with adversity. Other crises will occur at the times of nursery-school age, school age, the development of pubescent changes and the associated adolescent problems, vocational rehabilitation, and the assumption of more mature responsibilities as the child approaches adulthood. At each of these points, the physician has a unique role to play. He can be particularly helpful in guiding the family to the appropriate utilization of other professional services and agencies in the community. Thus, we may conceive of a sequence of services as each child moves from a predominantly medical setting in early life to the setting of education, occupational training, and, later, training for some independent responsibilities and for a community life. Throughout, the physician's guidance and counseling functions can play a constructive role, if he is well informed about the available agencies and institutions.

A continuing emphasis in this presentation has been on the contributions that the physician may make through prevention and early detection. It has been estimated that as many as 50 per cent of the cases of retardation may stem from preventable causes. Unfortunately, there is no one approach to prevention that will be effective for all cases. This, therefore, suggests that physicians individually and in organized groups might appropriately direct their efforts at preventive approaches on a broad front.

When retardation does occur, early detection by the physician can play a significant role in minimizing a handicap and maximizing the ultimate functioning of the child. Early detection can be accomplished uniquely by the physician, since health services constitute the only organized professional services available to most families during the period of infancy and early childhood, when it is hoped most cases of retardation might be detected. This will involve considerably more effort in medical education to prepare physicians to do more effective developmental appraisals as part of their general neurologic appraisal of the infant and young child. The neurologic examination should include an evaluation of sensory function. Although the observation of developmental lag in early life does not permit absolute prediction concerning later functioning, it does alert the physician to the possibility that the child may experience difficulty. Through his continued management and suggestions for appropriate care and stimulation, the doctor can help to minimize later difficulties.

It is apparent that this problem presents great challenges to the medical profession. The profession, however, has responded to other challenges fully as complex with considerable success. We expect that the attention that is being directed at this problem currently will provide us with knowledge and practices that will go a long way toward minimizing the human incapacities resulting from mental retardation. Perhaps no problem taxes the resourcefulness and the imagination of the physician in dealing with other professional agencies and groups as does the management of the child and the family when retardation is present.

## REFERENCES

BETTYE M. CALDWELL and LEONARD HERSHER, "Mother–Infant Interaction during the First Year of Life," *Merrill-Palmer Quarterly*, X (1964), 119–128.

BETTYE M. CALDWELL and JULIUS B. RICHMOND, "Programmed Day Care for the Very Young Child—A Preliminary Report," *Journal of Marriage and Family*, XXVI (1964), 481.

J. LEROY CONEL, *The Postnatal Development of the Human Cerebral Cortex* (Cambridge, Massachusetts: Harvard University Press, 1939–1959), Vol. I–VI.

MARTIN DEUTSCH (Ed.), "Papers from the Arden House Conference on Pre-School Enrichment," *Merrill-Palmer Quarterly*, X (1964), 207–209.

STERLING D. GARRARD and JULIUS B. RICHMOND, "Diagnosis in Mental Retardation" and "Mental Retardation without Biological Manifestations," in Charles H. Carter (Ed.), *Medical Aspects of Mental Retardation* (Springfield, Illinois: Charles C Thomas, 1965), pp. 3–31, 32–72.

STERLING D. GARRARD and JULIUS B. RICHMOND, "Factors Influencing the Biological Substrate and Early Psychological Development," in Ralph H. Ojemann (Ed.), *Iowa University Committee on Preventive Psychiatry: Recent Research on Creative Approaches to Environmental Stress* (Iowa City, Iowa: State University of Iowa, 1963a), pp. 11–37.

STERLING D. GARRARD and JULIUS B. RICHMOND, "Psychological Aspects of the Management of Chronic Diseases and Handicapping Conditions in Childhood," in Harold I. Lief, Victor F. Lief, and Nina R. Lief (Eds.), *The Psychological Basis of Medical Practice* (New York: Hoeber, 1963b), pp. 370–403.

LEO KANNER, *A History of the Care and Study of the Mentally Retarded* (Springfield, Illinois: Charles C Thomas, 1964).

EARLE L. LIPTON and ALFRED STEINSCHNEIDER, "Studies on the Psychophysiology of Infancy," *Merrill-Palmer Quarterly*, X (1964), 103–117.

*Mental Retardation: A Handbook for the Primary Physician.* Report of the American Medical Association Conference on Mental Retardation, Reprinted from the *Journal of the American Medical Association*, CXCI (1965), 183–232.

ROBERT G. PATTON and LYTT I. GARDNER, *Growth Failure in Maternal Deprivation* (Springfield, Illinois: Charles C Thomas, 1963).

PRESIDENT'S PANEL ON MENTAL RETARDATION, *A Proposed Program for National Action to Combat Mental Retardation* (Washington, D. C.: Government Printing Office, 1962).

SALLY PROVENCE and ROSE C. LIPTON, *Infants in Institutions* (New York: International Universities Press, 1962).

JULIUS B. RICHMOND, "Observations of Infant Development: Clinical and Psychological Aspects," *Merrill-Palmer Quarterly*, X (1964), 95–101.

JULIUS B. RICHMOND and SEYMOUR L. LUSTMAN, "Total Health—A Conceptual Visual Aid," *Journal of Medical Education*, XXIX (1954), 23.

WORLD HEALTH ORGANIZATION, *Deprivation of Maternal Care—A Reassessment of Its Effects,* Public Health Papers, Number 14 (Geneva: World Health Organization, 1962).

# 3

# The Neuropathology
# of Mental Retardation

## NATHAN MALAMUD

Until recent times, the neuropathology of mental retardation was essentially a descriptive science. Modern experimental, genetic, and biochemical investigations have exerted a significant influence in bringing about a more dynamic approach. As a result, a better understanding of the mechanisms and causes of changes in the central nervous system associated with mental retardation is gradually evolving. In general, pathologic investigations in this field have attempted to deal with three fundamental questions: (1) what types of pathology are encountered in the various conditions included under the term "mental retardation"? (2) do the pathologic findings reflect specific causes and mechanisms? and (3) are there structural changes in the central nervous system in all these conditions, or are there forms of mental deficiency "without organic pathology?"

The first question involves the problem of classification—that is, can we classify the many and complex changes in the brain that have been reported in the literature in a way that is meaningful in the search for their causes and mechanisms? For this purpose, the study of large samples that can be treated statistically might make it possible to identify fundamental types of disorder that, despite many variables, possess common characteristics distinguishing them from other types having different features. Such a classification is illustrated in Table 3–1, which is based on a series of 1,410 consecutive autopsies performed at California state hospitals for the mentally retarded.

Four fundamentally different types of disorder are here distinguished:
1. *Malformations,* in which the brain shows evidence of having under-

TABLE 3–1. *Classification of Neuropathologic Data in Mental Retardation*

| TYPE OF PATHOLOGY | NUMBER OF CASES | PER CENT |
|---|---|---|
| malformations | 920 | 65.0 |
| destructive processes | 359 | 25.5 |
| metabolic disorders | 66 | 5.0 |
| neoplastic disorders | 29 | 2.0 |
| no definite pathology | 36 | 2.5 |
| TOTAL | 1,410 | 100.0 |

gone an arrest or disturbance in its development, in the absence, as a rule, of any demonstrable lesion. It may be assumed that such inhibition of development occurs largely prenatally or congenitally, implying that the causes may be sought in genetic or intrauterine environmental factors. This was by far the largest group in the series here presented, comprising almost two-thirds of the cases.

2. *Destructive processes,* in which the changes in the brain are dominated by acquired lesions and there are no signs of anomalous development. With few exceptions, these changes can be said to have occurred at a time when the brain was already fairly well developed, that is, at birth, in infancy, or in early childhood. Although the lesions vary greatly in pattern and location, depending on their precise causes, they have in common the feature of being end-stages of once active disorders. This group comprised approximately one-fourth of the cases in this series.

3. *Metabolic disorders,* characterized pathologically by a progressive degeneration of tissue, in contrast to the static nature of the lesions in the former group. This is a heterogeneous group of disorders that have in common hereditary transmission and specific biochemical defects. They are the so-called inborn errors of metabolism and represent disturbances in the metabolism of fats, proteins, carbohydrates, and so forth. Though it includes only a small percentage of cases of mental retardation (5 per cent of the series), this group has been much investigated in recent years and promises to be of increased importance in future research.

4. *Neoplastic disorders,* in which developmental disturbances are associated with progressive tumor formation and in which hereditary transmission is, as in the previous group, a common feature. This, the rarest of the four types, comprised 2 per cent of the cases in the series.

As previously suggested, this type of classification can serve as a starting point in the search for specific causes and mechanisms, each category serving as a model for research. The group of malformations presents the greatest challenge, since, numerically, it includes the great bulk of mentally retarded persons, while, at the same time, it is etiologically the most obscure. Pathologically, the malformations may be classified according to stages of arrested fetal development in order to explore the operation of either genetic or intrauterine factors that act at or before certain definite periods of time. Experimental teratology has provided some information concerning the timing of effects of various environmental factors on the developing fetus, for example, the work on radiation by Samuel Hicks (1953) and on anoxia by Theodore Ingalls *et al.* (1950). However, in only a relatively small number of cases has a definite relationship been demonstrated between malformation of the brain in humans and maternal disorders occurring during pregnancy. This relationship has been noted in reports on maternal rubella by N. McAlister Gregg (1941) and by Charles Swan (1949), and on pelvic irradiation by J. Zappert (1927) and by Douglas Murphy, Margaret Shirlock, and Edgar Doll (1942). Nathan Malamud *et al.* (1964) have reported a statistically significant history of vaginal bleeding or threatened abortion and a somewhat less common history of maternal infections and the use of unusual drugs during pregnancy in a large number of cases associated with malformations of the brain. The studies of the National Institute of Neurological Diseases and Blindness (Masland, 1962) point in the same direction. The etiologic significance of these factors remains undetermined. According to Samuel Hicks (1953), thus far, the application of the findings in experimental teratology to human malformations has not been established.

Following the method of classifying the malformations in accordance with arrest at certain stages of fetal development, a group of specific anomalies may be distinguished from a group of nonspecific anomalies, as outlined in Table 3–2.

TABLE 3–2. *Classification of Malformations*

| TYPE OF PATHOLOGY | | NUMBER OF CASES | PER CENT |
|---|---|---|---|
| Specific | | 162 | 18 |
| Nonspecific | | 758 | 82 |
| with mongolism | 251 | | |
| with phenylketonuria | 9 | | |
| other types | 498 | | |
| TOTAL | | 920 | 100 |

The group of *specific malformations* comprises gross anomalies of the brain that may be related to inhibitions of development occurring during the first trimester or the first half of pregnancy. Included are, for example, gross disturbances in the formation of convolutions, such as pachygyria and micropolygyria; local failures in closure of the neural tube, such as porencephaly, encephalocele, and meningomyelocele; and agenesis of specific structures such as the corpus callosum and the vermis of the cerebellum. In any of these malformations, the failure in development has had to occur at an early period of embryonic life in order to account for the specific anomaly. There are recorded instances in which maternal rubella or other infections occurring during the first trimester of pregnancy may be related causally to such disturbances in development. Although in the majority of these malformations the etiologic factors remain unknown, further investigations in experimental teratology can be expected to yield increasingly more information.

The group of *nonspecific malformations* is characterized grossly by subtle or "mild" structural deviations of development, such as a moderate microcephaly, disproportion in size between the different lobes of the brain, discrepancies in the relative amounts of gray and white matter, or slight cyto-architectural anomalies. As shown in Table 3–2, these are much more common than the specific malformations, in a ratio of approximately four to one. The morphologic pathology in this group has been controversial, to the extent that some investigators have denied altogether the existence of organic changes as a basis for mental retardation. Yet it is among the nonspecific malformations that one encounters such disorders as mongolism and phenylketonuria. From the standpoint of anatomic pathology, there is no fundamental difference in the gross appearance of the brain in cases of mongolism, phenylketonuria, and so-called undifferentiated mental deficiency.

It is now common knowledge that the two major developments in the study of mental retardation in recent years have been the discovery by A. Fölling (1934) of phenylketonuria and the discovery by Jérôme Léjeune *et al.* (1959) of the chromosomal abnormalities in mongolism.

Phenylketonuria (PKU) has been regarded as the most common type of metabolic error associated with mental subnormality, although it accounts for only about 1 per cent of institutionalized mental defectives. It is caused by an autosomal recessive gene that determines the absence of the liver enzyme phenylalanine hydroxylase, which normally converts the amino acid phenylalanine to tyrosine. The absence of this enzyme results in the accumulation of phenylalanine in the blood and its excretion in the urine, largely in the form of phenylpyruvic acid. The manner in which the associated, often severe, retardation occurs remains unexplained, but the beneficial therapeutic effect of a phenylalanine-free diet suggests that a direct relationship exists between the metabolic disturbance and the cerebral symptoms. Nevertheless, one of the most puzzling features of the disorder has been the observation by many pathologists of negative or insignificant and inconsistent neuropathologic findings in PKU (Jervis, 1963). Some have reported a slightly reduced brain weight (Crome and Pare, 1960); some, a lag in the normal development of myelin (Alvord *et al.*, 1950); others, a gliosis suggesting a process of dysmyelination (Scholz, 1957; Poser and van Bogaert, 1959); while still others have noted actual demyelination (Benda, 1952; Corsellis, 1953; Jervis, 1954; Crome, 1962). The latter change was observed usually in adult cases, but was variously interpreted by the investigators cited. Clemens Benda regarded it as the direct result of the enzymatic defect, whereas George Jervis and L. Crome considered it to indicate the coincidental occurrence of two unrelated disorders, namely, Schilder's disease and PKU.

A series of nine brains of patients with PKU who came to autopsy at ages ranging from six to forty were examined by this author. In all cases, gross inspection of the brain showed mild nonspecific stigmata of arrested development, such as reduction in weight, changes in configuration of the convolutions, and a relative decrease in the amount of white matter. Microscopically, however, a significant change was observed in the myelin of the cerebral white matter in all cases, differing in character and degree, more or less, with the age of the patient at the time of death. In six of the brains from patients ranging in age from six to twenty, the white matter appeared somewhat reduced, but otherwise grossly normal. Microscopically, scattered areas showed a characteristic spongy state in which the myelin sheaths were interspersed with small vacuoles that seemed to separate them mechanically without actually destroying them. These varied in extent from small foci to extensive diffuse involvement and were found in the cerebral hemispheres, cerebellum, optic tracts, brain stem, and spinal cord. In the brains of three adults who ranged in age at the time of death from twenty-six to forty there was gross evidence of degeneration of myelin as indicated by gross focal or diffuse grayish discoloration of the white matter. Microscopically, spongy areas similar to those found in the younger brains were seen to merge imperceptibly with areas of active demyelination. That this represented an actual disintegration of myelin was confirmed by the presence of fat-breakdown products and by a reactive dense gliosis.

The above findings suggest that a slowly progressive destruction of myelin takes place in PKU. In keeping with such a view is a report by L. Crome *et al.* (1962) of a biochemical analysis of the brains of four patients with PKU. These investigators found that the water content of the brain was higher and the lipid content lower in PKU than in controls. In the one adult case in which they noted gross demyelination, they found that along with these pronounced physico-chemical changes there was an accumulation of cholesterol esters, indicating that active demyelination had in fact occurred.

It seems likely that among the early effects of PKU on the central nervous system may be hydration, accounting for the vacuolation of the tissue, followed by increasing destruction of myelin. Further investigation, both biochemical and with the electron microscope, ultimately may demonstrate the earliest changes. It is reasonable to assume also that adequate therapy administered early in life may arrest the initial biochemical effect before it leads to irreversible structural damage. What is of particular interest is that PKU, originally observed only to be associated with a mild and nonspecific arrest of brain development, may now be recognized as an active disorder of brain metabolism. The investigation of other nonspecific malformations for similar findings is a logical next step.

The brain of a patient with mongolism, like that of one with PKU, appears, at first glance, to be only mildly malformed—being slightly reduced in weight and possessing slight nonspecific anomalies in convolutional and cyto-architectural pattern. But here, too, certain patho-anatomic features suggest fundamental metabolic disturbances. It is well known that the mongol brain tends to undergo calcification more frequently than does the brain associated with other forms of mental retardation. Of particular interest is a tendency of the mongol brain to develop in middle age changes characteristic of so-called senile brain disease. First pointed out by George Jervis (1948), these findings have been observed consistently in the present study (Table 3–3). The changes are characterized by the formation of senile

TABLE 3–3. *"Senile" Brain Changes in Mongolism*

| AGE AT DEATH (YEARS) | NUMBER OF CASES | "SENILE" BRAIN CHANGES | | |
|---|---|---|---|---|
| | | MILD | MODERATE | SEVERE |
| below 37 | 279 | 0 | 0 | 0 |
| 37–66 | 29 | 4 | 2 | 23 |
| (average age 50) | | | | |

plaques and neurofibrillary lesions that, when occurring in middle age in the normal population, have led to a diagnosis of presenile dementia or Alzheimer's disease. But though of unknown cause, such changes suggest the operation of some specific metabolic disturbance that becomes structurally apparent in the mongol only in adult life.

In the group of destructive processes, one is dealing, as mentioned previously, with end-stages of disorders that were acquired during perinatal and postnatal periods of life. It is with these processes, especially, that precise correlation of clinical and pathologic data can lead to more adequate formulations of etiology and pathogenesis. It is well known that in cases where often incomplete and misleading retrospective clinical histories have led to erroneous and arbitrary diagnoses, careful pathologic analysis has, in many instances, demonstrated distinct pathologic patterns that are characteristic of specific causes and mechanisms. In particular, the pathologic sequelae of birth trauma, kernicterus, and certain viral and parasitic forms of encephalitis have become more clearly outlined through adequate clinico-pathologic correlations. An extensive literature about mental retardation associated with destructive processes has accumulated, and it is anticipated that these processes will become increasingly better defined through the broad studies in cerebral palsy and mental retardation being carried out by the National Institute of Neurological Diseases and Blindness.

In conclusion, I should like to draw attention to the final question posed at the outset, namely, "Is there a patho-anatomic substrate in all cases of mental retardation?" As noted in Table 3–1, only 2.5 per cent of this large series of brains showed no demonstrable pathology. Of greater importance, many of the conditions classified as nonspecific malformations have been considered by other authors to be cases of "mental defect without definite pathology." As pointed out previously, this same misinterpretation was made of PKU before its metabolic nature became known; and this can be assumed to be true also of other conditions included here as nonspecific malformations. Some investigators have distinguished low- from high-grade defectives on the basis of an assumed difference existing between pathologic and subcultural forms, respectively. Such an analysis of material in the present study is illustrated in Table 3–4. It can be seen that in all

TABLE 3–4. *Correlation of Types of Pathology with Severity of Mental Retardation*

|  | LOW-GRADE RETARDATES (IQ BELOW 50) | HIGH-GRADE RETARDATES (IQ ABOVE 50) |
|---|---|---|
|  | NUMBER OF CASES | NUMBER OF CASES |
| specific malformations | 115 | 7 |
| nonspecific malformations | 554 | 85 |
| destructive processes | 273 | 27 |
| TOTAL | 942 (89%) | 119 (11%) |

categories of pathology, including the nonspecific malformations, the entire range of mental subnormality was represented in these patients. It is true that 89 per cent of the patients in the series exhibited low-grade, and only 11 per cent high-grade, retardation; but this is to be expected in any series of autopsied cases, on the basis of the shorter life span of the more severely retarded patients. However, the question of whether or not there is any pathologic condition in the brain of the high-grade defectives can be answered in the affirmative, as aptly stated by Richard Masland (1958), who remarked,

> I consider it likely, however, that the factor of brain injury can operate throughout the whole range of intelligence, and in fact, that minor degrees of injury are far more common than are the severe and grossly evident ones (Masland *et al.*, 1958, p. 11).

REFERENCES

ELLSWORTH C. ALVORD, JR., LEWIS D. STEVENSON, F. STEPHEN VOGEL, and RALPH L. ENGLE, JR., "Neuropathological Findings in Phenyl-pyruvic Oligophrenia (Phenyl-ketonuria)," *Journal of Neuropathology and Experimental Neurology*, IX (1950), 298–310.

CLEMENS E. BENDA, *Developmental Disorders of Mentation and Cerebral Palsies* (New York: Grune and Stratton, 1952).

J. A. N. CORSELLIS, "The Pathological Report of a Case of Phenylpyruvic Oligophrenia," *Journal of Neurology, Neurosurgery and Psychiatry*, XVI (1953), 139–143.

L. CROME, "The Association of Phenylketonuria with Leucodystrophy," *Journal of Neurology, Neurosurgery and Psychiatry*, XXV (1962), 149–153.

L. CROME and C. M. B. PARE, "Phenylketonuria, A Review and a Report of the Pathological Findings in Four Cases," *Journal of Mental Science*, CVI (1960), 862–890.

L. CROME, V. TYMMS, and L. I. WOOLF, "A Chemical Investigation of the Defects of Myelination in Phenylketonuria," *Journal of Neurology, Neurosurgery and Psychiatry*, XXV (1962), 143–148.

A. FÖLLING, "Über Auscheidung von Phenylbrezträubensäure in den Harn als Stoffwechselanomalie in Verbindung mit Imbezillität," *Zeitschrift für physiologische Chemie*, CCXXVII (1934), 169–176.

N. MCALISTER GREGG, "Congenital Cataract Following German Measles in the Mother," *Transactions of the Ophthalmological Society of Australia*, III (1941), 35.

SAMUEL P. HICKS, "Developmental Malformations Produced by Radiation; a Timetable of Their Development," *American Journal of Roentgenology*, LXIX (1953), 272–293.

THEODORE H. INGALLS, FRANCIS J. CURLEY, and RICHARD A. PRINDLE, "Anoxia as a Cause of Fetal Death and Congenital Defect in the Mouse," *American Journal of Diseases of Children*, LXXX (1950), 34–45.

GEORGE A. JERVIS, "Early Senile Dementia in Mongoloid Idiocy," *American Journal of Psychiatry*, CV (1948), 102–106.

GEORGE A. JERVIS, "Pathology," in Frank L. Lyman (Ed.), *Phenylketonuria* (Springfield, Illinois: Charles C Thomas, 1963), pp. 96–100.

GEORGE A. JERVIS, "Phenylpyruvic Oligophrenia (Phenylketonuria)," in *Genetics and the Inheritance of Integrated Neurological and Psychiatric Patterns*, Research Publications of the Association for Research in Nervous and Mental Disease, XXXIII (Baltimore, Maryland: Williams and Wilkins, 1954), 259–279.

JÉRÔME LÉJEUNE, MARTHE GAUTIER, and RAYMOND TURPIN, "Études des chromosomes somatiques de neuf enfants mongoliens," *Comptes Rendus Académie des Sciences, Paris*, CCXLII (1959), 1721–1722.

NATHAN MALAMUD, HIDEO H. ITABASHI, JANE CASTOR, and HARLEY B. MESSINGER, "An Etiologic and Diagnostic Study of Cerebral Palsy," *Journal of Pediatrics*, LXV (1964), 270–293.

RICHARD L. MASLAND, "Current Knowledge Regarding the Prenatal Environmental Factors in Mental Deficiency," in B. W. Richards (Ed.), *Proceedings of the London Conference on Scientific Study in Mental Deficiency, 1960,* I (Dagenham, England: May and Baker, 1962), 55–76.

RICHARD L. MASLAND, SEYMOUR B. SARASON, and THOMAS GLADWIN, *Mental Subnormality, Biological, Psychological, and Cultural Factors* (New York: Basic Books, 1958).

DOUGLAS P. MURPHY, MARGARET E. SHIRLOCK, and EDGAR A. DOLL, "Microcephaly Following Maternal Pelvic Irradiation for the Interruption of Pregnancy," *American Journal of Roentgenology,* XLVIII (1942), 356–359.

CHARLES M. POSER and LUDO VAN BOGAERT, "Neuropathologic Observations in Phenylketonuria," *Brain,* LXXXII (1959), 1–9.

W. SCHOLZ, "Contribution à l'anatomie pathologique du système nerveux central dans l'oligophrénie phénylpyruvique," *Encephale,* XLVI (1957), 668–680.

CHARLES SWAN, "Rubella in Pregnancy as an Aetiological Factor in Congenital Malformation, Stillbirth, Miscarriage and Abortion," *Journal of Obstetrics and Gynaecology of the British Empire,* LVI (1949), 591–605.

J. ZAPPERT, "Über röntgenogene fetale Mikrocephalie," *Archiv für Kinderheilkunde,* LXXX (1927), 34–44.

Acknowledgment is made to the staffs of Sonoma, Pacific, and Porterville State Hospitals (California Department of Mental Hygiene) for the autopsy material that made the study illustrated in Table 3–1 possible. Parts of this chapter originally appeared in Harvey A. Stevens and Rick Heber, *Mental Retardation,* © 1964 by The University of Chicago, published by the University of Chicago Press.

# 4

# The Clinical Neurology
# of Mental Retardation

## ARTHUR L. DREW

By ancient and honorable tradition, clinical neurology and the neurologic sciences have been given a clear mandate to play an important role in the field of mental retardation. Their charter dates back to the fifth century B.C., when Hippocrates wrote an essay "The Sacred Disease" in which he pled for recognition of the importance of the brain, much as the modern clinical neurologist.

> It ought to be generally known that the source of our pleasure, merriment, laughter and amusement, as of our grief, pain, anxiety and tears is none other than the brain. It is specially the organ which enables us to think . . . . diseases which attack the brain are the most acute, most serious, and most fatal, and the hardest problem in diagnosis for the unskilled practitioner (Chadwick and Mann, 1950, pp. 190, 193).

It might be added that they represent difficult problems for any practitioner, skilled neurologist or not.

Today, clinical neurology is in a unique position to help bridge the gap between those workers in the behavioral sciences who view mental retardation as subnormal behavior and those workers in the biologic sciences whose concern is with the fundamental biologic phenomena that determine the form and function of the "organ of mind." The neurologist views mental retardation not as a discrete symptom but as one of many associated indicators of malfunction of the central nervous system, rarely occurring as an isolated neurologic finding. Further, the neurologist's primary concern with central nervous system function makes the influence of socio-cultural

33

and other environmental factors on neural performance of as much interest to him as the results of biochemical or structural defects. In computer jargon, input and output are of as much importance to the clinical neurologist as the hardware, in his evaluation of the problems of mental retardation.

In the area of mental retardation, most neurologic work is with children. However, the basic concern of the neurologist is neurologic function, and his knowledge of it tends to give him a wide perspective and facilitates his drawing on knowledge and experience with central nervous system disease that, although not directly concerned with mental retardation, may be of value in dealing with the retarded patient.

The time-honored methods of examination and history-taking continue to provide valuable diagnostic information. Since the causes of mental retardation are myriad, the neurologic history of a person suspected of being mentally retarded must be elaborated in detail and in areas of inquiry beyond those in the "routine" history. It is convenient to seek for possible etiology in the preconception period, the trimesters of pregnancy, the perinatal, neonatal, and postnatal periods. Each period has certain unique features, evaluation of which may lead to more complete diagnostic understanding of the mentally retarded child with neurologic disease or damage.

A careful genetic history should be a part of every diagnostic appraisal. Each epoch of development of the nervous system is attended by certain fairly specific hazards. An adequate and carefully taken genetic history can lead to the diagnosis of a wide variety of inherited disorders of the nervous system in which mental retardation is an important feature. A positive or negative family history should be documented or else identified as inadequate or not available. Where indicated, relatives and especially siblings should be examined.

Detailed history of the pregnancy with special attention to maternal health, medication, exposure to infection, and chemical or physical teratogens, is mandatory. Information concerning the delivery and the perinatal period cannot be too detailed. Neonatal and infant history of disease and behavior should be stressed. All too often, inquiry into the behavior of infants and children is neglected in the more stereotyped neurologic history.

The history of maternal health and the course of the pregnancy may reveal the etiology of a wide spectrum of developmental defects as well as intrauterine insults to the potentially normal central nervous system. Subsequent examination of the child may reveal extracephalic developmental defects that, when fitted into the timetable of embryologic development, will point to a fairly specific period of intrauterine development. In this case, every effort should be expended to obtain a more detailed history of the pregnancy. Obstetrical, perinatal, and postnatal histories will give important clues to acquired insult to the central nervous system. It should not be forgotten that problems during this period may complicate already existing genetic or teratogenic defects of the central nervous system.

Neurologic examination of the infant and the young child, especially if mentally retarded, requires quite a different approach from that afforded by the well-established methods used in the adult neurologic examination. It is essential that the infant or young child be observed carefully prior to any attempt at active examination. General appearance and presence or absence of facial, auricular, ocular, and digital anomalies must be carefully noted. Configuration as well as size of the cranium is an important clue to the condition of the cerebrum. Careful inspection for asymmetrical development of face and extremities often leads to the detection of significant neurologic deficit. Because of the large number of neurocutaneous conditions associated with central nervous system deficit and mental retardation, the skin must be examined carefully. Observation of spontaneous movement and posture should precede actual testing. When the patient is disturbed for testing, the responses to manipulation should be recorded. Parents, nurses, and others in close attendance on the infant and young child may report valuable observations of the spontaneous behavior of the patient under varying conditions, with special reference to seizure phenomena, infantile spasms, and tonic neck reflexes.

The actual examination of infant and young child involves the eliciting of a number of reflexes in addition to those usually elicited in the reflex examination of the adult. The Moro reflex, the Landau response, and tonic neck responses all are observed. Chvostek's sign and lip, rooting, abdominal, and anal reflexes are elicited. Muscle tone and consistency on the musculo-skeletal system and the placing and stepping responses will give information about the integrity of both upper and lower motor neuron systems. Sensory examination necessarily is limited to an attempt to establish gross evidence of loss of pain and, less reliably, touch sensation. Examination of the cranial nerves should include light reflexes, response to sound, and careful inspection of cranial nerve-motor function. Optokinetic responses and visual field defects may be looked for. Funduscopic examination is essential.

In older children, the neurologic examination approaches the format used with adults. However, it should be stressed that the various developmental scales, psychologic tests, and neuropsychologic evaluations are integral parts of the neurologic appraisal of children. The behavioral aspects of neural function more often indicate neurologic malfunction than do the aspects revealed by more traditional methods of neurologic examination. Hyperactivity, short attention span, rapid fluctuations of affect, poor concentration, and transient fluctuations in alertness may be observed, and strongly suggest organic neurologic involvement.

However, more elaborate techniques are required in the neurologic appraisal of the mentally retarded. The neurologist, like all clinicians, owes a great debt to colleagues in diverse basic research disciplines. Modern diagnostic methods in neurology are derived increasingly from methodology in biochemistry, electrophysiology, psychology, and psychiatry. Particularly in the field of mental retardation, the clinician must draw heavily on a variety of biologic disciplines. Among these, human genetics, embryology, teratology, and psychology and psychiatry are the most prominent. Perhaps nowhere in medicine is such a wide diagnostic armamentarium required as in the field of mental retardation.

Specific laboratory aids to the definite diagnosis of neurologically determined mental retardation often are suggested by history and examination. Where extracerebral developmental anomalies are present, chromosome-culture and karyotyping are indicated, unless the clinician is able to make a specific syndrome-diagnosis, and knows that previous cytogenic investigation has failed to reveal the gross chromosome aberrations detectable by currently available techniques. One or more affected siblings in the presence of a well-documented family history that shows other members to be unaffected suggests the operation of a recessive gene, as does a history of parental consanguinity. About twenty inborn errors of metabolism can be diagnosed by demonstration of amino acid abnormalities in urine and blood. The accurate differentiation of this group of diseases is essential if therapeutic measures are to be instituted. Genetic counseling and carrier-detection also depend on these biochemical studies.

A second group of neurologic disorders with a recessive pattern of inheritance is that of the progressive cerebral degenerations. Electroencephalography may be helpful in establishing the presence of a degenerative process. Electroretinography may permit the process to be identified as belonging to the cerebro-retinal group of progressive dementias. Spinal fluid electrophoresis to determine abnormalities in the globulin fractions is a useful laboratory procedure, as is the search for metachromatic granules in the urine. Biopsy of cerebrum, peripheral nerve, and rectum is often the only way in which a premortem differential diagnosis may be established. Biopsy should be seriously considered if a firm basis for genetic counseling and prognostication is to be established and our knowledge of these diseases expanded.

Radiographic study of skull and vertebral column should be carried out in a search for intracerebral calcifications and developmental anomalies. Ventriculography, pneumoencephalography, and arteriography are indicated where gross anatomic or vascular pathology is suspected. The electroencephalogram and various activating procedures should be used to detect complicating convulsive seizures, the treatment of which is of paramount importance in any habilitative program.

Additional techniques of evaluation are directed less toward etiologic diagnosis and more toward establishing the functional status of the nervous system, including intellectual function. Developmental testing, appraisal of social quotients, and detailed psychologic evaluation not only may permit the ascertainment of current intellectual level of function, but, to a lesser degree, may give some indication of potential. Together with a psychiatrically oriented history of child-rearing practices, these measures aid in the evaluation of the relative clinical importance of often coexisting organic neurologic factors and nonorganic psychogenic determinants of behavior.

With some important exceptions to be noted, the neurologist deals primarily with severely retarded persons. These patients present associated nervous system abnormalities, so that as a rule in clinical practice, mental retardation is only one of a cluster of signs and symptoms associated with nervous system malfunction. The contributions of the neurologist consist not only in the accurate diagnosis and prognosis of specific disease processes and abnormalities of the central nervous system but also in the frequently more difficult appraisal of the effect of associated neurologic signs and symptoms on intellectual performance. Such appraisal ranges from the detection and treatment of complicating convulsive disorder to the proper weighting of dysphasic deficits in a brain-damaged, mildly retarded child. Central nervous system dysfunction may be manifested by many signs and symptoms. The association of various neurologic deficits may lead the clinician to suspect a specific disease or structural defect. Only by continued search for specific causes can therapy and prevention be accomplished.

Since the vast majority of diseases and structural abnormalities of the brain are, in children, associated with intellectual deficit of varying degree, an exhaustive discussion of differential diagnosis is beyond the scope of the present treatment of the subject. However, certain broad categories of disease will be discussed briefly. These include the inborn errors of metabolism, certain neuronal storage diseases, conditions involving white-matter degeneration, neuroectodermal dysplasias, various autosomal- and sex-chromosome aberrations, and neurologic conditions resulting from damage in the perinatal period.

Among the diseases in which the biochemical lesion is best understood are the inborn errors of metabolism associated with mental retardation. Phenylketonuria is the prototype of this group. An inborn error of metabolism may be suspected on the basis of the demonstration of a recessive genetic pattern and by observation of the nonneurologic manifestations of the metabolic error. Cataracts, skin lesions, abnormalities of hair, retarded growth and development, skeletal abnormalities, and visceral involvement in various combinations, together with seizures and organic mental retardation, indicate the need for more definitive biochemical study. For the most part, evidence of abnormal development is present at birth or shortly after.

A second group includes genetically determined diseases leading to progressive dementia that are presumed to result from inborn errors of metabolism, but in which the pathogenesis is less well delineated. The cerebral storage diseases that can be subdivided into the sphingolipidoses, the mucopolysaccharidoses, and the glycogen storage diseases are in this group. A number of other storage diseases are not as yet entirely classifiable from a biochemical point of view.

The sphingolipidoses include the cerebro-macular degenerations in which previously normal children begin to show visual and intellectual deterioration. The diagnosis is suggested by the detection of macular and retinal changes and is confirmed by cerebral or rectal biopsy. These conditions are inherited recessively and are classified as congenital (Norman), infantile (Tay-Sachs), late infantile (Bielschowsky), juvenile (Spielmeyer-Vogt), and late (Kuf's), with reference to the age of onset. They are uniformly fatal. Other lipid storage diseases leading to progressive dementia that are of importance in the differential diagnosis of neurologically retarded children are infantile cerebral Gaucher's disease, a juvenile form of cerebral Gaucher's disease, and infantile and juvenile forms of Niemann-Pick disease. Visceral enlargement serves to help differentiate these from the cerebro-macular lipidoses. For the sake of completeness, Farber's disease, Fabry's angiokeratoma corporis defusum, cerebral cholesterinosis, and, possibly, Heller's dementia infantalis should be added to the list of lipid storage diseases leading to progressive dementia. Hurler's disease (gargoylism) is a form of mucopolysaccharidosis that can be diagnosed by grotesque facies, radiographic abnormalities, and the demonstration of excess mucopolysaccharides in the urine. A number of variants of this disorder have been described. Familial progressive myoclonic epilepsy with retardation has been added to the group of mucopolysaccharidoses under the eponym of Lafora's disease. Finally, some forms of glycogen storage disease are associated with cerebral involvement and dementia.

Turning from the neuronal storage diseases to the white matter degenerations associated with mental retardation, the first group to be considered is that of the exogenous multifocal perivenous inflammatory demyelinating conditions that occur in association with infectious disease. The exanthema of childhood may lead to serious encephalopathy with mental retardation. Similar, but fortunately less frequent, acute demyelination may occur following immunization. More diffuse cerebral demyelination is represented by Schilder's encephalitis periaxialis diffusa and by subacute sclerosing leucoencephalitis. The latter condition may be suspected when there is a metronomic electroencephalographic pattern, myoclonic phenomena, and a strongly positive gold curve in the spinal fluid.

The term dysmyelinating has been applied to the group of myelin diseases in which a genetic factor is evident and an enzymatic interference with myelin metabolism is present, in contrast to the exogenous demyelinating diseases. Clinically, only two can be diagnosed without recourse to either cerebral biopsy or autopsy tissue examination. Metachromatic leucodystrophy may be diagnosed by the demonstration of metachromatic granules in the urine or metachromatic staining of peripheral or dental nerve. It is a sulfatide metabolic disorder. The ascertainment of a sex-linked recessive genetic pattern and neonatal nystagmus with progressive spasticity suggests Pelizaeus-Merzbacher disease, another form of diffuse sclerosis or leuco-dystrophy. Other members of this group of dysmyelinations require cere-bral biopsy for verification and are characterized clinically by progressive dementia and decerebration, with onset varying from infancy through late childhood.

Another large group of neurologic problems associated with mental retardation can be classified as neurocutaneous or neuroectodermal dyspla-sias. Since the nervous system and skin share a common ectodermal origin, it is not surprising to find a large number of conditions affecting both skin and central nervous system. Tuberous sclerosis, some instances of neurofi-bromatosis, and encephalo-trigeminal angiomatosis (Sturge-Weber) and its variants are the three most commonly encountered neurocutaneous syn-dromes with mental retardation. Xeroderma, icthyosis, follicular keratosis, angiokeratoma, telangectasia, hemangiomatosis, linear nevus sebaceus, and incontinentia pigmenti are more rare dermatologic conditions with nervous system pathology and mental retardation. An exhaustive eponymic or symptomatic listing cannot be attempted here. Genetic factors are involved in most of these disorders.

In addition to the four Down's syndrome karyotypes, Turner's syn-drome, and some forms of holo-prosencephaly, a number of other rare au-tosomal and sex chromosome aberrations associated with mental retarda-tion and other central nervous system defects have been described. These include Klinefelter's syndrome, the triple-x syndrome, and the autosomal trisomy syndromes 13–15 and 18. Except in the case of the translocation form of mongolism, there is every indication that the risk for subsequent involved sibs is very low in these disorders.

Together with the grosser structural malformations caused by cytogenic and morphogenic distortions of intrauterine development, these conditions are apparent at birth. Anencephaly, hydrocephalus, and microcephaly in various combinations with spinal dysraphism may have a familial incidence; and at least one, holo-prosencephaly with extracerebral malformations, has proved to be a chromosome trisomy.

However, the vast majority of schizencephalic and encephaloclastic congenital malformations of the central nervous system are of unknown etiology. Many probably represent the effects of a large variety of known, suspected, or as yet unidentified teratogenic agents, physical, chemical, and immunologic. Most will be found to have associated extracerebral develop-mental defects. This association must be borne in mind by pediatricians, orthopedists, plastic surgeons, cardiologists, and others who may be called on to treat various extracerebral anomalies, lest they fail to recognize they are dealing with a child who has significant central nervous system deficit and mental retardation.

Another category of heredodegenerative diseases of the nervous system in which mental retardation is of significant frequency has been described as the polymorphous neuroabiotrophies. These diseases are genetically determined, systematic degenerations of the nervous system about which little, if any, knowledge of the basic biochemical defect is presently available. The neurologist knows them as clinical complexes of signs and symptoms indicating involvement of specific neuroanatomic structures. The differential diagnosis becomes an exercise at the descriptive Linnean level. They are best classified according to the major neuroanatomic involvement. The basal ganglion diseases in which mental retardation and/or progressive dementia occur include the rare familial juvenile parkinsonism, Huntington's chorea of childhood, and hepato-lenticular degeneration (Wilson's disease). The latter is now, of course, better understood as a metabolic disease. The rare dysnergia cerebellaris myoclonia of Hunt, and Hallervorden-Spatz disease may be included here. The spinocerebellar and spinal syndromes with significant frequency of associated intellectual retardation include Friedreich's ataxia, Marinesco-Sjögren syndrome, and, occasionally, familial spastic paraparesis. Polyneuritis, ataxia, and retinitis pigmentosa (Refsum's syndrome) may have associated mental retardation of a mild degree.

The next group of neurologic conditions that often are associated with mental retardation includes those children who suffer damage in the perinatal period. The perinatal period is a dangerous one to the highly sensitive central nervous system. Trauma, hemorrhage, and, most importantly, hypoxia all will cause cerebral damage that, in a high percentage of cases, will result in mental retardation of varying degree. In addition, congenital infections such as syphilis, toxoplasmosis, and cytomegalic inclusion body disease may lead to significant cerebral destruction and, more often than not, to mental retardation. Blood-group incompatabilities also must be considered as hazards in the neonatal period. Certain maternal variables contribute importantly to perinatal central nervous system damage leading to retardation; age and parity, prematurity, postmaturity, inadequate prenatal care, precipitate or otherwise complicated delivery, and placental abnormalities all increase the likelihood that the newborn will suffer significant neurologic damage. From this point on, the brain may be subjected to a variety of infections and traumatic, metabolic, and neoplastic insults that can lead to permanent damage and to varying degrees of organically determined intellectual deficit.

A neurologist may deal with the problems of the mildly retarded, or, perhaps more accurately, intellectually handicapped child, as well as with more severely retarded children. The rubrics "brain damaged," "cerebral dysfunction," and others have been applied to children, and less frequently to adults, whose intellectual and behavioral performances are aberrant but not necessarily retarded, although academic achievement almost always is interfered with. Because of academic failure, such children often are considered mentally retarded or seriously disturbed emotionally or both. Certainly, continued academic frustration and misplaced parental and teacher pressures may lead to significant, complicating emotional disturbance. Also, erratic behavior, inattentiveness, hyperactivity, short attention span, and bewildering inconsistencies in performance may reinforce the impression of retardation. At the present time, facilities for the teaching of the nonretarded, brain-damaged child are even more lacking than they are for the frankly retarded.

The specific learning disabilities, the development dysphasias, dyspraxias, and perceptual motor disabilities that are responsible for the learning failures of these children can and should be suspected from neurologic history and examination. Often the obstetrical and perinatal history points to some delay in motor development. Colic, restlessness, poor sleep, and febrile seizures are frequent. Language development is slightly delayed or incomplete. Articulation defects of speech are a common complaint. Histories suggesting minor seizure disorders are common. Difficulty in learning to dress, to ride a bicycle, and to play hand–eye or rhythmic games is reported often. Driven behavior, hyperactivity, short attention span, and lack of concentration and inconsistent academic performance disturb and bewilder parents and teachers.

Rigid adherence to the traditional neurologic history and examination more often than not will result in failure to detect organic involvement in the minimally brain-damaged or dysgenetic child. Pediatric neurologists gradually are developing an appreciation of the so-called soft signs and symptoms that may indicate cerebral dysfunction. Careful observation and examination of this group of children produce a wide spectrum of neurologic findings. Taken out of the clinical context of performance and history, these varied neurologic signs can easily be dismissed as nonsignificant. They include awkward gait with abnormal carriage of the upper extremities and inequality of the normal associative arm-swing. Frequent stumbling, slight loss of balance on sudden change of direction, poor tandem-walking, and difficulty in standing on one foot alone complete the soft signs detectable by observing gait and station. As the child undresses (and later dresses), it may be observed that he has more trouble with buttons, sleeves, and shoelaces than would normally be expected for his age. Right and left shoes are confused, raising a suspicion of dressing dyspraxia. The child may have difficulty in comprehending instructions and may show motor perseveration or synkinesis. Rapid succession movements of both upper and lower extremities may be poorly done. Check and rebound are often slightly abnormal or asymmetrical. Minimal inequality of reflexes, pubo-adductor, tibio-adductor, and crossed adductor responses may be observed.

Examination of the cranial nerves may reveal minimal extraocular muscle weakness and difficulty in establishing or breaking ocular fixation. Awkward, incomplete control of tongue movements suggests tongue dyspraxia or cortical sensory involvement of the tongue. Sensory examination frequently points to problems in spatial orientation that may involve intrapersonal or extrapersonal space or both. Right–left disorientation; delayed face–hand discrimination; finger agnosia; difficulty in the reproduction of geometric figures; and alterations in weight, size, and shape discrimination may be detected. Further investigation often will show problems in coloring within outlines and directionality- and laterality-confusions in paper and pencil work. Mixed hand–eye–foot preference is often part of the picture but is not an essential component.

Evaluation with a wide variety of psychologic test instruments should be undertaken of children whose histories and examinations contain a number of the deviations noted above. Efforts to delineate more accurately and to ascribe proper significance to these subclinical findings are the conjoint task of neurologist and neuropsychologist. From such cooperative efforts come individualized programs of training or retraining. Probably no other area of neurology, psychiatry, psychology, or education suffers more from lack of firm basic information, on the one hand, and from hastily evolved, pre-conceived formulations, on the other. It is highly improbable that any currently proposed single technique of evaluation or system of training will prove to be a panacea for the brain-damaged child.

It is essential to bear in mind that the presence of neurologic deficit is not necessarily of major significance in the management of the immediate clinical problem. The proper weighting of organic and environmental factors becomes a very real obligation of the neurologist who, curiously enough, often can and should minimize the significance of organicity in the clinical management of the mentally retarded. However, from the point of view of furthering our understanding of cerebral function and its relation to intellectual performance, these same soft signs may be of great importance. This touches on an area of great concern to the neurologist in his efforts to understand better the organic substrate of intelligence or the lack of it. How do nature and nurture interact? What proportion of the variance of the polyvariant form of so-called socio-cultural retardation can be attributed to disturbed neural function? These are questions falling well within the field of the neurologic sciences and clinical neurology.

Clinical neurology always has been concerned with mental retardation, inasmuch as neurology, as a discipline, never has taken very kindly to a dualistic philosophy. Regardless of the religio-philosophic position, the evidence that the brain is, at least, the organ of the mind has been accumulating steadily for centuries. Certainly from a medical point of view, mental retardation cannot be divorced from the neurologic sciences and from clinical neurology.

### REFERENCE

JOHN CHADWICK and W. N. MANN (Trans.), *The Medical Works of Hippocrates* (Oxford: Blackwell Scientific Publications, 1950).

# 5

# Diagnosis in Infancy and Early Childhood

RICHARD A. KOCH

## Introduction

Past epidemics of typhoid fever, plague, diphtheria, smallpox, and the like have led to the development of high-caliber health services in the United States. With the resolution of many of the problems posed by contagious disease, members of the health professions have turned their attention to other fields, such as prenatal care, child health, mental health, and care of the aged. Within these programs, services to the mentally retarded have been provided as part of over-all health services to the family, but only during the past few years have comprehensive diagnostic services been made available for evaluation of the retarded child (Hormuth, 1957). This came about because of the realization that mental retardation is a chronic, handicapping condition affecting 3 per cent of the population, and is, thus, an important public health problem (President's Panel, 1962). The extension of diagnostic services to the mentally retarded by the Children's Bureau in 1954 was stimulated, in part, by the National Association for Retarded Children through the Maternal and Child Health Services of state and local health departments. The decision to place the use of mental retardation funds within this framework resulted from the recognition of the important role of high-quality prenatal care in the prevention of mental retardation and in the need for early identification and adequate evaluation of retarded children during their preschool years.

The physician is often the first professional person to suspect the presence of mental retardation in a young child (Illingworth, 1960; Levinson and Bigler, 1960). His initial approach to diagnosis is often crucial in initiating treatment, early parent-counseling, and use of proper community resources. Unfortunately, too often the physician does not know the cause for the mental retardation in any one child, can offer little, if any, specific therapy, and cannot forecast future development precisely. In such circumstances, it is natural for parents to seek further diagnostic help and counsel. The reasons for "shopping" for additional diagnostic help are many, but the two major ones are the dissatisfaction of the parents with the physician's initial appraisal of their child and the impact of mental retardation on a family in our society (Kirk *et al.,* 1955).

Diagnosis is not an end in itself. It is the beginning of realistic planning by parents and professionals. The skills of many disciplines are required for comprehensive planning for a handicapped child. An interdisciplinary approach (Gardner and Nisonger, 1962) to the problems posed by handicapped children, especially the mentally retarded, can offer integrated help to the parents at the community level. The core team needed for such an evaluation of a preschool child is composed of physician, psychologist, social worker, speech and hearing consultant, and public health nurse. Obviously, during the school years the skills of the special educator are essential.

Though most types of retardation are irreversible, a few preventable forms do exist and may respond to medical measures if treatment is begun early in infancy (Hsia, 1959). For this reason, a thorough medical evaluation performed by an experienced physician and including a careful medical history, physical examination, and certain laboratory procedures, is essential.

## The Medical History and Physical Examination

The medical history should focus on the known predisposing causes of mental retardation, such as familial factors, maternal age, prenatal rubella, Rh incompatibility, prolonged labor, and perinatal distress. Particular attention should be paid to gestational age, birth weight and length, condition of the placenta and cord, causes of neonatal anoxia, the need for resuscitation, and perinatal convulsion and lethargy. Infection, jaundice, respiratory distress, feeding difficulty, or listlessness often are early clues. Infants with mental retardation are classified often as "very good babies" because of their inactivity. The failure to attain the usual developmental landmarks may be the first sign to alarm parents. Age of smiling, rolling over, sitting alone, standing, walking, feeding self, talking, and toileting are usually well

remembered by parents, at least in relation to siblings or other children.
Lack of speech development, inattention to sound, and increased visual
alertness suggest the presence of a hearing disorder. Early smiling and
awareness, but slow motor development, usually indicates cerebral palsy.
Normal development, followed by regression at nine to eighteen months,
should alert the physician to degenerative, amino acid, or emotional disorders.

Although the history is of great value, it is often the physical examination that is of crucial importance. Measurements of head circumference,
transillumination, height, and weight should be recorded routinely. Head
shape is of importance in craniostenosis, subdural effusion, hydrocephalus,
and microcephaly. Visual defects are common, and examination of the
fundus must never be omitted. The presence of retinal degeneration, papil-
ledema, retinoblastoma, cataracts, or other ocular anomalies is of great importance. It must not be forgotten that the eye is simply another dimension
of the central nervous system.

Dental dysplasia should be noted. Changes of the enamel of only the
lower central incisors may indicate a prenatal insult of sufficient magnitude
to cause cerebral dysfunction. Dysplasia of the enamel of all incisors is
associated commonly with natal damage, and generalized enamel dysplasia
is usually a result of postnatal disease such as meningitis. Timing of significant events in the medical history by examination of the teeth in this manner can be helpful in counseling.

Webbing of the neck, widely spaced nipples, and undescended testes
may indicate a chromosome disorder. Certain syndromes, such as Down's
syndrome (mongolism), can be recognized by visual inspection of the face
or extremities. Two syndromes have been described that can be recognized
easily by visual inspection. The Cornelia de Lange, or Amsterdam Dwarf, is
characterized by odd facies, heavy eyebrows, limb anomalies, and profound
mental retardation. Similarly Rubenstein's syndrome includes abnormal
facies, flat thumbs, flat great toes, mental retardation, and ocular disorders.
These syndromes are genetic in origin, and proper recognition is important
for counseling of parents. The presence of one congenital anomaly—for
example, a cardiac anomaly—should alert the examiner to look for another. Hepatosplenomegaly is an important finding. A large liver, jaundice,
and cataracts indicate the need for examination of the urine for galactose to
validate a diagnosis of galactosemia, an enzyme disorder of carbohydrate
metabolism. Sometimes a large spleen is one of the earliest signs of Niemann-Pick, Tay-Sachs, or Gaucher's disease, or some of the chronic infectious diseases acquired prenatally, such as cytomegalic inclusion body disease and toxoplasmosis.

Careful examination of the extremities includes the palmar creases
and fingerprints. The so-called four-fingered line (a single crease across the

palm instead of the usual two) may be associated with such syndromes as Down's, *cri du chat,* and other central nervous system anomalies. Examination for fingerprint patterns is useful. Ten ulnar loops on the fingertips usually are found in association with Down's syndrome. An excessive number of arches is found in chromosome 18 trisomy and of whorls in the *cri du chat* or Deletion V syndrome. Skin changes are important. Eczema frequently is associated with phenylketonuria, telangiectasia with ataxia-telangiectasia syndrome, dry chapped skin with Down's syndrome or hypothyroidism, and adenoma sebaceum with tuberous sclerosis. Of course, neurologic changes are looked for in any child with mental retardation. It is beyond the scope of this chapter to detail the interpretation of various neurologic findings. Suffice it to say that the presence of such findings increases the physician's impression that the cause of retardation in the particular child is organic.

Other useful aids that should be utilized by the physician in judging the presence or absence of neurologic signs are the psychologic examination and the electroencephalogram. Developmental tests in younger children are helpful and, as interpreted by the psychologist, may suggest an organic base for mental retardation. Electroencephalographic changes are common in brain-damaged children; however, a normal electroencephalogram does not rule out organic brain damage, nor does an abnormal one necessarily indicate brain damage. Since the interpretation of the electroencephalogram varies with the interpreter, physicians are urged to utilize their clinical judgment and not to depend on any single examination.

## LABORATORY PROCEDURES

The use of laboratory procedures varies a great deal. In many clinics, a routine blood count, urinalysis, urine for phenylpyruvic acid, electroencephalogram, and skull roentgenograms are performed. In addition to these studies, it is our practice to perform a tuberculin skin-test, urine amino acid study, and an X ray of the wrist for skeletal bone age determination. If the bone age is retarded, a blood protein bound iodine test is performed to rule out the presence of hypothyroidism. Buccal smear and chromosomal analysis are not done routinely. Further diagnostic studies, such as spinal puncture, pneumoencephalogram, or ventriculogram, rarely are indicated unless progressive neurologic changes occur. A urine test for cytomegalic inclusion virus culture is obtained in infants with multiple defects. A toxoplasma dye test is done in infants and young children whenever indicated by history or suspicion of the family history. Table 5–1 outlines the relationship of the commonly used tests to specific abnormalities and certain disease states.

TABLE 5–1. *Relationship of Specific Laboratory Tests, Results, and Type of Disease Exhibiting Such an Abnormality*

| SPECIFIC LABORATORY STUDY | ABNORMALITIES | DISEASE ASSOCIATED WITH RETARDATION OF GROWTH OR DEVELOPMENT |
|---|---|---|
| routine blood count | severe anemia | (1) iron deficiency<br>(2) lead poisoning |
| fasting blood sugar | low (30 mg.%) | (1) hypoglycemia<br>(2) leucine-sensitive hypoglycemia |
| serum<br>  calcium and<br>    phosphorus | elevated calcium<br>elevated phosphorus<br><br>low calcium | (1) idiopathic hypercalcemia<br>(2) renal insufficiency<br><br>(1) tetany<br>(2) pseudo-hypoparathyroidism |
| nonprotein nitrogen | elevated | (1) renal insufficiency |
| blood-protein iodine | elevated (over 9 ug.)<br>low (less than 4 ug.) | (1) hyperthyroidism<br>(2) hypothyroidism |
| serum phenylalanine | elevated (over 15 mg.%) | (1) phenylketonuria |
| red-cell galactose-1-phosphate content | elevated | (1) galactosemia |
| urinalysis | galactosuria<br>albuminuria | (1) galactosemia<br>(1) Lowe's syndrome |
| urine phenylpyruvic acid | phenylpyruvic acid | phenylketonuria |
| aminoaciduria | gross | (1) phenylketonuria<br>(2) galactosemia<br>(3) Lowe's syndrome<br>(4) lead poisoning<br>(5) Wilson's disease<br>(6) Hartnup's disease |
| | specific amino acid abnormality | (1) maple syrup urine disease<br>(2) other rare diseases, such as histidinemia |
| urine polysaccharide test | positive | (1) gargoylism (Hurler's disease) |
| urine for virus culture | presence of specific virus | (1) cytomegalic disease |
| electroencephalogram | convulsive pattern<br><br>hypsarrhythmia | (1) convulsive disorder *grand mal, petit mal,* psychomotor, etc.<br>(1) myoclonic |

TABLE 5–1 (*continued*)

| SPECIFIC LABORA-TORY STUDY | ABNORMALITIES | DISEASE ASSOCIATED WITH RETARDATION OF GROWTH OR DEVELOPMENT |
|---|---|---|
| skull X rays | large | (1) hydrocephalus |
| | small | (1) microcephaly |
| skull X rays | calcifications | (1) toxoplasmosis |
| | | (2) cytomegalic disease |
| | | (3) craniopharyngioma |
| | | (4) tuberous sclerosis |
| | | (5) parasitic infestation |
| skull X ray | suture separation due to increased pressure | (1) brain tumor |
| | | (2) subdural hematoma |
| skull X ray | suture abnormality | (1) cranio-stenosis |
| skeletal bone X ray (wrist) | retarded bone age | (1) hypothyroidism |
| | cortical structure of bone | (1) Hurler's disease |
| skeletal bone X ray (wrist) | lead lines | (1) lead poisoning |
| | increased density | (1) hypercalcemia |
| skeletal bone X ray | absent fifth metacarpal | (1) Down's syndrome |
| X ray of pelvis | flaring of ilium | (1) Down's syndrome |
| routine tuberculin | positive | (1) look for tuberculous focus rule out early meningitis |
| electromyogram | abnormality | (1) myopathy such as glycogen storage disease |
| spinal puncture | increased cells | (1) occult infection |
| | increased protein | (1) degenerative disease |
| | decreased sugar | (1) hypoglycemia |
| pneumoencephalo-gram | cerebral anomaly | (1) congenital defect |
| cerebral angiogram | cerebral anomaly | (1) vascular anomaly |
| ventriculogram | cerebral anomaly | (1) brain tumor or congenital anomaly |
| chromosome analysis | | |
| trisomy 21 | abnormal facies, muscle tone, etc. | (1) Down's syndrome |
| trisomy 16–18 | multiple | (1) congenital anomalies |
| trisomy 13–15 | multiple | (1) congenital anomalies |
| partial deletion | abnormal cry | (1) *cri du chat* |

### The Developmental Evaluation of the Child Less Than Three Years of Age

In the preschool child who presents slow development, one of the formal developmental tests should be performed. The Gesell Scales are most widely used in the United States; a somewhat similar scale, the Griffith Scale, is used in England. The Catell Scale is useful also, although it professes to indicate the result by intelligence quotient (IQ), a practice that most workers dealing with preschool children have abandoned. In my opinion, the developmental test scores should not be considered to predict future intelligence quotients. So many factors affect intellectual progress that it is immediately apparent that it would be hazardous to judge future intelligence by applying any measuring technique during the early years. Stable home environment, good mental and physical health, personality, opportunity for intellectual stimulation, security, discipline, and so forth contribute to intellectual growth.

But in spite of the limitations on predictive accuracy, developmental testing is a useful procedure. It provides a method for judging the rate of progress of a young child, and this is particularly helpful in counseling parents. It is important to have documentary evidence of progress that is understandable to parents. In our clinic, one of the parents is asked to hold the child on his lap during testing and often to participate in the testing procedure. This provides maximal opportunity for the child to cooperate with the examiner. Often, it is obvious to the parents at what rate the child is progressing. Once a developmental age has been obtained in months, this value is divided by the chronologic age in months, and the result is multiplied by 100, giving a Developmental Quotient (DQ). The developmental age is a useful concept on which to base counseling concerning readiness for certain activities such as toilet-training, feeding methods, discipline, and other developmental tasks.

Developmental testing, when performed by a competent observer, can be utilized as a neurologic tool. Head control, hand–eye coordination, hand usage, coordination, presence of tremors, dominance, vision, hearing, vocalization, and personality can be observed during the testing. Which parent holds the child, the parental reaction to success or failure in various items, the child's satisfaction in accomplishment, attention span, and the ease with which rapport is established are also important observations. Ronald S. Illingworth (1960) has emphasized the value of developmental testing in assessing the rate of progress of mentally retarded children. For these reasons, the physician should utilize such tests in his physical examination procedures in order to appraise fully the child and his situation. In our clinic, both the pediatrician and the psychologist utilize these procedures.

Even the well-trained specialist in child development or the public health nurse will find certain items useful in judging developmental ability.

## The Interdisciplinary Approach

An accurate evaluation incorporates not only medical findings but also psychologic, educational, and social factors, enabling all concerned to view the patient and his family as presenting a single, though complex, problem. This makes the team approach more useful than a single-discipline approach, particularly when dealing with handicapped individuals, where many community, social, and health facilities necessarily are involved. The clinic team functions under the leadership of the pediatrician, each member contributing to the therapeutic experience of the child and family. The findings of the team are coordinated by the physician to provide comprehensive evaluation and diagnosis. He communicates the findings to the family and helps them to plan for continued care. He remains a source of continued contact for the family.

In our clinic the child psychiatrist and the neurologist are utilized by the pediatrician as consultants. The role of the child psychiatrist is to aid the pediatrician in diagnosis and in counseling. This is particularly helpful when both organic and behavioral factors complicate the evaluation of a child functioning at a retarded level. The older the child, the more imperative it is that psychiatric consultation be available to the primary physician. The psychiatrist helps not only to assess the seriousness of the emotional symptoms but also to implement a psychiatric referral if he himself is not available for therapeutic intervention. The psychiatrist also can play an important role in inservice education of the clinic staff by teaching members of other disciplines to be more aware of the importance of emotional factors and by explaining the dynamics involved in problem families.

The role of the clinical psychologist is to assess the mental capacity of the child by means of appropriate psychologic tests and to appraise the personality factors that are crucial in planning the habilitative program for a child. He may participate in counseling as indicated. The social worker helps the parents to find ways of solving problems of adjustment that they may not be able to solve by their own efforts. His role is a delicate one, for acceptance of the child's condition by the parents often results from his patience, sustained interest, and skill in enabling them to gain greater insight and understanding. In the initial evaluation of the child, the social worker contributes important knowledge of the functioning of the family in which the child lives and an assessment of the family's ability to carry out recommendations by the team. Invaluable to the family's morale are the visits of the public health nurse, whose contact with the parents of the men-

tally retarded child will encourage his best possible care and management at home. She also brings to the team an assessment of the home management of the child and assists the parents in carrying out team recommendations.

Neurologists, speech and hearing clinicians, nutritionists, teachers, physical therapists, laboratory technicians, and various medical specialists contribute their skills and knowledge to consideration of the problem. Although parents must be encouraged to accept all the responsibility that they can, the various professional disciplines must furnish integrated support if the child is to develop to his fullest potential. Since retarded children usually require care for many years beyond the span of normal childhood, parents who inform themselves as well as they can and attain objectivity about their children are in a better position to coordinate all of the facts and to apply them to the best advantage of the child (Yannet, 1956).

## THE TRAVELING CLINIC PROJECT IN SOUTHERN CALIFORNIA—A DEMONSTRATION DIAGNOSTIC CLINIC

As an outgrowth of a long-term study of the mentally retarded child and his family by the staff of the Child Development Project of the Children's Hospital of Los Angeles (Koch *et al.,* 1962), Children's Bureau funds were allotted to the Project to establish a traveling diagnostic clinic service to operate in public health settings. The service was designed not only to serve retarded children but also to demonstrate to local professional personnel ways of meeting the needs of the retarded child and his family in his own community. Utilizing consultation and service from the staff of the Project, local health departments in Southern California have begun to sponsor services to the mentally retarded in their jurisdictions (Leckner, 1964; Schild *et al.,* 1962).

The services being instituted in Southern California consist of demonstration clinics that are held in local communities and offer a diagnostic and evaluation service to the child and his family. The clinic team consists of pediatrician, social worker, psychologist, and public health nurse. Working closely with the team members are their professional counterparts in the local community. All clinic staffings are teaching clinics for local professional personnel. It is expected that the people of the community will be encouraged to assist the family to maintain the child in his home whenever feasible by these demonstrations of methods to help the retarded child and his family. As the demonstration period in each health jurisdiction ends, similar services are continued by local health personnel. To date, clinics have been established in Southern California cities within a hundred-mile radius of Los Angeles (for example, Santa Ana, Pasadena, Long Beach, San Diego, Van Nuys, South Los Angeles, and San Bernardino). In addition, services have been extended periodically to rural communities as much as 350 miles from Los Angeles, for example, Bishop, Bridgeport, Ridgecrest, and Santa Maria (Ragsdale *et al.,* 1961).

During the first five years of the demonstration, 705 children were evaluated. The average age at referral was two and one-half to three years. Most were referred to the clinic by physicians and health department personnel. The diagnoses made are too numerous to mention, except in broad categories (Table 5–2). Some significant facts, however, need further dis-

TABLE 5–2. *Various Diagnostic Categories in 705 Children Evaluated by a Multidisciplinary Diagnostic Team*

| CATEGORY | NUMBER OF CHILDREN | PER CENT OF TOTAL |
|---|---|---|
| normal | 50 | 7.1 |
| neonatal asphyxia | 19 | 2.7 |
| birth injury, mechanical | 9 | 1.3 |
| congenital cerebral defects | 137 | 19.4 |
| Down's syndrome | 122 | 17.3 |
| premature birth, with associated encephalopathy | 42 | 6.0 |
| encephalopathy (cause unknown) | 32 | 4.5 |
| familial mental retardation | 36 | 5.1 |
| environmental deprivation | 27 | 3.8 |
| normal intelligence: but with | | |
| 1) hearing handicap | 10 | 1.4 |
| 2) visual handicap | 4 | 0.6 |
| 3) maternal deprivation | 10 | 1.4 |
| 4) behavior disorder | 55 | 7.8 |
| major personality disorder (such as autism, schizophrenia) | 22 | 3.1 |
| mental retardation without encephalopathy (cause unknown) | 55 | 7.8 |
| miscellaneous diagnoses (kernicterus, Hurler's, PKU, etc.) | 75 | 10.7 |

cussion because they have implications for the kinds of diagnostic services needed for mentally retarded children. Congenital cerebral defects accounted for 19.4 per cent of the total number. Down's syndrome (mongolism) was the largest single entity in this group (17.3 per cent). More than thirty different diagnostic entities fell into the miscellaneous group, each of them containing fewer than five children. Phenylketonuria occurred in 0.7 per cent of the patients, hypothyroidism in 1 per cent, and hypoglycemia in 0.7 per cent.

Of special interest are conditions considered to be "psychogenic" in origin. Cultural–familial mental retardation accounted for 5.1 per cent (this figure is extremely low in relation to national figures and probably is related to our sources of referral as well as to motivational factors of this group in seeking care through usual medical channels). Environmental deprivation caused by hearing- or visual-handicaps accounted for 2 per cent; and functional mental retardation associated with or caused by emotional disturbances, 7.8 per cent. Mental retardation associated with or caused by psychotic disorders such as autism occurred in 3.1 per cent.

Of great importance to physicians are those diagnoses, 17 per cent of our case load, in which mental retardation is associated with encephalopathies resulting from prematurity, toxemia of pregnancy, postnatal injury, prenatal infections, and postnatal cerebral infections. Whereas direct cause-and-effect relationship between the prior condition and the retardation sometimes is difficult to establish, the diagnostic experience of the Child Development Project supports similar findings of other workers, suggesting that mental retardation is significantly associated with these conditions (Lesser, 1963). Public health workers already were concerned with these maternal- and child-health problems before mental retardation received its present emphasis in program planning. The recognition that mental retardation can be another unfortunate sequela of these conditions underlines the importance of maternal- and child-health programs (Knobloch *et al.,* 1956).

The diagnostic experience and the planning with families for the care of their children have impressed the clinic workers with the importance of three things: early and adequate diagnosis and evaluation; home care of the young retarded child; and expansion of health services, private and public, to prevent conditions with which mental retardation is associated.

## EARLY AND ADEQUATE DIAGNOSIS AND EVALUATION

The young child whose development is slow or who has a condition with which retardation may be associated should receive prompt medical evaluation. The evaluation should include psychologic assessment, and the family should be offered counseling and sustained support by the social worker and the public health nurse. When children have emotional problems, there is great need for knowledgeable psychiatric services. We learned that young children need to be seen over an average of eighteen months, for at least three clinic visits, before the presence of mental retardation can be established or disproved with certainty and the degree of retardation, if present, can be determined. Intelligent plans for the child's future cannot be made until this assessment is completed. Time is needed for performance of diagnostic procedures, institution of medical therapy, correction of associated handicaps, and parent-counseling. This permits the child to develop further and to demonstrate any benefits of parental and professional efforts. In addition, early diagnosis and treatment are absolutely essential for best results in those conditions, such as phenylketonuria, hypothyroidism, and craniosynostosis, where prevention of the associated mental retardation is possible. These points can best be illustrated by case histories.

A child with Apert's disease, an inherited syndrome consisting of coronal synostosis, cleft palate, beaked nose, exophthalmus, and syndactyly, was conceived during the mother's convalescence from infectious hepatitis. The child was first seen at nineteen days of age, at which time it was felt that surgical correction of the synostosis was possible. This was accomplished without incident. Subsequently, cleft-palate repair and multiple plastic procedures on the hands were performed. The parents were very distressed by the problem, and the social worker was able to help them work through their feelings about having a severely handicapped child who was also retarded. Other workers had not been so encouraging. One surgeon refused to perform plastic surgery, indicating that "it wasn't worthwhile"; institutional placement had been advised by other workers. With continued support from the clinic personnel, the family made a good adjustment. The child entered a special class for educable retarded children in the public school where she also received speech therapy. This case illustrates the good results of early diagnosis and evaluation, adequate medical treatment, and sustained support for the family. If untreated, the course of Apert's disease is usually one of progressive blindness and mental retardation as a result of craniosynostosis.

The parents of a child with congenital anomalies of the eyes, celiac disease, and seizures were discouraged to the point of considering placing the child outside the home. At eight months, the boy's weight was eight pounds; he had made little developmental progress; large malodorous stools were noted; synechiae between the cornea and conjunctivae had developed, with resultant scarring. When seen at the Child Development Clinic, he was hospitalized for eyelid surgery, placed on a diet for patients with celiac disease, and treated with phenobarbital for his seizures. His subsequent course was spectacular. He attended public school, was found to have an intelligence quotient of 120, and was seizure-free. Early and continued medical care uncovered the superior intellectual potential of this "pseudo-retarded" child.

The diagnostic experience of the Child Development Clinic parallels fairly closely experience in the rest of the nation with the problem of mental retardation, as outlined by the Report of the President's Panel on Mental Retardation (President's Panel, 1962). Most of the diagnoses do not, within our present state of knowledge, represent a clear-cut etiology that would indicate preventive measures or medical treatment. For these conditions we can offer only early diagnostic attention, habilitative measures when indicated, and support to the family. A small percentage of conditions, on the other hand (for example, phenylketonuria, galactosemia, and hypothyroidism), yield readily to treatment.

The conditions that do offer additional promise of prevention are those with which health services already are concerned. In our clinic experience, 17 per cent of the diagnoses made relate to prematurity, complications of pregnancy, postnatal infections, and postnatal injuries. That mental retardation, as well as other handicaps, is related to these problems is clearly recognized (Lesser, 1963; Poole, 1963). Also well recognized is the relationship of these conditions to the socio-economic level of the parents (Lesser, 1963). By and large, the women most likely to bear damaged children are the economically and culturally disadvantaged in our population. The people in these groups are almost entirely dependent on public medical and health services, if indeed they utilize any services.

One example from our case load will illustrate many of these points. This child, a thirty-month-old boy, may or may not have been retarded. He was found by a public health nurse who was making an epidemiologic investigation in his home. The parents were recent arrivals to the city from the rural South. Their educational level was low. The father worked as a day laborer. There were four children in the family, and the mother babysat with an additional seven children each day to augment the family income. The mother had no prenatal care during any pregnancy. The patient had a history of premature delivery resulting from *abruptio placenta*. At age four months, the baby was admitted to the hospital with severe diarrhea and was critically ill for one month. At one year, he was admitted again with meningitis. At this time, he was suffering with severe anemia resulting from his prematurity. The parents did not return for follow-up care after his discharge. He had cerebral palsy, a slow developmental pattern, and may be said to have been culturally deprived. Planning additional medical care was difficult as the family car had to be used to transport the father to work. The mother was immobilized by the difficulty of using public transportation while carrying the patient and accompanied by small children. In addition, the family could ill afford to give up the income from babysitting. The deterrents to medical care for the child were the same deterrents to prenatal care for the mother.

This case illustrates some of the difficulties in planning programs of prevention of mental retardation. However, more important, it dramatizes the need to consider the entire maternal- and child-health program as the service unit in planning programs for prevention for this group of culturally and economically disadvantaged families. Clearly, the complications of pregnancy can be helped by the obstetrician; but if the pregnant woman does not go to the physician, there is little that can be done. Well-child supervision by the obstetrician would help to prevent many of the health hazards of infancy and childhood; but the child must be seen, and the family must learn to value and utilize medical advice.

How can maternal- and child-health services be developed or better organized to provide preventive care to the populations most in need of it? Belle Dale Poole has considered this question:

> Changes in traditional public health services seem to require more intellectual and emotional energy than the initiation and development of completely new programs.
>
> It may be necessary for the health department to abandon the unrealistic concept of service to a large and undefined segment of the community and to concentrate on the application of available knowledge to specific groups in the community (Poole, 1963).

The experience described of providing diagnostic services to 705 mentally retarded children underlines the importance of early diagnosis and the need for new types of health services for especially susceptible segments of the population. Health services have the responsibility for case-finding, assistance with evaluation of the retarded child, assistance to families caring for retarded children at home, and planning better community services for the retarded, including prevention, correction of handicaps, and family guidance.

## REFERENCES

William I. Gardner and Herschel W. Nisonger, "A Manuel on Program Development in Mental Retardation," *American Journal of Mental Deficiency* (Monograph Supplement), LXVI (1962), 1–192.

Rudolph P. Hormuth, "Community Clinics for the Mentally Retarded," *Children,* IV (1957), 181–185.

David Y-Y. Hsia, *Inborn Errors of Metabolism* (Chicago: The Yearbook Publishers, 1959), pp. 107–112, 132–137.

Ronald S. Illingworth, *The Development of the Infant and Young Child, Normal and Abnormal* (Edinburgh and London: E. & S. Livingstone, 1960).

Samuel A. Kirk, Merle D. Karnes, and Winifred D. Kirk, *You and Your Retarded Child* (5th ed.; New York: Macmillan, 1955).

Hilda Knobloch, Rowland Rider, Paul Harper, and Benjamin Pasamanick, "Neuropsychiatric Sequelae of Prematurity, A Longitudinal Study," *Journal of the American Medical Association,* CLXI (1956), 581–585.

Richard Koch, Betty Graliker, Karol Fishler, and A. H. Parmelee, Sr., "Mental Retardation in Early Childhood: A Study of 143 Infants," *Postgraduate Medicine,* XXXI (1962), 169–177.

Eleanor J. Leckner, "The Public Health Nurse in a Program for the Mentally Retarded," *Children,* XI (1964), 70–74.

A. J. Ledden, "Current Problems of Maternity Care." The First Annual Jessie
    M. Bierman Lecture in Maternal and Child Health, University of Califor-
    nia, Berkeley, May 1963.

Abraham Levinson and John A. Bigler, *Mental Retardation in Infants and
    Children* (Chicago: The Yearbook Publishers, 1960).

Belle Dale Poole, "What of Tomorrow, Maternal and Child Health Pro-
    grams," Paper presented at the Third Biennial Public Health Nursing Con-
    ference on Mental Retardation, Children's Hospital of Los Angeles, May
    1963.

President's Panel on Mental Retardation, *A Proposed Program for Na-
    tional Action to Combat Mental Retardation* (Washington, D. C.: Govern-
    ment Printing Office, 1962).

Nancy Ragsdale, Sylvia Schild, and Richard Koch, "The Child Develop-
    ment Project," *California's Health,* XVIII (1961), 177–180.

Sylvia Schild, et al., *A Demonstration Project Utilizing Child Development as
    the Focus for Community Interaction with a Local Health Department*
    (Washington, D.C.: U.S. Department of Health, Education, and Welfare,
    1962).

Herman Yannet, "Mental Deficiency," in S. Z. Levine (Ed.), *Advances in
    Pediatrics,* VIII (Chicago: The Yearbook Publishers, 1956), pp. 217–257.

This work was supported in part by a grant from the Children's Bureau and the
Mental Retardation Branch of the United States Public Health Service, Department of Health, Education, and Welfare, Washington, D.C. I wish to express my
appreciation to several members of the staff of the Child Development Clinic of
the Children's Hospital of Los Angeles for their assistance in the preparation of
part of this chapter.

# 6

# Recognition of Mental Retardation in the School-Age Child

## EDGAR A. DOLL

Under compulsory universal education all children attend school during some part of their life. In some states the compulsory age limits are from eight to sixteen years, in others from six to eighteen years. Permissive age limits may be from six to twenty-one years and may include children of kindergarten age or even nursery-school age. Thus, the range of ages for public schooling may be from as low as two or three years to as high as twenty-one years. If the school district conscientiously enforces compulsory education, or is generous in its program of permissive attendance and services, all but the most severely handicapped children will attend school during childhood and adolescence. Some school districts, alert to the problems of new enrollments, conduct pre-enrollment surveys. Others, still more alert, provide preschool evaluation and home advisory services as early in life as a significant disability may have been detected by physicians, parents, or other agencies. Provision for public education thus is extended to all children of school age, including many types of handicapped children such as those with visual impairments, hearing loss, orthopedic and neuromuscular disabilities, emotional disturbances, and mental retardation. This means that all mentally retarded children are seen by the schools at some time prior to maturity, except, perhaps, the most severely retarded or those with severe multiple handicaps.

The mentally retarded child is assumed to have been delayed in his

mental development or to be in the process of such delay. This delay may
be evident in some instances at birth and in others not until late in the
school career. Typically, the severe varieties of retardation, such as those
with cranial malformations, gross physical disabilities, or readily recognizable diagnostic syndromes will be evident at birth or in early infancy. These
conditions usually will have received pediatric attention, and some of these
patients may be so severely retarded that the possibility of public-school
attendance is substantially nil. Children with teratoid anomalies, for example, rarely enroll at school. Other severely retarded children, including
some from the categories just mentioned, may be capable of school attendance with varying degrees of profit. Still others, and these constitute the
majority, will not be detected as retarded until the time of school enrollment, while a smaller group will not be diagnosed until early adolescence.
Secondary or adventitious circumstances leading to mental retardation,
such as accident or illness (trauma, infection, deprivation), may occur at
almost any time in the developmental period.

Provision for mentally retarded school children varies widely from district to district and from state to state. Even where provision is adequate,
enforcement may be lax. For example, New Jersey makes mandatory provision for "children who are educable, those who are trainable, and *those
who are neither.*" The last group, presumably, permits no children to be
bypassed. Yet, even in New Jersey, the enforcement of this provision depends on the resources provided by the communities and the counties to
carry out the intent of the law.

Although our schools today are increasingly conscious of their social
responsibilities, they generally do not favor the enrollment of retarded children with marked physiognomic embarrassments. The presence of such
children at school is distressing to other pupils, to teachers, and to the retarded themselves. Neither are many schools enthusiastic about enrolling
children with very severe degrees of retardation. For centuries, the philosophy of education has been essentially academic. Many districts merely tolerate the even marginally mentally retarded because they constitute a drag
on the regular classroom or require exceptional provisions that yield only
meager academic returns.

Mental retardation is a condition with many facets, and effective treatment requires the collaborative resources of many scientific disciplines.
Each discipline tends to conceptualize mental retardation in terms of its
own special knowledge and professional purposes. Thus, the public schools
tend to see mental retardation in terms of reduced educability. However,
educability is likely to be conceived traditionally or provincially. In spite of
a half-century of vigorous progress in this area, there still is reluctance to
acknowledge and discharge our educational responsibilities toward the
mentally retarded child of school age. This is partly because of limited
awareness of the nature of mental retardation, its prevalence among school

children, and its sometimes obscure symptomatology. The teacher has no difficulty in discovering the academic slow learner, but encounters many subtleties in determining the causes of poor learning. Being literate herself, she finds it difficult to identify with people who prove unresponsive to literate instruction. Accustomed to accepting intelligence as a universal trait, she is puzzled by its lack in some pupils. The slow learner may be judged lazy or stupid. The ordinary school child is assumed to be academically able, a characteristic that hardly describes the mentally retarded pupil.

It is easy to see why teachers might have little patience with those students who profit little from academic instruction. The teacher somewhat grudgingly admits, if pressed, that some learning may take place independently of formal literate instruction in the classroom; but she tends to disparage such learning and to call it training. In the systematic philosophy of education, there are clear differences between education and training as discrete modes of learning. By education the teacher usually means the acquisition of formal knowledge, the ability to generalize, to transfer learning from one modality to another, the creative or imaginative aspects of learning, the ability to deal with abstractions, the capacity for thinking. In contrast, training is considered to be a mode of learning that is characterized by concreteness, repetition, and drill, without necessarily any increase in knowledgeability, insight, or generalization. In fact, both these kinds of learning are parts of the total process of education. We like to think that the majority of us are educable as defined above; whereas, in fact, most of us lean toward being only trainable.

Mental retardation in the schools should receive just as conscientious and competent interdisciplinary attention as in any other social setting. If we define the mentally retarded person as one who, by reason of constitutionally determined subnormal mental development, will be incapable at maturity of self-direction and support independently of guardianship or supervision, then the need to establish a prognostic as well as a diagnostic determination of the condition becomes apparent and imperative. We may formulate a series of criteria to be satisfied before a diagnosis of mental retardation is to be established.

*Social Inadequacy*　This is the point of departure without which our professional concern would be merely academic. Until this criterion is satisfied in fact, rather than by assumption, the diagnosis is only tentative. This criterion can be satisfied in a number of ways, of which the use of the Vineland Social Maturity Scale has been demonstrated to be practicable, quantitative, and verifiable.

*Mental Inadequacy*　It must be showed that the social inadequacy derives from mental inadequacy and, more specifically, from inadequacy of intelligence and the faculties of judgment and reasoning. The measurement must be valid, or presumed to be so, on the basis of psychometry that is adequate in terms of reception and expression as will be described later in relation to pseudoretardation. The measurement also must be prognostic of ultimate maturational attainment.

*Developmental Immaturity*  The mental functioning must be developmentally (maturationally) delayed or arrested during the normal period of growth and development. This requirement distinguishes amentia from dementia and allows for the vagaries of maturational irregularity.

*Obtaining at Maturity*  Since social and mental adequacy are functions of age and maturation, their determination prior to maturity requires prognostic interpretation. We consider children to be socially dependent until their assumption of full personal responsibility at maturity (early adulthood). Such prognosis must reckon with those etiologic and environmental influences that determine or affect the course of personal maturation, barring untoward events that cannot ordinarily be foreseen.

*Constitutional Origin*  The maturational criteria (social, mental, developmental) are presumed to be grounded in the biologic structure and function of the organism as a stable whole. Traditionally, mental retardation has been viewed as a relatively stable condition that can be assessed or predicted within certain limits by sufficiently sophisticated workers employing proper procedures. This essential stability, disregarding minor temporal instability, is presumed to derive from the constitutional (organic) structure of the person, as opposed to adventitious environmental circumstances, except as the latter influence the constitutional attributes more or less permanently.

*Irreversibility*  In the light of present knowledge, mental retardation is essentially irreversible. This does not deny the possibility of prevention or amelioration; but though many therapies and other maneuvers have been hailed, few have survived the test of time. Preventive measures—especially preconceptional, prenatal, natal, and early postnatal—have had some limited success; but adequately diagnosed mental retardation probably never is reversed to normal.

School people tend to oversimplify the recognition of mental retardation at school, emphasizing intelligence and effort as the only crucial factors in learning, without recognizing the importance of the other maturational aptitudes of the person. By relying too strongly on the measurement of intelligence and grossly oversimplifying its interpretation through such devices as the IQ, we underestimate the importance of special abilities or disabilities such as language, visual and auditory perception, neuromuscular facility, psychodynamic integrity, and, in general, the over-all neuropsychology of learning. We divide the mentally retarded into the educable and the trainable, with an ingenuous disregard for the contradictions involved. Typically, we are not concerned with the clinical differentiation of various types of mental retardation (other than, perhaps, Down's syndrome), but base our "diagnoses" on cut-off scores of continua for particular traits, rather than on the syndromic synthesis of those scores and traits. Prognoses are based too often on a fallacious theory of IQ constancy that, although approximately true for the average, does not apply to individuals. The very use of "educable" and "trainable" is implicitly invidious, and there is an obvious disparagement of the latter as compared with the former. We ignore the overlapping of specific traits in dissimilar categories, and lightly change our "diagnoses" from category to category with incidental changes in trait-ratings, so that the "educable" become "trainable" or vice versa with the rise and fall of IQ.

Typically, the mentally retarded public school child is deficient in academic learning. This deficiency is attributed implicitly to a corresponding deficiency in intelligence. But, although the retarded are slow learners, the obverse may not be true, even in the presence of poor intelligence. Many school psychologists are equipped inadequately to make differential syndromic diagnoses and to determine etiologies. Yet prognosis and treatment require these clinical differentiations. These are achieved under school auspices through a descriptive inventory of manifold measurements, utilizing all testing methodologies appropriate in the psychologic examination, interview data, and histories.

Among the characteristics of the mentally retarded are their general inability to deal with abstractions, generally limited resourceful judgment, low degree of imagination, and impoverished capacity for purposive thought. These are prime requisites for learning and adjustment in the public-school setting. The experienced teacher is alerted quickly to shortcomings in these qualities as revealed in the classroom. She recognizes the retarded child as one in need of individual attention, but she also finds him only feebly responsive to personal counsel or instruction. Several courses of action are open to her. She can carry the child along as a slow learner, without analysis or attempts at effective remedy or support. This course results usually in a "promotion" or transfer to some other teacher. She can give the retarded pupil individual attention during or after normal classroom hours. This is usually only palliative and merely delays more specific action. It also cheats the other members of the class by using time and energy properly due them. She may assign the dull child to some bright child for special support or tutorial assistance. She may request his transfer to a room of generally slower pace than her own. She may make an "evaluation," using educational procedures suitable for diagnostic teaching, such as standardized achievement tests to provide information for educational concentration. Any or all of these maneuvers only postpone the day of reckoning for the retarded child. As a result, he may be graduated from the eighth grade without being recognized as retarded, or he may become a drop-out or may be excused or suspended or even expelled for lack of suitable progress. Such pupils are embarrassments and hindrances in regular classrooms. Without special facilities, school administrations often become desperate enough to evade responsibility.

However, if the school has special education resources, including, perhaps, school psychologists, school social workers, speech therapists, nurses, and remedial teachers, the alert teacher, on finding a slow learner, reports this to her principal. They confer and review the pupil's cumulative record, including medical reports and other specialists' reports. If there are no medical reports, the nurse seeks to obtain them, including pediatric, ophthalmologic, audiologic, dental, neurologic, and psychiatric records, as may be desirable or feasible. The social worker canvasses the family situation and musters agency support if indicated.

Ultimately, the pupil and these data reach the school psychologist whose primary interest in mental retardation is its relation to poor learning and adjustment at school. His function is to validate the evidence gathered about the learning and behavior of the possibly retarded child, for purposes of remedy. He analyzes the data retrospectively and currently, observes the child, administers various aptitude tests, collates reports that may substantiate the referral problem, analyzes possible general and specific etiologies, and proposes a regimen designed to bypass, mitigate, or overcome the apparent difficulties.

The school psychologist's review of the problem develops a number of psycho-educationally relevant hypotheses. He explores these through observation, inference, and estimation, and then amplifies them by applying pertinent standardized evaluation procedures. He assures himself that the ordinary avenues of experiential reception and expression are intact in the child or that they are impaired. The evidence obtained, for example information about sensory adequacy, language facility, intellectual adequacy, dynamic freedom, motivation, energy output, skills, subject-matter attainment, and the like, may itself contribute to the ultimate diagnosis.

The school psychologist will look for explanations in terms of diagnostic categories as well as inaptitude and disability inventories. He is alert to the possibility of pseudoretardation, which includes the following symptom-patterns that resemble or simulate mental retardation. *Subcultural status,* a marginal level of normal adequacy, is related to familial inheritance and reinforced by cultural-economic deprivation or social "disadvantagement." *Academic retardation,* which is unsuccessful scholastic or literate attainment, results from specific verbal symbolic learning inaptitudes loosely or falsely identified as mental retardation. *Language deficiency* is a limited aptitude for abstract verbal facility in ideational communication exchange. This oligophasia or dysphasia may obscure or distort the valid estimation of intelligence that typically is accomplished through literate verbal psychometry. Language deficiency also reduces the effective understanding of and response to conversation, printed, or written interchanges. *Neurologic disorders,* which include central nervous system interference with normal organic function, may disrupt the ordinary stimulus–response mechanisms. *Psychopathologic manifestations,* such as the broad categories of mental disorder, belong to the realm of neuropsychiatry. These mental disturbances may be manifested by such symptoms as agitation, confusion, depression, autism, or any of a long list of conditions that mask or misrepresent sound mental measurements and functional learning or behavior. *Orthopedic conditions,* which are neuromuscular impediments to normal behavioral expression, conceal potential through imperfect coordination. *Sensory deprivations,* which reduce or prevent the reception of sensory experience, may therefore prevent appropriate reactions. Mild sensory impairments are easily overlooked and their consequences inadvertently discounted. *Somatic embarrassments* impose health and low vitality barriers on the usual "drive" or normal behavior. These include nutritional and metabolic (including endocrine) influences on personal adequacy. These categories are not mutually exclusive. They overlap, not merely as multiple handicaps, but as intricately correlated variables, and may, of course, be present in persons who also are genuinely mentally deficient.

How are these differentiations accomplished? All determinations deal first with particular behavior symptoms. The number, the degrees, and especially the patterns, presumptive origin, and course of these symptoms constitute the symptom-complex. This usually is not determined by one or even a few pathognomic indications. We are not concerned with functional mental retardation independent of clinical mental deficiency. Functional mental retardation might be determined by simple psychometry that provides an IQ score, but this might be invalid because of any of the obscuring factors noted above. An IQ might provide no reliable index for diagnosis, etiology, or prognosis, and does not justify an otherwise unproved diagnosis.

The business of the schools is instruction. That business is seriously embarrassed by psychobiologic obstacles to learning. Sensory imperception, psychodynamic distortions, receptive and expressive difficulties in language are only a few of these obstacles. The tendency toward categoric labeling also adds to the confusion. Terms such as "brain damaged," "emotionally disturbed," or "neurotic" seem to offer more help than they really do. Moreover, these labels do not belong in the school psychologist's book; they belong to the neuropsychiatrist. There is no real substitute for a point-by-point evaluation of all aptitudes and disabilities developmentally perceived. Mental retardation rarely exists merely as simple intellectual subnormality. As an over-all constitutional hypoplasia, it encompasses many other aspects of developmental maturation. This is true even in the absence of the more severe accompaniments, such as associated cerebral palsy, epilepsy, mental disturbances, diabetes, rheumatic fever, and so on.

Traditionally, our schools have been committed to an open-ended system of education, designed to prepare for living and a livelihood, but without specific parameters. In the case of the mentally retarded, the outlook for successful living and livelihood will be limited. Current talk about preparing the mentally retarded for independent competitive living refers only to the psychometrically subnormal and not to the clinically mentally deficient. We have obscured the essential social inadequacy of the mentally deficient retarded by combining them with the psychometrically dull normal retarded. In all our history, the prime criterion of mental deficiency has been social insufficiency at maturity. In attributing this limitation to intelligence alone, we have combined the socially inadequate retarded with the socially adequate retarded. There is appreciable overlapping in the various criteria that delineate the differences between these two groups.

The teaching of the retarded child requires attention to (1) learning mechanisms, (2) education versus training, (3) realistic goals, (4) future transition to adult living, (5) detection of special abilities to be exploited and disabilities to be bypassed. Both an appreciation of the clinical syndrome and an inventory of the assets and deficits of the individual child are required to meet the needs of effective educational planning and a suitable prescription of curriculum, methods, and materials. The clinically deficient child ultimately will require social guardianship; whereas, the merely psychometrically retarded may enter competitive employment and pursue independent living. The mentally retarded pupil will deal with concrete ideas and learn from repetitive drill and example; whereas the merely dull child will master simple generalizations, will learn from precept as well as example, and will have compensating occupational aptitudes for his scholastic inaptitudes. In short, the curriculums will differ in their objectives as well as in the dynamics of classroom discipline.

The educational management of the mentally retarded child should be based on a prediction of educability that may hold true from school entrance until school separation, or may be revised in course. Because of the slow learning and the frequently associated maladjustments that are characteristic of the mentally retarded school child, it is impracticable to provide for him in ordinary classrooms. To do so is unfair to the normal students, to the teachers, to the retarded children themselves, and to the parents of both groups. Special class placement need not be derogatory, nor does it limit the prospect of the child's profiting from instruction. On the contrary, such special placement enables the retarded pupil to achieve a sense of belonging, to experience success, to maintain social self-respect, and to benefit profitably from instruction suited to his needs. Such instruction will be vocational and social, as well as academic.

The education of the more severely retarded will emphasize the training aspects of self-help and the mastery of certain social amenities. Such academic education as is offered may be in the nature of training, as in the acquisition of work-recognition skills or the rote of arithmetic. The so-called educable student also will benefit from training. He does not have a great capacity for insight in the comprehension of scholastic knowledge, and, for him, a work-experience program is indicated that will increase the likelihood of successful, semicompetitive, supervised employment.

## Summary

We have indicated how a referral for evaluation is usually made from the classroom teacher and the principal, relating to a problem that is most commonly one of learning or behavior, and that requires special study of manifestations and etiologic factors. This referral is processed through (1) teacher interview, (2) cumulative school record, (3) parent interview (and usually home visit), (4) psycho-educational examinations for achievement, social adequacy, intellectual level, dynamic and perceptual deviations, language facility, and so on. As the evaluation proceeds, the resources of other disciplines are called on as needed, for example, family physician or pediatrician, ophthalmologist, audiologist, speech pathologist, and school social worker, and the other representatives of the "clinical team."

In this program, the "team" is not formally organized as a conventional group (which might not include specialists critical to a given case, such as orthopedist, dentist, cardiologist, neurologist). Nor do these specialists confer as a team staff. Rather, the referrals to specialists are made as required by the more general members of the group, and the reports are rendered to them. In some instances, referrals are received for preschool children and in others from agencies other than school personnel (family physician, specialist, welfare agency, court). In the former instance, the child is treated as a prospective pupil and, in both instances, is processed through school channels as a pupil with problems.

Obviously, the most serious problem is how to obtain early referrals. Too often the referral is not made until unhappy consequences have become so grave as to constitute a crisis for the child and the family. This is often too late for effective management, and much preventive or ameliorative treatment time has been lost. This represents a problem of continuing public education, not only for school personnel, but for specialists and agencies who might find the school a source of ancillary treatment or at least a help in avoiding aggravation of problems. The schools are learning gradually that the old stitch in time may save even more than the classical nine. The child with sensory impairment in vision or hearing, with remediable health problems, with predisposition to behavior difficulties or emotional involvements is in need of early detection and sympathetic management even before actual school enrollment.

The current nation-wide movement for attention to the mentally retarded has many antecedents in the history of modern education. That such attention has thus far been insufficient need not weaken our hope that the

time may come when the retarded child will be welcome at all schools and
will receive the optimum benefits of the education to which he is entitled in
a democracy. The public school stands as a major rallying center for all
aspects of child health and development, not merely mental health and
mental retardation. Let us use it to the fullest advantage.

# PART II

## The Emotional Impact
## of Mental Retardation

# 7

# The Mentally Retarded
# and The Family

## MICHAEL J. BEGAB

In its diverse forms and complex dimensions, mental retardation is probably first and most importantly a family problem. To some families it is a tragedy of utmost magnitude, and its effects are disillusionment, despair, and disruption. To other families it is a crisis, more serious than most perhaps, but capable of resolution in time and without harmful self-sacrifice. To still others, it is not a problem in itself, but is merely one element among many in the daily struggle for social survival.

Parents of the mentally retarded come from every walk of life, although the large majority are among our most disadvantaged people. Whatever their status or the severity of the child's handicap, almost invariably we may predict a significant and lasting effect, not necessarily adverse, on the lives of other family members. Even the child whose parents are no more intelligent than himself is a source of potential conflict in the home or community that may further chain the family to its deprived living conditions.

Neither mental retardation nor parenthood, then, has the same meaning to all parents. Even husband and wife may differ in outlook. In assessing the impact of mentally retarded persons on family life and selecting the treatment plan that seems most promising, each situation must be handled individually. Much depends on parental experiences during their own childhood; on their income, education, and culture; on their religious beliefs and value system; and, perhaps most important, on the stability of their marital relationship. The appearance of the child, too, his degree of disability, and the pattern of his behavior will influence family adjustment. Nor can the attitudes of relatives, neighbors, and the larger community be overlooked,

These variations in families, children, and communities, and the countless combinations in which they interact point up the folly of stereotyped approaches to mental retardation problems. Even where clinical conditions are identical—for example, with mongoloids of the same age, mental ability, behavior pattern, and physical health—the response and adaptation of families may differ widely. Many want to and can keep the child at home, while some will find daily care of a child with gross stigmata too disturbing. Special medical needs may be resolved by one family through private residential care; another may lack the resources for such placement and may be unwilling or unable to secure public care. And, more often than not, the area where a family lives and the resources available in that community will dictate the course of action to be followed.

With these qualifications in mind, the problems presented by retarded individuals, as they relate to family life, can be categorized in various ways: (1) psychologic and emotional reactions and their impact on family stability, (2) practical problems of care and management, (3) educational needs in guidance and training, and (4) planning for future care. The problems that will predominate in a specific family depend on the factors mentioned earlier. For many, several effects bear down with equal impact on family stability and integrity.

## EMOTIONAL PROBLEMS

Most of the literature and research on the emotional problems associated with mental retardation has been done in medical or psychiatrically oriented settings. Clinical observations and findings have focused primarily on the severely impaired or on the less handicapped with central nervous system damage (Farber *et al.*, n.d.; Group for the Advancement of Psychiatry, 1963). In nearly all instances, the intellectual disparity between parents and retarded child is marked. The reactions noted bear little resemblance to those in families in which the child's mental endowment approximates that of other members.

Disregarding the latter families for the moment, what does the birth of a retarded child mean to average parents and to their normal children? In a child-centered culture such as our own, the meaning of parenthood is influenced greatly by social values and the expectations that we have for our children. Our emphasis on physical and intellectual prowess causes a retarded child to represent a threat to the self-esteem of his parents, placing them at a distinct disadvantage in facing many of life's routine experiences. In the "backyard" comparison of infant development and achievement, these parents have few sources of gratification and many sources of anxiety and embarrassment. When the reasons for the child's developmental lags are not fully understood, the child may be consciously or unconsciously punished for his comparative deficiencies, pushed toward achievements beyond his capacities, or overprotected to such a degree that growth is stifled.

Parents think of children as extensions of themselves, and they are assailed with feelings of self-doubt and guilt when their offspring is glaringly imperfect. Although guilt may not be the universal reaction it sometimes is purported to be, it is extremely common; few persons reach the stage of parenthood completely free of guilt-producing experiences. Seldom does a child reach adulthood without earning his parent's disapproval and a consequent sense of unworthiness. Sex behavior, in particular, because of our cultural taboos and the need to repress both our thoughts and activities in this area, is an important source of guilt feelings. The relationship to mental retardation is aptly expressed by Benjamin Spock:

> And sex also happens to be the origin of babies. So the inevitable guilt left over from childhood—about touching the genitals, about sex play with others in early childhood, about petting in adolescence, about sexual thoughts in all stages of childhood—is stored up in a compartment of our conscience, all ready to beset us if there is anything wrong with our child . . . As if this weren't enough, the conscientious obstetrician adds another link to the chain of potential guilt by prohibiting intercourse for such a long period before childbirth that a fairly large percentage of couples probably find themselves disobeying occasionally (Spock, 1960, p. 25).

The physician and other professionals toward whom parents are likely to turn for help should recognize that guilt and its common corollaries of shame and depression are not verbalized or elicited readily. But the symptoms are there for the careful and patient observer to see. They are evident in the withdrawal of parents and child from social contacts, in the parents' extreme overprotectiveness and overindulgence, in their pervasive mood of lethargy, chronic sorrow, hopelessness, and immobility. Parental guilt often is most intense when the retarded infant is the product of an unplanned and unwanted conception. In this situation, unlike similar pregnancies resulting in normal children, defenses tend to crumble. Hostility toward the child or toward each other, where either parent was an unwilling partner to pregnancy, gives rise to excessive and unrealistic guilt.

The ability of parents to mobilize their energies in constructive ways, to make use of medical prescriptions and recommendations about various aspects of care and training, frequently rests on the successful resolution of these feelings. A single counseling session, especially when feelings are deeply rooted or long enduring, will hardly ever suffice. Reassurance that the child's handicap is not hereditary (where this is, in fact, the case) or the result of any acts of commission or omission by the parents can be of help, but this usually requires several interpretations and opportunity for ventilation and possibly vindication. This takes time. So do other efforts at assuaging guilt, such as universalizing the problem, emphasizing the therapeutic potentialities of their child's condition, and redirecting their energies toward emotionally rewarding activities. Sometimes these objectives can be facilitated by referral to a local association of parents of mentally retarded children. Knowing that they are not alone and that others have found successful solutions to seemingly insurmountable problems can markedly change the parents' outlook.

It is not uncommon for parents to harbor death wishes toward their retarded child or to wish otherwise to be rid of him, especially as he gets older and the problems more burdensome. The repression of such feelings may be manifested by psychosomatic complaints. Or, reaction formation in the form of overprotectiveness toward the child may take place. The physician can be a convenient scapegoat should he appear unconcerned about a minor illness in the child. An irritable response by the physician, justifiable and very human in other circumstances, can reinforce this unhealthy adaptive mechanism. It is important that he understand the underlying dynamics involved and help the parents recognize that their wish to be rid of their child is neither unusual nor unacceptable.

Another common reaction to mental retardation, especially during the initial phase of adjustment, is to deny that the handicap even exists (Kanner, 1953). Denial is a basic form of self-protection against painful realities. Some parents literally close their minds to the child's limitations. "He is lazy; he doesn't care; he could do more if he really tried." Denial symptoms are expressed in many ways, and they often are potential sources of exasperation to the physician. Some parents are preoccupied with the one or two things the child does well and completely ignore all other functions performed poorly. Others cannot "hear" the diagnosis despite repeated interpretation, ask skeptical questions, and shop around from clinic to clinic looking for magical cures. Still others stress the child's associated physical defects and are oblivious to his mental limitations.

The "hope that springs eternal in the human breast" is frequently a corollary to the denial mechanism. Hope and reality are not necessarily incompatible. Even when the outlook for the child's future progress is dim, interpretation must be tempered with sympathy and understanding. Failure to do so may drive parents to further "shopping" and to depression. True, unrealistic hope can make parents the target of charlatans; but, properly harnessed, it can be a force for positive action. They must be protected from today's unfounded claims, yet assured that when an effective therapy is discovered, they will be the first to be informed.

In the face of severe and prolonged handicap, denial may become completely irrational and self-blame too threatening to endure. The tendency is to project blame elsewhere: to the obstetrician for an allegedly incompetent delivery or prematurely induced labor, to the pediatrician for improper treatment of infection or injury, or to the teacher for deficiencies in education and training. Nor are the parents themselves "target free," especially when an unstable marital relationship antedates the child's defect. The husband blames the wife; the wife, the husband, and no suspect apple on the family tree escapes accusation. Such projections are a potential source of friction between parents and physicians, or other professionals. The parents can become so absorbed in this scapegoating process that they have little energy remaining to meet the child's needs. Feelings must be resolved if treatment is to progress. Recognition that the anger of parents against professional workers is not personal can prevent counter-hostility. In an accepting climate, the parents can regard the question, "Why did this happen to me?" with greater detachment and can accept the generally true observation that "It can happen to anyone."

Not all of the feelings and defenses outlined here are experienced by all parents, nor are they characterized by the same intensity or duration. For the most part, these reactions are not pathologic, but are normal responses to intense ego-frustrating experiences. In time, many parents are able to acknowledge maturely their child's condition and to adjust satisfactorily. Much depends on their ability to compromise on limited goals, on their emotional and spiritual reserves, and on the help that they get from professional and community resources.

The range of parental attitudes is influenced also by etiologic factors and the time that the symptom of retardation first appears. An important distinction may be made between genetic causes and "environmental accidents." Although in both instances parents may fear future pregnancies, in the former the fear has a more realistic basis and can be predicted mathematically. Genetic counseling can be of help, not only to the parents, but as it may relate to the as yet unborn offspring of their normal children. Some parents may regard the "odds" to be too risky. Adoption is often a suitable alternative. Knowledge of and referral to reputable child-placing agencies by the physician can be highly therapeutic. The time of onset of symptoms is also important. The child who is born physiologically normal but becomes damaged later in life still may arouse guilt feelings in his parents. This is not associated, however, with the dynamics of "creation," and is generally less deep-seated and is therefore easier to handle. They may, however, need considerable help in accepting their child's severely reduced capabilities and in modifying their goals and expectations.

A primary, though exaggerated, concern of parents to which professionals frequently contribute is the effect of a retarded child on other children in the family. Advice to place the child away from home in the interest of the normal children is made too routinely and often is ill-founded. True, many instances can be cited of the harmful effect of a retarded child on his brothers or sisters, but these are in the minority. Positive effects on the normal child also have been noted (Kramm, 1963). Children largely reflect the feelings of their parents. If the parents are unashamed of the retarded child, the normal children are likely to be so, too. In one study, only 15 per cent of the families reported significant emotional disturbances among the normal children (Holt, 1958). Some of these children were extremely resentful of the attention given the retarded child; others resorted to attention-seeking devices; and still others withdrew from social contacts or attempted to compensate for feelings of deprivation by total absorption in their schoolwork. Rarely was parental rejection of the normal child complete. And, considering how often the danger of imitative behavior is proposed as a basis for placing the retarded child outside the home, it is significant that in this same study only one family out of 201 reported this to be a problem.

The attitudes of parents and siblings toward the retarded child are the most crucial to family adjustment, but the imprint of the larger community cannot be ignored. Feelings of aversion and nonacceptance toward the retarded still characterize public thought and discourage families from social contacts. Neighbors stare and make unkind, if unwittingly so, comments; complain about the retarded child's behavior; and refuse to let their normal children play with him. And, of course, friends of the retarded child's siblings can be equally heartless in their remarks and actions. The emotional hurt experienced by some parents is difficult to endure. Many seek escape from painful and embarrassing questions in social isolation, sometimes self-imposed. If they can be drawn into church- and civic-sponsored social activities, these problems can be lessened.

These comments on the psychologic reactions and social problems of families of retarded children suggest the potentially disruptive impact of these children on family life. But this is by no means the entire problem. Problems in care and management, too, sometimes distinct from, yet often interrelated with, feelings and attitudes, often are involved.

## CARE AND MANAGEMENT

The problems presented are directly related to the degree of dependency in the child. Among the severely handicapped, many require nursing care around the clock. They cannot walk, bathe, dress, or feed themselves. Some require constant care, not only during waking hours, but also at night. Such burdens cannot be long endured by parents without help. The health of the mothers, who usually bear the brunt of care, can be affected drastically. They may suffer from chronic fatigue, and occasionally verge on mental breakdown. Sometimes older sisters are pressed into service as "second mothers" to share the burden. The effect can be character-building, but there is also the risk of denying the normal child the usual pleasures and activities of childhood.

The care of children with associated physical defects and continuing medical needs is a severe financial drain. Extra costs are involved in seeking medical advice and treatment for some, and training and recreational opportunities for others. Even the cost of board and lodging, from which parents of normal children usually obtain relief when the children are grown, may continue indefinitely. Not uncommonly, the depletion of the family's resources may have far-reaching consequences on its mobility, earning power, and education level. Problems of care are heightened also in many instances by the unwillingness of parents to leave their retarded children in the care of strangers. In such circumstances, husband and wife seldom go out together and have little chance for relaxation and relief. The behavior and developmental growth patterns of the profoundly and severely retarded often present management problems, as well. Sensorimotor handicaps may interfere with the development of self-care skills, and bowel- and bladder-training may be difficult, not only because of the child's limited comprehension, but also because his nervous system has not matured sufficiently to permit voluntary control over these functions.

Management techniques based on concepts of normal growth patterns, even with a modified timetable, are likely to prove unsuccessful in many instances. While these children generally follow the normal basic sequence of sitting, crawling, walking, and talking, they do so at different rates, and some developmental steps may be missed entirely. Concepts of normal growth are even less appropriate when applied to psychologic, social, and sexual frames of reference. The severely retarded seldom progress beyond a mental age of four years. Often their psychosocial development, too, is fixed approximately at this level. Their common preoccupation with bodily needs, masturbatory behavior, temper outbursts, and negativism are characteristic of the behavior of young children. Some are wholly oblivious to common dangers. All of this is a source of anxiety and embarrassment to parents, and it cannot be remedied easily by the corrective measures and diversionary tactics that succeed with young normal children. Constant supervision is a physical impossibility for most parents. In some respects, the management of the severely handicapped is less burdensome than that of the less retarded child. For the most part, problems are confined to the orbit of family life. With rare exceptions, the severely retarded are not a threat to the safety of others, have little sex drive or interest, and usually lack the capacity for reproduction. Whatever management problems they present stem largely from their prolonged and total dependency and need for constant protection and supervision.

No clear lines of demarcation can be drawn in problems of care and management between subgroups of retarded persons based on intellectual criteria alone. Nevertheless, behavioral dimensions tend to expand as intelligence increases, bringing into play a host of additional factors such as personality, interest, motivations, likes, and dislikes. The presence or absence of central nervous system pathology can be another important factor. Where pathology exists, behavior is often excitable, unpredictable, or uncontrollable. Frequently, the individual is hyperactive, aggressive, or destructive, and has difficulty in conforming to externally imposed controls. Not all brain-damaged children, however, exhibit this so-called classical syndrome of behavior. Many are placid, hypoactive, responsive, and tractable and can be taught acceptable conduct. Most are self-centered, have low tolerance for frustration, and tend to seek immediate satisfaction of needs. Some strive constantly for attention or are demonstratively affectionate. These traits are common but are neither universal nor inevitable. The management problems presented can be corrected by some of the same techniques used in modifying similar behavior in young normal children (Dittman, 1959).

Concern about delinquent behavior or sexual misconduct in moderately retarded adolescents or adults seldom is well founded. These individuals, in contrast to many of the mildly retarded, do not understand the impropriety of such behavior or foresee its consequences. Where damage to persons or property is involved, their behavior is more likely to be unintentional than willful. In more serious crimes, rarely repeated, the behavior usually can be traced to instigation by more intelligent peers. Sex misbehavior also is relatively uncommon in this subgroup. The moderately retarded young man is seldom sexually assaultive; the young girl, infrequently an object of exploitation. Many never mature sexually and have little interest in or understanding of heterosexual relationships. Some of these persons do show normal development and desires, however. Because of their poor judgment and controls, they need close supervision for the protection of themselves and others. Successful management of this behavior, as is the case also with more favored peers, occasionally requires residential placement.

## Guidance and Training

Many of the family problems described thus far apply primarily, but not exclusively, to the young retarded child, to the period following recognition of the child's defect, whatever his age, or to the older child whose underdevelopment places him behaviorally in the preschool age group. The educational needs of parents, however, especially as they relate to guidance and training, are in a state of constant flux. As the child passes each developmental milestone, new crises may arise. School brings new social relationships, competition, and for the mildly retarded whose mental impairment is not yet identified, frustration, and failure. Puberty and adolescence, troublesome for most youngsters, may present special problems for the parents of the mildly handicapped, yet paradoxically few for parents of the severely handicapped. Adulthood poses new demands for economic and social self-sufficiency and other obstacles that the retarded person and his family must hurdle.

Parents lack the guidelines by which to measure a retarded child's growth and are additionally handicapped in child-rearing by the uneven rate of development that characterizes many of these children. They are puzzled when their ten-year-old compares physically to others his age, reasons like a five-year-old, behaves socially on a seven-year-old level, yet responds emotionally with the temper tantrums of a three-year-old. None of the usual bases for assessment—chronologic age, mental age, social maturity—suffice by themselves to guide the parent–child relationship. Consequently, expectations often are unrealistic, and the child is pushed beyond his capacities or is needlessly held back.

Many young retarded children need special guidance, not only in learning to care for personal needs, but in the improvement of their physical appearance and social mannerisms. Such guidance is a function of all parents, but their ability to fulfill it in these cases may be sorely taxed. To teach the retarded child good grooming, the social amenities, proper habits, and self-care skills requires patient supervision, repetitive training, a high level of frustration tolerance, and considerable energy. The burden of early training rests primarily with the mother, but not all are equal to the task. In these families, the father and older siblings frequently must share the responsibility. In this total family involvement, focus on the retarded child to the exclusion of the interests of other family members must be avoided, but neither must the retarded child be shoved into the background. Achieving the proper balance of the needs of all is not a simple matter and may require professional intervention. The public health nurse and the child welfare worker are especially well suited to this task.

Guidance for the parents is no less vital than for the child himself, for it is within the orbit of family life that the child is taught the "social-mindedness" characteristic of later life. Here he learns right from wrong, consideration of others, respect for property, and how to share. To create an atmosphere most congenial to this development, parents need educational as well as therapeutic services to help them carry out their child-rearing functions. Attention to these problems in the early phases of family adjustment can prevent more serious difficulties later in life.

The slower growth rate of retarded children often means an unchanging role for the parents. For example, the normal child of six to twelve begins to identify with his playmates in behavior, dress, grooming, and language. He forms secret clubs and in every way practices social organization and group living. Although he still looks to his parents for basic security and moral guidance, the influence of the school, church, and other social institutions becomes more and more important. Acceptance by and responsibility to the group become of fundamental value. In contrast, retarded children lack the social and emotional maturity at this age to form group identifications. Even when social relationships are available, too frequently they are painful and frustrating rather than character-building. This places an even greater burden on parents in the promotion of healthy personalities, a burden that they must continue to carry beyond early childhood.

For many parents, the onset of puberty in their child is a signal for panic. If the adolescent has few constructive outlets outside the home and is bored, the problem of parental supervision is amplified. Should there be a heightened interest in boy–girl activities, parental concern for the youngster's protection is understandable. Parents wonder how much, if anything, the child should be told about sex, and often they tell him nothing, thereby sometimes unwittingly contributing to the problem. Neighbors may express uneasiness about the youngster even when his overt behavior is above reproach. That these concerns stem from uninformed parental and social attitudes is apparent, but this makes the problem no less real.

Parental constraint about sex education seems to be shared by schools, institutions, and professionals as well, for seldom is sex hygiene and development or heterosexual relationships a part of the formal curriculum. Yet it is wholly unrealistic to expect these individuals, especially those with mild retardation, to understand proper codes of conduct with the opposite sex without some form of preparation. Most of the retarded can learn about menstruation and other bodily functions, the development of secondary sex characteristics, social responsibilities, masturbation, and acceptable dating behavior. The professional counselor can help parents discharge these educational functions or can assume the role himself where insecurity, lack of understanding, or anxiety does not permit the parents to do so.

The likelihood of sexual misconduct among the retarded is probably more pronounced in the disadvantaged family, particularly if the behavior of the parents is itself suspect. The retarded youngster is not likely to incorporate society's codes when these conflict with the observed patterns of his parents. Here, intensive efforts at character re-education are essential. But even when parental behavior is acceptable, the environmental stress to which retarded children are exposed heightens their vulnerability. In an atmosphere of impoverishment and limited outlets for status and acceptance, sex can easily be equated with affection and recognition. This, too, can be corrected, but the solution does not lie in outmoded concepts of segregation and control. Treatment and guidance aimed at building up self-esteem and inner controls are more likely to have constructive consequences. Although the risks are real, the fear of sexual misconduct among retarded adolescents and adults is highly exaggerated. The important consideration is that such behavior stems from a wide range of environmental hazards rather than from low intelligence in itself. Viewed in this context, this particular family problem may cause less alarm.

## Planning the Future

Many mildly retarded youngsters, especially those who are free of neurologic defects or serious emotional pathology, leave school, find jobs, get married, become parents, and lose their identification as retarded persons. Some make a final vocational adjustment and need outside help only during periods of social stress. For the less capable, however, the future seems full of uncertainty to the parents. The prospect that they will achieve some measure of financial security and social prestige, even with ample education and training, is remote.

The trend toward keeping the retarded in their own homes and communities, although desirable, is, nevertheless, a source of chronic stress to the parents. Even for the most adequate parents, today's successes often are marred by tomorrow's uncertainties. "Who will look after my retarded child's interests when I am gone or can no longer do so myself?" The deep concern and anxiety reflected in this often-repeated question are well founded. Parents of retarded children realize perhaps better than anyone else the self-sacrifice and dedication often entailed in their care. They cannot expect, nor indeed are many willing, to burden other members of the family with the often trying responsibilities of supervising a retarded adult. They hesitate to seek the assistance of friends and fear to rely on strangers, whom they regard as lacking in personal interest and understanding.

With advances in the medical sciences resulting in an increased life expectancy of the retarded, more and more parents are faced with the likelihood that their children will survive them. The problem is compounded by technologic advances in industry, automation, and the frequent movement of families from one community to another. These social changes, taxing the capacities of the handicapped adult for independent functioning and social usefulness, have brought into sharp focus the need for safeguards in case of parental death, disablement, or inadequacy. It is apparent that even some of the less disabled cannot be expected to conduct many commonplace activities, for example, negotiation of contracts or decisions regarding medical care, employment, and marriage, with "ordinary prudence and judgment." These individuals need social and legal protection and personal guidance.

Various plans are available to parents, and all of them are to be preferred to premature placement that deprives the retarded child of valuable growth-promoting experiences. Some parents can work out satisfactory arrangements with private institutions for lifetime care by setting up trust funds to cover support and other costs. Others have joined large-scale group insurance programs to provide for the child's future maintenance. Still others recognize the need for guardianship of person and estate, and they make such designation by last will and testament.

Sometimes the need for guardianship stems not only from the incapacities of the retarded person but also from the inadequacies of his parents who are still living. Some parents lack the skill or resources to meet the physical, emotional, or behavioral problems of their retarded child and are not responsive to professional guidance. Where these conditions prevail, society, through its established agencies and social institutions, has a responsibility to protect the individual's interest and rights. The need for guardianship in these cases should be evaluated carefully and reviewed periodically, not only with respect to the retarded person's changing capacity for self-reliance, but also to the environmental circumstances that may have dictated the arrangement in the first place. Guardianship is one of the least often employed, yet perhaps most effective, protections of the retarded person's future. Properly applied, it can shield parents from needless anxiety and enable them to mobilize their energies toward the resolution of immediate and pressing family problems (Begab and Goldberg. 1962).

## The Limited Family

Many of the emotional and practical problems discussed earlier do not apply to the large number of retarded children whose intellectual defects do not set them apart from other family members. The problems encountered in these families are attributable largely to deficiencies in child-rearing and external pressures of the community. Here, guilt seldom is evident in parents and there is little anxiety, ego-threat, or despair about the future, at least for the reasons described earlier. Problems are more likely to be precipitated by the child's failure in school, conflicts with neighbors, child neglect and abuse, and limited work skills and earning capacity. These problems are the core, the cause, and the consequence of many of our social ailments. Mental retardation is considered to be of secondary importance by these deprived families, and, in truth, other factors often are more debilitating. These children seldom are brought to medical attention because of mental retardation, but, because of their deprived living circumstances, are especially vulnerable to illness and are frequent visitors to clinics and hospitals. While their problems are largely social, physicians can play an important preventive role by ensuring adequate nutrition and health supervision and by referring the child, when protective intervention is indicated, to appropriate agency and legal authorities.

Help to the child in the absence of family-oriented services, however, may fall considerably short of desired goals. It is questionable, for example, whether several hours of mental stimulation in a preschool setting can compensate for deprivation during the remainder of the day. Family problems require family solutions. If children are to be taught new modes of thinking and communication, instilled with values different from those held by their parents, and inspired toward higher goals in life, then home and outside services must be brought closer together. Only as newly learned habits are reenforced and methods of training and discipline consistently applied can culture-conflicts be avoided and gains sustained.

Past efforts in working with deprived families often have been sabotaged by the negative conditions under which help is proffered. Parents who come to agency attention because of their own or their child's deficiencies regard offers of aid with suspicion and distrust. Many are social isolates. They seldom participate in civic group-activities, have few friends, and are therefore somewhat outside the influence of their neighbors. For these reasons, they have little concern for the community's attitude toward them, their desire for social approval is low, and little initiative is exerted to improve their child-rearing practices or poor living conditions.

Despite these apparent limitations, many of these parents want to do better but become apathetic in the face of repeated frustrations and community pressures. Their true need is for professional guidance and community support. Innovations in the anti-poverty program may provide new channels for aid to these parents in the art of homemaking and child care, budgeting, and the judicious use of time. Encouraged to broaden their sphere of activities and relationships and given the tools for achievement, they may be motivated to strive for self-improvement and to conform to society's values and standards.

## SUMMARY

Mental retardation as a family problem is, then, as diverse as the many causes that produce this condition and the differences in family and community situations that contribute to it. Each situation must be evaluated carefully. Only as the nature of the problem and the dynamics underlying it are fully recognized can appropriate solutions be undertaken and the retarded person's potentials realized. As the child progresses through life, his needs and those of his family assume new dimensions, calling for different services or professional skills. To the extent that these are adequately provided and properly coordinated, the mentally retarded will prove to be less of a threat to family stability. In time, society will be more than repaid for its investment.

## REFERENCES

MICHAEL J. BEGAB and HARRIET L. GOLDBERG, "Guardianship for the Mentally Retarded," *Children*, IX (1962), 21–25.
LAURA L. DITTMAN, *The Mentally Retarded Child at Home—A Manual for*

*Parents,* U.S. Department of Health, Education, and Welfare, Children's Bureau Publication Number 374 (Washington, D. C.: Government Printing Office, 1959).

B. FARBER, W. JENNE, and R. TOIGO, *Family Crisis and the Retarded Child,* Council for Exceptional Children, Research Monograph Number 1 (n.p.: n.d.).

GROUP FOR THE ADVANCEMENT OF PSYCHIATRY, *Mental Retardation: A Family Crisis and the Therapeutic Role of the Physician,* Report Number 56 (New York: Group for the Advancement of Psychiatry, 1963).

K. S. HOLT, "The Home Care of Severely Retarded Children," *Pediatrics,* XXII (1958), 744–755.

LEO KANNER, "Parents' Feelings about Retarded Children," *American Journal of Mental Deficiency,* LVII (1953), 375–383.

ELIZABETH R. KRAMM, *Families of Mongoloid Children,* U.S. Department of Health, Education, and Welfare, Children's Bureau Publication Number 401 (Washington, D. C.: Government Printing Office, 1963).

BENJAMIN SPOCK, "Parents' Feelings about Children's Handicaps," *Ladies' Home Journal,* May 1960, pp. 20–27.

# 8

# Developmental Problems of the Mentally Retarded Child

## NANCY BAYLEY

If we assume that a fair number of children are mentally retarded because their early life experience has been in environments that are inimical to the realization of their inherent capacities, then it becomes necessary for us to learn all we can about the kinds of environment in which infants develop. Furthermore, we should ask what, specifically, in the experience of a child with (say) a two-month or ten-month mentality will enhance or inhibit his continuing development.

## THE QUESTION OF ENVIRONMENTAL RETARDATION

Some of the early attempts to discover the nature of the retarding experiences have resulted in some general terms such as "environmental impoverishment," "maternal deprivation," and "institutionalism." However, these terms are too general and have resulted all too often in the assumption that the difficulties arise out of living in an institution or separation from the mother, as such. Efforts to investigate infants' environments in detail make it clear that although these conditions frequently are associated with retardation or behavior pathology, they need not be. It seems to me that it would be much better to put all of these terms into one large category that might be called "environmentally inappropriate" conditions. Then one could try to determine the specific ways in which the living situations and experiences of infants may be inappropriate.

Whether or not a specific environment is impoverishing may depend on

85

the age (or maturity) of the child. Harriet Rheingold (1961), for example, found that though three-month-old infants in an institution had many fewer interactions with persons or objects than did a control group of babies living with their own parents, the behavior of the two groups of babies was closely similar. In another study, Rheingold (1956) found that though six- to eight-month-old infants in an institution responded to her special care and became more social and outgoing, they did not advance in developmental status over a matched control group. What is more, a year after all of the babies had left the institution to return to homes, Rheingold and Nancy Bayley (1959) found no relevant discernible differences between the "mothered" babies and the controls. The mean intelligence quotients (IQ's) of the experimental and control groups at twenty months were 97 and 95, respectively.

It appears also that a bland, relatively unstimulating environment in the first year or two of life need not cause permanent retardation. The studies of Harold Skeels and his associates (Skeels, 1942; Skeels and Dye, 1939) are relevant. They found that thirteen orphanage children around two years of age with IQ's ranging from 35 to 89, when placed in an institution for the mentally retarded where they received stimulation in the form of loving care from the older female inmates, developed rapidly and soon achieved normal developmental status. Skeels (1965) revisited these people as adults and found them to be adequate members of their communities. They have responsible jobs, and many are married and have children with normal intelligence. One is a college graduate.

I have tested at four years, and again at five and six, a girl who lived her first nineteen months in the institution in which she was born, one of twenty babies who were cared for in one room by a succession of nursing assistants. The ratio was one assistant to ten babies. This child had never been fed solid food or allowed freedom to move outside her crib. She was not toilet-trained. She spoke not even one word. At nineteen months she was taken for adoption by an intelligent middle class couple. At four years and subsequently, her IQ was approximately 140, and she was and continues to be a remarkably likeable, socially perceptive child. Her mother reported that the child learned to walk and to talk in sentences very soon after nineteen months and that within two or three months she "just blossomed out."

In contrast to this child from a bland early environment is a boy I saw first at twenty-four months. He was the third child in a professional family in which the parents had advanced degrees and the older siblings had high IQ's. This boy cried, mostly screaming, while sitting on his mother's lap for the first half-hour of the testing session, and eventually, after three testing sessions in three days, earned an IQ of 63. He impressed me as a sensitive, vulnerable, unhappy child. The parents quickly accepted and intelligently acted on advice that they lower their expectations, gear their demands to his level of functioning, and put their efforts into making the child happy and secure. On successive annual retests, his IQ rose, until at six years when he participated in the tests shyly but happily, he earned an IQ of 99. Relevant to this kind of change in IQ are the studies of A. D. B. and Ann M. Clarke (1960), who found marked increases in IQ among children who had been removed from adverse home conditions. The amount of increase was related both to the degree of adversity of the prior environment and to the length of time since removal from it.

These cases illustrate several points. One is that the effects of early lack of appropriate stimulation, if not unduly prolonged, need not prevent later normal intelligence. Another is that emotional factors may prove to be very important. A third point is that, in our efforts to advance growth in the retarded child, the level of difficulty should be low enough and the complexity of demands made on the child should be simple enough to ensure a high incidence of success in his responses. That is, adequate motivation and the development of skills in problem-solving can occur only if a child experiences a fair proportion of successes as the result of his efforts.

## The Problem of Early Diagnosis

Another problem of pervasive importance is the difficulty in early diagnosis of mental defect or retardation. It has been demonstrated repeatedly that test scores on behavior development in the first year or so of life do not predict later intelligence, except in cases of extreme retardation (Bayley, 1949). The lack of correlation between early mental scores and later IQ is illustrated for the Berkeley Growth Study sample in Figure 8–1. The IQ's earned by the children at sixteen, seventeen, and eighteen years (average of three test scores) are correlated with their IQ's at each of thirteen earlier age levels, starting at one month of age. Each age level includes all tests given the children at three consecutive ages. The correlations are for boys and girls separately. It is clear that, for these samples, global mental-test scores in the first eighteen months are entirely unrelated or even, for the boys, are negatively related to intellectual status (IQ) in young adulthood.

If, as these correlations indicate, we cannot predict school-age IQ from tests given to healthy infants under two years of age, then how can we detect potential mental deficiency in the very young? Clearly we need to know more about the nature of early mental development.

### Inherent Changes in the Nature of Mental Functions

Many efforts to analyze the characteristics of early behavior point to discontinuities in the nature of the mental functions that develop at different

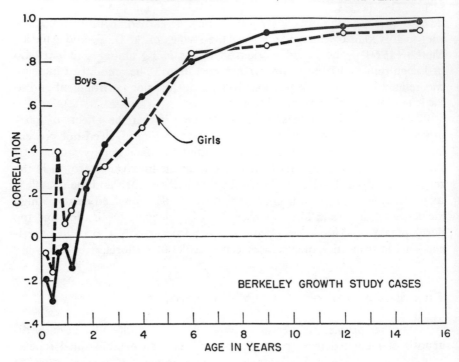

**Figure 8–1.** Correlations of earlier mental-test scores with 16–18-year scores. (After Bayley and Schaefer, 1964.)

ages. In the first few months of life, infants develop sensory acuity, muscular strength, and sensorimotor coordinations. They rapidly acquire experience that is the basis for perceptual discriminations among objects and occurrences. These are the basic tools or building blocks of mental function. Gradually, these sensory and motor capacities are utilized in more complex adaptive mental processes. However, it does not logically follow that proficiency in these simple acuities and skills will result in proficiency in the later more complex thinking processes.

Studies involving item analysis of the infant scales have been oriented toward selecting either individual items or clusters of items that will be correlated with later IQ. In these analyses, so far, few items or factors have been found to correlate with a criterion such as IQ at five years or at eighteen years, and none of these correlations is at a sufficiently high level to be useful in predicting mental capacity for a given child. This is so, even though the items themselves are valid and reliable measures of the child's status in infancy.

### Early Diagnostic Criteria

These general analyses have been made on tests given to unselected samples, that is, to "normal" infants. We may, however, obtain useful diagnostic criteria from test scores of populations selected for their high incidence of mental retardation. Such populations may range from defectives such as mongoloids to possibly neurologically damaged and premature babies.

Marjorie P. Honzik, John J. Hutchings, and S. Robert Burnip (1965) gave the revised research form of the Bayley Mental and Motor Scales to eight-month-old infants whose birth records indicated likelihood of central nervous system damage. In comparison with a control group, the "suspect" babies tested significantly lower on several items involving attentiveness, problem-solving, eye–hand coordination, and ability to sit alone, to creep, or to try to walk. Also, on the Bayley behavior profile these suspect babies were more often rated as having short attention span and meager interest in the toys, as being flaccid or hypertense, either very inactive or hyperactive, and easily upset emotionally. The combination of such items into an "impairment score" may prove to be useful in diagnosis. However, we do not yet have tests of the predictive capacity to later ages of these differentiating eight-month items.

## HEREDITARY–ENVIRONMENTAL INTERACTIONS: EVIDENCE FROM THE BERKELEY GROWTH STUDY

In our efforts to understand the nature of early shifts in mental status, we have made further analyses of the Berkeley Growth Study cases (Bayley and Schaefer, 1964) and have found patterns of behavioral relationships that may prove to be important for understanding some aspects of the etiology of environmental retardation. An analysis of a complex array of mother–child relationships during the growth of the children has shown clear relations between emotionally-toned behavior and IQ's as well as clear sex differences in the patterns of correlation. It is hypothesized that, although there are wide within-sex differences, in general, females are inherently more resilient than males in recovery from the effects of strong environmental impacts. Although we cannot go into the details of these analyses here, a discussion of some of the relevant patterns of correlation that led to our hypothesis will be useful.

### Age Changes in Relation to Socio-economic Status

It has long been common knowledge that intelligence is correlated with socio-economic status. However, these correlations are not present until children are three or four years old. Figure 8–2 presents for five parental

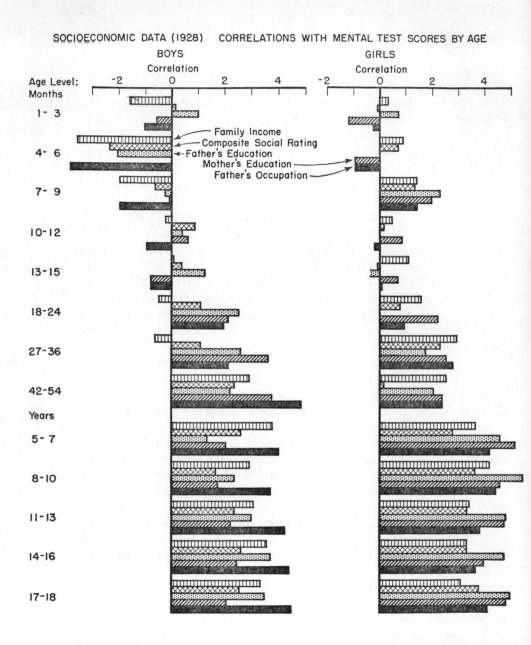

**Figure 8–2.** Correlations of socio-economic data with mental-test scores by age at testing (one month to 18 years). (After Bayley and Schaefer, 1964).

socio-economic variables (family income, composite social-rating, father's education, mother's education, and father's occupation) at the time the children in the Berkeley Growth Study were born, the correlations with the boys' and the girls' IQ's from one month through eighteen years.

In Figure 8–2, the boys' correlations, on the left, present a picture of a negative relation with parental status at four to six months. The correlations become positive only around two years of age. The relationship at school age is highest with father's occupation. The girls' correlations remain essentially zero for the first two years and become strongly positive at five years. Their school-age correlations are highest with parents' education.

In comparing these two sets of correlations, it appears that, like the children's self-correlations with their eighteen-year intelligence, the boys' scores are negatively correlated at around six months, while the girls' early scores show no effects of parent–child relations. However, by school age, the girls' IQ's are more highly correlated than are the boys' with both the mothers' and the fathers' education. These differences are small, but other data indicate that they may be actual and not chance.

### Age Changes in Relations between Mother–Child Behavior

Figure 8–3 shows a series of correlations between an array of maternal variables and ratings of their infant's happiness at ages ten to thirty-six months (Schaefer and Bayley, 1963). The mother's behavior was rated from notes made at the times that her infant was tested and measured, on about twenty visits when the children were one to thirty-six months old. The items of behavior are arranged in an order of neighboring, based on their intercorrelations. They fit into a circular pattern of consecutively related behavior variables (a Guttman Circumplex), with two orthogonal factors that have been named *love versus hostility* and *autonomy versus control*. As arranged in this chart, the maternal behavior is ordered from granting autonomy through accepting, loving behavior that becomes increasingly controlling, into increasingly hostile behavior, to ignoring, the latter being related to granting freedom and autonomy. We can see here that mothers who are positively evaluating, equalitarian, and affectionate tend to have happy babies; while punitive, rejecting mothers have unhappy babies. (Negative correlations are represented by bars extending to the left of the center line for each sex.) The only sex differences are in the dimension of autonomy–control, where there is a tendency for controling mothers to have happy daughters but unhappy sons.

This is only one example of the kind of concurrent mother–child relation found for the behavior studied. In general, the mother–child correlations were high in the maternal love–hostility dimension and low in the autonomy–control dimension. The important point for our present discussion, however, is the sex difference in persistence of the relationships.

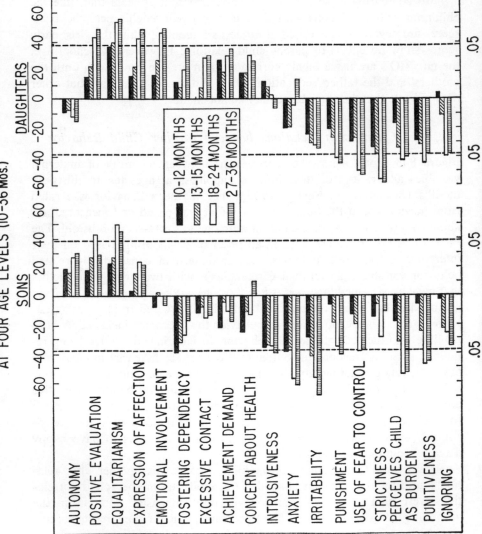

**Figure 8-3.** Correlations of maternal-behavior ratings with ratings of children's happiness at 10–36 months. (After Schaefer and Bayley, 1963.)

Figure 8–4 summarizes this sex difference. It represents averages of the amount of correlation between maternal and child behavior for each age level (Bayley, 1964). In Part A, maternal love–hostility as observed in the first three years is correlated with a series of ratings and scores on the sons' and daughters' behavior at all ages, ten months to eighteen years. These averages represent amount of correlation, whether negative or positive. From eighteen to forty-two months, the mother–daughter correlations are greater, but after three-and-one-half years, it is the mother–son correlations that are greater. Part B shows insignificant degrees of correlation with early maternal autonomy–control except with the sons at adolescence. The correlations with another set of maternal ratings on the same variables, made when the children were nine to fourteen years, are summarized in Parts C and D. The curves in C show even more strongly the higher relations between maternal love–hostility and the sons' behavior after the children are three years of age. At this later age, the maternal autonomy–control dimension, seen in Part D, shows a relationship only to the daughters' behavior in adolescence.

To generalize from these behavioral interrelations, the pattern that is presented repeatedly is one in which the daughter's behavior often is related to concurrent maternal behavior, but the correlations do not persist as the interval increases between the time of the maternal behavior and the time of the child's behavior. On the other hand, the mother–son relationships do persist, and maternal behavior in the sons' first three years continues to show correlations with the boys' behavior into late childhood, and for some variables, even at adolescence.

## Relations of Maternal and Child Behavior to IQ

With these patterns of behavioral relations in mind, let us examine their correlation with the children's intelligence (Bayley and Schaefer, 1964). Figure 8–5 shows the correlations between maternal behavior and children's mental scores on twelve tests given at months one through twelve. Each type of maternal behavior is correlated with four consecutive sets (average of three test ages) of the children's mental scores. The correlations with the girls are what might be expected. From the patterns of correlation shown in Figures 8–2 and 8–5, we may say that loving and controlling mothers have happy daughters who make high scores, while the daughters of punitive-rejecting mothers make low scores. The boys present, however, a very different picture. It appears that happy boy babies with loving mothers make low scores while the unhappy boys with hostile mothers make high scores.

After the first year, however, the picture changes. The preschool (thirteen- to fifty-four-month) correlations are shown in Figure 8–6. The correlations for the girls remain pretty much the same through three years. But

Averages of Correlations (regardless of sign) between Maternal and Child Behaviors

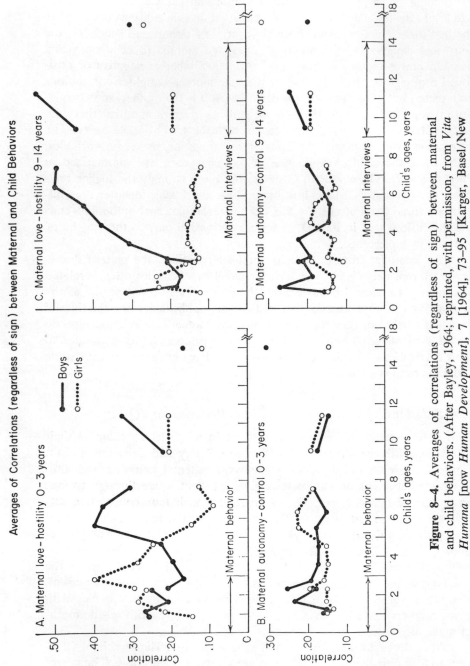

**Figure 8–4.** Averages of correlations (regardless of sign) between maternal and child behaviors. (After Bayley, 1964; reprinted, with permission, from *Vita Humana* [now *Human Development*], 7 [1964], 73–95 [Karger, Basel/New York].)

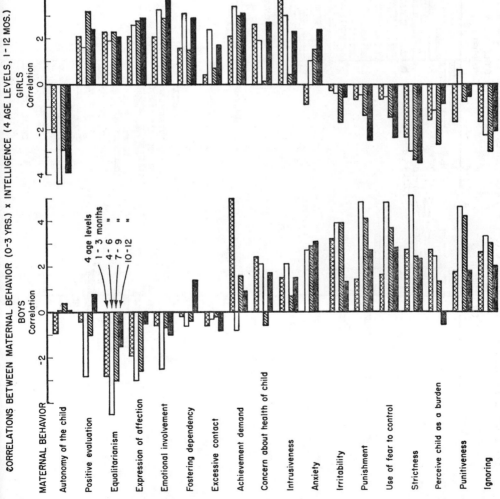

**Figure 8-5.** Correlations between early maternal behavior and children's intelligence at four age levels, 1–12 months. (After Bayley and Schaefer, 1964.)

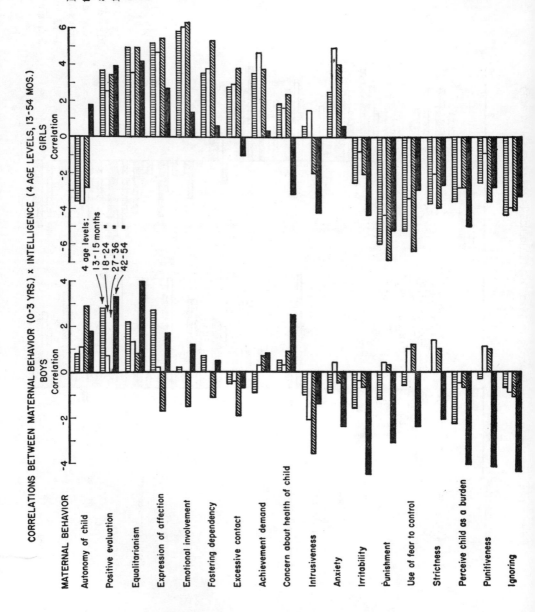

**Figure 8-6.** Correlations between early maternal behavior and children's intelligence at four age levels, 13–54 months. (After Bayley and Schaefer, 1964.)

CORRELATIONS BETWEEN MATERNAL BEHAVIOR (0-3 YRS.) x INTELLIGENCE (4 AGE LEVELS, 13-54 MOS.)

GIRLS

BOYS

Correlation

Correlation

4 age levels:
13 - 15 months
18 - 24 "
27 - 36 "
42 - 54 "

MATERNAL BEHAVIOR

Autonomy of child
Positive evaluation
Equalitarianism
Expression of affection
Emotional involvement
Fostering dependency
Excessive contact
Achievement demand
Concern about health of child
Intrusiveness
Anxiety
Irritability
Punishment
Use of fear to control
Strictness
Perceive child as a burden
Punitiveness
Ignoring

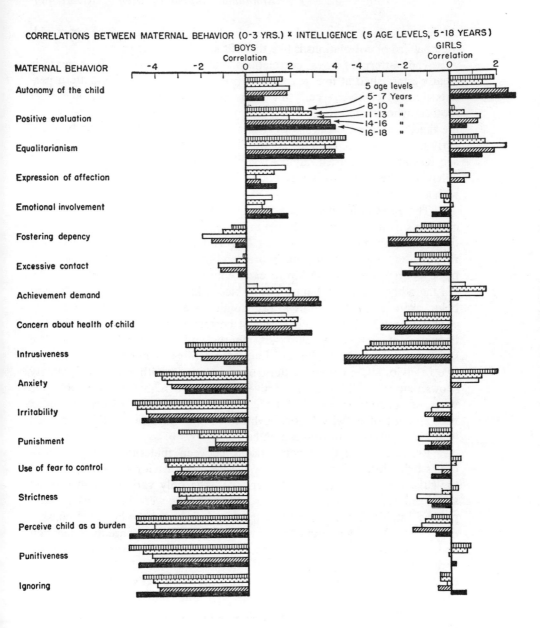

**Figure 8–7.** Correlations between early maternal behavior and childrens' intelligence at five age levels, 5–18 years. (After Bayley and Schaefer, 1964.)

the boys are in a process of change; by the time they are four years old, their pattern of correlations is like that of the girls at three years.

The pattern of boys' correlations that appears first at four years is clearly established at five years. As we see in Figure 8–7, this pattern persists through eighteen years, the entire school-age period. The boys with mothers who treated them well as infants, even though they scored low at the time, are now the ones with high scores, while the correlation between early maternal hostility and later IQ is clearly negative. The girls' school-age IQ's are, by contrast, almost completely independent of early maternal behavior. The one possible exception is the series of negative correlations with maternal intrusiveness.

These sex differences are apparent also in the correlations between the children's own early behavior (ten to thirty-six months) and their IQ's over time (one month to eighteen years). This is illustrated in Figure 8–7 for the rating of happiness. Happy girl babies tend to score high in intelligence, but by school age the relationship to early emotional state becomes negligible. On the other hand, the happy boy babies, who exhibit a tendency toward below-average mental scores at six months, are the ones who more often earn higher IQ's later. Their strongest correlations are between ratings of happiness at eighteen to thirty-six months and IQ after four years. The same patterns of correlation are found for ratings of positive versus negative behavior. A complex pattern of correlations with ratings of activity shows that for both sexes the active babies have high IQ's through three years, but (and more clearly for the boys) later IQ is negatively correlated with amount of activity before eighteen months and positively correlated with it at eighteen to thirty-six months.

Repeatedly, in these comparisons between maternal behavior, children's behavior, and mental scores, the correlations for the boys, but not the girls, were found to persist over time. The only variables that showed significant relations with the girls' school-age IQ's were indicators of their parents' intelligence, and for these the correlations for the boys are consistently lower. We have noted these in Figure 8–2 for the parents' education and occupation. Also, ratings of the mothers' IQ's, made from the notes on early maternal behavior, correlated about .50 with the girls' IQ's at five to eighteen years, and only around .30 with the boys' IQ's. Thus, it appears that, in comparison with the boys', the girls' intellectual functioning is less permanently affected by emotional factors in the environment and is more clearly related to their inherited potential.

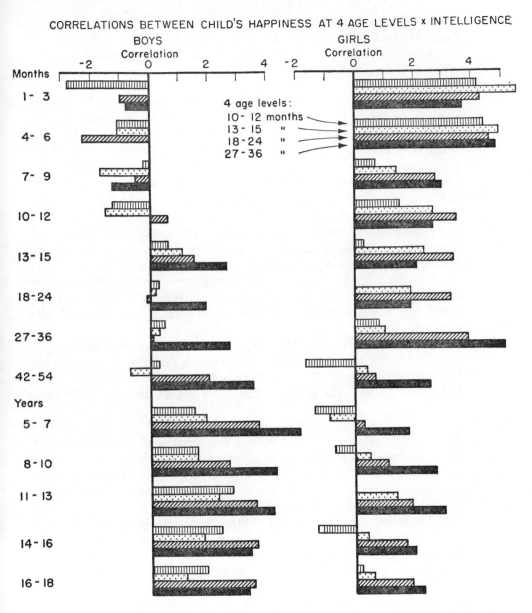

**Figure 8–8.** Correlations between children's happiness at four age levels (10–36 months) and their intelligence 1 month through 18 years. (After Bayley and Schaefer, 1964.)

## Sex Differences in Parent–Child Correlations in Ability: The Evidence from Other Studies

The sex differences in the correlates of intelligence are so pervasive in this sample that it has seemed worthwhile to explore other reported sex differences of this type in an attempt to determine their prevalence. So often, in the literature, there are reports of significant findings in experimental studies for males but not for females. Could these differences result from inherent sex differences in reaction to the environment, as well as from differences in the nature of the environments experienced by boys and girls?

One test of such a difference is to determine the prevalence of those sex differences in correlation with parental intelligence that might be at least partly genetically determined. In a series of studies, Jerome Kagan and Howard Moss (1959; Moss and Kagan, 1958) reported similar sex differences in the behavioral correlates of intelligence for the Ohio children studied at Fels. They also reported higher parent–daughter than parent–son correlations between children's IQ's and both parents' education and parents' IQ's.

A further search of the literature has yielded several additional sets of parent–child correlations in intelligence in which the data are available for boys and girls separately. Five of these studies are summarized in Figure 8–9. They are arranged approximately according to the ages of the children studied.

In the first study, by Florence Goodenough (1927), IQ's of two-, three-, and four-year-olds tested twice, a few weeks apart, on the Kulhman-Binet are compared with their parents' education. (These $r$'s are computed for samples of thirty-one to forty-one children.) Although the differences are not consistent, in nine of the twelve pairs, the parent–child correlations are higher for the girls than for the boys.

The Kagan and Moss study (1959), shown next, gives correlations of the children's Stanford–Binet IQ's at ages three, six, and ten years with the parents' education and with the parents' Otis IQ's. (Sample sizes range from thirty-six to fifty-nine.) In this instance the correlations are higher for the girls in ten of the twelve pairs. There are no other clear trends in these correlations, except that for both boys and girls the relation tends to be stronger with the mothers' than with the fathers' education.

The third study, by John Marks and James Klahn (1961), reports correlation of fathers' occupation with scores on the Wechsler Intelligence Scale for Children for 106 children of eight and eleven years. Computations were made separately for scores on the Verbal, the Performance, and the Full scale. Whether the comparisons with fathers' occupations are for either of the subscales or the Full scale, for each age or both ages combined, the

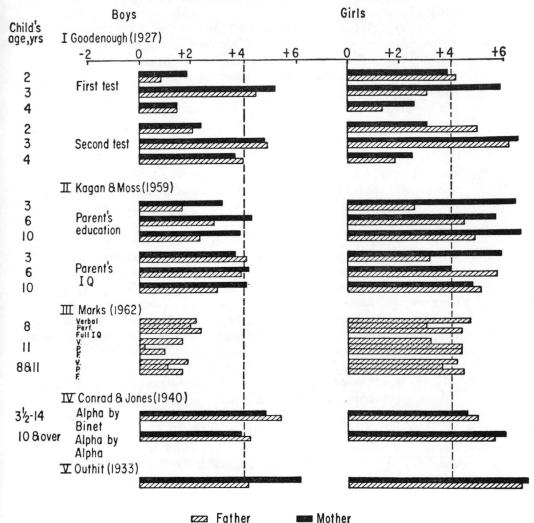

**Figure 8–9.** Parent–child correlations in ability (IQ, education, occupation) by sex. (Based on data from Florence Goodenough [1927]; Jerome Kagan and Howard Moss [1959]; John Marks and James Klahn [1961]; H. S. Conrad and Harold Jones [1940]; and Marion C. Outhit [1933].)

father–daughter *r*'s are higher than the father–son *r*'s. The authors report that the sex differences for the total sample on the Full scale are highly significant.

In the H. S. Conrad and Harold E. Jones study (1940), there are two broad age groupings, and two different tests were given to the children. The parents all were given the Army Alpha (N's range from ninety-seven to one hundred and twenty-eight). For the group of children aged three and one-half to fourteen years who were given the 1916 Stanford–Binet, the father–son correlations are higher than the father–daughter correlations, though they are closely similar for the sexes. For the sample ten years and older, in which both parents and children were tested on the Alpha, the girls again correlate more highly with each of their parents than do the boys. In this second Conrad and Jones sample, because its scores are based on the same test and because it includes no one under ten years, we may assume greater stability in children's IQ's and, hence, a more adequate measure of parent–child correlation.

Marion C. Outhit (1933), in an early study, tested parents and children of fifty-one families. She gave the Army Alpha to everyone over eleven years and the Stanford–Binet to children under twelve years. She reported slightly higher parent–daughter than parent–son correlations, computed from average scores of the sons and the daughters in each family. Because Outhit published her individual data, they are available for other computations. In forty-five of her families, at least one son and one daughter were tested. This selected sample permits a comparison between the IQ's of the same parent population and those of their sons and their daughters. By using the IQ of the oldest tested son and daughter from each family, the age difference between parent and child at the time of testing was reduced, and the proportion of relatively stable scores among the children and the number of parent–child pairs tested on the same scale were increased. The resulting correlations (the last set in Figure 8–9 are, again, higher for the daughters than for the sons. The mother–daughter *r* is .68, the father–daughter *r* is .66; the mother–son *r* is .61, and the father–son *r* is .44. The fact that the parents in this sample are the same for both sons and daughters makes this a potentially crucial test. Tests of significance (the brother–sister *r* is .55) indicate that these differences in father–child correlation approach significance at the .05 level.

Two studies not represented on the chart reported similar sex differences. Marjorie P. Honzik (1963) correlated parents' education with children's IQ's and found higher parent–daughter than parent–son correlations for samples of eighty-three to one hundred and fourteen cases tested repeatedly at twelve ages between twenty-one months and fifteen years. The highest correlations were between fathers and daughters. She found even stronger sex differences in the same direction for the siblings of these cases with sample sizes of sixteen to thirty-three at each of four age levels, covering the same age span.[1] C. B. Hindley (1962) presented regression lines on four ages (six months, eighteen months, three years, and five years) for three social classes for forty-three boys and thirty-seven girls tested at all four ages. He used the Griffith Scale at the first two ages and the 1937 Stanford–Binet at the two later ages. Mean scores of girls display a class order from eighteen months onward which, according to Hindley, is highly significant from the age of three years. Among the boys, the trends do not start until three years and are then only moderate.

In these two studies, there is evidence that the relation of girls' scores to socio-economic status is not only stronger but stabilizes at a younger age than in boys. Several of the other studies also show this trend for earlier stability in the girls' intellectual functioning. In the Berkeley Growth Study, it is manifested in the correlation between the children's early test scores and their own eighteen-year IQ's. A careful study of the patterns of correlation in the several studies cited here leads one to hypothesize that at least two types of sex difference are operating. One of these is the difference in the degree of correlation at ages when the relationships are relatively stable. If we can assume that the preponderance of higher correlations of parents with daughters (78 per cent of sixty-three $r$'s) than with sons is a true difference, then we may say that not only do these parent–child correlations in mental ability appear earlier, but once established, they are stronger with daughters than with sons.

The last and perhaps most impressive of our parent–child comparisons is the set of correlations (Figure 8–10), based on the Marie Skodak and Howard Skeels (1949) report of one hundred children, forty boys and sixty girls, who were placed in adoptive homes before they were six months of age. For these children there are 1916 Stanford–Binet IQ's at four testings (at ages averaging two and one-fourth, four and one-fourth, six and one-half, and thirteen and one-half years), and also 1937 Form L Stanford–Binet IQ's for sixty-three of the true mothers, and education of ninety-one of the true mothers, sixty of the true fathers, and all of the adoptive mothers and fathers. In Figure 8–10, the upper set of correlations gives the relations with the true parents. The top bar represents the correlation with true mother's IQ, next is true mother's education, then true father's education. The same comparisons are repeated for each age level and test. The shifts in correlation with age are very similar to those found for the Berkeley sam-

[1] Another set of correlations reported by Marjorie P. Honzik (1963) between fourteen- and fifteen-year IQ's of the Guidance Study cases and the IQ's of their own children at six age levels, two to ten years, are not in accord with this general trend. For these samples of fifteen to thirty-three cases, the parents' IQ's correlate with the five- to ten-year children's IQ's more highly with sons than with daughters. However, these data are not comparable to the other studies that are based on adult status of the parents. The "parents" were younger at the time that they were evaluated and the parent sample contained either a father or a mother of a child, but not both.

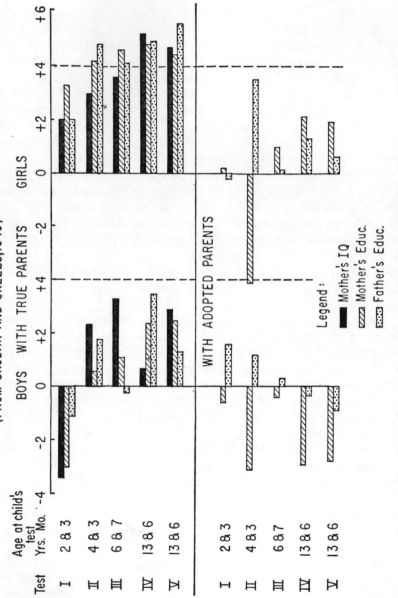

**Figure 8–10.** Correlation of boys' and girls' IQ's with education of true and adoptive parents and IQ of true mothers.

ple. Again, the girls' correlations are higher with all three measures of the natural parents. This is the more impressive because these parents had few or no interactions with their children. The correlations with the adoptive parents' education, given in the lower half of the chart, are in striking contrast. These correlations appear to be randomly distributed around zero, or possibly even to show a negative correlation between the abilities of adoptive mothers and sons.

If the intellectual stimulation afforded by higher status home environment plays a significant role in boys' mental functioning, one might have expected moderately high positive correlations between the boys' IQ's and their adoptive parents' education. On the other hand, if the Berkeley patterns of correlation are representative, then the boys' intellectual functioning may not be affected so much by parental ability as by parental behavior in the dimension of love–hostility. This hypothesis cannot be tested in the Skodak and Skeels material because it does not include information about behavior of the adoptive parents.

## POSTULATION OF A GENETIC SEX DIFFERENCE IN RESPONSE TO ENVIRONMENTS

The findings in the Berkeley study of higher parent–daughter correlations in mental abilities, contrasted with higher mother–son relationships between maternal behavior and children's mental abilities, have led to a hypothesis of a genetic sex difference in resistance to, or resilience in recovery from, environmental influences. This sex difference may be selective, and the effects of the environment may be either enhancing or depressing for a given structure or function. Our data show not only different patterns of positive and negative correlation between variables of maternal behavior and the IQ's of boys and of girls but also different patterns of correlation with parents' abilities. It is only the boys who show, for both maternal and child behavior, persistent correlation between early behavior and later IQ. Furthermore, not only in this study, but in others for which data by sex of the child are available, the girls' IQ's more frequently correlate higher than boys' with measures of parental intelligence or ability.

The sex differences noted here are in accord with a number of observed physical sex differences. For example, it is well known that the infant mortality rate is greater for boys than for girls, and boys have repeatedly been found to be more susceptible to physical trauma. An example of the latter is seen in studies of the effect of the Hiroshima and Nagasaki atomic bombings on child survivors. William Greulich et al. (1953), from studies of measures and X rays of several hundred first-graders who were examined two years after the bombings, found boys to be significantly more retarded than girls in both size and skeletal age. Two years later, the girls had recovered further and were near the norms for height of Japanese children, while the boys continued to be retarded. In another study of children in the Marshall Islands, who were accidentally exposed to radioactive fall-out, Robert A. Conrad *et al.* (1957) found that two years later, growth in height of boys was two inches less than expected, but the girls' heights were not affected. The studies of effects of such inhibiting conditions as poor nutrition on sex differences in growth, in height, and in weight are conflicting, evidently because some comparisons are made with concurrent observations when the girls are affected, while others involve measures made at some time after the inhibiting factor has been corrected. J. J. Van der Werf ten Bosch, who has noted this difference, says:

> Could it be that the relatively short-term response of girls to adverse environmental conditions, as expressed in altered height and weight development, constitutes a homeostatic mechanism which serves long-term purposes . . . ? The male hormone would be responsible for higher vulnerability because it fails to make the body respond to changes in the environment through alterations in body growth (Van der Werf ten Bosch, 1962, p. 189).

Bayley and Schaefer have proposed a genetic basis for these sex differences.

> Whether or not the male hormone [or some other sex-determined biochemical enzymatic process] is the effective agent, some pervasive physical differences in adaptability might also be reflected in behavioral flexibility and capacity for a given organism to return to its own homeostatic norm. Obviously we need more carefully controlled studies of these variables. At present they are suggestive rather than definitive. Also, the relations are probably very complex and their behavioral manifestations are often indirect as well as varying in degree (Bayley and Schaefer, 1964, p. 29).

## RELEVANCE OF RESEARCH FINDINGS TO PROBLEMS IN MENTAL RETARDATION

### Sex Differences

What can we learn from these studies concerning the problems of the mentally retarded? Several things stand out clearly. First, the emotional climate in which the infant develops is important, and this importance is more evident for the boys. Boys appear to be less able than girls to recover from hostile, rejecting treatment; but they may also profit more, in the long run, from understanding, loving acceptance. If these relationships show up in a small, presumably normal sample, then we may very well find a fair number of potentially adequate boys among the mentally retarded who comprise the least adequate portion of a large heterogeneous population. This type of etiology may have its greatest incidence among those retarded who are classed as "familial." The Berkeley Growth Study findings show relatively more hostile behavior among the low socio-economic status mothers of boys than of girls (Bayley and Schaefer, 1960). But even when parents' education was controlled, the relation between maternal hostility and sons' IQ's remained. Also, in the Berkeley Growth Study both boys and girls showed a higher incidence of low IQ among those who were responsive to persons and also had relatively hostile mothers. Because of the small number of cases, these findings can be only suggestive. However, the pattern of relations makes sense, and it seems to be well worth exploring further.

### Age Changes in the Nature of Intelligence

From the study, a second finding of relevance to the problem of mental retardation is the change in the nature of intellectual functions around the second to third year. With its shift in the correlates of mental-test scores, this age appears to be crucial in the development of later intellectual ability. Its significance may be a function of a complex pattern of concurrently developing processes. It is the period when language develops, when the processes of communication become (or fail to become) established between the child and others. It is the time when not only language but motor controls, competence in self-care, and ability to carry out simple commands normally are established. Furthermore, children's mental growth by the second and third year has reached a stage of maturity that enables them to form stable response-tendencies and motivational orientations that are determined largely by their parents' customary attitudes and by rewards and punishments for given behavior.

### Relevance of the Nature of Intellectual Function to Training Procedures

These two findings, on sex differences and age changes, taken together may point to the importance for the child of our understanding his drives and abilities, gearing our demands and opportunities for learning to his level of functioning, and encouraging rather than punishing or ignoring behavior that may lead to further achievement. This may be the area in which environmental impoverishment and lack of emotional security are most significant. The second and third year of life may be the period in which the establishment of object-relations and of free interpersonal communication is crucial.

It is true also, of course, that some children will remain incapable of intellectual progress beyond these simple concrete processes of the two-year-old. My point is that this may very well be the period that will determine for many whether normal mental development will continue. The period may be more crucial for boys because of their tendency toward greater vulnerability, and perhaps also because of a tendency among some classes of mothers to be more harsh and less understanding of their boys than of their girls.

The findings from research on mental development, when considered together, indicate a complex process of interaction between inherited potentials as they mature, and environmental pressures as they become relevant with maturation. The impact of the environment on intellectual function varies with the environment and with the genetic potential of the individual. There is evidence to indicate that even though it might some day be possible to bring up each child in an environment that is optimal for him and, thereby, to raise the general level of intelligence, there still would be individual differences in children's intellectual adequacy.

REFERENCES

NANCY BAYLEY, "Consistency and Variability in the Growth of Intelligence from Birth to Eighteen Years," *Journal of Genetic Psychology,* LXXV (1949), 165–196.

NANCY BAYLEY, "Consistency of Maternal and Child Behaviors in the Berkeley Growth Study," *Vita Humana* (now *Human Development*), VII (1964), 73–95.

NANCY BAYLEY and EARL S. SCHAEFER, "Correlations of Maternal and Child Behaviors with the Development of Mental Abilities: Data from the Berkeley Growth Study," *Monographs of the Society for Research in Child Development,* XXIX, Number 6 (1964).

NANCY BAYLEY and EARL S. SCHAEFER, "Relationships between Socioeconomic Variables and the Behavior of Mothers toward Young Children," *Journal of Genetic Psychology,* XCVI (1960), 61–77.

A. D. B. CLARKE and ANN M. CLARKE, "Some Recent Advances in the Study of Early Deprivation," *Journal of Child Psychology and Psychiatry and Allied Disciplines,* I (1960), 26–36.

H. S. CONRAD and HAROLD E. JONES, "A Second Study of Familial Resemblance in Intelligence: Environmental and Genetic Implications of Parent–Child and Sibling Correlations in the Total Sample," in *Intelligence, Its Nature and Nurture,* XXXIX *Yearbook* of the National Society for the Study of Education (Chicago: University of Chicago Press, 1940), pp. 99–141.

ROBERT A. CONRAD, CHARLES E. HUGGINS, BRADFORD CANNON, AUSTEN LOWREY, and JOHN B. RICHARDS, "Medical Survey of Marshallese Two Years after Exposure to Fall-out Radiation," *Journal of the American Medical Association,* CLXIV (1957), 1192–1197.

FLORENCE L. GOODENOUGH, "The Relation of the Intelligence of Pre-school

Children to the Education of Their Parents," *School and Society,* XXVI (1927), 1–3.

William W. Greulich, Catherine S. Crismon, and Margaret L. Turner, "The Physical Growth and Development of Children Who Survived the Atomic Bombing of Hiroshima or Nagasaki," *Journal of Pediatrics,* XLIII (1953), 121–145.

C. B. Hindley, "Social Class Influences on the Development of Ability in the First Five Years," in G. Nielson (Ed.), *Child Education: Proceedings of the XIV International Congress of Applied Psychology,* III (Copenhagen: Munksgaard, 1962), 29–41.

Marjorie P. Honzik, "A Sex Difference in the Age of Onset of the Parent–Child Resemblance in Intelligence," *Journal of Educational Psychology,* LIV (1963), 231–237.

Marjorie P. Honzik, John J. Hutchings, and S. Robert Burnip, "Birth Record Assessments and Test Performance at Eight Months," *American Journal of Diseases of Children,* CIX (1965), 416–426.

Jerome Kagan and Howard A. Moss, "Parental Correlates of Child's I.Q. and Height: A Cross-Validation of the Berkeley Growth Study Results," *Child Development,* XXX (1959), 325–332.

John B. Marks and James E. Klahn, "Verbal and Perceptual Components in WISC Performance and Their Relation to Social Class," *Journal of Consulting Psychology,* XXV (1961), 273.

Howard A. Moss and Jerome Kagan, "Maternal Influences on Early I.Q. Scores," *Psychological Reports,* IV (1958), 655–661.

Marion C. Outhit, "A Study of the Resemblance of Parents and Children in General Intelligence," *Archives of Psychology,* XXIII (1933), 1–60.

Harriet L. Rheingold, "The Effect of Environmental Stimulation upon Social and Exploratory Behavior in the Human Infant," in B. M. Foss (Ed.), *Determinants of Infant Behaviour* (New York: John Wiley Sons, 1961), pp. 143–171.

Harriet L. Rheingold, "The Modification of Social Responsiveness in Institutional Babies," *Monographs of the Society for Research in Child Development,* XXI, Number 2 (1956).

Harriet L. Rheingold and Nancy Bayley, "The Later Effects of an Experimental Modification of Mothering," *Child Development,* XXX (1959), 363–372.

Earl S. Schaefer and Nancy Bayley, "Maternal Behavior, Child Behavior and Their Intercorrelations from Infancy through Adolescence," *Monographs of the Society for Research in Child Development,* XXVIII, Number 3 (1963).

Harold M. Skeels, "A Study of the Effects of Differential Stimulation on Mentally Retarded Children: A Follow-up Report," *American Journal of Mental Deficiency,* XLVI (1942), 340–350.

Harold M. Skeels, "Effects of Adoption on Children from Institutions," *Children,* XII (1965), 33–34.

Harold M. Skeels and Harold B. Dye, "A Study of the Effects of Differential Stimulation on Mentally Retarded Children," *Proceedings of the American Association on Mental Deficiency,* XLIV (1939), 114–136.

MARIE SKODAK and HAROLD M SKEELS. "A Final Follow-up Study of One Hundred Adopted Children," *Journal of Genetic Psychology*, LXXV (1949), 85–125.

J. J. VAN DER WERF TEN BOSCH, in A. MERMINOD (Ed.), *The Growth of the Normal Child during the First Three Years of Life*, Modern Problems of Pediatrics, International Children's Center, VII (Basel: S. Karger, 1962).

# 9

# Children, Mental Retardation, and Emotional Disorder

IRVING PHILIPS

## Introduction

In 1958 funds were furnished by the National Institute of Mental Health to develop a program at the Langley Porter Neuropsychiatric Institute to train psychiatric personnel in the field of mental retardation. From 1958 to 1963, 170 families were referred to the Institute for diagnostic study and evaluation of retardation. Children with mental retardation of all degrees of severity and ranging in age from nine months through adolescence were studied, and each child's condition was evaluated as fully as possible. Psychiatric evaluation was part of each study. At the beginning of our program, we hoped to see retarded children whose intellectual deficit was not complicated by emotional disorder. We contacted pediatric, public-health, social-welfare, and psychiatric facilities to request referral of children who were mentally retarded but had no emotional disorder.

We did see a few children who were making an adequate adjustment and whose parents only wished help with future plans and someone with whom to discuss current problems. Tom B., an oriental youngster thirteen years old, was seen at our clinic because his parents wanted a re-evaluation and help with further planning. Mr. and Mrs. B. remarked that Tom had been evaluated periodically, and there was no question concerning his retardation. They felt that he was doing as well as he could. Tom was always slow in developing. Examination revealed an extremely small head, consistent with the diagnosis of mental deficiency owing to microcephaly. Despite his appearance, his adjustment was good. He spoke freely and easily to

111

members of the clinic staff, with little apprehension or anxiety. His vocabulary was consistent with his IQ of 55. His adjustment in school was reported to be good, and he was mastering the "three r's" at simplified levels. He had many friends, played sports with his peers, rode a bike on trips, belonged to the Boy Scouts, and helped his father in the family business. He talked with pride of his accomplishments and related how he used to be teased at school but since he stood up and fought back, he is now part of the group.

It was uncommon, however, to see a retarded child who presented no emotional maladjustment of moderate to severe degree as part of his clinical picture. This report summarizes the work of this program in relation to emotional problems of the mentally retarded. It will discuss what we have come to consider some common misconceptions concerning emotional disorders in retarded children, as well as particular emotional difficulties occurring during the developmental years.

The mentally retarded child is, in all periods of his life, more vulnerable to the development of maladaptive behavior than the normally endowed child. He is handicapped by lowered intellect, sometimes complicated by other anomalies, that results in a delay in and a slowed rate of personality development. Although he may be more or less comparable with his normal peers in physical stature, his ability to cope with situations of everyday living is impaired. In addition, his disappointed family may find it difficult to give him the emotional nurturing and support that they would give a normal child. Society offers him fewer of the environmental supports afforded normal children. Often he is placed in special schools, shunned and avoided by his peers, excluded from much of community life. It is assumed that he can make little contribution to the society in which he lives. He is referred to as a "child" even though he may be a young adult. In effect, the retarded child's unfavorable conception of himself is doubly reinforced by his family's disappointment and by society's attitudes toward him.

## MISCONCEPTIONS ABOUT RETARDATION AND BEHAVIOR

There are three related misconceptions about maladaptive behavior in the retarded child. First, it is often thought that the maladaptive behavior of the retarded child is a function of his retardation rather than of his interpersonal relationships. Second, it is assumed that emotional disorder in the retarded is different in kind from that in the normal child. And, third, it is thought that certain symptoms and specific maladaptive behavior patterns in a retarded child are the result of organic brain damage that produces these particular symptoms.

The constitutional endowment of any child is not the only factor determining his ability to learn and to develop. The child may have ultimate limitations in his capacity to develop, but his life experiences may interfere with the fullest development of this innate potential. Organic defect resulting from injury, metabolic abnormality, congenital anomaly, infection, and so forth may limit the level of function. However, emotional disorder developing from such experiences as emotional deprivation, frustration, separation, traumatic experience, and the like also may inhibit or distort function (Philips *et al.*, 1962). The child, then, who is retarded because of organic defect may also evidence emotional disorder that interferes with his maximal development. We recognize that although deficiency or disease may be a major contributing stress, the child's emotional disorder probably is not an organically inevitable concomitant of his defect, but is, rather, a function of the same kinds of processes that give rise to emotional disorder in children who have no definable "disease" (Boatman and Szurek, 1960).

Thus, disturbed behavior in the retarded is not primarily the result of limited intellectual capacities, but is related to delayed, disordered personality functions and interpersonal relationships with meaningful people in the environment. In addition, epidemiologic studies have indicated that in 85 per cent of retarded children, the primary etiology of the retardation is related to psychologic, social, and cultural factors (Tarjan, 1962). By our present means and knowledge of diagnosis, no abnormalities can be found in physical or laboratory examinations of the majority of these 85 per cent. These are the mildly retarded, who come from lower economic groups living in deprived areas with poor medical care; they demonstrate retarded functions as they develop, rather than at birth. A number of studies have indicated the influence of culture and family life on intellectual development. Hilda Knobloch and Benjamin Pasamanick (1961) reported a controlled study of infants in which they found no significant Negro–white differences in developmental quotient at birth. At three years of age no significant differences in motor function were observed in the two groups, but significant differences were noted between the Negro and white populations in adaptive social behavior. In addition, most child psychiatric clinics report that over 40 per cent of child psychiatric patients are referred for problems related to learning disturbances. Learning inhibition resulting from interpersonal and psychologic factors may result in a lowering of the testable IQ even though evidence within the test performance indicates higher potentials for learning.

The second misconception is that emotional disorder in the retarded is of a different nature than that seen in the normal child. In our experience during the past five years, we have seen in retarded children the gamut of psychopathology seen in children with normal intellectual endowment. We have seen transient disorders, psychoneurotic, character, personality, psychophysiologic, and psychotic disorders. The following examples illustrate some of these.

Mr. and Mrs. W. sought help for their thirteen-month-old child who was diagnosed as having Down's syndrome. They had been to many clinics. Mrs. W. requested gastrointestinal X rays of the youngster because he was constantly spitting up. Mr. W. reported that his wife had become more upset, suspicious, and sleepless since the birth of the child. She remarked that the boy's vomiting, often projectile in nature, took place with every feeding. He banged his head and rocked constantly in his crib; sleep patterns were reversed. At the end of a four-week study, in which Mrs. W. was seen weekly for interviews, she seemed to feel better. She discussed her feelings and was relieved by the thoroughness of our examination of the child. The child's symptoms disappeared except for occasional head-banging.

Jimmy, a three-year-old boy with mongolism, was impulsive and assaultive to his peers, difficult to manage at school, and almost impossible to control at home. A local nursery school for the retarded was ready to expel him—a decision never made with any other child in the history of the school. The father, a former prominent athlete, maintained unrealistic expectations and felt his son would be slow but could finish high school and work in his business. He discussed with pride his son's "cute" and "all boy" impulsivity and destructiveness.

Billy, a six-year-old, mildly retarded boy with an IQ of 68, was sullen and morose, spent most of his free time by himself, had no friends, and peered off into space in school, giving little attention to his work and consequently not learning. In the course of our study, he became quite agitated as he revealed his very active fantasy life. He presented the clinical picture of a schizoid personality.

Helen, a seventeen-year-old adolescent, was socially isolated and withdrawn in her behavior. Her IQ was 68 and her school repeatedly reported that she could do better in her work, but was withdrawn and disturbed. Her mother spent all of her free time with Helen, fearful that her daughter would get into trouble, that perhaps she would be sexually attacked or be induced to troublesome behavior. Helen developed a phobia about being touched. She avoided crowds, bathed frequently, and washed her hands throughout the day.

The third misconception is that certain symptom-complexes and maladaptive behavior in retarded children result from organic brain damage that produces these particular symptoms. Symptoms often mentioned are hyperactivity, short attention span, distractibility, and impulsive irrational behavior. Although we have seen some children with brain damage who have these symptoms, we have seen also the same symptoms in a number of children with both low and high IQ's, but without demonstrable organic brain disease. We have seen children described as hyperactive and destructive who are inhibited and overcontrolled in the playroom. We have seen children whose distractibility and inattentiveness could be related to interpersonal interactions occurring at particular moments. Although these children are difficult to treat, we have had some therapeutic success in working with them.

For example, Jim W., a youngster of ten years with a right-sided hemiplegia and convulsive episodes, was referred to our clinic by his school because of his impulsive, hyperactive behavior. Repeated intelligence tests indicated an intellectual deficit in the low 60's. He had poor concentration and gave brief and abortive attention to tasks at hand. If he was not immediately successful at any task, he would race around the room and not return to his work. His teacher felt he could do better at school. His parents related that he had frequent temper tantrums when frustrated, and that it was impossible to reason with him. He often was involved in dangerous pursuits, such as climbing out of an upper-story window and walking along the ledge, or running into the street, just avoiding passing cars. He was always a school problem and posed great difficulty to his teacher. He and his parents were seen for weekly psychotherapeutic interviews. Initially, he was a problem to his therapist because of his hyperactivity. As therapy progressed, he began to play and talk more freely about his troubles. He began to show marked improvement in school and at home and made friends. He began to work up to his level and learned to read, write, and do arithmetic. He obtained a job delivering papers. In the playroom near the end of treatment, when he was frustrated with a puzzle, he reared back to throw it and smiled at his therapist as he relaxed and said, "I know you want me to say it and not throw it."

## RETARDATION AND EMOTIONAL DEVELOPMENT

As was noted earlier, the retarded may be divided into two groups on the basis of etiologic factors. Eighty-five per cent are mildly retarded, with etiologies primarily involving social, cultural, and psychologic factors. Fifteen per cent of the retarded have severe to moderate deficit associated with primarily organic etiologies; these include injuries, microcephaly, mongolism, phenylketonuria, and cerebral agenesis. The disorders of children in this group usually are diagnosed early in life, often at birth. The appearance of these children, complicated by various stigmata, distinguishes them from other children and they readily appear to parents, peers, and community as being different. These two groups will be discussed separately, but similar emotional problems appear in both.

The child whose retardation is diagnosed early in life often presents great difficulty to his family. The human infant is characterized by a long period of total dependence on other persons. The interpersonal reactions of the parent with the infant may influence the child's development. The warm tender relationship experienced by the infant with his mother may foster a sense of confidence and eventual trust in his world. There is probably no more tragic experience for a parent than to be told that his child is mentally defective. The parent, faced with this disappointment, may react to his child in a variety of ways, from withdrawal to guilty over-solicitude. If the parents are depressed and disappointed, inconsistent in their care, hostile and angry, inhibited and frightened, the infant may react with symptoms indicating distortions of personality development. He may view the world with a sense of distrust and suspicion, becoming too frightened to try new tasks or angry in retaliation.

Several studies, such as those by René Spitz (1945), William Goldfarb (1947), and Sally Provence and Rose Lipton (1962), have demonstrated the effects of maternal deprivation on infant personality development. The parent who withdraws from a child may be unable to provide those experiences necessary for growth. Deprivational experiences may result in increased autoerotic play, infant depression, defects in intellectual development, delayed speech, and severe ego deficits. Also, there may be associated changes in growth patterns as evidenced by slow motor and social adaptive behavior.

During infancy, various symptoms may indicate pathologic personality development. These include vomiting and spitting up, frequent episodes of infection and diarrhea, head-banging, blanket- and finger-sucking, rocking, and sleep disturbances. Weaning problems are noted frequently as well as difficulty in adjusting to changes in diet from liquid to solid foods.

During the first years of life, the retarded child exhibits a delay in reaching developmental landmarks; and all skills, such as bowel and bladder control, locomotion, language skills, and adaptive behavior, develop late. Although he may be similar to his peers in physical size, he has not the motor control necessary to compete. While other children are engaging in parallel and later in cooperative play, he has difficulty keeping up with his age mates. When he is physically ready to play, he has outgrown in age and size those children with whom he might profitably engage in play. The younger children find it hard to play with him. His difficulty in play may be a further crippling factor, intensifying his sense of inferiority. Self-isolation and an inhibition from attempting new or competitive tasks may result.

When he reaches normal school age, the regular classroom may not admit him. He leaves the mainstream of community life and becomes a segregated citizen. Usually he does not enter school until the age of eight. Although there may be beneficial effects of preschool experiences for the development of social skills of retarded youngsters, the opportunities for preschool experience for most retarded children are limited or nonexistent. The child may have to remain at home and may need continuous parental supervision, which further intensifies parental disappointment and causes the child to feel increasingly more isolated and unworthy. The experience of entering school may present difficulties to any child who has had earlier problems in life. The retarded child may be more vulnerable in this situation. He may tend to consider himself different and unwanted and set himself apart from others. Thus, he may be shunned and teased by his peers, called names and taunted, be the fall guy for the class bully, and the victim of jokes. Neighbors may forbid their children to play with him. In reaction to his inability to solve his environmental and internal conflicts, he may develop a variety of symptoms of emotional disorder. These run the gamut from simple transient behavior problems to severe neurotic, delinquent, and schizophrenic disorders.

Adolescence, beginning with the onset of puberty and the development of secondary sexual characteristics, poses a new challenge. During adolescence the conflicts inherent in earlier life experiences are reawakened with increased intensity. The added pressure of physiologic changes may cause a recrudescence of dormant emotional conflicts and result in symptoms. The more complete the resolution of the developmental tasks of earlier periods of life, the less difficult the adolescent period. The retarded child who is hampered in his early development meets the pressure of adolescence additionally handicapped. The task of fulfilling his needs for identification with a group, for social outlets, recreation, vocational choice, and some separation from his parents may be fraught with difficulty. Society may offer him little opportunity to achieve some solution. The result is further isolation. He may become more dependent on his parents, fearful of his own impulses, withdrawn and isolated, or he may react with increased aggressivity, sexual indulgence, and delinquent behavior. Sexual development, often normal, is a cause of concern for the parent. It is necessary to help the child deal realistically with his own impulses and offer him whatever controls are needed. If the child is confronted with parental fear, dread, disgust and panic, he will be more frightened and also more likely to "taste the forbidden fruit" in a destructive and self-defeating manner. It is important to note that delinquent, perverse, and anti-social behavior is no more frequent in the retarded population than in the general population. Delinquent acts are determined, not by intellectual abilities, but more likely by social, economic, cultural, and, most of all, family attitudes.

## THE MILDLY RETARDED: A VITAL PROBLEM

The second group to be considered is that of the mildly retarded, or the 85 per cent whose retardation is related primarily to social, cultural, and psychologic factors. This is a population generally not familiar to most professional workers, a little-studied group for whom services traditionally are minimal. Families often are broken and parents or parent surrogates are concerned largely with the harsh economic realities of staying alive or subsisting; their energies are not devoted to verbal communication and learning endeavors. Problems in this group come from parental indifference and apathy, culturally developed distrust and suspicion, and socio-cultural isolation. These factors often result in poor and inhibited school performance.

In this group are children not diagnosed as mentally retarded at birth, who may or may not manifest slow development. They usually are diagnosed as retarded by the schools. They learn slowly, show little interest, and are poor in language and communication skills. When tasks of reading, writing, and arithmetic are demanded, they fall behind. There is usually much absenteeism for repeated minor illnesses. These youngsters manifest inattention to school tasks, immaturity in school behavior and personality development, slowed language development, and low achievement-test scores. They fall behind in school subjects, and each term their academic distance from their peers increases. On standard achievement tests, they score in the mildly retarded range and sometimes are placed in special classes. Their discouragement increases, apathy becomes more apparent, and learning is increasingly more difficult. They may present a variety of behavior problems in reaction to their indifference. In adolescence, they may become school drop-outs, ill-prepared in either academic or vocational skills. They may become chronically unemployable or exhibit delinquent anti-social behavior. They have few satisfactions in living.

In this group also are the children with learning inhibition. Test results may indicate mild retardation, but a wide scatter in performance indicates higher potential for learning. If a child does not read, his ability to perform in school is severely impeded, and he will fail in most school subjects. The advent of the nuclear age has placed a great emphasis on achievement and performance and has stressed competition. In our clinic, there has been, during the past decade, an increase in referrals of children with specific learning disabilities. These children often are inhibited and withdrawn, and frequently present a clinical picture of a schizoid personality. They may have associated somatic problems such as eczema, asthma, malnourishment or obesity, ulcers, and frequent infectious diseases.

## CHILD PSYCHOSES DIFFERENTIATED FROM RETARDATION

The psychoses or the schizophrenic reactions of childhood often appear in the 85 per cent of the mildly retarded. Many centers working with these children are investigating methods of differentiating the psychotic child from the retarded child whose deficiency is a result of organic causes. This is often a difficult task. When psychosis or mental deficiency (uncomplicated by emotional disorder) occurs as a separate entity, the distinction is not so difficult. The difficulty in distinguishing the child with severe emotional disorder from the child with mental deficiency is that psychotic reactions may occur superimposed on the deficiency.

The childhood psychosis may be defined as follows: "A disorder (so pervasive) that almost all affective expression is distorted and the capacity to experience real satisfaction and to learn at age level is impeded" (Boatman and Szurek, 1960). The child appears to be unresponsive to people, often is withdrawn and isolated, and relationship with peers is almost non-existent. He is negative in his approach to learning tasks, including the basic skills of feeding, dressing, and toileting; speech may be totally absent or garbled; a few do have speech that is more meaningful, but still is grossly defective in quality, quantity, tone, and content. Learning is accompanied by negativism and inhibition, with some level of functional retardation. Standardized tests often are useless in determining IQ scores, since the child may not respond to the test items. The child presents a picture of vacuous stupidity, with isolated moments of bright-eyed eagerness. This clinical description presents a well-defined clinical entity, yet the psychotic reactions of childhood are characterized by great variability and exhibit a range of symptoms of maladaptive and self-defeating behavior so pervasive that effective, everyday living is hindered. For a more complete description, reference should be made to Stanislaus Szurek (1956), Maleta Boatman and Stanislaus Szurek (1960), and Lauretta Bender (1953).

Psychotic children with and without mental deficiency evidence a greater or lesser degree of retardation. The psychotic child and the defective child with psychosis present similar clinical syndromes; and to differentiate them definitively is, in many cases, difficult. Among the clinical signs that may be helpful are the child's performance on psychologic tests or in psychiatric interview and play, his activity in a group, and his fine and gross motor behavior. Islands of integrated behavior in play or scattered performance on psychologic tests with some scores at age level may indicate underlying normal intelligence. The psychiatric examination of the psychotic child may reveal these isolated areas of normal intelligence and integrated behavior consistent with or beyond his age level despite the functional retardation. For example, a severely disturbed, mute, three-and-a-half-year-old, in play with a train, tried repeatedly to hook an engine to a train car, but the hook of the engine was bent and could not connect with the tightly screwed eye. He became upset with trying to complete the task and threw the toys against the wall. Later in the hour, he surreptitiously loosened the eye, quickly connected the cars, and disregarded them as he silently stared off into space. Of course, this is a task usually performed by a five-year-old, and indicated the superior intellectual potential of this youngster. The psychotic child appears retarded because of his learning inhibition and negativism, symptoms of his disorder, whereas the defective child's psychotic symptoms are superimposed on his limitation in learning.

The behavior of the child in a group may offer clinical clues for the differentiation. In groups of retarded children at nursery schools or state hospitals, the psychotic child may stand out like a "sore thumb." The children with mental deficiency, regardless of etiology, relate quickly to the examiner, play meaningfully with toys and objects, and relate to each other. The psychotic child is part of the group, but never in the group. He is the "loner." He may play with the toy and never look at it, but spin it, twirl it, mouth it, or disregard it, much as he does other personal or impersonal objects. At times his behavior may become chaotic and self-hurtful. He is at the periphery while the others are in the circle. Often, the behavior disorder in the child with mental deficiency is not so intense, and there is frequently greater relatedness. However, if the emotional disorder is of psychotic proportions, the differentiation may not be possible on the basis of behavior in a group.

Finally, the neuromuscular development of the psychotic child without mental deficiency often is unimpaired. The child is skillful in his use of tools, except when negativism interferes with the task. One psychotic child hospitalized in our ward discovered how to unscrew all locks and light switches adeptly and quickly. Many a staff member was surprised to sit on a chair and have it collapse because the screws were removed. Complex twiddling or continuous, repetitious bouncing on a trampoline or swinging on a swing may indicate motor behavior consistent with age and not usually attained by the defective child.

There are instances in which the differentiation is not possible, and a clinical trial of psychotherapy with the child and his parents may delineate one condition or the other. If there is some resolution of the emotional disorder, it is then possible to define more clearly the intellectual potential of the child. For example, a three-and-a-half-year-old youngster was referred to the Institute because of slow development, mutism, and severely disturbed behavior. He had banged his head and rocked in his crib since age nine months. He showed severe, self-hurtful, and destructive behavior, temper tantrums, many fears, and marked retardation, with difficulty in dressing and feeding himself. His family situation was difficult, with great turmoil between the parents. Since we were uncertain whether he was a child with only severe emotional problems or was mentally defective as well, the boy and his parents were seen for weekly psychotherapeutic interviews. As he became more responsive, the staff felt there was little question of his normal capacity. Psychologic tests measured his IQ at 43 at the beginning, 63 at age four-and-a-half, 80 at five, and 91 at seven-and-a-half. There was little doubt that he could eventually score within the higher average range.

In contrast, Jim, a severely disturbed youngster of six, was mute, delayed in his motor development, and extremely self-destructive. He would bang his head, slam the door with his fingers caught in the jamb, and was aggressive and hurtful to other children. The boy and his parents were seen for weekly interviews while Jim was an inpatient. On the ward the pressures associated with demands for performance beyond his capacity were not there. He related well to the ward staff. As his symptoms became less severe, he became more responsive. His performance was similar to that of a three-year-old, with rather concrete and immature performance. Repeated psychologic tests indicated little change in his achievement during the course of his treatment.

## SUMMARY

In summary, the individual is a product of all the experiences that have occurred in his life, both the integrative and disintegrative. The retarded child is vulnerable to defects in personality development not only because of constitutional endowment but also because of his interpersonal experiences with his environment. Emotional problems are the same as those occurring in children with normal intelligence. His symptoms may be influenced by his retardation, but can be understood in relation to his life experiences. If he is overwhelmed by his condition or encumbered by emotional disorder, he may live in solitude and despair, often hopelessly dependent on his parents, with neither his nor their feeling fulfilled in the promise of life. The potential of the child may never be realized; he may be victimized by his conflicts, with resulting self-depreciation, inhibition, and withdrawal, or he may react in retaliation with explosive aggressive behavior that demands control and custody.

The retarded child, because of special vulnerability in the area of personality development, needs special help. If this is given, he may develop successfully and be able to live a satisfactory life within his limitations. The mentally retarded require early and continuing good interpersonal relationships and a variety of opportunities for optimal personality development.

## REFERENCES

LAURETTA BENDER, "Childhood Schizophrenia," *Psychiatric Quarterly*, XXVII (1953), 663–681.

MALETA J. BOATMAN and STANISLAUS A. SZUREK, "A Clinical Study of Childhood Schizophrenia," in Don D. Jackson (Ed.), *The Etiology of Schizophrenia* (New York: Basic Books, 1960), pp. 389–440.

WILLIAM GOLDFARB, "Variations in Adolescent Adjustment of Institutionally-Reared Children," *American Journal of Orthopsychiatry*, XVII (1947), 449–457.

HILDA KNOBLOCH and BENJAMIN PASAMANICK, "Some Thoughts on the Inheritance of Intelligence," *American Journal of Orthopsychiatry*, XXXI (1961), 454–473.

IRVING PHILIPS, MARY JEFFRESS, EHUD KOCH, and MALETA J. BOATMAN, "The Application of Psychiatric Clinic Services for the Retarded Child and His Family," *Journal of the American Academy of Child Psychiatry,* I (1962), 297–313.

SALLY PROVENCE and ROSE C. LIPTON, *Infants in Institutions* (New York: International Universities Press, 1962).

RENÉ A. SPITZ, "Hospitalism," *The Psychoanalytic Study of the Child* (New York: International Universities Press, 1945), Vol. I, pp. 54–74.

STANISLAUS A. SZUREK, "Psychotic Episodes and Psychotic Maldevelopment," *American Journal of Orthopsychiatry,* XXVI (1956), 519–543.

GEORGE TARJAN, "Research and Clinical Advances in Mental Retardation," *Journal of the American Medical Association,* CLXXXII (1962), 617–621.

# PART III

## Prevention of Mental Retardation

# 10

# Recent Advances in Mental Retardation

## HARRY A. WAISMAN

Many professions have contributed to our progress in dealing with the mentally retarded child, and it is now well recognized that the physician who first sees the mentally retarded child must, of necessity, depend on the paramedical and nonmedical professions for both diagnosis and treatment. To relate the recent developments in research to the goal of prevention is an awesome task, and what follows is, in the exact sense, an overview. No more than a nod can be given to some areas, but perhaps greater recognition can be given to some of the biologic factors that have attracted attention. For prevention of mental retardation, we must utilize the increasing body of data gathered by all the professions so that the child can receive the maximum benefit of all our efforts.

## HISTORY OF RESEARCH IN MENTAL RETARDATION

Some of the first observations of mentally retarded patients were made years ago in the middle of the eighteenth century when children who could not learn or who were damaged at birth came to the attention of certain interested physicians and educators. These early investigators described these children and began to classify them into various groups. Later, the development of testing procedures and evaluation of children according to their ability made possible a comparison of their performance with that of their peers. Progress was made in classification and in measurement of motor performance, speech performance, and classroom-learning in those

children who failed to develop normally. Since the turn of this century, we
have become increasingly aware of the importance of genetic differences
that affect the intelligence of children.

Meanwhile, studies by neurologists and anatomists also were proceeding rapidly. Other workers studied the sense organs and the significance of
sensory deprivation. The recognition of social influences, the greater application of language development, and the role of environmental impoverishment and affectional deprivation was concurrent with the recognition that
the emotional problems of the retarded child and his family could be
treated properly by psychologists, social workers, psychiatrists, and understanding family physicians. Increasing awareness of the significance of
learning methods and procedures, the importance of nursery school, daycare-centers, and the like were other important interests of nonbiologic researchers.

## Biologic Research and the Mentally Retarded

It has been presumed, on the basis of some evidence, that prematurity is an
important cause of mental retardation and that any research designed to
reduce the incidence of prematurity will do a great deal to decrease the
unfavorable maturational and perinatal factors that have played a major
role in the etiology of mental retardation. The United States Public Health
Service is now completing a collaborative study of approximately 60,000
pregnancies in order to evaluate those factors that cause abortions, early
fetal deaths, and neonatal mortality, and those etiologic factors that are
responsible for cerebral palsy, mental retardation, and complex neurologic
disorders in the survivors of these pregnancies.

In premature infants of low birth weight (1,500 grams or less), Lula O.
Lubchenco and coworkers (1963) showed that the IQ is related inversely
to birth weight, and these workers are convinced that poor performance in
school is a result of prematurity. On the other hand, children who tested as
normal performed poorly in a school situation because they had reading
difficulties, hearing losses, immaturity in behavior, and so forth. Margaret
Dann *et al.* (1964) compared premature children with their own siblings
and found that the premature were somewhat retarded. In blind children,
the IQ was variable. The data of Lubchenco show that many of these children with retrolental fibroplasia had lower IQ's than the general population
and that of sixty-three children, twenty-five had IQ's below 90.

The question of prematurity and its influence on IQ has not been resolved. A. D. McDonald (1964) showed that children with a birth weight
of not more than four pounds were not mentally inferior to the general
population. Whereas it was true that some premature females weighing less
than three pounds had lower IQ scores than those weighing between three
and four pounds, this finding could not be confirmed for the males, and this

inconsistency raises a question about the correlation between IQ and birth weight.

Not all infants of low birth weight are premature. Twins of markedly different birth weights were compared to determine the effect of low birth weight that is not owing to prematurity (Babson *et al.*, 1964). The smaller twin presumably had a less favorable prenatal environment than the larger twin. The intellectual attainment of the "runt" was found to be less than that of the normal-sized twin. The nonruns as a group had more than six points higher average IQ than the runts, and these differences were significant for both identical and fraternal twin pairs. Unhappily, invoking statistics for these small differences clouds the significance of emotional and social factors that also may determine learning efficiency in these children.

S. H. Reisner *et al.* (1965) studied ten sets of twins in which only one was hypoglycemic, and they found that the hypoglycemic twin was invariably the smaller twin. The hypoglycemia was proposed as a possible cause of mental subnormality and slow development in the smaller as compared with the larger twin.

J. Yerushalmy *et al.* (1965) studied both birth weight and length of gestation of newborn infants. They found that small infants of long gestation had more severe anomalies than small infants of short gestation. However, infants of mothers who smoked were about seven ounces lighter at each gestational age and this decrease in size was not associated with any increase in anomalies or in survival when compared with other infants of the same gestational age (Yerushalmy, 1964).

Obviously, disagreement exists, and the need for additional data is apparent. From the data it could be deduced that prematurity is hazardous because the immature central nervous system is more subject to damage when myelin is being deposited around nerves and when internuncial and glial connections are being formed.

A number of factors are of great importance to the completion of a normal pregnancy, and research on the following has enlarged our knowledge.

*Uterine Physiology* Premature labor, for example, is an important cause of prematurity. Studies such as those by Rubén Laguens and José Lagrutta (1964) and Roberto M. Pinto *et al.* (1964) of the structural and biochemical changes of the uterine musculature at various stages of pregnancy will help to clarify the causes of premature labor.

*Bacteriuria in Pregnancy* Edward H. Kass (1962a) has discovered that there is an asymptomatic bacterial infection of the genitourinary tract in 6 per cent of all pregnant women. It was found that a prematurity rate as high as 27 per cent occurred in pregnant patients with bacteriuria in contrast to 7 per cent in those who were treated to eliminate the infection (Kass, 1962b). In a double-blind controlled study of antibacterial drugs in pregnancy, Priscilla Kincaid-Smith and Margaret Bullen (1965) found that women with bacteriuria had a higher incidence of fetal loss, prematurity (defined by weight), and pre-eclamptic toxemia. Successful treatment of the bacteriuria did not reduce the frequency of complications. They suggest that bacteriuria in pregnancy is often a manifestation of underlying chronic renal disease and that this is the cause of the complications. P. J. Little (1965) found no significant increase in prematurity in patients with bacteriuria, but more than one-third of the fifty-two women with untreated bacteriuria developed pyelonephritis compared to 4 per cent of the treated women. William E. Schamadan (1964) and Witold A. Hoja *et al.* (1964) have not found an increase in prematurity associated with bacteriuria. Some workers are more concerned about the deleterious effects of the antibiotics than about the prematurity, and it is thus obvious that additional data are necessary to resolve this polemic.

*Anemias of Pregnancy*   A premature birth rate of 42 per cent was found for patients whose hemoglobin at the time of delivery was 7.4 grams–per cent or less (Macgregor, 1963). The neonatal mortality was increased, but no more so than for other infants of comparable weight. The average birth weight increased and the premature birth rate fell when the patients were given iron routinely before the thirtieth week of pregnancy.

*Toxemias of Pregnancy*   Studies have shown that toxemia in pregnancy is associated with uterine asphyxia, and good evidence exists that some substance that causes an increase in blood pressure accounts for the pre-eclampsia and eclampsia. This vasopressor agent has been found in the placenta, and it seems likely that it is formed also in the placenta (Berger and Cavanagh, 1963). When the causes of toxemia are better understood, it will be easier to find methods to prevent this condition.

*Fetal Congenital Anomalies*   Abnormal intrauterine development is frequently the result of an abnormal chromosomal pattern. These abnormal fetuses often are rejected by spontaneous abortion. Spontaneous abortion fetuses have been examined and chromosomal patterns were found to be abnormal in approximately 50 per cent of these unborn children (Thiede and Salm, 1964). Most of them showed elevated chromosomal counts above the normal number of forty-six. A. E. Szulman (1965) found chromosomal abnormalities in sixteen of twenty-five cases of spontaneous abortion. Six of these were trisomies, five were cases in which only one of the sex chromosomes was present (45-X0), and five were cases of triploidy. No mammalian triploids have been known to survive, but triploid cells occasionally are found in mosaics.

*Virus Diseases*   Virus diseases always have been suspected to be a cause of prematurity, brain damage, and formation of congenital anomalies. But only within recent years, when methods for the study of viruses have progressed to the point where identification, characterization, and isolation of the viruses have become more exact, has there been meaningful progress in this area. German measles during pregnancy has been believed to cause intrauterine damage to the fetus, giving rise to congenital abnormalities and most often deafness in the newborn child. Recent studies (Sever *et al.,* 1964) showed that of 600 pregnant women, 17.5 per cent had no antibodies against German measles and that the presence or absence of antibodies could not be correlated with a history of rubella as given by the pregnant women. These investigators previously had used tissue-culture-grown virus to produce clinical rubella in volunteers who had no antibody to the disease. The virus could be re-isolated from these individuals. These volunteers developed antibodies and were thought to be immune to the disease. It is likely that antigens soon will be prepared that can be used to immunize those women who have no antibody to this disease, and one can foresee the time when all pregnant women will be tested for the presence of one or more antibodies or be given an immunization against German measles or other viruses that threaten the developing fetus. The administration of polio vaccine and measles vaccine is now so routine that one might expect that proper preparations soon would be available also for other virus diseases.

It should be pointed out that it is strongly suspected, because of recent research, that Coxsackie virus, herpes-simplex virus, cytomegalic inclusion disease virus, and perhaps many others account for some fetal deaths and intrauterine brain damage.

*Toxoplasmosis* Much attention has been paid to infection by the intracellular protozoan parasite, *Toxoplasma gondii*. This organism has long been known as a cause of mental retardation accompanied by such signs as microcephaly, intracranial calcifications, and chorioretinitis. Harry A. Feldman (1958) summarized a large number of congenital toxoplasmosis cases and found that 31 per cent were born prematurely and 27 per cent of these died. Fifty-six per cent had some degree of psychomotor retardation. Earlier it was thought that once the mother had had an infection with *Toxoplasma,* sufficient antibodies were formed to prevent the re-occurrence of this disease in subsequent pregnancies, but recent data (Langer, 1963) have demonstrated that more than one case of toxoplasmosis can occur from a mother so infected.

Recent research on experimental toxoplasmosis in rats and its influence on subsequent pregnancies has provided important data, even though in another species. George Wildführ (1954) investigated the influence of *Toxoplasma* infections in mother rats on the young in the first and second generations. The mother was infected near the end of the pregnancy, about the eighteenth to nineteenth day of gestation. No rat in the first generation showed any symptoms, and there were no deaths. In the second generation, only one rat had a significant toxoplasmosis titer, and another died after one month of age. Therefore, it seems likely that the female rat has the ability to transmit the infection to the young in subsequent generations, although the number of young infected is small.

*Anoxia* Significant work has been done on quantitating the effects of controlled asphyxia in fetal and newborn rhesus monkeys. These experiments by H. N. Jacobson and William F. Windle (1960), Windle (1964), and Windle *et al.* (1962) simulated the circumstance of anoxia in infants. Fetal monkeys were delivered by caesarean section under local anesthesia without rupturing the fetal membranes. Asphyxia was controlled by leaving the fetus within the membranes until respiration was initiated by opening the sac. If resuscitation was required, this was accomplished by endotracheal catheterization and intermittent positive pressure insufflation of the lungs with oxygen. Using this technique, it was possible to obtain information on the resistance of near-term monkeys to asphyxia of eleven to seventeen minutes' duration. Asphyxiated fetuses began to breathe spontaneously after intervals varying from six minutes to seventeen minutes from the time that resuscitation began. There was a direct correlation between this length of time and the length of the interval (three to seven minutes) between the last gasp and the beginning of resuscitation. In contrast, in nitrogen-asphyxiated newborn monkeys that survived, spontaneous respiratory movements occurred as soon as oxygen was administered. All asphyxiated monkeys showed functional defects, but these were temporary in those that began to breathe unaided. Some of the monkeys were severely crippled neurologically. The later effects of the anoxia *in amnio* were studied by Sue V. Saxon (1961b) who showed gross behavioral effects in those monkeys that were not crippled (Saxon, 1961a). From the data provided by Jacobson and Windle, it seems that ten minutes may be the critical length of time that the central nervous system of the monkey can withstand oxygen deprivation without great damage and resulting neurologic and intellectual damage. However, a three-year follow-up of normal and anoxic human newborns (Graham, Ernhart, and Thurston, 1962) showed that only slight effects on intelligence were caused by anoxia. Anoxia per se cannot be considered a major source of severe brain damage in infants.

*Other Studies*    A number of factors that influence placental physiology now are being investigated. Studies are in progress also of the role of tobacco-smoking in the production of infants of lower birth weight and on the influence of poor diet, toxins, radiation, and so forth.

A heartening awakening has taken place in the recognition of the social and economic factors that influence prenatal care, provide optimum conditions for normal delivery, and so forth. As a result of these studies, it is hoped that proper medical care will be provided for the portion of our population that is now culturally and economically deprived and from which large groups of mentally retarded children are derived.

## GENETIC AND BIOCHEMICAL CAUSES OF MENTAL RETARDATION

An increasing number of genetic and biochemical causes of mental retardation have been identified. Studies of these have provided the most exciting approaches to the treatment of children with a variety of types of mental retardation. It should be pointed out that genetic and biochemical errors account for perhaps 10 to 15 per cent of the mentally retarded in institutions. This is a sizable number, and prevention of retardation in this group would do much to reduce the institutionalized population. There is sufficient information to suppose that we are now at a threshold of new developments in this area. Just as we hope to prevent mental retardation by greater attention to factors that cause prematurity, it is now firmly believed that mental retardation often can be prevented by specific attention to those individuals who possess some hereditary abnormality or abnormal gene complement.

The story really began with a notion first proposed by Archibald E. Garrod (1908) more than fifty-five years ago in England. This concept of inborn errors of metabolism received support only after the same disease was discovered in several members of the same family. The abnormal chemical process was a defect in the biochemical pathway caused by an absence of an enzyme system. Suffice it to say that recent research in enzyme biochemistry has brought about a greater understanding of these diseases. Each gene or part of a gene controls the synthesis of an enzyme. It is now possible to identify the enzyme that is deficient in each of a number of diseases. Work on the genetic code has helped us understand how certain hereditary traits are established in cells by the desoxyribonucleic acid (DNA) in each cell, and to understand the role of the ribonucleic acid (RNA) that is elaborated by information obtained from the DNA. Specific proteins are formed that determine such important factors as intelligence, memory, learning, recall, and retention. In the future other fascinating information is likely to come from studies of some of these newly described diseases.

*Phenylketonuria*　This has become perhaps the best known of the inborn errors of metabolism since it was discovered in 1934 by A. Fölling (1934) in Norway. This disease was first thought to have an incidence approximating one in 40,000 births. Recent studies in Massachusetts, which is one of the states that has compulsory testing for phenylketonuria in newborn infants (others are Rhode Island and New York, as of this writing), have shown that the incidence is about one in 10,000 live births. Whether compulsory testing is the best way to identify phenylketonuric children, or whether education of physicians is a preferable way remains to be determined.

During the past eight years it has been possible for us to study newly identified children with phenylketonuria (Berman *et al.,* 1961). A low-phenylalanine diet was provided shortly after diagnosis was made. This long-term study is now being summarized, and it is quite clear that improved intellectual performance can be obtained by careful supervision of the diet, by careful control of the plasma level, and by close cooperation between the physician, the social worker, the dietician, and the parents. When the parents understand the disease in all its aspects, their cooperation in providing optimum conditions for treatment is one of the most important factors enabling the child to develop with a good potential. The earlier the diagnosis is made, the better the outcome. From our data (Figure 10–I) we obtain the distinct impression that the diagnosis should be made early if an optimum IQ is to be obtained. Our long-term study has shown us the im-

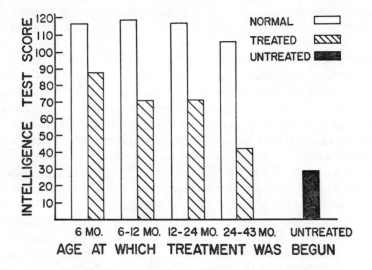

**Figure 10–1.** Age at which treatment was begun.

portance of doing serial developmental or intelligence quotients, not only on the child with PKU, but also on his normal siblings and on his untreated siblings with PKU who were diagnosed too late for therapy. There is a clue in our data that suggests that a mother who is a heterozygote for PKU and whose IQ is low-normal may fail to recognize that her child is not developing normally, and this may delay the time when the diagnosis is made and when the diet is begun.

It is now possible to simulate PKU in the rat, so that an appropriate experimental model is available for biochemical and behavioral studies (Wang and Waisman, 1961). The value of this model should be apparent, for experiments now can be performed on PKU rats rather than on children with this disease (Waisman and Harlow, 1963). These rats with PKU have high blood-phenylalanine levels, excrete phenylketones, and perform water-maze tests poorly as compared with rats fed normally (Polidora, Boggs, and Waisman, 1963). This model has been improved by using the monkey (Waisman *et al.,* 1962). The ability to simulate PKU in this subhuman primate (Waisman and Harlow, 1965) closely related to man has made possible more accurate behavioral experiments, brain biopsies, and meta-bolic studies that provide information not possible to obtain from children with this disease.

In brains of phenylketonuric rats (Waisman *et al.,* 1964), there was an increase in the glial cells in the cortical gray matter. In the white matter, myelin formation seemed to have been retarded or interrupted. From very preliminary data with the electron microscope, mitochondria of the glial cells of a phenylketonuric monkey were found to be enlarged and there was a loss of cristae. At the present time, it is not possible to correlate brain enzyme activity with the morphologic changes, and more data are desirable.

*Histidinemia*    This disease is a curious inborn error of metabolism that may or may not be related to mental retardation. It was observed that children with this disease excreted histidine in the urine and also had high levels in the plasma. This work was done by H. Ghadimi *et al.* (1961), Victor H. Auerbach *et al.* (1962), Angelo M. DiGeorge and Victor H. Auerbach (1963), Theo Gerritsen (1964), and Harry A. Waisman (1964). The only uniform clinical symptom that these children have is poor speech. Placing these children on a low-histidine diet seems unneces-sary if there is no mental retardation, although the plasma-histidine level can be reduced by a low-histidine diet. Speech-correction therapy may help a great deal in overcoming speech problems. Apparently, this is a mild in-born error of metabolism with relatively little brain damage in contrast to many other diseases in which damage is severe.

*Homocystinuria*    This inborn error of metabolism was discovered in-dependently in my laboratory by Gerritsen *et al.* (1962) and Gerritsen and Waisman (1964b), and in Ireland by Nina A. J. Carson and W. D. Neill (1962) and Carson *et al.* (1963). These patients have homocystinuria, subluxated lenses, mental retardation, convulsions, genu valgum, fine sparse hair, and tend to develop thrombosis. Subluxated lenses and excre-tion of homocystine are the key findings in these children. The brain dam-age is quite extensive so that mental retardation is obvious. Some patients have had Marfan's syndrome (Gibson, Carson, and Neill, 1964), and our patient had spongy degeneration of the brain (Waisman and Gerritsen, 1964). Sections of this child's brain showed hypoplasia of the corpus cal-losum, a micropolygyric cortex, and also changes that are characteristic of van Bogaert-Bertrand type of spongy degeneration. Very weak reactions with sulfhydryl and disulfide stains indicated that certain sulphur-contain-ing proteins were not present in this child's brain (Chou and Waisman,

1965). This decreased staining is probably the result of the enzyme deficit. The enzyme that is absent in homocystinuria (Mudd *et al.,* 1964) is cystathionine synthetase, and it is found ordinarily in the liver. This enzyme converts homocystine and serine to the next metabolic product, cystathionine. The lack of this enzyme in the liver probably is responsible for the inability to deal with this sulfur amino acid. We were able to show (Gerritsen and Waisman, 1964a) that the brain from our patient had no cystathionine. It seems likely that cystathionine is important for normal brain development and is not part of the brain structure itself, but can be found free in the brain tissue.

How can homocystine patients be treated? This is not known, but since patients with homocystinuria cannot form cystathionine, one might suppose that the administration of cysthathionine would provide normal growth and development of intellectual processes.

*Cystathioninuria*   Still another rare condition is a defect in the methionine-cysteine pathway that results in the excretion of abnormal amounts of cystathionine. One patient was a sixty-four-year-old, moderately retarded woman (Harris, Penrose, and Thomas, 1958–1959) and the other was a forty-four-year-old man with acromegaly, deafness, some emotional disorder, and normal or low-normal intelligence (Frimpter, Haymovitz, and Horwith, 1963). Both patients had normal relatives who excreted moderate amounts of cysthathionine.

*Hyperglycinemia and Hyperglycinuria*   This disease, in which the simple amino acid glycine is excreted in large amounts, is rarer than most of the others thus far mentioned. However, it has been found in many parts of the world. Cases have been found in the United States by Barton Childs *et al.* (1961); William L. Nyhan, Margaret Borden, and Barton Childs (1961); and William L. Nyhan, Julian J. Chisholm, and Roy O. Edwards, Jr. (1963); in Japan by Keiya Tada *et al.* (1963); in England by W. Cochrane, C. R. Scriver, and V. Krause (1963); in Germany by K. Schreier and W. Müller (1964); and in the Netherlands by H. K. A. Visser, H. W. Veenstra, and C. Pik (1964). It will be necessary to study additional cases to explain how this simplest of all amino acids is concerned with brain damage. These patients are severely retarded and show signs of severe neurologic damage, cerebral spastic appearance, and failure to develop. A new type of hyperglycinemia with hypo-oxaluria has been discovered by Theo Gerritsen, e. Kaveggia, and Harry A. Waisman (in press).

*Hypersarcosinuria*   This error of metabolism was found in a one-year-old boy who was only slightly retarded (Gerritsen and Waisman, 1965), and it is not certain that the error of metabolism is the cause of the retardation.

*Urinary Excretion of 3, 4-Dihydroxyphenylalanine (DOPA)*   Two five-year-old boys were examined because of short stature (Copps *et al.,* 1963). Both boys appeared to be neglected and malnourished, and both were mentally retarded. The excretion of DOPA was higher than normal, but decreased when the boys were fed an unrestricted diet. Since this has not been noted previously in malnutrition, there may be some other factor that contributes to this condition.

*Succinicaciduria*    A metabolic defect in the urea cycle results in the production of this unusual excretory product. Argininosuccinase was absent in two siblings with the disease and was significantly decreased in the parents and two of the three normal siblings. It was absent also in another patient with the disease (Tomlinson and Westall, 1964). The disease apparently is a result of an autosomal recessive gene. Approximately seven children with this disease have been reported in the literature by Nina A. J. Carson and D. W. Neill (1962); Marvin D. Armstrong, Kerin N. Yates, and M. G. Stemmermann (1964); B. Levin, H. M. M. Mackay, and V. G. Oberholzer (1960); and R. G. Westall (1960). The patients have moderate to severe mental retardation and an aminoaciduria in which the argininosuccinic acid is the primary abnormality. Three other severely retarded siblings with argininosuccinicaciduria have been reported (Wallis, Beer, and Fischl, 1963). However, the amounts of argininosuccinic acid excreted by these children were much less than in the other cases, and it is not yet clear if the etiology of the disease in these children is different from that in those originally described.

*Citrullinuria*    This metabolic defect has been identified in only one child who had severe mental retardation. Although the data suggested a block in the normal metabolic utilization of citrulline, urea excretion was in the normal range (McMurray *et al.*, 1962). The enzymatic defect has not yet been defined (McMurray *et al.*, 1963).

*Hartnup Disease*    A defect in the transport of tryptophan has been suggested as the cause of Hartnup disease. These patients have photosensitivity, a pellagra-like rash, and marked cerebellar ataxia. The aminoaciduria is characterized by a generalized aminoaciduria, hyperindoluria, and hypertryptophanuria (DeLaey *et al.*, 1964). Although mental deterioration was present in the Hartnup family, studies on other patients have shown that mental retardation is not significant in this disease (Jepson and Spiro, 1960).

*Hydroxykynureninuria*    This error of tryptophan metabolism has been described by G. M. Komrower and his coworkers (1964) in an eight-year-old moderately retarded girl.

*Maple Syrup Urine Disease*    Maple syrup urine disease has now been found in more than fifty children, each of whom has severe mental retardation, vomiting, muscular hypertonicity, and onset of symptoms very early in infancy. Death usually occurs in untreated patients before one year of age. Diet therapy has improved the outlook for these patients (Snyderman *et al.*, 1964). The defect is apparently in the oxidative decarboxylation of the

branched chain α-keto acids, so that keto acids of valine, leucine, and isoleucine can be found in the urine and in the blood. These keto acids are
identified easily by the dinitrophenylhydrazine test.

The so-called Oasthouse urine disease is considered by some workers
to be a variant of maple syrup urine disease because of similar clinical
features in the one patient thus far reported (Smith and Strang, 1958), but
too few biochemical findings have been made to describe it as a separate
syndrome.

*Hypervalinemia*   Idiopathic hypervalinemia was discovered by Yoshiro Wada and his coworkers (1963–1964) who described a child with
vomiting, failure to thrive, drowsiness, and hypervalinemia. This child also
resembled those with maple syrup urine disease, but the levels of leucine and
isoleucine in blood and urine were normal. The electroencephalogram was
mildly abnormal and the karyotype was normal. These workers suggested
that the block in valine metabolism lies in an early step of degradation, but did not name the suspected enzyme deficit.

*Hyperprolinemia*   Two types of hyperprolinemia have now been
identified by Mary L. Efron and her coworkers. One type apparently is
caused by a deficiency of proline oxidase (Efron, 1965a) and has been
found in two families (Efron, 1965b). The defect was found in four children in each family, and two other children in each family were normal. In
each family, only one of the four affected children was retarded, and this
retarded child also had hereditary renal disease. A second type of hyperprolinemia has been found in only one patient, and it apparently is a result
of a deficiency of pyrroline-5-carboxylate dehydrogenase. The patient was
mildly retarded and there was no evidence of renal disease.

*Joseph's Disease*   Proline occurs in the urine in Joseph's disease, but
proline levels in the blood apparently are normal. This disease is much
more serious than hyperprolinemia. It was found in three retarded siblings
(Joseph *et al.,* 1958) who had convulsions that began in the first month of
life. The first child died at ten months of age and the second at two years.
The third child was still living at eight months.

## OTHER INBORN ERRORS OF METABOLISM

A host of inborn errors of metabolism undoubtedly will be identified in
the future by careful screening and evaluation of patients with specific birth
defects who show mental retardation and failure to thrive. Careful attention
to the excretion of amino acids by children must take into account the
excretion of free amino acids by normal children, and this baseline information has been presented in part by H. H. Van Gelderen and L. J. Dooren
(1964). A review of the aminoacidurias brought up to date has been presented by Efron (1965a). Additional diseases associated with errors in

sugar metabolism probably will be found also. Unusual cases of lactosuria, sucrosuria, xylosuria, and pentosuria have been described already. Not only sugars and amino acids but also, perhaps, fats and fatty acids are involved. In diseases such as Hurler's disease, abnormal fat-sugar complexes are found that may be the cause of the disease. Other types of lipodystrophy and lipochondrodystrophy also may be found to be caused by inborn errors of metabolism.

*Maternal Phenylketonuria (PKU)* Since women with phenylketonuria are able to have children, it is important to know the effect that this condition may have on the offspring. Charlton C. Mabry *et al.* (1963) described three phenylketonuric mothers who had seven retarded children among them. Seven other children in one of these families died in infancy of unknown causes. R. Wendell Coffelt (1964) described a phenylketonuric mother of normal intelligence who had two mildly retarded children. An editorial in *Lancet* ("Maternal Phenylketonuria," 1964) suggested that mothers of children with epilepsy or mental deficiency should be examined for phenylketonuria, as this might be the cause of some of these abnormalities. Robert Guthrie (1964) stated that a mother with PKU was found because of high phenylalanine levels in her infant, and the test on the newborn is therefore of value in finding occult PKU in the mother. He believes that follow-up tests should be done whenever the blood phenylalanine of the newborn is as high as four milligrams–per cent. A phenylketonuric mother with normal intelligence has been found who has had two phenylketonuric children, and it is not surprising that both of these children were retarded (Partington, 1962). Normal children also can be born to mothers with PKU. Michael W. Partington and Elizabeth J. M. Lewis (1963) stated that at least eleven normal children from five families have been born to phenylketonuric mothers, and Charlton C. Mabry *et al.* (1963) listed seven known phenylketonuric mothers with apparently normal offspring. Four of these mothers were of normal or low-normal intelligence, and three were retarded.

Although phenylketonuric mothers can have normal offspring, the risk of retardation in the offspring is extremely high. Another important factor is the genetic make-up of the husband of the phenylketonuric mother. If he also has PKU, all of the children will have PKU. If he is a heterozygote, approximately half of the children will have PKU and half will be carriers; and retardation would occur only as a result of the maternal PKU. This problem is becoming more important as girls with treated phenylketonuria grow up and will be able to marry and have children. Many of these women may prefer to adopt children instead of having children of their own. Others may prefer to try a diet low in phenylalanine and hope that the offspring will be normal, but probably it is unrealistic to believe that these pregnant women will adhere to a low-phenylalanine diet.

Animal studies also can contribute to our knowledge about maternal

PKU. Boggo and Waisman (1964) fed high levels of phenylalanine to pregnant rats and found that fetal plasma-phenylalanine levels were twice as high as the maternal levels. It seems likely that the fetal brain would be damaged by such high phenylalanine levels, but no gross abnormalities were noted. Kerr and Waisman (unpublished) fed high levels of phenylalanine to pregnant monkeys (*Macaca mulatta*) and found that the birth weight was equal to that of babies from normally fed mothers. The babies appeared to thrive, and only further behavioral and learning tests will divulge their intellectual ability.

*Congenital Anomalies*  These frequently are associated with mental retardation. Apparently the occurrence of anomalies in the skin, ears, hands, teeth, and so forth indicates generalized ectodermal involvement, and so it is not surprising that brain tissue which arises from ectoderm also is profoundly affected. Suffice it to say that the congenital anomalies are associated frequently with aberrations in chromosomes (Marden, Smith, and McDonald, 1964). Whenever an abnormal chromosome is identified, mental retardation usually is an important accompanying sign of disease. In mongolism there is usually an extra autosomal chromosome, but some sex-linked extra chromosomes are found also to cause mental retardation, as in Klinefelter's disease. Several autosomal diseases are known to be a result of trisomy of selected chromosomes, that is, a third chromosome is added to a chromosome pair, and this is represented by trisomy 18 (Smith *et al.*, 1960) and trisomy D. It is not yet possible to prevent some of the chromosomal aberrations, but with more information it may become so.

## SUMMARY

Progress is being made in the biologic disciplines as well as in the paramedical areas. Those who are studying various aspects of behavior and sensory and affectional deprivation have interesting opportunities for further research. Understanding of social and cultural deprivation will provide ways by which our young citizens can become more productive and no burden on society. Research in language development, research on teaching methods, and research on special educational procedures are all being done. It should be pointed out also that this research concerns not only retarded children but also certain retarded adults. Training programs and vocational rehabilitation are important aspects with which research in this specialized field is now concerned.

Greater cooperation between bio-medical and nonmedical behavioral investigators should be worked out so that research findings can be applied more meaningfully. Animal research and basic brain biochemistry undoubtedly will provide information that will be helpful in better treatment of retarded children in the future.

REFERENCES

MARVIN D. ARMSTRONG, KERIN N. YATES, and M. G. STEMMERMANN, "An Occurrence of Argininosuccinic Aciduria," *Pediatrics*, XXXIII (1964), 280–282.

VICTOR H. AUERBACH, ANGELO M. DiGEORGE, ROBERT C. BALDRIDGE, CHARLES D. TOURTELLOTTE, and M. PRINCE BRIGHAM, "Histidinemia: A Deficiency in Histidase Resulting in the Urinary Excretion of Histidine and of Imidazolepyruvic Acid," *Journal of Pediatrics*, LX (1962), 487–497.

S. GORHAM BABSON, JOHN KANGAS, NORTON YOUNG, and JAMES L. BRAMHALL, "Growth and Development of Twins of Dissimilar Size at Birth," *Pediatrics*, XXXIII (1964), 327–333.

MAX BERGER and DENIS CAVANAGH, "Toxemia of Pregnancy," *American Journal of Obstetrics and Gynecology*, LXXXVII (1963), 293–305.

PHYLLIS W. BERMAN, FRANCES K. GRAHAM, PETER L. EICHMAN, and HARRY A. WAISMAN, "Psychologic and Neurologic Status of Diet-Treated Phenylketonuric Children and Their Siblings," *Pediatrics*, XXVIII (1961), 924–934.

DALLAS E. BOGGS and HARRY A. WAISMAN, "Influence of Excess Dietary Phenylalanine on Pregnant Rats and Their Fetuses," *Proceedings of the Society for Experimental Biology and Medicine*, CVI (1964), 407–410.

NINA A. J. CARSON, D. C. CUSWORTH, C. E. DENT, C. M. B. FIELD, D. W. NEILL, and R. G. WESTALL, "Homocystinuria: A New Inborn Error of Metabolism Associated with Mental Deficiency," *Archives of Disease in Childhood*, XXXVIII (1963), 425–436.

NINA A. J. CARSON and D. W. NEILL, "Metabolic Abnormalities Detected in a Survey of Mentally Backward Individuals in Northern Ireland," *Archives of Disease in Childhood*, XXXVII (1962), 505–513.

BARTON CHILDS, WILLIAM L. NYHAN, MARGARET BORDEN, LESLIE BARD, and ROBERT E. COOKE, "Idiopathic Hyperglycinemia and Hyperglycinuria: A New Disorder of Amino Acid Metabolism, I," *Pediatrics*, XXVII (1961), 522–538.

SHI-MING CHOU and HARRY A. WAISMAN, "Spongy Degeneration of the Central Nervous System. Case of Homocystinuria," *Archives of Pathology*, LXXIX (1965), 357–363.

W. COCHRANE, C. R. SCRIVER, and V. KRAUSE, "Hyperglycinemia-Hyperglycinuria Syndrome in a Newborn Infant," *Abstracts of the Society for Pediatric Research*, Atlantic City, May 1, 1963, p. 102.

R. WENDELL COFFELT, "Unexpected Finding from a PKU Newborn Screening Program," *Pediatrics*, XXXIV (1964), 889–890.

STEPHEN C. COPPS, THEO GERRITSEN, DAVID W. SMITH, and HARRY A. WAISMAN, "Urinary Excretion of 3,4-dihydroxyphenylalanine (DOPA) in Two Children of Short Stature with Malnutrition," *Journal of Pediatrics*, LXII (1963), 208–216.

MARGARET DANN, S. Z. LEVINE, and ELIZABETH V. NEW, "A Long-Term Follow-Up Study of Small Premature Infants," *Pediatrics*, XXXIII (1964), 945–955.

P. DeLacy, C. Hooft, J. Timmermans, and J. Snoeck, "Biochemical Aspects of the Hartnup Disease. Part I. Results of Intravenous and Oral Tryptophan Loading Tests in a Case of Hartnup Disease. Part II. Some Observations on Rats About Trytophan Metabolism. Part III. General Discussion and Conclusions," *Annales Paediatrici,* CCII (1964), 145–160, 253–262, 321–331.

Angelo M. DiGeorge and Victor H. Auerbach, "The Primary Amino-acidopathies: Genetic Defects in the Metabolism of the Amino Acids," *Pediatric Clinics of North America,* X (1963), 723–744.

Mary L. Efron, "Aminoaciduria," *New England Journal of Medicine,* CCLXXII (1965a), 1058–1067, 1107–1113.

Mary L. Efron, "Familial Hyperprolinemia. Report of a Second Case, Associated with Congenital Renal Malformations, Hereditary Hematuria and Mild Mental Retardation with Demonstration of an Enzyme Defect," *New England Journal of Medicine,* CCLXXII (1965b), 1243–1254.

Harry A. Feldman, "Toxoplasmosis," *Pediatrics,* XXII (1958), 559–574.

A. Fölling, Über Auscheidung von Phenylbrenzträubensäure in den Harn als Stoffwechselanomalie in Verbindung mit Imbezillität," *Zeitschrift für physiologische Chemie,* LLXXVII (1934), 169–176.

George W. Frimpter, Asher Haymovitz, and Melvin Horwith, "Cystathioninuria," *New England Journal of Medicine,* CCLXVIII (1963), 333–339.

Archibald E. Garrod, "The Croonian Lectures on Inborn Errors of Metabolism, I, II, III, IV," *Lancet,* II (1908), 1–7, 73–79, 142–148, 214–220.

Theo Gerritsen, "Histidinemia and Mental Retardation," in Jakob Oster (Ed.), *Proceedings of the International Congress on the Scientific Study of Mental Retardation* (Copenhagen, 1964), pp. 94–95.

Theo Gerritsen, e. Kaveggia, and Harry A. Waisman, "A New Type of Idiopathic Hyperglycinemia with Hypo-Oxaluria," *Pediatrics* (in press).

Theo Gerritsen, James G. Vaughn, and Harry A. Waisman, "The Identification of Homocystine in the Urine," *Biochemical and Biophysical Research Communications,* IX (1962), 493–496.

Theo Gerritsen and Harry A. Waisman, "Homocystinuria: Absence of Cystathionine in the Brain," *Science,* CXLV (1964a), 588.

Theo Gerritsen and Harry A. Waisman, "Homocystinuria, An Error in the Metabolism of Methionine," *Pediatrics,* XXXIII (1964b), 413–420.

Theo Gerritsen and Harry A. Waisman, "Hypersarcosinemia, a New Error of Metabolism," *Federation Proceedings,* XXIV (1965), 470.

H. Ghadimi, Michael W. Partington, and A. Hunter, "A Familial Disturbance of Histidine Metabolism," *New England Journal of Medicine,* CCLXV (1961), 221–224.

J. B. Gibson, Nina A. J. Carson, and D. W. Neill, "Pathological Findings in Homocystinuria," *Journal of Clinical Pathology,* XVII (1964), 427–437.

Frances K. Graham, Claire B. Ernhart, and Don Thurston, "The Relationship of Neonatal Apnea to Development at Three Years," in *Mental Retardation,* Research Publications of the Association for Research in

Nervous and Mental Disease, XXXIX (Baltimore, Maryland: Williams and Wilkins, 1962), 159–168.

ROBERT GUTHRIE, "Routine Screening for Inborn Errors in the Newborn: 'Inhibition Assays,' 'Instant Bacteria' and Multiple Tests," in Jakob Oster (Ed.), *Proceedings of the International Congress on the Scientific Study of Mental Retardation* (Copenhagen, 1964), pp. 495–499.

H. HARRIS, LIONEL S. PENROSE, and D. H. H. THOMAS, "Cystathioninuria," *Annals of Human Genetics,* XXIII (1958–1959), 442–453.

WITOLD A. HOJA, JAMES D. HEFNER, and MELVIN R. SMITH, "Asymptomatic Bacteriuria in Pregnancy," *Obstetrics and Gynecology,* XXIV (1964), 458–462.

H. N. JACOBSON and WILLIAM F. WINDLE, "Responses of Foetal and Newborn Monkeys to Asphyxia," *Journal of Physiology,* CLIII (1960), 447–456.

JOHN B. JEPSON and MARY JANE SPIRO, "Hartnup Disease," in John B. Stanbury, James B. Wyngaarden, and Donald S. Fredrickson (Eds.), *The Metabolic Basis of Inherited Disease* (New York: McGraw-Hill, 1960), pp. 1338–1364.

R. JOSEPH, M. RIBIERRE, J.-C. JOB, and M. GIRAULT, "Maladie familiale associant des convulsions à début très précoce, une hyperalbuminorachie et une hyperaminoacidurie," *Archives Françaises de Pediatrie,* XV (1958), 374–387.

EDWARD H. KASS, "Maternal Urinary Tract Infection," *New York State Journal of Medicine,* LXII (1962a), 2822–2826.

EDWARD H. KASS, "Pyelonephritis and Bacteriuria, A Major Problem in Prenatal Medicine," *Annals of Internal Medicine,* LVI (1962b), 46–53.

PRISCILLA KINCAID-SMITH and MARGARET BULLEN, "Bacteriuria in Pregnancy," *Lancet,* I (1965), 395–399.

G. M. KOMROWER, VERA WILSON, J. R. CLAMP, and R. G. WESTALL, "Hydroxykynureninuria: A Case of Abnormal Trytophan Metabolism Probably Due to a Deficiency of Kynureninase," *Archives of Disease in Childhood,* XXXIX (1964), 250–256.

RUBÉN LAGUENS and JOSÉ LAGRUTTA, "Fine Structure of Human Uterine Muscle in Pregnancy," *American Journal of Obstetrics and Gynecology,* LXXXIX (1964), 1040–1048.

HEINRICH LANGER, "Repeated Congenital Infection with *Toxoplasma gondii,*" *Obstetrics and Gynecology,* XXI (1963), 318–329.

B. LEVIN, H. M. M. MACKAY, and V. G. OBERHOLZER, "Argininosuccinic Aciduria: An Inborn Error of Amino Acid Metabolism," *Archives of Disease in Childhood,* XXXVI (1960), 622–632.

P. J. LITTLE, "Prevention of Pyelonephritis of Pregnancy," *Lancet,* I (1965), 567–569.

LULA O. LUBCHENCO, FREDERICK A. HORNER, LINDA H. REED, IVAN E. HIX, DAVID METCALF, RUTH COHIG, HELEN C. ELLIOTT, and MARGARET BOURG, "Sequelae of Premature Birth. Evaluation of Premature Infants of Low Birth Weights at Ten Years of Age," *American Journal of Diseases of Children,* CVI (1963), 101–115.

CHARLTON C. MABRY, JASPER C. DENNISTON, THOMAS L. NELSON, and CHOON D. SON, "Maternal Phenylketonuria: A Cause of Mental Retardation in Children without the Metabolic Defect," *New England Journal of Medicine,* CCLXIX (1963), 1404–1408.

A. D. MCDONALD, "Intelligence in Children of Very Low Birth Weight," *British Journal of Preventive and Social Medicine,* XVIII (1964), 59–74.

MARGARET W. MACGREGOR, "Maternal Anemia as a Factor in Prematurity and Perinatal Mortality," *Scottish Medical Journal,* VIII (1963), 134–140.

PHILIP M. MARDEN, DAVID W. SMITH, and MICHAEL J. MCDONALD, "Congenital Anomalies in the Newborn Infant, Including Minor Variations," *Journal of Pediatrics,* LXIV (1964), 357–371.

"Maternal Phenylketonuria," *Lancet,* I (1964), 598.

W. C. MCMURRAY, F. MOHYUDDIN, R. J. ROSSITER, J. C. RATHBUN, G. H. VALENTINE, S. J. KOEGLER, and D. E. ZARFAS, "Citrullinuria. A New Aminoaciduria Associated with Mental Retardation," *Lancet,* I (1962), 138.

W. C. MCMURRAY, J. C. RATHBUN, F. MOHYUDDIN, and S. J. KOEGLER, "Citrullinuria," *Pediatrics,* XXXII (1963), 347–357.

S. HARVEY MUDD, JAMES D. FINKELSTEIN, FILADELFO IRREVERRE, and LEONARD LESTER, "Homocystinuria: An Enzymatic Defect," *Science,* CXLIII (1964), 1443–1445.

WILLIAM L. NYHAN, MARGARET BORDEN, and BARTON CHILDS, "Idiopathic Hyperglycinemia: A New Disorder of Amino Acid Metabolism. II. The Concentrations of Other Amino Acids in the Plasma and Their Modification by the Administration of Leucine," *Pediatrics,* XXVII (1961), 539–550.

WILLIAM L. NYHAN, JULIAN J. CHISOLM, and RAY O. EDWARDS, JR., "Idiopathic Hyperglycinuria. III. Report of a Second Case," *Journal of Pediatrics,* LXII (1963), 540–545.

MICHAEL W. PARTINGTON, "Variations in Intelligence in Phenylketonuria," *Canadian Medical Association Journal,* LXXXVI (1962), 736–743.

MICHAEL W. PARTINGTON and ELIZABETH J. M. LEWIS, "Variations with Age in Plasma Phenylalanine and Tyrosine Levels in Phenylketonuria," *Journal of Pediatrics,* LXII (1963), 348–357.

ROBERTO M. PINTO, ROBERTO A. VOTTA, ESTEBAN MONTUORI, and HÉCTOR BALEIRON, "Action of Estradiol 17$\beta$ on the Activity of the Pregnant Human Uterus," *American Journal of Obstetrics and Gynecology,* LXXXVIII (1964), 759–769.

V. J. POLIDORA, DALLAS E. BOGGS, and HARRY A. WAISMAN, "A Behavioral Deficit Associated with Phenylketonuria in Rats," *Proceedings of the Society for Experimental Biology and Medicine,* CXIII (1963), 817–820.

S. H. REISNER, A. E. FORBES, and M. CORNBLATH, "The Smaller of Twins and Hypoglycaemia," *Lancet,* I (1965), 524–526.

SUE V. SAXON, "Differences in Reactivity between Asphyxial and Normal Rhesus Monkeys," *Journal of Genetic Psychology,* XCIX (1961a), 283–287.

SUE V. SAXON, "Effects of Asphyxia Neonatorum on Behavior in the Rhesus Monkey," *Journal of Genetic Psychology,* XCIX (1961b), 277–282.

WILLIAM E. SCHAMADAN, "Bacteriuria during Pregnancy," *American Journal of Obstetrics and Gynecology,* LXXXIX (1964), 10–15.

K. SCHREIER and W. MÜLLER, "Idiopathische Hyperglycinämie (Glycinose)," *Deutsche Medizinische Wochenschrift,* LXXXIX (1964), 1739–1743.

JOHN L. SEVER, GILBERT M. SCHIFF, and ROBERT J. HUEBNER, "Frequency of Rubella Antibody among Pregnant Women and Other Human and Animal Populations," *Obstetrics and Gynecology,* XXIII (1964), 153–159.

A. J. SMITH and L. B. STRANG, "An Inborn Error of Metabolism with the Urinary Excretion of α-hydroxy-butyric Acid and Phenylpyruvic Acid," *Archives of Disease in Childhood,* XXXIII (1958), 109–113.

D. W. SMITH, K. PATAU, E. THERMAN, and S. L. INHORN, "A New Autosomal Trisomy Syndrome: Multiple Congenital Anomalies Caused by an Extra Chromosome," *Journal of Pediatrics,* LVII (1960), 338–345.

SELMA E. SNYDERMAN, PATRICIA M. NORTON, ELLEN ROITMAN, and L. E. HOLT, JR., "Maple Syrup Urine Disease, with Particular Reference to Dietotherapy," *Pediatrics,* XXXIV (1964), 454–472.

A. E. SZULMAN, "Chromosomal Aberrations in Spontaneous Human Abortions," *New England Journal of Medicine,* CCLXXII (1965), 811–818.

KEIYA TADA, TOSHIO YOSHIDA, TOSHIO MORIKAWA, AKIBUMI MINAKAWA, and YOSHIRO WADA, "Idiopathic Hyperglycinemia (The First Case in Japan)," *Tohoku Journal of Experimental Medicine,* LXXX (1963), 218–226.

HENRY A. THIEDE and SANDRA B. SALM, "Chromosome Studies of Human Spontaneous Abortions," *American Journal of Obstetrics and Gynecology,* XC (1964), 205–215.

SOPHIE TOMLINSON and R. G. WESTALL, "Argininosuccinic Aciduria. Argininosuccinase and Arginase in Human Blood Cells," *Clinical Science,* XXVI (1964), 261–269.

H. H. VAN GELDEREN and L. J. DOOREN, "The Excretion of Free α-amino Acids in Children," *Archives of Disease in Childhood,* XXXIX (1964), 261–264.

H. K. A. VISSER, H. W. VEENSTRA, and C. PIK, "Hyperglycinaemia and Hyperglycinuria in a Newborn Infant," *Archives of Disease in Childhood,* XXXIX (1964), 397–402.

YOSHIRO WADA, KEIYA TADA, AKIBUMI MINAGAWA, TOSHIO YOSHIDA, TOSHIO MORIKAWA, and TOSHIRO OKAMURA, "Idiopathic Hypervalinemia: Probably a New Entity of Inborn Error of Valine Metabolism," *Tohoku Journal of Experimental Medicine,* LXXXI (1963-1964), 46–55.

HARRY A. WAISMAN, "Histidinemia. Un Error Congenito del Metabolismo," *Pediatria,* VII (1964), 206–213.

HARRY A. WAISMAN and THEO GERRITSEN, "Homocystinuria: A Metabolic Defect Associated with Mental Retardation," in Jakob Oster (Ed.), *Proceedings of the International Congress on the Scientific Study of Mental Retardation* (Copenhagen: 1964), pp. 507–518.

HARRY A. WAISMAN, K. HABLE, HWA L. WANG, and K. AKERT, "Some Ultrastructural Changes in the Brain of Phenylketonuric Rats and Monkeys," *Progress in Brain Research,* IX (1964), 207–212.

HARRY A. WAISMAN and HARRY F. HARLOW, "Experimental Phenylketonuria in Infant Monkeys," *Science,* CXLVII (1965), 685–695.

HARRY A. WAISMAN and HARRY F. HARLOW, "The Biochemical Induction of Phenylketonuria in Monkeys and Rats," in S. Karger (Ed.), Second International Congress on Mental Retardation, Vienna, 1961, *Proceedings, Part I. Organic Bases and Biochemical Aspects of Imbecility* (Basel-New York: S. Karger, 1963), pp. 54–61.

HARRY A. WAISMAN, HWA WANG, GAIL PALMER, and HARRY F. HARLOW, "Experimental Phenylketonuria in Infant Monkeys," in B. W. Richards (Ed.), *Proceedings of the London Conference on the Scientific Study of Mental Retardation, 1960* (Dagenham, England: May and Baker, 1962), pp. 126–141.

K. WALLIS, S. BEER, and J. FISCHL, "A Family Affected by Argininosuccinic Aciduria," *Helvetica Paediatrica Acta,* XVIII (1963), 339–348.

HWA WANG and HARRY A. WAISMAN, "Experimental Phenylketonuria in Rats," *Proceedings of the Society for Experimental Biology and Medicine,* CVIII (1961), 332–335.

R. G. WESTALL, "Argininosuccinic Aciduria: Identification and Reactions of the Abnormal Metabolite in a Newly Described Form of Mental Disease, with Some Preliminary Metabolic Studies," *Biochemical Journal,* LXXVII (1960), 135–144.

GEORG WILDFÜHR, "Tier experimentelle Untersuchungen zur Frage der diaplazentaren Übertragung der Toxoplasmen beim vor der Gravidität infizierten Muttertier," *Zeitschrift für Immunitätsforschung und Experimentelle Therapie,* CXI (1954), 110–120.

WILLIAM F. WINDLE, "Respiratory Distress: Relation to Prematurity and Other Factors in Newborn Monkeys," *Science,* CXLIII (1964), 1345–1346.

WILLIAM F. WINDLE, H. N. JACOBSON, M. I. ROBERT DE RAMIREZ DE ARELLANO, and C. M. COMBS, "Structural and Functional Sequelae of Asphyxia Neonatorum in Monkeys" (*Macaca mulatta*), in *Mental Retardation,* Research Publications of the Association for Research in Nervous and Mental Disease, XXXIX (Baltimore, Maryland: Williams and Wilkins, 1962), 169–182.

J. YERUSHALMY, "Mother's Cigarette Smoking and Survival of Infant," *American Journal of Obstetrics and Gynecology,* LXXXVIII (1964), 505–518.

J. YERUSHALMY, BEA J. VAN DEN BERG, C. L. ERHARDT, and H. JACOBZINER, "Birth Weight and Gestation as Indices of 'Immaturity,'" *American Journal of Diseases of Children,* CIX (1965), 43–57.

# 11

# Notes for a Sociology of Prevention in Mental Retardation

## STEWART E. PERRY

Perhaps the most significant social element in mental retardation appears in the basic ideas that we use to signal and describe mental retardation. These ideas themselves are social creations and arise in part from experiences not related to mental retardation. That is, to understand one sort of poorly formulated experience, we agree to use our formulated knowledge of quite unrelated sorts of experiences. We choose a set of ideas arising from these other experiences and apply it as an analogy, metaphor, or model to understand the phenomena that we wish to study, and then we check it out empirically. Frequently, side by side with one idea or set of ideas, another quite contradictory idea may be in use, and it, too, may have empirical evidence adduced for it.

In the instance of mental retardation, whole sets of implications immediately stem from beginning with the idea that mental retardation is a clinical phenomenon. For example, there is an immediate implication that somehow, if sufficient knowledge can be mobilized, the condition can be treated successfully or prevented. Yet, this implication of preventability is contradicted by the currently held conception that intelligence is "normally distributed" in the human population—a conception for which there is strong evidence. With the ideas inherent in the conception of a normal distribution, one must, by statistical reasoning, expect universally a certain percentage of cases of relative mental retardation and conclude that an inescapable portion of the Gauss curve will describe the lower, handicapped levels of intelligence in the population. As in quality controls in industry,

145

with this concept one must expect a certain percentage of errors or rejects
—the imperfectly intelligent, the retarded. In other words, prevention of the
"normal" errors of mental retardation is not really possible, if it is true that
the distribution of intelligence is, in the absence of distorting influences,
describable by the well-known bell-shaped curve for IQ distribution.

Unfortunately, the field of mental retardation is so undeveloped that it
is somewhat difficult to clarify this and other apparent contradictions in the
notions by which it is currently approached. For this reason, it is particularly important for the student of the phenomenon to examine carefully the
preliminary conceptions with which he begins his inquiries; they are particularly susceptible to the entrance of social influences. And though all ideas
are historically limited in the end by the social conditions in which they
arise and operate, it is yet the task of science to try to present a model that
may transcend the times.

One of the models or metaphors by which the sociologist can approach a question about human behavior conceptualizes the social data as
something on the order of a manufacturing concern. This model envisages a
kind of system that exists or arises in the process of putting out a product;
the product is manufactured by virtue of the intake of persons, materials,
and ideas from the environment, and their organization in particular ways to
accommodate their intake and generate an output. The metaphor has advantages and limitations like all conceptual models; but for the purposes of
this chapter, I shall use it as a heuristic device—a convenient way of putting mental retardation in a sociological framework and deriving from that
framework some implications for prevention.

However, let me first take the precaution of pointing out that this
model, too, is a social invention and stems clearly from our common experiences, in an industrialized society, of the production line and its philosophy. In industry, for example, cost accounting helps to determine the point
at which it no longer makes sense to try to prevent errors in the manufacturing process, a point at which it does not make sense to strive further to turn
out a more perfect product. At that point, new preventive measures for the
reduction of errors are no longer introduced, according to budgetary reasoning. In human affairs one has to be on guard against such reasoning.
Therefore, I shall use the metaphor of the manufacturing concern as a way
of considering the production of mental retardation rather than as a way of
considering how normally bright or even brighter children are turned out in
our society. Thus, the "errors" in production, in my scheme, are the children *without* handicaps, children who somehow escaped from being shaped
into the mentally retarded condition that is produced by the system. In this
conception I hope it will be more difficult to lapse into the position of accepting a minimum rate of the mentally retarded as somehow not preventable. I believe that this is an important preliminary in the use of any social-
science framework for the prevention of mental retardation.

## SOME GENERAL FEATURES OF THE
## PRODUCTION SYSTEM

If we are to ask, sociologically, how we can prevent mental retardation, we must examine each aspect of the production system that produces this something that is labeled mental retardation. Note that the product is not necessarily (or at least exclusively) mentally retarded persons. Rather, the product is compounded of the same sorts of elements that the system has ingested—that is, materials, persons, and ideas (including schemes of evaluation and attraction as well as cognition). In this way, one can understand how it is that the system produces persons who are not necessarily mentally retarded but who may nevertheless be so labeled. That is, the system produces mentally retarded persons, but it also produces a way of looking at the world (a scheme of ideas and their related behaviors) such that one is enjoined to label this person "mentally retarded," that person "not mentally retarded"—and perhaps this third person "indeterminate."

The social order of mental retardation clearly turns out people as a product, as well as ideas. But it involves people also as workers, designers, distributors, and even, of course, as raw material. Although it may be an intellectually interesting and useful, if shocking, pursuit, I shall not systematically describe all the ways in which we in the field and others in our society are organized for these roles, each with his (unintended) task in the production system that I want to abstract or construct from all else that goes on. Nevertheless, it is absolutely necessary to except no one from scrutiny, including those professionals whose task it is to prevent mental retardation. If we are to understand how a social order participates in the unintended manufacture of the mentally retarded, we cannot arbitrarily except from inquiry any part of that interconnected order. I shall describe, therefore, briefly in one instance and more extensively in another, how the clinical and other professional workers do their part as personnel in this unwelcome production.

Finally, this sociological frame of reference also requires the sociologist to consider the material conditions that are socially (that is, in an organized way) produced or transmuted from the physical environment. Since this may be a somewhat confusing notion, let me give three different types of social transmutation of the physical world by the production system. Some apparent transmutations are purely fictional—such as the way in which certain genetic materials are ingested in the work of some analysts and then returned to the environment as "declining national intelligence." Other materials are combined in ways that increase or intensify their material importance—as when the social impetus to assortative mating augments the incidence rate of cretinism. And, finally, changes wrought by social influences on the human physical equipment may be rather generalized—as when the incidence of a whole range of physiologic handicaps accompanied by mental retardation rises in direct ratio to the degree of racial and class segregation in the United States.

As the reader may gather, therefore, the sociological frame of reference in use here provides a rather thoroughgoing means of looking at every sort of evidence of mental retardation, including physiologic, philosophic, and other evidence. By no means does this suggest that a sociological analysis will explain the evidence fully. On the contrary, it can explain and describe only one aspect of that evidence—the sociological. One must consider whether or not that explanation and description merits, for a current scientific or practical purpose, more attention than some other analytically abstracted aspect—the physiologic, for instance. It is, of course, my contention that in many respects possible sociological explanations have been too long ignored and too little understood and that efforts to prevent much mental retardation will succeed only with a recognition of the significance of the social element in all of mental retardation.

Because, indeed, sociological analysis is relevant to mental retardation in any of its forms, including those that are, like cretinism or birth injuries, so clearly physiologic (genetic or acquired) in etiology—because, as I say, the sociological frame of reference may be used for illuminating any evidence of mental retardation, this chapter can do no more than briefly review the potentials for such analysis. First, I shall present a general and very brief overview of a number of different ways in which social processes can be understood as participating in the production of mental retardation, and I shall indicate a few ways in which prevention may take the form of social change. Second, I shall take up one topic in detail—the relevance of American class structure as a social process participating in the incidence of mental retardation; I intend to indicate the ramifying implications of just this one social feature of mental retardation, and thereby to illuminate the interlocking character of the production system and indicate how each feature reinforces and stabilizes other aspects so that there appears to be a rather long-term stability despite any developing changes. I also suggest the necessary preventive perspective that the clinician must take if he is to deal with the sociological production of mental retardation.

## Producing Mental Defectives in America

To examine the process of production of mental retardation in our society, I will take up successively as foci one sort of product (the culturally deprived child); one aspect of the organization of personnel (the pattern of clinical services); one feature of our use of material resources (the disposition of wastes); and, finally, one class of ideas (the static concept of intelligence in the self-fulfilling diagnosis or prophecy of mental retardation). Each of these parts of the production line can be reviewed to see how it might be changed and put to other tasks.

### Cultural Deprivation

The most important feature of the production line and certainly the most prominently recognized factor today produces the so-called culturally deprived child.[1] Essentially, these are children whose entire career of socialization has not included the kinds of experiences that prepare the growing human being for participation in the broad midstream of American society. These children may be considered "deprived" on the ground that participation in that broad midstream is virtually required for a self-satisfying and valuable life in the United States. The reasoning behind such a judgment seems sound if one emphasizes the phrase, "in the United States"—but aside from that, the absence of certain sorts of social and personal experiences can add up to a relatively stable intellectual handicap for participation in the basic American style of life. This handicap, especially by virtue of the reinforcing effects of later experiences that are promoted by the handicap, rushes the child into adulthood along an assembly line process after which the finished product cannot be rebuilt.

Perhaps the most easily grasped example of this sort of train of events in our own lives is the way in which, for one reason or another, one comes to think of oneself as rather good in "arithmetic" but poor in "languages," mainly because of a differentiated experience with stimulating or depriving classes in the two distinct subjects in, say, the third grade. The school child of average intelligence and performance thus comes to sort himself out in various ways and to select one sort of later experience rather than another on the basis of such self-definition; moreover, these same definitions are encouraged, and indeed may have originated in the evaluations of a teacher or parent. So instead of an elective in French in high school, the student may be channeled into an economics course.

If this kind of concatenation of reinforcements so influences the ordinary child, how much more intensely influenced is the child who comes to his elementary school for the first day without ever having seen a book or magazine in his home, or a letter being written by his mother, or a bill being paid by check by his father, and so on. Such limitations of experience are likely to be accompanied by a number of other related ones—instead of color in clothing and blankets, drabness and fadedness; simpler toys, rather than those having a movable part; the pervasiveness of vegetable cooking

[1] A useful discussion may be found in a work written from the standpoint of workers in public-school programs (Riessman, 1962).

odors, but not the momentary wafts of perfume from a vase of flowers; and so on. The round of life is filled with one class of experience of cultural objects and empty of another, and it leads to an adulthood in which the latter class is meaningless or threatening and to be avoided.

The recognition of this train of events has suggested the use of a cultural tooling-up period for underprivileged children, in which, like their middle-class cohorts, they too go to a nursery school that hopes to develop their sensibilities while relieving their families of some responsibility for care. The prevention of mental retardation that occurs out of cultural deprivation probably can be accomplished by such new socializing institutions, but they imply increasingly ramifying reorientations and reorganizations of community patterns of life. In contrast to earlier, more individualistic concerns, the community as a whole, rather than the family, would begin to assume immediate responsibility for the care and training of younger and younger children for longer and longer periods throughout the day and the year. Thus new problems are produced by the new social assembly lines, but this epitomizes one means to the social prevention of mental retardation in the instance of the culturally deprived child.

Cultural deprivation is combined often with physical deprivation, and the condition of mental retardation may indeed stem primarily from the physical or physiologic history of the person. The train of physiologic events can be distinguished clearly from underdevelopment of the person's cultural capacities, and in examining some physiologic events, I take up a second and a third feature of the production line, a second and a third social organization of processes that produce mental retardation. In these instances, the social patterns indirectly produce mental retardation by producing physiologic events leading to mental deficit.

## Social Pattern of Clinical Services

In its simplest form, the second aspect of the production line can be described as a pattern of inadequate clinical services. But this description is quite misleading, for it tends to suggest that all that is needed is more money, more staff, more equipment, and so on. In truth, the pattern of inadequate clinical facilities in the sense that I mean here is much more complicated. It means the reinforcing social conditions in clinical services that deprive the mother and child, the adult and infant, of crucial clinical-welfare resources, such as obstetrical or prenatal care—just at those points at which the risks of physiologically induced mental retardation are greatest.

There are two ways in which the clinical-welfare system particularly promotes the incidence of mental retardation by social means. One is the lack of fit between styles of life of clinical clients and of clinical professionals,[2] and the other is the actual organization and interrelation of different kinds of clinical service.[3]

For example, the style of life of the mother from lower socio-economic levels sets up barriers against her even thinking about continuous prenatal and postnatal supervision. Thus, either the primipara whose child is more likely to suffer a birth injury or the older mother of many children whose constitution is (according to a clinical hypothesis about some forms of mongolism) depleted of the chemical resources for normal fetal development may produce a retarded child in the absence of the clinical attention that is not a part of her style of life.

Moreover, her style of life contrasts so sharply with that of the clinic physician, the nurse, and the social worker that these professionals' own natural ways set up barriers to their services being utilized fully by many lower-class mothers who manage somehow to reach the clinic. For example, the nurse, the doctor, the social worker, and their colleagues may have such difficulty understanding the meaning of successive illegitimate pregnancies to a mother that, through unintended revulsion at her life, they are deterred from providing the necessary care of the woman who stirs them to a shocked "Not again!" In turn, the mother is repelled by both the technical and the interpersonal experiences that she encounters in the hands of her would-be helpers.[4]

Aside from the difficulties involved in the coming together of two divergent ways of life in the free or low-cost clinic, there is another characteristic of the giving and receiving of clinical assistance in our nation that produces, in the same indirect manner, the higher incidence of mental retardation in the lower classes. This is the fragmentation in services—as a great many medical people are painfully aware—that often defeats the most sophisticated and persistent clinician and patient. For example, the number of persons, agencies, clinics, and offices that must be contacted, cajoled, bearded, bullied, or seduced by both the clinic staff member and the patient to obtain a variety or adjunctive services is in itself a social barrier to

[2] The conceptualization of this lack of fit has received the term "culture conflict" in an early discussion by Otto Pollak (1956).

[3] Some critics insist that it is a case of no organization rather than of a particular type of organization of resources. For a sociological view of the lack of working relationships among social agencies, see Walter B. Miller (1958). For a discussion of problems of coordination in setting up new clinical facilities, and for some basic bibliographic references on health and welfare coordination, see Ray H. Elling (1963). For a generalized critique, see Peter Nokes (1960). Of particular importance are studies (to this date very infrequent) of the internal processes and organization of the residential institution for the mentally retarded. However, I shall not deal with this problem area. For a recent research report, see Robert B. Edgerton (1963).

[4] Esther Lucille Brown provides an excellent review of all the ways in which social and cultural differences between patients and staff interfere with optimum patient care (Brown, 1965).

adequate clinical care. As Leona Baumgartner has insisted, the form of American health and welfare services is "a many-splintered thing." [5] And mental retardation is one result.

The organization, then, of the services that prevent mental retardation by prenatal and postnatal care of the infant and his family requires considerable revision in order that such reorganization will have positive implications for more problems than mental retardation; and in fact it may well be undertaken, if at all, under the impetus of other medical needs than those related to mental retardation. As a social tool, such reorganization can have broad-scale effects on the prevention of many social-iatrogenic disorders like mental retardation—disorders that arise out of the current unintegrated pattern of clinical services in which agencies do not serve each other. [6]

The sociological analysis of organizational problems in the provision of health services suggests that there is no easy technical solution for the present lack of integration among them. Bringing all facilities under one administrative roof helps to avoid the definition of a person as someone else's client. It has certain advantages as a way of resolving some of the hesitancies about offering help to a patient who enters the clinical maze by one door, but also needs assistance that is conventionally available only to a patient who has entered from another portal. However, everyone's experience with the large organization in any realm of life is not reassuring enough for one to assume that integrated governmental medicine on the local level is a full solution; making two offices ultimately, but only distantly, responsible to the same chief does not thereby make them ready to cooperate in the pursuit of adequate service to the client-patient.

The techniques of integration of services must include a large variety of social inventions. For example, new types of facilitating roles may have to be developed. The Soviet Union provides an instructive example. In the Soviet Union, a general lack of administrative integration was somewhat neutralized by the informal development of a new, though illegal, role— that of the trouble-shooter who facilitates the meshing of needs and services in the manufacturing or agricultural sectors of the economy. These outlawed "brokers" specialize illegally, for a fee, in cutting red tape for subadministrators in their relations with other subadministrators in the far corners of the country. The new social role provides the necessary integrating mechanism to mesh the many diverse production- and supply-establishments. Similarly, one can expect that our current hodgepodge of health and welfare services will spawn a number of different and perhaps unsettling

[5] Leona Baumgartner has made this point many times. The phrase comes from her Address at the Symposium on the Hospital and Community, on the occasion of the 150th anniversary of the founding of the Massachusetts General Hospital, Boston, February 1, 1961.
[6] My own experience of this came as a staff member of a psychiatric home-treatment service (Perry, 1963).

techniques for attaining the degree of integration that is increasingly demanded. Perhaps specific, systematic, and rational sociological attention can raise necessary questions about the efficiency of "outlawing" one or another technique just because it does not fit ideologic preconceptions—in the way that the "brokers" of the Soviet Union were outlawed because their function was not ideologically rationalized. Thus, for example, in the United States the bugaboo of socialized medicine should not be permitted to scare off efforts to resolve by governmental means some of the fragmentation problems of the health services. The resolution of such problems can make possible a decreased incidence of mental retardation and other morbid conditions.

In summary, I have conceptualized the pattern of clinical services as a sociological factor in the inducement of physiologic deficit leading to mental retardation. Of course, the provision of clinical service is also—and more importantly—a means of preventing mental retardation, but here I have suggested its part only in actually producing mental retardation of a physiologic etiology. The means most likely to be effective in dismantling this feature of the production line entail, first, a new look at the career socialization process undergone by health professionals so that they may be relieved of interpersonal and cultural handicaps for dealing with those persons whose children are most likely to become mentally retarded, and, second, sociological analysis of problems of organization and bureaucracy impeding the integration of our available health facilities.

## Social Use of the Material Environment

The social patterns with which our material resources are used also have an indirect influence on the production of mental retardation. In this instance, the significant personnel are not those immediately concerned with clinical service; the only clinicians involved are perhaps the public health people, but they are joined by the full range of the general population. I shall mention here a single aspect of our American way of using the material environment—namely, the disposition of wastes. The disposal of wastes, like the inefficient organization of clinical-welfare services, is perhaps less important as a factor in the production of mental retardation than in the production of other human ills.[7] Nevertheless, it must be recognized as a significant problem—and as a problem that, with increasing population and therefore increasing amounts of waste, will be increasingly serious. It

[7] It is relatively easy to establish the relevance of pollution of the air in urban areas and of the water to differential and seasonal variations in incidences of the various casualties of the human organism. What is perhaps less easy is to balance the cost of one more frequent class of casualty (mortality rates of aged or other vulnerable populations in smoggy weather) against that of another less frequent class (such as prematurities with associated mental defect).

may be useful to concentrate briefly on this aspect of our use of the physical environment to see how it might suggest means of preventing mental retardation.

Much preventive effort would require no intensive social scientific study. For example, the United States Children's Bureau did not require an extensive study of child behavior in a small enclosed space to determine that light-duty magnets were the safest way to hold refrigerator doors closed, so that even abandoned, a refrigerator would not be so dangerous to small, exploring children. Changes in the manufacture of refrigerators easily prevent the cases of neurologic or other damage from near suffocation and heart stoppage of children trapped in a refrigerator. Similarly, a few moments' thought can suggest the best way to prevent the toxicologically-induced mental retardation owing to inhalation of fumes from a burning auto battery—that is, to make batteries out of non-combustible, yet equally cheap, materials. But not all such problems can be solved so easily on a physical and economic basis, and here, of course, the public health professional must confront established social patterns of life that promote accidents, ill health, or other physiologic conditions leading to mental retardation.

The icebox abandoned in a vacant lot and the batteries dumped where people scavenge for fuel are minor features of the social patterns of waste disposition that have posed the danger of cases of mental retardation in the past. To what greater extent the disposition of atomic wastes—deliberate and necessary from the laboratories and manufactories of atomic materials, or unintended, unnecessary, and sometimes unexpected, in the emissions from underground tests or free dispersal through open-air tests— contributes to an increased incidence of genetically-determined retardation remains a statistical speculation from unpublicized studies. Yet the social organization and cultural definition of waste disposal is surely as much at stake in the field of atomic energy as are any of the more obvious problems of international security. Moreover, the pollution of air through industrial smoke and gaseous wastes and of the rivers and other waters of the nation through industrial and residential sewage looms high among the other pathogenic features of our ways of handling wastes. In fact, they are probably more difficult to prevent than the atomic pollutants, since our ways of dealing with the latter are a more recent, less integrated part of the culture. In any event, the production of mental retardation can be clearly linked with our whole system of waste disposal. And waste disposal itself is only one subsystem of our whole social pattern of using the material resources available to our society. The analysis of "accidental" and any other etiologic classification of mental retardation must not overlook this pattern if we are to find all the possible means for the prevention of mental retardation.

### Ideas about Intelligence and Mental Defect

The production and maintenance of certain kinds of ideas also may lead to mental retardation among vulnerable segments of the American population. The sociologist can describe a system in which, by virtue of the ideas in vogue about human behavior, mental retardation, and other matters, the condition of mental retardation is produced as a kind of self-fulfilling prophecy. The best established example of this process is the way in which the Negro population has been disadvantaged intellectually because Negroes have been considered less intelligent than whites. On the basis of the idea that the Negro race is less intelligent, actions are founded that deny Negroes adequate scholastic and other opportunities. Having been denied those opportunities, the Negro cannot perform as well in the scholastically-related tasks that may be used as tests of intelligence.

The identical process has occurred with early diagnosis of the mentally retarded. That is, on the basis of a conclusion that a child or infant is mentally retarded certain actions may be founded that will deprive him of the opportunities to develop his intellectual capacities. For example, delay or refusal of adoption used to occur quite routinely on the grounds of simple mental retardation; thus, those unadopted infants (whose psychometric scores were insufficient) were consigned to institutional life or to a succession of temporary adoptive homes, both of which have been established as usually tending to depress intelligence-test performance, with a consequent ratification of the prediction of mental retardation. Similarly, in the instance of other infants diagnosed early as mentally retarded, the parents may be urged by the physician to institutionalize the child as early as possible. If the child is incorrectly diagnosed, the results of early institutionalization certainly help to bear out the erroneous diagnosis.

Changes in practices of recommending institutionalization and of adoption have occurred with changes in conceptions of the development of intellectual capacities. Thus, for example, it seems quite likely that physicians of various specialties—pediatricians, obstetricians, and general practitioners—may be less likely to recommend early institutionalization nowadays than a very few years ago.[8] Nevertheless, there seems to remain the same erroneous conception of intelligence and of mental retardation that has underlain these practices and that will engender the identical self-fulfilling prophecy in a variety of guises. Namely, there is the conception of intelligence (and therefore mental retardation) as a basically static phenomenon. Such changes in a person's intelligence as can be observed are, then,

[8] See *Institutionalizing Mentally Retarded Children: Attitudes of Some Physicians* (Washington, D. C.: U. S. Department of Health, Education, and Welfare, Welfare Administration, Children's Bureau, 1963). This pamphlet reprints four short articles by Simon Olshansky and various collaborators on attitudes of general practitioners, pediatricians, obstetricians, and interns and residents.

conceptualized as somehow epiphenomena, accessory to the intelligence, but not really related to it—phenomena owing to error, to crude instrumentation, to environmental distortions, and so on. In other words, the mental operations used in the determination of intelligence run something like this: "Go through the chosen procedures for determining intelligence, and accept the results as final if you are fairly confident that no error is involved, if you feel your procedures are sufficiently sophisticated for your current purpose, and if you do not know of any environmental distortions that have occurred." The obvious dangers in such a procedure should not draw attention away from the fundamental idea on which it is based—namely, a static conception of intelligence.

So long as workers in the field of mental retardation continue to use, deliberately or unwittingly, a static conception of intelligence, this idea will govern social actions that will encourage the verification of the idea. The static conception of intelligence leads to other sorts of ideas, or has other sorts of ideas implicit in it. Here, particularly, is the hard-to-eradicate but spurious distinction between a class of mental retardation that is related to some materiality (for example, tissue deterioration owing to birth injury, or developmental anomaly owing to a sportive gene) and retardation that is somehow not considered material but related to psychogenic or sociogenic factors. Insofar as this distinction is made, one is likely to be able to trace it back to the notion that somehow or other the materially-based intelligence is static, and the mental retardation owing to psychologic or sociologic distortions is an artifact that overlies the static, materially-based level of intelligence. This will be true even in the writings of those workers who are most concerned with the social and psychologic factors in mental retardation.[9]

I find myself falling into that thought pattern from time to time and believe it very difficult to maintain the conceptual framework in this field that requires one to see any process as merely an abstracted quality and all processes—"material" or "nonmaterial"—as interactive. In the third edition of one of the best texts in mental retardation, Seymour Sarason (1959) has added a monograph written jointly with Thomas Gladwin, an anthropologist, that illustrates the ease with which one may fall into the pattern of thought I have criticized. Although in the two previous editions of the text, Sarason avoided a conceptual commitment by the time-honored textbook writer's practice of examining and contrasting various points of view and their related research studies, in the third edition he and his coauthor say they "insist" on distinguishing "mental retardation" (that is, culturally de-

---

[9] See the otherwise very informative review of some recent basic studies, Hilda Knobloch and Benjamin Pasamanick (1961), especially pp. 454 and 468. Mercer (1965) argues that the clinical perspective per se interferes with an adequate grasp of social factors in the mental-retardation problem, but I would suggest that even the sociological perspective can suffer from a static conception of intelligence and retardation as human attributes.

termined mental subnormality) from "mental deficiency" (that is, mental subnormality associated with demonstrable central nervous system pathology). Now, there is all the need in the world for distinguishing crucial nervous system pathology from crucial social and psychologic pathology, but the fallacies of setting up classifications of the mentally retarded on the basis of whether or not there is *demonstrable* nervous system pathology are no different from the general semantic fallacy of such diagnostic classification thought patterns described long ago by F. G. Crookshank (1938). I need only mention here the difficulty with which one may struggle in an attempt to distinguish pathologic function from pathologic structure, while recognizing that there are pathologic functions with which, at least today, we cannot associate pathologic structure—and vice versa.[10] Much of our difficulty in conceptualizing the phenomena of mental retardation can be traced to the comforting but misleading notion that somehow there is a stable quality of intelligence, structurally determined in the material of the body, however difficult it may be for us hard-working scientists to describe it today.

I might add that the process approach to mental retardation has implications also for problems of clinical management and vocational placement. That is, the situational determinants of performance, for example, are likely to be overlooked or underemphasized when the worker is caught in the static frame of reference. It is this frame of reference, I believe, that inhibits the professional person from decisions and actions that will maximize the rather surprising capacities of mongoloid children, for example, which have only recently been better recognized.

In summary, so long as workers who have the notion that intelligence is substantial and stable are produced out of the training sequences in psychology, sociology, medicine, and so on, just so long will these workers participate in producing mental retardation. They will do so by acts that will fulfill their prophecies of mental retardation, as adoption practices, institutionalization recommendations, and so on have in the past. The prevention of mental retardation rests, in this instance, on the careful analysis of ideas propagated in the training of specialists and others. I would suggest that one of the most crucial social features of these training sequences that fosters the reification of intelligence and other constructs of science is the departmentalization of the training itself. The social organization of education that conveys the message that certain subject matter is the property of a particular group of workers and may be considered only by them or only with their permission assists in the hypostatizing of the subject-matter processes. Departmentalization of the clinical services following this pattern leads to further hypostatization, and so we have mental retardation

---

[10] I was made aware of this problem (as it appears in the genetics of mental deficiency) by Gordon Allen, M.D., and discussed it in Stewart E. Perry (1954) which is reprinted in abridged form as Chapter 21 of the present volume.

clinics staffed by people who deal with a reified mental retardation. I shall try to indicate how ideas, including changing ideas, of mental retardation are related to the social structure of our society and to the resultant clinical services for the mentally retarded. I hope, in this way, to point the way toward what is the most central possibility for prevention of mental retardation, when one begins from the sociological point of view.

## The Middle Class and Mental Retardation in America[11]

Now I want to present a point of view about the history of some changes in the field of mental retardation, linking them to the American social structure and its processes, and outlining a perspective for a program of preventive action. This perspective is influenced by an often reprinted yet strangely ignored paper by Kingsley Davis, "Mental Hygiene and the Class Structure." [12] Davis suggested that the ethos of the American culture provides a limited notion of mental health and blinds the mental hygienist to the social sources of mental illness embodied in the American class structure. I shall argue correlatively that there are middle-class sources of differential attention to problems of mental retardation and of differential action taken on those problems.

There are two important topics that I want to consider first. These are not ordinarily treated but seem to be crucial: first, the sociology of the expert or worker in the field of mental retardation[13] and, second, the sociology of the layman in the field of mental retardation. I shall deal with these two topics as two parts of a single question: what social behavior goes along with ideas about mental retardation? That is, how do people—either experts or laymen—behave when they deal with the idea of mental retardation?

### The Experts

Mental retardation has been a field much neglected by mental-health specialists—an apology that seems to begin most reviews. The result of such neglect is, of course, that this is a subject about which very little is known. One must deal, then, with the behavior of experts struggling with their own

[11] This section, to the end of the chapter, is a revision of an article previously published as "The Middle Class and Mental Retardation in America," *Psychiatry*, XXVIII (1965), 107–118.

[12] His insights lay fallow for almost twenty years until the revival of interest following the Hollingshead-Redlich study (Hollingshead and Redlich, 1958).

[13] Lewis A. Dexter (1958; 1962) is probably the only writer to have examined elements in the culture of the worker in mental retardation to see their influence on developments in the field.

ignorance; and where there is the least information, there is likely to be the most controversy. So it often happens that even a serious discussion of mental deficiency may become an argument or controversy about those questions that are still difficult to handle—such as, exactly what brings about the mental-defective condition in the instances not marked by observable physiologic signs? Any interest in this question is apt to take a very partisan shape. For example, the two camps in the study of mental deficiency have, in the past, been divided on the basis of whether or not the condition is curable, and the answer to this question usually is based on the person's conception of the etiology of the condition.[14]

The more pessimistic workers usually have believed that the condition is primarily an organic one, either inherited or acquired; the more optimistic workers have considered hereditary, organic factors to be less important and incline toward environmentalist, functional explanations of the condition. There are minor exceptions to this rule, and the social conditions of work in the field can affect one's position on the question.[15]

If a general lack of development in the field of mental deficiency contributes to an emotional view of the field, then that view will be revealed in a variety of ways in the behavior of the specialists, even though controversial and emotional behavior in connection with scientific topics is antithetical to the mores of science and its practitioners. One generally expects clinical scientists and other scientific experts to be above that kind of emotionality, to be secure in the objectivity of their knowledge. That is a general expectation. So when we do not have much knowledge (and sometimes even when we do), the language and behavior of controversy somehow must be handled, suppressed, and redirected into channels congruent with the scientific posture. The adjustment techniques of the scientist or scientific clinician as a social being come into play here. Thus, much controversy can be swept under the table by an adroit scientific formulation. For example, today we are less involved in the old nature-nurture controversy about intelligence or other basic human characteristics primarily because behavioral scientists have closed ranks pretty solidly with a controversy-reducing, but not necessarily fruitful anodyne: we all say today, "It's an interaction."

[14] Mental deficiency is not a disease, but a name for a condition that may or not be associated with some disease. So, of course, it is not strictly correct to talk about "curability."

[15] For example, with the increasing tendency to keep the higher-level performer within the community, the residential mental-retardation institution becomes more and more a hospital and less and less a training school. The staff of such institutions must work with more of the severe and relatively hopeless conditions; and the rewards of this sort of work are quite different from those of work with trainable children. This must have significant consequences for the conception of mental retardation held by such staff—as well as many other consequences for recruitment of staff, and so on. For a general treatment of social influences in the work situation of researchers and scientists in psychiatry, see Stewart E. Perry (1966).

And that usually settles the question. No one need push matters any further. Our relative lack of information is covered over with a slogan—interaction—that hides the need for further inquiry.[16] Instead it permits us—and, of course, I include myself here—to go into other questions that are more fashionable.

Mental retardation as a field of inquiry always has lagged a bit behind in picking up the fads and fashions currently running through the experts' culture in social-science and mental-health studies. So it was that as short a time ago as 1953, in a survey of views and the status of the field that I made for the National Institute of Mental Health, it seemed as if the nature-nurture controversy were still under way. We were still in an era of emphasizing organic, inherited types of causes of mental retardation, but the nature advocates were being pressed hard by the nurture advocates. The significance of new evidence collected over the previous decade, say 1940 to 1950, perhaps dating earlier from the work of Harold M. Skeels and others,[17] was beginning to be understood in a climate of opinion more and more open to environmentalist interpretations. The great years of the intelligence test as the final arbiter of a child's lifelong potential were the 1920's in America, but by the early 1950's, other ideas and other evidence were crowding the psychometricians, even in the field of mental retardation. In fact, we had passed through a turbulent period of about twenty years in which the influence of culture on personality (and intelligence) was an especially fashionable topic for investigation.

The ideas of the experts in mental retardation (or of those not at all expert people whose opinions nevertheless were asked for) tended to lag behind what was being said elsewhere in social science and psychiatry. Today it is no longer considered bad form to regard the most frequent cause of cases of mental retardation to be social, cultural, and interpersonal deprivation. Today many if not most interested physicians are quite ready, for example, to verbalize this point of view; but even ten years ago, that was not true.[18]

---

[16] The concept of interaction does not in itself inhibit further study, of course; but since it laid to rest the controversy between hereditarians and environmentalists, a singular motivation that had stirred so much work was also laid to rest. Interaction seems to be an accurate conceptual description of the relations between genetic and environmental processes, but we do not seem to be motivated to see in what ways this interaction takes place.

[17] See, for example, Harold M. Skeels and Harold B. Dye (1939); Skeels (1942). The latter study was especially significant in the context of Otto Klineberg's careful analysis of intelligence test changes in Negroes moving to the North (Klineberg, 1935).

[18] In the second edition (1953) of *Psychological Problems in Mental Deficiency*, first published in 1949, Sarason still reported, "Despite the well-nigh perfect correlation between the garden-variety of mental deficiency and unfavorable social conditions, the consensus among workers in the field is that cultural factors are relatively unimportant" (p. 134). The third edition (Sarason, 1959) was unrevised but included a mono-

I am afraid, however, that today's verbal recognition of the importance of social and other deprivations has not been accompanied by any clear thinking about what to do about it. The ignorance of the experts in mental retardation is plastered over with satisfaction that now, indeed, we recognize an important source of mental retardation in the deprived sociocultural experience of the child. But aside from muttering something about giving the mentally retarded child enough stimulation to overcome the deprivation, the expert worker in the field usually devotes his attention to something else that remains more fashionable today, and leaves to newcomers the task of dealing with socio-cultural problems.

## The Laymen

To understand what remains the important focus today in mental retardation, so far as the interest of most of the experts is concerned, I must turn to the sociology of the layman in the field of mental retardation and his influence on the experts and scientists.

It is well recognized that fashions within a scientific field, built on some new and undigested discovery, often create fashions within society at large. This was true, for example, of Darwin's evolutionary theories and discoveries, which were perverted into a way of thought for reactionaries and conservatives in the political life of this and other nations. However, influence runs quite often in the other direction. That is, the interests of the public at large push scientific research in a particular direction to the exclusion of other scientific work. Take, for example, the development of atomic weapons; it has had top priority even over other war research, to say nothing of peaceful research interests, from America to China. This same public influence operates in the medical field, of course—for example, in the development of the polio vaccines (Wilson, 1963).

The present state of the field of mental retardation in America is understandable only when one recognizes the importance of the National Association for Retarded Children (NARC) and similar organizations. Today that group, in a most striking repetition of history, has been playing a part similar to that of the National Foundation for Infantile Paralysis, including eliciting the support of a president who interested himself in mental retardation almost as much as Franklin Roosevelt interested himself in polio. In 1953, when the National Institute of Mental Health decided to make a survey in order to plan program development in mental retardation, the clamor of the parents' groups, such as the NARC, was just beginning to be heard. As a matter of fact, my own job was occasioned by the emergence of that organization as a politically significant group with important sympa-

graph, written with an anthropologist, that illustrated the increased attention being given to social considerations in mental retardation.

thizers in Congress among whom was a Congressman, recently turned junior Senator from Massachusetts. The influence of the NARC has continued to increase and of course that influence was amplified enormously by the election and administration of President Kennedy some years later.

The NARC is an organization of parents and friends of retarded children, including specialists in the field. As such, it naturally represents the immediate interests of its members more closely than the general scientific perspective of the field. That is, it is concerned especially with the provision of services for the care of mentally retarded children, as exemplified by the children of its members, and with the prevention of mental retardation, again as exemplified by the conditions of the children of its members. There is nothing whatsoever to criticize in this outlook—which is, in fact, perhaps somewhat broader than I have stated it here.[19] On the other hand, it is necessary to recognize the meaning of this NARC perspective within the field of mental retardation in America.

The joining of a relative ignorance among mental retardation professionals about socio-cultural deprivation with militant and socially responsible as well as politically influential parents' organizations has resulted today in a concentration on those aspects within the field of mental retardation that most clearly meet the needs and understandings of people like ourselves in the field and like those represented by the membership of those organizations—that is, the middle and upper classes of America.[20]

The focus in the field of mental retardation as a professional arena is then the most visible mental defective—the child of middle-class or upper-class parents, or children similar to that child. The mentally retarded child of the privileged social classes in America ordinarily exhibits one or another rather definite clinical picture involving organic etiologies of some kind—mongolism, birth injuries, metabolic disturbances, and so on. The care of such children and the prevention of such conditions in future births remain the most salient interests of the field today, despite the recognition, in verbal formulas at least, of the importance of quite different groups of mentally retarded children—that is, those crippled intellectually by social, cultural, and interpersonal deprivations.

The problem with this is that the kinds of conditions that are most visible socially actually account for a minority of the cases of mental retardation. Insofar as diagnoses of all cases admitted to public institutions have been made, they permit one to estimate that anywhere from 55 to 75 per cent of all the mentally retarded in and out of institutions do not fall into

[19] For an authoritative illustration of the views of the organization, see a book by a former executive officer of the NARC (Dybwad, 1964).

[20] I should emphasize here that the increase in attention to mental retardation of any sort is likely to spill over into increased attention to mental retardation of all sorts. There is, therefore, an unplanned but nevertheless effective increase in concern with problems quite distant from middle-class concerns, even though middle-class concerns remain uppermost.

the constitutional or organic categories of brain infection, mongolism, birth injuries, phenylketonuria, and the other clear nosologic groups with organic etiology.

The disregarded majority of cases are, of course, those to whom the hypotheses about socio-cultural deprivation are most applicable. We do not pay attention to those cases today, for the most part. We selectively inattend the problem of these children, for they become visible only for a relatively short period of time and then disappear again. They are socially visible during the period in which they pose problems for the public-school system that our middle-class society has developed for itself. At that time, it is clear that they fit poorly the requirements of academic life; but, luckily, in a few years they can leave school and can begin relatively productive lives as skilled, unskilled, or semiskilled workers and, in the instance of women, as housewives.[21] Only if they happen to become more visible by violation of some other rules of our society do these mentally retarded children or adults raise questions for us about their mental capacity. For example, some kind of delinquency or criminality brings them and their retardation problem to the fore; the delinquency or criminality may not be even their own, may indeed be that of their parents, but it can lead to a focusing on the mentally retarded condition of the child and a labeling of him for shipment to an institution for defectives. But for the most part, persons thus singled out do not have the organic involvements that characterize the middle-class mental defective who is, in fact, usually much more crippled intellectually than lower-class retarded children.[22]

As workers concerned with the field of mental retardation, we are subject to a number of social and cultural influences that make us define our professional problems in certain ways. We need to be aware of these factors in our intellectual and professional work, and we need to know where they stem from. We must recognize, first, that we still are a long way from understanding anything at all useful about the majority of the mentally retarded that will enable us to improve their intellectual status. Second, our

[21] A recent study of the progress of ex-students of public-school classes for the mentally retarded will be described in a forthcoming paper by Jacob Schonfield and Simon Olshansky.

[22] The reason for this is, of course, the simple absence of culturally-deprived subnormal persons in the middle classes, for it is these and others similar to them that make up the greatest proportion of the higher levels of the mentally retarded. The severe conditions of retardation are ordinarily considered to be distributed normally through all classes (Penrose, 1963, p. 45 *et passim*). A recent study in the United States indicated that perhaps the lower classes have a higher incidence of severe defects as well; but this finding is interpreted in the light of social theory more than genetic theory about class differentials in morbidity. That is, differential access to resources that offset the influence of seasonal variations in temperature apparently leads to a higher incidence of premature births associated with mental defect, and so on. See the studies summarized in Hilda Knobloch and Benjamin Pasamanick (1961).

attention has focused on the types of mental retardation that are most socially visible, and only when they have become quite visible. Workers in the
psychologic and medical fields did not pay much attention even to the so-
called middle-class conditions of mental retardation with organic etiology
until they were brought to our attention by such people as the members of
the NARC. Further, much potential intellectual or scientific controversy in
the field of mental retardation today is virtually stilled by our preoccupation
with cases of mental retardation that do not raise the most troublesome
questions.

In this context, it redounds to the credit of President Kennedy and the
members and consultants of his panel on mental retardation that a truly
path-breaking government document was issued, *A Proposed Program for
National Action to Combat Mental Retardation* (President's Panel on Mental Retardation, 1962). Ordinarily, a governmental or quasigovernmental
report on a problem area is likely to be rather mealy-mouthed. It is, after
all, the distillate of the opinions of a wide range of people with opposing
points of view; and, in the end, it may be a compromise document that will
offend no one, but also sits motionless in the middle of the road. This
lowest-common-denominator kind of thinking is illustrated most unfortunately by the report of the Joint Commission on Mental Illness and
Health,[23] from which our nation will garner little that is new in the years to
come. The President's Panel report, on the other hand, is a rousingly forth-
right statement from which a wide variety of significant actions can derive.
What I shall have to say about action in this field, though it does not itself
derive from that report, cannot differ greatly from it.

President Johnson, by proposing a war against poverty, uses the ideas
inherent in the Kennedy Panel report as a springboard for a generalized
attack on social etiologic factors in mental retardation. In fact, under the
aegis of this anti-poverty program, one can almost say that the current
process of redefinition of mental retardation will reach its ultimate stage in
reconceptualizing a certain category of the mentally retarded. They become, in the eyes of both laymen and experts, economic and political victims instead of clinical cases. I move past the current evidence to suggest
that while the recent process of reconceptualizing the field of mental deficiency began with middle-class sources of resistance to that reconceptualization, it will end with new ideas inherent in a program of action stemming
from sources within that same class perspective.[24]

---

[23] Joint Commission on Mental Illness and Health, *Action for Mental Health* (New
York: Basic Books, 1961). The same criticism ought not to be directed toward most of
the subsidiary expert reports that came out of the Commission's work.
[24] In a personal communication, Arlene Daniels has pointed out to me the relevance
of the middle-class concern for the "slow learner" at the expense of the gifted child
in public-school programs. See Richard Hofstadter (1963, especially Part 5).

## CHANGES IN THE REIGNING IDEAS
## OF MENTAL RETARDATION

Before moving into the matter of action to prevent mental retardation, it is imperative to review carefully some specific features of our ideas about mental retardation as a social and cultural phenomenon, especially as these ideas have changed up to the issuance of the President's Panel report. Perhaps the place to begin is with a recognition of the traditional view of mental deficiency as, on the whole, a rather hopeless condition. This has been the consensus of most of the workers in the field; it has also character-ized the ordinary layman's viewpoint. And no one has wanted to enter a hopeless field. Yet, from 1949 on, there have been gathering indications in the literature and in clinical work in the field that we had been considering mental deficiency from an inappropriate viewpoint all along. There have begun to be glimmerings of a complete revision of our ways of looking at deficiency. By 1953, these were still just glimmerings, and today much of the thinking in the field still has not changed.[25]

The traditional and generally held view of mental deficiency has been based on the ideas that (1) deficiency is incurable, (2) it is of organic etiology, (3) it is primarily a problem of subnormal intellectual capacity, and (4) defectives are much more alike than they are different from each other. This traditional viewpoint or frame of reference has been challenged on both practical and scientific grounds.

The practical grounds were that the diagnostic groupings that we tradi-tionally used had not been helpful in learning more about the individual mental defective. Everyone who works with defectives knows that there is a variety of conditions associated with subnormal intellectual functioning. Some of these are rather easily differentiated, and thus certain of the diag-nostic categories have been meaningful and have led us to further informa-tion about the patients who can be thus diagnosed—for example, those with phenylketonuria. On the other hand, a great number of defectives could not be adequately diagnosed in any way. At the time of the 1953 NIMH survey, some 55 per cent of the first admissions to public institutions for the men-tally retarded were diagnosed as "undifferentiated" or "familial." The latter accounted for about 30 per cent and gave us very little more information about those so classified than did the "undifferentiated" label, which gave us nothing.[26] "Familial" merely meant that someone at some time, for either

[25] For example, the following passage from a recent reference work:
. . . a percentage of retardates are potentially capable of normal performance and are retarded because of purely functional reasons, but this is certainly a very small percentage of the total retarded population (Spitz, 1963).
[26] One of the problems with "undifferentiated" as a category is that it is used in an undifferentiated way for instances in which some physical stigmata are observable

good or poor reasons, decided that at least one member of the patient's family had at some time also been mentally retarded; the implication was, of course, that there was an inherited defect.

When we could say, by means of our classification scheme, virtually nothing about over half of the cases of newly institutionalized mental deficiency, then there was obviously something lacking in the way in which the patients were being viewed scientifically. Obviously, the curious investigator had to begin looking for some other way to analyze the information that we could get about mental deficiency. On the basis of a number of conversations and interviews with such investigators and workers in the field, I could report back to NIMH in 1953 that a revolution was brewing:

> It appears more and more likely that future investigators will start out with a frame of reference very different from the traditional one. Instead of considering all mental defectives to be more significantly alike than they are different, newer workers will be more interested in their differences. Instead of being a condition of the intellect, mental deficiency will be viewed as a situational complex of many processes, of which the intellectual ones are only a very small part—and sometimes a rather unimportant part. Instead of primarily organic etiologies as the focus of interest, workers in this field will try to abstract many other different kinds of processes from the mental defective complex as being important etiologically. Instead of considering mental deficiency as hopeless, it will be considered as amenable to significant improvement.[27]

In a sense, it was as if workers put all kinds of mental deficiency back into an undifferentiated group, and attacked the problem of describing what went on in any individual case by a different classification scheme. Instead of dividing defectives into diagnostic categories, one could then make use of analytic or process categories. Figure 11–1 illustrates the difference. Each of the categories of processes in Scheme B is not necessarily in the same realm of discourse as another; nor are they necessarily on the same level of abstraction. The logical task of making such distinctions is not necessary until one begins to try to relate the processes; in the meantime, the categories are signposts for new choices of method or approach to the general problem. They can enable the investigator to pull into the spotlight evi-

---

without clear etiology and for instances in which there is nothing but a diagnosis of "mental deficiency" based on a history of incompetence in social and scholastic matters.

[27] NIMH staff report (1953). See also Stewart E. Perry (1954), especially p. 46. One of the most unexpected fruits of refusing to lump even apparently similar defectives together occurred in the study of mongolism, in which it recently appeared that certain differentiable instances of the mongoloid problem are more related to genetic faults than to intrauterine experience. The evidence is reviewed in Lionel Penrose (1963).

dence, data, and hypotheses that have nothing to do with mental retardation itself but are part of the frames of reference of those working in physiology, sociology, or whatever. In fact, a revolution occurred in the classification of individual cases of mental retardation out of the use of evidence and work seemingly unrelated to it.

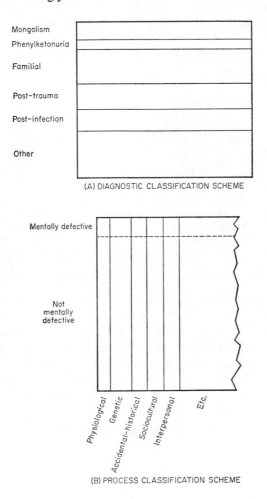

(A) DIAGNOSTIC CLASSIFICATION SCHEME

(B) PROCESS CLASSIFICATION SCHEME

**Figure 11–1.** Diagnostic and process classification schemes.

Insofar as this revolution involved social-science data and studies, it can be seen quite dramatically in the later statistical reports prepared by NIMH. Table 11–1 summarizes the pertinent first admissions data. The first thing that hits the eye in this table is the fact that sometime in the years between 1949 and 1961 there was obviously a change in the classification

TABLE 11–1, *Clinical Classification of First Admissions to Public Institutions for the Mentally Retarded**

|  | 1949<br>(N = 7,800) | 1961<br>(N = 8,804) |
|---|---|---|
| organic signs apparent† | 40% | 61% |
|   for example: mongolism | (11%)‡ | (10%) |
| uncertain (presumed psychologic etiology) |  |  |
|   without organic signs apparent | NU | 33% |
|   for example: cultural-familial | NU | (13%) |
| familial | 31% | NU |
| other forms (not organic nervous disease) | 4% | NU |
| undifferentiated | 25% | NU |
| unclassified | NU | 3% |
| no mental retardation | NU | 3% |
|  | 100% | 100% |

* These figures can be considered only grossly comparable for a variety of reasons. In each of the years, differing numbers of institutions made usable reports for these census purposes; some of the classifications used in one year were *not used* in the other (NU); definitions of classifications have changed in some respects. For other cautions, see the reports for the years 1949 and 1961, *Patients in Mental Institutions*, published by the U. S. Public Health Service, from which this table was adapted.
† This is the only classification used in this table that is not virtually verbatim from the source tables.
‡ A percentage in parentheses refers to a subcategory of the previous percentage in the same column.

system and, in fact, in 1959 a new diagnostic classification scheme was published.[28] It was a radical revision of the old terminology and specifically recognized some etiologic processes not recognized in the old terminology. For example, a broad category was instituted to include the whole range of causative processes that were not body-oriented, but mind-oriented (that is, psychosocial). One of the mind-oriented subcategories, "cultural-familial,"

[28] Rick Heber (1959). A second edition, "A Manual on Terminology and Classification in Mental Retardation," appeared in April 1961. Compare Rick Heber (1961). Somewhat earlier (1957), the Committee on Nomenclature of the American Association on Mental Deficiency published a fourth edition of the manual for classification to be used by institutions for mental defectives, but this was explicitly considered an interim measure, pending the publication of the new manual in 1959. The 1957 publication was indeed an interim phenomenon: the "familial" category was described in it as referring to a group of normally occurring polygenetic factors which, however, produce low intelligence in "accumulation"; but "other associated factors" of a psychosocial nature, the manual went on, "most commonly . . . add to the [polygenetic] causative mechanism." Plainly, this category had become a catch-all to bridge the two periods of thought on the subject. See American Association on Mental Deficiency (1957, p. 14).

replaced the body-oriented category of "familial," maintaining the word but completely changing its meaning.

Comparing the statistics for 1949 with those for 1961, the first year in which there were enough reporting institutions (using the new classification scheme) to make the figures roughly comparable,[29] one can see the following. (1) The cases of the old category of "familial" look as if they have ended up in the "uncertain-psychologic" category, and not just in the "cultural-familial" subcategory. (2) For the first time it is clearly recognizable that the institutions for mental defectives admit a sizable percentage of persons who are not mentally retarded.[30] (3) As might be expected, the rates for clearly distinguished and long recognized syndromes or disorder pictures—such as mongolism—remain rather constant. (4) The increase in the percentage of institutionalized patients with "organic signs apparent" is not accompanied by a decrease in those patients "without organic signs apparent." (Note that this is not necessarily the result of an elimination of the "undifferentiated" category—unless one assumes that better diagnostic services and facilities have transferred all of the undifferentiated patients into those categories with organic signs apparent, and unless we disregard the recent tendency to avoid institutionalization of the higher-level defective, who is ordinarily without apparent organic signs.)

In summary, changes in conceptions of mental retardation and the institutions for its care are at stake here, rather than any change in actual incidence of the condition. The conceptual changes are visible in the new title of the pertinent section of the statistical report. Instead of "institutions for mental defectives and epileptics," there are "institutions for the mentally retarded." This mirrors the terminology in the name of the National

[29] It happens that, as of the date of this writing, 1961 is also the latest year for which statistics are presently published.

[30] By virtue of other information not detailed here, it seems that these are not the mentally normal epileptics, who often in the past were admitted (and continue to be admitted) to institutions for the defective. Moreover, it is instructive to avoid the easy explanation of "error" for the admissions of those who are not mentally retarded. The error, if any, often seems to have rather clear social and psychologic sources and arises from the same cultural patterns as other social fictions about the distinctions between the mentally retarded and those who are not mentally retarded. For example, Lionel Penrose remarks on the negative correlation in the United States and in the Union of South Africa between the number of admissions to mental retardation institutions and the number of prisoners consigned to penitentiaries within administratively bounded areas; he attributes the relationship in part to differences in the way whites and Negroes are dealt with administratively. "More attention is paid to the problem of mental defect among the white than among coloured delinquents" (Penrose, 1963, p. 261). Erving Goffman has questioned whether consignment to the mental institution is a more lenient outcome than to be remanded to prison when questions of mental capacity are brought up (Goffman, 1961). Merely raising this question highlights the social, cultural, and psychologic parameters in our ideas about mental retardation.

Association for Retarded Children.[31] Moreover, a recognition of our relative lack of information is mirrored in the change from the 1949 term, "clinical diagnosis," as the classifying scheme to the more cautious 1961 term, "medical classification" with "supplementary terms."

Partly, these changes are a result of increased public and scientific attention paid to mental deficiency, but certainly they are partly a result of social-science data and studies filtering into the field of mental deficiency. At this point, I shall recall briefly some of the data and studies that led to this conceptual revolution, but that have not been exploited fully as yet. What appears to be one of the most promising areas for investigation is that of the interpersonal aspects of the mental-defective complex. Whereas very few persons interested in mental deficiency have been interested also in the interpersonal processes in mental deficiency, a good deal of work has been done with regard to nondefective persons that is quite pertinent to these processes in the mental-defective situation. One of the uses of this way of viewing mental deficiency is that the same sorts of investigation with nondefective persons can be seen in the same context. In this connection, among the early investigators who come immediately to mind are René A. Spitz, John Bowlby, William Goldfarb, and Harold M. Skeels. Their work has demonstrated over and over again how subnormal intellectual functioning can grow out of the experiences and attitudes with which a child is met in his very early life. In short, the kinds of interpersonal experiences that a person undergoes will affect his intellectual operating level for better or for worse.

In the light of these studies, it is possible to develop a hypothesis of mental deficiency that characterizes it as something like a defense mechanism—an adaptive response—of an interpersonal nature. Such a hypothesis fits tolerably well into our growing knowledge and conceptualization of the psychodynamics of behavior—the person-behaving-in-a-situation. The concepts of psychodynamic social psychologies offer various ways in which such a hypothesis can be stated and explored. The same sort of approach to the analysis of problems of human behavior was responsible for our beginning to understand what schizophrenia is all about. Before we tried to look at schizophrenia from the developmental interpersonal viewpoint, it remained a completely mystifying condition, cut off from ordinary behavior.[32] The same sort of approach may be able to do the same thing for manic-depressive psychosis.[33]

I cite these instances of the fruitfulness of such an approach in solving

[31] The emotional as well as connotative differences between "retarded" and "defective" or "deficient" or "subnormal," and so on, should be recognized. However, I am using all of these terms interchangeably here.

[32] This was, of course, the signal contribution of Harry Stack Sullivan. See the recent definitive collection of his early papers (Sullivan, 1962).

[33] I refer here to the preliminary indications introduced by the work of Frieda Fromm-Reichmann, Mabel Blake Cohen, and others. See Cohen *et al.*, 1954.

the mysteries of behavior deviations as an indication of the feasibility of the same approach in regard to mentally defective behavior. In both of these instances, it should be pointed out that the problem had first been formulated as a defect (in reactive capacity, in capacity for affective response, or what not). Once the traditional concept was discarded and the behavior viewed in terms of common human defenses, rather than uncommon defects, something could be done about it.

One can conclude, then, that certain mental-defective situations can be understood only if we try to look at them from the angle that children can be brought up to be mentally retarded, just as they can be brought up to be schizophrenic or manic-depressive. Furthermore, if it is true that the girl child is, in general, supposed to be brought up (in a society that values males more than females) as less smart than the boy child, there is no difficulty in considering that, within certain other disadvantaged groups in our society, both sexes can be reared to be stupid, or at least more stupid than an advantaged group. The most striking example is, of course, the overproportional incidence of mentally dull people in the Negro community.[34] Yet, caught early enough, this sort of induced, trained mental incapacity can be reversed, as Skeels demonstrated experimentally.

Mental dullness arising from deprivation is, then, not only understandable as an interpersonal phenomenon, but also as a matter of the social and cultural conditions of life for whole groups of people. This means that we must not stop at an interpersonal analysis of any mental-defective situational complex. We must look at it also within the framework of the broad social analysis of the social scientist. If, in the analysis of deprivation, we stop at the level of the interpersonal and its concept of a defensive adaptive mechanism that is diagnosable as mental retardation, we are apt to think that the preventive and curative measures must be interpersonal. Most clinicians will be tempted to stop at this point, for among the skills that the clinician often has to offer are the interpersonal skills of the therapeutic interview, for example. Yet those skills will be of little avail in many of the instances of mental retardation that the clinician comes in touch with if he hopes to achieve a definitive improvement in the person's performance or to prevent the deprivation that arouses the response of mental retardation.

By the time that he ordinarily comes to the clinician, the mentally defective person is usually set in his pattern; for the clinician will not see him until he makes trouble for society somehow; and usually the retarded

[34] Well-presented and dependable evidence on the relationship between admission to a hospital and social and ethnic status is available in a paper by George Sabagh and collaborators (1959). Their admissions data and a provocative attempt to understand sex differences in admissions (Churchill, 1964) offer a clear expression of the effects of differential evaluation of skin color, sex, and social position when it comes to questions of mental retardation. Charles Windle (1962) summarizes the relevant evidence with respect to prognosis, in a monograph that is a valuable analysis of a wide literature.

child will not make trouble for a society bigger than his family—if that—until he has been in school for a while and disturbs the teacher by his slow progress. At the earliest, he usually will be at least five to seven years old. Of course, not every seven-year-old retarded child will be immune to the clinician's best effort to open the doors for him to intellectual normality, but all too many will have been too deprived of mental nourishment to be returned to that state of curiosity and lively interest in the details of the world and their interrelations that we call normal intelligence. Correcting the intellectual diet for these children would have certain unfortunate analogies to beginning to correct the protein diet of the phenylketonuric retarded child at age five, or six, or seven.

Prevention, rather than cure, is the only answer here, at least at our present stage of knowledge. But how is that to be accomplished? Is someone going to teach these parents (deprived themselves) how to bring up a child who will be undeprived and normally intelligent? That might indeed be a function for the public health nurse, for example. But does that nurse have the necessary time or even the professional mandate to do so, or will she ever have that kind of time and mandate? Probably such teaching will be done mainly with parents of very special groups of intellectually handicapped children—for instance, with parents of those children whose physical handicaps (such as cerebral palsy) may lead to the parental overprotection that stunts intellectual development; or perhaps with parents of those children whom we call autistic or schizophrenic whose parents for some reason were unable to mother them. Again, these will ordinarily be the children of the middle class, whose parents are more accessible to clinical facilities.

Few of these services get to that great group of mentally retarded children who are not differentiated from each other, and who were differentiated in the old days from the other mentally retarded only by the term "familial." Here Sarason's comments are worthy of repeated citation:

> Despite the well-nigh perfect correlation between the garden-variety of mental deficiency [what used to be called familial] and unfavorable social conditions, the consensus among workers in the field is that cultural factors are relatively unimportant (Sarason, 1953, p. 134).

That statement is not at all true today, as the NIMH statistics show, for we distinguish a "cultural-familial" group, for example. We are now convinced that cultural factors are important, but even so, we turn our attention elsewhere. Thus, it remains true that we selectively inattend that "well-nigh perfect correlation." Partly, we do so because we are baffled about what to do with it. I do not think it need baffle us if we are willing to think a bit more freely and dangerously.

If we seek to prevent pathologic genetic processes in mental retardation by genetic means, if we seek to prevent pathologic physical processes in mental retardation by physiologic means, if we seek to work on pathologic interpersonal processes in mental retardation by interpersonal means, then we must attack the pathologic socio-cultural processes in mental retardation by socio-cultural means.

The largest single class of mental-retardation phenomena can be wiped out if we are willing to attack the social and cultural conditions that produce them. In this connection, I should emphasize again that these adverse social and cultural conditions may be indicted for a great many cases of mental retardation besides those owing to mere cultural deprivation. The incidence of mental deficiency owing to birth injuries, postnatal traumas, infections, and so on, is also higher in the culturally deprived communities of our nation (Pasamanick, 1955).

If clinicians are interested in doing something quite broadly about mental retardation, to prevent the greatest number of cases from ever happening, they must, as clinicians, become concerned with radical changes in our social order. We shall have to raise our eyes from time to time from the individual mentally retarded child with whom we deal and look at the vicious social order within which he has been produced. This order produces mental deficiency by poverty; racial discrimination; tax protection of the advantaged classes to the handicap of the disadvantaged; public-school programs designed, not for the culturally deprived, but only for the articulate and influential families of the middle class and the rising members of the working class; and all other public programs of little meaning within the subculture of the lower class.

For example, in my own city, the city and state recently appropriated a considerable sum of money to restore a beautiful temporary fair building that originally had been deliberately and especially designed so as to fall gradually into lovely ruins when the fair was closed fifty years ago! And at the same time, funds were refused for a free birth-control clinic at the city hospital. This sort of contrast in values can be found throughout our social order in America. As members of the privileged classes, you and I benefit from this social order in many ways. It is true that the San Francisco Palace of Fine Arts is more immediately important to me as a denizen of middle-class San Francisco than a free birth-control clinic. But we pay a price for these benefits. Part of the price is the wholesale production of mentally retarded children whom we ignore in favor of something else.[35] Yet that process of ignoring the social sources of mental retardation can be transcended. Once before, American medicine redefined a clinical entity as social pathol-

---

[35] I can find no better illustration of this than in Lewis A. Dexter's recent analysis of American schools. He shows, in the simplest terms, the price we pay for our scholastic system (Dexter, 1964).

ogy—in the instance of tuberculosis—and by so doing organized the first lay campaign against a specific disease in the history of medicine.[36]

If we expect to do something really meaningful about mental retardation, we shall have to reconsider our silent acceptance of an invidious structure of preferences built into our social order. This will be true for clinicians, as well as for any others genuinely concerned with the prevention of mental retardation. The clinician who expects to do something major about mental retardation must move on the broad scale of public health and social reform. He must not think that it is not appropriate to a clinical profession. He must not bury his head in the clinical sand of conventional work with a few patients, when every day more and more are needlessly born into a life of mental deprivation. Attending to the individual needs of the mentally retarded child or adult who comes today to the office, the clinic, the hospital, is basic to the clinician's professional responsibility; but paying attention to that one child or adult must not rule out our responsibility to look at those ranks of the unborn mentally retarded of the future who mutely, invisibly stand in supplication just behind the patient we see today.

## REFERENCES

AMERICAN ASSOCIATION ON MENTAL DEFICIENCY, Committee on Nomenclature, *Statistical Manual* (4th ed.; Willimantic, Connecticut: American Association on Mental Deficiency, 1957).

ESTHER LUCILLE BROWN, *Newer Dimensions of Patient Care* (New York: Russell Sage Foundation, 1965).

LINDSEY CHURCHILL, "Sex Differences among Mildly Retarded Admissions to a Hospital for the Mentally Retarded," *American Journal of Mental Deficiency*, LXIX (1964), 269–276.

MABEL BLAKE COHEN, GRACE BAKER, ROBERT A. COHEN, FREIDA FROMM-REICHMANN, and EDITH V. WEIGERT, "An Intensive Study of Twelve Cases of Manic-Depressive Psychosis," *Psychiatry*, XVII (1954), 103–137.

F. G. CROOKSHANK, "The Importance of a Theory of Signs and a Critique of Language in the Study of Medicine," in C. K. Ogden and I. A. Richards, *The Meaning of Meaning* (5th ed.; New York: Harcourt, Brace, 1938), Supplement II, 337–355.

KINGSLEY DAVIS, "Mental Hygiene and the Class Structure," *Psychiatry*, I (1938), 55–65.

LEWIS A. DEXTER, "Selective Inattention in Social Science: With Special Reference to Mental Deficiency," *Social Problems*, VI (1958), 176–183.

LEWIS A. DEXTER, "The Role of the Professions in Evaluating Retardation," *Journal of Mental Subnormality*, VIII (1962), 2–12.

[36] The historian Donald Fleming has called this "one of the decisive events in the involvement of the whole of mankind in the making of their own history" (Fleming, 1954, p. 144).

LEWIS A. DEXTER, *The Tyranny of Schooling: An Inquiry into the Problem of "Stupidity"* (New York: Basic Books, 1964).

GUNNAR DYBWAD, *Challenges in Mental Retardation* (New York: Columbia University Press, 1964).

RALPH B. EDGERTON, "A Patient Elite: Ethnography in a Hospital for the Mentally Retarded," *American Journal of Mental Deficiency*, LXVIII (1963), 372–385.

RAY H. ELLING, "The Hospital-Support Game in Urban Centers," in Eliot Freidson (Ed.), *The Hospital in Modern Society* (New York: Free Press of Glencoe, 1963), pp. 43–111.

DONALD FLEMING, *William H. Welch and the Rise of Modern Medicine* (Boston: Little, Brown, 1954).

ERVING GOFFMAN, *Asylums* (Garden City, New York: Doubleday, 1961).

RICK HEBER (Ed.), "A Manual on Terminology and Classification in Mental Retardation," *American Journal of Mental Deficiency* (Monograph Supplement), LXIV (1959), 3–111.

RICK HEBER, "Modifications in the Manual on Terminology and Classification in Mental Retardation," *American Journal of Mental Deficiency*, LXV (1961), 499–500.

RICHARD HOFSTADTER, *Anti-Intellectualism in American Life* (New York: Knopf, 1963).

AUGUST B. HOLLINGSHEAD and FREDRICK C. REDLICH, *Social Class and Mental Illness* (New York: Wiley, 1958).

*Institutionalizing Mentally Retarded Children: Attitudes of Some Physicians* (Washington, D. C.: U. S. Department of Health, Education and Welfare, Welfare Administration, Children's Bureau, 1963).

JOINT COMMISSION ON MENTAL ILLNESS AND HEALTH, *Action for Mental Health* (New York: Basic Books, 1961).

OTTO KLINEBERG, *Negro Intelligence and Selective Migration* (New York: Columbia University Press, 1935).

HILDA KNOBLOCH and BENJAMIN PASAMANICK, "Some Thoughts on the Inheritance of Intelligence," *American Journal of Orthopsychiatry*, XXXI (1961), 454–473.

JANE MERCER, "Social System Perspective and Clinical Perspective: Frames of Reference for Understanding Career Patterns of Persons Labelled as Mentally Retarded," *Social Problems*, XIII (1965), 18–34.

WALTER B. MILLER, "Inter-Institutional Conflict as a Major Impediment to Delinquency Prevention," *Human Organization*, XVII (1958), 20–23.

PETER NOKES, "Purpose and Efficiency in Humane Social Institutions," *Human Relations*, XIII (1960), 141–155.

BENJAMIN PASAMANICK and ABRAHAM M. LILIENFELD, "Association of Maternal and Fetal Factors with Development of Mental Deficiency. 1. Abnormalities in the Prenatal and Perinatal Periods," *Journal of the American Medical Association*, CLIX (1955), 155–160.

LIONEL S. PENROSE, *The Biology of Mental Defect* (3rd ed.; London: Sidgewick and Jackson, 1963).

STEWART E. PERRY, "Home Treatment and the Social System of Psychiatry," *Psychiatry,* XXVI (1963), 54–64.

STEWART E. PERRY, *The Human Nature of Science: A Study of Researchers at Work in Psychiatry* (New York: Free Press, 1966, in press).

STEWART E. PERRY, "Mental Retardation and the Middle Class in America," *Psychiatry,* XXVIII (1965), 107–118.

STEWART E. PERRY, "Some Theoretic Problems of Mental Deficiency and Their Action Implications," *Psychiatry,* XVII (1954), 45–73.

OTTO POLLAK, *Integrating Sociological and Psychoanalytic Concepts: An Exploration in Child Psychotherapy* (New York: Russell Sage Foundation, 1956).

PRESIDENT'S PANEL ON MENTAL RETARDATION, *A Proposed Program for National Action to Combat Mental Retardation* (Washington, D. C.: Government Printing Office, 1962).

FRANK RIESSMAN, *The Culturally Deprived Child* (New York: Harper, 1962).

GEORGE SABAGH, HARVEY F. DINGMAN, GEORGE TARJAN, and STANLEY W. WRIGHT, "Social Class and Ethnic Status of Patients Admitted to a State Hospital for the Retarded," *Pacific Sociological Review,* II (1959), 76–80.

SEYMOUR B. SARASON, *Psychological Problems in Mental Deficiency* (2nd ed., 3rd ed.; New York: Harper and Row, 1953, 1959).

HAROLD M. SKEELS, "A Study of the Effects of Differential Stimulation on Mentally Retarded Children: A Follow-Up Report," *American Journal of Mental Deficiency,* XLVI (1942), 340–350.

HAROLD M. SKEELS and HAROLD B. DYE, "A Study of the Effects of Differential Stimulation on Mentally Retarded Children," in *Proceedings and Addresses of the 63rd Annual Session of the American Association on Mental Deficiency,* XLIV (1939), 114–136.

HERMAN H. SPITZ, "Field Theory in Mental Deficiency," in Norman R. Ellis (Ed.), *Handbook of Mental Deficiency* (New York: McGraw-Hill, 1963), pp. 11–40.

HARRY STACK SULLIVAN, *Schizophrenia as a Human Process,* with introduction and commentaries by Helen Swick Perry (New York: W. W. Norton, 1962).

JOHN ROWAN WILSON, *Margin of Safety* (Garden City, New York: Doubleday, 1963).

CHARLES WINDLE, "Prognosis of Mental Subnormals," *American Journal of Mental Deficiency* (Monograph Supplement), LXVI (1962), 1–180.

# 12

# Genetic Counseling and Eugenics

## ROBERT W. DAY

### INTRODUCTION

Mental retardation is a symptomatic result of many pathologic processes. Past and continuing efforts point to an ever increasing number of disorders that can result in mental retardation, some with genetic determinants. In this chapter we shall examine the nature of inheritance, the types and characteristics of genetically determined abnormalities leading to mental retardation, and the ways in which genetic knowledge can be used in the control of mental defects. However, any discussion of the genetic aspects of mental retardation draws most heavily on the subject matter of human genetics, with specific examples chosen from those disorders associated with impaired intellectual functioning. For this reason the reader is referred at the outset to more general and extensive treatments of the problem (Stern, 1960; Knudson, 1965) and, in addition, to several recent articles and books detailing specifically the genetics of mental defect (Penrose, 1964; Anderson, 1964; Knobloch and Pasamanick, 1962; Breg, 1962). It must be emphasized that the key to an understanding of the role of genetic abnormality in the etiology of mental defect is an understanding of genetics.

Two approaches are used to determine the role of genetic factors in the causation of both normal and pathologic human variation. The first is an *ad hoc* assessment, beginning with an index case or proband through whom the abnormality is first determined, followed by an extensive family investigation. A pedigree is thus constructed, and, by pooling pedigrees representing similar clinical disorders, the mode of inheritance or the risk of the disease among relatives, by the degree of relationship, is calculated. Appropriate index cases for *ad hoc* studies can be drawn from a variety of sources. The emphasis is on the accuracy of the pedigree information, including verification of clinical diagnoses and extensive searching for the disease among all relatives available for study. With proper analysis of the assembled pedigrees, this method is very powerful and is the source from which most of the current information of immediate clinical genetic usefulness has been derived.

A second approach to measuring the impact of genes on human variation begins with complete assessment of all similar cases in a defined population group. This method draws on the first in assigning conditions ascertained in the study population to the appropriate genetic etiology. However, the emphasis is more on achieving an understanding of how the disease and, thus, the gene or genes involved are maintained in the population. Procedures followed in this population technique are, first, complete ascertainment of all cases of a similar condition and, second, analytic treatment of the data collected to reveal the roles of mutation, selection, reproductive advantage of carriers of abnormal genes, and other biologic behavior that will explain the observed distribution of the disease or variant within the population.

A set of rules describing the general behavior of genetically determined diseases or traits based on pedigree and population approaches is shown in Table 12–1. Application of these rules to a number of human

TABLE 12–1. *Criteria Suggesting Genetic Factors in the Determination of a Trait**

---

1. an elevated risk in relatives compared with the general population
2. greater concordance of the trait in identical than in fraternal twins
3. an excess consanguineous parentage for a presumed recessive trait
4. failure of the trait to "spread" to nonrelated individuals
5. onset at a characteristic age without a known precipitating event
6. variation among populations in the incidence of the trait
7. occurrence of a homologous, inherited condition in other animals

---

* After Morton, "Segregation and Linkage," in W. J. Burdette, ed., *Methodology in Human Genetics* (San Francisco, Calif.: Holden-Day, Inc., 1962), pp. 18–19.

traits[1] demonstrates that several distinct genetic mechanisms can be recognized according to the behavior of a condition within families and defined

[1] In this discussion, a trait is defined as either normal or abnormal variation for some characteristic such as intelligence, height, blood group, and so forth, and thus covers a variety of situations both continuously distributed and discrete. A malformation is defined as a structural abnormality present from birth, but ranging from molecular to anatomically visible. In this sense, the term malformation includes what many authors designate as congenital anomalies, that is, structural abnormalities not grossly apparent. A disease is a pathologic trait, when inherited, and may or may not be a malformation or anomaly, depending on how completely the mechanism is understood.

population groups. These mechanisms are listed in Table 12–2. Genetically determined disorders associated with mental retardation have been identified for each of the five mechanisms shown. Individual conditions are, however, rare, with frequencies between one per 10,000 and one per 100,000 newborns for the single gene traits and variably higher in the remaining four categories. Some 5 to 6 per cent of all live-born children have at birth or will develop during life a disease or malformation with a recognizable genetic etiologic component. Some portion of this 5 to 6 per cent will have mental retardation associated with the genetically determined disability.

TABLE 12–2. *Genetic Mechanisms Determining Diseases, Malformations, and Human Variations*

---

1. single genes
   a. autosomal dominant
   b. autosomal recessive
   c. X-linked recessive
2. chromosomal abnormalities
3. complex malformations
4. incompatibilities
5. segregating traits
6. polygenic traits

---

Brief consideration of several genetic and epidemiologic principles and observations provides a framework on which to construct a more detailed treatment of methodology and specific applications. For instance, the phenotype, or observable and often measurable characteristics of any person relative to some particular trait, is the sum of all the genes (the genotype), the environment, and the interactions between the two. The following equation summarizes the preceding:

$$\text{phenotype} = \text{genotype} + \text{environment} + \text{interactions}.$$

Controversy has long endured between those subscribing to a predominantly environmentalist approach to human variation and those advocating the primary role of genotype in the determination of phenotype. In no area has this controversy consumed greater energy than in debates about the shaping of intelligence. This presentation will disregard any environment–genotype argument. Instead, a more profitable concept approaches diseases as having genetic components on a spectrum. At the one end are disorders in which the abnormal genotype is the major determinant of an abnormal phenotype. Phenylketonuria (PKU) is such a condition. Absence of the enzyme phenylalanine hydroxylase results in rapid increase in the blood level of phenylalanine which, because of this enzyme disorder, cannot be metabolized by the normal conversion to tyrosine. Current information indicates that the majority of patients with PKU rapidly will develop irreversible mental defect, unless the environment is altered by the provision of a special diet that is low in phenylalanine. However, some proportion of patients with high phenylalanine levels do not show brain damage. The protective mechanism by which damage is mitigated is not known. One such mechanism could involve an as yet unidentified interaction of genes or of genotype and environment. At the other end of the spectrum lie conditions such as hydrocephalus and other neural-tube anomalies. These diseases aggregate in families, and the risk of recurrence is higher among relatives of patients than among nonrelated persons. Nevertheless, epidemiologic observations show differences in the distribution of these malformations by space, time, and host characteristics. These extrinsic variations support an etiologic role for environmental factors interacting in some as yet unknown way with susceptible genotypes to produce the anomalies.

In any discussion of human genetics, heritability is a concept of major importance. Since the science of genetics begins with a consideration of why related individuals resemble each other more than they resemble nonrelated persons, and since the amount of resemblance is proportional to the degree of relationship, the heritability of a trait is used to express the extent of this resemblance. As defined by experimental methods, heritability can be expressed mathematically in terms of correlations. The concept is important, however, even without the appropriate experimental situation, and, in the case of man and clinical genetic knowledge about man, the following general rule applies: human genetic analysis is maximally powerful where heritabilities are high. In other words, the importance of abnormal genes and the risks involved for relatives of patients are most clearly demonstrated for the single gene determined diseases (category 1, Table 12–2) where the heritabilities are high. On the other hand, relative risks owing to genotypic variations are far less well understood and evaluated where heritabilities are low, as among the complex malformations and segregating traits (categories 3 and 5 of Table 12–2).

Clinical and epidemiologic studies of mental retardation have demonstrated to date an important dichotomy according to the degree of retardation. Generally, patients with low IQ's (below 50) are more likely to be so affected for organic, including genetic, reasons. Likewise, single etiologic categories of disease frequently are identified in association with the retardation. On the other hand, multiple or interacting causative forces are found more often among patients with higher IQ's (above 50). Cultural and other complicated environmental factors are heavily involved, as attested by the disproportionately higher rates of the milder forms of mental retardation among children from lower socio-economic environments. These general points are illustrated in Table 12–3.

TABLE 12–3. *Associations between the Degree of Mental Retardation and the Occurrence of Genetically Determined Abnormalities*

|  | IQ LOW ($<50$) | IQ HIGH ($>50$) |
|---|---|---|
| presence of etiologically abnormal genotypes | frequent | infrequent |
| heritabilities (single specific causes) | high | low |
| relative importance of complex, cultural-environmental factors in etiology | low | high |

## GENETIC ANALYSIS

Methods of genetic analysis offer some powerful techniques for the study of diseases. The following section describes the application of these methods to the categories of genetically determined diseases listed in Table 12–2.

### Segregation Analysis

Segregation analysis in human genetics is based on Mendelian principles. For purposes of segregation analysis, conditions with recognizable heritability that are transmitted from parent to offspring in discontinuous fashion are studied. The explanation of segregation lies in the nature of the genetic material and in the manner in which such material is transmitted from parent to child. Briefly, current genetic theory states that the individual units of heredity, the genes, are molecules of desoxyribonucleic acid (DNA), showing unique structural specificity. Each functional unit directs the formation by appropriate intermediary steps of cellular proteins that, in turn, determine the growth, reproduction, regulation, and other aspects of cellular function.

The genes are present in the chromosomes of the cell nucleus. One role of the chromosomes is that of distributing equal amounts of genes and other genetic information during the formation of progeny. This is accomplished by transmission of one set of chromosomes in the sperm for union with another set present in the ovum. To maintain equal contributions from both parents the diploid chromosome set of the adult human is halved from forty-six to twenty-three during the formation of the sperm and ova, or gametes. For this purpose, the specialized cell-divisions of the meiotic process, occurring only in the reproductive tract, result in one member of each of the twenty-three chromosome pairs arriving in the functional gametes. At fertilization, the new organism is thus composed of two members of each pair, one of paternal and the other of maternal origin. The normal diploid chromosome number, forty-six, is reconstituted by this process.

If, in a given mating, one parent possesses a distinct trait (Phenotype A), owing to the presence of one gene (A) carried on one member of the appropriate chromosome pair; and the other gene at this particular location (the A locus) on the homologous chromosome has an alternative form (A′), this parent is called a heterozygote (AA′). The mechanics of meiosis are such that the chromosome with gene A and the homologue with gene A′ are equally likely to be included in any functional gamete. If such a heterozygote AA′ (phenotype A′) mates with a homozygote A′A, both of whose A loci are occupied by the A′ gene, the resulting offspring will occur with a segregation ratio of one-half AA′ and heterozygous, and one-half A′A′ and homozygous. In this situation, the A gene is termed dominant to A′, since the presence of at least one A gene confers the A phenotype.

In the above example of dominant inheritance, it was assumed that the parents were equally likely to be of the heterozygote genotype (AA′) and the resulting segregation products to be equally distributed among the sexes. Any distortion of the segregation pattern away from the above would occur only if the locus under consideration were on the X chromosome. In man, twenty-two of the chromosome pairs are autosomes and the remaining pair are the sex chromosomes, the female having two X's and the male one X and one Y.

On the basis of these considerations, a set of rules that describes the segregation pattern and characteristics of autosomal dominant inheritance can be derived. A similar approach can be applied to segregation analysis of the other classes of single genes listed in category 1, Table 12–2, autosomal recessive, and sex-linked or X-linked recessive. Maintaining the notation used above, A for dominant and AA′ for deleterious recessive genes, the appearance of homozygotes A′A′ offspring occurs only in matings between two heterozygotes (AA′). Again, segregation is assumed to result in equal ratios of A and A′ gametes. At fertilization the probability of an A′A′ conception or zygote is one-quarter, the product of the A′ gamete probabilities of one-half for each parent.

Rules governing the segregation pattern of autosomal genes are shown in Table 12–4. Of special interest is the high frequency of relationship or consanguinity between the parents, both carriers, of children with rare diseases due to homozygosity for abnormal autosomal recessive genes. The importance of consanguinity lies in the much higher likelihood that related parents carrying an abnormal recessive gene both will have received that gene from a common ancestor. By application of a series of calculations based on the frequency of the gene and the frequency of first cousin and other degrees of relationship between parents, it can be shown that a high proportion of children homozygous for rare deleterious recessive genes will be the products of consanguineous matings.

TABLE 12–4. *Segregation Characteristics and Modes of Inheritance of Single Gene-Determined Rare Traits*

---

1. AUTOSOMAL DOMINANT
   a. Except for mutation, all affected offspring have an affected parent.
   b. The two sexes are equally affected.
   c. Offspring from matings between an affected heterozygote and a normal homozygote are affected with the segregation frequency of one-half.
2. AUTOSOMAL RECESSIVE
   a. All relatives except siblings of affected individuals are usually normal.
   b. The two sexes are affected equally.
   c. Offspring from matings between two normal heterozygotes are affected with the segregation frequency of one-quarter.
   d. Consanguinity of parents of affected children is more common than in the general population.
3. X-LINKED RECESSIVE
   a. Except for male relatives in the female line, parents and other relatives usually are normal.
   b. Except for mutants, all affected sons have carrier mothers.
   c. Affected males have normal sons, but their daughters are all carriers (heterozygotes).
   d. Carrier (heterozygous) females have normal and affected sons and carrier and normal daughters with segregation frequencies of one-half for each.
   e. Chromosomally normal affected females are the offspring of matings between an affected father and a carrier mother.

---

Although the two X chromosomes of the female are homologous—that is, similar loci are present—and thus show gene behavior similar to that observed for autosomal genes, the X and Y chromosomes of the male are not homologous. The Y chromosome is male-determining; however, evidence of specific traits owing to the genes carried on the Y chromosome is almost completely lacking. An important aspect of X-linked or sex-linked genes results from the nonhomology of the X and Y chromosomes. Whereas an abnormal recessive X-linked gene in the female can be carried in heterozygous fashion because of the presence of the two homologous X chromosomes, any deleterious X-linked recessive present in the male will have full expression. There is no homologous locus on the Y chromosome to counteract the effect of the abnormal gene. As a result, males will be affected much more frequently than females. Further, segregation analysis for X-linked recessive genes predicts the ratio of carrier to normal to affected female offspring and the ratio of normal to affected male offspring from various mating types. Segregation properties of X-linked recessive genes also are shown in Table 12–4. Extension of the rules developed to explain simple modes of inheritance to traits determined by a series of alleles such as the A, B, and O genes of the ABO blood groups, or to the case of two separate gene loci with two or more alleles at each locus, can be treated by extension of segregation analysis. Further applications and generalization of segregation analysis have been developed for maximal utilization of the accumulated familial and population information (Morton, 1962). Currently, such techniques are efficient where the trait under study exhibits high heritability, although reduced penetrance and variable expression also can be accommodated. Of immediate interest are recent developments in segregation analysis leading to estimates of the number of loci involved among phenotypically similar traits, that is, severe mental defect (Dewey *et al.,* 1965).

### Chromosome Abnormalities

Within the past six years, improvements in tissue-culture techniques have made possible simple methods for studying the human chromosomes. Until 1956, the normal number of human chromosomes was held to be forty-eight. Gal Hin Hijo and Albert Levan (1956) were first to correct the figure to forty-six, and the importance of deviations from this number has become apparent by the many associations now known between abnormal chromosome number and mental retardation. Present techniques permit the study of the human chromosomes from all body cells that will grow after explanting to a tissue-culture system. The most commonly employed cells are the leukocytes; however, skin and bone marrow also are obtained relatively easily for culture. Direct methods of chromosome study, direct in that no tissue culture is involved, are possible also, provided that a suitable proportion of the cells used are already in division at the time of removal from the body.

     Probably the single most impressive accomplishment of human chromosome study to date is represented in knowledge about mongolism or, better, Down's syndrome. First described in 1866 by the British physician Langdon Down, this malformation constitutes the single most common specific diagnostic category identifiable among the mentally retarded. Some 10 to 15 per cent of institutionalized mentally defective patients have the disorder. The over-all frequency among newborns is estimated to be between one per 500 and one per 1,000 live births. Because a distinctive combination of physical abnormalities is present as part of the syndrome and because both prevalence and incidence are high for a serious congenital problem, this disorder has been investigated intensively during the past half-century. Notable contributions have been made by Jakob Oster (1953) and Lionel S. Penrose (1961a), among others. As a result of clinical, genetic, and epidemiologic studies, the etiology was considered until recently to include a combination of genetic and environmental factors. However, Jérôme Léjeune and coworkers (1959) first described and others soon confirmed the presence of an extra small chromosome in cells obtained by tissue culture from patients with Down's syndrome.

The resolution of much of the accumulated and often confusing genetic, clinical, and ecologic information about Down's syndrome by the discovery that extra chromosomal material is characteristic of the condition represents an important step toward understanding this type of malformation and mental retardation. Further, this discovery and the subsequent developments to be discussed present an important synthesis between observation and mechanisms that may be repeated in the future for many other complex malformations in which evidence of combined genetic and environmental etiology exists, but without any common denominator to explain the various observations. Table 12–5 presents a summary of the clinical, genetic, and epidemiologic information accumulated about Down's syndrome prior to 1959. Parallel notation describes the association between these observations and the chromosomal finds. Comprehensive reviews have been prepared by John L. Hamerton (1962) and by Jérôme Léjeune (1964).

TABLE 12–5. *Comparison of Genetic and Epidemiologic Observations on the Etiology of Down's Syndrome (Pre-1959) and Current Cytologic Explanations*

| PRE-1959 | POST-1959 |
| --- | --- |
| maternal age effect | trisomy-21 |
| maternal age, independent group | translocation |
| equal ratio of affected to normal offspring of affected mothers | meiosis with trisomy-21 |
| 100 per cent concordance in identical twins; near 0 per cent in fraternal | one versus two contiguous trisomic zygotes |
| familial aggregations greater than expected | translocation carrier parents genetic influences on nondisjunction parental mosaics somatic or germinal gonosomic |

Detailed examination of certain of the genetic and epidemiologic observations of Down's syndrome (Table 12–5) will show some of the characteristics of genetically determined traits shown in Table 12–1. For example, in the few recorded instances of mothers with Down's syndrome having offspring, the ratio of affected to nonaffected among the progeny is about one to one. This finding suggests autosomal dominant inheritance. On the other hand, nearly all children with Down's syndrome are the offspring of normal parents and are born into families without previous, known cases. The explanation for this observation would stress an autosomal dominant mutant, the mutation representing a single abnormal gene arising from a normal gene present in either parent. Mutation or genetic newness in this sense must be invoked in this particular explanation, since patients with Down's syndrome show not only generally depressed fertility but also much reduced viability. However, point or gene mutations occur with an average frequency of between 0.5 and 1.5 per 100,000 loci per generation (Penrose, 1961b). With an average frequency of Down's syndrome estimated at one per 1,000 live births or more, the mutation argument is not tenable.

The chromosomal findings in Down's syndrome provide, however, an explanation for the observed results in offspring of affected mothers. A female with Down's syndrome will have an extra chromosome, by definition a number 21 and one of the smallest autosomes, giving a total of forty-seven chromosomes, with three 21's. At meiosis, one-half of the ova formed will contain two of these number 21 chromosomes, and one-half will have only one number 21. Fertilization of those ova having two 21's by a normal sperm containing a single 21 will result in children with trisomy-21, forty-seven chromosomes and clinical Down's syndrome. Lacking the specific evidence of extra chromosomal material in Down's syndrome, the pre-1959 situation, the observed ratios of affected to nonaffected progeny of affected mothers suggested a genetic mechanism. The chromosomal evidence, when combined with the expected types and frequencies of ova produced in a trisomic-21 female, provided a satisfactory explanation.

Other evidence of genetic factors operating in the etiology of Down's syndrome included the results of twin investigations. In human genetics, studies on twinning have long had special importance. Only in identical or monozygotic twins are all genes similar. Because of social and other factors, it is not possible in man to manipulate the mating system. Therefore, degrees of genetic similarity that can be produced experimentally by sib–sib and other mating systems generally are not available among humans. A comparison of trait frequency in identical and in fraternal twins can suggest the importance of the genotype in determining the presence of the trait under study. Similarity in a twin pair is expressed as concordance and dissimilarity as discordance. For concordance, the frequency with which the co-twin of an affected twin also is affected is used. For discordance, the measurement describes the frequency with which the co-twin of an affected twin is not affected. A high percentage of concordance among identical twins, in comparison with fraternal twins, suggests that some genetic component is involved in the causation of the trait.

Results of twin studies in Down's syndrome consistently suggested that genetic factors were etiologically important. With few, but currently explainable, exceptions, the concordance in identical twins approaches 100 per cent; the concordance in fraternal twins is about 0 per cent. The explanation for this twin-evidence, based on the chromosomal findings in Down's syndrome, is as follows. The majority of patients with this syndrome have an extra number 21 chromosome. The origin of this extra chromosome is an accident of meiosis. Whereas in normal gamete formation only one member of each chromosomal pair proceeds to a functional sperm or ovum, an occasional gamete is formed by the abnormal process of nondisjunction, in which both members of the parental pair of homologous chromosomes are present. Fertilization by a normal, complementary gamete then results in a conception or zygote with the excess chromosome, a trisomic. All subsequent cell division, mitoses, needed for growth and replacement will include the extra chromosome, and all cells of the body will be trisomic.

In identical twinning, a single zygote is formed that, during an early division, separates to form two cell masses that develop independently into two individuals. The chromosomes of these two identical persons, having a common origin, also are identical. If the original zygote is trisomic-21, so also are the resulting identical twins. Nonidentical or fraternal twins, on the other hand, result from simultaneous fertilization of two ova and have no greater genetic similarity than two sibs, although they share a common maternal environment during gestation. On the average, the probability that both fraternal twins will have trisomy-21 is very small—at first approximation the square of the population incidence.

A familial aggregation is the presence of multiple cases within a sibship or family in excess of the random occurrence of such aggregation as calculated from the population incidence. Familial aggregations of Down's syndrome have been observed repeatedly. About 1 per cent of patients have a similarly affected sib. About .004 per cent would be expected. Recent chromosomal discoveries have pointed to at least two mechanisms that explain some proportion of these observed aggregation frequencies. Five per cent or less of patients with Down's syndrome have forty-six rather than the characteristic forty-seven chromosomes. Excess number 21 chromosomal material is present; however, the mechanism is one of chromosomal rearrangement rather than a change in chromosome number. Translocations have been identified in which a number 21 chromosome and another autosome undergo breaks and rejoin so that a composite chromosome results. This translocation product contains most of the number 21 material as well as the major part of the other autosome involved. Although most translocation forms of Down's syndrome occur spontaneously, a proportion are inherited from a parent who carries the translocation. The chromosome complement of these carriers includes two 21 chromosomes, one independent and one as part of the translocation. With two sets of genes located on the equivalent of two 21 chromosomes present, the carrier is genetically balanced and therefore phenotypically normal. At meiosis, however, certain carriers or translocation heterozygotes will form gametes that are genetically unbalanced. The types and frequencies formed by the carriers vary, depending on the morphologic characteristics of the translocation and the sex of the carrier. Selection against certain classes of unbalanced gametes or zygotes also occurs. The most clinically important carrier is the female with forty-five chromosomes, the D/G translocation heterozygote. Theoretically, one-third of all offspring from a mating between a female D/G translocation heterozygote and a normal male will have Down's syndrome; one-third will be translocation heterozygotes like the mother; and one-third will be both phenotypically and chromosomally normal.

A proportion of patients with Down's syndrome have mosaic chromosome complements. By definition, mosaicism is the simultaneous presence of two or more cell populations in the same individual, these cell populations differing in chromosome number. Mosaics with clinical Down's syndrome include patients with a proportion of cells with forty-seven chromosomes, trisomy-21, a proportion with forty-six chromosomes including two 21's, and other cell populations with possibly forty-eight chromosomes, tetrasomic for number 21, and so forth. By analogy, a few phenotypically normal parents of trisomic-21 patients have been identified as mosaics, with cell populations that include both disomic and trisomic-21 chromosome complements. If, in a parent with mosaicism, a portion of germinal cells also included trisomic-21 complements, the risk of such a parent producing unbalanced gametes would be very high.

A study of many pedigrees in which there is more than one patient with Down's syndrome offers evidence that the observed familial aggregations result from many causes. In addition to the translocation carrier and mosaic parents, some evidence suggests that other factors such as genetic influences and subtle chromosomal rearrangements can account for multiple cases within a sibship. Techniques of chromosomal analysis are still relatively crude. Technical improvements no doubt will be available shortly. The results from a more refined technology may suggest other disruptions of normal disjunction and gamete formation that will account for the majority of patients with Down's syndrome.

The factor most commonly associated with the incidence of Down's syndrome is the maternal-age effect, or the direct increase in frequency of the condition as a function of the mother's age. Paternal age shows no such association. Although no proven explanation for this effect is presently available, maternal aging in some manner influences the rate of nondisjunction and does so very strongly, especially after the ages of thirty to thirty-five years. For example, at a maternal age of under thirty years, the over-all incidence of Down's syndrome is about one per 2,000 to one per 3,000 live births. At ages forty-five and over, the rate is one in 40. This method of measuring maternal-age effect is an important aspect of genetic and epidemiologic analysis. Applied to other autosomal trisomies, the effect has been identified, and may be regarded as a sign of nondisjunctional and subsequent chromosomal imbalance causing the condition under study. Current explanations for the maternal-age effect are based on the very different mechanism of gamete formation in the human female and the human male.

The preceding discussion of how the genetic and other analyses of Down's syndrome have been reconciled and extended in view of recent chromosomal discoveries stressed the importance of technical improvements as well as specific application of several of the evidences for genetic etiology presented in Table 12–1. In addition to clarifying much that had been described about Down's syndrome, the application of chromosome technology to a variety of malformations associated with mental defect has resulted in the description of two other autosomal trisomy syndromes, the D and the E trisomies. Both are much more severe malformations in comparison with trisomy-21, resulting in extreme selection and a very short life span. Another important application of chromosomal techniques has resulted in better understanding of the etiology and pathogenesis of abnormal sexual development. Although the relationship between intersex states and mental retardation is confused currently, basic biologic discoveries about sex determination have been made. Two types of sex-chromosome abnormality, XXY Klinefelter males and XXX or Triple-X females, are observed among institutionalized populations of mental defectives. The total frequency for the former is about 1 per cent of institutionalized males. Based on an incidence at birth of 0.25 per cent, this four-times excess compares closely with the excess noted for XXX females. Other studies suggest that less severe mental retardation may be more commonly associated with certain of the sex-chromosomal anomalies (Ferguson-Smith, 1962).

### Incompatibilities

The incompatibilities, category 4, Table 12–2, are important genetic mechanisms that can result, if untreated, in mental defect. The best known example is Rh incompatibility, and the genetics are straightforward. A mating between an Rh negative mother and an Rh positive father will result in all or a portion of the offspring being Rh positive, depending on the paternal genotype, since Rh positivity is dominant. An important environmental component also is involved. As the Rh antigen of the Rh positive fetus can enter the maternal circulation and result in the production of anti-Rh antibody, the extent of antibody-response is related to the amount of exposure. Thus, the larger the number of incompatible pregnancies, the stronger the antibody response will be. Maternal anti-Rh antibody will complex with the fetal red cells, producing hemolysis and the features of erythroblastosis fetalis. The condition is treatable by exchange transfusion of the newborn, and recent technical improvements have shown it to be possible also to prevent fetal loss by amniocentesis to determine the extent of red-cell destruction and by fetal transfusion to provide enough additional intrauterine growth so that a live-born infant may be delivered prematurely by caesarean section. Without exchange transfusion, the erythroblastotic infant will develop kernicterus and consequent irreversible brain damage and mental retardation. Further rapid advances in the prevention of hemolytic disease of the newborn by preventing sensitization of the Rh negative mother are imminent. If, as has been suggested, the fetal Rh positive red cells enter the maternal circulation at the time of birth of the first Rh incompatible child, destruction of these sensitizing cells by immune globulin may prevent immune responses in subsequent pregnancies.

### Complex Malformations and Segregating Traits

These categories of genetically influenced pathologic traits (3 and 5, Table 12–2) represent situations in which neither pedigree nor population studies have produced evidence thus far for any consistent and testable genetic etiologic mechanism. Rather, the role of abnormal genotypes in the production of these traits is suggested by observations such as familial aggregations, twin evidence, and incidence differences in different population groups. Further, the general severity of these disorders often serves to limit or exclude reproduction in affected persons and, thus, eliminates any possibility of testing a genetic etiology by studying the offspring of patients with the disease.

Where the effect of an abnormal genotype is lethal, leading to abortion or very early loss, techniques have not been developed so far for estimating the genotypic contribution. However, observable chromosomal abnormalities have been implicated in about 20 per cent of a series of randomly collected spontaneous abortions (Carr and Lpool, 1963). Positive identification of the aberrant karyotype is of obvious advantage in the study of chromosomal abnormalities. To date, positive identification of abnormal genes requires some form of mating test. Future developments, especially techniques demonstrating abnormal gene products not first identified by segregation procedures as heritable, will suggest the importance of genetic mechanisms in the production of many malformations and diseases associated with mental retardation. The segregating traits differ from the complex malformations in that manifestation is generally later in life, and the reproductive behavior in affected individuals, although reduced, is probably less decreased than among patients with the complex malformations.

### Polygenic Traits

I include here another category, the continuously distributed traits including intelligence, blood pressure, and others (category 6, Table 12–2). This is undoubtedly a mixed group. Pathologic states, currently believed to represent the extremes of a continuously distributed trait, may be shown to have an origin independent of or superimposed on a multifactorial genetic base. Scientific advance has served to separate subgroups on the basis of specific causes or processes. An excellent illustration is provided by the distribution of IQ's, which is a normally shaped curve throughout most of the range, with an excess at the lower end (Dingman and Tarjan, 1960). The etiologic implications of this observation have been described in Table 12–3. Much of this excess can be explained on the basis of a large number of genetic and environmental conditions that are so extremely deleterious to the development of the potentially normal intelligence as to overwhelm such developmental mechanisms completely and result in severe defect.

Current theories explaining the manner of inheritance of intelligence can be used to illustrate the genetic analysis of continuously distributed traits. The model for such traits postulates a different notion of gene action on human variation than has been presented in connection with major traits controlled by single or a very few abnormal genes at one or a small number of loci. A different type of gene, the polygene, is involved. By definition, any one of a series of polygenes individually will have a very small effect on the variation within a trait. The phenotype is determined by the average of all the polygenes involved, and the number of loci active in trait specification is large a priori. Furthermore, the environmental contribution to the variation observed in the trait is large also. Study of polygene effects and behavior utilizes correlation analysis for measurable differences between relatives with, if possible, randomized environmental components. In man, the difficulties of manipulation for the control of the environment and for study of large numbers of offspring from closely inbred matings have been persistent drawbacks to the study of polygenic inheritance. The inherent difficulties of measurement of the traits under study also have been formidable.

The IQ test as a reproducible measurement, presumably culture-corrected or stabilized where comparisons between individuals of similar socio-cultural backgrounds are undertaken, has provided a tool for investigating the genetic component of human intelligence. Although often claimed to be highly important in determining intellectual ability, the relative effect of genotype on IQ remains in dispute. Some compromises in theories of the nature of intelligence have been proposed. For example, the result, the IQ, represents the play of environment interacting with a genetically determined range of potential ability. On the extremes, an environmentalist approach would conclude that any genetic component to intelligence would have to be proved; a predominantly genetic argument would impose a similar demand or burden of proof on the proponent of major environmental determinants of the IQ.

If a genetic determination of intelligence is accepted, certain phenomena may be expected. For instance, greater reproductive rates among parents with lower than average IQ's would result in a lowering of the average population IQ within a generation. Although the number of offspring per mating is known to be greater among the group with lower socio-economic status, extensive study has thus far failed to show a decline in the population average IQ. This hypothesis also depends on a direct association between socio-economic status and IQ, a highly complex interrelationship that may be difficult to demonstrate because of confounding, cultural and otherwise.

In summary, the evidence favoring genetic determination of IQ is open to question. The arguments in support of environmental determination also present major problems in documentation. At present, an interaction between intrinsic and extrinsic components can be assumed. In practical terms, environmental manipulation has been shown to influence test scores and achievement. Where an adverse environment obscures the development of a potentially adequate or high level of intelligence, changes in the environment are warranted. As the issue of IQ determination is not closed, opportunities for further investigation, especially for evaluation following environmental changes, should be utilized.

## PREVENTION AND TREATMENT

Prevention of disease can be approached on two levels, primary and secondary. Primary prevention is aimed at stopping completely the initiation of a deleterious process or event. Secondary preventive measures concentrate on early case-finding and treatment such that consequences of the abnormal process do not appear. The application of genetic knowledge to the prevention of mental retardation takes both forms.

### Primary Prevention: Genetic Counseling

At present there is no way of altering genotype or of influencing the selection of gametes, other than by controlled insemination from a presumed genetically normal donor. Artificial limitation of reproduction thus provides the only means of preventing the formation of genetically abnormal zygotes. An assessment of the risks of producing abnormal offspring with or without further implementation constitutes genetic counseling. Enlarged to include pregnancy terminations, where and when permitted, this statement also summarizes primary prevention applied to genetically determined diseases.

Many books and articles have been written about genetic counseling (Motulsky and Hecht, 1964). Although almost no information is available about the effectiveness of counseling, certain rules for good counseling practices can be stated. The condition for which the couple or individual is segregating should be fully diagnosed and verified. The risk of abnormal offspring should be evaluated completely, taking into account all pertinent and available information. The management of those seeking the counseling should be skilled and should include a full description of the problem with all necessary support. Since limitation of family size is so often needed, skilled birth-control information forms an important adjunct to counseling services.

The procedures involved in counseling are those of high-quality medical care. Since genetic problems do not respect the traditional categories of medical practice, availability of supporting services is necessary for adequate counseling. With the rapid increase in diagnostic procedures, laboratory facilities are of major importance. Thus, the appropriate setting for counseling is the medical center. Additionally, follow-up and supporting services have value in the implementation of the counselor's advice. The impact of a malformed or otherwise imperfect child, coupled with the possibility of repeat occurrences in subsequently born children, and the implications, including limitation of further reproduction, pose obvious psychologic difficulties to parents. Full support to the family, compatible with the severity of the situation, forms an important aspect of the counseling process. Rapid assimilation of unfavorable information by those seeking advice is the exception. For this reason, among others, a full and clear statement of the problem to the family's primary physician will enable him to give continuing support.

All advances in human genetics have important bearing on the skill with which genetic counseling can be delivered and on the effectiveness of this approach. The relative risk of subsequently affected children varies according to the genetic mechanism involved. For autosomal dominant and recessive autosomal and X-linked genes, such risks are high depending on pedigree and clinical or laboratory evaluation of carrier states among the parents. For instance, some serious abnormalities associated with mental retardation behave as autosomal dominant mutants. If such a mutation has occurred and the parents are normal, the risk of recurrence is probably very low. However, a proportion of deleterious autosomal dominant genes is nonpenetrant or, stated otherwise, can be carried without producing any disease. Recognition of nonpenetrance is thus of great importance and often can be suggested by careful pedigree-taking and analysis. Should one of the parents carry the gene in question in nonpenetrant form, the recurrence risk to children born subsequently would be much higher than in the case of a single mutant. Evidence that relatives had had the abnormal gene would offer strong evidence of nonpenetrance.

When the mental retardation is associated with a disease or process with complex etiology—that is, when heritability is low—the prognosis is generally good. The risks of subsequently born affected children are calculated empirically, since no theoretic risk can be assumed in the absence of etiologic information. Review of large collections of pedigrees identified by the presence of at least one affected person will support a number of genetic hypotheses, but without consistency. Therefore, the empiric risk is averaged over the entire group. If heterogeneous etiologic mechanisms are present, the calculated risk figures are not very meaningful in any specific family. The obvious need is for more understanding of the mechanisms involved, more research, and, through this process, substitution of theoretic for empiric risk estimates.

The advances made recently in understanding the role of chromosomal abnormalities in the etiology of Down's syndrome can be used to illustrate these points. It was stated before that, on empiric grounds, about 1 per cent of all patients with Down's syndrome would have an affected sib or close relative. In terms of recurrence risks, however, several groups of families, ascertained through the presence of at least one case of Down's syndrome, can be recognized. In one group, where the patients have maternally inherited D/G translocations, the theoretic risk is one in three. Further, these patients are born more frequently to young than to older mothers. In contrast, with trisomy-21, the transmission of a chromosomal translocation should be independent of maternal age. Chromosomal study of the affected child and the parents will show in which group of recurrence risks a given family belongs. For mothers under thirty years of age at the birth of the first child with Down's syndrome, the empiric recurrence risk can be calculated at one in 100 or less. If, however, chromosomal studies show a maternally inherited D/G translocation in the affected child, the theoretic recurrence risk is advanced to one in three or at least thirty-three times higher. On the other hand, if the child is trisomic-21 and the parents are chromosomally normal, the recurrence is much less than one in one hundred (Day and Wright, 1965: Petersen and Luzzatti, 1965).

Another genetic technique of great potential value in counseling is an understanding of linkages between various genes. When a parent carries a deleterious gene, is heterozygous AA′, and is heterozygous at another locus, BB′, four classes of gametes are equally possible: AB, A′B, AB′, A′B′. If, however, the A and B loci are located sufficiently close together on the same chromosome two types of gametes will occur more frequently—the frequency depending on this distance or the closeness of the linkage. Thus, the deleterious gene A′ may be found in viable offspring most frequently with the B gene and the A with the B′. Recognition of these linkages makes it possible to predict the risk that an unaffected sib of the carrier parent or a sib of an affected patient will carry the abnormal gene. Linkages have been described most completely for loci on the X chromosome; however, several have been identified on autosomes. Interpretation of linkages involves a difficulty in that, at meiosis, genes are exchanged between homologous chromosomes—the phenomenon of crossing-over. Any prediction of carrier state and risk based on linkage information must take into account also the crossing-over frequency.

## Secondary Prevention

Increasingly effective secondary preventive measures have become available recently. A number of inborn metabolic errors leading to mental defect have been identified, appropriate treatments have been developed, and mass screening methods have been worked out. The aim is early detection to ensure maximally effective treatment for prevention of mental retardation. The best current example is phenylketonuria (PKU) screening, in which tests for elevated serum phenylalanine have been applied to large numbers of newborns (Guthrie and Whitney, 1964; Hsia *et al.*, 1964). The advantages of this approach over urine-testing include (1) greater sensitivity in that fewer false negative test results are obtained; (2) earlier time of diagnosis because blood phenylalanine becomes elevated after one to two days of milk-feeding, whereas diagnostic urine products may not be present until several weeks after birth; (3) better assurances that all children will be tested, since a high percentage of children born in hospitals are available for testing prior to discharge. Presumably, diagnosis of PKU early in the newborn period, followed by prompt treatment, results in the control of mental retardation from this cause.

Newborn screening for metabolic disorders leading to mental retardation can be extended to a number of already recognized conditions. Collection of small specimens of blood and urine during the newborn period, the application of automated testing methods to these specimens, and an extension in the number of diseases that can be diagnosed and treated early in life offer important new approaches. Equally valuable are techniques such as registries and linkage procedures that can identify high-risk infants very early in life. Such approaches are being developed with the aid of high-speed data-processing equipment and programming for the increasingly large amounts of genetic information daily collected on the population from sources such as newborn screening programs, medical care and insurance schemes, reportable diseases, and others (Newcombe, 1962).

Another secondary preventive measure is treatment of erythroblastotic newborns by exchange transfusions. Kernicterus with resulting permanent brain damage is thus prevented. Newborns at risk of kernicterus can be identified by jaundice at birth. Matings at high risk of having erythroblastotic offspring can be identified by Rh blood-typing of both parents and determinations of the maternal anti-Rh antibody level during pregnancy.

## EUGENICS AND THE FUTURE

The total amount of mental defect owing primarily to abnormal genes cannot be estimated accurately. Even in the rare and specific traits showing simple locus control, some of which have been discussed here, variations in gene behavior (incomplete penetrance and variable expression) would put in question any such estimate. Further, the role of polygenes in determining the distribution of IQ's, including that portion of the lower end of the scale that may be defined as pathologic, is by no means clear. On the other hand, the importance of various genotypes in determining intellectual function is undoubtedly great. With further research, the list of genetically caused mental-deficiency states will be extended. Information about specific etiologies will aid the development of methods for early detection and treatment. It would appear that, since mental retardation is a symptom of many pathologic processes, the attack on this problem will require multiple weapons. Within our current understanding of the problem, no single discovery is likely to eliminate mental retardation. Rather, the successful approach will combine identification of entities, understanding of etiology, prevention or early diagnosis, and successful treatment. Advances over the past hold out every reason to view the future with hope. As has been shown already, an abnormal genotype does not necessarily condemn an individual to serious and irreversible consequences.

Treatment of genetic abnormalities does, however, raise important questions for coming generations. Whereas patients with PKU if not treated have been infertile in the past, widespread institution of very early diagnosis and therapy will result in an increase in the abnormal gene because these patients will now be able to reproduce. Phenylketonuria is used as an example; there are other sublethal traits now mitigated by treatment, many of which are unrecognized because of low heritability or present difficulties in identifying genetic mechanisms involved that might show behavior similar to that described for PKU. Complete prevention of mental and physical defects in all patients with PKU will result in one generation in a 1 per cent increase in the gene frequency and a 2 per cent increase in the number of homozygotes. Similar increases in successive generations will result in a gradual build-up of the abnormal genes; however, it will be some thirty generations before the gene frequency is doubled. Unquestionably, more efficient methods of treatment will be available, not to speak of the anticipated revolutionary advances of human biology expected in the next six hundred years. Nonetheless, eugenic considerations remain. Even if artificial limitation of reproduction of persons with treated phenylketonuria were completely effective, the disease frequency would remain at present levels because of mutation. Only identification and either limited or controlled reproduction of the one in fifty in the population who are heterozygotes would result in a decrease in frequency of the abnormal gene.

A number of inherited diseases are similar to PKU, and thus the probability that every person carries at least one recessive gene that produces a deleterious homozygote is unity. Realistic approaches to the control of hereditary diseases have been outlined above. Recognition of the universal carrier state in the population merely underscores the wisdom of control measures presently in use. Further, the knowledge that might justify mass fertility limitation according to genotype is not available. Questions about the beneficial or harmful effects to carriers that these deleterious, individually rare genes may confer have not been answered. Conversely, there is every indication that appropriate environmental manipulations may lower the frequency of mental retardation. Techniques are available to facilitate these manipulations in accordance with recognized social goals. This is not to depreciate in any way the already very great contribution of advances in human genetics to the control of mental defect, especially those conditions for which preventive and therapeutic measures are firmly established. In fact, it is in just such situations that genetic counseling is most needed and most appropriate. Rather, the power of genetic analysis and the applicability of genetic knowledge, within the obvious limitations imposed by the present situation, have been stressed. There is every expectation that genetic efforts to understand and to control mental retardation will continue to increase productively and cooperatively with research and control measures contributed from many other fields.

REFERENCES

CARL HENRY ALSTROM, "A Study of Inheritance of Human Intelligence," *Acta Psychiatrica et Neurologica Scandinavica*, XXXVI (1961), 175–202.
V. ELVING ANDERSON, "Genetics in Mental Retardation," in Harvey A. Stevens and Rick Heber (Eds.), *Mental Retardation: A Review of Research* (Chicago: University of Chicago Press, 1964), pp. 348–394.
W. ROY BREG, "Genetic Aspects of Mental Retardation," *Quarterly Review of Pediatrics*, XVII (1962), 9–23.
DAVID H. CARR and M. B. LPOOL, "Chromosome Studies in Abortuses and Stillborn Infants," *Lancet*, II (1963), 603–606.
ROBERT W. DAY and STANLEY W. WRIGHT, "Down's Syndrome at Young Maternal Ages: Chromosomal and Family Studies," *The Journal of Pediatrics*, LXVI (1965), 764–771.
W. J. DEWEY, I. BARRAI, N. E. MORTON, and M. P. MI, "Recessive Genes in Severe Mental Defect," *American Journal of Human Genetics*, XVII (1965), 237–256.
HARVEY F. DINGMAN and GEORGE TARJAN, "Mental Retardation and the Normal Distribution Curve," *American Journal of Mental Deficiency*, LXIV (1960), 991–994.
M. A. FERGUSON-SMITH, "Sex Chromatin Anomalies in Mentally Defective Individuals," *Acta Cytologica*, VI (1962), 73–80.
ROBERT GUTHRIE and STEWART WHITNEY, *Phenylketonuria: Detection in the Newborn Infant as a Routine Hospital Procedure*, U.S. Department of Health, Education, and Welfare, Children's Bureau Publication Number 419 (Washington, D.C.: Government Printing Office, 1964).

JOHN L. HAMERTON, "Cytogenetics of Mongolism," in John L. Hamerton (Ed.), *Chromosomes in Medicine,* Little Club Clinics in Developmental Medicine, Number 5 (London: William Heinemann, 1962), pp. 140–188.

GAL HIN HJIO and ALBERT LEVAN, "The Chromosome Number of Man," *Hereditas,* XLII (1956), 1–6.

DAVID Y-Y. HSIA, JULIAN L. BERMAN, and HERMAN M. SLATIS, "Screening Newborn Infants for Phenylketonuria," *Journal of the American Medical Association,* CLXXXVIII (1964), 203–206.

HILDA KNOBLOCH and BENJAMIN PASAMANICK, "Mental Subnormality," *New England Journal of Medicine,* CCLXVI (1962), 1045–1051, 1092–1097, 1155–1161.

ALFRED G. KNUDSON, JR., *Genetics and Disease* (New York: McGraw-Hill, 1965).

JÉRÔME LÉJEUNE, "The 21 Trisomy—Current Stage of Chromosomal Research," in Arthur G. Steinberg and Alexander G. Bearn (Eds.), *Progress in Medical Genetics,* III (New York: Grune and Stratton, 1964), pp. 144–177.

JÉRÔME LÉJEUNE, MARTHE GAUTIER, and RAYMOND TURPIN, "Les chromosomes humains en culture de tissues," *Comptes Rendus Académie des Sciences,* CCXLVIII (1959), 602–603.

N. E. MORTON, "Segregation and Linkage," in Walter J. Burdette (Ed.), *Methodology in Human Genetics* (San Francisco: Holden-Day, 1962), pp. 17–52.

ARNO MOTULSKY and FREDERICK HECHT, "Genetic Prognosis and Counseling," *American Journal of Obstetrics and Gynecology,* XC (1964), 1227–1241.

H. B. NEWCOMBE, "Population Genetics: Population Records," in Walter J. Burdette (Ed.), *Methodology in Human Genetics* (San Francisco: Holden-Day, 1962), pp. 92–113.

JAKOB OSTER, *Mongolism* (Copenhagen: Danish Science Press, 1953).

LIONEL S. PENROSE, "Mongolism," *British Medical Bulletin,* XVII (1961a), 184–189.

LIONEL S. PENROSE, "Mutation," in Lionel S. Penrose (Ed.), *Recent Advances in Human Genetics* (Boston: Little, Brown, 1961b), pp. 1–18.

LIONEL S. PENROSE, *The Biology of Mental Defect* (New York: Grune and Stratton, 1964).

DAVID PETERSEN and LUIGI LUZZATTI, "The Role of Chromosome Translocation in the Recurrence Risk of Down's Syndrome," *Pediatrics,* XXXV (1965), 463–469.

CURT STERN, *Principles of Human Genetics* (2nd ed.; San Francisco: W. H. Freeman, 1960).

ALAN C. STEVENSON, "The Load of Hereditary Defects in Human Populations," *Radiation Research,* Supplement 1 (1959), 306–325.

PERCY STOCKS and MARY N. KARN, "A Biometric Investigation of Twins and Their Brothers and Sisters," *Annals of Eugenics,* V (1933), 1–55.

# PART IV

## Comprehensive Care of the Mentally Retarded

# 13

# Medical Treatment of the
# Mentally Retarded

## PETER COHEN

Mental retardation is a manifestation of a diverse group of conditions, some a result of biochemical disorders with genetic determination. There are others with genetic implication, such as familial microcephaly or stenosis of the aqueduct of Sylvius, which produces hydrocephalus. Still others are associated with chromosomal abnormalities. Some result from abnormal conditions that operate during the prenatal period. Perinatal factors, such as birth injury or anoxia, may cause brain damage. Prematurity and hemolytic disease of the newborn are other conditions with which high risk is associated. Injury or disease of the brain during infancy or childhood also may result in mental retardation. Some patients may need treatment with appropriate diet for an inborn error of metabolism or substitution therapy for hormonal deficiency. Some may require neurosurgical intervention because of an anatomic defect or space-occupying lesion that affects the brain. Others may require blood replacement in the newborn period for hyperbilirubinemia.

    In anticipation of treatment, it is first necessary to provide for diagnosis and evaluation in order to determine the cause and degree of retardation. If the cause is known, it may suggest specific therapy; if the degree is known, it can aid in counseling and planning an educational or training program.

METABOLIC DEFECTS

A number of biochemical disorders have been recognized as causes of mental retardation (*Mental Retardation Handbook,* 1965) (Tables 13–1 and 13–2) but, unfortunately, few are preventable except by recognizing the eugenic factors that may be involved. Early recognition of some of the conditions, for example, phenylketonuria and maple syrup urine disease, may lead to amelioration of the consequences by appropriate treatment.

*Phenylketonuria*   This condition is produced by a metabolic defect that results from the failure of the hepatic enzyme, phenylalanine hydroxylase, to convert phenylalanine to tyrosine. Affected individuals are normal at birth but, with the continuing ingestion of food that contains phenylalanine, there is increased accumulation of phenylalanine in the blood, resulting in progressive failure of mental development. This may not be recognized until a number of months have elapsed, by which time the damage may be permanent. The condition occurs in approximately 1/10,000–20,-000 of the population and is a hereditary disease due to an autosomal recessive gene.

A few children with the disease appear to be of normal intelligence, but most of them fall into the severely retarded group. The physical manifestations usually include blond hair, blue eyes, dry skin, irritability, hyperactivity, and convulsions, and there is a characteristic odor to the urine. Early diagnosis is imperative and can be accomplished by testing the blood for phenylalanine by the Guthrie bacterial-inhibition test (Guthrie, 1961); or the method of Bert N. LaDu and Patricia J. Michael (1960); or the urine with ferric chloride for phenylketones, which usually appear between two and six weeks after birth.

Dietary treatment has been most effective in preventing brain damage in the very young child and includes the use of a specially devised formula in which reduced amounts of phenylalanine are supplemented with natural foods—essentially fruits and vegetables. By careful calculation of the diet and appropriate intake, the phenylalanine level in the blood can be kept so low that damage will not occur (Kleinman, 1964; Knox, 1960; Kang *et al.,* 1965). Other reports (Centerwall *et al.,* 1961; Berman *et al.,* 1961) emphasize that those who are treated early (between two and six months of age) are significantly more intelligent than those whose treatment is started at a later age.

*Maple Syrup Urine Disease*   This is another metabolic condition that appears to be helped by dietary treatment (Holt *et al.,* 1960). It is a rare familial anomaly that seems to be transmitted by an autosomal recessive gene. It results from a failure of oxidative decarboxylation of the branched chain amino acids: leucine, isoleucine, and valine. The corresponding keto-

TABLE 13-1. *Identifiable Biochemical Disorders Often Associated with Mental Retardation, Characterized by Elevated Blood Amino Acids\**

| DISEASE | AMINO ACID ACCUMULATED IN BLOOD | CHIEF CLINICAL FEATURES IN PATIENTS WITH BIOCHEMICAL DEFECT |
|---|---|---|
| phenylketonuria | phenylalanine | mental retardation<br>convulsions<br>eczema<br>fair hair and skin |
| maple syrup urine disease | valine<br>leucine<br>isoleucine | mental retardation<br>spasticity<br>myoclonic seizures |
| tyrosinosis | tyrosine | myasthenia gravis |
| hyperprolinemia | proline | congenital genitourinary tract anomalies<br>renal disease<br>photogenic epilepsy<br>mental retardation |
| hydroxyprolinemia | hydroxyproline | mental retardation<br>microscopic hematuria |
| histidinemia | histidine | delayed speech development<br>mental retardation |
| citrullinuria | citrulline | mental retardation<br>convulsions<br>vomiting |
| hyperglycinemia | glycine | mental retardation<br>ketosis after leucine ingestion<br>neutropenia, thrombocytopenia<br>hypogammaglobulinemia |
| homocystinuria | methionine<br>(homocystine in urine) | mental retardation<br>seizures<br>dislocated lenses<br>thromboembolic phenomena |
| Oasthouse urine disease | valine<br>leucine<br>isoleucine<br>methionine<br>phenylalanine<br>tyrosine | mental retardation<br>white hair<br>edema<br>unpleasant odor of urine |

\* Modified from Efron, M. L., *et al.* (1964).

TABLE 13–2. *Identifiable Biochemical Disorders Often Associated with Mental Retardation, Characterized by Increased Urinary Amino Acid but Little or No Increase in Blood Concentration**

| DISEASE | CHIEF CLINICAL FEATURES | AMINO ACIDS IN EXCESS IN URINE |
|---|---|---|
| Hartnup disease | mental retardation<br>ataxia<br>pellagra-like rash | "neutral" amino acids<br>many |
| Joseph's syndrome | infantile convulsions<br>increased cerebro-spinal<br>  fluid protein | proline<br>hydroxyproline<br>glycine |
| argininosuccinic-aciduria | mental retardation<br><br>convulsions<br>friable hair<br>ataxia | argininosuccinic acid |
| cystathioninuria | mental retardation<br>congenital anomalies<br>psychosis<br>pituitary disease | cystathionine |
| hypophosphatasia | bone disease<br>low alkaline phosphatase | phosphoethanolamine |
| glycinuria, with nephrolithiasis | neophrolithiasis | glycine |
| galactosemia | mental retardation<br>jaundice, cataracts | many |
| hepatolenticular degeneration | cirrhosis<br>tremor | many, especially cystine<br>  and threonine |
| cystinosis | vitamin D-resistant rickets<br>acidosis<br>dehydration<br>early death | all plasma amino acids |

* Modified from Efron, M. L., *et al.* (1964).

acids seem to form normally, but further degradation is blocked. Then they accumulate in the serum and cerebrospinal fluid and are excreted in large quantities in the urine. Plasma levels of the respective amino acids are elevated also. The urine has a characteristic odor from which the disease acquires its name, and has a positive reaction on testing with 2, 4-dinitrophenylhydrazine. The ferric chloride test usually produces a navy blue color.

A fairly adequate intellectual development in patients with this disease has been achieved by R. G. Westall (1963), who used a diet containing minimal amounts of leucine, isoleucine, and valine. He started treatment on the sixth day of the patient's life with an artificial diet consisting of fresh skimmed cow's milk as a source of the required amount of leucine, isoleucine, and valine, with a small supplementation of valine. The other L-amino acids were given in proportions and amounts similar to those in a full milk diet. Arachis oil was used as a source of fat, and sucrose for carbohydrate. A mineral mixture was added. When the patient was ten and a half months of age, the skimmed milk was replaced with fresh whole cow's milk supplemented with Heinz Junior foods. At thirteen months of age, the child's mental and neurologic development was considered to be normal.

*Galactosemia*    This is a disorder of carbohydrate metabolism. In this, galactose is not utilized readily because of an enzymatic defect of galactose-1-phosphate uridyl transferase, which converts galactose to glucose. Toxic effects result from the accumulation of galactose-1-phosphate in the tissues that results from the inadequate breakdown of galactose to glucose. This defect is transmitted as an autosomal recessive trait.

Infants who suffer from this disease often show evidence of nutritional failure associated with vomiting, enlarged liver and, sometimes, icterus. Usually growth is markedly impaired, and some children develop cataracts and mental retardation. Estimates of galactose-1-phosphate uridyl transferase levels in the blood may confirm the suspected heterozygocity, and family studies may reveal the presence of hereditary galactosemia (Hansen *et al.,* 1964).

There is prompt improvement after treatment with a galactose- or milk-free diet (available as lactose-free nutramigen). Cataracts may disappear if they have not persisted too long; but if mental damage has already occurred, it is not likely to be improved (Donnell *et al.,* 1960). David Hsia (1961) reported success with a lactose-free diet in forty-six galactosemic patients. On the appropriate diet, 71 per cent maintained intelligence in the normal range: whereas on the improper diet, there were only 28 per cent in this range.

*Cretinism*    This results from a lack of thyroid hormone and produces a characteristic picture. If the disease is present at birth, the infant appears inactive, eats poorly, is cold and constipated, the skin is pale with a dusky mottled appearance, and the tissues are loose and flabby. Growth is very slow and the body remains short, stocky, and infantile in proportions. The forehead is low; the base of the nose is broad and flat, the eyes appear wide apart; the eyelids are puffy and wrinkled; the lips are thick; and the tongue usually protrudes. The child has a deep, hoarse cry; teeth are slow to erupt; the abdomen becomes large and pendulous with poor muscle tone; and umbilical hernia is often present. Mental retardation is a significant accompaniment.

Early recognition of this disease and treatment with appropriate amounts of thyroid hormone produce a significant physical and mental response. The intellectual improvement, however, sometimes is not so apparent as the physical improvement. The greater the delay in treatment, the less chance there is for significant mental development (Smith *et al.,* 1957).

*Defects of Lipid Metabolism* These include Tay-Sachs disease, Niemann-Pick disease, Gaucher's disease, gargoylism, and the progressive leukoencephalopathies. The only approach possible to their prevention is a eugenic approach.

## Chromosomal Abnormalities

The *chromosomal abnormalities* associated with mental retardation include mongolism, trisomy-13–15, trisomy-17–18, and Klinefelter's syndrome.

Mongolism (Down's syndrome) is the most common condition in this category, and there are aspects of prevention based on the age of the mother and on the type of trisomy involved. The most common occurrence of mongolism is toward the end of the mother's childbearing years, when it usually results from trisomy associated with nondisjunction. The chance of having a mongoloid increases markedly as the woman gets older. In the younger woman the condition may be associated with translocation of chromosome 21. The mother has an empiric risk, then, of one-third for Down's syndrome, one-third for a normal child who carries the translocation, and one-third for a clinically and chromosomally normal offspring.

There is little indication that trisomy-13–15 or 17–18 will reappear in a family. There is no evidence to indicate that abnormalities involving the sex chromosomes, such as Klinefelter's syndrome (XXY or XXX), tend to recur in subsequent siblings. Therefore, the risk is low.

## Other Genetic Defects

Certain types of retardation are related to genetic factors, and a careful evaluation may determine whether such factors play a role. Where there is a clear-cut hereditary basis, the facts can be presented to the parents about the risk of a similarly affected child in a subsequent pregnancy.

If the disorder is due to a recessive gene, the chance of recurrence for each successive pregnancy is 25 per cent. If a dominant gene appears in a parent's parent, a parent's sibling, or other relative, the approximate risk of mental defect in each child is 25 per cent; if the parent is affected, the risk is 50 per cent. If a child develops a disorder that is considered to be dominant (for example, tuberous sclerosis or neurofibromatosis), and there is no family history of a similar condition, the disorder is probably due to a new mutation, and the risk for recurrence is less than 10 per cent.

A sex-linked recessive trait is recognized by the characteristic pattern of transmission through the mother to the sons, of whom 50 per cent will be affected; the daughters will be normal, but 50 per cent will be carriers.

One of the most common causes of hydrocephalus is stenosis of the aqueduct of Sylvius, which usually is transmitted genetically and produces early and severe hydrocephalus. Many of these patients have other developmental anomalies. Hydrocephalus may result from obstruction anywhere within the cerebrospinal fluid system. In older children, it sometimes results from tumors located in the third ventricle near the aqueduct, the fourth ventricle, or in the cerebellum. These produce obstruction of the cerebrospinal fluid system and interfere with the flow of fluid. Hydrocephalus may result also from post-inflammatory or post-traumatic obstruction of the basilar system, particularly in the region of the tentorium, or from progressive fibrosis of the arachnoidal pathways at the base of the brain, with eventual obliteration of the routes for extraventricular circulation and absorption of the cerebrospinal fluid. The presence of a block and the size of the ventricles can be confirmed by means of a pneumoencephalogram or ventriculogram.

Appropriate treatment consists of removing the block to the cerebrospinal fluid system, although it is not always possible to treat hydrocephalus by direct surgical intervention. Ingenious shunting procedures have been developed that produce temporary and, in some cases, lasting improvement; but they are designed to divert the spinal fluid to a system outside the brain —for example, to the cisterna magna or into the heart, peritoneum, or ureter (Laurence and Coates, 1962; Scarff, 1963).

In a study of treated and untreated patients with hydrocephalus, David Yashon (1963) compared the outcome of fifty-eight nonsurgical cases to sixty-nine with a variety of operations. Of thirty-one survivors in the untreated group, ten were considered to be nearly normal mentally; of the treated cases, twenty-nine were alive; and of these, sixteen were considered to have normal or nearly normal motor and sensory function.

## OTHER PRENATAL FACTORS

Metabolic and endocrinologic disorders in the mother that may affect the infant include diabetes mellitus, myasthenia gravis, idiopathic thrombocytopenic purpura, and hypothyroidism.

Infants born to diabetic mothers have a higher morbidity and mortality rate and a higher incidence of congenital abnormalities and brain abnormality. Good control of diabetes during pregnancy is imperative, not only for the mother's welfare, but also for that of her infant. The mother with hypothyroidism requires adequate treatment during pregnancy in order to prevent congenital malformations and mental retardation in her infant. The widespread use of drugs during pregnancy must be avoided in order to prevent teratogenic effects of damage to the fetus. Drugs that have an effect on the fetus and the neonate are shown in Table 13–3.

TABLE 13–3. *Effects of Medication on the Fetus and Newborn Patient*

| MATERNAL MEDICATION | FETAL OR NEONATAL EFFECT |
|---|---|
| potassium iodide | |
| propylthiouracil | goiter and mental retardation |
| methimaxole | |
| aminopterin | |
| methotrexate | anomalies and abortions |
| chlorambucil | |
| bishydroxycoumarin | |
| ethyl biscoumacetate | fetal death; hemorrhage (?) |
| salicylates (large amounts) | |
| phenobarbital (excess amounts) | neonatal hemorrhage |
| quinine | thrombocytopenia |
| antibacterial agents | |
|   sulfonamides | kernicterus |
|   novobiocin | hyperbilirubinemia |
|   nitrofurantoin | hemolysis |
| vitamin-K analogues (excess amount) | hyperbilirubinemia |
| phenothiazines | hyperbilirubinemia (?) |
| intravenous fluids | |
|   (unphysiologic quantities) | electrolyte abnormalities |
| heroin and morphine | neonatal hypoxia |

Infection during the prenatal period has a significant influence on the developing fetus in the production of brain damage, as well as an effect on other organs.

N. McAlister Gregg (1941) first recognized the influence of rubella on the fetus. The 1964 epidemic in the United States emphasized its seriousness. It is estimated (Horstmann, 1965) that at least several thousand children with major congenital defects—and probably many more with less severe handicaps—have been born as a result of this epidemic. The prevention of this disease awaits the development of a vaccine. In the meantime, a physician can encourage childhood exposure of females to the disease, even while recognizing the danger of its spread to others. The use of gamma globulin to prevent the infection in exposed pregnant women has not proved to be of value.

Other viral infections are not known to produce teratogenic effects. However, if these infections occur in the last trimester, they may lead to prematurity or transmission of the infection to the fetus, thereby producing serious illness and sometimes death. Cytomegaloviruses may be present in the asymptomatic mother and produce serious disease in the infant. Toxoplasmosis, a protozoan infection that may be transmitted from the asymptomatic mother to the fetus, can cause serious damage to the brain, eyes, and other organs. Congenital syphilis is preventable by routine prenatal testing to detect the infected mother. She can then be treated to protect the fetus from infection. Table 13–4 summarizes maternal infections affecting the fetus and newborn.

TABLE 13–4. *Maternal Infections Affecting the Fetus or Newborn*

| MATERNAL DISEASE | EFFECTS ON FETUS OR NEWBORN | PREVENTION |
|---|---|---|
| Acute bacterial infection | prematurity | early treatment |
| Tuberculosis | congenital tuberculosis | separation from mother early treatment |
| Specific viral infections | | |
| rubella | malformation | (see text) |
| influenzae | malformation (?) | immunization during epidemic (?) |
| poliomyelitis | polio in newborn | maternal immunization |
| Herpes simplex | Herpes in newborn | isolate asymptomatic infant from mother |
| chickenpox | chickenpox in newborn | isolate asymptomatic infant from mother |
| mumps | not established | isolate asymptomatic infant from mother |
| measles | stillbirth; abortion | maternal immunization |
| vaccinia | vaccinia | maternal vaccination contraindicated |
| cytomegalic inclusion virus | microcephaly, chorioretinitis, etc. | none |
| Nonspecific viral infections | | |
| upper respiratory infections | none | none |
| severe viral infections | prematurity (?) | none |
| Spirochetal infections | | |
| syphilis | congenital syphilis | prenatal serology and treatment |
| Protozoan infections | | |
| toxoplasmosis | microcephaly, chorioretinitis, etc. | none |

There is ample evidence of the teratogenic effect of ionizing radiation in therapeutic doses. The low levels of radiation encountered with diagnostic X ray procedures carry small hazard. Generally, it is recommended that elective X ray study be performed only in the first ten days following onset of a menstrual period, and there should be adequate shielding of the pelvis. Routine X ray pelvimetry is not recommended. Newer techniques are being developed to minimize the amount of exposure to radiation, such as the use of ultrasensitive films and image intensifiers. Radioactive isotopes are not recommended for use in the pregnant woman.

## Natal Period

The high correlation of brain damage with prematurity emphasizes the importance of finding ways to reduce its incidence. The physician plays an important role by recognizing the factors that lead to prematurity and by protecting his patient from these factors. The health of the mother and the medical care that she receives are not the only important determinants of prematurity. It is associated also with poor socio-economic status. The variables related to this make it difficult to know whether the retardation found in some premature infants is a factor of the prematurity or of the socio-economic status.

Neonatal asphyxia is generally accepted as a cause of brain damage and mental retardation. Studies of infants (Schachter and Apgar, 1959), as well as animal experimentation (Windle, 1958; Barley and Windle, 1959), support the contention that anoxia at birth leads to mental impairment. Anoxia may result during the birth process if the placenta separates too soon, if the umbilical cord kinks, if the child aspirates amniotic fluid, or if the child does not breathe immediately. The physician must be alert to these events and to methods of resuscitation.

During the birth process, the physician must be aware of the complications that might lead to birth injury and that are associated with hemorrhage in and around the brain. Birth injury can result also from precipitous birth and abnormal breech and transverse presentations, where the risk of injury or suffocation to the baby is great.

Subdural hematoma, which results from hemorrhage and effusion into the subdural space, can follow birth trauma or head injury of any kind. In children under two years of age, the findings may resemble those of hydrocephalus (an enlarging head, prominent anterior fontanelle and superficial scalp veins). The hematoma may act like a slowly expanding intracranial lesion and, if not recognized and treated, results in cortical atrophy from the pressure on the underlying cerebrum (Hollenhorst *el al.,* 1957). Treatment consists in aspiration of the accumulated subdural fluid. In long-standing cases, when a membrane forms and results in re-accumulation of fluid, the membrane must be removed, since aspiration alone will not successfully relieve the condition.

Francis D. Ingraham and Donald D. Matson (1954) reported a fourteen-year follow-up of 222 patients treated with subdural taps and craniotomies. After surgery, between 70 per cent and 80 per cent appeared to develop normally for their age (or close to it). Post-operative convulsions were rare, and residual neurologic signs, other than generalized hyperactivity of the deep tendon reflexes, were not common. The retarded and deficient children usually had large chronic hematomas and marked atrophy of the hemispheres by the time the membranes were removed. There was reformation of subdural hematoma that required a second craniotomy in ten cases.

Hemolytic disease of the newborn is another condition for which the physician should be prepared, since it is now possible to prevent the serious brain damage that might occur from it. This condition results from blood incompatibility of the mother and her unborn child. The most common blood factor involved is the Rh factor. Antibodies are produced in the mother that destroy the red blood cells in the infant. In the resulting breakdown of these cells, bilirubin is elaborated, builds up to a toxic level, and produces encephalopathy. Treatment by exchange transfusion has been most successful in preventing kernicterus, associated athetosis, high-frequency deafness, and mental retardation (Sass-Kortsák, 1961). Unfortunately, some are so seriously affected at birth by the Rh sensitization of the mother that they do not survive.

Termination of pregnancy before the expected date of confinement in order to protect the fetus from prolonged exposure to Rh antibodies has resulted in a reduction in the perinatal mortality rate (Goplerud, 1963; Boggs et al., 1963). The development of a spectrophotometric method of examination of amniotic fluid has led to more accurate prediction of the severity of the disease and the detection of cases for early termination of pregnancy (Bowman and Pollak, 1965). For babies severely affected before thirty-four weeks of gestation, a technique for intrauterine transfusion has been developed to protect them *in utero* until they are large enough to survive delivery (Liley, 1961). Since the first successful transfusion of this type was reported by A. W. Liley (1963), there have been a number of successful transfusions (Bowman and Friesen, 1964; Duggan and Taylor, 1964; Queenan, 1965; and Liley, 1965).

## POSTNATAL PERIOD

The growing child is subject to infections, accidents, and poisons that may affect the brain and cause mental retardation. The bacterial meningitides such as those due to Hemophilus influenzae and tuberculous meningi-

tis often show neurologic sequelae. Viral encephalitides also may be re-
oponoiblo for brain damago,

Preventive measures include early recognition and prompt treatment of
the bacterial meningitides and tuberculosis case-finding by routine tubercu-
lin-testing. A child whose tuberculin test converts should be treated. Measles
vaccine, if used on a wide scale, will eliminate the problem of measles encephalitis. Accidents continue to be a significant cause of death and morbidity in childhood. It is important to educate parents to protect their children
from the dangers of their environment. The use of automobile seat-belts
and the provision of safe play areas are important means of preventing
accidents. The danger of poisoning should be stressed in the education of
parents. Lead poisoning may lead to mental retardation and clearly is preventable. It often is found associated with lowered socio-economic status.

There is an increasing awareness of the "battered-child syndrome"
(Kempe *et al.,* 1962), which appears in children who have been beaten by
their parents or guardians, often with resulting head injury. Laws have been
passed in many states requiring the reporting of such cases when suspected
by the physician. Child protective services should be informed of such cases
whenever this condition is suspected by the doctor, whether required by law
or not.

## Psycho-Socio-Cultural Factors

In addition to the biologically determined conditions, psycho-socio-
cultural factors may interact with any of the above conditions or be directly
responsible for apparent intellectual inadequacy. There is good evidence to
indicate that these factors are responsible for a large percentage of retardation of mild degree in children who usually are not recognized as retarded
until they enter school, are unsuccessful in their school performance, and
manifest acting-out behavior. These children often come from economically
and socially depressed families. Their parents often have limited educational backgrounds, and other members of the family may exhibit subnormal intelligence or social inadequacy. These individuals are usually absorbed into the community as semiskilled or unskilled workers when they
reach adulthood. Certain minority groups are overrepresented.

The physician may not be in a position to change the multiplicity of
factors operating to depress the intellectual potential of children who live
under conditions that are less than adequate. He can be aware of them,
however, and act as a community leader in developing resources for families who are at a disadvantage and cannot obtain private care. Emphasis
should be placed on continuity of care and the need for care for adolescent
girls, women with fertility problems, and other high-risk pregnancy groups
(Table 13–5).

TABLE 13–5. *High-Risk Infants**

---

FAMILY HISTORY

presence of mutant genes                    previous defective sibling
central nervous system disorders            parental consanguinity
low socio-economic group                    intrafamilial emotional disorder

MEDICAL HISTORY OF MOTHER

diabetes                                    cardiovascular or renal disease
hypertension                                thyroid disease
radiation                                   idiopathic thrombocytopenic purpura

PREVIOUS OBSTETRICAL HISTORY OF MOTHER

toxemia                                     high parity
miscarriage immediately preceding           prolonged infertility
    pregnancy
size of infants

PRESENT PREGNANCY

maternal age < 18 or > 38                   radiations
multiple births                             anesthesia
polyhydramnios                              maternal rubella in first trimester
pyelonephritis                              diabetes
out-of-wedlock pregnancy                    toxemia
oligohydramnios                             fetal-maternal blood-group
medications                                     incompatibility

LABOR AND DELIVERY

absence of prenatal care                    precipitate, prolonged, or complicated
prematurity                                     delivery
postmaturity-dysmaturity                    low Apgar score—5 min.

PLACENTA

massive infarction
amnion nodosum
placentitis

NEONATAL

single umbilical artery                     convulsions
jaundice                                    failure to regain birth weight by ten
                                                days
head size                                   manifest congenital defects
infection                                   disproportion between weight or length
                                                and gestational age
hypoxia                                     survival following meningitides
                                                encephalopathies, and traumatic
severe dehydration, hyperosmolarity,
    and hypernatremia

---

* Adapted from Proceedings of the White House Conference on Mental Retardation, Washington, D. C., 1963.

Women in these lower socio-economic groups are less likely to obtain adequate prenatal care, the lack of which may lead to contributory factors that produce mental retardation. Inadequate prenatal care results from many causes: inadequate awareness of its value as well as social and ethnic attitudes that cause the pregnant woman to shun medical care, negative administrative policies in social and health agencies, inadequate medical facilities for those in community care programs. The physician can influence all of these by apprising himself of the facts and taking appropriate steps with the aid of community agencies.

## ASSOCIATED CONDITIONS

Mental retardation is only a part of any condition associated with brain damage; for example, it occurs in 50 per cent of children with cerebral palsy. One may be faced, then, with the treatment of mental retardation, as well as of the associated condition. For these children, treatment should provide the benefits to be derived from physical, occupational, and speech therapy. The intensity and duration of treatment should depend on the degree of the physical handicap, the associated mental retardation, and the goals desired. Bracing and surgical intervention also may be helpful in some cases.

Epilepsy may be a manifestation of brain damage. In most epileptics, seizures can be controlled with appropriate treatment. Prompt treatment is essential, however, if the retarded individual is to obtain the maximum benefit from whatever program is instituted.

Drug therapy is recommended for the mentally retarded child who is hyperactive and a behavior problem. This includes the use of anticonvulsants, amphetamines, and the group of ataraxic drugs. The most effective drug may have to be found by empiric use, since hyperactive children vary so widely in their response to drugs.

## MANAGEMENT

The discovery that a child is different from normal produces a tremendous impact on a family. The parents hope that the apparent retardation is only temporary and that some simple explanation, when recognized, will allow treatment that will permit the child to catch up (Bryant and Hirschberg, 1961; Wright and Tarjan, 1963).

After appropriate evaluation, when the parents finally realize that their child is truly retarded, it is natural for some of them to develop guilt feelings. Since they are responsible for the child's conception, it appears to them that one or the other must be solely responsible for his defects. Sometimes guilt feelings result in projection of the blame onto someone else, for example, the doctor who delivered the child. The physician must give the parents an opportunity to give vent to any guilt feelings or any projection of them that might fall on others. Clarification of these feelings will have a beneficial effect on the milieu in which the child is raised.

As their defective child grows older, the parents may react to the burden of care by an unconscious wish to be rid of their problem. This often results in overcompensation in the form of excessive care, protection, and concern. When their demands for the needs of the child are not met, they sometimes develop bitter hostility toward relatives, doctors, neighbors, the school, or the community in general. Such attitudes have a deleterious effect on the affected child and can influence his behavior and attainments so that he becomes more inadequate in social behavior and cannot achieve his potential.

Sometimes, because of significant emotional problems superimposed on the problem of mental retardation, psychotherapy can help make the child more effective and help him achieve his potential. The physician must recognize also that although some parents realize the slowness of the child at the moment, they hope that he will somehow catch up after adequate treatment—particularly with schooling. It is the responsibility of the physician to project the child's development into the future to the best of his ability, so that the parents can plan accordingly and have no false illusions about what to expect. Institutionalization may be one of the alternatives to be considered in the future management of the child. The physician should assist the parents to make this decision, rather than make it for them.

In the interpretation of the nature of the retardation and in counseling the parents, the physician must be sympathetic toward the retarded child and forbearing toward the parents. Many parents resent the physician who informs them bluntly—often with too little examination or investigation—that their child is retarded and that nothing can be done.

When physicians use the phrase, "He will never be any better," they mean that the relationship between the mental and chronologic age will remain constant. The parents interpret this, however, to indicate that the child will make no intellectual progress whatever, and they become even more discouraged. Later, when the child shows signs of progress, the parents begin to feel that the doctor was wrong in his prognosis and nurture the hope that the child will begin to develop normally. This produces a lack of confidence and trust in the physician because of his own earlier, hasty interpretation.

A series of office visits may be necessary to answer the many questions of parents. The physician should adopt an "open door" policy to questions that pertain to the progress of the child and his physical needs. The physician continues to be of vital importance to the family of the retarded child long after the diagnosis is established and the immediate needs are satisfied.

He must plan with them in relation to the crises that inevitably will occur. When the diagnosis has been established, plans for school must be made. Parents will raise questions about sibling relationships. Family crises will occur in connection with the illness of a parent, a move to another community, or other pregnancies. When the child reaches puberty, the parents will be concerned about sexual matters; later there will be a need for vocational placement or marriage. There is always the possibility of a decision to place the child out of the home, and problems will arise because of reactions to separation that may occur following such placement.

For many of these situations, the physician should be aware of the wide range of services from a variety of professions and organizations that assist in the care of the retarded individual during his lifetime. There is increasing emphasis on living in the family, where the retarded child can receive stimulus, care, and encouragement to realize more of his potential. Only 4 per cent of the retarded population is now in institutions; the others live out their lives in the community. This requires an array of community facilities to provide the necessary services. Government aid will enable many communities to speed up their planning for these citizens. (*Mental Retardation Handbook*, 1965). Public health nurses can assist in directing the parents to appropriate follow-up for their infant. The child who requires a special diet can be controlled more adequately by the visit of a nurse who knows the family. She can ensure the care and protection from illness that all infants deserve. All retarded children deserve the same pediatric care as normal children to keep them in the best physical condition. They must be protected from communicable diseases for which immunization is available, especially diphtheria, whooping cough, tetanus, smallpox, polio, and measles. A residential nursery may be necessary for some children. A homemaker to assist the mother with her family chores when the care of the affected infant becomes a burden beyond her physical and emotional endurance, or babysitter services, may give the mother an opportunity to satisfy her personal needs.

A nursery school may provide further enrichment for the child of toddler age and also serve as a meeting ground for the parents to meet others with similarly affected children. For the child with associated defects, cerebral palsy, hearing defects or epilepsy, appropriate treatment can be instituted and continued there. When the child reaches school age, he can enter the class most suited to his ability—one for the educable retarded or one for the trainable retarded. Some may be so severely handicapped that it would be unrealistic to enroll them at all in such classes. For them, day-care programs may provide necessary sensory stimulation.

Where appropriate recreation programs are available, retarded children may fit into organized youth activities, such as scouting or camping under the auspices of parents' groups. Religious education should be provided within the family unit. For the youth and young adult, programs are available for vocational counseling, personal adjustment training, or occupational training that may lead to competitive employment. Sheltered workshops have been developed to train and to provide work opportunities adapted to the skills of the retarded individual. Counseling, psychotherapy, and social services often are available in the community.

As the retarded individual grows older, guardianship plans must be developed for the time when parents no longer are available to supervise them. Boarding homes can provide an opportunity for continued social supervision. In addition to old-age assistance benefits, such benefits as Aid to the Totally Disabled provide for their needs and make it possible for these individuals to remain in the community.

Psychiatric services may be necessary throughout the life of the affected individual. Homemaker and home-nursing services also may be necessary. Each community should provide a valuable service known as "respite." When the parent cannot take care of the affected child because of his own illness, or an emergency from illness or death of a relative, or the need of a family for a vacation without the extra care of the retarded individual, local residential facilities should be available for varying lengths of time. The severely retarded child probably will require public or private institutionalization for long-time residential care.

Family agencies, both denominational and nondenominational, can be helpful in counseling. In addition, most communities have organized parent groups that provide great emotional support and give the parents an outlet for shared experience.

## SUMMARY

Mental retardation requires the physician's awareness of the many factors that lead to it, in order that he may do what he can in the field of prevention. When retardation appears to be present, a careful evaluation should be made to determine its cause and degree so that appropriate treatment and planning can be provided. The physician should be aware also of the community facilities available for his retarded patients. The major part of the physician's service to the retarded child and his family is his counsel and guidance.

## REFERENCES

CLARK J. BAILEY and WILLIAM F. WINDLE, "Neurological, Psychological and Neurohistological Defects Following Asphyxia Neonatorum in the Guinea Pig," *Experimental Neurology*, I (1959), 467–482.
PHYLLIS W. BERMAN, FRANCES K. GRAHAM, PETER L. EICHMAN, and HARRY

A. WAISMAN, "Psychologic and Neurologic Status of Diet-treated Phenylketonuric Children and Their Siblings," *Pediatrics,* XXVIII (1961), 924–934.

THOMAS R. BOGGS, JR., JOHN MOORE, HARRY FIELDS, and S. LEON ISRAEL, "Early Termination of Pregnancy in Rh Sensitization," *Obstetrics and Gynecology,* XXI (1963), 334–338.

JOHN M. BOWMAN and RHINEHART F. FRIESEN, "Multiple Intraperitoneal Transfusions of the Fetus for Erythroblastosis Fetalis," *New England Journal of Medicine,* CCLXXI (1964), 703–707.

JOHN M. BOWMAN and JANET M. POLLAK, "Amniotic Fluid Spectrophotometry and Early Delivery in the Management of Erythroblastosis Fetalis," *Pediatrics,* XXXV (1965), 815–835.

KEITH N. BRYANT and J. COTTER HIRSCHBERG, "Helping the Parents of a Retarded Child. The Role of the Physician," *American Journal of Diseases of Children,* CII (1961), 52–66.

WILLARD R. CENTERWALL, SIEGRIED A. CENTERWALL, VIRGINIA ARMON, and LESLIE B. MANN, "Phenylketonuria II. Results of Treatment of Infants and Young Children. A Report of 10 Cases," *Journal of Pediatrics,* LIX (1961), 102–108.

GEORGE N. DONNELL, WILLIAM R. BERGREN, and ROBERT S. CLELAND, "Galactosemia," *Pediatric Clinics of North America,* VII (1960), 315–332.

E. R. DUGGAN and WALTER W. TAYLOR, "Fetal Transfusion in Utero. Report of a Case," *Obstetrics and Gynecology,* XXIV (1964), 12–14.

MARY L. EFRON, DEAN YOUNG, HUGO W. MOSER, and ROBERT A. MACCREADY, "A Simple Chromatographic Screening Test for the Detection of Disorders of Amino Acid Metabolism," *New England Journal of Medicine,* CCLXX (1964), 1378–1383.

C. P. GOPLERUD, "Preterm Delivery for Sensitized Rh-negative Mothers," *Journal of the American Medical Association,* CLXXXIV (1963), 626–630.

N. MCALISTER GREGG, "Congenital Cataract Following German Measles in the Mother," *Transactions of the Ophthalmological Society of Australia,* III (1941), 35–46.

ROBERT GUTHRIE, "Blood Screening for Phenylketonuria," *Journal of American Medical Association,* CLXXVIII (1961), 863.

R. G. HANSEN, R. K. BRETTHAUER, JARY MAYES, and J. G. NORDIN, "Estimation of Frequency of Occurrence of Galactosemia in the Population," *Proceedings of Society for Experimental Biology and Medicine,* CXV (1964), 560–563.

ROBERT W. HOLLENHORST, HAROLD A. STEIN, HADDOW M. KEITH, and COLLIN S. MACCARTY, "Subdural Hematoma, Subdural Hygroma and Subarachnoid Hemorrhage among Infants and Children," *Neurology,* VII (1957), 813–819.

L. E. HOLT, JR., SELMA E. SNYDERMAN, JOSEPH DANCIS, and PATRICIA NORTON, "The Treatment of a Case of Maple Syrup Urine Disease," *Federation Proceedings,* XIX (1960), 10.

DOROTHY M. HORSTMANN, "Rubella and the Rubella Syndrome. New Epidemiologic and Virologic Observations," *California Medicine,* CII (1965), 397–403.

DAVID Y-Y. HSIA, "Inborn Errors of Carbohydrate Metabolism," *Diabetes,* X (1961), 260–268.

FRANCIS D. INGRAHAM and DONALD D. MATSON, *Neurosurgery of Infancy and Childhood* (Springfield, Illinois: Charles C Thomas, 1954).

ELLEN S. KANG, JOSEPH L. KENNEDY, JR., LORRAINE GATES, IDA BURWASH, and ANN MCKINNON, "Clinical Observations in Phenylketonuria," *Pediatrics,* XXXV (1965), 932–943.

C. HENRY KEMPE, FREDERIC N. SILVERMAN, BRANDT F. STEELE, WILLIAM DROEGEMUELLER, and HENRY K. SILVER, "The Battered-Child Syndrome," *Journal of the American Medical Association,* CLXXXI (1962), 17–24.

DAVID S. KLEINMAN, "Phenylketonuria. A Review of Some Deficits in Our Information," *Pediatrics,* XXXIII (1964), 123–134.

W. EUGENE KNOX, "An Evaluation of the Treatment of Phenylketonuria with Diets Low in Phenylalanine," *Pediatrics,* XXVI (1960), 1–11.

BERT N. LA DU and PATRICIA J. MICHAEL, "An Enzymatic Spectrophotometric Method for the Determination of Phenylalanine in Blood," *Journal of Laboratory and Clinical Medicine,* LV (1960), 491–496.

K. M. LAURENCE and S. COATES, "A Natural History of Hydrocephalus. Detailed Analysis of 182 Unoperated Cases," *Archives of Disease in Childhood,* XXXVII (1962), 345–362.

A. W. LILEY, "Intrauterine Transfusion of Foetus in Haemolytic Disease," *British Medical Journal,* 5365 (1963), 1107–1109.

A. W. LILEY, "Liquor Amnii Analysis in the Management of the Pregnancy Complicated by Rhesus Sensitization," *American Journal of Obstetrics and Gynecology,* LXXXII (1961), 1359–1370.

A. W. LILEY, "The Use of Amniocentesis and Fetal Transfusion in Erythroblastosis Fetalis," *Pediatrics,* XXXV (1965), 836–847.

*Mental Retardation: A Handbook for the Primary Physician,* Report of the American Medical Association Conference on Mental Retardation. Reprinted from the *Journal of the American Medical Association,* CXCI (1965), 183–232.

JOHN T. QUEENAN, "Multiple Intrauterine Transfusions for Erythroblastosis Fetalis," *Journal of American Medical Association,* CXCI (1965), 943–945.

ANDREW SASS-KORTSÁK (Ed.), *Kernicterus. Report Based on a Symposium Held at the IX International Congress of Pediatrics, Montreal, July, 1959* (Toronto: University of Toronto Press, 1961).

JOHN E. SCARFF, "Treatment of Hydrocephalus: An Historical and Critical Review of Methods and Results," *Journal of Neurology, Neurosurgery and Psychiatry,* XXVI (1963), 1–26.

FRANCES F. SCHACHTER and VIRGINIA APGAR, "Perinatal Asphyxia and Psychologic Signs of Brain Damage in Childhood," *Pediatrics,* XXIV (1959), 1016–1025.

DAVID W. SMITH, ROBERT M. BLIZZARD, and LAWSON WILKINS, "The Mental Prognosis in Hypothyroidism of Infancy and Childhood. A Review of 128 Cases," *Pediatrics,* XIX (1957), 1011–1022.

R. G. WESTALL, "Dietary Treatment of a Child with Maple Syrup Urine Disease (Branched-Chain Ketoaciduria)," *Archives of Disease in Childhood,* XXXVIII (1963), 485–491.

WILLIAM F. WINDLE (Ed.), *Neurological and Psychological Deficits of Asphyxia Neonatorum* (Springfield, Illinois: Charles C Thomas, 1958).

STANLEY W. WRIGHT and GEORGE TARJAN, "Mental Retardation. A Review for Pediatricians," *American Journal of Diseases of Children,* CV (1963), 511–526.

DAVID YASHON, "Prognosis in Infantile Hydrocephalus," *Journal of Neurosurgery,* XX (1963), 105–111.

# 14

# Mental Retardation and Psychotherapy

STANISLAUS A. SZUREK

IRVING PHILIPS

For many years some psychiatric clinicians have included mentally retarded patients among those who can benefit from psychotherapy or other psychologic efforts—such as those subsumed under milieu therapy, which involves nurses, technicians, occupational therapists, and teachers in psychiatrically directed hospital work. These are the clinicians who have made serious efforts to distinguish clearly between the clinical phenomena and symptomatology of emotional or mental disorder and those of intellectual deficiency. The frequent complex interrelations between the two conditions are familiar to them. They know that sometimes patients with mental deficiency have little or no appreciable emotional disorder but that, probably much more often, moderate or mild degree of intellectual deficiency is complicated by some measure and varying forms of emotional disorder. They are aware that the most severe emotional disorders, especially the psychotic maldevelopments of personality in early childhood, are accompanied regularly by signs of some degree of retardation.

At best, reliable measurement of intelligence is difficult and, in a certain proportion of such psychotic children, to estimate the degree of mental retardation on initial clinical study is practically impossible. On the other hand, clinicians experienced in this field also find that many children with recognizable emotional disorders manifest varying degrees of retardation either focal or generalized. Further, they have seen children's intellectual functioning and testable intelligence decrease over a span of years when living in particularly adverse circumstances. Conversely, they have seen a rise in the testable intelligence and improvement in academic work of children whose symptoms of emotional disorder have subsided with psychotherapy.

Louis B. Fierman's statement (1965) that it is a clinical myth to hold that psychotherapy is ineffective with patients who have below-average intelligence is a truism to these clinicians. For them the following discussion of psychotherapeutic experience with mentally retarded persons probably will bring little that is new. It has been said that most psychiatrists, particularly child psychiatrists, have shown little if any clinical interest in mentally retarded patients and their families (Potter, 1964). That this has not been true of all child psychiatrists seems evident (Tarjan, 1962; Kerr and Szurek, 1950; Philips *et al.*, 1962; Gunzberg, 1958; Finch, 1960). The clinical examples that are included here represent only a small portion of the available evidence to support this statement. For those who may have succumbed unwittingly to the aforementioned myth, we hope that what follows will be of some interest and value in reconsidering the question.

## Encephalitis, Mental Deficiency, and Personality Development

Over twenty-five years ago, one of us (S.A.S.) had a still vividly remembered clinical experience with a mentally retarded boy over a period of seven or eight years. This experience clarified several principles now more widely known and accepted concerning the distinctions between the clinical phenomenology of mental retardation and that of personality development. The boy was seen first in a psychiatric clinic for children at the age of seven or eight because of severe weeping and tantrum-like periods of disturbance when in school or on leaving home for his second- or third-grade class with his twin brother. His most remarkable and obvious characteristic was a peculiar dyskinesia, choreo-athetotic in character, involving the muscles of his face, neck, and shoulders. These were particularly evident when he spoke, at which time an unusual incoordination became evident. He seemed to be inhaling while trying to speak, which tended to reduce the volume of his voice to a whispering squeak, and appeared to be due to a spasm of respiration with a deadlock in articulation. This required a deep inspiration, partial expiration, and a repetition of another similar sequence. According to his parents, this symptomatology appeared sometime after an attack of Von Economo's encephalitis when he was four years of age, with fever, somnolence, and reversal of the sleep cycle.

His parents, of lower middle socio-economic status, were not surprised that psychometric testing (IQ in the middle 60's) had corroborated the clinical impression of a moderate degree of mental deficiency, since they had noted that his development and learning rate slowed after his illness below that of his twin, with whom he had kept pace until then. Both the boy and his parents, and later his twin, impressed the examiners as friendly, amiable people, considerate toward each other; in short this was a sturdy, realistic, well-integrated family. They were concerned about the boy's emotional difficulty regarding school and were interested in whether anything could be done for his general condition. They were concerned also, but not deeply anxious, about his possible need for care and guidance after their own disability or death. Examination of the patient's twin brother revealed his intelligence to be just average and his school performance adequate. The two boys did not share enough similarities physically (including fingerprints and hair whorls) to be considered identical twins. The mother recalled a little uncertainly that there were two placentas at their delivery.

After careful review of all the findings, the staff could only suggest excusing the patient from required school attendance (there were no special programs for the retarded then available) and trial of the hyoscine-atropine class of drugs for the dyskinetic symptoms. There also was considerable staff debate as to whether or not institutionalization should be recommended, particularly to reduce the danger of impulsive, anti-social, self-destructive behavior or sexual misconduct after puberty. The immediate examiners argued that there was as yet insufficient indication of such difficulty and that there would be sufficient time to consider such a move later if such problems appeared. The family seemed in no way concerned about his behavior, nor did they wish institutionalization for the boy. Periodic visits of the boy and his parents to the clinic were undertaken to assess the results of the boy's withdrawal from school and the effects of medication, and to observe any untoward behavioral difficulties.

During the following two years, these visits, regularly scheduled every few weeks and after some months at lengthening intervals, were kept faithfully and produced some interesting information. None of the drugs prescribed had any noticeable effect on the dyskinetic symptoms. Yet, later, when regularly scheduled appointments seemed no longer necessary, the boy appeared occasionally at the clinic to ask the psychiatrist for prescriptions, sometimes after having had no drugs for weeks at a time. It became clear that although he emphasized that he wanted only the prescription, he seemed to benefit from the contact and at times discussed some relatively minor trouble or disappointment. Such occasional visits continued until he was over sixteen years of age and until the psychiatrist left to enter military service.

The more striking developments during the period of contact with this boy and his family concerned their mutual adaptation and the boy's general behavior. All of the emotional turmoil disappeared when the stress of school work was removed. The parents emphasized what a good-natured and industrious boy he was throughout this period. He attended church regularly with his family; he got along well with his siblings and other children in the neighborhood; and he showed no special interest in girls. He was consistently helpful to his mother and married sister, doing errands and all sorts of household chores. Eventually he obtained small odd jobs from the local merchants, milk men, and vendors of produce. He saved his money carefully and even became a money lender to his siblings. Finally, on his own initiative when eligible in age, he obtained admission and went to one of the federally provided work camps for boys, but became lonely after a few months and resigned to return home to look for local work.

It was not until his twin brother enlisted and was accepted by one of the branches of the military service, during World War II, that the patient became progressively more disturbed. He then came repeatedly to the clinic complaining of severe headaches, insomnia, and restless nervousness. He did not seem clearly to relate his turmoil to his own rejection for military service. Psychotherapeutic discussions and eventually mild sedation were ineffective, as were efforts to discuss the problem with his parents. Finally, they found the increasing severity of his disturbance beyond their ability to tolerate at home, and he was admitted to a state hospital operated largely for persons with the post-encephalitic disorders that were then so numerous as a result of the epidemics of the 1920's. It is regrettable that circumstances prevented learning of later developments in this boy's life.

## MENTAL RETARDATION RESULTING FROM MALINTEGRATIVE EXPERIENCE

In addition, we have had experience in common with other clinicians (Skeels, 1965; Skodak and Skeels, 1949; Freud and Burlingham, 1944; Provence and Lipton, 1962; Clarke, 1958; McCandless, 1964) with children, seen because of adverse life experiences, who suffered increased disturbances in learning with subsequent lowering of the testable IQ but without any evidence of intervening somatic disease. We have seen parentless children whose foster-home placements have been changed repeatedly or children with other adverse home situations, whose intellectual performance and IQ ratings on testing have slowly but perceptibly declined. This has led clinicians to recognize that the IQ level is subject to variation, not only because of disease, but because of malintegrative social and family experiences as well.

For example, Rose, the only daughter of a mother whose life adjustment was always borderline and of an industrious but alcoholic father, was in a special class for slow learners at age fifteen. For the first year of the girl's life, the parents reported a happy and fruitful marriage. For reasons not clear, the father's alcoholism became chronic when the child was three and one-half, and he deserted the family when she was four. The mother's behavior became more erratic, and she was seen repeatedly at psychiatric clinics. She was sexually promiscuous, often living openly with men in her home. The mother's course became more difficult as the years passed. At the start of school, the child was considered precocious and could do intricate puzzles. In the first grade her IQ was 125, and she was reading at the second-grade level. She was in a class for gifted children in second grade. In the third grade she was two years advanced in grade in reading. In the fourth grade she began having trouble with her studies; her tested IQ was 110. In the sixth grade she was considered a slow learner, reading at the 5.9 grade level. In the eighth grade she was doing poor work, and her IQ was 101. Two years later, on entering high school, she was placed in a special class for slow learners; her IQ was 87. There was no evidence of intervening somatic disease.

## MENTAL RETARDATION WITH MENTAL DISORDER

We have recognized the converse, as well—that is, that individuals with relatively high IQ's have responded with improved and sometimes superior intellectual performance after a change in their circumstances of living or after resolution of emotional difficulties. Among other findings, George Kriegman and Josephine R. Hilgard (1944) illustrated, with a carefully studied group of thirty children, that there is a significant relationship between IQ level and symptom improvement when psychotherapy of the child and his parents has successfully resolved concomitant conflicts. This study involved above-average, normal, and retarded children.

During the past eighteen years, in the study of childhood schizophrenia at the Langley Porter Neuropsychiatric Institute, many children have been seen whose emotional disorder was so severe that all learning was greatly complicated by negativism and inhibition. In these children, retardation was frequently a part of the clinical picture. The differentiation of children with mental deficiency complicated by emotional disorder from children with severe emotional disorder but normal intelligence was sometimes difficult. In a few instances psychotherapy that produced some reduction of conflict made the distinction possible. For example, Jane, a five-year-old, white, female child, was admitted to the Children's Ward for study and evaluation. She was a severely emotionally disturbed child who was difficult to manage from early in life. The parents reported that the pregnancy and delivery were without incident. Breast-feeding was attempted but stopped at three weeks because of the mother's poor milk supply. As a small baby Jane never seemed to notice adults, and at six months she actively turned her face away when people came near her crib. She sat alone at nine months and walked at eighteen months. Although she uttered sounds and said, "Mama" and "Dada," there was no further communicative speech. She learned poorly, and each developmental task was accompanied by much frustration and difficult disturbed behavior. By the age of five she was mute, affectively unresponsive, ate dirt and grass; at moments of frustration she would rip off her clothes, made no effort at self-care, and was destructive and withdrawn in behavior. The results of physical, neurologic, and laboratory examinations were within normal limits. Formal intelligence tests were not possible. It was the impression of the examiner that she was an acutely disturbed child. Because of her history and delayed development, there was some suspicion of mental deficiency—of what degree it was impossible to estimate. She was seen for individual therapy three times per week during the next three years of hospital treatment. She developed a limited vocabulary, became more communicative, related more easily to others, and learned to care for herself, with a reduction of her destructive behavior and need to eat dirt. At school, she seemed more attentive. Her ability to learn was limited, despite the reduction of her emotional disorder. Her parents decided that she was too difficult to control at home and applied for her admission to the local state hospital for the retarded. Some children were seen who had obvious deficiency with learning problems or difficulty in social adaptation. Psychotherapy with these children sometimes reduced the emotional conflict, with resulting better adaptation.

In 1958, a training program supported by funds from the National Institute of Mental Health was developed at the Langley Porter Neuropsychiatric Institute to enhance the experience of psychiatric trainees with mental retardation. We have had, therefore, the opportunity to observe even more fully the results of psychotherapy with mentally retarded children with emotional disorders and their parents. Experiences during these seven years with mentally retarded children in many clinical situations have substantiated further our previous impressions.

## RATIONALE OF METHODS OF PSYCHOTHERAPY WITH THE MENTALLY RETARDED

Psychotherapy with the child and parents can be effective in the reduction of conflict in the mentally retarded child. On the basis of other studies (Gunzberg, 1958; Bergman *et al.*, 1951; Beier, 1964) and as noted elsewhere in this volume (Chapter 9), the range of psychopathology is probably as broad as the categories represented in the American Psychiatric Association *Diagnostic and Statistical Manual* (1952). Experience has demonstrated to us the usefulness of concomitant psychotherapy with emotionally disturbed retarded children and their parents. We have found that psychotherapy leading to reduction of conflict is helpful in delineating diagnostic problems as well as in producing symptomatic improvement of emotionally disturbed retarded children. With the reduction of conflict, energy is freed for learning, with consequent better adaptation.

> The child begins to learn with whatever genetically given capacities he has, from his unique developmental history and particular current life situations, with progressively greater freedom from retaliatory anxiety and hence with greater spontaneity and creativity (Szurek and Berlin, 1956, p. 4).

The result is greater ego development, arising from the child's more integrative experiences in living with less hopeless dependency, disappointment, and despair.

The experience of our staff in working with mute, autistic children, whose condition so often negatively affects learning in all aspects of everyday living, has helped us to utilize similar treatment methods in psychotherapeutic work with the retarded child and his parents. Also, we have found that treatment methods that are effective for children with normal intelligence are equally useful for work with the retarded child. In essence, we try to meet the child at whatever level of development, physical and emotional, he has achieved, to help him reduce those elements of conflict that interfere with learning and/or social adaptation. We try to help him express in words or play, rather than in action, feelings associated with conflict or frozen, inhibited distortions of these same feelings that lead to self-defeating behavior, leaving less energy available for the learning of skills.

We have learned that lack of speech or little speech is not a contraindication for work in the playroom. Such psychotherapeutic work does not involve speech only, and the behavior of the child may be understood by close, attentive observation of motivational conflicts resulting in either action or obsessive inhibition. If the behavior is fully understood eventually, through repeated observations of characteristic sequences, appropriate verbal or behavioral response by the therapist may have a modifying influence that in itself may be effective in producing change.

> This attentiveness can be described as both vigilant and relaxed: depending on what is therapeutically indicated, it may be a readiness to restrain destructive behavior; or it may be an "active," inaction, as in silent, "permissive" behavior, which may be at once observing and interpretive. Relaxed attentiveness will permit, with repetition and in time, accurate observation of all details in every sequence of behavior, whether manifested in speech, sound, movement, or in any observable visceral changes. Such careful, regular observation of all details in every sequence of behavior and of any variations in a given pattern of behavior eventually may make sequences understandable to the therapist . . . close, careful, sequential study of ac-

tion, even in the absence of speech, may elucidate motivation, which is the essence of psychological study. Moreover, close observation of persons with mental disorder can reveal *conflicting* motivation, which is the goal of psychotherapeutic work (Szurek and Berlin, 1956, p. 2).

We try to help the child achieve satisfactory solutions to such self-defeating conflicts so that more productive living is possible. We try to maintain an interested, attentive attitude toward all aspects of his behavior in order to understand the nature of his difficulty as well as to enable the child to experience his own self-worth in the therapeutic relationship. We consider concomitant work with both parents to be essential. We try to help each parent understand his situation and to work through any inhibited feelings of remorse, grief, and disappointment, as well as to reduce those conflicts that interfere with his ability to help himself, his child, and his mate to achieve the best possible solution.

For example, after eight years of unsuccessful effort to have a child, Mr. and Mrs. W. adopted two children near birth, the first a girl and two years later a boy, John. A month after the boy's adoption, the family noticed that he had a hemiplegia of the right side of his body. The father insisted that they return the boy, but the mother thought that this was "God's will"; and with some pressure from the agency both parents agreed to keep the boy. He was a difficult infant and child, and his developmental history revealed a characteristic slow development consistent with a later tested IQ in the low 60's. At the age of three he had his first convulsion, and epileptic seizures continued periodically up to the time of admission to the clinic. His parents were always concerned about his health, hesitant to censure him in the management of his behavior, and doubted their ability to help him. The family made many financial sacrifices for the boy, including great medical expenses, to obtain the best care for him. These expenditures further strained a precarious financial situation. His schooling was difficult. At the age of ten, he was referred to our clinic at the insistence of the school. He was in a special school for the physically handicapped, but his hyperactive behavior, poor concentration, and brief attention span made him a difficult problem for his teachers, and little learning seemed to occur. He often was involved in dangerous pursuits, such as climbing out of a second-story window and walking on the ledge, or running into the street just avoiding passing cars. His parents stated that they were helpless to control him. They felt criticized by the school and neighbors and would do anything suggested to them.

At the start of therapy, Mr. W., aged forty-eight, had had two myocardial infarctions requiring hospitalization and was in poor health. He had worked as a postal clerk all of his married life, with little financial reward. He was orphaned early in life, had completed high school, and had prepared for the priesthood, but left because he did not feel fully committed.

He was extremely overcompliant, ready to obey all suggestions and make any sacrifice necessary.

Mrs. W., aged forty-five, also orphaned early in life, was a registered nurse who stopped working to care for her two children. She expressed her worry about her husband's health and her obligation to nurse and protect him. She felt guilty and fearful that she had not done all that she might have done for her son. After a psychiatric study in which each parent was seen for four interviews, they eagerly accepted the suggestion that treatment might be helpful for them as well as a means of answering some of their questions about their son.

In the course of therapy, John was seen by a female therapist, Mrs. Smith. His behavior in the playroom was like that described in the classroom. He was impulsive, manipulative, and continually tested limits. He asked many questions and wanted to know all about the personal life of the therapist. In the second interview, he quickly preceded the therapist into the playroom, locked the door and would not let her enter for the first fifteen minutes. He remarked that he was not going to be bossed by a woman and spent the remaining hour defying limits set, alternately complying with the rules and breaking them, then restarting the activity. This behavior continued until the seventh interview, when he became preoccupied with play that continued periodically for many interviews thereafter. He painted a picture of a small boy caught in a tornado. He was preoccupied with tornadoes, volcanoes, and explosive storms. In his fantasy, the boy was overwhelmed, was unable to help himself, and was a passive victim of the violent natural phenomena. The therapist remarked in the tenth hour that perhaps the little boy could get out and was not as helpless as he appeared. The storms would not hurt him. Efforts to encourage discussion of John's feelings for some time had no effect. In fact, contrariwise he often wanted to leave the play or unzip his trousers and pretend to urinate in the sink.

In the eleventh hour, he seemed to be more orderly and calmer and wrote on the blackboard "color—freedom—Smith." He became more inquisitive about the therapist, frequently asking many personal questions about her life, family, and interests. He made some abortive efforts to try to touch and kiss the therapist. During the twelfth interview he related a dream. It was summer and he was on vacation. While swimming in a pool, he saved a boy from drowning but almost drowned himself. While he was there, he played with a girl in the water and noticed that both of them had forgotten to put their swimming suits on. A teacher was there and told everybody to behave since she was the boss. The little boy liked her and did favors for her. At the conclusion of the dream, he began to ask many personal questions and with some embarrassment remarked that he liked the therapist very much and wanted to marry her. Following this display of tenderness, he became upset and began to unzip his trousers and to run out of the room. The therapist remarked that they could be friends and like each other without being married and wondered if he might be running away because he had told her that he liked her. John became furious and violent and threw things about the room. It took many minutes for him to calm down.

In successive interviews, he continued to draw tornadoes with a boy caught in the middle, hoping to be saved. In these interviews, the tornadoes involved not only the boy but also a boy and a girl who were caught in a tornado and who eventually saved each other. He also related many dreams and nightmares that he had, often with animal figures, some that were born deformed, others that had their heads bashed in, but always with accompanying themes of mothering, injury, salvation, and protection. The therapist tried to talk to him about his feelings about himself, his condition and handicap, and how he could do better despite his injury. He began to talk about his parents, especially his father and some of the difficulties he had with him concerning discipline, control, and help to do better. As John became more trusting, he seemed to do better in school. The teachers remarked that his behavior was more relaxed and also more productive.

In the playroom, whenever his behavior was unruly, he was restrained and told to talk about his feelings rather than become so upset. He tried periodically to see whether he could mess up the playroom; but with each occasion of verbal restraint, he relaxed more quickly. After these abortive episodes he would continue in his play, often writing on the blackboard such pleas as "stop me," "make me wise up," or "please, please, help me climb up in the sunlight." Whenever he was disappointed by the therapist's being absent from the clinic, being on vacation, or by some disruption in therapy, he would become quite angry, and the hour would be extremely difficult because of his impulsive and destructive outbursts. Sometimes he would accompany this by writing verbal invectives on the board, such as "Smith stinker." Throughout the therapeutic process, the therapist tried to get John to verbalize his feelings rather than act on them. As she became more precise in recognizing when outbursts were likely to occur, she was able to control them much more quickly, often by a word or a knowing glance.

In the twenty-fifth interview, John rushed into the playroom and locked his therapist out. He allowed her in after ten minutes. She was angry and told him that this was not the best way to spend the time with her. John became quite remorseful. He began to wonder why "I get these crazy ideas." He began to talk about his low self-esteem, expressed by the feeling that his brain gets jammed up, that he cannot behave right. The therapist suggested that perhaps he would be able to control his behavior if he could see that there were many things that he could do right. John began to smile and began to relate to the therapist the many things that he could do and do well. In the next interview, he came to the interview with his good arm in a cast, having broken it in a fall from a playground slide. He began to talk about his incapacity and his feeling of helplessness in having two bad arms. Impulsively he took out a crayon and began making scribbling marks on the wall. The therapist was quite firm and tried to encourage him to state verbally what he was feeling. He became remorseful and began to clean off the wall the best he could with his frail arm. When he was unable to do so, he began to cry for the first time. He related how angry he was with himself for getting into such a silly situation and began to talk about his accident, his carelessness, and his foolhardy behavior.

Each parent was seen weekly for psychotherapeutic interviews. In the initial part of her work, Mrs. W. was uneasy in talking about herself. She was able to describe how she was repeatedly caught by her wish to help John, but was unable to discipline or to support him. She felt that her son was too incapable and could only be pitied. As a former nurse, she felt responsible for her son's failure and her husband's failing health. Any display of anger was alien to her. She was often victimized by salesmen, storekeepers, and her husband's whims for compulsive purchases. As she talked of her anger at others and her impatience with herself about stating her wants and wishes, she began to see that she was less helpless than she imagined. She began to encourage her son and to talk things over with him, seeing him as a growing boy with special problems. She insisted that her husband take more responsibility for himself and for the care of his health and not expect her to assume responsibility for something over which she had little control. She no longer accepted passively all of his impulsive purchases, but was able to express herself more directly. In order to help the family finances, she returned to nursing and accepted a part-time job, expecting everyone, including John, to assume more responsibility at home. John responded by doing chores at home for the first time, as well as seeking after-school work.

Mr. W. did all he could to please the therapist, rarely mentioned any problem, voiced excessive gratitude for the interest of the clinic, and saw his situation as "fine, just fine." Slowly, he began to voice concern about John, his hesitation about keeping him, and the sadness in his life. He talked of his fear of failing health and his inability to deal with people directly and firmly, always maintaining his Irish charm and humor despite adversity. As he voiced his discontent and helplessness, he began to see how he might do more for himself. He began to expect more from his son, to apply sanctions, and to enforce them without having to indulge John in order to make up for disciplining him. It became possible for him to express genuine affection for his son without the usual obsequious and self-righteous overtones. John, in turn, became more affectionate toward his father. Mr. W.'s self-concern and disappointment with himself turned toward more constructive solutions. He began to make demands on other people as well as being more forthrightly self-assertive against repeated attempts at exploitation by others in connection with his work and buying habits. He began to think

more of himself and considered how he could care better for his heart condition by following medical advice and by reducing his worry and anxiety.
He felt closer to his family and openly discussed with his wife his concerns
about the future.

For approximately the next eighty-five hours, John continued to show
improvement in the direction of greater integration, greater productivity,
and increased interest in schoolwork. It was no longer necessary for him to
attend a special school for the physically handicapped; but, on the school's
insistence, he entered a special class in junior high school where he did very
well. His time in therapy also became more productive. His close relationship with his therapist became more intense, and he began to work out
some of his anxiously rebellious and fearful feelings toward authority, especially as represented by parental figures. He was able to deal more realistically with his handicap, talk about his limitations, and display many new
strengths. Conferences with his school revealed that he was doing extremely
well in his social adjustment, making friends and joining school activities and
the Boy Scouts. He also secured a paper route and was earning money by
doing family errands as well as conducting the small business. Since his
parents felt that things were going very well with John and themselves, therapy was discontinued after one hundred and ten hours. The family adjustment had improved considerably, John's behavior was becoming more integrated, and he seemed to be finding his place in the community. Psychologic
tests showed little change in his IQ during the course of treatment, and he
tested consistently in the low 60's.

This example further illustrates that the retarded child who often is
believed to be unimaginative is quite capable of expressing conflict in creative and symbolic form such as play, dreams, and verbalizations.


## PSYCHOTHERAPY WITH PARENTS OF INFANTS AND VERY YOUNG CHILDREN TO REDUCE OR PREVENT DISORDER

Personality development is determined basically and primarily by the
degree of integrative experience of the child with his parents and family and
is not primarily a matter of innate intellectual endowment. The emotional
impact of the retarded child on the family has been described by many
clinicians (Group for the Advancement of Psychiatry, 1963; Bryant and
Hirschberg, 1961; Begab, Chapter 7 this volume). From our own experience, it seems probable that, even in the best integrated families, the birth
of a moderately or severely retarded child often interferes with parental
ability to be as helpful to the child as the parent may wish. We have seen
the overt expression of symptoms in parents after such births, in interference with parental ability for "mothering" and "fathering" and mutual

emotional support in this crisis. The child, in turn, may develop symptoms of an emotional disorder with distortion in personality development. Psychotherapy of parents in these situations, especially during infancy and very early childhood of their offspring, may be best directed toward helping the parents resolve their difficulties so they can provide less ambivalent and conflicted care for the child.

For example, Mr. and Mrs. M. sought help for their thirteen-month-old child who was diagnosed as having Down's syndrome. Mrs. M. requested gastrointestinal X rays for the youngster because he was constantly spitting up. Mr. M. reported that his wife had become more upset, suspicious, and sleepless since the birth of the child. The history revealed that the boy's frequent vomiting often was projectile and took place with every feeding. He banged his head and rocked constantly in his crib. Sleep patterns were reversed. In the course of a four-week evaluation of the child, the parents were seen weekly for interviews. The father discussed his grief about the birth of this child and his indecision about what to do about, for, and with him. He was more concerned about the condition of his wife and her increasing suspiciousness. Mrs. M. discussed her feelings of failure and disappointment. She seemed to feel better as a result of her experience with the patient, noncritical attitude of the physician, who was thorough in the examination of the child as well as attentive to her situation. At the conclusion of the study, the parents remarked that they were able to discuss frankly and openly their concern as well as some of their mutual indecision about what to do for the child. Both parents seemed to feel less anxious about their plight. In the course of the study, the child's symptoms disappeared except for occasional head-banging.

The following example illustrates the converse, that is, the positive aspects of the family on personality development. A married woman in her early thirties with two preadolescent children, a son and a daughter, was seen for several years in psychotherapeutic sessions, three and then two sessions per week. Among many other symptoms, she had experienced great difficulty in rearing both of her children almost since their birth. The son, the elder of the two, was rather withdrawn, doing much less well in school than his teachers thought him capable of doing, and unable to persist for long in any of his many interests. The daughter was given to frequent severe temper tantrums, was violently rebellious toward her mother about many matters of self-care, eating habits, and promptness. Her schoolwork was spotty and inconsistent.

Slowly, with numerous recurrences of many of her symptoms and recrudescence of difficulties with the children, the patient improved considerably, as did her children. She became pregnant and was very happy, and quite certain that mothering the third child would be a much more satisfying experience for her than it had been with the previous two. She was correct in her expectations. The infancy and early life of the third child, a daughter, was smooth for both mother and child. This course continued despite the increasingly apparent fact that the child's developmental rate was about half or less than normal for each landmark. The mother was sadly realistic in her estimates of the child's deficiency and was able to see clearly the importance of the child's emotional development. She continued to be gently, tenderly, and firmly nurturant in her attitudes until the child could be accepted in her fourth year in a nearby special boarding school for the retarded. The mother visited frequently and took the child home overnight or for a weekend when it was not too inconvenient for everyone else in the family. This child's disposition remained sunny and friendly, with evidence of eagerness to learn everything up to her limited capacity, for as long as the therapist had contact with this family.

This instance illustrates the relative independence of the factors determining personality development and those underlying mental deficiency. By the same token, the presence of emotional disorder in a mentally deficient child indicates that parental attitudes have been sources of conflict in their rearing of such a child. The determinants of the parental conflicts may or may not include their reaction to the child's deficiency.

### BRAIN DAMAGE WITH RETARDATION; ASSOCIATED PSYCHOGENIC HYPERKINETIC SYNDROME REDUCED WITH PSYCHOTHERAPY

Brain damage by itself does not lead necessarily to hyperkinetic symptoms or to other behavioral difficulty unless the learning handicap produced by disease negatively affects with sufficient severity the individual's ability to cope with or perform in his life situation, and then only if there are parent–child conflicts. For example: Bill, an eleven-year-old boy with mental deficiency, spent six and one-half years on the Langley Porter Neuropsychiatric Institute Children's Service Ward, in treatment for a severe emotional disorder. At the time of his admission at age four, his parents were concerned about his loss of speech, soiling and wetting, hyperactive and destructive behavior, and *petit mal* and minor motor seizures. These complaints started some four to eight months after a severe head injury at the age of twenty-six months. The prenatal and natal history was within normal limits. Speech development was normal, and he spoke simple words at twelve months and simple sentences at twenty-four months. His motor development was normal except for some awkwardness in walking at thirteen months. When his tripping, weaving, and falling persisted to eighteen months, a family physician was consulted. He was impressed by Bill's increased activity and "nervousness" and prescribed Thorazine. At about this time the boy's father was fired from a job for alleged thefts, and there was heightened tension and silence between the parents. At twenty-six months, Bill fell twenty-five feet onto a lawn and suffered multiple skull fractures and fracture of the left femur. However, he never lost consciousness, and, at the hospital, he recovered rapidly without apparent neurologic involvement. He continued to acquire new skills in speech and self-care.

Bill's neurologic and emotional development began progressively to deteriorate about four months after the accident. One year after the accident, when he was three, he developed minor motor seizures requiring medication, and he gradually lost the ability to speak. Ataxia, tremulousness, and a short attention span were described by his pediatrician. An electroencephalogram thirteen months after the accident, at age three and one-half, revealed a *petit mal* variant, and psychologic testing indicated that his developmental quotient was at a two-year-old level with no apparent speech.

During this time there was heightened marital stress. The father developed a laryngeal and pharyngeal cancerophobia and paranoid fears about his wife's fidelity. The mother was upset by her husband's disturbed behavior and threatened divorce.

At the time of admission to our service, Bill was four years old. He had a wide-based gait, right-sided neurologic signs (Babinski, weakness, and hyper-reflexia), with incontinence and little skill in self-care. Minor motor seizures were noted as well as an occasional right-sided Jacksonian and *grand mal* episode. Approximately one hundred and fifty electroencephalograms were performed over the next six and one-half years. The original records were thought to represent a hypsarhythmia. Over the years the hypsarhythmia disappeared, and, in the opinion of the electroencephalographer, these records suggested a deep and diffuse abnormality. Neurologic signs shifted from week to week, and, at the time of his discharge at the age of eleven, awkwardness and motor incoordination seemed to be present, but without specifically identifiable neurologic signs such as the right-sided signs originally noted. Three pneumoencephalograms were within normal limits. The results of spinal fluid examination, funduscopic study, chromosomal studies, and many other examinations were also within normal limits.

The emotional disturbance at the time of admission was that of a severely regressed boy with suggestion of "autism" or "childhood schizophrenia." However, as the emotional disturbance over the years began to improve with treatment, the residual picture was that of a mentally deficient child. During this six-and-a-half-year period, Bill was seen for more than six hundred weekly individual psychotherapeutic playroom sessions, and his parents were seen in individual psychotherapy for more than two hundred hours. In addition, a special program involving a nursery school and a close relationship with a nurse was instituted.

Two main phases characterize Bill's period of hospitalization and residential care. First, there was the period of gathering the data from all of the various disciplines involved. Second, after it was established that nonprogressive neurologic disease was present, there was the long psychotherapeutic experience with marked reduction in psychopathology in both Bill and his parents. The father's phobias cleared, and his paranoid fears and jealousy about his wife lessened. At the time of Bill's discharge, the father had greatly improved his occupational status and became a leader in a community social club. The mother became less angry and felt less guilt-ridden about her feelings of responsibility for her son's condition. Her relationship with her husband improved, and she felt less threatened by his concerns about his body and her faithfulness. Bill demonstrated marked improvement in his capacity to respond positively to staff with a lessening of his ritualistic and stereotyped play, becoming the most outgoing child on the ward. His hyperactive and destructive behavior disappeared, and he was able to learn self-care skills such as dressing and toileting. Once the emotional disorder lessened, the residual intellectual defect was apparent. The therapist was able to clarify with the parents alternatives for care, and they decided in favor of state-hospital placement.

## PSYCHOTHERAPEUTIC REDUCTION OF EMOTIONAL DISORDER IN MENTALLY DEFICIENT CHILD WITH DOWN'S SYNDROME

Intellectual performance of the child is only one factor in social adaptation. We have seen children and adults with average and superior intellect whose adaptation was so impaired that fruitful everyday experience was limited. Conversely, we have seen children and young adults with IQs in the 50–70 range who made a good adjustment in the community, were gainfully employed, and secured satisfaction in their daily pursuits. Yet the myth of the direct relationship of adaptation and intellectual performance persists.

If psychotherapeutic work reduces the patient's emotional disorder, the underlying intellectual defect may simply remain the same or may become more obvious. When such work is accompanied by an improvement in intellectual functioning, it is clear that the disorder previously had affected learning negatively—so-called affective pseudostupidity. Psychotherapy may or may not result in an increase in testable IQ. Certainly, reduction of emotional disorder often increases learning rate whether or not the tested IQ is increased. This learning may be primarily of social skills and of self-care, or of skills likely to be interpersonally—that is, socially and possibly economically—important rather than a symbolic or academic type of learning. In any case, a more integrated personality development of the child (aided further by parents less in conflict) increases the probability that less self-destructive social living will follow.

Mark, a three-and-one-half-year-old boy with Down's syndrome, was referred to the clinic because of his impulsive and assaultive behavior. He was difficult to manage in nursery school and almost impossible to control at home. He broke many objects around the house, pulled up the plants and flowers, and frequently ran out into the streets. At nursery school, he paid little attention to tasks at hand and socialized poorly. During the psychiatric study when he was first introduced to the psychiatrist, he reached for his glasses, and attempted to pull them off and toss them to the floor. Although he seemed to relate quite easily, he vacillated between aggressive outbursts and efforts at ingratiation. In the playroom he was quite active with the hammer block, pounding vigorously and intensely. His play with dolls was characterized by putting them in his mouth, biting, spitting, and stomping on them. After he finished with a toy, he would throw it on the floor or against the wall. He made frequent attempts to strike the examiner, and, after being controlled momentarily, would begin again. His play and aggressive outbursts were associated with much anxious tension. His use of language had a memorized automatic quality, and it was uttered with little feeling or meaning. There were isolated words but no sentences, and those words that he did use often were difficult to understand.

The parents' marriage was fraught with difficulty long before the boy was born, including many marital infidelities by both partners. The father often was assaultive, and the mother, in turn, tended to berate him and to laugh at any of his efforts. At moments of heightened tension the father suffered from impotence, which his wife used in order to ridicule him. The father accepted the boy in an unrealistic manner, expecting him to follow in his footsteps, finish high school in the lower part of his class, but make up for his deficiency by participating in athletics and later working in the family business. The mother saw the boy as an opportunity to hold the marriage together, at the same time using him to point out the father's inadequate and unrealistic ambitions. Both parents looked on the impulsive behavior of the boy or any sign of developmental progress as evidence of the fulfillment of their hopes.

At the conclusion of the study, psychotherapy for this boy and his parents was recommended. The boy was seen for weekly playroom sessions, and his parents for individual interviews. The following vignette describes the first fifty-seven playroom interviews over a span of twenty months. The work with the parents will not be described in detail, but there was a close relationship between the boy's symptoms and improvement and the parents' history and the lessening of tension in a difficult marital situation.

In the early therapy hours, Mark engaged in much random activity, with destructiveness and aggressive outbursts that the therapist tried to control by verbal admonitions and physical restraint. In the sixth interview, he was physically restrained from scattering crayons and clay and throwing them at his therapist. Angry, frightened, and hurt by the restraint, he climbed to the top of the dollhouse and sat there making faces at the therapist, stuck out his tongue, grimaced, and smiled ingratiatingly. He began to suck his thumb, but quickly pulled it out of his mouth. As he repeated this behavior, the therapist remarked that maybe someone had told him that he should not suck his thumb. The boy looked plaintively at the therapist and replied "yes." As he began hesitantly to make motions of placing the thumb in his mouth and withdrawing it, the doctor gently took the hand and moved the thumb toward the boy's mouth. He began to suck with relaxed pleasure. The next moment he climbed down from the dollhouse and wandered peacefully around the playroom. He began to play with the crayons in the box without throwing them about the room aimlessly and wantonly. In subsequent hours a rule was established that no new activity would begin until he had placed all of the toy objects of the previous activity back on the shelf. He began to enjoy upsetting the crayon can and then retrieving the crayons one by one. He seemed to be delighted with this game and often repeated it at moments when he seemed anxious. As he seemed to gain better control, he became more trustful of his therapist and liked to sit near him, although this activity was marked always by some hesitancy and tension. Sometimes Mark would spit or kick at him when the therapist seemed less attentive to his play or activity. In the nineteenth hour, after he had received a penicillin injection for an upper respiratory infection, he was able to accept the offer of the therapist's lap for the first time and lay there almost the whole playroom session. He listened to the therapist's stories and songs and tried to imitate him. In the next hour, he came to the therapist and said "kiss," and the therapist cuddled and held him. Following this interlude he said his first sentence quite clearly and distinctly, pointing to an upper shelf of the cabinet and saying, "I want to get up there."

As therapy progressed, physical outbursts could be restrained with gentle physical control or often by a word. He began to use toys more appropriately, often using the crayons to color on paper, or chalk on the blackboard. His vocabulary increased considerably, and he enjoyed using his improved ability to communicate appropriately.

Toward the end of therapy, the therapist informed him that he was leaving the clinic, and Mark immediately responded, "Oh, no, Doctor W——." As the therapist verbalized what the boy might be feeling, Mark began to smile, move close to the therapist, and thereafter began to demonstrate in play and speech much of what he had accomplished throughout the past year and a half. His school reported behavior paralleling the activity of the playroom. He was more responsive, played well with other children, and actively participated with his school group in learning training tasks. At the start of therapy, his initial testing indicated an IQ of 70, which, because of his play and manner, was thought to be an overestimation resulting from his advanced physical coordination and memorized vocabulary. Later tests were in the range of the high 30's and low 40's, which was more consistent with his abilities.

## Pseudoretardation and Psychotherapy

As previously mentioned, emotional disorder in the retarded child occurs frequently and may distort development further. Emotional disorder in itself may reduce further the already lessened capacity to learn. The retarded child in his life experience is often confronted with: (1) parental crisis, (2) negative community attitudes—fear and apprehension of the community, with lowered expectations of the retarded person and resulting isolation and segregation, (3) a longer period of dependence—slowed attainment of developmental landmarks, poor physical coordination of skills, and need for longer period of total care. This may be one source of conflict in parents. The longer dependence of the child may cause a greater burden and result in guilt about their impatience and rejective impulses, and this may intensify other sources of conflict. (4) Conflicts of adaptation may be experienced—learning deficiency, lowered self-regard, and lessened self-confidence, reinforced by derogatory or contemptuous attitudes of others; difficulties in play with age-mates; repeated discouragement and disappointment. (5) Limited resources may be available in the community for help for his special needs and problems—nursery schools, public-school classes, recreational opportunities, vocational training, and job opportunities, as well as medical and psychologic help.

All of these factors in turn may inhibit further whatever innate capacity he has for satisfying living. When effective in the reduction of conflict, psychotherapy may increase learning both qualitatively and quantitatively and may be reflected in a rise of the testable IQ. For example, during an individual treatment session, Mrs. C., who was being seen in concomitant psychotherapy with her husband and schizophrenic son, mentioned hesitantly that she was concerned about her younger boy, Jim, age six. She was fearful that he was retarded since he had developed slowly and was poor in school achievement. He had many morbid fears, such as of sirens and loud voices, of balloons, dogs, and water. He cried easily when teased by other children or scolded by his parents. He was afraid to attend school, and his attendance was very poor. A psychiatric study was suggested by Mrs. C.'s therapist, but time was not immediately available. As Mrs. C. talked of her many difficulties, she experienced some relief and Jim's school attendance became more regular with fewer absences. When time was available for the study, Jim, six and a half, was a fearful youngster who was shy, withdrawn, and meticulously neat and tidy in appearance. His teacher informed us that he was timid, insecure, easily distracted, and concentrated poorly. His many fears interfered with his schoolwork. He was isolated and inhibited and often negative about attempting new tasks. His parents stated that the pregnancy and delivery were uncomplicated, but early in life they noted that his development was retarded; he sat alone at one year, walked at nineteen months, and did not climb stairs until three. He said a few words at about age two, but soon stopped, and he did not speak again until one year later. Physical examination revealed a right internal strabismus, pigeon-toed gait, and a supernumerary toe. Psychologic tests indicated that his IQ on the Stanford-Binet was 59, with no scatter. He seemed to do as well as he could. The Bender-Gestalt indicated possible organic disturbance. In the playroom during the evaluation, the boy was extremely fearful and made little attempt to play with toys, but if he did he promptly washed them and returned them to the shelf. If he marked the blackboard, he would immediately wash and clean it compulsively. He consistently avoided touching or playing with doll figures, but was more interested in impersonal toys such as trucks, trains, and blocks. The psychiatrist's impression was that this was a mentally deficient child whose emotional problems inhibited his performing up to his full potential.

Jim and his parents were seen for psychotherapy. Mr. C. was born in the Orient and spent his early years there before immigrating to the United States with his family. He had a college education and majored in engineering. His income was always far below his educational level. He developed a peptic ulcer following his marriage. He had much repressed anger and many obsessive-compulsive symptoms and phobias. Mrs. C., although born in the United States, spent her first seven years in the Orient. She married her husband after completing high school. She always felt depressed and isolated from her peers. Soon after their marriage, a son was born, followed three years later by Jim. During the first six years of Jim's life, she worked in her father-in-law's laundry to supplement the family income. There were many marital infidelities by the husband during this period. When Jim was two, his father had a gastric resection for a bleeding ulcer. The mother reported that her depression was so severe that she often contemplated suicide. It was at this time that the boy stopped talking.

In the course of treatment, Mrs. C. was helped to see herself as less helpless, and she was able to control her household situation better. She gave up her work in the laundry, spent more time at home with her boys, and insisted that her husband be more involved with his family. She gained considerable relief. Mr. C. was initially more silent in treatment. As he began to talk about his disappointment in his boy's development, he also related his many fears and internal threats. At this time, he was seeking more gainful employment as well as spending more time with his family.

Jim was seen by three therapists, each for a six-month period. Jim's first therapist saw him for a total of seventeen weekly sessions. During the first two months of treatment, Jim made a few tentative gestures toward engaging the therapist in play, but generally treated him as if he were not in the room at all. He seemed impervious to most interventions. In the ninth session, he made some chalk marks on the wall, but immediately and fearfully erased them. He began to clap the eraser on the table top and seemed to enjoy the activity, but soon became distraught, looking furtively for reassurance. It was difficult to encourage him to continue to play. In subsequent sessions he was more untidy. In the twelfth hour he made many marks and figures on the blackboard and asked the therapist to lock the door of the playroom so he could not leave; the therapist encouraged greater freedom in play. During the next hour Jim began to eye the fingerpaints, unscrewing the cap, and gazing at the colored paint, but never inserting his fingers. As the therapist began to use the fingerpaints, Jim used a tongue depressor and tentatively placed a bit of the paint on paper. In the next hour he began to use his hands to paint, although very daintily. He was concerned with his dirty fingers and washed his hands thoroughly and repeatedly. He did not respond to the therapist's efforts at encouragement or invitations to return to play. During the next visit he seemed more cheerful and sang a song he had learned in school. He handled a dog puppet and had it bite a piece of wood, but, with some fear, he placed the dog in the cupboard, saying "bad dog." Toward the end of this brief therapy, Jim was told by his therapist that he would be leaving the clinic and a new doctor would take his place. Jim became quite distant and for the next two hours had very little to do with the doctor and returned to his earlier forms of play.

He was seen by his next therapist for a total of twenty visits during a period of six months. In the first three or four interviews, he adopted the same kind of play patterns that were noted early in treatment, but he seemed to respond more quickly to the therapist. By the sixth hour he was more involved in play with clay, cars, and trucks. He also became preoccupied with time and clocks and spent much of his time checking to see how much time was left. In the ninth interview he began to fingerpaint again and seemed to use the paints more freely. In the tenth hour he began to investigate the dollhouse and, for the first time, played with the doll figures. He was preoccupied with the mother, father, and baby. Generally, in this play, the father was put behind a bureau and not seen, and the mother seemed to be involved in changing the baby's diapers, taking care of the baby, and sending it to school. In the sixteenth interview he took out the male doll and said that it was his father. He put him into an ambulance and drove to the hospital, commenting that his father was sick. In the seventeenth hour, three hours before termination with this therapist, he wondered if the doctor would be leaving and asked who his new doctor would be. At this time, one year after his first test, Jim was retested, and his performance on the Stanford-Binet showed definite improvement; his over-all IQ had increased from 59 to 79. There was again little scatter of the items. Difficulty still was apparent on tasks requiring the combination of visual and motor abilities.

His figure drawings showed improvement both intellectually, with additional body parts, and emotionally, the figures appearing happy. His third therapist saw him for thirty-two sessions during the next nine months. Jim elaborated many of the problems that were apparent during the first thirty-seven sessions. His school reported that he was doing better, but still did not seem to be doing as well as he could. His behavior had improved considerably and, although still a shy and withdrawn child, he seemed to be doing better in social activities. One year later, at the termination of therapy with his third therapist, his full-scale IQ on the Wechsler Intelligence Scale for Children was 89 and the Bender reproductions were oversimplified with considerable difficulty in angle formations.

## IMPORTANCE OF THERAPISTS' ATTITUDES IN WORK WITH THE MENTALLY RETARDED

In psychotherapeutic work with children and parents, it is obvious to clinicians that it is desirable that the therapist himself be as free as possible of conflict to increase the chance that resolution of conflict will occur in his patients. If he is aware of his own prejudices and recognizes those myths of his culture that may pervade his thinking, there will be less interference with his therapeutic skill. Most therapists have little experience with the retarded in their training or life experiences. The characteristics of intellectual deficiency are in marked contrast to the usual high intellectual performance, verbal facility, and levels of abstraction encountered in their own experience and modes of thinking. Often the therapist may find working with the retarded less interesting and may say, "what have you after you resolve the problem," "the retarded are not treatable," "shouldn't they be best cared for in institutions?" One therapist remarked that his greatest difficulty in working with a young boy with Down's syndrome was the reactions of his colleagues that reinforced some of his own doubts. Once he was able to recognize his own pessimistic feelings, he began to observe the youngster more closely and to help him deal more effectively with his impulsive behavior. He noted that when he was fully attentive to the boy, the child responded more appropriately, with fewer sudden "unexplainable" outbursts. Frequently the therapist may feel that the methods he has learned in working with other patients are not adaptable to the retarded since they would not be understood by the patient.

Debbie Jones, a twenty-one-year-old, white, well-developed, bright-eyed, excessively and irritatingly talkative young lady, was referred to the Institute for inpatient hospitalization because of loud psychotic-like verbalizations, erratic performance, and general disruptive behavior at her sheltered workshop, at home, and to passers-by on the street. She had been attending a local work-training center for the past year. When Debbie was evaluated at the clinic, the staff thought that she would do better as an outpatient. For two years she was seen weekly by three successive therapists, each for a period of from six to nine months. In the course of therapy Debbie described herself as a "high-class joker" and talked considerably about the latest adolescent fads, told familiar jokes repetitiously, talked loudly and excitedly, and made very little contact with her therapist. The therapists, in turn, felt futile about the situation and tried various techniques to reach her, but with little success. There were frequent complaints to supervisors that little could be done for this girl and that it seemed a waste of their training time to see her. Nevertheless, her work at the training center seemed to improve, although her behavior continued to be difficult to manage. Her fourth therapist saw her for the next six months and began to talk to her more realistically about her current and future plans as well as about what made it so difficult for her at the center. Debbie seemed to be somewhat more responsive, and her behavior in the waiting room seemed to quiet down to some degree. The following therapist at an initial treatment review voiced the feeling that everyone at the clinic seemed to treat Debbie as a twelve-year-old, which was pretty much the way she dressed, acted, and looked. He suddenly realized that she was now twenty-five, a young lady actively engaged in the adult workshop, mixing with adults, yet treated like a child. He wondered if she were not, in part and with unconscious revengefulness, fulfilling the parents' expectations and the clinic staff's discouragement. At his next meeting with her, he began to call her Miss Jones rather than using the nickname of Debbie. He voiced his expectation that she could behave more like an adult and would feel better doing so. In subsequent interviews, her behavior at the clinic had changed considerably. She began to talk less of records, jokes, and teenage fads. Her dress and manner changed. She no longer wore bobby socks and became neater in her appearance and much calmer in her behavior. She also began to talk about some of the difficulties she experienced in working as well as about her wish for greater freedom. The work-training center remarked at this time that she began to show an increased level of performance in her work. Her IQ of 51 (verbal 65, performance 39) remained essentially the same during the course of therapy.

## SUMMARY

In summary, psychotherapeutic experience with retarded children and their parents has been described to illustrate the following.

1. Mentally retarded individuals can benefit from psychotherapeutic efforts for the resolution of emotional disorder. Emotional disorder may

inhibit learning, distort development, and impair social adaptation. Reduction of conflict may free energy that can be used for learning of academic or social skills that are socially and economically important.

2. The technique and methods of psychotherapeutic work with the retarded are the same as those utilized with children of more normal intelligence. Concomitant work with the parents of the child is useful in the psychotherapy of the child. Therapy of parents, disturbed by signs of retardation or deficiency in their infant or very young child, may prevent or reduce the development of more serious disorder in the child. If such therapy is successful, more integrated personality development may ensue.

3. Some clinical experience has been presented to suggest that brain damage by itself does not lead necessarily to particular behavioral symptomatologies. These result from motivational conflicts arising from parent–child malintegrative experiences. Such conflicts and resulting symptoms may be resolved with successful psychotherapy. Psychotherapy with the mentally retarded may improve their skills in living and allow fuller realization of whatever potential the retarded may have, even though a subsequent rise in the IQ does not occur. Emotional disorder may affect learning negatively, with resulting pseudostupidity that may be relieved by successful therapy.

4. The attitudes of the therapist about retardation as a hopeless condition may detract from the success of the psychotherapeutic work with the child and his parents. The therapist who can find work with the retarded satisfying and not be encumbered by the myths of his culture may contribute significantly to therapeutic success.

5. In recent years there has been increasing emphasis on the care and treatment of the retarded. Often the retarded are limited in utilizing those opportunities that are available. Emotional disorder frequently interferes with their obtaining those benefits that may make living more fruitful. Psychotherapy for the child and his parents may facilitate better adaptation and greater satisfaction in living.

## REFERENCES

AMERICAN PSYCHIATRIC ASSOCIATION, COMMITTEE ON NOMENCLATURE AND STATISTICS, *Diagnostic and Statistical Manual, Mental Disorders* (Washington, D. C.: American Psychiatric Association, 1952).

DELTON C. BEIER, "Behavioral Disturbances in the Mentally Retarded," in Harvey A. Stevens and Rick Heber (Eds.), *Mental Retardation: A Review of Research* (Chicago: University of Chicago Press, 1964), pp. 453–489.

MURRAY BERGMAN, HEINZ WALLER, and JOHN MARCHAND, "Schizophrenic Reactions during Childhood in Mental Defectives," *Psychiatric Quarterly*, XXV (1951), 294–333.

KEITH N. BRYANT and J. COTTER HIRSCHBERG, "Helping the Parents of a Retarded Child, The Role of the Physician," *American Journal of the Diseases of Children,* CII (1961), 52–66.

A. D. B. CLARKE, "Genetic and Environmental Studies of Intelligence," in Ann M. Clarke and A. D. B. Clarke (Eds.), *Mental Deficiency, The Changing Outlook* (London: Methuen, 1958), pp. 84–121.

LOUIS B. FIERMAN, "Myths in the Practice of Psychotherapy," *Archives of General Psychiatry,* XII (1965), 408–414.

STUART M. FINCH, *Fundamentals of Child Psychiatry* (New York: W. W. Norton, 1960), pp. 197–205.

ANNA FREUD and DOROTHY BURLINGHAM, *Infants without Families* (New York: International Universities Press, 1944).

H. C. GUNZBURG, "Psychological Assessment in Mental Deficiency," in Ann M. Clarke and A. D. B. Clarke (Eds.), *Mental Deficiency, The Changing Outlook* (London: Methuen, 1958), pp. 257–291.

WILLIAM J. KERR, JR., and STANISLAUS A. SZUREK, "Effect of Glutamic Acid on Mental Function: Pilot Study," *Pediatrics,* V (1950), 645–648.

GEORGE KRIEGMAN and JOSEPHINE R. HILGARD, "Intelligence Level and Psychotherapy with Problem Children," *American Journal of Orthopsychiatry,* XIV (1944), 251–265.

BOYD R. McCANDLESS, "Relation of Environmental Factors to Intellectual Functioning," in Harvey A. Stevens and Rick Heber (Eds.), *Mental Retardation: A Review of Research* (Chicago: University of Chicago Press, 1964), pp. 175–213.

GROUP FOR THE ADVANCEMENT OF PSYCHIATRY, *Mental Retardation: A Family Crisis—The Therapeutic Role of the Physician,* Report Number 56 (New York: Group for the Advancement of Psychiatry, 1963).

IRVING PHILIPS, MARY JEFFRESS, EHUD KOCH, and MALETA J. BOATMAN, "The Application of Psychiatric Clinic Services for the Retarded Child and His Family," *Journal of the American Academy of Child Psychiatry,* I (1962), 297–313.

HOWARD W. POTTER, "The Needs of Mentally Retarded Children for Child Psychiatry Services," *Journal of the American Academy of Child Psychiatry,* III (1964), 352–374.

SALLY PROVENCE and ROSE C. LIPTON, *Infants in Institutions* (New York: International Universities Press, 1962).

HAROLD M. SKEELS, "Effects of Adoption on Children from Institutions," *Children,* XII (1965), 33–34.

MARIE SKODAK and HAROLD M. SKEELS, "A Final Follow-up Study of One Hundred Adopted Children," *Journal of Genetic Psychology,* LXXV (1949), 85–125.

STANISLAUS A. SZUREK and IRVING N. BERLIN, "Elements of Psychotherapeutics with the Schizophrenic Child and His Parents," *Psychiatry,* XIX (1956), 1–9.

GEORGE TARJAN, "Research and Clinical Advances in Mental Retardation," *Journal of the American Medical Association,* CLXXXII (1962), 617–621.

The authors wish to thank their colleagues and trainees on the Children's Service of the Langley Porter Neuropsychiatric Institute for the use of their clinical notes in the preparation of this chapter: John Langdell, M.D., for the case of Jane; Olga Shkurkin, P.S.W., for the case of John W.; Alfred Gianascol, M.D., Charles Graham, M.D., Raymond Reedy, M.D., and Murray Persky, M.D., for the case of Bill; Robert Wald, M.D., for the case of Mark; Stephan Schoen, M.D., Carroll Brodsky, M.D., and Jan Pierce, Ph.D., for the case of Jim. Their diligent work and compilation of notes made this chapter possible. The many therapists who worked with the parents of these children are not listed by name, because of space, but their work and help are also acknowledged by the authors.

# 15

# Preschool Programs for the Retarded

## HERBERT GOLDSTEIN

There are strong indications that the next major development in the education of the retarded will be the preschool program. More and more, attention of educators and psychologists is turning to concepts of development and their role in the treatment complex. Much of the recent research and program activity is based on the notion that early intervention will elevate the intellectual and social functioning of children. Researchers and program developers alike contend that preschool education may reverse the debilitating effects of culturally or psychologically limiting environments. For example, Samuel A. Kirk (1958) attacked the problem directly in his study of young retarded children in socially and psychologically disadvantaged settings in communities and in an institution for the retarded. He achieved noteworthy success with the experimental groups who participated in a highly individualized preschool program. Other investigators have employed an indirect approach by providing preschool treatment for children in high-risk neighborhoods under the assumption that relevant compensatory treatment would manifest its effectiveness by reducing the proportion of the retarded usually contributed to the school-age population from these disadvantaged neighborhoods. This design is, in a sense, basic to Project Head Start.

RESEARCH AND EXPERIENTIAL BACKGROUND

Accepting the evidence that there is merit in early educational experience for retarded children, we must turn our attention to the content of preschool programs as it relates to any educational program for the retarded. Since the preschool program is one segment of the educational continuum, it would be appropriate to examine closely standard procedures in the established aspects of this continuum.

If there is any lesson to be learned from past experience, it is that programs for the school-age and post-school-age retarded generally have developed as a reaction to problems rather than from anticipation, thoughtful planning, and action. As a result, many programs are markedly expeditious and are modelled after those established in regular classes. Thus, curriculum, methodology, evaluation, teacher-preparation, and administrative procedures represent somewhat watered-down and truncated versions of those for regular classes. The outcome of years of reaction to mainly logistic issues has been the development of programs for the retarded that are not so clearly superior to traditional educational provisions as they need to be. Other than a reduced teacher–pupil ratio in elementary-school programs, there is little that can be identified clearly as being directly responsive to the broad range of learning and behavioral characteristics of the retarded.

In general, preschool programs already display a history of vagueness arising out of expediency and speculation. Pauline S. Sears and Edith M. Dowley (1963), in a thorough review of the literature, point out that the primary objective of preschool education frequently has been the welfare of persons other than children. They list, among others, pre-parental education, teacher-training, research, teacher-employment, and custodial care for children of working mothers as the main objectives of nursery schools in the past and, in some instances, in the present. Some settings have stressed habit-training in daily routines as a prelude to more subject-centered activities in the child's future, although others see the school as an extension of the child's home and, therefore, a supplement to other experiences and relationships.

Over the years, the nursery schools have focused on intellectual, social, and emotional development. If considerable control is not imposed, these could become adopted as the goals of preschool education for the retarded. If this happens, there is a good possibility that preschool education for the retarded will come to be of more value to other persons than to the children involved. On the other hand, early comprehensive planning may result in programs of value to both.

Results of research on preschool programs for the retarded indicate that it would be a serious mistake to think of existing concepts of preschool education as being directly applicable and fruitful for the retarded. Filling gaps in social and cognitive experiences, extending family experiences, and providing group and individual activities not usually a part of the child's ordinary milieu have not been markedly successful. In Samuel A. Kirk's study (1958), for example, a concentrated program, aimed at children's limitations, showed clear-cut superiority over the usual experiences of control children at home. When the controls entered the first grade, however, they gained intellectually and socially so that earlier differences were reduced considerably by the end of the first year of school. Other studies have had similar results insofar as the effects of the first year of school are concerned. L. L. Smith and J. B. Stroud (1960) found that the six-year-olds in their study gained 5.6 points in Binet IQ during their first year in school. Herbert Goldstein, Laura Jordan, and James Moss (1965) found that six-year-old educable mentally retarded children in both experimental and control groups gained over 7 points in Binet IQ by the end of their first year in school, irrespective of special class or regular first-grade experience. These and other studies suggest that the real test of preschool education is in the ability of the preschool program, first, to increase children's rate of social and intellectual development beyond that which would ordinarily occur with the first exposure to formal schooling at the traditional school-entering age, and, second, to develop in children skills and abilities that are meaningful within the developmental continuum of schooling and post-school adjustment and to develop these so effectively that long-term retention takes place.

One might conclude that ordinarily most preschool programs, regardless of specificity, will fulfill the first goal. M. E. Walsh (1931) found that children attending nursery school gained more in social attributes, independence, and curiosity than matched nonattenders. Merl E. Bonney and Ertie Lou Nicholson (1958) found that preschool attenders located in kindergarten, first, second, and third grades had higher sociometric scores than nonattenders. Gregory B. Allen and Joseph M. Masling (1957) found similar results beginning to appear during the second grade; classmates of preschoolers saw them as more prestigeful and more intelligent. These and other studies suggest that children with these attributes could be expected to develop intellectual styles and abilities beyond what might be expected of children coming from less stimulating environments.

Harold E. Jones (1954), in the course of his discussion of the literature on environmental effects on mental growth, stated that one could expect gains in intelligence among children whose environment is changed from static, unstimulating routines to one that is fresh, dynamic, and consonant with developmental phenomena. In response to the contention on the part of naturists that such changes are regression effects, he points out that, in most instances, children moving from static to dynamic environments are low in IQ. Thus, something besides regression is at work.

The Iowa Studies conducted by Beth Wellman (1940) and her colleagues are a good case in point. The results of the work at the Iowa Child Welfare Research Station in the 1930's and 1940's brought into focus the nature–nurture controversy. Although this work has attracted much cogent criticism, developmentalists generally have leaned toward the nurture side of the argument in their work and writing. J. McV. Hunt (1961), after reviewing the controversy, concludes that there is much to support the position that impoverishment of experience during the early months can slow the development of intelligence, as represented by IQ, and can inhibit the development of basic criterion capacities of individuals that might have developed under environmental conditions more in harmony with the intellectual structures developing in the child. On a more optimistic note, he points out that there is evidence that the average level of intelligence in the population might possibly be increased substantially if we understood better the way encounters with environment foster the development of intellectual capacity.

It is becoming more and more clear, then, that early intervention can be effective if the intervention has relevance to the developmental characteristics of the child. The old notion that change alone will suffice needs rigorous assessment. Where children present developmental deficiencies and imbalances associated with aberrant physical and intellectual conditions, the degree of consonance between the child's characteristics and the substance of the program of intervention becomes the keystone to the program. Thus, factors beyond etiology and social class need to be taken into account in structuring and implementing a preschool program for the retarded, if it is to be effective in developing skills and abilities that have meaning for performance at maturity.

## GUIDELINES IN PROGRAM DEVELOPMENT

The long-range effectiveness of any educational program, in whole or in part, can be judged by its participants' assimilation into the next immediate setting in the progression, be it the next grade, the next school level, or into post-school settings. Education is better at evaluating its effectiveness intramurally than extramurally. This can be attributed to better, more reliable within-school measurement devices as well as greater control over the subject population from preschool through secondary school. Nevertheless, it is the extramural evaluation that is crucial if any assessment of the effectiveness of the educational program is to be meaningful.

Historically, inferences about the effective educational program for the retarded have been drawn from follow-up studies. These have focused on the social and occupational attributes of the educable retarded compared with their more or less normal peers. The results of these studies have had little discernible impact on educational programs beyond some gross modifications in curriculum and the organization of secondary programs.

One of the major problems in follow-up studies arises from the mobility of the moderately retarded. In most cases, the inability of the researcher to locate more than what he hopes is a representative sample of the total initial group limits the extent to which he can assess the educational program as being accountable for the success or failure of the retarded in postschool settings. For this reason, we can focus on the severely retarded adult whose mobility is more limited and whose identity is more discernible. This in no way suggests that we are dismissing the moderately retarded from our thinking, nor does it suggest that the principles underlying the goals of education for these persons are different.

Most would agree that in the case of the severely retarded, the goal of education is to develop in each individual those skills and abilities that make for adequacy in the home and community as well as in a supervised work setting. The most visible and accessible segment of this twofold goal is found in the accomplishment of the retarded in the supervised or sheltered work setting. Their performance at work is a reasonable basis for projecting back to the preschool program in order to establish the need for and nature of the content of the programs.

The psychologic literature on the effects of formal and informal experience on the maturing child leads us to believe that the social and occupational performance of the mature retarded person reflects, at least in part, the outcome of his experience or lack of experience prior to and during this workshop tenure. We can assume also that his pre-workshop experiences contribute more to his social and work status in the long run than does his workshop-learning, because of when, how, and for how long they occur. If, through objective or subjective assessment, we find that workshoppers are functioning at a level below what could reasonably be expected, we might assume that the discrepancy in performance could be the result of lack of preparatory experience. True, some may be so handicapped physically or emotionally as to defy present systems of treatment. The large majority are responsive, however, to appropriate educational treatment to a noteworthy degree.

If we observed workshops for the severely retarded in this country and abroad with social and occupational performance in mind, and if we laid these abilities out in two distributions representing (1) a continuum of ability to cope with complex sensorimotor tasks, and (2) a continuum for social adjustment, and if we compared the U.S. with the European distributions, we probably would find significant differences in social performance in the home, neighborhood, and work setting. In the distributions of sensorimotor abilities, there probably would be a sizable overlap, but we likely would find that the upper limits of the distribution are the province mainly of the European retarded. This would be reflected in the capacity of the sheltered workshop to contract for a broader range of work, more diversity in work-assignment possibilities, and, of no small importance, greater earning power for the workshop and workshoppers. Thus, we would see many severely retarded adults performing tasks similar to those found in our own workshops. But we would also see a noteworthy proportion doing work involving the use of power tools, soldering equipment, and cutting and grinding equipment. Others would be engaged in intricate assembly and sorting tasks. With a few exceptions, these activities are not common in our own sheltered work settings.

These very important differences can be traced to differences in pre-workshop experiences. Characteristically, the American retarded do not get involved in formal education experiences until they can measure up to certain administrative criteria. And when they finally do, the educational program is, more often than not, designed to make them more palatable socially to others, rather than to enhance sensorimotor, as well as social, skills.

With reference to the criteria in this country for admission to public educational programs for the severely retarded, these are concomitants of a policy that says, in effect, if the severely retarded child is to participate in an educational program, he needs to conform to the requirements of existing public-school policy and facilities. Thus, like all children, he must be at least six years of age, be able to communicate, be toilet-trained, be reasonably mobile, and so forth. For the severely retarded child, these criteria for admission are paradoxical. Most agree that these criteria would not exist if the policy were to fit program and facilities to the characteristics of the severely retarded rather than the reverse. Delayed language development and multiple disabilities that limit mobility and toileting are concomitants of severe mental retardation and must be taken into account as factors for amelioration in the educational program rather than as bases for elimination from the program.

Characteristically, then, the American retarded are some place other than in a program designed to enhance communication and motor skills during that time when they probably could make the most progress, quantitatively and qualitatively, and, at the same time, lay a substantial foundation for further growth and development. When at long last they enter school, they participate in a curriculum that emphasizes social learning with a little emphasis on practice in whatever motor skills have been developed along the way.

Thus, the more or less typical picture of the severely retarded child in this country is one of a youngster who must wait for schooling until he can measure up to administrative criteria that have little bearing on pedagogy or on his learning and adjustment needs. He may, if he is fortunate, find himself in a parent-operated or supported preschool setting where his language, motor development, and social development get some attention. Once he is toilet-trained, communicative, and mobile enough to accommodate the distances between his classroom and certain important school locations, he is admitted to a formal educational program. Here he is instructed in many activities designed to make him more helpful and more skilled in looking after himself. Depending on the elaborateness of school provisions, he may stay in the program to sheltered-workshop age, when he is screened and, if considered suitable, is accepted into a sheltered workshop.

We certainly would find the picture very similar for many European retarded. But for those who have received early intensive educational treatment, the results seem to be dramatically different insofar as skills basic to important occupational sensorimotor and social performance are concerned. There are in some European countries comparatively long histories of educational provision for the severely retarded, commencing with pre-school programs. The programs are found in a variety of physical settings and administrative arrangements. Staffing varies from volunteer workers under professional supervision to professional staff throughout. Regardless of physical or administrative arrangement, most agree that early education of the severely retarded is a necessary procedure, among others, in the amelioration of developmental imbalances.

## Characteristics of the Preschool Program

It is difficult to disregard the contribution of educational programs within the total context of development of the retarded. At the same time, it has become abundantly clear that educational programs that deal superficially with the physical and cognitive characteristics of the retarded offer limited returns to the retarded in ability to cope with social and occupational environments. The evidence suggests that an educational program should have two important characteristics. First, the program should involve the retarded child at the earliest possible age so that gaps, imbalances, and insufficiencies in cognitive and perceptual development can be anticipated and accommodated. Second, the program should be aimed continuously and directly at the factors in the growth and development of the retarded that impinge on social and occupational characteristics at maturity. These characteristics may materialize if the development and implementation of the preschool program take into account the following: administrative principles, diagnosis, staffing, curriculum, and facilities.

### Administrative Principles

Administratively, the preschool program for the retarded must be put into proper perspective among the existing models for program structure. Familiar criteria must be placed alongside the characteristics and needs of the retarded and evaluated in accordance with the extent to which each contributes to or inhibits the effective implementation of the program. For example, admission age as a criterion should be considered, not within the context of tradition, but as an important factor in the learning of retarded children. School location plans must take into account the fact that young retarded children will be more dispersed than regular class pupils. We may have to turn to centralization of classes as the best answer to transportation, staffing, and servicing problems of a comprehensive program. Beyond these, there are implications for administrative decision in the topics to be discussed below.

## Diagnosis

An important part of the information basic to curriculum development and the management of children in the preschool program is derived from diagnostic procedures. The extent to which the knowledge gained through diagnosis gives direction to educational planning and action is determined often by the extent to which biomedical and psychologic data are comprehensive. For example, a medical diagnosis that does not go beyond the differentiation of central nervous system involvement and a recitation of the evidence is of little value to the educator and psychologist.

Two kinds of data are required from the physician if educational planning is to be more than speculative. First, planning for teaching will be facilitated if the behavioral components of physical disability are a part of the diagnostic report. The existence of visual or auditory disabilities, for example, should be reported as specifically as possible and in terms of their implications for behavior. This will go a long way toward tracking down perceptual disorders as they impinge on specific kinds of learning and will provide a foundation for the planning of remedial procedures in the preschool by psychologists and teachers. Secondly, management of children individually and in groups requires that the teacher have complete information about the physical status of children insofar as it has implications for activities in the classroom and school. Prior knowledge of the physical restrictions and liabilities of children is important to teachers in the preliminary plans for deploying children in the many activities during the school day. This information helps to reduce in number and effect the occasions when plans need to be modified in mid-operation. Since retarded children of preschool age are relatively nonverbal, the main source of information in this area, other than the obvious and undesirable deterioration of the child's behavior, is in the comprehensive medical report.

Likewise, psychologic diagnosis should go beyond the traditional estimate of intellectual status. In particular, teachers need to know the learning characteristics of children in terms of their specific abilities and disabilities in perception and cognition. Along with this, they need an assessment of the child's emotional status as it may affect his classroom functioning. Within the area of learning disabilities, it is important that there be information concerning the specifics of the disability as it relates to the receptive-cognitive-expressive sequence in learning as well as the relationship of one disability to another within the context of learning. The latter is an important aspect of diagnosis because of the frequency of multiple disabilities among the severely retarded.

### Curriculum

Curriculum for preschool classes for the retarded is a logical outcome of medical-psychologic information. With these data available, the preschool staff can plan a more direct attack on developmental abnormalities and deficiencies as they become obvious in the course of the education program. In preschool classes for the severely retarded, for example, a program of sensorimotor development specific to the status of each child can be devised if it is based on appropriate information and consultation derived from medical sources. Parallel programs in language and cognitive development can be devised in similar fashion with the level of instruction determined by the status of the child. When and where indicated, these can be coordinated with programs in social and personal development.

It is important to recognize that the relevance and timeliness of teaching decisions are determined, in great part, by the nature and amount of information basic to decision-making. One of the major problems in classes for preschool and school-age retarded children stems from either a complete absence of medical-psychologic information about children or reports that are so sparse or ambiguous as to have no bearing on the teacher's planning and action. We can see the results of this in the rather random, limited programs in classes for the school-age retarded where there is an imbalance between social and mental-health activities and the kinds of learning that lead to skillful sensorimotor and cognitive performance. The former occupy the better part of the learning day simply because almost any activity that is nonspecific to individual psychophysical development is easily classified as a social or mental-health activity.

For the severely retarded preschool child, curriculum probably should begin with the basic stages in mobility, perception, eye–hand coordination, and language development. Instead of confining the activities of the classroom to the traditional mid-range activities such as cutting, pasting, finger-painting, and simple rhythmics, the curriculum should provide training and practice in earlier developmental skills associated with mobility and perception. As gross skills are mastered and as neurologic evaluation gives guidance, more specific motor and perceptual tasks can be introduced into the teaching–learning sequence. Language development, guided by the child's history in this area and his performance, should parallel the sensorimotor program. The program in language development should take into account early stages in vocalization such as babbling and echolalia and can best be guided by a specialist in language development. As the child shows readiness for socialization, this program should be initiated. The foundational activities are, however, essentially sensorimotor in orientation and are supplemented by language and social learning.

The educable mentally retarded preschool child probably should be engaged in a curriculum that contains similar areas of learning, but with different emphasis. Language–concept development and social learning can be exploited to a greater degree by these children than by severely retarded preschool children of the same chronologic age. Helen C. Dawe (1942) found that children engaged in a program stressing comprehension and concepts made significant gains in vocabulary and social information and were more prepared for reading. She found increases in verbal IQ.

Since there is a sizable literature showing that the motor skills of school-age retarded children are inferior to those of normal peers, early experiences in sensorimotor development should constitute an important part of the program. The level at which sensorimotor training should start can be indicated by a comprehensive medical evaluation prior to preschool admission. Progress and alterations in the program should be evaluated similarly.

### Staffing

Staffing patterns for preschool programs must be responsive to the structure and substance of the program rather than to existing models for other types of preschool or school-age children. Whereas the teacher of preschool normal children can be comparatively self-sufficient, the teacher of preschool retarded children requires much highly specialized information and consultation. In a complete preschool program, the teacher probably will need to work individually with children and will require the assistance and cooperation of a teaching aide. This is particularly indicated in preschool classes for the severely retarded where intensive, directed individual instruction in sensorimotor and language development is necessary. A competent teacher's aide can be working effectively with the small group in self-care and social learning while the teacher works with one child at a time. Thus, management procedures will not detract from teaching procedures, and the preschool session will more nearly approximate total effective utilization.

Regardless of how teaching staff is deployed, and there are many ways, the competence of the teacher will determine the extent to which the educational program is realized. In considering the competencies of the preschool teacher, we must realize that there is no reliable model available as a criterion. Certainly, the traditional regular- or special-class teacher hardly fits the preschool picture when competencies derived from the teacher-preparation programs are considered. The traditional nursery-school teacher comes a bit closer. Here too, however, the preparation program does not take into account sufficiently the dynamic ties between ordinary developmental phenomena, developmental imbalances or insufficiencies, and the kinds of teaching procedures that are required by each. Certainly, existing educational programs for the severely retarded show that an expeditious approach to teacher staffing has few, if any, desirable results.

In all probability, the preparation of the preschool teacher, unlike that of others, will demand an interdisciplinary endeavor with psychiatric, neurologic, and psycho-educational staff laying substantial groundwork for preparation of pedagogy. This means that medical and psychologic faculty must become para-educational in orientation if developmental factors are to be sufficiently understood by the teachers to form the matrix for an effective attack on learning disorders.

Assuming appropriate teacher preparation, the important interactions between the teacher and other staff require that close and continuing coordination and supervision be an integral part of the preschool program. Coordination and supervision not only will enhance the communication between advisors, prescribers, and teachers but also will provide for quick assessment of many of the experimental and exploratory procedures typical of new programs. Such assessment is an important ingredient in special classes of all types where evaluation of the effectiveness of teaching procedures and materials is almost entirely subjective.

It would be a serious oversight not to recognize that teachers of special classes, particularly preschool classes, have few, if any, organized and structured guides in curriculum areas. Theoretic and experimental literature abounds, but is far removed contextually from classroom application. Therefore, teachers are called on to translate obscure and esoteric constructs into dynamic interactions. Each teaching decision, then, has as many alternatives as teacher ingenuity, creativity, and insight can conjure up. A knowledgeable observer, the supervisor, can enter into the decision-making process and the evaluation of the effectiveness of procedures and materials. Thus, the supervisor, through his role in the coordination of staff activities, the dissemination of information, and the evaluation of procedures, is an important link in the combination of diagnostic, consultative, administrative, and teaching staff. In a preschool program where the success of the program hinges on the close cooperation of medical and psychologic specialists in child development with teaching and administrative staff, knowledgeable coordination and supervision are indispensable.

The form that coordination and supervision should take will be determined by the program as a whole. Where there are a number of classes, dispersed or centralized, a professional worker well versed in the diagnostic-administrative-pedagogic elements of the program may act as an important link. Where one or two dispersed classes constitute the program, coordination may be achieved by a procedure rather than by a person. Regular and frequent meetings between the teachers and supporting-guiding staff will help staff see the nature of roles and contribution basic to the program.

## Facilities

Historically in this country, programs for retarded children and the children themselves have been required to fit into available educational facilities. This is understandable to some degree in light of serious shortages in educational buildings and of the limitations in financial support of public education in many communities. This practice has distorted and vitiated educational programs in many important ways and has imposed irrelevant selection criteria for designating who will be admitted to programs.

Teachers have had to eliminate important parts of the curriculum because of the location or physical characteristics of the classroom or school building. Children are denied admission to classes because they cannot meet the criteria for mobility or self-care in buildings designed for regular classes. It is paradoxical that children who could profit from special education are rejected or limited in program because there is little, if anything, special about the special education facilities.

If present policies in the designation of special classes are to continue in decision-making about the location of preschool classes and if the regular classroom is to be the model for the preschool class, we can expect an increased proportion of rejectees as well as an increase in the number of irrelevant programs. These policies cannot help but persist if we continue to subscribe to the notion that directed learning can take place only in the traditional classroom in the traditional school building. Programs for the severely retarded in a number of communities have demonstrated that special classes in churches, community centers, and the like, permit flexibility in programming and in admission practices often missing from traditional settings.

Obviously, the characteristics of the preschool child and the nature of the preschool program must be taken into account when planning for the classroom. The classroom could be in a traditional school building, providing its distance from critical facilities and its accessibility to children are such that children are not penalized. If, however, the classroom is on the third floor or just behind the boiler room and if it is so constructed that it will not permit the flexibility and equipment needed in working with preschool-age children, a more appropriate location for the classroom should be found. The growing interest of school architects in facilities for handicapped students is a healthy sign. With suites for secondary-level programs for the retarded now a matter of fact in many communities, specially designed facilities for school-age and preschool retarded children soon may materialize.

It is important to keep in mind that the five elements of the special educational program for the preschool-age retarded discussed here can be separated only for purposes of discussion. In planning and structuring a program, each has to be considered as it relates to and affects all other elements. This has to be done within the context of the administrative unit within which the program will function. Thus, although the principles of administrative, diagnostic, curriculum, staffing, and facilities design obtain in all administrative units, the specific procedures emanating from the principles will be peculiar to the size, constituency, population, distribution, and financing provisions of each administrative unit, be it a public-school district, a volunteer organization, or an institution for the retarded. In all cases, however, the point of departure in identifying specific procedures is a thorough understanding of the characteristics of the preschool retarded within the administrative unit.

Our present state of knowledge about the retarded precludes our crystallizing current beliefs and procedures into dogma. The ferment in all areas of research and treatment indicates that we are, at best, only beginning to get below the surface aspects of the learning problems of the retarded. Presently, workers in education and psychology, after long years of ruminating about individual differences, are beginning to act on these differences. Research in the diagnosis and remedy of learning disabilities is beginning to provide a foundation for procedures in diagnosis that will result possibly in quantitative and qualitative data that can lead to definitive educational procedures. Within this context, the age of the retarded learner is an important factor. Thus, early education based on programs appropriate to the developmental status and needs of the retarded is indicated.

## SUMMARY

Assumptions underlying preschool classes can be stated thus: (1) Preschool classes for the retarded will provide these children with stimulation and enrichment otherwise denied them in disadvantaged environments. Such stimulation and enrichment will raise intellectual levels quantitatively and qualitatively so that in-school and out-of-school functioning will be enhanced commensurately. (2) Preschool classes for the retarded will make modifications possible in the child's developmental schedule so that gaps that may hinder learning and adjustment may be closed. (3) Preschool classes for the retarded have noteworthy mental-health value in that they offer parents a period of freedom from the usual child-stimulated pressures. They also signify to the parents a measure of extra-family interest and concern.

These assumptions are, as they stand, logically and psychologically sound, but only if we assume further that the retarded are homogeneous in those variables susceptible to preschool treatment. Thus far, observation and research indicate that every preschool program, experimental or functional, makes the assumption of homogeneity and does so on the basis of either an oversimplification of the research bearing on the learning of infants or on a short-sighted assessment of the results of this research, or on both.

Samuel A. Kirk (1958) pointed out that the results of his study do not shed light on why certain children gain and others do not while in the same setting. If we laid out the distributions of all such studies, we probably would find the same question implicit in the data irrespective of mean differences. The one point that all such studies make with considerable clarity is that a broad, undifferentiated program has a low probability of making a difference in the development of retarded children. The alternative to a traditional preschool program is one that is carefully thought through from (1) administrative principles, (2) diagnosis, (3) staffing, (4) curriculum, and (5) facilities.

In the case of substantive aspects of the program, past research indicates that a predominantly social information orientation is insufficient. In the past, we have concentrated on self-care, socialization, and economic usefulness as the keystones of the program. Results of this emphasis are so negligible as to indicate that a balanced program is needed. Assuming that there are discontinuities and imbalances in the physical-intellectual development of the retarded, it would seem logical to attack these deficiencies in a paired or parallel physical-intellectual program wherein children are required to be both active and perceptive in a managed, purposeful relationship.

The program, with respect to administrative and staffing factors, requires the participation of interested disciplines. Program has to be organized by educator, psychologist, and medical specialists if diagnosis and curriculum are to acquire meaning. A meaningful diagnosis requires a thorough medical evaluation that will go beyond the usual statements of etiology and condition. Those responsible for curriculum could profit from the physician's impressions about physical and sensory assets and liabilities, as well as recommendations for management. These must be as definitive as possible if they are to become data for use in the program. The psychologist has to elicit and discuss more than psychometric and gross behavioral phenomena. A picture that portrays nature and rate of development is essential if an approach to optimal teaching is to be achieved. Educational diagnosis should take place within the context of the preschool program so that individual and group activity will be consonant with the sequence and rate of program administration.

The continuity and integrity of the preschool program depend on enlightened supervision and coordination. Local conditions will help to determine the nature of this facet of the program. Thus, administration, diagnostic services, staff, curriculum, and facilities will, in one way or another, be drawn into a continuous relationship.

## REFERENCES

GREGORY B. ALLEN and JOSEPH M. MASLING, "An Evaluation of the Effects of Nursery School Training on Children in the Kindergarten, First and Second Grades," *Journal of Educational Research,* LI (1957), 285–296.

MERL E. BONNEY and ERTIE LOU NICHOLSON, "Comparative School Adjustments of Elementary School Pupils with and without Preschool Training," *Child Development,* XXIX (1958), 125–133.

HELEN C. DAWE, "A Study of the Effect of an Educational Program upon Language Development and Related Mental Functions in Young Children," *Journal of Experimental Education,* XI (1942), 200–209.

HERBERT GOLDSTEIN, LAURA JORDON, and JAMES W. MOSS, *The Efficacy of Special Class Training on the Development of Mentally Retarded Children* (Urbana, Illinois: University of Illinois Press, 1965).

J. McV. HUNT, *Intelligence and Experience* (New York: Ronald Press, 1961).

HAROLD E. JONES, "The Environment and Mental Development," in Leonard Carmichael (Ed.), *Manual of Child Psychology* (New York: Wiley, 1954), pp. 631–696.

SAMUEL A. KIRK, *Early Education of the Mentally Retarded* (Urbana, Illinois: University of Illinois Press, 1958).

PAULINE S. SEARS and EDITH M. DOWLEY, "Research on Teaching in the Nursery School," in N. L. Gage (Ed.), *Handbook of Research on Teaching* (Chicago: Rand, McNally, 1963), pp. 815–864.

L. L. SMITH and J. B. STROUD, *Effects of Comprehensive Opportunity Program on the Development of Educable Mentally Retarded Children* (Mimeographed), (Iron City, Iowa: College of Education, State University of Iowa, 1960).

M. E. WALSH, "The Relation of Nursery School Training to the Development of Certain Personality Traits," *Child Development,* II (1931), 72–73.

BETH L. WELLMAN, "Iowa Studies on the Effects of Schooling," in Guy M. Whipple (Ed.), *Intelligence: Its Nature and Nurture,* 39th Yearbook of the National Society for the Study of Education (Bloomington, Illinois: Public School Publishing Co., 1940), pp. 377–399.

# 16

# The School Years—
# Program Design

## GEORGE BRABNER, JR.

### INTRODUCTION

This chapter will describe some of the major problems, needs, and controversial issues associated with the design of public-school programs for educable mentally retarded children[1] and will suggest a somewhat different approach to one of these problems—curriculum construction— from those previously employed in more conventional programs.

The specific areas of interest and the order in which they will be considered are as follows: (1) the definition of mental retardation and the implications for the school program of the explicit or implicit acceptance of a particular definition; (2) the problem of diagnosis, what it entails medically, psychologically, and educationally, and its significance for program-planning; (3) the need for clarification of the role of the teacher, a matter that eventually must be resolved in teacher-preparation programs, but that calls for decision-making now by the administrator; (4) the need for incorporation into the curriculum of recent technologic advances in education; (5) the segregated versus the integrated program—a long-standing controversy in the education of the mentally retarded; and (6) the pressing need

[1] *The educable mentally retarded child* is one who, because of slow mental development, is unable to profit to any great degree from the programs of the regular schools, but who has these potentialities for development: (1) minimum educability in reading, writing, spelling, arithmetic, and so forth; (2) capacity for social adjustment to a point where he can get along independently in the community; and (3) minimum occupational adequacy such that he can later support himself partially or totally at a marginal level (Kirk, 1962, p. 86).

for fresh approaches to curriculum development for the retarded. Following brief discussions of the first five topics enumerated above, a more detailed presentation of a suggested approach to curriculum construction will be made.

## PROBLEMS, NEEDS, AND ISSUES IN PLANNING SPECIAL CLASS PROGRAMS

### The Problem of Definition

It is rather odd that after some 150 years, commencing with Jean M. G. Itard, special educators and psychologists still have not reached accord on a definition of mental retardation. Unfortunately, "mental retardation" continues to remain about as useful a concept to these professionals as does "mental illness" (Szasz, 1960) to the psychiatrist and the clinical psychologist. Indeed, in connection with mental illness, we find a terminologic schism paralleling that in mental retardation and one raising similar problems. For example, the limitations inherent in the psychosis–neurosis dichotomy remind one of similar dichotomies that abound in the area of mental retardation: subcultural–pathologic, trainable–educable, mentally retarded–mentally deficient, and so forth. Curiously, mental retardation has stubbornly resisted all attempts to contain it within our traditionally restrictive definitions (Doll, 1941) or within the more flexible definition proposed by the American Association on Mental Deficiency (Heber, 1961).

An excellent discussion of the two most prominent positions being taken today with respect to the defining of mental retardation has been set forth by Arthur Benton (1964). According to him, one group of professionals divides the mentally retarded into two categories, first, those in whom there is evidence of underlying organic defect or some genetically based inadequacy of the central nervous system that accounts for the low intelligence and maladaptive behavior (this is "true" or "real" retardation, and is more or less permanent), and, second, those who exhibit no detectable central nervous system pathology and whose low intelligence and maladaptive behavior are attributed to emotional disturbance, sensory defects, sensory deprivation, cultural deprivation, and so forth (this is "functional" or "pseudo" retardation, possibly amenable to treatment).

A second group of professionals (for example, those who would subscribe to the American Association on Mental Deficiency definition) prefer to view the term "mental retardation" as a description of the current status of the individual. That is, in contrast to the definition described before, wherein certain mentally retarded behavior is regarded as predetermined by a "structural defect" and irreversible, the second definition considers such behavior to be potentially responsive to treatment—medical, psychologic, or educational—even though such treatment may not as yet be known.

A third but less popular point of view is illustrated in a cogent article by Frank Garfunkel (1964) who raises serious questions about our ability to identify mental retardation as a behavioral entity at all and, therefore, about the justification for the existence of this field for scientific study. This position holds that the mentally retarded are an "administratively defined subset of children who are functioning at an arbitrarily subnormal level of functioning" (p. 46). That is, whether or not a child is mentally retarded is determined by administrative fiat. Furthermore, it is maintained that the population of mentally subnormal children (all those exhibiting subaverage intelligence) cannot be meaningfully divided into the retarded and the nonretarded in any other way than administratively and that even this procedure is confused because of differences in geographic location, laws, socioeconomic factors, and educational practices within communities.

In summarizing his remarks on the mentally subnormal, Garfunkel makes the following points:

> The mentally retarded are an administratively defined subset of children who are functioning at an arbitrarily subnormal level of functioning. There are many subnormal children who are not retarded because they have not been assigned to an institution or to a special class. The number of these children varies considerably but it is rather certain that it represents a fairly large proportion of the subnormal. On the other hand, there are many retarded children who, although subnormal, have general personality problems to such an extent that it can be safely said that their chief problem is not intellectual, and the basis for placement can be said to be only trivially related to intelligence test performance. The picture is further complicated by the mentally subnormal children with brain damage, hard of hearing and deafness, partial sightedness and blindness, childhood psychosis and a great many other labels that involve children who score low on intelligence tests (Garfunkel, 1964, p. 51).

Whether or not a director of special education, a special class teacher, or a psychologist subscribes to one of these or to some other definition or viewpoint—although such subscription may not always be overt—may be an important factor determining the objectives and direction of a special-class program as well as the individual actions of personnel who have contact with the children. A conflict of definitional viewpoints within a program can create divisive forces detrimental to the program as a whole. For example, if, in the same program, one teacher of the retarded believes that she should exert every effort to improve a child's social and academic performance so that he can return eventually to the regular grades, while another teacher feels that such efforts and subjectives are unrealistic and even harmful for the retarded, then there exists a fundamental conflict in educational goals that requires resolution. Similarly, if an administrator believes that mental retardation is not more or less permanent but can be prevented or even reversed completely or partially at a later date through educational intervention, his conception of a curriculum for the retarded will differ radically from that of the administrator who accepts the former view and, consequently, tends to favor a more traditional approach.

### The Diagnostic Problem

It is conceded generally that a sound procedure for diagnosing mental retardation is basic to any modern educational program for the retarded, and yet there are few aspects of the program about which there is greater confusion. Interpretations of what is involved in making a diagnosis of mental retardation vary considerably. The view that it is essentially the examination procedure employed by a pediatrician or a psychiatrist is implied, if not stated, in a number of state laws. Sometimes a diagnosis of mental retardation is considered to have been made when a trained psychologist has administered an intelligence test to a child and has obtained an IQ score below some arbitrary cut-off point. At the other extreme are those who deplore such "solo" diagnoses and insist that no individual, regardless of the training provided in his discipline, is qualified to make a diagnosis of mental retardation. They maintain that such a diagnosis properly is carried out in a mental-retardation clinic staffed expressly for this purpose by professionals representing a variety of disciplines, all of whom, if need be, can bring their skills to bear on the diagnostic problem. They point to the need in some cases for extensive and highly technical laboratory tests, as well as neurologic, psychologic, social, and sometimes educational data.

Critics of this multidisciplinary approach contend that it is an ideal seldom attained in practice, and point out that such clinics came into being primarily as a result of pressure applied by parents of trainable children and not because of any genuine need springing from the problems of retarded children in public-school programs. They assert that the vast majority of these children are only mildly retarded and, being free, for the most part, from the severe neuropsychiatric and metabolic disorders afflicting a much higher proportion of the trainable mentally retarded, do not require intensive and expensive diagnostic workups. These same critics contend that few preschool mildly retarded children can be diagnosed as such because, for the most part, they are neurophysiologically normal and probably test in the low-average range prior to school entrance at six or seven years of age. At the time of entrance, however, they test as retarded on instruments such as the Stanford-Binet because these measure "conventional school aptitude," and it is in this complex of abilities and attitudes that these children are most deficient because of their predominantly lower socio-economic backgrounds.

In essence, proponents of this point of view maintain that the school situation "makes" these children mentally retarded because of the culture-alien demands that it imposes on them. As further evidence supporting this belief, the results of follow-up studies of graduates of special classes are cited. Most of these studies seem to suggest that the majority of these graduates become indistinguishable from the general population, and, by marrying, holding down jobs, and staying off the relief rolls, meet the minimal demands of cultural acceptability.

Seymour Sarason (1960) has called attention to the need for community diagnostic facilities and to the failure of professionals to provide parents with a realistic understanding of the retarded child's capacities, preparation for anticipated future problems, and a formulation of concrete programs of action. In a perceptive article, Wolf Wolfensberger (1965) is highly critical of the diagnostic process now used to identify mental retardation and demonstrates that some of the problems mentioned by Sarason are still with us. He identifies five practices that he labels "embarrassments" to the field:

> (1) Diagnosis is quite often a dead-end for the family. Instead of leading to a meaningful service assignment it frequently results only in a frustrating series of fruitless cross-referrals. (2) Many diagnostic centers do not provide adequate feedback counseling, considering their duty done the moment the diagnostic process is completed *to their satisfaction.* (3) Diagnostic services are often overdeveloped in comparison to other available resources. (4) According to theory and cliché, it is of utmost importance that diagnosis take place as early as possible. In practice, however, early diagnosis can be a disaster. . . . A child diagnosed as retarded at or near birth may never find the crucial initial acceptance and may be viewed with conflicted attitudes which prevent the formation of deep parental love. (5) I contend that we really have no strong empirical basis for claiming even a fraction of the benefits attributed to the team evaluation in vocational prediction (pp. 29–30).

Like Sarason, Wolfensberger calls for a family-centered attitude on the part of the diagnostic team rather than the traditional staff-centered one. Furthermore, he believes that an examination of practices and needs in the "much hailed but often rather stereotyped team approach" is long overdue.

Sarason, who contends that no person can diagnose mental retardation, has suggested the following as essentials to an "ideal" clinical evaluation of mental subnormality—ideal in the sense that an awareness of these essentials may tend at least to minimize reckless diagnoses: (1) an intellectual and social assessment of the present functioning of the child; (2) data relating to the development of major problems in the life of the child (these may be psychosocial, physical, medical, and so forth); and (3) an evaluation of the neurologic status of the child. Sarason also feels that the teacher can make an important contribution to diagnosis since she is one of the few adults who has an opportunity to observe the child in a learning situation and a peer-comparison situation. Because no one functions at a measured IQ level at all times and in all situations, the teacher's observations may be significant ones.

In any event, a diagnosis must not be treated casually, for it may not only label a person for life, but it also may affect the course of that life by determining the program or training for the future; moreover, it unquestionably will affect the life of the family unit. The diagnosis should identify the etiologic factors involved, for knowledge of etiology is important in the prevention of such conditions in others. In addition, the diagnosis should suggest the "treatment" to be employed, which may be psychologic, medical, educational, or all of these combined. Some of the more important questions to be asked in making a diagnosis are the following: Is the child functioning effectively with what he possesses intellectually? What is the child's conception of himself in relation to those around him? How has the child affected the family, and how has it, in turn, affected the child? With respect to the last question, it should be noted that one is interested not only in the retarded child but also in the problem confronting the family. The most severe problems arise when the parents accept the negative views of society toward their child, and it is these negative parental attitudes that ultimately will prevent the child from utilizing effectively what capacity he does have.

## The Need for Clarification of the Role of the Teacher

Special educators agree that the role of the special-class teacher of the retarded should not be one of mere "baby-sitting," but beyond this point there is considerable divergence of opinion. Should she work closely with each child and as much as possible on an individual basis, or should she group for instruction as best she can and take care of the needs of individual children when she can? Should she, like the Montessori teacher, be nondirective and less verbal, rather than directive and verbal, making herself available but not obtrusive? Should she minimize pressure for learning and achievement, but maximize pressure for promoting sound emotional development?

Where and how does programmed learning fit in? One psychologist-educator has claimed that the "teaching machine" is no more likely to replace the teacher in the classroom than the automatic washing machine has replaced the housewife in the home. In certain quarters, however, there is a nagging suspicion that, although the teacher may not be replaced, her role eventually will be so drastically altered through the introduction of automated instruction into the classroom that it will be unrecognizable as that of a teacher in the traditional sense. Some of the above issues are not, of course, restricted to the education of retarded children, but neither are they divorced from it. They serve to emphasize the involvement of program considerations for the retarded with the entire educational ferment that is characteristic of the times.

There is not space in this chapter to treat all of the issues raised here; nevertheless, let us examine one that is related fundamentally to philosophy and practice in the special class. Because retarded children fail so frequently in learning tasks, should the teacher tend, generally, to structure the learning situation to allow little or no room for failure, or is there a place for the selective application of the latter? That this is not an easy question to answer, but one that surely deserves thorough exploration, is indicated by studies conducted by Rick Heber (1957), William I. Gardner (1958), James W. Moss (1953), Irving Bialer (1960), and Martin B. Miller (1958). The findings of these studies suggest, to some degree, that on a variety of learning tasks performed in a negative reinforcement setting, the mentally retarded appeared to try harder, even in face of possible failure.

This research led to the development of the personality construct of "locus of control," that is,

> success is only meaningful to the person who succeeds if he can see himself as having been *instrumental* [controlling, not being controlled] *in achieving* success. Similarly for failure. That is, failure as an *experience* can occur only if a person is actively seeking some goal, some reinforcement, and he "knows" that his own ineffectiveness is the reason he doesn't achieve that goal (Miller, 1964).

Somewhat related to the construct of locus of control is the psychologic construct of stress. G. Orville Johnson (1962) contends that learning can be made more purposeful and meaningful for retarded children in special classes by the introduction into the learning situation of "realistic stress." Stress, he maintains, can serve as the drive or motivation to learn.

A similar thesis has been advanced by Bergen R. Bugelski (1956), who believes that anxiety as an "attention-getting" drive can be used effectively to aid learning. In fact, he goes so far as to assert that the art of teaching is made up largely of techniques for controlling the development of degrees of anxiety or curiosity. Similarly, on the basis of the work of Zeaman and House in discrimination learning with the mentally retarded and on the theoretic models of Donald O. Hebb and Alfred Strauss and Laura Lehtinen, Halbert Robinson and Nancy Robinson (1965) draw the conclusion that the "management of attention is possibly the most valuable contribution a teacher can make." Again, as was implied earlier, much of what the teacher actually will carry out in practice in the classroom is contingent on her own definition or conception of mental retardation. Postulated effects of automated instruction on the role of the special-class teacher have been mentioned. A definite possibility exists that the role of the teacher as what the learning psychologist calls the "eliciting stimulus" eventually will vanish.

## The Need for Incorporation of Recent Technological Advances in Education into the Curriculum

It is becoming increasingly obvious to educators that many traditional methods of education are inadequate to cope with present quantitative and qualitative requirements for instruction, and nowhere in the public-education system is there a stronger need for greater efficiency and quality of instruction than in programs for the mentally retarded. This is true primarily because so much must be taught so well in so little time, for the majority of the retarded probably will continue to leave special-class programs at or near sixteen years of age. In addition, the physical and psychologic abberations that can interfere with learning are probably far more numerous than in a regular grade class; therefore, grouping for efficient instruction is quite often not feasible or is at best a crude compromise.

Advances in educational technology in recent years have been exciting —new uses for open- and closed-circuit television, "single-concept" and programmed films, nonverbal films and films that motivate, automated electric talking typewriters, group tutorial instructional systems, computer-assisted instruction, "teaching machines," and so forth—but the incorporation of many of these innovations into public-school programs for retarded children has moved at a snail's pace. Part of this lag undoubtedly can be attributed to the understandable reluctance of some administrators to adopt sometimes expensive methods and equipment that have not been properly investigated and evaluated. Much of the lag can be accounted for by pessimistic attitudes concerning the capacities of the retarded, lack of imaginative thinking, and a general inertia traceable to a multiplicity of factors.

Fortunately, there are indications that interest in the new technology is beginning to quicken. Lawrence M. Stolurow (1960) has discussed the gains that can be anticipated through automation in special education and has made substantial contributions through his own research using teaching machines with retarded subjects. Leslie F. Maplass *et al.* (1962) also have demonstrated the effectiveness of certain automated teaching procedures for retarded children, and Murray Tondow (1964) has discussed the potential applications of computers in special education, suggesting a variety of ways in which they may be employed. A. Edward Blackhurst (1965) has discussed the implications of technology in special education and has advocated the utilization of a student-subject matter interface ("any device that is used by the student in interaction with subject matter") that could provide information about the learning performance and characteristics of the retarded. Computer-based instructional facilities now make such provision for individual differences in the education of the retarded technologically feasible.

In reply to critics who feel that automated instruction will take the "human element," presumably more crucial to the retarded even than to the nonretarded, out of teaching, advocates of increased use of the new technology in special classes have some strong rejoinders. They point out that what we label the "human element" is a double-edged sword not always having a salutary effect on retarded children. Prejudice, ridicule, sarcasm, irritation, and impatience will not be exhibited by an automated device. In certain situations, shy or distractible children may be better taught in the absence of others, including the teacher, whose presence, when the pupil makes errors, may serve only to inhibit or hinder learning. Automated devices also can control certain critical time intervals in instruction more precisely; for example, they can provide immediate rather than delayed reinforcement. More accurate standardization in the administration of various formal and informal educational tests also can be achieved.

One of the greatest voids in educational technology is that existing between the self-teaching materials devised by Maria Montessori and the "talking typewriter" of O. K. Moore. The commercial manufacturer of "educational" toys and games has attempted to fill this void, a void that should have been filled by the efforts of creative teachers provided with the proper encouragement, knowledge, and equipment necessary to develop meaningful self-educational materials. Happily, federally sponsored centers for the storage and development of special educational materials now are being organized at several universities (McCarthy, 1965).

With the development of a new and more sophisticated educational technology, significant benefits can be brought to the retarded as well as to other exceptional children, but special educators can and should be leaders, not followers, in exploiting the full range of these benefits.

## Segregated versus Integrated Facilities for the Retarded

No discussion of problems and controversies associated with programs for the mentally retarded would be complete without some comment on segregated versus integrated programs for these children. Although the controversy has diminished in intensity in the last twenty years or so, special educators of the mentally retarded are still far from agreement on whether the retarded are better provided for in separate schools, classes, or other facilities not an integral part of the regular school program for nonretarded youngsters, or in "integrated" facilities in the same school setting with the regular grade children.

Some educators are opposed to integration for the trainable mentally retarded, but favor it for the educable retarded. Others are opposed to the integration of the retarded with "normal" children in any circumstances, although this point of view is held by probably a steadily decreasing minority. Some treat the matter as an academic question, taking the position that, since some states already have endorsed the inclusion of special classes in the regular school program as being the most "democratic" procedure, it is highly doubtful that this trend ever will be reversed. They also point to the successful efforts of parents of trainable retarded children to have their children enrolled in public-school special classes as evidence of an irreversible trend.

In describing the controversy at its height (up until the mid-1940's), Ignacy Goldberg and Leonard S. Blackman (1965) have stated the issue of segregated versus integrated facilities for the retarded as follows:

Pro-Integration

(1) the integrated classes conformed more closely to democratic values and principles; (2) the mentally retarded children would profit, both academically and socially, from opportunities for frequent association with normal children; and (3) the normal children would acquire a better understanding of and a greater respect for individual differences.

Anti-Integration

(1) administratively and pedagogically the special school could provide more efficient and higher quality services; (2) the application of auxiliary services such as psychology, guidance, and speech would be facilitated; and (3) the absence of an "unhealthy" competitive environment would be both academically and emotionally beneficial to children poorly equipped to compete (p. 30).

Regardless of whether this controversy has waned or is merely dormant, it seems that some of the assumptions associated with either position can and should be subjected to experimental verification. Assumptions two and three in the first category and three in the second seem to lend themselves to such verification.

It would be helpful for special-class administrators to view integration as a belief, a policy, and a process. The

nature of the actual process of integration is as yet poorly understood and is probably a phenomenon, or more probably several phenomena, which can be most appropriately investigated within a conceptual framework derived from social psychology (Brabner, 1964, p. 109).

In retrospect it would appear that the time, effort, and money that have been devoted in the past to research studies comparing the relative merits of special-class placement and regular grade placement for retarded children might have been as well spent in assessing, for example, the effects of "stressful" learning climates on classroom performance.

## *The Need for New Approaches to Curriculum Development*

I have viewed with growing concern the proliferation of curriculums that have been developed for the retarded in communities all over the nation. The range of educational philosophies, emphases, and the obsolescence of the programs is great, and the disparities among them often are casually explained away as quite understandable in light of the unique social, economic, political, or physical factors operating within the respective communities.

The following are some statements typical of those voiced by educators involved in the day-to-day planning and implementation of these curriculums:

> Because we in Community A have a local economy that is predominantly agricultural, most of our children do not require the particular emphases in content areas x, y, and z recommended in Community B's program for the retarded.

> In an upper middle-class community, it would be pointless to stress training for certain low-skilled nonmanual jobs in the curriculum, as is done in Big City's program. The parents would object to it as training for lower social class status—in fact, they already are insisting on more emphasis on the academic subjects—and besides, there aren't many jobs of that type in the community, anyway.

> The ability to perform simple routine tasks effectively is what makes these children happy—the kind of tasks that more intelligent individuals find boring and monotonous. After all, someone must do these jobs in any society.

> These children have experienced so much failure in their lives and have acquired so many maladaptive behaviors that a focus in the program on sound mental hygiene must take precedence over every other consideration.

These statements not only reflect a tremendous diversity in programmatic emphasis and prediction, but also are surface manifestations of what, in all probability, are profoundly differing approaches to the education of retarded children. Considering the constantly increasing population mobility in this country, particularly from the southeastern portion of the United States to the northern urban areas and from these urban areas to the suburbs, it would not be at all surprising if many mentally retarded children are being exposed to a variety of very different educational climates exhibiting little, if any, thread of continuity from one to another.

Two questions are pertinent to this discussion. In view of the large-scale population movements, the rapidity with which technologic change and consequent social and economic change are occurring in our society, the explosion of information (doubling man's knowledge every fifteen years), and the ever growing demand on the individual for competence in specialized skills in everyday pursuits, can a special educator in a given community seriously entertain the view that he and his staff can select the curriculum content to provide for the acquisition of that knowledge and those skills that are prerequisite to personal, social, and occupational adequacy in the future life of any person? If the answer to this question is negative, then the second question to be asked is, Is there an alternative to curriculum diversity to provide an underlying principle for all programs for the retarded, or must individual programs be so altered to meet the "requirements" of local communities as to have in common only the type of child for whom they are devised?

One might be urged to resort to the use of a university curriculum laboratory for inspiration for an alternative procedure. But, other than furnishing information of some vague historic interest, this highly touted educational resource has proved consistently to be a sterile source of fresh ideas and program models for the retarded. Regrettably, many of the documents produced in these laboratories, purporting to be bona-fide curriculums or curriculum guides, turn out on closer inspection to consist of not much more than a number of rather arbitrarily selected educational objectives under which are listed—sometimes at great length and in great detail—numerous examples of what are considered to be appropriate activities for attaining these objectives. Generally, these objectives and activities are virtually indistinguishable from those employed with nonretarded children. Whether these "laboratories" serve better as wellsprings of creative program design than as repositories of the accumulated ignorance of schoolmen is debatable.

Where, then, can one turn for a fresh approach to curriculum construction for the mentally retarded? Certainly, bold new experiments in various subject areas of curriculums for nonretarded children have been undertaken in recent years, starting with the contribution of the Physical Science Study Committee in the 1950's. Moreover, with the passage of Public Law 88–164, Title III, and the Elementary and Secondary Education Act of 1965 (Public Law 89–10) that authorize construction of experimental schools and the redesign of existing schools for research objectives, there is now at least the financial wherewithal for the encouragement of imaginative curriculum experimentation.

I suggest that consideration be given to a concept that has great merit as a potential guiding principle for program development. Sad to say, this concept is being noised about to such an extent that it is in grave danger of meeting the same fate as Dewey's "learning-by-doing" principle, that is, of being so distorted and used so indiscriminately as to become an empty slogan, devoid of any real meaning. This is the idea of "learning to learn," which is simultaneously the principal goal of the curriculum and the guiding principle determining the content of the curriculum.

The concept of learning to learn, though it can be stated in a rigorous experimental manner, as Harlow has done in his studies of learning sets in monkeys, also can be interpreted more broadly as the fostering of the ability to learn, thus encompassing the host of attempts by psychologists in the laboratory and by psychologist-educators in the classroom to investigate and to develop the cognitive processes of children. The names of Jerome S. Bruner, O. K. Moore, Richard Hess, Jean Piaget, and W. Fowler are familiar to many special educators. In the history of special education for the mentally retarded, the closely allied concept of the educability of intelligence has long been prominent in the thinking of distinguished special educators. Alfred Binet, who tried to develop the higher mental processes of retarded children in his "mental orthopedics" curriculum, Maria Montessori and her "didactic materials," and, more recently, Samuel A. Kirk, who attempted to educate the intelligence of preschool retarded children, are only a few such educators.

Some of Samuel A. Kirk's former students have reported the results of a two-month educational program for young, mildly retarded children (Olson *et al.*, 1965). This program was based on psycholinguistic skills of the type measured by the Illinois Test of Psycholinguistic Abilities. The children were enrolled in the curriculum on the basis of their linguistic strengths and weaknesses. The results of the study indicated that in constructing a curriculum for young retarded children there is a need for differential emphasis of cognitive areas. This is an example of a highly specific model for curriculum construction for the mentally retarded and one that is probably too limited in scope for other than a phase of the total curriculum, but it serves as an interesting illustration of one departure from long-established classroom practices.

Another approach—this time with nonretarded children—that may provide a different philosophy and a stimulus to thinking in the area of the retarded is exemplified by the Valley Winds School in suburban St. Louis. The following description of the Valley Winds program is not intended to be a model for a curriculum for the retarded. It is offered primarily for its general philosophic flavor and its stress on the development of children who think independently. The writer feels that these two elements are far from being incommensurate with the design of programs for the retarded, although traditional programs typically have tended to minimize the latter as an educational objective.

The ultimate goal at Valley Winds is the aim also of most educators, to turn each child into an independent thinker who can teach himself. In contrast to traditional elementary schools, where most youngsters spend 90 per cent of their time being taught by a teacher, Valley Winds allows its nine- through-ten-year-olds and even some of the younger children to spend at least half of their school day with little or no instruction. After each youngster has acquired the basic skills of reading, writing, and arithmetic, he is expected to pick out topics in science, social studies, and literature and to plan his own projects and work out his own school-day study schedule. He can work alone or with a friend, and if he likes, he can spend the entire day studying the subject that interests him. (There are no bells or buzzers at Valley Winds.) After he has completed the Basic Skills Division (ages six to eight) and the Transition Division (ages eight and nine), he is placed in the Independent Study Division (ages nine to twelve), where he is provided with special instructors. In addition to being nongraded and taught by teams of teachers, a child can call on a wide variety of electronic and me-chanical self-teaching devices, from tape recordings to teaching machines, to movies, and educational television. In effect, at Valley Winds School, children as young as seven are following learning procedures that usually are reserved for college students. But, whereas many colleges boast a select student body, the children at Valley Winds Elementary represent a true cross-section of lower middle-class suburbia and have an over-all IQ average of 108, just a shade above the national norm.

Charles Mansfield, the thirty-three-year-old principal at Valley Winds, explains it this way:

> Because of the rapid expansion of knowledge, much of what a child will learn in class will be out of date when he graduates. If he goes to college, he will either have to be able to learn on his own or get out. For these reasons we are trying to teach children how to learn, how to be responsible for themselves (Black, 1965, p. 81).

Denis Brogan (1960) also maintains that we should not attempt to educate the pupil for the world that he is going to enter because we have no way of knowing what that world will be. The only certainty is that in a normal lifetime it will change in ways that we cannot now predict. O. J. Harvey, David E. Hunt, and Harold M. Shroder (1961) have expressed opinions similar to these with respect to educational objectives. They believe strongly that the major goal is to foster the development of higher conceptual levels to increase the learner's adaptive capacity and flexibility. I concur fully with this view and contend that increasing the child's ability to adapt to change should be the central concern of the educator of the retarded and of the nonretarded alike.

Mansfield's remark quoted above to the effect that if a child goes to college "he will either have to be able to learn on his own or get out" applies equally to the educable mentally retarded child, for when he enters the proverbial "college of hard knocks" he, too, will have to be able to learn or get out. In fact, Herbert Goldstein (1964) believes that the available evidence indicates that the post-school situation is becoming so critical for the retarded that it may be necessary, in the not too distant future, to establish sheltered workshops for these children, just as we have for the trainable mentally retarded.

The concept of "adaptive behavior" that Rick Heber (1959) has proffered is another heartening example of forward-looking thinking that is keenly cognizant of the limitations of an approach to the retarded, either educational or psychologic, that tends to focus too narrowly on the dimensions of measured intelligence or of academic achievement. Lee J. Cronbach (1964), too, has become interested in problems related to the concept of learning to learn. Although he prefers the term "aptitudinal transfer," it is clear that he is talking about transfer to instructional situations rather than a student's unaided performance in mastering the criterion task. Cronbach believes that an approach to curriculum in which the selection of content is of secondary concern is prerequisite to preparing an individual for lifelong learning. Emphasis on aptitude as an educational objective is one possible way of achieving this desired state, and he offers as a tentative definition of aptitude "those abilities that affect rate of learning in a specified task or class of tasks under a specified instructional procedure."

Whether a single comprehensive model can be developed for a learning-to-learn curriculum for the retarded, or whether one will evolve that combines, for example, a psycholinguistic model like the Illinois Test of Psycholinguistic Abilities with specific cognitive development exercises based on Piaget's theory of intelligence, plus, perhaps, activities suggested by Guilford's "structure of intellect," or even O. K. Moore's "automated responsive environment," is yet to be determined; however, there are strong indications that the time for rethinking and decision is at hand. Probably all that can be said for curriculums for the retarded up to the present time is that, by and large, they have proved to be irrelevant. If radical curriculum experimentation is required to eliminate the stagnation that exists in the special classes and the quiet desperation that compels conscientious but guilt-ridden teachers to emphasize academics because they are skeptical of the educational value of the proposed alternatives, then let us get on with it.

## Summary

Six areas of interest illustrating problems, needs, and issues associated with special class programs for the retarded during the school years have been discussed. These areas are the problem of definition of mental retardation, the problem of diagnosis, the segregated versus the integrated program, the need for clarification of the role of the teacher, the need for incorporation into the curriculum of recent technologic advances in education, and the need for fresh approaches to curriculum development for the retarded.

It is suggested that a shift to a learning-to-learn approach, stressing increasing effectiveness of adaptability to change and the development of independence of thought and action, may be worth investigating as an alternative to curriculum approaches that traditionally have been content-oriented.

## REFERENCES

ARTHUR L. BENTON, "Psychological Evaluation and Differential Diagnosis," in Harvey A. Stevens and Rick Heber (Eds.), *Mental Retardation: A Review of Research* (Chicago: University of Chicago Press, 1964), pp. 16–56.

IRVING BIALER, "Conceptualization of Success and Failure in Mentally Retarded and Normal Children," Unpublished doctoral dissertation, George Peabody College for Teachers, Nashville, Tennessee (Ann Arbor, Michigan: University Microfilms, 1960).

HILLEL BLACK, "A School Where Children Teach Themselves," *Saturday Evening Post* (June 19, 1965), pp. 81–85.

A. EDWARD BLACKHURST, "Technology in Special Education—Some Implications," *Exceptional Children,* XXXI (1965), 449–456.

GEORGE BRABNER, "Integration and the Special Class Administrator," *Journal of Education,* CXLVII (1964), 105–110.

DENIS W. BROGAN, *America in the Modern World* (New Brunswick, New Jersey: Rutgers University Press, 1960).

BERGEN R. BUGELSKI, *The Psychology of Learning* (New York: Holt, Rinehart, 1956).

LEE J. CRONBACH, "Aptitudes as an Outcome of Instruction," Unpublished paper presented at the Center for Advanced Study in the Behavioral Sciences, Stanford, California, June 1964.

EDGAR A. DOLL, "The Essentials of an Inclusive Concept of Mental Deficiency," *American Journal of Mental Deficiency,* XLVI (1941), 214–219.

WILLIAM A. GARDNER, "Reactions of Intellectually Normal and Retarded Boys After Experimentally Induced Failure," Unpublished doctoral dissertation, George Peabody College for Teachers, Nashville, Tennessee (Ann Arbor, Michigan: University Microfilms, 1958).

FRANK GARFUNKEL, "Probabilities and Possibilities for Modifying Behavior of Mentally Retarded Children: Tactics for Research," *Journal of Education,* CXLVII (1964), 45–52.

IGNACY GOLDBERG and LEONARD S. BLACKMAN, "The Special Class—Parasitic, Endophytic, or Symbiotic Cell in the Body Pedagogic," *Mental Retardation,* III (1965), 30–31.

HERBERT GOLDSTEIN, "Social and Occupational Adjustment," in Harvey A. Stevens and Rick Heber (Eds.), *Mental Retardation: A Review of Research* (Chicago: University of Chicago Press, 1964), pp. 214–258.

O. J. HARVEY, DAVID E. HUNT, and HAROLD M. SHRODER, *Conceptual Systems and Personality Organization* (New York: John Wiley and Sons, 1961).

RICHARD F. HEBER, "Expectancy and Expectancy Changes in Normal and Mentally Retarded Boys," Unpublished doctoral dissertation, George Peabody College for Teachers, Nashville, Tennessee (Ann Arbor, Michigan: University Microfilms, 1957).

RICK HEBER (Ed.), "A Manual on Terminology and Classification in Mental Retardation," *American Journal of Mental Deficiency* (Monograph Supplement), LXIV (1959), 3–111.

RICK HEBER, "Modifications in the Manual on Terminology and Classification in Mental Retardation," *American Journal of Mental Deficiency,* LXV (1961), 499–500.

G. ORVILLE JOHNSON, "Special Education for the Mentally Handicapped—A Paradox," *Exceptional Children,* XXIX (1962), 62–69.

SAMUEL A. KIRK, *Educating Exceptional Children* (Boston: Houghton Mifflin, 1962).

LESLIE F. MAPLASS, A. S. GILMORE, M. W. HARDY, and C. F. WILLIAMS, *Automated Teaching for Retarded Children: A Summary Comparison of Two Procedures.* Project Number 1267 Cooperative Research Project (Washington, D. C.: Department of Health, Education, and Welfare, 1962).

JAMES J. MCCARTHY, "A Special Education Instructional Materials Center," *Mental Retardation,* III (1965), 26–28.

MARTIN BERT MILLER, "Locus of Control, Learning Climate, and Climate Shift in Serial Learning with Mental Retardates," Unpublished doctoral dissertation, George Peabody College for Teachers, Nashville, Tennessee (Ann Arbor, Michigan: University Microfilms, 1958).

MARTIN BERT MILLER, "Locus of Control and Effective Behavior," Paper presented at the Second Annual Meeting of the American Academy on Mental Retardation, Lynchburg, Virginia, October 1964.

JAMES W. MOSS, "Failure-Avoiding and Success-Striving Behavior in Mentally Retarded and Normal Children," Unpublished doctoral dissertation, George Peabody College for Teachers, Nashville, Tennessee (Ann Arbor, Michigan: University Microfilms, 1953).

JAMES L. OLSON, HANS R. HAHN, and ANITA L. HERMANN, "Psycholinguistic Curriculum," *Mental Retardation,* III (1965), 14–19.

HALBERT B. ROBINSON and NANCY M. ROBINSON, *The Mentally Retarded Child: A Psychological Approach* (New York: McGraw-Hill, 1965).

SEYMOUR B. SARASON, "Aspects of a Community Program for the Retarded Child," in James F. Magary and John R. Eichorn (Eds.), *The Exceptional Child* (New York: Holt, Rinehart and Winston, 1960), pp. 105–110.

LAWRENCE M. STOLUROW, "Automation in Special Education," *Exceptional Children,* XXVIII (1960), 78–83.

THOMAS S. SZASZ, "The Myth of Mental Illness," *American Psychologist,* XV (1960), 113–118.

MURRAY TONDOW, "Computers in Special Education—An Introduction," *Exceptional Children,* XXXI (1964), 113–116.

WOLF WOLFENSBERGER, "Embarrassments in the Diagnostic Process," *Mental Retardation,* III (1965), 29–31.

# 17

# Consultation and
# Special Education

## IRVING N. BERLIN

The teachers of mentally retarded children face some of the most difficult and serious problems in the schools. As a mental-health consultant to several school systems, I have come to understand the particular burdens of teachers of retarded children, their position in the school, and the small amount of help available to them in coping with the serious problems that they face daily.

## TEACHERS' PROBLEMS AND SATISFACTIONS IN TEACHING RETARDED CHILDREN

Problems arise from having to teach severely intellectually handicapped children who resist learning and change, with resulting minimal satisfactions for teachers in their work. Most of these youngsters are severely emotionally disturbed; in fact, some are psychotic children whose intellectual functioning cannot be assessed, and they are therefore placed in classes for the retarded. These youngsters create bedlam in the classroom. Their aggressive, restless, unpredictable behavior is not only difficult to manage, but also takes so much time and energy that little is left for the less disturbed child who could learn. Even the not so emotionally disturbed child usually has been poorly disciplined and trained at home, so that his willfulness and inability to take care of personal hygiene place other burdens on the teacher. The parents of many retarded children hope that each class or experience will change their child dramatically; in fact, they hope it may rid

279

him of his retardation. Their demands on the teacher, which stem from their own feelings of guilt and other emotional problems that will be discussed later, place additional pressure on the teacher to be effective with every child.

As a school consultant, I have slowly learned how my particular training in child psychiatry, that is, family psychiatry, can be used to help teachers of retarded children with some of these problems. For most of us, the satisfaction and gratification that we obtain from our work come from seeing the fruition of our efforts, the tangible results of our labors. For teachers, and now I speak also as a teacher of child psychiatrists, satisfaction comes from evidence that their students have learned what they have to teach and have been caught up in the exciting process of learning and mastery of subject matter, and from the pleasure in learning that they manifest in their behavior. All of us are thrilled by the outstanding, brilliant students whose quick grasp of subject matter—be it reading, arithmetic, physics, or personality dynamics—gives evidence of our effectiveness as teachers. Such experiences renew our energy and devotion to teaching and are among the most important rewards that keep teachers satisfied and stimulated in their work.

Teachers of retarded children, both mildly and severely retarded, rarely have these professional satisfactions. Infrequently, the patient, persistent, and warm efforts of a teacher may so affect a psychotic youngster who functions at a retarded level that he blossoms out and begins to learn, to socialize, and to behave more appropriately in school and at home. The teacher has been largely responsible for a minor miracle, with all the job and personal satisfactions that such a vivid transformation deserves. However, such dramatic change occurs rarely. Patient, persistent efforts at teaching the rudiments of preschool reading readiness, or the basics of personal grooming, or social behavior at the table or in class result in only minor observable increments of learning and require an interminable length of time, the patience of Job, and the disposition of an angel. Or, as one teacher remarked to me after an especially trying and apparently fruitless day, "You really need to be an early Christian Martyr to teach these kids."

How can one get satisfaction from teaching retarded children? Where does one's sense of achievement come from? As in work with psychotic youngsters and underprivileged children, expectations of how much the child will learn and how soon must be scaled down considerably. This, of course, most teachers of the retarded know or are taught. They are aware that increments of knowledge will occur in very small quantities and over a long period of time. However, they are not taught to be aware of and to search out the accompanying manifestations in the child's attitudes and behavior that show the teacher that the retarded student is beginning to learn and that encourage the teacher to continue the long process.

For example, one teacher reported with discouragement her long and persistent effort to help a ten-year-old, hyperactive, silly, giggling, retarded boy to recognize different shaped and colored objects in learning the alphabet—a red Apple, and so forth. As she described the tedious repetition over many weeks with little result, she mentioned, in passing, that the only effect of her continued efforts seemed to be that whenever she took out the letter cards, pictures, and blocks, the boy came eagerly to her side and ceased his silly talk and hyperactive running around the classroom. When I mentioned that this in itself was a monumental step and indicated the beginning of the child's readiness to settle down and his pleasure in the learning experience with her, the teacher at once recalled that there had been a gradual reduction of disruptive activities, especially in individual teaching sessions, but also somewhat in the group sessions. It is important to look for and to recognize all behavior changes associated with the learning efforts, since these indicate readiness to learn and also that, although the subject matter is not being learned so rapidly, the child is learning about the setting and conditions necessary for learning. He also realizes that the teacher will persist in helping him learn. This latter, the feeling that someone will stick with you, despite disruptive behavior that discourages others, until you do begin to learn, may be a new experience for many children.

## School Problems of the Retarded Child

The behavior problems of the retarded child are the problems most frequently brought to consultation by teachers. Most teachers who work with both the educable and the trainable groups complain that their primary stumbling block is the negativistic, stubborn, hyperactive, hostile, destructive, and sometimes assaultive behavior of these children. Occasionally they express concern about the less frequently encountered, very apathetic, listless, and withdrawn students. Certainly, the teacher of the mentally retarded who teaches a group composed of microcephalic or hydrocephalic and severely dysplastic children has ample grounds to ask whether their disturbing behavior results from the amount of brain damage that is so apparent in these conditions. This raises the frequent and persistent question of whether education of any kind can take place in face of so much brain damage. Should these youngsters be refused admission to these classes despite parental pressure? How does one account for such behavior in those retarded children in whom there is no obvious evidence of organic deficit and the signs of minimal brain damage are not very clear from neurologic examination, electroencephalograms, and skull X rays.

In this area, what we have learned from psychotherapeutic work with severely psychotic, retarded children and their parents may be relevant. When teachers raise these questions, I often describe instances in which there was a question of how much of a child's retardation was due to brain damage or cerebral dysfunction and how much to severe emotional disturbance resulting in a psychotic picture and severe behavior problems. These questions often could be answered only by a therapeutic trial. The efforts of the ward staff, child psychiatrist, teacher, occupational therapy worker, and work with the parents sometimes resulted in the gradual reduction of the "crazy" behavior, greater ability to relate to adults and children, genuine playfulness, and more appropriate expression of all emotions. Then it was possible to delineate the residual deficit in mentation. Interestingly enough, the work with child and parents that made clear the degree of mental deficiency present and clarified the child's potential for learning also revealed the severity of the emotional disturbances in child and parents, which often had made it impossible to obtain a clear picture previously.

Timmy, a seven-year-old boy with mongolism who looked four years of age, was brought to the Mental Retardation Clinic of the Children's Service at Langley Porter Neuropsychiatric Institute because of his combative, aggressive behavior, running away, and prolonged tantrums that only his father could control. His mother spent most of her days with Timmy because his assaultiveness toward other children, aggressiveness, and tantrums had made it impossible for him to remain in a nursery school for retarded children. Psychologic evaluation was impossible because of his tantrums, but the psychologist guessed he was severely retarded and not educable on the basis of the Vineland Social Maturity Scale, with the mother and the nursery-school teacher as informants. His own observations confirmed the extremely low level of functioning of the child. It soon became clear that the parents were in severe conflict with each other and that Timmy's birth had been an effort to patch up their marriage. The parents were unable to talk with each other about their disappointment in having a mongoloid child. They were unable, also, to accept his severe limitations in learning and were very angry at the physician who advised early placement of Timmy. Since his birth, the parents' social life had been seriously curtailed—as if Timmy were evidence of some defect in them, and they did not want to face their friends. The isolation was reinforced when, from age one and one-half, Timmy's behavior could not be controlled by babysitters. On physical examination, Timmy was found to be a healthy, typical mongoloid child. Psychologic evaluation could not be done because he was so restless and negativistic.

In response to a firm attitude in the playroom and repeated physical restraint with every tantrum, Timmy began to play, to mouth and to use toys, to show interest in water play, and to be able to sit and listen to instructions from his therapist. It became clear that despite his monosyllabic speech, Timmy understood much of what he heard and, in the playroom, began to carry out simple instructions.

The mother felt especially helpless with Timmy and blamed his aggressiveness and tantrums on the father, who seemed both to encourage and to enjoy this "masculine" behavior, but could also control it by physically holding Timmy or, occasionally, by a spanking. Early in the individual psychotherapeutic work with the parents, the mother's angry feelings at being saddled with this retarded boy came out. She was able to express her anger with the father for not being home more to help control Timmy and for encouraging his tantrums. She blamed the father for Timmy's mongolism, stating there was no taint in her family.

Finally the father was able to talk about his disappointment at having a retarded child, especially a boy. He had hoped that his son would follow in his footsteps as an outstanding athlete and would share his interest in fishing, hunting, and sports. He felt the mother was to blame for Timmy's temper outbursts because she made no effort to stop him physically, thus encouraging his aggressive behavior. He also resented the mother's turning over all care for Timmy to him when he came home. The father wondered, too, about the cause of Timmy's deficit and felt it was his wife's fault because she had refused to have any children for the first twelve years of their marriage and only became pregnant to save the marriage when she was in her late thirties.

The therapist encouraged the mother to be more firm and demonstrated how Timmy could be restrained if necessary. Primarily, he helped her to realize how much easier her life would be if she could convey to Timmy by her attitude, tone, and words that she meant what she said and was determined to follow through. One result of these efforts with the mother was that Timmy became toilet-trained and no longer wet his pants. Timmy became easier to handle at home. His parents were less angry with each other and used him less as a weapon against each other. As a result of his being helped in his play therapy and his settling down at home and becoming interested in a wider variety of objects in his environment, Timmy was able to spend more time at play, listening to stories, and so forth. It then became possible to try him in a school program for the retarded. There it became clear that Timmy was educable, and his intelligence, which had not been measured because of his restless, combative behavior, was finally evaluated as being in the low 60's with some evidence that this was a minimal evaluation. Finally, Timmy's behavior was sufficiently improved so that the parents not only could leave him with a babysitter for evenings out, but could leave him with a relative for a week so that they could have their first vacation together in over seven years.

I tried to help teachers see a child's behavior as not only a manifestation of his brain injury with resulting limitations in perception, cognition, and motor abilities, but also as a manifestation of how he felt about himself and the adults around him and how they, particularly his parents, had regarded him. Thus, when in one instance I asked a teacher of a trainable class what she felt a ten-year-old boy's assaults on her and other children might be expressing, she at once responded with, "Will you permit me to behave in this dangerous way?" When I asked what she did, she replied that, as soon as he began hitting or kicking anyone, she grabbed him and held him tightly until he relaxed. He responded rather rapidly to her firm expression of determination that such behavior could not be tolerated in the classroom. She said that she never knew when it would happen. We then talked about what she said to him after such an episode. The teacher related that she told him she could not stand such behavior and that he might not be allowed to stay in the class if it continued. We then tried to reconstruct such a tantrum. It became clear that there were several associated events. These explosions occurred most often before lunch, though sometimes in the afternoon, and they almost always happened when the teacher was engaged in helping several other children, mostly girls, learn how to prepare desserts from packaged mixes. Having described these associated events, the teacher recalled that after she held the boy and he stopped fighting, he relaxed and nestled in her arms until she felt a bit awkward about holding such a gangling ten-year-old and let go of him. After this discussion, the teacher decided to watch the boy more carefully before lunch, to notice his beginning restlessness, and to keep him close to her, perhaps with a hand touching his from time to time during the "cooking" exercise. One of the unspoken problems that came up repeatedly had to do with how to deal with the child's sensual and sexual needs and expression. This was never talked about explicitly.

When I next talked with the teacher about this child, she said that although there had been a reduction in these violent episodes near lunch time, they were now occurring later in the day when she was involved with all the children in clay and coloring activities at the table. The boy would lash out suddenly at the nearest child or at her. She remarked that she already had looked at the associated events and could not find any other besides the ones mentioned. I wondered how she had let this boy know what he could do if he wanted or needed her attention, or if he felt a hungry yearning for an undefined something and disappointment that it was not forthcoming. Or, if he suddenly felt angry, upset, or excited, how such feelings could be expressed without hurting someone and making her angry or being hurt himself, as had happened when one of the children retaliated by hitting the boy on the head with a mallet after being hurt by a vicious kick.

The teacher first doubted that this severely disturbed and retarded child could understand this kind of communication, and, furthermore, she was not sure what to substitute for the expression of anger and other feelings. We tried to find words to describe very simply how the boy might be feeling at particular moments. We described fear and anger in terms of tight, grinding, hurting feelings in his stomach or chest or muscles. Also, that before these feelings he might feel a hungry, wanting-something feeling. We also talked about some ways in which he could let her know he felt this way. Since he used only garbled speech, the teacher recalled the word "go," which he sometimes used to tell her when he needed toileting. We also talked about how angry, hurt feelings could be discharged by pounding clay rather than striking out, and that sensual feelings could be enjoyed by kneading and working clay, since there seemed to be a lack of any opportunity for expression of sensual pleasures in any of his activities. This child's response to firm holding after a tantrum by snuggling also suggested perhaps both a cause for such behavior, in the emergence of an unexpressed and possibly unexpressable feeling, and a way of obtaining close, warm, and sensual feelings from another.

For the next two meetings, at two-week intervals, this teacher brought up problems with other children, mostly concerned with how to help a tiny microcephalic girl protect herself from the more aggressive, larger children. Here again, the main problem seemed to center around the expression of angry, hostile feelings and behavior and its handling. When we examined this girl's behavior, certain provocative and teasing aspects became evident. After describing these factors, the teacher began to think out loud about how she might anticipate the previously unattended provocative behavior and deal with it as a bid for interaction and close, warm, physical contact with someone. She talked also about how repulsive this child was, physically, with her odd, dwarfed body, tiny head, and constant drooling. Thus, her bids for human contact were difficult to respond to. The teacher had learned that these were problems also for the parents. We then talked about how difficult it is to pretend feelings that one does not feel. I described my own learning experience with a cachexic, anorexic girl who demanded affection and declarations that she was lovable and attractive despite her skeleton-like appearance. It was only after I could say to her and to myself that she was not attractive or very lovable in this state, but that I was willing to work with her and that perhaps, in the process, I might feel differently, that some of my own guilt for not being able to respond or to pretend liking was reduced. The teacher then was able to talk briefly of her own guilt about many children whom she felt obliged to like and respond warmly to, but whose appearance or behavior made it difficult for her to feel and to express warm and affectionate feelings. On a subsequent visit, the teacher talked of Ted, the first child, and of Alice, the microcephalic girl, and how much easier she was with them and they with her. She described the evolution of her firm attitude toward hostile, aggressive, destructive behavior that was less tinged with guilt as she felt both less sorry for these severely handicapped youngsters and less helpless about assessing their capabilities and expecting them to behave in ways more compatible with living with others. She was also beginning to expect them to learn what they could in her setting.

As teachers of the retarded feel less guilty about their own reactions toward these youngsters and are able to expect more adaptive behavior from the child, they begin to feel greater satisfaction in their teaching. They see more progress and are able to assess more realistically the behavior changes and amount of subject-matter learning that occurs. One teacher described her enthusiastic delight as one youngster began to call the other children by name and to ask for things instead of his previously assaultive grabbing and calling everyone "hey you." Or, in another instance, it was clear that a twelve-year-old girl finally understood the concepts of one and more than one instead of rote counting without comprehension. She was able to indicate the difference between herself as one and the rest of the class as many. The time, energy, and ingenuity required to help this child make such a distinction were enormous, but the teacher's glowing face showed plainly that it had been worthwhile. It became clear that the rewards were at hand for teachers, providing that obstacles in the form of exaggerated self-expectations and guilt and helplessness about working with such difficult and often not very likable children could be overcome. As teachers began to scale down their self-expectations about how much, by magic or hard work, they "should" be able to accomplish with each child, they found that they made more progress with most children.

## TEACHERS' WORK WITH PARENTS

In addition to the difficulties in working with retarded children who present a variety of severe behavior and learning problems, the teacher is burdened also by parental pressures. It became clear in consultation with the teachers of the classes for the retarded and with the director of the program that the more parental pressure, the more emotionally disturbed was the child concerned. With rare exceptions, teachers found these pressures unbearable and became angry with parents who demanded so much, and often seemed not to want to do very much themselves. The implicit demand was, cure my child of his deficiency—you could if you only wanted to. The appeal to the omnipotence of the teacher was difficult to resist initially by many teachers. When few and miniscule changes did occur, they felt both guilty and angry at the parents' continued demand for miracles. For some teachers, dealing with the parents became a greater burden than teaching the children.

As we discussed particular children's parents, certain patterns emerged that increased our understanding of the parents' problems and helped us to plan ways of understanding and reacting to the parents' demands, so that they became less of a burden. We began to recognize that each demand also carried an implicit request for help with the parents' feelings about the child and often, also, a request for help in dealing with the child's behavior at home.

In many instances, the family's life is centered around the retarded child because of the parents' acute disappointment that the child cannot fulfill their own hopes and ambitions. They may feel such anger at the child and need to blame someone or something for the retardation that often they cannot face the reality of the situation. Parents frequently feel guilty about the anger they feel about and toward such a child, so that they are not able to set limits for unacceptable behavior. Often parents find that these feelings make it difficult for them to spend much time with the child, helping him learn what he can. Many parents express their disappointment and anger with every physician, psychiatrist, or psychologist who confirms the diagnosis of retardation and holds out little hope for much change. Each time such a diagnosis and prognostic statement is made, it may be felt as a statement that something is also terribly wrong with the parents who produce a defective child. The guilt, anger, and feelings of being no good or biologically inferior as the parents of a defective child usually are not dealt with by professional persons who diagnose and recommend treatment or placement, so that these families keep hunting for someone who will give them hope or promise of a cure. The teacher is, therefore, often vested with the last futile hope. Perhaps education has some magic to change their child into a normal boy or girl. Unless teachers understand the turmoil, unhappiness, disappointment, and self-blame of these parents, they either hold out false hopes, fearing to disappoint the crushed parents, or may be hostile and brutal in giving "factual" information about the limits of educational efforts, angering the parents further.

A variant of this pattern occurs in families where tensions between parents were great before the birth of a retarded child. The presence of the child aggravates the parental conflicts to such a degree that only the retarded child may hold them together in a common cause. These parents unite around the child in the face of the outside world, but at home the child's upbringing and care may become the vehicle for their acute conflicts. The child in need of parental control, steadiness, clear delineation of limits, and other parameters important for living in society, is confused by the conflicting attitudes, violent emotions, and unpredictable behavior of his parents and, thus, becomes violent, unpredictable, uncontrolled, and rarely learns self-care or what is expected of him in social situations. His retardation and the limitations it places on him are frustrating enough. Additional problems are created when unrealistic expectations are imposed on the child by his conflicted parents, who may alternately expect nothing in the way of adaptive social behavior, learning, self-care, and so forth, and then suddenly expect or demand that the child learn something quite difficult. The anger and acute disappointment expressed by parents who both demand more and expect less than the child can do perplex the child and add to his unbridled, impulsive behavior. The child soon learns that hostile, destructive behavior produces attention, concern, and often guilty oversolicitous efforts to placate the child in a tantrum. The parents, in acute conflict with each other, often try to force the teacher to solve their problems by insisting that the teacher assume responsibility for the emotional as well as for the learning problems of their child. They appear helpless, unable to do anything with the child, and often may say that the teacher is their last hope, as if their childlike helplessness and faith in the omnipotence of the teacher must result in their being helped and their child cured.

Parents of the dysplastic child often need to protect themselves against their own distaste at his appearance, the easily understood death wishes that, if realized, would relieve them of the burden of the child, and of anger at the fate that burdened them so. Their guilt about these feelings makes them watchful that no one else express the revulsion that they may feel. They are extremely defensive about their child and often minimize the child's incapacities to others and paint an unrealistically bright picture of their child's abilities. They may become hostile if it is pointed out to them that these attributes are unreal and nonexistent when the realities of the child's actual capacities and attainments are talked about. The parents who need such defenses rarely are satisfied with the best efforts of the teacher, in contrast to parents who have been able to accept their own feelings and the realities of the child's retardation. Parents who have made their peace with their own feelings usually have tried to help their child to attain social attitudes and behavior within his capacities, and they are delighted with the progress shown in school.

One of the most distressing experiences for teachers of the retarded occurs when they have helped the child to increase his learning skills, only to find that the parents, mostly mothers, are furious that the teacher could accomplish something that they could not. In these instances, it becomes clear that the child is involved in some of the parents' neurotic conflicts and that the teacher is damned whether she succeeds or fails.

It must be clear that—since for all of us our children serve as extensions of ourselves, at least into posterity if not as living realizations of our unrealized desires and ambitions—the parents of the retarded child have a realistically difficult burden with which few professional people help them.

## METHOD OF HELPING PARENTS OF THE RETARDED

In the face of the aforementioned serious problems confronting the teacher, how can she be helped to do some of the job not undertaken by other professionals with parents? One of the areas discussed repeatedly by teachers with me was how one handles the pressures and expectations of parents so that the teacher's efforts will relieve them of this burden. We discussed the need we all have to relieve someone of his anxieties about problems by promising something we know cannot be fulfilled. We talked also about our own reactions in childhood to such promises by our parents, the promise to buy something one desperately wanted when there was no money available, the promise to make whole or replace a broken object, to patch up a disrupted relationship. All of us have experienced the relief that the parent has taken the problem off our shoulders and will deal with it in some unknown adult way. However, we soon realize that omnipotence is not there—that often the promises are made, not with the intent of fulfilling them, but to placate us. We then feel disillusioned, bitter, and let down. We feel that it would have been better if the promises were not made, and, finally, we learn not to make unrealizable requests, partly to avoid our own hurt and disappointment, but also to avoid causing our parents to need to dissemble, tell us untruths, and feel discomfort and loss of face and stature when they cannot make good their promises.

Similarly, the parents of retarded children who plead for or demand promises of major changes in their child usually know that any such promises are unrealistic. They may be cheered momentarily by the implication that omnipotent help is available, but reality soon reasserts itself, and they feel angry at being deceived, even though they forced the deception. Further, having been promised the moon, they are not content or pleased with the small changes that are possible and that do occur.

Out of our discussion we evolved a method in which the teacher made no promises, no matter what the pressures, before getting to know the child. She made an appointment to see all new parents four to six weeks after the child's entry into the class. At that time the teacher had made some assessment of the child's present functioning and had a few ideas about potential capacities and where she was going to try initially to focus her work. Also, because of her classroom experience, she was able to ask intelligent questions about the child's integration in the home, the kinds of expectations the family had for the child, and how they handled certain problems that might be helpful to the teacher in the classroom. She would seek also to obtain the help of the mother, particularly in understanding the meaning of certain kinds of behavior and how it had evolved. Thus, the teacher tried to engage the parents in a joint venture, as collaborators. She indicated in a variety of ways her need for the parents' help and for information about the way the classroom affected the child at home. The teacher also stressed the need for the delineation of small, discrete, and attainable goals in her work with the child so that the youngster could experience success and the pleasure that came with it.

In some instances, the recurring pressures and demands from parents required repeated meetings in which the same kind of material was discussed over and over until the parents finally understood from the teacher's concerned and firm attitudes that she could work only toward realistic goals and hoped for the parents' collaboration in this. During these sessions with parents, the value of ventilation of parental hostility became evident. Those teachers who were able to listen to the parents' anger toward all medical authorities, to bear up under the apparent attacks on them, to express sympathetic understanding of the problems, and still return to a discussion of the job to be done, found that after a period these parents were able to listen more and to talk with less anger. Parents finally were able to recognize the value of the teacher's efforts with their child and to consider what they might do at home to complement the school experience.

Many of the disturbing behavior problems in the classroom were problems at home also. Parents whose disappointment, hurt, anger, and guilt made it difficult for them to be firm and set clear limits with their child were helpless to be firm and set limits now. They had no such previous experience with this youngster, and every abortive effort ended when the child's temper tantrum aroused anxiety in them, so that they resorted to the old methods of placation and giving in. It was thus reassuring to parents to hear that the teacher had similar difficulties, and that only persistence and living through the tantrums to a different end, that is, the adults' firm insistence that the child behave or do what he needed to do, would set the pattern for gradual reduction of tantrums and greater social adaptability at home and in school.

Many parents felt terribly angry that no one would share or help them with their overwhelming burden of caring for a severely retarded child. Thus, when the teacher could make clear her willingness to do her part, parents felt less abandoned and seemed more willing to understand their child's limitations and also his potential for better functioning. Parents then began to see themselves as part of a collaborative effort and discussed and examined more frankly their moments of discouragement and impasse in their daily life with their child. After such open discussion of problems, parents seemed better able to consider suggestions for dealing with their difficulties, and their efforts often met with some success. Also, they gradually expected fewer miracles from the teacher.

One of the most rewarding experiences reported by teachers of the retarded occurred when they helped parents to recognize the unrealized potential of the child and to engage in collaborative efforts to expect more of the child in areas in which he could be effective, rather than previous unrealistic expectations often coupled with no real effort to help the child to do what he could. One seriously explosive twelve-year-old mongoloid girl responded to the united efforts of teacher and parents so that after one and one-half years she was able to set the table, wash dishes, serve food, do the laundry, and mop the floors. Her personal grooming also improved so much that the parents were less ashamed of her. Her help with the household tasks, which relieved the mother of many onerous jobs, resulted in much praise and expressed satisfaction from the teacher and mother. Subsequently, her explosive outbursts became relatively rare. In social situations at home, she rarely needed to create a fuss to gain attention and concern from adults. The teacher's home visit revealed the extent to which this girl had become an asset to the household and how much they depended on her to keep the home running smoothly. The father said both he and the mother felt ten years younger and were able to attend to their other child with less guilt and few tantrums from their retarded daughter.

For the parents of the dysplastic, unlovely, poorly coordinated, and severely retarded child, the teacher's willingness to work with the child, and, especially, her lack of defensive need to prove she likes the child or to reassure the parents about the child's appearance, since they cannot be so reassured, seems to be helpful. One disturbed mother, who was hostile to the teacher and defensive about her hydrocephalic youngster, was greatly reassured by the teacher's matter-of-fact and nondefensive assessment of what this boy could learn. Later this mother was able to talk about her acute embarrassment when in public places with the boy, her hatred toward people who stared at him, and finally how repulsive she found him in comparison with her handsome other children. She found herself unable to be around him very much, so that he clung to her desperately when she was around. When she noted the expectations the teacher had of the boy and that he responded to such expectations with greater effort toward self-care and less clinging, she began to expect more of him at home and found him more tolerable.

The sequence of reduced self-expectations by the teacher—clear evaluation of the child's present functioning, with some planning for the next step to be taken; understanding of parental demands and hostility without giving way to them; presenting clearly the teacher's aims with the child and the need for close collaboration with the parents; repeated spelling-out of these points and indicating how the teacher's fair firmness over a period of time helped the retarded child to function better—began to reduce the magnitude of the parental problems to the teacher.

In consultation with teachers of the mentally retarded, the two large areas that we needed to work on continuously were the ways in which teachers get satisfaction in their work and manage to live with the disturbed and disturbing behavior of both their students and the parents. As we helped teachers to get a sense of accomplishment from every aspect of change in the child's behavior and even minute increments of learning, they were able to assess more accurately the present functioning and potential of their students. As they reduced their own self-expectations of being able to effect major shifts in their students' capacities, they also began to attend more to the behavior and adaptive aspects of the child's functioning that retarded his learning. They became more attuned to the possible meaning and requests implied in the child's disruptive, isolating, or destructive behavior. Teachers became better able to handle the unexpressed or distorted expression of the child's needs by finding more suitable means of gratification, sensual pleasure, and, finally, pleasure in learning, pleasing someone else, and becoming a more meaningful person to both the teacher and the group.

The parents' demands, hostility, unreal assessment of their child, and their charged feelings were dealt with by offering time to discuss their child, by listening with understanding to their angry complaints and demands, and by presenting realistic assessment of present functioning and a hopeful but realistic assessment of what could be done in the next step toward learning and social adaptation in school and at home.

Many disturbed parents began to identify with the teachers' attitudes toward their child, especially the teachers' firmness, their clear expectations in areas in which the child could be successful, and their prompt reward of success by personal warmth and approval. In time, teachers learned to sit through the initial hostile attacks and demands, bolstered by their knowledge that the understanding and acceptance of these feelings often formed the groundwork for teacher–parent collaboration in the service of the child, the family, and the school.

## REFERENCES

ALICE V. ANDERSON, "Orienting Parents to a Clinic for the Retarded," *Children,* IX (1962), 178–182.

CLEMENS E. BENDA, N. D. SQUIRE, JOHN OGONIK, and ROBERT WISE, "Personality Factors in Mild Mental Retardation. Part 1. Family Backgrounds and Sociocultural Patterns," *American Journal of Mental Deficiency,* LXVIII (1963), 24–40.

IRVING N. BERLIN, "Teachers' Self Expectations: How Realistic Are They," *The School Review,* Summer (1958), pp. 134–143.

IRVING N. BERLIN, "Mental Health Consultation in Schools as a Means of Communicating Mental Health Principles," *Journal of the American Academy of Child Psychiatry,* I (1962), 671–679.

HERBERT G. BIRCH, *Brain Damage in Children* (New York: William & Wilkins, 1964).

LAURA DITTMAN, "Home Training for Retarded Children," *Children,* IV (1957), 89–94.

LEON EISENBERG, "Psychiatric Implications of Brain Damage in Children," *Psychiatric Quarterly,* XXXI (1957), 72–92.

LEO KANNER, "Parents' Feelings about Retarded Children," *American Journal of Mental Deficiency,* LVII (1953), 375–383.

SAMUEL A. KIRK, *Early Education of the Mentally Retarded* (Urbana, Illinois: University of Illinois Press, 1958).

HILDA KNOBLOCH and BENJAMIN PASAMANICK, "Mental Subnormality," *New England Journal of Medicine,* CCLXVI (1962), 1045–1051, 1092–1097, 1155–1161.

J. G. LYLE, "Some Factors Affecting the Speech Development of Imbecile Children in an Institution," *Journal of Child Psychology & Psychiatry and Allied Disciplines,* I (1960), 121–129.

ARTHUR MANDELBAUM and MARY ELLA WHEELER, "The Meaning of a Defective Child to Parents," *Social Casework,* XLI (1960), 360–367.

WILLIAM A. OGLE, "Psychotherapeutic Treatment in Mental Deficiency. Report of a Case," *Canadian Psychiatric Association Journal,* VIII (1963), 307–315.

IRVING PHILIPS, "Common Misconceptions Concerning Mental Retardation," in Irving Berlin and Stanislaus A. Szurek (Eds.), *Mental Retardation and Psychophysiological Disorders,* Child Psychiatry Series Volume 3 (Palo Alto, California: Science and Behavior, in press).

IRVING PHILIPS, MARY JEFFRESS, EHUD KOCH, and MALETA J. BOATMAN, "The Application of Psychiatric Clinic Services for the Retarded Child and His Family," *Journal of the American Academy of Child Psychiatry,* I (1962), 297–313.

S. L. SHEIMO, "Problems Encountered in Dealing with Handicapped and Emotionally Disturbed Children," *American Journal of Occupational Therapy,* III (1949), 303–310.

STANSILAUS A. SZUREK, "Concerning the Sexual Disorders of Parents and Their Children," *Journal of Nervous and Mental Disease,* CXX (1954), 369–378.

STANISLAUS A. SZUREK, "Emotional Factors in the Use of Authority," in Ethel L. Ginsburg (Ed.), *Public Health Is People* (New York: Commonwealth Fund, 1950), pp. 206–225.

DAVID VAIL, "Mental Deficiency: Response to Milieu Therapy," *American Journal of Psychiatry,* CXIII (1956), 170–173.

THOMAS G. WEBESTER, "Problems of Emotional Development in Young Retarded Children," *American Journal of Psychiatry,* CXX (1963), 37–43.

# 18

# Vocational Rehabilitation and Mental Retardation

## MICHAEL M. GALAZAN

### REHABILITATION AND INITIAL DIAGNOSIS OF RETARDATION

A diagnosis of mental retardation often creates such a substantial barrier of negative associations for the diagnostician that it may severely limit the possibility of results from vocational rehabilitation for the patient. The advice and suggestions given by the physician or psychologist depend on his knowledge, beliefs, and attitudes. Many professionals view pessimistically the socio-economic potential of the moderately and severely retarded. Frequently, they consider the future of such persons to be hopeless and are not aware of the progress made in rehabilitation of the retarded in recent years. They also frequently are unaware of community resources available to assist them in evaluating the potential of the retarded child and in formulating a plan for his future based on present knowledge and resources.

Many educational programs are undertaken by parent groups and professional associations to acquaint professional disciplines with new concepts in the field of retardation. These focus on the potential of the retarded as indicated by results of vocational rehabilitation programs. If the benefits that vocational rehabilitation offers to the retarded are recognized at the time of initial planning for the retarded child, such planning must relate to evaluation of potentials that can be enhanced by training in the home, in the school, and through other community resources.

Once the initial assumption is made that the mentally retarded person can achieve a meaningful level of independence and self-support, factors to be evaluated include the ability of the family to care for the child, the effect on the other children in the family situation, and the resources available in the community to serve the child. These must be related to the final goal and weighed fairly. Thus, deficiencies and impaired functioning do not receive the major emphasis. It is essential that the physician, the primary resource for the family in the initial diagnosis of retardation, know of the vocational rehabilitation and social adjustment potentials of the retarded so that he may take these into consideration in helping the family to give the child the necessary opportunities for development.

## Preparation for Independence — A "Continuum"

Living in maximum independence, which is the goal for the retarded person, can be achieved only if it is approached through a continuum of preparation. During the preschool years, the establishment of self-care skills and responsibility are most critical. During the early school years, academic skills, individual and social responsibility, acceptable habit patterns, and effective incentives should receive major emphasis. Carefully structured patterns of rewards or reinforcements can contribute substantially to the strengthening of desirable personal habits and improved social relationships. During adolescence, prevocational orientation and experience, as well as continued academic instruction and habit-pattern training, including family participation, will improve the potential for independence. Community resources should be available to provide opportunities for the achievement of satisfactory social relationships.

Our value system for the middle class emphasizes grades in school, expensive cars, homes, and occupational roles in the professions and business. This may be discouraging for the retarded. College education as a major prerequisite for vocational success becomes the obvious symbol of his inevitable failure. The current anti-poverty program has found that there is minimal motivation to achieve independence among the economically deprived. The large proportion of the retarded who are educationally and socially deprived have little incentive to develop independent attitudes and habit patterns. Therefore, motivating the retarded person becomes extremely difficult. It can be done, however, if the value system that is built for him emphasizes achievable objectives. These should include independence, activities within his abilities, and social relationships that give him satisfaction and pleasure. The principal objective of his rehabilitation is to prepare him to develop his full potential to meet the responsibilities of community living, including employment. If that can be made a basic part of his value system so he can have a feeling of self-esteem, he will be motivated to work, to conform to rules of behavior, and to suffer the frustrations of learning new and difficult tasks. The lack of a realistic, motivating value system is often the cause of the failure of the retarded person to fulfill his potentialities.

## EARLY OVERPROTECTION AND ITS EFFECT ON VOCATIONAL REHABILITATION

Clinical practice in the field of vocational rehabilitation of the mentally retarded has indicated that the initial parental attitude of overprotection established during the diagnostic process and early period of development seriously handicaps the child's future development of independence and self-support. Overprotection presents a most difficult problem in work with the retarded. The concept that the retarded are always children and never adults is reflected in the vocabulary referring to the retarded. The national organization working with the retarded is called the National Association for Retarded Children. Local groups frequently follow the same pattern, and professional and lay speakers who discuss retarded adolescents and adults often refer to them as children.

In the face of such attitudes, even in the most informed lay and professional groups, it is difficult to establish the necessary parental attitudes that will encourage the development of independence and responsibility. Overcoming this major handicap arising from his early experience in the home, in the community, and in school is an almost hopeless task for the retarded person. The normal child "fights" his parents for opportunities to establish his independence. The support that he receives from his peers gives him the strength to break the parents' restraints on his freedom to enter the danger-laden world of the adult. The first independent crossing of the street, the first independent trip on public transportation, the first independent use of the car, all of these anxiety-ridden experiences that present both parent and child with major challenges must be available to the retarded as well as the normal. In the struggle for independence, the retarded child gets no help from his peers. In most instances, the retarded have little relationship with each other, except in the school setting, and therefore are of little help to each other in their social adjustment. The peer group is frequently a handicap because any child who tends to move in the direction of more independence will encourage envy, jealousy, and a feeling of hostility from parents of other retarded children.

Parents of retarded children face an almost impossible task in helping their children achieve independence. Parents of normal children draw on the experiences of their own parents, their friends, and neighbors. Parents of retarded children have no such guides or support to give them the security to allow their retarded children to assume the risks that are inherent in assuming responsibilities. Responsibilities around the home, such as running errands and doing household chores, contribute substantially to the development of normal children. They are even more critical in the development of the retarded child. These responsibilities become important training opportunities to establish the basis for future programming in the field of vocational rehabilitation. They are the initial vocational training programs.

The school itself must overcome a protective attitude toward the retarded child and provide activities requiring increasing independence and responsibility. School programs for the retarded are frequently in centrally located areas far from the homes of the retarded children. Travel, which is one of the most important areas of independent activity, is arranged in a manner that provides the retarded child with a continuing crutch, not withdrawn even when he becomes an adolescent or an adult. School systems now are extending programs for the retarded to the age of twenty-one and still are transporting these retarded adults by bus. Mobility-training, using techniques developed for the blind, as well as some developed specifically for training of the retarded, is needed. Broader programs are required to develop communication skills that will make the retarded child more effective in his relationships with others. He needs to be helped to develop internal control, self-competition, self-criticism, self-motivation, and to have experiences in coping with failure. Other experiences, such as errands, homework, responsibilities around the school area, and shop work, are part of the learning opportunities of our normal adolescents, but not usually of the retarded.

Certainly there are risks involved in allowing a retarded child to assume such responsibilities, but such risks exist for the normal child as well. They must be faced with the full understanding that no child can become an independent adult without facing dangers during the growth process. Since the schools are institutions that cannot pioneer in the areas where danger exists without parental approval, the schools will depend, to a great extent, on the physician to support them so that these risks may be taken. The physician ought to be as much concerned about the lack of development and use of the psychologic mechanisms on which the retarded adult will depend as an independent, self-supporting adult, as he is about the care of the physical organism. If a child were not allowed to walk because there was danger that he might fall, or not be allowed to climb or perform other normal physical activities, the physician would be concerned; if a child is not allowed to assume normal responsibilities for developing independence and responsibility, so that he will lack these patterns of behavior on which his future functioning as an independent adult depends, the professional must be even more concerned.

## PARENTS AND VOCATIONAL REHABILITATION

The normal dependency of the infant is increased and prolonged in the retarded infant by his disability. The parents' capacity to understand and meet his needs is reduced appreciably by anxiety and frustration stemming from the child's retardation. This stress creates other family problems that represent additional restrictions on parental ability to meet the basic nurture and developmental needs of the retarded child. The anxiety of the parent and his inadequacies in helping his child to meet daily difficulties diminish the retarded child's most important source of support when he reaches adolescence and adulthood. The parents have expended so much of their energy in the care of the child during his earlier years that they are satisfied, even relieved, to let the school or the workshop assume complete responsibility. When they do cooperate, they may establish standards and goals that are far beyond the potential of their child. Their concern with social status interferes with the achievement of a realistic vocational goal by the retarded adolescent. The extreme difficulty in working with parents, the demands that they make on the profession, their distrust and hostility, and the complicated problems they present frequently interfere with adequate programming for them. The difficulty in motivating parents, especially those in the lower economic groups, to participate in a program presents additional difficulties. As a result, substituting the counselor for the parent is a common practice. The frequent decision to eliminate parents from an active role has serious consequences for the final outcome of the rehabilitation process.

Although in vocational programming for the normal adolescent and adult, participation of the parent is extremely helpful, it is vital for the retarded. The initial part-time job and the final placement on a job with other workers who are normal create great stress, anxiety, and many frustrations. At adolescence and young adulthood, the retarded need their parents' help in moving out of the sheltered environment of the home and the special school into the real world of work and relationships with nonretarded adults. The importance of the parents in the social adjustment of the retarded person and the final attainment of the vocational rehabilitation objective is recognized in the literature. It rarely is emphasized in practice. Methods, means, techniques, and incentives must be found that will allow greater involvement of the parents. A research and demonstration program undertaken by the United Association for Retarded Children, Inc., and the Jewish Vocational Service of Milwaukee is experimenting with all types of incentives, including prizes and special rewards. Parents' participation is so vital that any effort or any incentive that achieves that goal is justified.

## THE PREVOCATIONAL PROGRAM

In the development of an adequate rehabilitation program, the re-tarded youngster should begin to be exposed to prevocational training at about the same age as the normal youngster, about fourteen years of age. He should have a complete vocational assessment, including testing and counseling, pre-employment physical examination, and an opportunity to test himself in many types of vocational activities. Through this assessment process, it will be possible to develop an exploratory prevocational program that will not allow the vocational development to be structured on the basis of preconceptions of the teacher, vocational worker, or parent. Because the retarded child has had so little opportunity to explore his capabilities, this type of prevocational program is extremely important. It offers the retarded increased opportunity for development of independence. Concurrently, it provides an opportunity for parents to evaluate the risks involved, to expe-rience the initial anxiety with regard to such risks, and to handle these anxieties. Without such prevocational programs, the retarded adolescent is kept a dependent child with minimal opportunities for developing the pat-terns of independent behavior available to the normal child.

In order to strengthen prevocational programming, the Vocational Rehabilitation Administration has encouraged the development of coopera-tive programs between the public school, the vocational rehabilitation agen-cies, and the sheltered workshops. These programs are based on a research and demonstration program developed by the Jewish Vocational Service of Milwaukee in cooperation with the United Association for Retarded Chil-dren, Inc. in Milwaukee.

This program consists of half-day academic work in public school and half-day work experience in the sheltered workshop for each retarded ado-lescent, beginning at the age of fifteen. Although the original program in-cluded no one below the age of fifteen, many retarded young people of fourteen could benefit from a program of this type. These retarded young people receive credit for their work experience and may continue in the joint academic–work experience program until they have achieved their maximum academic potential. This type of school–work program includes a close working relationship between the public-school teacher and the workshop staff so that the academic program may be made meaningful in terms of the retarded adolescent's development in the work program. Em-phasis on special academic training, attitudes, patterns of behavior, or rela-tionships with coworkers and supervisors may receive the attention of both the school and the workshop to assure maximum progress. The school cur-riculum, which is changing continuously in order to meet more effectively the needs of the retarded, is tailored to the needs of each student on the basis of the maximum amount of information available about his potential and his educational needs for vocational adjustment.

Other types of specialized programs should be included in the prevocational development of the retarded. These include prevocational orientation to acquaint them with work opportunities in the community and visits to industrial plants and business organizations as well as to government agencies that may offer work opportunities.

## Vocational Adjustment, Evaluation, and Training

The line between the prevocational and the vocational development of the retarded adolescent is indistinct and cannot be specifically stated in terms of age. Some school systems that previously discontinued the education of the retarded at sixteen years of age now are keeping the students until they are twenty-one. One must be aware, however, that when the retarded young adult has been exposed to a prevocational program, he will have developed a large part of his potential for vocational adjustment. Without it, he leaves school as a child, with minimal strength to undertake the responsibilities of independent adulthood. There is no way to evaluate how much potential has been lost.

In order to evaluate thoroughly the present development of the retarded youngster and his potential for the future, the rehabilitation agency, cooperating with the school, usually makes a complete assessment, including medical, social, psychologic, vocational, and educational factors. The parents and the rehabilitation counselor, and the child himself, when feasible, jointly develop a plan of training that is best suited to his needs and capacities.

Many resources eliminate retarded persons from their programs because they claim that the retarded cannot achieve the objective for which the particular program has been established. The State Division of Vocational Rehabilitation, whose aim it is to prepare the retarded for productive employment, eliminates many because they do not appear capable of industrial or sheltered employment after training. It is the responsibility of the physician to join with other professional groups in the community to point out that the capacities of the retarded who have received minimal training cannot be measured adequately. A retarded person must be given an opportunity to participate in rehabilitation programs before such measurement is undertaken. This conclusion is based on the following assumptions: first, that maximal development has not taken place without such training and exposure, and second, that the protective attitudes of the parents, the schools, and all other social resources in the community have handicapped the retarded person additionally, so that his measurable potential for vocational rehabilitation has been lessened rather than increased.

For those who have not had the benefit of prevocational training, maximum resources, including State Vocational Rehabilitation agencies, workshops, and family counseling services, should be available to develop whatever potential is still intact, so that they can achieve maximum independence despite the delay in the initiation of adequate vocational rehabilitation and training.

## Types of Training

The vocational-rehabilitation training programs available to the retarded young adult who has left school include training programs in sheltered workshops and on-the-job training facilities, as well as training programs in vocational schools. Manpower-development training programs of the Department of Labor and anti-poverty training programs also include the retarded.

Various types of training are utilized to develop the retarded adult's potentials for vocational adjustment. For the minimally retarded adult, training in specific skills, such as simple machine operation in factory or office, and in maintenance and service occupations, has proved extremely effective. This type of training has been given in vocational schools, public schools, and sheltered workshops. Occupations for which the retarded have been trained are discussed in several studies. For the moderately and severely retarded person, training in a specific skill has been found to be less important than training in job habits and work behavior, for example, speed, grooming, work quality, and interpersonal relationships with fellow workers and supervisors. This type of training has taken place in work settings in sheltered workshops or work-adjustment centers. In these centers, actual work is done and, in the process of working, the retarded are taught the work habits needed in business and industry.

Most training programs are of limited duration, ranging from six weeks in some programs under the Manpower Development Program of the United States Department of Labor to a limited number lasting nine months in sheltered workshops. The length of the training programs available to the retarded is extremely significant since it is known that the more severe the retardation, the slower the absorption of training concepts. It is important to emphasize that the retarded need to be exposed to the maximum amount of training in order to become independent. This is especially true for those who have not had an adequate prevocational program. State Departments of Vocational Rehabilitation, whose funds are extremely limited, are forced to restrict the length of the training program. They frequently discontinue training too early, so that no meaningful result is achieved and the retarded person returns to his home and loses the benefit of the investment that has been made. Federal funds are necessary in order to extend the period of training for the retarded so that a greater number may become both vocationally and socially independent. A federal program of increased support for an extended period of training for the retarded is now under consideration.

The severely retarded who cannot work a full day because of a limited attention span, productivity, or lack of behavior control, have training programs available to them in social adjustment and activity centers. Here they are helped to develop habits and patterns of behavior that make it possible for them to become employees in sheltered workshops and thereby to contribute partially to their own self-support and to achieve greater independence.

## PLACEMENT

After training, the retarded adult must be helped to obtain work. This requires intensive assistance in getting a job, not just exposing him to employment opportunities. The more severely handicapped find communication difficult and do not indicate their true work potential to prospective employers. The employer, too, suffers from the overprotective attitude of the community and needs reassurance that the retarded worker has as much right to face minimal danger of a job in his plant as the normal worker. After trained retarded workers are helped to obtain employment, they are found to be capable of carrying out the responsibilities of jobs and impressing employers with skills and attitudes that they were not able to verbalize when seeking employment.

The moderately retarded individual frequently needs individualized placement services; the severely retarded always do. The lack of individualized placement services results in the retarded worker's not being able to utilize the training he has been given. He returns to his home, remains inactive, and loses all of the benefit derived from the training program. Many who had previously been considered unemployable have been trained for employment and have found jobs. Although most jobs are in maintenance and service occupations, jobs in all types of industries and business now are open to the retarded. A new program of employing such workers in federal civil-service jobs has opened increased opportunities for trained retarded individuals.

## Keeping a Job

The initial phase—the first day, first week, first month—of adjustment on the job is a critical period. The adjustments to be made are frequently both difficult and threatening. The frustrations faced in relating to normal workers, as well as the traumatic experiences that he may encounter, frequently result in the retarded worker's losing the job after a substantial investment made in training and placement. At the present, there are limited resources available to help during the initial period on the job. Most training and placement services assume that once the retarded worker has been placed on a job, his need for continuing help is minimal. They indicate their availability for help, but do not actively seek to offer the help so vitally needed. On the other hand, if the retarded individual is having serious difficulties, he hesitates to seek help because he feels he should be able to succeed independently, and is reluctant to admit his difficulties. His old pattern of failure appears to be re-establishing itself and he reacts by withdrawing from the situation.

At this critical time there should be the greatest investment in service and resources in order to assure his continuing successful adjustment. Because of the failure of our agencies to provide such resources, in a large majority of instances the retarded worker does not keep his job and does not seek additional help. Follow-up services from rehabilitation agencies must be available to assist in making the initial adjustment. The parent is an important resource at this point.

## The Sheltered Workshop — Relationship of Training and Sheltered Work

When placement in private industry is not practical or feasible, it is important that the retarded person have an opportunity to work in a sheltered workshop. Sheltered workshops have been established in increasing numbers because of the recognition by communities that this is the most constructive method of serving severely retarded persons. It gives them a feeling of self-worth and contribution to the community and is the most economical method of providing the care and supervision required. Many states have established methods of financing such sheltered workshops to assist private philanthropic groups in developing programs. The Vocational Rehabilitation Administration has encouraged the development of such resources and has made funds available for building and staffing. Interest in this field has given rise to an increasing literature describing the administration and programs of sheltered workshops for the retarded.

The importance of sheltered workshops for the retarded cannot be

overemphasized. As more and more severely retarded are given an opportunity to train for independence, a significantly high proportion of them will
be unable to move into industrial jobs and will need sheltered-workshop
opportunities. Even the current limited training opportunities for the retarded are creating a need for sheltered workshops that cannot be met. It is
vitally necessary to correlate training opportunities and sheltered-workshop
opportunities so that we are not training the retarded, only to shatter their
hope for work because no opportunity is available to utilize their training.

## RECREATION AND SOCIAL ADJUSTMENT

Although work is the major focus of the vocational rehabilitation
process, recreation and social adjustment are extremely important aspects
of adjustment for the retarded. Many retarded who have achieved a level of
skill that makes it possible for them to find employment fail because they
are unable to make a social adjustment.

During his early development, the retarded child has increasingly limited opportunities to make friends. Usually he has been in a neighborhood
with normal children who have rejected or made fun of him. He has had
negative experiences that have seriously affected his relationships with
others. Because retarded adults frequently are thought of as children, recreational activities often are set at a child's level, without recognition of adult
needs. It is important to emphasize the establishment of adult recreational
activities. It is essential not to overlook the development of social adjustment and skills that make it possible for the retarded to establish interpersonal relationships with others of similar interests.

In order to develop the retarded adult's social adjustment opportunities, it is necessary to provide him with the normal experience of making a
friend. In too many instances, social-adjustment programs have been primarily recreational, so oriented that the retarded person related more to the
activity than to the people involved. He may, therefore, have learned a skill
such as bowling or baseball, but not learned how to relate to others in a
continuing and meaningful way. Frequently, as one observes the participation of such a person in a recreational or social situation, one sees him
functioning as an isolated individual without interaction with others in the
group. Emphasis in social-adjustment programs must, therefore, be placed
on the development of interpersonal relationships, starting with an individual relationship and expanding to include relationships in a group setting.
There should be opportunities to make such relationships and encouragement to continue them, so that the retarded do not live as isolates in the
community. Parents can help in this type of training and should be encouraged and given the information and help that will make it possible for them
to participate. The retarded also must be taught to use community re-

sources and facilities at their own levels of understanding and participation.

For those who cannot work even in a sheltered workshop, social activity and interpersonal relationships on whatever level possible become the major emphasis of programming. Work activities as well as recreational activities can be included in such programs, but the major emphasis should be on increasingly effective social-adjustment skills to lessen dependence on families and to create the least amount of tension in the home and in the community.

With proper use of resources in vocational rehabilitation, recreation, and social adjustment, the life of the retarded can become meaningful, and the parents of retarded adults will be better able to carry the responsibility of keeping them at home and continuing to be responsible for them without having family adjustment and personal health affected.

## COMMUNITY EDUCATION

In order to effect the goals of vocational rehabilitation and social adjustment, it is necessary that the community be prepared to offer the retarded the opportunity to utilize the skills they develop. Although extended programs of community education have been undertaken by parent associations, the medical profession, the teaching profession, and the government, the most effective method of education is still minimally available. The retarded still are segregated and isolated in the community so that most children and adults have little opportunity to relate to a retarded individual, except as a "freak." It is not unusual today for adolescents in a normal public-school system to be frightened of the retarded, or for workers in industry to treat them as "dummies." This situation affects a large proportion of the moderately and all of the severely retarded.

To achieve real understanding of the retarded in our communities, we should attempt to overcome the handicaps arising from segregation. Although it may be necessary to segregate the retarded in most subject areas in school, it should be possible to desegregate them for social activities, games, and some subject areas where students of normal intelligence could learn to understand them and relate to them. During prevocational programs for the retarded, efforts should be made to involve them in vocational programs with individuals of normal intelligence, as well as in programs in the community that will expose them to relationships with people of normal intelligence. In the training programs, it will be necessary to expose workers in industry to the retarded so that when placement is made, they are no longer strange individuals who create feelings of fear and rejection. Although European communities have established special communities for the retarded, this type of segregation is not accepted in the American philosophy and there is a need for a constructive program to eliminate segregation.

SUMMARY

Effective knowledge about rehabilitation and the potential of the retarded is extremely important to the physician or the professional who
initially makes the diagnosis. The future that he envisions for the retarded
child colors his development of a plan and sets the limits of the opportunities
for the retarded child to develop his potential. Preparation for living with
maximum independence can be achieved only if all aspects of the retarded
child's development receive proportionate and appropriate attention. Early
overprotection is a great handicap to vocational rehabilitation; it is necessary to expose the retarded to the normal dangers inherent in learning to be
independent and responsible.

Parents must support the retarded child, adolescent, and adult in his
development toward independence. They must be motivated and given support to help the child face the danger of independent activity. They must be
helped also to achieve the necessary skills and the knowledge so that when
the retarded child needs help, they are willing and able to give it.

The initial evaluation of the retarded child's potential for prevocational and vocational training must make special learning opportunities
available to him and not deny these because he is considered unemployable.
He needs a prevocational program that will help him to develop his capacity for work and to achieve a value system that will make him want to work
and to tolerate the frustrations that he must face. Vocational rehabilitation
training helps him to develop work habits, attitudes, and sometimes skills as
necessary preparation for a job in the community. Training resources must
allow him sufficient time to develop fully his potential. Once he is trained,
he must be helped to find a job through a good placement program and
to maintain that job through an adequate job maintenance program.

Community education must include exposing the community to frequent contact with the retarded. Concurrently, the retarded must be helped
to achieve a good social adjustment so that they are not isolated in the
community, but make friends and are able to continue warm and ongoing
human relationships. These are the ordinary satisfactions that every human
being must have and that the retarded deserve in their pursuit of happiness.

REFERENCES

ANNA G. BASS, JUDITH G. STANN, and BENJAMIN WACHS, "Guidance and Place-
    ment," *Occupational Education,* VIII (1951), 153–176.
ALLEN BOBROFF, "Economic Adjustment of 121 Adults, Formerly Students in
    Classes for Mental Retardates," *American Journal of Mental Deficiency,*
    LX (1956), 525–535.

JULIUS S. COHEN, "Employer Attitudes toward Hiring Mentally Retarded Individuals," *American Journal of Mental Deficiency*, LXVII (1963), 705–713.

NATHAN M. COHEN, compiler, *Vocational Training Directory of the United States* (3rd ed.; Arlington, Virginia: Potomac Press, 1958).

SALVATORE G. DIMICHAEL, "Northeastern Institute on Clinical Services for the Retarded and Counseling of Parents," *Personnel Guidance Journal*, XXXV (1957), 454–456.

JACK W. FLEMING, "Understanding the Retarded Client," *Journal of Rehabilitation*, XXXIX (1963), 21, 62, 63.

WILLIAM A. FRAENKEL, *The Mentally Retarded and Their Vocational Rehabilitation—A Resource Handbook* (New York: National Association for Retarded Children, Inc., 1961).

ABRAHAM JACOBS, JOSEPH T. WEIGOLD, and MAX DUBROW, *The Sheltered Workshop: A Community Rehabilitation Resource for the Mentally Retarded* (New York: New York State Association for Retarded Children, Inc., 1962).

OLIVER P. KOLSTOE and ALBERT J. SHAFTER, "Employability Prediction for Mentally Retarded Adults: A Methodological Note," *American Journal of Mental Deficiency*, LXVI (1961), 287–289.

H. MICHAL-SMITH, "A Study of the Personal Characteristics Desirable for the Vocational Success of the Mentally Deficient," *American Journal of Mental Deficiency*, LV (1950), 139–143.

# 19

# The Mentally Retarded Adult
# in the Community

## ELIAS KATZ

This chapter will outline some basic considerations in program development for mentally retarded adults in the community. It is hoped that this may provide an approach to an admittedly serious and complex problem. Current heightened interest in the mentally retarded has focused largely on programs for retarded children and on the prevention of mental retardation, with little emphasis on the retarded adult. A growing concern for retarded adults—especially for those who live in the community—is manifested in various ways, for example, in the development of community rehabilitation workshops, recreational and residential programs for retarded adults. There are many gaps in these programs, and much remains to be done to provide necessary coordination.

Relatively little is available in the literature on the subject of program development for the adult retarded in the community. To be sure, much has appeared on program development for all mentally retarded persons, including adults, and some has been published on vocational rehabilitation of the retarded adult (Fraenkel, 1961). Perhaps it has been assumed that program development for *all* mentally retarded persons would provide programs for adults. In practice, however, programming for all the mentally retarded has focused on retarded children. Furthermore, vocational rehabilitation of the retarded adult can be extended in practice only so far, in attempts to meet the varied needs of retarded adults and their families. By and large, vocational rehabilitation services are not extended to more severely handicapped retarded clients, and certain services such as medical care, on-going subsistence, and job placement may not be available as a vocational rehabilitation service.

## DEFINITIONS

It is essential to define the "mentally retarded adult in the community," a process that will highlight some of the difficulties in this field. First, as to the "mentally retarded" part of the term, we accept the American Association on Mental Deficiency (AAMD) definition, "mental retardation refers to subaverage general functioning which originates during the developmental period and is associated with impairment in adaptive behavior" (Heber, 1959, p. 3). Unfortunately, there are problems in implementing this definition since there are no standardized methods as yet of sharply defining "adaptive behavior." One problem concerns the "borderline" level, which includes those with IQ 70–84 (Level I of AAMD definition) (Heber, 1961). Many adults with measured IQ scores below 84 hold jobs, marry, raise families, and seem to engage in normal adult pursuits without apparent need for special programs on their behalf. In terms of the AAMD definition of mental retardation, this chapter is concerned primarily with those retarded adults for whom special community programs are needed. Here, too, the concept of "visibility" of the adult retarded is involved. This has been aptly put:

> . . . (it is) general knowledge that the mentally retarded individual is less apparent in adult society. Whether it is the individual who is not apparent is as yet an unanswered question. It may be that a characteristic of a wholesome society is that the mentally retarded become more and more a part of the stream of normal living. On the other hand, it might be possible that such loss of identification is due to the fact that no specific services are available to which the mentally retarded can turn for help . . . (California Study Commission, 1965, p. 27).

In any case, we are here concerned with those retarded adults who require special services and programs to meet their needs, since there are many with the same measured intelligence who do not require or use these services.

To continue our definition of "mentally retarded adult in the community," for purposes of this report "adult" will include those who have passed the chronologic age of compulsory school attendance, which in most states is sixteen (or eighteen) years. In some states, such as California, special education has been mandatory for pupils classified as "educable mentally retarded" since 1947, and as "trainable mentally retarded" since 1963 (California Study Commission, 1965, p. 59). Although such a definition of "adult" has many inadequacies, it emphasizes that the program of special education in schools is available for the retarded during the period of childhood and youth and stops being available when most persons (except those going to college) leave school and enter productive employment, thus becoming "adult."

In this connection, a large percentage of mentally retarded students in high school and junior high school do not remain in school until the end of the period of compulsory attendance, being exempted, expelled, dropped out, or being given earlier "graduation." By the present definition, despite their need for special programs, persons below sixteen or eighteen years and not attending school would not be classified as "mentally retarded adults" since they technically are eligible for special education in the public schools and are therefore not considered in this chapter.

As for the mentally retarded adult *in the community,* this report differentiates them from those who are housed in the state hospitals for the retarded. According to California State Department of Mental Hygiene reports, in 1964 the total resident population of all ages in the state hospitals for the retarded was 12,648, and an additional 2,555 patients were outside the state-hospital setting. Similar statistics are reported from most states. Using relatively low-incidence percentages, the California Study Commission on Mental Retardation estimated that in California, with a population of approximately eighteen million, there were more than 175,000 mentally retarded adults over seventeen years of age. Over the years, some retarded adults have been placed in the community from the state hospitals; some who are in the hospital leave for community placement; and some will be committed to the hospital from the community. In the aggregate, it would seem that the institutionalized adult retarded population in California constitutes less than 2 per cent of the total number of retarded adults, the remainder living in the community (California Study Commission, 1965, p. 28). In this chapter, we will limit consideration to the institutionalized retarded adult, a topic deserving extensive treatment in its own right.

## NEEDS OF MENTALLY RETARDED ADULTS IN THE COMMUNITY

In planning for the retarded adult in the community, one may approach the problem from any number of viewpoints. I believe a fruitful clinical approach would involve defining the individual needs of the retarded adult and then discussing the provision of programs in the community to meet these needs, either by expanding or modifying existing programs or by developing new ones. The needs of retarded adults may be classified as "physiologic" and "psychosocial," although it is widely accepted that there is a vital interaction between bodily needs and the social setting in which the individual lives. Physiologic needs are more easily defined and include those that must be satisfied if the person is to survive, such as need for air, food, water, glandular secretion, waste elimination, and protection from pain, extremes of heat and cold or noxious substances, popularly described as needs for "food, clothing, and shelter." Psychosocial needs are more difficult to define since there is a considerable variation from culture to culture. We can assume that, broadly speaking, in our American culture, the major psychosocial needs are a feeling of security, a feeling of adequacy, a need to love and to be loved, and a need to come into contact with the physical world around one, as expressed in curiosity and reality-testing. Howard Kelman has stated that

> the fundamental needs of mentally retarded children are the same as those of other children. Briefly, the requisites are: a stable, financially secure, and accepting family group; appropriate school and recreation facilities; and preparation and training for work. . . . (Kelman, 1962, p. 130).

For the retarded adult this may be paraphrased as a stable, financially secure, and accepting family group, appropriate counseling and recreational facilities; and training and opportunities for work in terms of vocational potential.

Current thinking about the physiologic needs of the retarded adult suggests that many earlier beliefs that the retarded are subject to early fatal diseases and that they are markedly inferior to others in such characteristics as height and weight have not been substantiated. However, until contrary evidence is presented, it is likely that there is a higher incidence of mental retardation among the economically and socially deprived and that, among those who are economically and socially deprived, there is likely to be a higher incidence of disease as well as some inferiority in such characteristics as height and weight (President's Panel, 1962). In any case, one can postulate that the physiologic needs of the retarded do not differ from those of others, but, in practice, because more retardation is found in populations that are socially and economically deprived, the needs of the retarded in these populations are likely to be met just as poorly as are the needs of other deprived persons in these populations. In other words, retarded adults may well have physiologic needs that are not well satisfied because they live among people whose physiologic needs are inadequately met.

Whereas consideration must be given to defining the physiologic and psychosocial needs of the retarded adult in the community, in any one individual these needs are manifested as a characteristic complex of forces interacting within a social and cultural environment. This implies that in meeting individual needs consideration must be given to the "whole person" as well as to specific needs in limited areas. To a large extent, the mentally retarded as a group have been victims of a tendency to focus on some specific aspect of their needs. They usually are treated as though their only problem were mental retardation; whereas mental retardation may be only a part of their problem, although of course inextricably linked with such matters as poor training, physical handicaps, low socio-economic level, and lack of opportunities for recreation, employment, and so forth. Translating this thought into program development, it would appear that the retarded adult in the community needs to be provided with services that are broad and comprehensive, as well as highly specific, if his needs are to meet at all.

## NUMBER OF RETARDED ADULTS IN THE COMMUNITY

In view of the difficulties in defining the term "mentally retarded adult in the community," prevalence figures in this group can be only estimated. Of some interest is the idea advanced by the California Study Commission on Mental Retardation that there are times in a person's life when he would be considered mentally retarded—such as when in childhood he is placed in special classes for the retarded; whereas in adulthood, if he could make a satisfactory social and occupational adjustment without the need of special programs, he would not be considered mentally retarded. This leads to the concept that during his lifetime the person would blend into the general population, moving in and out of the mentally retarded group with variations in his need for and use of services provided in the community. This concept, when translated into incidence figures, yielded estimates of per cent of population estimated to be retarded (in California) of 0.5 per cent for those under five years, 2.2 per cent for five to seven years, 3.0 per cent for eight to sixteen years, 2.0 per cent for seventeen to fifty-four years, 1.5 per cent for fifty-five to fifty-nine years, 1.0 per cent for sixty to sixty-nine years, and 0.5 per cent for seventy and older, with an average incidence of 1.83 per cent for the total population of California (California Study Commission, 1965, p. 16–21). There is something intriguing about the notion that a person could be mentally retarded at some period of life and not mentally retarded at other periods, since intelligence usually is considered to be a relatively fixed trait (or group of traits). However, this concept is compatible with recent studies (Kirk, 1958; and others) which claim that intelligence may be modified by special training, and that, for each retarded person, there may be wide variations in the components of intellectual functioning manifested according to time of life and situational factors.

Even if one adopts a limited estimated percentage of mental retardation in the population, it appears that in California alone those in the group above seventeen years of age substantially outnumber those below seventeen years of age by almost two to one, with an estimated 250,000 persons in the over-seventeen-year-old group by 1970, the bulk of whom will be below fifty years of age. This sobering estimate suggests the vast dimensions of this problem on a national basis in numerical terms alone.

## SOME CONSIDERATIONS IN PLANNING PROGRAMS FOR THE ADULT RETARDED IN THE COMMUNITY

A comprehensive program to serve the considerable number of mentally retarded adults in the community must be rooted in a number of basic considerations. These may be summarized as follows.

1. *Planning for the mentally retarded adult must be related to community planning for all citizens and for all handicapped persons.* It would appear to be inefficient and ineffective to develop a community plan for the mentally retarded adult without reference to other handicapped persons and without reference to general community services programs, but this procedure is not uncommon. For example, I have known of communities where a small group of highly motivated parents of severely retarded adults moved ahead rapidly to establish a sheltered workshop for their own severely retarded children, giving little thought to the nature of the program to be provided, needs of the group to be served, the community resources available, and so forth. Fortunately, this approach is becoming less common, and even where parents of the retarded provide the motivation for establishing a workshop program, there is a greater tendency to work with others. This is in line with recent policies of the National Association for Retarded Children, Inc. (NARC), which now requires member units to devote their energies to "obtaining" services rather than "providing" services for the retarded (*Statement of Policy, 1964*).

2. *Planning for the retarded adult must be related to planning for the retarded child.* As pointed out above, one can arbitrarily separate the adult from the retarded child—using eligibility for public-school attendance as the dividing line—but in practice there is no sharp demarcation. The retarded person is usually slow in maturing into adulthood from adolescence, unless retardation is so severe that adulthood is never attained. Furthermore, although there are phases in physical and social development from childhood to adulthood, there are no clear breaks or abrupt changes. It is the same person who is living through the successive experiences, and the basic personality traits do not greatly change.

Separation of services for the retarded child is reinforced by arbitrary assignments of governmental and private agencies and professional workers for serving the retarded. As an example, one finds that prevocational education for the retarded child is largely the province of the public-school program, but vocational rehabilitation services are, by legislative mandate, available only for the retarded adult. Vocational education in public schools and vocational rehabilitation counseling provided by a state rehabilitation agency are separate in administrative structure, financial support, and methodology. Only during the past few years has progress been made in bringing the public-school programs and vocational rehabilitation counseling together into a meaningful relationship so that the retarded client can have the benefit of continuing service from school to the post-school period. An excellent contribution to progress in bridging the gap between the school and post-school period has been made by joint meetings such as those sponsored by the U. S. Office of Education and the U. S. Vocational Rehabilitation Administration, and reported in *Preparation of Mentally Retarded Youth for Gainful Employment* (U. S. Department of Health, Education and Welfare, 1959).

3. *Planning for the retarded adult in the community should provide for participation in the planning process by those who provide services (such as social workers, physicians, psychologists, and other professional workers), as well as by those who are to receive services (the mentally retarded person and his family).* This presupposes a collaborative process in program development involving both providers and users of services, a process that does not exist in most communities. Generally speaking, professional workers in public and private agencies provide services to those who can use these services in accordance with policies and procedures established by the agency's governing board or head, and with funds available. Total responsibility for program-planning and implementation generally rests with the agency, with little or no participation by the users of services. An example of exclusion of the user of services from participation in program-planning is the present manner of providing public-welfare services to welfare recipients, where determinations of need and decisions as to the nature and amount of services and grants for welfare clients are made entirely by professional staff of the welfare department. What is true of services and funds provided by welfare departments to welfare recipients is true to a greater or lesser degree of publicly available services provided for the retarded adult in the community. What little is available in the way of education, counseling, residential, and recreation programs is provided with little or no participation in the planning and operation of the program by the retarded adult or his family.

That the present approach to providing programs to those who need them has many weaknesses has been recognized for some time. However, with the enactment of the Economic Opportunity Act of 1964, whose goal is to combat poverty in the United States, the central concept has been established that a community action program to combat poverty is one "which is developed, conducted, and administered with the maximum feasible participation of residents of the areas and members of the groups served" (Public Law 88–452, 1964). The implementation of this concept in relation to eliminating poverty poses serious difficulties, especially since it represents such a break from present practices, and, in some communities, a struggle has been taking place between the advocates and the opponents of this approach. Whatever the outcome of this conflict, if there is any validity to the idea that the poor should participate in programs to eliminate poverty, then there is equal validity to the proposition that retarded adults and their families should participate in programs to help the mentally retarded adult.

It is of some interest to observe how parents of the retarded, organized in hundreds of active chapters throughout the United States and affiliated with the National Association for Retarded Children, Inc., have been able to make their influence felt so far as programs for the retarded are concerned. This influence has been manifested in a variety of ways: by support of legislation and budgets on federal, state, and local levels; by support of research and professional education; by literature; by consultation services; and by individual units establishing and operating programs of service to retarded children, retarded adults, and their families. It is noteworthy that most of the sheltered workshops for the retarded have been founded and are now being operated by member units of the NARC. The parents of the retarded in their own organizations have had the experience of developing and implementing programs to meet the needs of their retarded adult children.

This leaves an interesting question—could the retarded adult in the community himself participate in program-planning and -implementation? Although the idea is novel (and perhaps disturbing to some), it is necessary to consider two points: first, there may be many retarded adults in the community who would be capable of participating in program-planning and -implementation, especially in cooperation with their parents and with professional assistance where necessary, and, second, reports of family group therapy with retarded adults have indicated that these adults can participate effectively in developing significant programs involving themselves and their families (Segal, 1964). As some retarded adults develop in maturity and social competency, they may well demonstrate capabilities for planning and self-direction in programs that could contribute to their own independent living in the community.

4. *Planning for the retarded adult in the community must provide for preparation of professional workers, for research, and for program evaluation.* One may well ask whether efforts to develop programs for the retarded adult in the community can be successful without well-trained staff to carry on the job. As is the case in virtually all the health, education, and welfare professions, there is a marked shortage of well-trained, experienced workers, with every prospect that this shortage will increase rather than diminish. What needs to be done in relation to training of workers with the adult retarded in the community applies equally well to others. Prospective workers must become interested early in their careers; they must be provided with stimulating and satisfying assignments and remunerated appropriately.

The closest approximation to professional training in one aspect of services for the adult retarded in the community is the graduate training program for rehabilitation counselors sponsored by the Vocational Rehabilitation Administration (VRA) in twenty-seven colleges and universities. A similar arrangement is available in university schools of social welfare where field work in agencies serving the retarded is provided. The New York City Association for the Help of the Retarded, the Devereux Schools, and Columbia University have, with VRA support, been offering summer programs on the subject of rehabilitation of the retarded. Beyond these limited efforts, I know of no professional training for workers who directly serve the retarded adult in the community.

The paucity of research in relation to the retarded adult in the community has been noted before. Systematic investigations must be conducted in their personal adjustment, earning, social and vocational potentials, and achievement. Those concerned with the effectiveness of community programs seeking to bring amelioration of the condition of the retarded adult might consider some of the pitfalls involved in evaluating such efforts before embarking on such studies (Herzog, 1959).

5. *There must be some coordinating mechanism in the community that makes it possible (a) for retarded adults to obtain available services and (b) for those providing services to retarded adults to coordinate their work most effectively and efficiently.* The need for coordination of services for the adult retarded has found expression in several forms. Two general approaches to coordination, the Los Angeles and the San Francisco plans, will be described. In Los Angeles, the concept of a "joint powers agreement" has developed, making it possible for public agencies to coordinate services for the retarded. This is expressed in the following recommendation of the Welfare Planning Council, Los Angeles Region:

> . . . To promote coordination of services to the retarded, to foster communication among agencies rendering such services, and to stimulate development of additional services necessary to provide a comprehensive continuum of care of the retarded, it is recommended that the County's public agencies establish a Mental Retardation Services Board under the terms of California Government Code, Sections 6500 *et seq.*, which provide for joint exercise of powers by public agencies. The functions of the Board will be coordination of existing services, development of standardized procedures that would facilitate better planning of services and serve to eliminate duplication of diagnostic services, promotion of interdisciplinary in-service training programs, and assisting the schools and other social agencies to develop a cooperative plan for filling the post-school "vacuum" in service to the retarded (Welfare Planning Council, 1965).

In 1962, the San Francisco Coordinating Council on Mental Retardation (SFCCMR) came into existence as a voluntary group of professional workers from many disciplines and agencies, with the goal of improving services for the retarded. The SFCCMR provided a focus for coordination of mental-retardation programming and service in the community. It must be emphasized that the SFCCMR's objective has been to stimulate agencies and organizations and individuals to conduct programs for mentally retarded. Conducted in 1964–1965, the Pre-Planning Study of the SFCCMR (financed by a VRA grant) highlighted many areas in which services for mentally retarded adults must be provided, including vocational training, job placement, counseling and related services for adults, and an urgent need for professional training on all fronts.

The SFCCMR was influential in establishing the "Information and Referral Service for the Mentally Retarded" (financed by the National Institute of Mental Health) as a function of the Community Mental Health Services of the San Francisco City and County Public Health Department and has been sponsoring imaginative plans to coordinate and expand services for the retarded in San Francisco ("Coordinating Council on Mental Retardation," 1965).

## COMPREHENSIVE PROGRAMMING FOR THE MENTALLY RETARDED

Even before federal legislation was passed in 1963 providing funds for comprehensive planning for facilities for the retarded (Public Law 88–164, 1963), a number of plans had been developed; but with the availability of these funds, almost every state has been busily engaged in devising and implementing its plans. The *Monograph on Program Planning in Mental Retardation* of the American Association on Mental Deficiency suggests that a comprehensive program should include the following elements:

Service Aspects—

    (1) diagnosis, treatment, parent-counseling
    (2) training and education
    (3) vocational (re) habilitation and placement
    (4) day and residential care
    (5) recreational opportunities
    (6) long-term supervision and guidance

Supportive Aspects—

    (1) research
    (2) training of personnel
    (3) case-finding
    (4) public education

(Gardner and Nisonger, 1962, p. 40.)

Although a good part of the AAMD monograph is devoted to a more detailed description of these components of a comprehensive program for all retarded, it may be appropriate to indicate which aspects of the program would be applicable to the retarded adult in the community.

## COMPREHENSIVE EVALUATION OF THE RETARDED ADULT

There is little disagreement on the importance of comprehensive evaluation of the retarded for purposes of planning services to meet individual and group needs, and on conducting such evaluations using the "team" approach, with professional workers such as physicians, psychologists, social workers, and teachers. There are, however, wide variations in thought as to how, when, where, and by whom such evaluation should be done. Some subscribe to the position that since the physical health of the retarded child is the responsibility of the pediatrician, comprehensive evaluation of the retarded should be medically oriented and supervised by a pediatrician supported by a team of professionals (Giannini, 1957). Others believe that community mental-health centers that might provide comprehensive evaluation of the retarded "must be free to take advantage of demonstrated leadership capability from whatever source it may come—medical or nonmedical (Brayfield, 1965). Still others favor psychiatric supervision:

> The Psychiatric Center for Children's first responsibility would be that of comprehensive differential diagnosis followed by the development of a treatment plan based on the concept that the patient is first a child and only secondarily afflicted with an abnormality (Group for the Advancement of Psychiatry, 1959, p. 16).

Some of these viewpoints, it will be noted, tend to stress the retarded *child,* leaving open the whole problem of comprehensive evaluation of the adult. This may be because the retarded adult's major problems (in addition to medical problems he may have in common with other adults) are focused on social and occupational adjustment.

A number of possible approaches remain to be explored for purposes of comprehensive evaluation of the needs of and services for retarded adults. For example, in California, the state Department of Rehabilitation was authorized by the state legislature to establish residential centers offering comprehensive evaluation services for handicapped adolescents and adults in relation to their social and vocational adjustment. Another direction may be in the enrichment of services in community rehabilitation workshops so that comprehensive evaluation, counseling, and social adjustment services are available for workshop clients who need them. Still another lies in better coordination of information on individual clients through the use of a procedure such as the Rehabilitation Codes. As the manual accompanying the Rehabilitation Codes (Riviere, 1962) indicates, this is a system of classification of information essential to the rehabilitation process. It provides a serial case record of the disabled person's status at given dates from first contact through service and follow-up in the community, to closure. Information about the client's personal history, health history, impairment (etiology, disability, handicap, capabilities, achievements, and potentialities) is entered on a cumulative record form starting with the first evaluation case conference and is changed when re-evaluation is undertaken.

## VOCATIONAL TRAINING AND REHABILITATION SERVICES FOR THE RETARDED ADULT

The emergence of a massive effort to meet the vocational needs of the retarded adult in the community is the result of many forces, some of which can only be surmised. For one thing, there is a social concern for the growing number of retarded youth who have received special education in the public schools and who leave school at the age of eighteen years, with no jobs or opportunities for normal social living. Special education for the retarded is more costly than general education for most children because of the need for smaller class sizes to provide proper training. This more costly special education may be considered society's investment in the preparation of the retarded child to function as an adult after leaving school. Although the preponderance of special-class graduates may be making an adjustment in the community, many are unemployed, some are delinquent, and many require public assistance from tax funds. Some taxpayers have wondered whether their investment in special education is indeed paying off, and, if not, what should be done. One suggestion is to improve the early identification of those retarded needing vocational rehabilitation and to provide these services as early as possible in order to accomplish the transition from school to adult living.

A second source of interest in developing vocational services for retarded adults is that many are capable of being more independent and productive within their mental and physical limitations. This has been demonstrated by their performance in sheltered workshops, on semiskilled and unskilled jobs in business, industry, and civil service, and in their response to rehabilitation counseling services. The harnessing of this productive contribution to our economy would amply justify efforts to do so. In this connection we may well salute the leadership that the Vocational Rehabilitation Administration (VRA), United States Department of Health, Education, and Welfare, has provided through support of basic state vocational rehabilitation services and through support of research and demonstration programs in the general field of handicapping conditions, including mental retardation (Doyle, 1965).

Much information has been accumulated about the vocational adjustment of the retarded adult in the community. Numerous follow-up studies have been made of retarded pupils who have attended public-school classes and of retarded patients on leave from state hospitals for the retarded. Those who have evaluated these studies have tended to be somewhat pessimistic about the significance of the findings. For example, in his review of follow-up studies of retarded pupils who have attended school classes for the retarded, Samuel Kirk concluded that ". . . until we obtain well controlled studies of a longitudinal nature, our opinions about the benefits or detriments of special classes will remain partly in the realm of conjecture" (Kirk, 1964, p. 63). In a similar vein, Charles Windle found, after reviewing and evaluating the literature on the prediction of success of mentally retarded adults following release into the community from state hospitals for the retarded, that "The most that can be accepted from the previous literature is a number of suggestions, best estimates and reasonable hypotheses" (Windle, 1962, pp.133–134).

Since the late 1950's, as vocational rehabilitation services for the retarded became more available, information has begun to accumulate about retarded adults who have been clients of community sheltered workshops, as well as about retarded adults who have been provided with vocational rehabilitation services by state rehabilitation agencies. No comprehensive study has been made of the vocational adjustment of retarded adults who have been attending workshops, although there have been reports emanating from individual workshops (Association for the Help of Retarded Children, 1957) and from state agencies that have studied workshops within their state (Nelson, 1962).

Information about the vocational adjustment of one group of retarded adults in the community has been reported by the Division of Statistics and Studies of the United States Vocational Rehabilitation Administration, which undertook a study of the socio-economic and other characteristics of this group. Among the findings were the following:

> Over 7,000 mentally retarded persons were rehabilitated in fiscal year 1963 . . .
> Persons with mental retardation constituted 5/4 percent of all rehabilitants. Over two-thirds of the mentally retarded rehabilitated were under the age of 20 . . .
> Only 5 percent of the retarded had dependents. . . .
> Nearly all of the retarded were capable of activity outside the home without help. . . .
> The largest single source of referral for retarded clients was educational institutions. . . .

Before receiving rehabilitation services, three-quarters of the retardates were primarily dependent on family and friends for support. Seventeen percent were being supported by public funds. . . .

Approximately 90 percent were not earning wages before receiving rehabilitation service. . . . After receiving service less than 10 percent of the retarded were not wage earners. . . .

Approximately 40 percent of the mentally retarded entered service type occupations, 20 percent were classed as unskilled workers and 17 percent became semiskilled employees. . . . (U. S. Vocational Rehabilitation Administration, 1965).

Although there are limitations to studies of this type, especially in view of the wide variations among states in their definitions of the terms "mentally retarded" and of "successful" rehabilitation, the efforts being made with retarded adults appear to be justified from a financial point of view. In addition, the increasing number of retarded clients referred on graduation from school (50 per cent of all retarded referrals in 1963) points to a great need to coordinate school and post-school services.

In this connection, Salvatore DiMichael (1964) has described a comprehensive longitudinal approach to vocational rehabilitation services for the retarded from early years to adulthood. He indicates (Figure 19–1) that there is a regular progression in training programs and vocational services at various age levels, appropriate to the retarded individual's degree of mental handicap.

## DEVELOPMENTS IN SAN FRANCISCO

The program that has been emerging in San Francisco during the past few years will illustrate the development of vocational rehabilitation services for the retarded adult, although it is impossible to present a complete panorama or to acknowledge the contributions of all who have participated. From 1951, when San Francisco Aid Retarded Children, Inc. (SFARC), was established, one of its first programs was a sheltered workshop for young adults operated by parent volunteers. The program included simple jobs, like stacking and bundling rolls of newspaper, as well as social activities like games and recreational experiences. In 1953, the sheltered workshop was granted a full-time staff member by the Adult Education Division of the San Francisco Unified School District to conduct a program that would more adequately meet the needs of the enrollees. Under the supervision of the director, it was possible to provide some psychologic testing, to focus more on training, and to engage the enrollees in a longer work-day. In 1956, SFARC was awarded an "Extension and Improvement Grant" by the United States Office of Vocational Rehabilitation (now the Vocational Rehabilitation Administration). The effect of this grant was to establish psy-

Outline of Plan to Provide Maximum Vocational Opportunities for Mentally Retarded Adolescents and Adults*

| SCHOOL PLACEMENT† | AGES 14+ | 15+ | 16-18+ | 19+ | ADULT PLACEMENT |
|---|---|---|---|---|---|
| **A. Higher tracks† (Educable)** | | | | | |
| 1. *Competitively employable* | Unit in occupational exploration | Job-sample try-outs in class | Training as trade-assistant with special class for job-related fundamentals | Supervised on-the-job training (half to full time) | Competitive employment |
| 2. *Marginal competitively employable* | Prevocational unit; personal-social development in group projects | Unit in occupational exploration | Training in broad occupational area & class in job-related fundamentals | Supervised on-the-job training (half to full time) | Transitional sheltered employment |
| | | | Job-sample try-outs in class; general shop (men), homemaking (women) | Extended in-school training (broad occupational area) | |
| **B. Lower tracks (Trainable)** | | | | | Long-term sheltered employment |
| 3. *Sheltered employable* | Self-help and interpersonal skills, communication, family living | Prevocational exploration, personal-social development in group projects | General shop (men) Homemaking (women) | Sheltered workshop and school program | |
| 4. *Marginal sheltered employable* | Same aims as above but lower skills | same as above | same as above | Adult activity center, and school program | Adult activity center (short- or long-term) |

Prospects for semi-skilled work

Prospects for unskilled work

\* Program assumes foundation of personal and social skills, and their continuing development into adulthood. The program includes occupational exploration, self-evaluation, evaluation and plan for adult-preparation, individual counseling, group counseling, parent counseling, vocational training, ½-school + ½-work experience, evaluation and plan for adult-readiness, job placement, follow-up, and counseling for adult living.

†Interchange of student from one "track" to another may be made whenever desirable.

**Figure 19–1.** Outline of plan to provide maximum vocational opportunities for mentally retarded adolescents and adults. (After DiMichael, 1964, p. 12.)

chologic evaluation services and social casework and groupwork services on a very limited basis as an integral part of the sheltered workshop, in addition to work experiences. The program was enlarged to include more enrollees.

During this period, other sheltered workshops for the mentally retarded, including those in New York City (Association for the Help of Retarded Children, 1957) and Tampa, Florida (Ferguson, 1959), had developed sheltered workshops that became prototypes for VRA "selected demonstration projects." From 1957 to 1961, SFARC was awarded a VRA grant to establish and to demonstrate a work-training center for mentally retarded adults. The major objective of this program was to demonstrate that those mentally retarded adults who had been considered to be "non-feasible" for vocational placement would be enabled to get jobs through appropriate work adjustment. Among the findings of the project were (1) that work adjustment and work-training in a sheltered workshop could lead to the placement of retarded adults on jobs, and (2) that certain types of clients in the population served by the program were not likely to get jobs in the community, and for them special services would be necessary (Katz, 1961). One result of the work-training center project was the establishment of a position for a vocational rehabilitation counselor in the San Francisco district office of the state Department of Rehabilitation, devoted to full-time counseling of the mentally retarded.

Toward the close of the work-training center project, steps were taken by SFARC to insure continuation of services for retarded adults in community programs along lines developed by the project. The group of retarded adults who were considered "vocationally feasible" by the state Vocational Rehabilitation Service (VRS) and who required short-term evaluation, counseling, and work adjustment prior to job placement were referred by the state VRS for such services to the San Francisco Community Rehabilitation Workshop, the cost of services being financed by VRS fees. A second group, identified in the work-training center project as those who could tolerate a full work-day in a sheltered setting, was placed in a long-term sheltered workshop that later became a component of the San Francisco Community Rehabilitation Workshop. Services for this group are being purchased from the San Francisco Community Rehabilitation Workshop by San Francisco Aid Retarded Children, Inc. The Adult Training Center (or Social Development Center) was established as a long-term program for a third group of severely handicapped retarded adults. Here the enrollees were provided with an opportunity to do some kind of productive work for a short time each day, according to their capacity; and the remainder of their day was devoted to recreation and social activities. This program was operated and financed by SFARC. In addition, it was recognized that there was a group of more seriously handicapped retarded adults requiring intensive evaluation, counseling, and treatment, together with counseling for their families. To demonstrate some of the problems and methods for working with this group, the Independent Living Rehabilitation Program (ILRP) was established by SFARC in 1961, with a VRA grant, with a view to making these retarded adults more independent in daily living (Katz, 1964).

The goals of the ILRP were to help seriously handicapped retarded young adults to make the transition from school to adulthood; to help retarded patients on leave from state hospitals for the retarded to make a better adjustment to community living; to reduce the waiting list for commitment to state hospitals for the retarded by providing a productive alternative to commitment; and to help the enrollee's family participate in the development of personal, social, and vocational competencies, in cooperation with the social service staff.

To accomplish these goals, a therapeutically oriented, interdisciplinary rehabilitation-team approach was used, including work-training of enrollees and social services with enrollees and their parents. Referrals came from the San Francisco public schools, county Department of Public Welfare (now county Department of Social Services), state Department of Mental Hygiene, and state Department of Rehabilitation. Prior to the enrollee's admission to the program, an eight-week evaluation was conducted by the staff, during which time the enrollee was observed at work and play. His parents were interviewed and involved in the program. If the staff decided that he should continue in the program, he engaged in a daily individualized program, including at least two hours in a sheltered workshop, at a minimum salary of fifteen cents per hour, with the rest of his day spent in homemaking, crafts, leisure-time activities, recreation, travel-training, and training in reading and writing. Social services included individual casework interviews, as well as extensive group work in social clubs, parent groups, and family-counseling.

One finding of the ILRP was that some enrollees who had been considered previously to be "non-vocationally feasible" became employable in sheltered workshops or as helpers in service occupations. Almost none of the enrollees had to be committed or returned to a state hospital for the retarded. Many developed a markedly improved self-image and greater independence. For many who were admitted after graduation from public-school classes, the ILRP provided an excellent transition from school to more adult functioning. However, some presented personal or social problems of such magnitude as to make it impossible for the staff to help them appreciably.

Although progress has been made in developing a comprehensive and coordinated program of vocational rehabilitation services for the adult retarded in San Francisco, reinforced by local, state, and federal help, it would be unwise to assume that other communities necessarily move in the same direction, since there are great variations in the conditions and factors influencing such developments. However, this illustration of what has occurred may be helpful to others dealing with similar problems in vocational services for the retarded adult in the community.

## COUNSELING PARENTS OF THE RETARDED ADULT

Counseling for parents of retarded adults represents a gap in community services. The retarded adult living at home may have many problems that can best be ameliorated by counseling his parents. This principle is observed in child psychiatry clinics, where it is recognized that the disturbed child in the family can be helped best if the parents are seen concurrently in therapy. An application of this principle occurred in the ILRP project, where eligible adult retarded clients were admitted only when parents agreed to participate in counseling with the social service staff while their child was enrolled in the program. This arrangement brought about better understanding of the retarded adult's problems by his parents and generally provided a more receptive attitude by parents of the growing social competency and independence of their child (Segal, 1964).

Parents of retarded adults who live at home face a disturbing problem: "What will become of my child after I am gone?" This question demands extensive parent-counseling, involving long-range planning and study of available resources. There are vast changes taking place in community programs for the adult retarded, so that solutions that were appropriate a few years ago, such as institutionalization, are no longer the best alternatives. Indeed, the number of alternatives favoring retention of even severely handicapped adults in the community seems to be increasing.

Still another consideration has to do with the extended period during which parent-counseling may be necessary. It is true that many family difficulties can be resolved through short-term counseling, but the problems presented by the retarded adult may well remain with him during his entire adulthood, and his parents may need help for a long period of time. This can be provided best by making counseling available as needed.

## LIVING ARRANGEMENTS

The problems surrounding the provision of day care and residential care in the community for retarded adults are largely unexplored. In the past, the general approach to housing the more severely mentally handicapped was to place them in state hospitals. In recent years overcrowded state hospitals and long waiting lists, coupled with an increasing improvement in community services, including special education for retarded children and adolescents, have altered considerably the idea that the state hospital is the best place even for moderately and severely retarded adults. As pointed out above, parents' desire to keep their retarded children out of state hospitals for the retarded has had a considerable influence on this trend. As a consequence, more attention is being directed to the question of living arrangements for the adult retarded in the community.

Several factors bear on this problem. These include age, sex, and severity of mental handicap, the presence or absence of parents and family, the availability of foster homes in the community, and whether the retarded adult is a patient on leave from the state hospital. It seems obvious that the wide variation in these factors among retarded adults would suggest a need for great flexibility in developing living arrangements for this group.

Among possible living arrangements for the adult retarded in the community are (1) living totally independently, (2) living at home with parents or responsible relatives, (3) living in a foster home or a family-care home (for patients on leave from state hospitals), and (4) living in a "halfway house." These are not conceived, necessarily, as a sequence of levels, since a given living arrangement could well be permanent for many individuals.

The "halfway house" took its name from its being a steppingstone for the mentally ill patient "halfway" from the hospital back to the community, in recognition of the need to provide a transition from institutional life. In recent years this idea has been extended to the mentally retarded patient who is on leave from a state hospital and who does not return to his own home. However, there are differences in the behavior, attitudes, and abilities of mentally ill and mentally retarded adult patients on leave from state hospitals that suggest that halfway houses for the retarded adult may have to be somewhat different from those for mentally ill adults. In this connection, it is of interest that the Conard House in San Francisco has been conducting a successful demonstration program of a halfway house in which mentally retarded, mentally ill, and normal young adults live in the same residence. The implications of this program are provocative (Mikels and Gumrukcu, 1963).

## RECREATION FOR THE RETARDED ADULT IN THE COMMUNITY

Recreation for the handicapped adult, including the retarded, has been increasingly recognized as an unmet need, but only recently has any substantial progress been made. Starting in the early 1950's, various parent groups sponsored or operated summer-camp programs for the retarded, usually including adults. By 1965, in California alone over twelve summer-camp programs for the retarded were listed. Although such activities are beneficial, only a small fraction of those who could profit from this experience were able to attend, and they represent only a part-year activity, with a long hiatus from summer to summer.

To fill the gap there has been a growth of interest in organized recreation programs. County and local recreation agencies have assumed some responsibility for programming on a year-round basis. In some communities, specialists in recreation for the handicapped have been added to park and recreation departments; whereas in other communities, coordinating councils for the handicapped have undertaken the recreation assignment.

In connection with recreation services, familiar questions arise, such as, "Should the retarded be given recreation programs independently of the average participant, or should they be worked into groups engaged in recreation activities?" "Should special recreation workers be assigned to handle the retarded or should the retarded be handled by regular recreation workers who might be given some special training in working with this group?" "Should regular recreational facilities provide for the retarded, or should special facilities be built?"

## LONG-TERM SUPERVISION AND GUIDANCE IN THE COMMUNITY

There is little question that for many parents of retarded children one of the greatest appeals of the state hospital for the retarded is its provision for permanent supervision and care, especially when parents are no longer able to provide such care. For these parents, the availability of the state hospital provides a sense of future security not otherwise possible. This does not mean, however, that parents prefer the state hospital. A survey by the Subcommittee on Mental Health Services, California Assembly Ways and Means Committee, indicated "that about half the families with children on the current waiting list for state hospitals for the retarded would not place their children in a state hospital if other alternatives were available" (California Legislature, Assembly Ways and Means Committee, 1965, p. 63). This finding suggests that many parents of retarded children would be satisfied to keep them in a community program if permanent supervision and adequate care were possible.

The paradox of this situation is that, in many states, the retarded adult becomes eligible for long-term supervision and guidance in the community *after* he has been committed to a state hospital for the retarded and subsequently placed on leave from the state hospital. In several cases, retarded adults living in San Francisco in very difficult family situations could be helped only by being committed to a state hospital for the retarded, then placed on leave back in San Francisco, thus becoming eligible for family care, social casework services, and medical services as a patient on leave from the hospital. One danger in this obviously wasteful and circular process was the possibility that the patient might be "lost" in the large state hospital and remain there indefinitely. To circumvent this problem, the subcommittee proposed that "the State shift its responsibility from the time when the child enters the state hospital to the time when expert diagnosis establishes the fact that special care is needed that the family cannot afford." This approach would, in effect, make it possible to provide necessary guidance and financial help to retarded adults in community programs rather than having to go to state hospitals to accomplish the same purpose.

Numerous proposals are being advanced to make possible long-term guidance and supervision of the retarded adult in the community. These take various forms, such as state guardianship of the retarded adult, whether through the state Department of Mental Hygiene or the county Welfare Department, guardianship of retarded adults by private agencies (including parent groups), or their becoming permanent clientele of diagnostic and counseling centers run by the state or county. As yet the best way to manage this problem has not appeared, but experience with a variety of methods should provide a basis for the best future plan.

## SUPPORTIVE SERVICES

The AAMD monograph on program development has grouped "research, training of personnel, case finding and public education" as supportive services that are necessary for strengthening the direct services provided for the retarded (Gardner and Nisonger, 1962). Although such an approach has many values for purposes of clarification, in practice it would be difficult to find sharp demarcation between direct services and supportive services. For example, research studies on the attitudes of retarded adults toward work have implications for direct vocational counseling services provided them. The training of social workers to work with retarded adults is best accomplished when field-work training is provided in an agency that furnishes a high level of professional services. Case-finding is a process that is strongly associated with service, since interviews may be essential to case identification, and some counseling may take place in the course of referral. Public education is a continuing program in which a constant orientation to mental retardation must be maintained, associated with demonstrable evidence of adequate service to the retarded client.

The immediately preceding observations are not intended to minimize the importance of intensive efforts along each of these lines. So far as research on the adult retarded in the community is concerned, almost every statement in this chapter raises questions demanding systematic investigation. One might mention such problems as the dearth of evaluation instruments, the absence of evidence about learning in the retarded adult, and the paucity of sociologic study of the adult retarded in community settings, to give some indication of the rich potential for research. Little is known about the maturational processes of the retarded from childhood to adulthood, and only recently has light been thrown on the impact of the retarded child in the family setting (Farber, 1960). The increasing availability of research funds from federal, state, and private sources should do much to build a body of knowledge that could provide a basis, not only for better future service, but also for extending more basic understanding of the functioning of all persons.

## PROFESSIONAL TRAINING

The training of professional personnel for studying and working with the retarded has been expanded greatly by federal funds. A milestone in such legislation was Public Law 88–164, which included funds for the construction of "centers for research on mental retardation and related aspects of human development," "university affiliated facilities for the mentally retarded," "community facilities for the mentally retarded," funds for the training of teachers of the retarded and other handicapped children, and research and demonstration projects relating to the education of handicapped children. The present and future availability of training funds from governmental sources should not be interpreted as minimizing the scholarships that have been and continue to be made available by private groups, notably the Parent-Teachers Associations, which for years have provided scholarships for teachers to receive special training to teach the retarded. However, it should be noted that with the few exceptions pointed out earlier in the chapter, there has been virtually no preparation of professionals for working with the retarded adult in the community. Rehabilitation counselors, adult education instructors, physicians, social workers, psychologists, and other professionals serving retarded adults in the community have no specialized training for these assignments.

## CASE-FINDING

The problem of detecting retarded adults in the community and referring them to appropriate programs would not appear to present a serious problem because there are so few programs available for retarded adults, and these are either overcrowded or have long waiting lists. This does not mean that those who actually make use of a program such as a sheltered workshop are necessarily the ones who can profit the most from it. For example, certain more able retarded adults may be retained indefinitely in a sheltered workshop because there is no other employment in the community for them; whereas others (including some who might live nearby) would not even be aware that such a program existed. There is little question that case-finding for specific programs becomes easier as a program becomes better known to the general public because potential clients (retarded adults and/or their parents) then find it easier to contact the program directly.

The techniques of case-finding have been described in detail elsewhere. Public education, adequate services, and professionally trained staff are all necessary to conduct good case-finding. An important resource often overlooked is the public health nurse who actually visits families in which there is a retarded child. Increasingly, public health nurses are being trained to recognize the retarded child.

In 1965, two laws were passed in California that will have an important impact on case-finding. First, each newborn baby must be tested for phenylketonuria (PKU), an inborn error of metabolism that afflicts one out of every 20,000 children born and leads to retardation unless an appropriate diet is prescribed. Aside from finding potential and actual retarded children, this may open the way to early identification of the three out of one hundred who may be retarded. Second, each school district must conduct a census of handicapped children to plan for their educational needs. This also should identify many retarded children.

## PUBLIC EDUCATION

Little can be accomplished to improve community services for the adult retarded without an enlightened public attitude. Over a long period, folklore about mental retardation has grown up that is based on assumptions not yet verified by scientific investigation. Among these are the following:

> The IQ (score is) regarded as a highly efficient predictor of an individual's level of vocational and social adjustment, and of his ability to profit from an education and rehabilitation program.
>
> Some assume that the retarded show a rapid turnover in jobs, while others believe that a retarded individual once placed on a job tends to remain in that position indefinitely.
>
> The retarded demonstrate a lack of persistence.
>
> The mentally retarded are highly suggestible.
>
> The mentally retarded are accident prone. (U. S. Department of Health, Education, and Welfare, 1959).

The knowledge available about these and related matters should be communicated to the public, since the negative attitudes implied by the stereotyped ideas effectively block support for community services.

One of the most impressive approaches to public education is to bring persons who do not ordinarily have contact with retarded adults into direct contact with programs in which they are productively engaged. A well-run recreational program or sheltered workshop for the retarded will do more to show the visitor the potentialities of even seriously mentally handicapped adults than a vast amount of literature and lectures, although all media of communication obviously should be employed.

## SUMMARY

Some basic considerations have been stated on planning programs for mentally retarded adults in the community related to their psychosocial needs. Stress has been placed on relating services for the retarded adult to total community programming for other handicapped adults and for retarded children. It has been proposed that, wherever possible, the retarded adult and his parents (as users of services) participate in program development with professional workers and agencies providing services. Professional training, research, and coordination of services should be provided.

It appears that a significant development of programs for retarded adults in the community has occurred in relation to vocational rehabilitation services. The needs for such services as recreation, residential care, and parent-counseling have been for the most part unsatisfied. Developments in program-planning for retarded adults in San Francisco have been described, and it is likely that great strides will be made as more federal, state, and local support is provided to meet the needs of retarded adults in the community.

## REFERENCES

ASSOCIATION FOR HELP OF RETARDED CHILDREN, INC., *A Sheltered Workshop Operation for the Mentally Retarded* (New York: Association for the Help of Retarded Children, Inc., 1957).

ARTHUR H. BRAYFIELD, "Community Mental Health Centers 'Staffing' Legislation," *American Psychologist,* XX (1965), 429–430.

CALIFORNIA (State) LEGISLATURE, ASSEMBLY WAYS AND MEANS COMMITTEE, *A Redefinition of State Responsibility for California's Mentally Retarded,* Report by the Subcommittee on Mental Health Services, Assembly Interim Committee Reports, XXI (Number 10), 1963–1965 (Sacramento, California: Office of State Printing, 1965).

CALIFORNIA (State) STUDY COMMISSION ON MENTAL RETARDATION, *The Underdeveloped Resource, A Plan for the Mentally Retarded of California,* A Report to the Governor and the Legislature (Sacramento, California: Office of State Printing, 1965).

"THE COORDINATING COUNCIL ON MENTAL RETARDATION—What It Is, What It Does," *Mental Retardation Bulletin,* I (1965), (Published at 1600 Scott Street, San Francisco, California).

SALVATORE G. DiMICHAEL, "Providing Full Vocational Opportunities for Re-
    tarded Adolescents and Adults," *Journal of Rehabilitation,* XXX (1964),
    10–12.
PATRICK J. DOYLE, "New Horizons in Rehabilitation of the Mentally Ill and
    Mentally Retarded," *Journal of Rehabilitation,* XXXI (1965), 14–15.
BERNARD FARBER, "Family Organization and Crisis," *Monographs of the Society
    for Research in Child Development,* XXV, Number 1 (1960).
ROBERT G. FERGUSON, *Habilitation of Mentally Retarded Youth,* Part I and
    Part II (Tampa, Florida: MacDonald Training Center, 1959).
WILLIAM A. FRAENKEL, *The Mentally Retarded and Their Vocational Rehabili-
    tation—A Resource Handbook* (New York: National Association for Re-
    tarded Children, Inc., 1961).
WILLIAM I. GARDNER and HERSCHEL W. NISONGER, "A Manual on Program
    Development in Mental Retardation," *American Journal of Mental De-
    ficiency* (Monograph Supplement), LXVI (1962), 3–192.
MARGARET J. GIANNINI, "Diagnostic Approach in Mental Retardation," New
    Jersey State Department of Health, *Public Health News,* XXXVIII (1957),
    322–332.
GROUP FOR THE ADVANCEMENT OF PSYCHIATRY, *Basic Considerations in Mental
    Retardation: A Preliminary Report,* Report Number 43 (New York: Group
    for the Advancement of Psychiatry, 1959).
RICK HEBER (Ed.), "A Manual on Terminology and Classification in Mental
    Retardation," *American Journal of Mental Deficiency* (Monograph Sup-
    plement), LXIV (1959), 3–111.
RICK HEBER, "Modifications in the Manual on Terminology and Classification
    in Mental Retardation," *American Journal of Mental Deficiency,* LXV
    (1961), 499–500.
ELIZABETH HERZOG, *Some Guide Lines for Evaluative Research, Assessing Psy-
    cho-Social Change in Individuals,* U. S. Department of Health, Education,
    and Welfare, Social Security Administration, Children's Bureau Publication
    Number 375 (Washington, D. C.: Government Printing Office, 1959).
ELIAS KATZ, "An Independent Living Rehabilitation for Seriously Handicapped
    Mentally Retarded Adults," *The Training School Bulletin,* LXI (1964),
    34–44.
ELIAS KATZ (Ed.), *Final Report, Work-Training Center for the Mentally Re-
    tarded,* U. S. Vocational Rehabilitation Administration Project Number 205
    (San Francisco: Aid Retarded Children, Inc., 1961).
HOWARD R. KELMAN, "Social Needs of Retardates: How Are They Determined
    and How Can They Be Met?" *The Training School Bulletin,* LVIII (1962),
    128–135.
SAMUEL A. KIRK, *Early Education of the Mentally Retarded* (Urbana, Illinois:
    University of Illinois Press, 1958).
SAMUEL A. KIRK, "Research in Education," in Harvey A. Stevens and Rick
    Heber (Eds.), *Mental Retardation: A Review of Research* (Chicago: Uni-
    versity of Chicago Press, 1964), pp. 57–99.
*Mental Retardation Activities of the Department of Health, Education, and
    Welfare* (Washington, D.C.: Government Printing Office, 1965).
ELAINE MIKELS and PATRICIA GUMRUKCU, "For the Former Mental Patient:

A Therapeutic Community Hostel," *Journal of Rehabilitation,* XXIX (1963), 20–21.

NATHAN NELSON, *Workshops for the Mentally Retarded in California,* Vocational Rehabilitation Service, State Department of Education (Sacramento, California: Office of State Printing, 1962).

PRESIDENT'S PANEL ON MENTAL RETARDATION, *A Proposed Program for National Action to Combat Mental Retardation* (Washington, D. C.: Government Printing Office, 1962).

MAYA RIVIERE, *Rehabilitation Codes: Development and Field Testing of an Operational Tool for Serial Recording of the Rehabilitation Process: Five Year Progress Report, 1957–1962,* Special Project U. S. Vocational Rehabilitation Administration, Department of Health, Education, and Welfare, Number RD-788 (New York: Rehabilitation Codes, 1790 Broadway, New York, New York, 1962).

ARTHUR SEGAL, "Social Work with Mentally Retarded Adults in a Rehabilitation Setting," *Social Casework,* XLV (1964), 599–604.

*Statement of Policy on Services for the Mentally Retarded, Opportunities for Professional Preparation in the Field of Mentally Retarded Children* (3rd ed.; New York: National Association for Retarded Children, Inc., 386 Park Avenue South, 1964).

U. S. DEPARTMENT OF HEALTH, EDUCATION, AND WELFARE, *Preparation of Mentally Retarded Youth for Gainful Employment,* U. S. Office of Education, Bulletin 1959, Number 28 and U. S. Office of Vocational Rehabilitation Service Series Number 507 (Washington, D. C.: Government Printing Office, 1959).

U. S. VOCATIONAL REHABILITATION ADMINISTRATION, *The Rehabilitated Mentally Retarded: Selected Characteristics of Mentally Retarded Clients Rehabilitated by State Vocational Rehabilitation Agencies in Fiscal Years 1958–1963* (Washington, D. C.: U. S. Department of Health, Education, and Welfare, 1965).

WELFARE PLANNING COUNCIL, LOS ANGELES REGION, MENTAL RETARDATION JOINT AGENCIES PROJECT, *The Mental Retardation Survey of Los Angeles County: Summary of Findings, Conclusions, Recommendations* (Los Angeles, California: Mental Retardation Joint Agencies Project, 1965).

CHARLES WINDLE, "Prognosis of Mental Subnormals," *American Journal of Mental Deficiency* (Monograph Supplement), LXVI (1962), 1–180.

# 20

# Changing Concepts of
# Residential Care

## DONALD M. BRAMWELL

There are a multitude of changing concepts in the comprehensive care of the mentally retarded; new developments in diagnosis and prevention, in care and treatment, in education, training, and vocational programs, and in the many problems involving the patient and his family. Change is certainly not new, but in recent years the tempo has been greatly accelerated. Many of the changes occurring in residential care of the mentally retarded can be attributed directly to new concepts developing in the community. Since World War II, there has been a dramatic change in public attitude toward mental retardation—an understanding and acceptance of the retarded individual, his family and their problems, and a growing awareness of their many needs. Gunnar Dybwad has stated,

> Historically, mental retardation has been viewed, for the most part, as a static, unchanging, incurable condition. Although there were some brilliant thinkers and gifted practitioners who envisioned the potentials of training and treatment for the retarded, the idea "once retarded, always retarded," led over the years to the general practice of providing humane treatment with little hope that the afflicted individuals could ever participate in the competitive world of employment and civic responsibility. . . . Since that time, we have become aware that mental retardation is not a single entity but rather a complex problem resulting from many causes and having many ramifications. . . . An individual is a complex personality, with many skills and weaknesses, which vary from person to person. . . . An individual does not remain static. He either progresses or falls behind as time passes, depending upon attitude and actions, society's, the home's, and,

334

eventually, his own. Whether an individual is retarded or not depends, a
great deal, on what is demanded of him (Dybwad, 1964).

If the community demands and expects more of an individual, including one who is mentally retarded, then the community must assume responsibility for providing adequate opportunities and facilities for that individual.
The changed attitude of the community has been vital in the development
of myriad community programs, which in turn have had a profound
effect on residential care. With changes in attitude and awareness of needs
has come the realization that residential care in a state institution is not the
sole solution, nor even the best. The belief that the mentally retarded
should be isolated and detained in special institutions, schools, and colonies
resulted from humanitarian and social concern throughout the nineteenth
century. It has given way, during the last two decades, to a generally accepted assumption by the members of the helping professions and of parent
organizations, reflected in recent federal and state legislation, that the person with mental retardation should be a member of the community. Therefore, the community must take the necessary measures to meet the social,
emotional, and economic needs of its mentally retarded population through
an expansion, both in numbers and variety, of residential care facilities located in the community. It is important also for the community to consider
the social demands that are placed on the mentally retarded person at
different stages in his development and to remember that these demands
will have an effect on his ability to adjust to the expectations held for him.
This will require a different approach to each individual and, in turn, will
necessitate the development of various types of residential placement. We
must keep the individual in mind, rather than the diagnosis.

Michael Begab (1964) has stated, "Although the overwhelming majority of the retarded have always lived in the community, only recently has
the philosophy been accepted that they do, indeed, belong there, and that
they can be productive and law-abiding members of society." Not many
years ago, a retarded person was kept in his own home, where he assisted
with chores and simple household duties, or, if he became a burden or
problem to the family or the community, he was placed in a state institution. There were few alternative types of residential placement. The principle at that time was one of segregation and control; and the philosophy,
one of "out of sight, out of mind." In spite of a much more enlightened
attitude in the community in recent years, it has been reported by the National Institute of Mental Health (*Mental Health Statistics,* 1965) that the
trend of small but steady increases in the resident patient population in
public institutions for the mentally retarded continued into 1964. In that
year there were almost 180,000 patients in the 134 such public institutions
in the United States, an increase of about 40,000 since 1954. In addition to
these residents in institutions for the retarded, an estimated additional

40,000 mentally retarded were resident patients in the state and county mental hospitals. The number of admissions for the first time exceeded 15,000 in one year, resulting in an admission rate of eight patients per 100,000 civilian population. However, this was only 109 patients more than in 1963. The steady increase can, of course, be attributed directly to the increase in total population of the United States. More institutions now are admitting patients regardless of age. Many institutions previously limited admissions to patients six to twenty-one years of age, but now are admitting infants and young children as well as adults who were cared for at home until the parents were no longer able to provide this care.

The expansion of residential care facilities in the community is one of the major changes in residential care. Although most retarded individuals still reside in their own homes, many other facilities now are becoming available for the retarded person in the community. These include such facilities as foster homes, nursing homes, day care-centers, nursery schools, private schools, private institutions, and sheltered workshops, as well as state institutions. Almost all of the mildly and most of the moderately retarded now reside in some type of residential care facility within the community, including their own homes. Some of those remaining in their own homes attend special classes, either in public or private schools. Others who live in foster homes may also attend public or private schools. Older patients may live at home and work in a sheltered workshop or supervised work-placement. Thus, many of the mildly and moderately retarded individuals living in the community now are provided work opportunities and special education.

The Office of Education of the Department of Health, Education, and Welfare (1964) reports that the nation today is providing special education for approximately 1,670,000 children and young people, the largest number that our schools ever have served. Education programs are available to serve many types of exceptional children, including blind, partially seeing, deaf, hard-of-hearing, speech-impaired, socially maladjusted, emotionally disturbed, mentally retarded, gifted, crippled, and those with special health problems. These children receive instruction in special day schools, special classes in regular schools, in residential schools, hospitals, and clinics, and, when no other plan is available, in their own homes. Special school programs are served by a variety of professional persons, ranging from itinerant teachers to speech and hearing specialists. Because of the diversity of their needs, some children attend school for a full day, some for only part of the day; some require special education for only short periods, perhaps only a few months; whereas, others require it for years. At the beginning of this century, few local school systems had any handicapped children in special-education programs. Since that time, there has been a steady increase in these local programs, and the increase has been further accelerated in the past quarter century. At least 90 per cent of the children now receiving special education are enrolled in programs administered by the local public-school system. Today the character of some institutions serving handicapped children appears to be changing in such a way as to make them an even more vital part of the total range of school services for the handicapped. More of the residential schools are providing diagnostic services and short-term remedial instruction, which can be especially valuable when there is a close relationship between the institution and the child's home community. For example, in California, the Department of Education reports that one hundred new classes for trainable mentally retarded pupils were established in California public schools in September 1964, bringing the total number of pupils to 5,252 now enrolled in 482 classes for the trainable mentally retarded. In the ten-year period from 1954 to 1964, the number of classes increased from fifty-six to 482, and the number of pupils enrolled from 628 to 5,252. In the 1963–1964 school year, the increase of one hundred classes was more than double the increase of any previous school year. The total number of pupils now enrolled in special classes in California public schools exceeds 50,000.

If the retarded individual can remain in his own home and attend special classes, he will be much better off. This is emphasized in a report by the Group for the Advancement of Psychiatry (1959), in which it is stated that:

> accepted psychiatric principles do not support the separation of any child from his family if the only purpose is to make an educational program available to him. In recent years more communities have developed special public school programs for the educable mentally retarded and some now also include provisions for the trainable children. When such facilities are available, the admission of a retarded child to a residential setting is determined by the severity of the other related factors—psychological, social or somatic. This trend, which has significantly altered the composition of institutional patient populations calls for a reconsideration of the aims, programs, facilities and personnel of such institutions. . . . A mildly retarded individual is seldom admitted to a residential center simply on the basis of his impaired intelligence. However, the disintegration of the family constellation, distorted sociocultural attitudes and lack of available community facilities and programs often result in further psychological impairment in the retarded child. He may then become a psychiatric casualty and, since adequate help is rarely available to him in his own community, placement in a residential facility becomes necessary even though it could have been avoided had other resources been available (pp. 13–14).

A number of traveling clinic programs have been established in an attempt to find a solution to the lack of community resources for the mildly and moderately retarded. One of these traveling clinics operates from the Sonoma State Hospital in California (Butler and Bramwell, 1964). Since

many patients are cared for satisfactorlly at home by their own families, but
need counseling, guidance, support, and reassurance, a traveling clinic
going to remote areas that do not have adequate facilities for diagnosis,
evaluation, counseling, and guidance can be of great assistance, not only to
these families, but also to supporting agencies in the local communities.
Traveling clinics can be an adjunct to the residential care of the child in his
own home or in a foster home. Therefore the traveling clinic offers another
alternative to institutional placement by making it possible for the family to
keep the retarded child at home. This concept has been stressed by Eleanor
F. Hawley (1963) in an article setting forth the contributions of the public
health nurse to families who have a retarded child. The public health nurse
may be a member of a diagnostic and evaluative clinical team, and often
serves as a liaison between an institution and the family. The Public Health
Nursing Service recognizes the physical, emotional, social, recreational, and
economic needs both of the family and of the retarded child and not only
attempts to meet these needs, insofar as possible, but also strives to utilize
existing community facilities to the maximum extent. Even though a diagnosis of mental retardation implies a need for special services, it must be
kept in mind that these children have the same basic needs as normal children. They need loving care and opportunities to seek and achieve success
based on their abilities however limited these may be. Every child, normal
or retarded, needs to be accepted as he is, rather than as the child we might
wish he were. Unfortunately, many conceptions associated with mental retardation are a result of ideas about what retarded individuals can *not* do
rather than what they *can* do. However, by meeting the basic needs of all
children, it is hoped the retarded child can be allowed to develop his individual potential within the environment most conducive to such development—namely, the home. With this goal in mind, the public health nurse
carries on a continuous educational campaign and concerns herself with
early case-finding of deviations from normal. By teaching home care of the
child and by making appropriate referrals, she can be of great assistance in
helping the family maintain a retarded child in his natural home.

The means by which many of the community residential facilities and
programs came into existence are relevant to changes in residential care.
For example, local, state, and federal governments are providing direct subsidies to parents, homemaker services, foster-home care, and care in private
institutions or nursing homes. Retarded individuals now institutionalized in
state hospitals in California may be placed in foster homes under a family-
care program subsidized by funds from the state Department of Mental
Hygiene. With this additional financial assistance, many mildly and moderately retarded can be placed in private boarding schools and private residential facilities. The more severely retarded or those with serious behavior
problems may be placed in private institutions. Many of these private
schools or institutions provide twenty-four-hour supervision and some pro-

gramming for these individuals. For the more severely retarded and physically handicapped person, the nursing home may be the residential facility of choice in the community, providing twenty-four-hour nursing supervision with medical consultation. In California, both a Study Commission on Mental Retardation and a legislative committee have recommended and are urging legislation to provide financial assistance for the purchase of care in the community for families who are unable to handle this expense without assistance.

The California Department of Mental Hygiene further indicates the need for development of residential rehabilitation centers. As previously stated, residential care for the mentally retarded includes residential schools, training facilities, boarding homes, and foster homes. Some of this care can be purchased; however, in addition to these facilities, residential rehabilitation centers are needed to provide care, training, and rehabilitation for retarded persons who do not require hospital care but who do need a protected living environment with a program of training and rehabilitation. These proposed state-operated residential rehabilitation centers should not exceed 500 beds, should be designed with small living units, and should provide an extensive program of training, education, and rehabilitation. The objective of this type of facility should be to prepare as many retarded persons as possible for community living. Some eventually would be able to leave the facility and maintain themselves; others might continue to live at the facility and have outside employment; and still others might live at home and come to the center for daytime training and education. Such residential rehabilitation centers would not be medical facilities, but would be rehabilitation and education facilities operated by persons skilled in the fields of education or rehabilitation. Every effort should be made to meet the needs of the individual close to his home and in such a way as to maintain his relation with his family and peers. With such programs being planned, it is likely that, in the future, fewer boys and girls will find themselves living in institutions merely because community resources are lacking, regardless of whether they are blind, deaf, retarded, or are medically, socially, psychiatrically, or otherwise impaired.

What is happening to the traditional state institution as a result of these changing concepts? We find that state institutions are now more and more becoming hospitals in the true meaning of the word, rather than schools, homes, or colonies. Only a little more than ten years ago, state hospitals for the retarded in California were called state homes. Even in those state residential institutions that still are oriented primarily to the concept and philosophy of providing educational and vocational programs, it is becoming increasingly necessary to provide more medical and nursing care. Many of these residential schools or colonies now are building acute medical units in close proximity to their present facilities. A Group for the Advancement of Psychiatry report (1959) states:

The aim of a modern residential institution should be to assist the patient in achieving maximum social, emotional and intellectual maturation and the earliest possible return to his own home. It is no longer valid to look upon the residential setting as a permanent abode for all mentally defective youngsters. Programs should include all the medical techniques together with such other services as our society commonly provides for the development of independent adults . . . the admission of any retarded child is almost always accompanied by an emotional upheaval in the family constellation. These facts in themselves point to the essential role which psychiatry must play in the development of programs for the mentally retarded. The more rapid movement of patient populations and the admission of patients with a specific therapeutic goal in mind clearly demand that residential institutions be viewed as medical facilities. Since it is advisable that this function be reflected in their title, such facilities should be designated appropriately.

This is not to say that many residential facilities are not fulfilling a vital need as residential schools or homes, but they should be recognized as such and serve the mildly and moderately retarded rather than the severely retarded with multiple physical handicaps. Because of the alternative residential placement possibilities now available within the community for the mildly and moderately retarded, most state institutions are receiving the more severely mentally retarded patients with multiple physical handicaps and concurrently are returning an increasing number of mildly and moderately retarded to the community. There has been an absolute increase in the number of these severely handicapped children in recent years as a result of the many new developments in modern medicine in the care and treatment of the premature and handicapped infant whose life is being preserved and prolonged. Only a few years ago, many of these children would not have survived even the first few weeks of life. The modern state hospital for the retarded provides the necessary resources to care for this type of patient.

Historically, the role of the residential state institution has been one of custodial care. There is now a progressive movement toward more intensive specialized treatment. With the admission of more severely handicapped children to state hospitals, however, constant vigilance is required to prevent custodial attitudes and philosophies. Where previously vocational training, education, socialization, and preparation for independent living in the community were goals to be sought for the mildly and moderately retarded, now the state hospital must be much more concerned with providing intensive medical and nursing care for the severely handicapped patient for whom operant conditioning has become a primary goal. Educational and vocational training for independent living is unrealistic for these patients. They should be admitted to state hospitals for the mentally retarded, thereby leaving the schools, homes, or colonies to handle the mildly and moderately retarded who require vocational, educational, and other types of rehabilitation and training.

As a result of the change in the patient population of state hospitals for the mentally retarded, it has become necessary to revise training programs to enable employees to care more adequately for the severely handicapped patient. Such training programs have received assistance and added impetus through federal funds provided by National Institute of Mental Health in-service training grants and hospital improvement programs. These employee training programs will be medical and nursing oriented, with emphasis on physical care, training, and habilitation. Basic nursing care must be augmented by other clinical disciplines, including physical therapy, orthopedic services, rehabilitation services, psychology, social service, and education. Each discipline is finding its role changing to adapt to the more severely handicapped patient. For example, psychologists must devise new tools for testing the potential of these patients, since present methods and techniques do not suffice in most instances. Rehabilitation services and the hospital school must devise new techniques and methods for training and teaching these patients to develop their abilities and potentials to the fullest. The various medical specialties, such as orthopedics, cardiovascular medicine, pediatrics, neurology, physical medicine, eye, ear, nose, and throat, and others, are becoming more concerned with the severely handicapped patient. Also, the need for additional clinical services has increased rapidly in areas such as clinical laboratory studies, electroencephalography, and X rays. Specialized tests and procedures such as karyotyping, biochemical tests for the various inborn errors of metabolism, and the use of radioisotopes have increased the need for additional clinical laboratory services. Albert J. Glass (1964) has stated that public mental hospitals including those for the mentally retarded, represent the largest and most readily available segment of mental health resources in this country. He recommended that they move out into the community even more actively, in order to exploit these resources to the fullest and provide additional treatment programs including increased residential treatment services for mentally disturbed and retarded children and adolescents. Although the need for state hospitals to be medical and nursing oriented residential care facilities is becoming more evident, this in no way diminishes the need for other types of residential facility. As more facilities are provided in the community, the need for standard-setting, licensing, and inspection of these facilities becomes increasingly important. Conflicting policies must be resolved and a single state agency made responsible for licensing.

As more and additional types of residential facility in the community are required for the retarded, the location of new facilities becomes increasingly important. Charles Cleland outlined the range of factors relating to site selection of new institutions for the retarded and emphasized the importance of economic and climatic conditions, labor resources, distances involved, and political pressures in relation to the functions of institutions as they affect patient care in the present and future.

> The ability of residential institutions to respond to changes occurring within the field of mental retardation is, in many instances, seriously impaired by their location. Unable to alter their environment by shifting to a new location, institutions, once situated, may exist throughout their entire history chained to a set of economic, geographic, and labor market conditions seriously handicapping their efforts to meet the objectives of service, production, research, and training. . . . Of the 476 public and private institutions for the retarded listed in the 1960 Directory of the American Association on Mental Deficiency, it is possible that as many as half are operating in such unfavorable locations. . . . The general improvement in institutional programs, the population explosion, urbanization, and increasing technology intensify the demand for residential facilities for the retarded, with the resultant likelihood that institutions will multiply during the coming decade. In view of the humanitarian and economic considerations involved in the establishment of such institutions and their relatively long life expectancy, favorable location of future institutions is increasingly important. . . . It is axiomatic that a viable institution must secure, hold, and sustain a professional staff capable not only of creativity, but of that ancillary accomplishment, utilization of the creative efforts of others. . . . The image of the institution develops—in the main—from the staff it holds and from those it loses. As the history of the poorly located institution extends and age brings physical plant deterioration, the image of the institution usually deteriorates correspondingly (Cleland, 1963, p. 127).

In considering the location of new state facilities for the mentally retarded, it must be recognized that the state hospital is now emerging as a major training center and resource for the therapeutic team. It is, therefore, quite important that new institutions for the mentally retarded be located close to large universities in order to promote training, research, and development of new programs. The gap between institutions of higher education and the state hospitals is now beginning to close, as faculty members of universities, colleges, and medical schools engage in teaching, training, and working within the state hospitals. Concurrently, members of state hospital staffs are on the faculties of colleges, universities, and medical schools. This interchange between the institutions of higher education and the state hospitals has emphasized the role of the state hospital as a teaching center. Another interchange between institutions of higher education and state hospitals is the development of rapidly expanding research departments in state hospitals. Many state hospitals are becoming major research centers, with a great increase in the number of full-time personnel working in research, particularly since funds have become increasingly available in recent years.

Many university faculty members are utilizing the clinical material and facilities of the state institutions for valuable research. Research is not restricted to basic research into the causes of mental retardation; applied clinical research projects are increasing to develop new methods and techniques for assisting the severely handicapped patient in achieving his full potential.

A concept that is not new but that is not usually considered of vital importance in residential care of the retarded is the use of volunteer programs. Of the many volunteers now working with the retarded, especially noteworthy are the teenage volunteers. A number of youth organizations such as Girl Scouts, Boy Scouts, Campfire Girls, Junior Red Cross, and teenage church groups are quite active in volunteer programs for the retarded, both in state hospitals and in community residential facilities. Volunteers bring with them hope, enthusiasm, and a renewed faith that the community does care, and they take back to the community a greater understanding and acceptance of the retarded. The volunteers are "ambassadors extraordinary" between the community and the residential-care facility.

In summary, there can be little doubt that the concept of residential care, both in the community and in the state institution, is in a transitional phase. We may anticipate many new developments in community facilities, including long-term care, resident school care, family homes, nurseries, day-care centers, and other private facilities. There has been a continuing increase in the number of these private facilities in recent years. In California, as of June 30, 1964, there were 240 private facilities with a licensed capacity of 3,512 for the care of the mentally retarded. The admission rate to private institutions for the mentally retarded was 9.9 per 100,000 population, while admission to the state hospitals during the same period was only 8.4. The average daily population rate for private mentally retarded patients was 14 per 100,000; for state hospitals, 67.9. Day-care patients accounted for one-fourth of the patient population in facilities for the mentally retarded, and 61 per cent of the patients resident in facilities for the mentally retarded were in the age group five to seventeen years, males outnumbering females. Facilities with less than fifty beds showed the greatest increase. With private institution admissions exceeding state hospital admissions by 275 in 1964 in California, the important role they play in this most populous state in the Union can be appreciated.

The aim of a modern residential institution should be to assist the patient to achieve maximum social, emotional, and intellectual maturation, and the earliest possible return to his own home. It is no longer valid or feasible to look on the residential setting as a permanent abode for all mentally defective youngsters. The movement is back, therefore, to the community, to smaller facilities closer to the patient's home, providing a variety of services to meet the needs of each mentally retarded person. The President's Panel on Mental Retardation (1962) reported,

The challenge to State institutions is how to accelerate the change from large isolated facilities to smaller units close to the homes of the patients and to the health, education, and social resources of the community; and the challenge to both State and private residential facilities is how to re-place the old concept of custodial care, wherever it still exists, with modern programs of therapy, education, and research. Institutional care should be restricted to those whose specific needs can be met best by this type of service. Institutions are but one facet in a continuum of care (p. 134).

There is still an urgent need for more residential facilities in the community, such as foster homes, nursing homes, private schools, private institutions, day-care centers, and clinics, and a need for more beds in small state-oper-ated facilities located close to the patient's home. These facilities, located in strategic areas, should probably be less than 500 beds and should be not only residential but also diagnostic and counseling centers. This will, of course, require money and trained personnel. With the increase in the num-ber of facilities for residential care in the community, the large state hospi-tals for the retarded should be able to reduce their inpatient population, reduce overcrowding, and eliminate waiting lists. The state hospitals, how-ever, still have a long way to go to meet the standards for state residential institutions for the mentally retarded established by the American Associa-tion on Mental Deficiency ("Standards for State Residential Institutions," 1964). At the present time, most state hospitals are pressed to provide even a minimum fifty square feet of floor space for each bed, although the Amer-ican Association on Mental Deficiency standards call for a minimum of seventy square feet of floor space. In most hospitals, bathing and toilet facilities are also totally inadequate according to these standards. The state hospitals have an obligation and a responsibility to make every effort to meet basic standards for residential care.

In the community there is still a shortage of physical facilities for many types of needed programs for the retarded. On this subject, the Presi-dent's Panel states,

High priority should be given, however, to construction of facilities for day and residential care and related community programs designed to express the new program concepts recommended in other sections of the report (p. 141). . . . Impetus should be given in the United States to the develop-ment of a wider range of diversified residential arrangements for those re-tarded persons who, for whatever reason, cannot live with their own or foster families; i.e., small units designed in program and structure to meet different needs (p. 146).

In conclusion, concepts are changing continually with respect to the residential care of the mentally retarded, and there is a great demand for new ideas, imagination, initiative, ingenuity, personnel, funds, and facilities, as well as courage of conviction. As Begab (1964) has succinctly stated, "We have come a long way toward meeting the long neglected needs of the retarded and mounting an all-out attack on mental retardation, but one decade of action cannot offset centuries of inaction. There is still much to be done" (p. 464).

## REFERENCES

Michael Begab, "Mental Retardation: The Role of the Voluntary Social Agency," *Social Casework,* XLV (1964), 457–464.

George A. Butler and Donald M. Bramwell, "From Trial and Error— How We Developed a Traveling Clinic Program," *Mental Retardation,* II (1964), 286–289.

Charles C. Cleland, "Locational Variables in the Establishment of Institutions," *The Training School Bulletin,* LX (1963), 123–129.

Gunnar Dybwad, *The Dynamics of Mental Retardation,* U. S. Department of Health, Education, and Welfare, Public Health Service Publication Number 1267 (Washington, D. C.: Government Printing Office, 1964).

Albert J. Glass, Keynote Address, Sixteenth Annual Mental Health Institute, Dallas, Texas, 1964.

Group for the Advancement of Psychiatry, *Basic Considerations in Mental Retardation: A Preliminary Report,* Report Number 43 (New York: Group for the Advancement of Psychiatry, 1959).

Eleanor F. Hawley, "The Importance of Extending Public Health Nursing Services to Retarded Children Living at Home," *Mental Retardation,* I (1963), 243–247.

*Mental Health Statistics,* U. S. Department of Health, Education, and Welfare, Public Health Service, National Institute of Mental Health (Washington, D. C., 1965).

President's Panel on Mental Retardation, *A Proposed Program for National Action to Combat Mental Retardation* (Washington, D. C.: Government Printing Office, 1962), pp. 134–135, 141, 146.

Office of Education, Department of Health, Education, and Welfare, *School Life* (Official journal of the Office of Education) (Washington, D. C.: Department of Health, Education, and Welfare, 1964).

"Standards for State Residential Institutions for the Mentally Retarded," *American Journal of Mental Deficiency* (Monograph Supplement), LXVIII (1964), 1–101.

# PART V

Community Aspects of
Mental Retardation

# 21

# Some Theoretic Problems of Mental Deficiency and Their Action Implications

## STEWART E. PERRY

This analysis is based on an extensive review of the literature and on informal consultations with many workers in the field of mental deficiency and in allied studies. It has two aims: first, to provide a theoretic frame of reference for viewing the study of mental deficiency and, second, to point out some of the different implications for practical activity in the field that stem from various theoretic concepts and from the current state of the field. The two aims are, of course, closely allied, for according to one's frame of reference in any situation, one draws particular deductions for action.

Offhand, one is inclined to consider mental deficiency as a relatively permanent human condition and to feel that the most to be done for the person so afflicted is training of a narrowly educational or vocational sort. One hopes that such training, if the defective person has sufficient mental capacity, will fit him for specific limited positions in his institution or the community at large. Such a conception of mental deficiency very nearly epitomizes the general professional opinion in the field—if one is to judge from what has been published in periodical and other literature. There are certain bases on which such a conception rests. They may be stated in the following terms: (1) Mental defectives are to be viewed from the standpoint of their common symptomatology (substandard intelligence); that is, all mental defectives are alike, except for degree of deficiency. (2) Mental deficiency is to be considered as a specific subnormal condition of the intellect. (3) Etiology of mental deficiency lies in its organic nature, either acquired or hereditary. (4) Once the condition appears it is irreversible and permanent.

These four general statements sum up more or less the point of view of most workers in mental deficiency; they seem also to sum up the general public attitude toward the condition. However, I think it will be obvious to the reader that these statements about mental deficiency are not couched in the same kind of terms as current statements in other areas of mental-health study. Thus formulated, this conception of mental deficiency does not coincide with present-day thinking in other branches of mental-health study. For instance, the psychotic is no longer viewed from the standpoint of his symptoms alone, without regard to the context of his total current situation and history. Juvenile delinquency is no longer considered a specific condition of a weak conscience or superego. Drug addiction and alcoholism are not studied primarily from the standpoint of the constitutional and organic bases and effects of these afflictions. Yet mental deficiency is still generally considered along the same lines already discarded in other areas of study. Of course, there is no a priori reason why the study of deficiency should be couched in the same sort of terms as the study of other mental disorders; nevertheless, the consideration of mental deficiency in its traditional frame of reference has not done justice to the possibilities for a better understanding of what happens and what has happened in the instance of any particular person who is defective. Some sort of revision is therefore in order.

As one becomes sensitive to these lacunae in the study of mental deficiency, one may see a trend in the literature that is challenging the generally held conception of mental deficiency. As Leo Kanner says, "It does indeed seem strange that after nearly a century of scientific occupation with 'feeblemindedness,' those best informed should still be wondering what they have been, and are, dealing with" (Kanner, 1948, p. 367). What appear to have been the first inklings of a need for a re-evaluation of mental deficiency were published in book form in 1949.[1] The basis for these attempts at re-evaluation lies, of course, in the same studies that brought about the current conception of other mental phenomena—that is, the dynamic interpretation of human behavior.

A dynamic interpretation of mental-deficiency behavior cannot be approached when one holds the traditional view of mental deficiency, for it requires a complete reassessment of the nature of mental deficiency—in effect a redefinition. Each mentally defective person must be considered, not as belonging to a homogeneous category called mental deficiency, but

[1] See the works cited in the acknowledgment following the references. The quarterly *American Journal of Mental Deficiency* has previously published a number of articles addressed to redefining mental deficiency.

as an individual;[2] his subnormal intellectual functioning must be looked on, not as an isolated phenomenon, but as part of his total presenting situation and history; his condition must be considered, not as constitutionally or organically determined, but as an interdependent complex of constitutional or physiologic processes, interpersonal processes, and socio-cultural processes; and from a research standpoint, the mental defective must be approached, not with an assumption of irreversibility and permanence, but with the assumption that benevolent intervention may lead to reversibility or improvement of the condition. Only with an approach based on such a frame of reference will it be possible to make progress in the study of mental deficiency.

These are the conclusions that seem to be indicated by current trends in the study of mental deficiency. In the succeeding sections of this chapter I hope to point out the basis for these conclusions and their usefulness.

## TRADITIONAL TERMINOLOGY AND CLASSIFICATIONS

The actual terms, words, phrases, and classifications in this field are quite confused in meaning and use. I have tried not to carry this confusion over into this chapter, and for purposes of clarification of the relationship between what is said here and what has been said elsewhere, some preliminary remarks on terminology are in order.

"Mental deficiency," "mental defect," "mental subnormality," and "mental retardation" are the four most commonly used terms, often used synonymously.[3] Some writers maintain a difference between them; mental

[2] That is, the individual defective, to be understood, will be seen as categorized in many ways, only some of which will have anything to do with deficiency per se. Significant groupings may have to do with variety and degree of defect, etiology, and prognosis, but also with processes evidenced in common with those persons mentally normal or above normal.

[3] Other more or less synonymous terms include the following: oligophrenia (used primarily on the European continent); amentia (an obsolescent term, now rarely used except in Great Britain); feeblemindedness (like the term idiocy, used in the last century, now in disrepute mostly for social and emotional reasons). In England, feebleminded is sometimes used to designate one group of defectives only, the high-grade or moron. Terminology is especially affected by the emotional tinges that have become attached to the words and phrases. "Retardation" is fast elbowing out "deficiency" and "defect," but this might be all to the good since the first term is less dogmatic. "Exceptional children" has been used also to include mental defectives along with physically handicapped, emotionally disturbed, and especially smart children. This term has its usefulness too (besides the euphemistic note), for in school administration it may not matter whether the exceptional child is super-bright or mentally defective; all "exceptional children" require special attention in a school system.

deficiency may mean "not enough mind originally" to be normally intelligent; mental defect, "an originally sufficient mind has been damaged" so that it is not normally intelligent; and mental retardation, merely any kind of permanent or temporary "delayed development of mental capacities" with resulting subnormal intelligence. These distinctions are not widely made, and indeed they serve little purpose. First, they are vague; and, second, it is practically impossible to differentiate patients sufficiently well in order to classify them thus, except in extreme cases. Therefore, all of these terms will herein be used synonymously. . . . It is significant that we have so many and such confused names for a condition that we can describe so poorly. . . .

In the past, mental deficiency has been distinguished from mental illness. It is a fairly useful distinction, but there are some indications that more progress could be made in this field if the distinction were not so tightly drawn as to exclude the probability of important processes common to both groups. To this date, we know scarcely more than is epitomized in John Locke's comment in 1689: "In short, herein seems to lie the Difference between Idiots and Madmen, that Madmen put wrong *Ideas* together, and so make wrong Propositions, but argue and reason right from them; but Idiots make very few or no Propositions, and reason scarce at all" (Locke, 1689, Book II, Chapter XI, Section 13).

Even if a satisfactory general term could be found, there would remain the problem of subclassifications. Almost every important worker in mental deficiency has tried his hand at this. Some classifications have been more satisfactory than others, but none has been really successful. The generally accepted dichotomous etiologic classification at this time is "endogenous" (inborn defect) and "exogenous" (acquired defect). The endogenous defective is distinguished supposedly by the "hereditary transmission of psychobiological insufficiency" (Doll, 1946), but he is very often organically indistinguishable from the normal. The exogenous defective has suffered some trauma, an injury or infection or other disturbance of the body system; generally, his organic condition makes it fairly easy to differentiate him from the normal. There are some defectives who simply do not fall into either of these groups, for instance, those with mongolism.[4]

From the standpoint of measured intelligence rather than etiology, defectives are classified as idiots, imbeciles, and morons, in ascending degrees of intelligence. These are analytic categories that shade into each other, no matter what frame of reference is used for their differentiation. Idiots are those who have an intelligence quotient below 20, or who are unable to take care of their own simplest body needs. Imbeciles are those who have an intelligence quotient of 20–50, or who are unable to profit from ordinary

[4] Almost all dichotomous divisions of deficiency offer the same distinctions and advantages as the exogenous-endogenous classification.

scholastic instruction. And morons are those who have an IQ of 50–75, or who are unable to use discretion and judgment.[5]

Table 21–1 provides a composite illustration of current diagnostic classifications in the United States. From Table 21–1 it may be noted that

Table 21–1. *Diagnosed First Admissions of Mental Defectives to Eighty-Nine Public Institutions for Mental Defectives and Epileptics in the United States, 1949* *

| DIAGNOSIS | NUMBER | PER CENT |
|---|---|---|
| familial | 2,399 | 30.7 |
| undifferentiated | 1,933 | 24.8 |
| mongolism | 862 | 11.1 |
| post-traumatic | 485 | 6.2 |
| with developmental cranial anomalies | 484 | 6.2 |
| postinfectional | 427 | 5.5 |
| with congenital cerebral spastic paralysis | 422 | 5.4 |
| other forms (miscellaneous) | 331 | 4.2 |
| with epilepsy | 180 | 2.3 |
| with endocrine disorder | 139 | 1.8 |
| with other organic nervous diseases | 118 | 1.4 |
| with tuberous sclerosis | 12 | 0.2 |
| with familial amaurosis | 8 | 0.1 |
| TOTAL | 7,800 | 99.9 |

* The table is adapted from a report, *Patients in Mental Institutions, 1949,* prepared by the National Institute of Mental Health; Washington, U. S. Government Printing Office, 1952 (Federal Security Agency, Public Health Service Publication No. 233). An additional 1,387 cases are included in the original table in a category labeled "unknown." This figure of 1,387 refers to cases that have not been reported by the institutions as diagnosed cases—one of the reasons for which seems to be that no medical person was available to make a diagnosis. The significance of changes in diagnostic terminology after the original publication of this paper is reported in Stewart Perry, Chapter 11.

less than fifty out of one hundred diagnosed first admissions of mental defectives are presently clinically differentiated. The differentiated group comprises mainly defectives who have some sort of apparent physical concomitant to the mental defect. The remaining 55 per cent or more are distributed into two categories, the undifferentiated and the familial, familial indicating a history of mental subnormality in the family, ordinarily with a presump-

[5] Approximately 75 per cent of all defectives are in the moron or borderline groups. The remaining 25 per cent is divided between the idiot and imbecile groups.

tion of inheritance. For the purposes of this analysis, this group of 55 per cent or so will be called unclassified. Sarason has called them simply garden-variety, but even this term may imply more homogeneity than exists. The unclassified defectives represent, of course, the ones about whom we need to know much more, especially since they make up more than half of the total number of defectives.

## Mental Deficiency as a Situation Complex

It is basic to important work in the field of mental deficiency that there be an adequate system of differentiation of various kinds of deficiency. Although all mental defectives may be seen as having arrived at the same end point—that is, a condition of subnormal intellectual functioning—one must find out the means by which each one arrived there in order to throw light on the individual case. The historic events that have led to mental deficiency are different according to the individual case.

It would seem a commonplace in the mental-health disciplines that each person be treated from the standpoint that he is an individual in terms of his past history; that is, that he is significantly different from the next person who is suffering from the same mental disorder. Yet this has not been the practice in mental deficiency. Kanner has said:

> The study of "feeblemindedness" seems at present to be entering upon a stage similar to that which existed with regard to the study of "insanity" about three quarters of a century ago.
>     At that time, protests began to be raised against the assumption of the homogeneity of the "Insane" . . . (Kanner, 1948, p. 365).

The problem that faces the worker is how best to understand the deficiency in each case and how to make the differences meaningful between one case and another. A unique event cannot be understood by itself; some of its essentials are understood by reference to the same essentials in other events. Since the one essential characteristic of mental defectives is insufficient, it is necessary to construct other significant subgroupings or categories—or to draw good analogies (Deutsch, 1952). Some other significant categories can be constructed by reference to similarities in the degree and nature of the subnormal functioning, but others will depend on an investigation of the total context of such functioning, both historically and in the present.

Thus, for the purposes of this analysis, mental deficiency will be considered as a total situation complex, integrated on the basis of presumed or observed subnormal intellectual functioning. The total situation cannot be studied at once, but approaches to the entire context are afforded by various methods of study. These methods are the several different sets of operations by which one determines the particular subnormality of the defective. No one set is adequate for all cases of deficiency; nor is any combination of them without limitations. It is with these sets of operations, their limitations, and their advantages that this study will seek to point out significant groupings of processes in the total mental-defective situation complex and the theoretic and practical implications of such groupings. . . .

In investigation of a particular problem formulated as a mental-defective situation, inquiry can be focused at two levels. The focus of attention may be on the defective himself in his particular total situation; or it may be on the situation itself. For instance, we may be interested in studying a mongoloid patient and his psychologic, physical, and social characteristics and activity. Or the focus may be on the mongoloid person merely as a part of the particular total situation, which may also include, for instance, his family's difficulties with him or society's problem in general with subnormal members. Because mental deficiency ultimately involves the study of the particular mentally defective person, it seems appropriate to proceed first on the individual-centered level of inquiry, and then on the more general situation-centered inquiry. Naturally, neither level is independent of the other, but for simplicity they may be dealt with separately as abstracting different aspects from the same complex and requiring somewhat different methodologic procedures.

In individual-centered inquiry, the way in which the worker views the mentally defective person will determine how the deficiency is defined. Moreover, the operations that the worker goes through in his inquiry into mentally defective functioning will determine which aspects of the individual he sees. Thus, in individual-centered inquiry, different approaches bring out different facts about the defective person. One may see the person as subnormally intelligent, which will imply intelligence-test procedures, or as socially incompetent, which will imply other procedures. Moreover, the methods of inquiry used may define which etiologic factors the worker is interested in. I will discuss briefly and generally how the mental defective as an individual may be looked at in terms of the methods used and the etiologic possibilities. These differ according to the individual studied.

## Mental Deficiency as Subnormal Intelligence

Almost by definition, one might say, mental deficiency is subnormal intelligence. Yet this is merely substituting one phrase for another, unless there is some specification of the way intelligence may be defined. Even though it is hard to get a broadly acceptable definition of intelligence, it is easy enough to use the operational definition that is acceptable for most purposes: intelligence is what the test tests. This is merely a shorthand way of saying that the test scores are highly correlated with certain criteria accepted as validating evidence of intelligence: (1) teachers' and psychiatrists' ratings of intelligence; (2) listings in *Who's Who;* (3) scholastic grades in primary and secondary school or in college; (4) scores on other intelligence tests; or (5) a combination of any or all of these. These are the means of validating intelligence tests, and the test is, of course, the quick, reliable technique for predicting and postdicting performance in terms of these validating criteria. These correlations with intelligence test scores would make the test sufficient for many purposes, such as determining college admissions. But presumably these criteria also correlate appropriately with whatever else is involved in what the layman calls intelligence. In other words, the tests work pretty well.

The standardized intelligence test has demonstrated its value as a relatively dependable technique for answering some of the questions about human behavior. However, the very ease and economy with which intelligence tests may be administered and their high degree of reliability for answering some questions have led to their overuse and abuse. In America, reliance on such tests to determine intelligence has been much more widespread than elsewhere (Sarason, 1953). As a matter of fact, in many cases, intelligence tests alone have been used to determine whether or not a person is to be called mentally defective and dealt with as such. Reliance on this single means of identifying the mentally defective person is, of course, related to the point of view that sees the defective merely on the basis of his symptomatology, as much as it is to the prestige of psychologic tests. The pitfalls in relying only on test scores in diagnosis of mental deficiency have been discussed by many others (Doll, 1941; Sarason, 1953). . . .

Limitations of the psychologic test in looking at mental deficiency may be mitigated to a great extent by intelligent use of the tests in conjunction with other ways of looking at the mental defective; and the most competent clinicians use these other ways also. However, there is a basic question involved here that has troubled psychologists a long time: granted that the intelligence test does not explain all aspects of a person's behavior, still does it not say what his fundamental capacity for intelligent behavior actually is? That is, by such a test is it possible to determine the given, constant human intelligence capacity for any particular individual, the gifts that he is born with?

A concept of a constant intelligence—as measured and observed—is basic to a concept of the constant character of mental deficiency. If one can determine the basic, constant[6] intelligence of a person, and the person's intelligence turns out to be subnormal, the person is predictably mentally defective for all his life. If, however, intelligence—again, as measured and observed—is regarded as a product of the hypothetical constant intelligence

[6] "Constant" here means constant relative to the developmental era.

gift, that is, innate biologic capacity, as well as the experience that the person has been through, then it is conceivable that differences in experience (as well as biologic gift) will help determine what is measurable and observable as intelligence. The idea that intelligence is a variable product of interaction and not a constant is becoming more prevalent.[7] That this concept of intelligence is gaining ground is merely another aspect of the scientific revolution of the twentieth century in ways of thinking about human and other phenomena—that is, as interaction processes rather than as discrete entities. This same sort of revolution in thinking about mental deficiency derives from the changing concept of intelligence as a product rather than a constant. Thus, the condition of mental deficiency as determined by a measure of intelligence cannot be considered constant.[8] It is also a product of the person's experience and his constitutional capacity. That the person's experience is important in the development of intelligence has only recently given impetus in America to the examination of other facets of the mental defective besides his psychologic test scores—of other aspects of his functioning that would cast light on his use of experience.

Outside of America, however, intelligence and its variant, mental deficiency, usually have been viewed rather broadly as social phenomena. As Harold M. Skeels and Harold D. Dye (1939) have pointed out, Alfred Binet, who first developed a consistent technique for measuring intelligence (especially in mental defectives), held that intelligence is a product of learning and therefore is dependent on the person's social experience. The history of American psychology shows that Binet's tools of intelligence measurement were accepted, but the conceptual framework on which they rested was commonly ignored. This difference in thinking about intelligence continues, and it is to be expected that workers in this country would have to take cognizance of it as an American cultural phenomenon. Depending on the concept of intelligence that is held, differences in a working program dealing with mental deficiency will result. For example, a program colored by the concept of a constant, constitutional, measurable intelligence will find its emphasis in spheres of activity that do not have to do with remedial efforts. In such a case there would be program emphasis on improvement of custodial care and vocational training for mental defectives as persons of limited basic capacities. On the other hand, an interactional concept of intelligence would show itself in an emphasis on what can be done to improve the operating level of mental defectives in a significant way—in effect, raising their intelligence operating level. The one concept implies making the most of what there is in the capacity of the subnormal person; the other

[7] For a discussion of the varying concepts of intelligence pertinent to this point, see the review of the subject by Florence Goodenough (1946), pp. 450–475.
[8] At the same time it must be recognized that the rates of change vary from individual to individual, and that change may be almost infinitesimal in a particular sampling of the development or deterioration of one person's powers.

concept implies seeing what can be done to intervene in his subnormal func
tioning.

Some other important action implications stem from these two concepts of intelligence and mental deficiency.[9] An interactional concept of
intelligence and mental deficiency gives more leads to the possibility of prevention. The use of the word "prevention" here is not meant to imply stav-
ing off an entity, deficiency; rather it is used in the sense of modification or
manipulation of some processes in a total situation. And some such modification or manipulation may be just as pertinent to the improvement of normal functioning as they are to the maintenance of normal functioning or the
improvement of subnormal functioning. Considering intelligence as a product of experience and constitution enables one to consider the possibility
of varying more of the influences or factors involved—variations that may
prevent the product which is mental deficiency. For instance, a modification
of the biochemical experience of the organism may prevent the product
called cretinism with its related mental defect. Or a modification of the
interpersonal or cultural experience of the organism may prevent the malevolent development of what may be nonphysiologically determined deficiency among the 55 per cent of unclassified deficiencies.

If, on the other hand, mental deficiency is considered as a constant—
irreversible and given—avenues of prevention are more limited. For instance, the only way to prevent mental deficiency in those of the unclassified familial type is presumably to prevent their being born in the first
place.[10] Here, prevention is entirely in the province of eugenics. Measures
of positive and negative eugenics (the facilitation of genetically favorable
births and the suppression of genetically unfavorable births) offer relatively
little hope. "The majority of geneticists . . . would not at present give
scientific support to a program of positive eugenics . . ." (American Eugenics Society, 1953). And negative eugenics in regard to this group of defectives poses scientific and cultural problems that are well-nigh insurmountable; for the familial cases, primarily high-grade, are capable of producing
normal or better than normal offspring, whereas normals may produce subnormal children. In the case of certain genetically determined syndromes,
such as phenylketonuria, eugenic measures would be and are useful. Such
cases as these make up but 1 to 2 per cent of the total number of defectives.

Action to prevent mental deficiency as acquired defect is not linked to
either of the above conceptualizations of intelligence. Efforts to prevent the
accidents and infections that cause mental deficiency are not specific to
either theoretic system. The proportion of these cases to the whole is, how-

---

[9] Of course, the presumed advantages or disadvantages for action programs of a
theoretic conception are not relevant to its scientific validity.
[10] Here it is significant that "prevention" is meant in terms opposite to what was just
previously noted.

ever, perhaps about one to nine;[11] so that from an action standpoint, the implications of the different theories of intelligence remain important.

A final point might be mentioned. The form of intelligence distribution sometimes has been taken to indicate the constancy of intelligence. That is, if one conceives of intelligence as always distributed in a normal curve, then, for instance, mental deficiency—the low end of the curve—will remain constantly distributed. Actually, even if intelligence distribution is best described by the Gauss curve—and there is some doubt about this (Wechsler, 1952)—the absolute distribution need not be conceived of as immutable. The pattern may remain the same, but the actual level may change. Just as the same description of height can be maintained although Americans become increasingly taller, so too the actual intelligence level may rise without disturbance of the form of its distribution. And control over the factors that make up intelligence may produce a different distribution.

It may appear that this analysis has devoted an excessive amount of attention to the concept of constant intelligence. But since the history of the study of mental disorder has been marked by a pessimistic attitude apparently related to the theory that the constancy and constitutionality of such disorders make them incurable, it seems appropriate to point out its relevance to implications for action in regard to mental deficiency. The history of the study of schizophrenia is pertinent to this point, for experimentation, research, and treatment languished so long as schizophrenia commonly was considered constitutional and irreversible.

### Mental Deficiency as Social Failure

With the use of an interactional concept of intelligence, then, the importance of situational factors in the definition of mental deficiency increases. The social situation of the person must be inquired into to determine whether or not the person is operating as a mental defective. Outside of America, mental deficiency has been more consistently viewed as a social phenomenon, as social failure, or incompetence.[12] That is, the mental defective is a person who cannot get along on the same level as other members of his society. If he is getting along all right, has a steady job, gets into no

[11] Some investigators have claimed that improved techniques for the diagnosis of birth injuries to the central nervous system would indicate that perhaps 50 per cent of deficiency is a result of such injuries. Such claims are, however, unsubstantiated as yet.

[12] See Alfred F. Tredgold (1952). However, as will be pointed out later, interest in social concomitants of mental deficiency has been related to the need for more inclusive description and is not at all a result of the use of an interactive concept of intelligence that views social processes as important in the nature of intelligence.

economic or legal trouble, and so on, he is not mentally defective no matter if his test scores would categorize him as deficient. Instead of relying solely on the test scores, the worker also looks at the patient's social adjustment.

It is difficult, however, to define social adjustment in terms of failure or incompetence so that it is exact enough to serve as an over-all criterion for mental deficiency. How is one to weigh, for instance, a steady, comfortable relationship with a spouse against a steady job in deciding the social level of the person concerned? Furthermore, if the person's situation changes—his wife dies or his job is redefined—will his abilities carry him through such a difficulty? Both problems, precise definition and possible situational change, are related, of course. If one could determine the social operating level of a presumed mental defective in an exact manner, it might be possible to predict with some success his level of performance within the probable situational changes that he might have to face. The clinician faced with a case must try to do this by reference to the patient's history, his test scores, and by personal observation of the patient. . . .

Although it is generally recognized that the psychologic test of intelligence should be supplemented by determination of the state of the whole person including his social behavior, it is still true that, in many school systems, only rudimentary recognition is given to other factors besides the psychologic test. Thus, the determination of whether or not a child is to attend school or be temporarily or permanently excluded from the public-school system may rest primarily on what score he may make on a test. Similarly, a decision is reached as to whether he should attend special classes. The evaluation of the teachers who have been in close contact with him is, of course, important anywhere and may in fact be the reason why he is given a psychologic test. But such evaluations are essentially clinical or impressionistic and depend on the insight and experience of the teacher, as well as on his ability and willingness to manage and teach a child who is operating on a subnormal level. The identification of subnormal children by a more inclusive approach and the administrative decisions that are dependent on such identification would be improved presumably by the development of social maturity measures. Of course this is an area in which not only the mentally defective child is concerned. The identification of "maladjusted" children in general is importantly involved in such social behavior scales.

Such scales may focus attention on the social concomitants of intelligent behavior for better diagnostic purposes; they have other practical advantages. A number of follow-up studies of persons who were supposed to be defective but who turned out to lead socially valuable lives on average and higher than average economic, social, and intellectual levels (Muench, 1944; Baller, 1936; Charles, 1953) indicates the importance of a more thorough examination of presumed defectives as well as a more tentative disposition that does not freeze the person into the category in which he is placed. Social behavior scales will point up the necessity to avoid such categorization.

At this point, it may be appropriate to mention that, historically, education has been more consistently concerned than any other discipline with the problems of mental deficiency. Whereas deficiency has suffered a varying fortune in regard to the amount of attention paid to it by medicine, psychology, and other concerned specialties (Haskell, 1944), the educator has been interested all along in the training and scholastic preparation of the defective for a more normal life.

For almost everyone in the United States or in the Western culture in general, school is the first important social contact outside of the family, and it is here that the child will come intimately to the attention of others besides his family who will discern deviations from expected behavior. Thus, the teacher is very likely to be the first person to be confronted with the problem of a mentally defective child, in the sense that the defective will fail this first test of social requirements. The social failure of the defective in meeting the demands of schooling is, in addition, an intellectual failure— an appearance of the lack of capacity by which most definitions of intelligence are reached; that is, through scholastic achievement. It was this problem that faced the French education authorities who commissioned Binet to do his pioneer studies in intelligence-testing.

The interest of workers in the problem of social failure or incompetence and its measurement has been a result of the attempt to provide symptomatic description, rather than to provide etiologic explanations or to indicate therapeutic prescriptions once the diagnosis of deficiency is established. Yet the collection of this sort of information on the social failure of the mental defective can contribute a good deal to an approach to intervention—such as the possibilities of psychotherapy—and to prevention—such as with respect to the social, cultural, and interpersonal preconditions of some presently unclassified deficiency. Thus, attention paid to the emotional experience as an etiologic factor can be an outgrowth of concern with mental deficiency as a social failure.

## Mental Deficiency as Organic Failure

Whereas the worker's interest in the aspect of social failure has had, historically, little relevance to questions of etiology, the reverse is true in regard to the worker's interest in the physiologic aspects of mental deficiency. Approaching mental deficiency with the methods of biology and physiology, one comes closer to an etiologic as well as symptomatic description of the condition. The patient who has had, for example, an encephalitic infection is examined from the standpoint that his physical condition (brought on by the infection) has resulted in his mental deficiency—barring other factors. The damage to the biologic substructure of human intelligence is considered the etiologic factor in such a case of mental deficiency; the implication is that in the absence of such damage the patient would have been normal in intelligence.

Indeed, one of the most frequent signs of mental defect is the appearance—mostly in low-grade defectives—of physiologic failure in the form of injury, disease, developmental anomalies, and so on. In such cases the physiologic equipment of the mental defective is demonstrably below par. And in these cases, generally to the extent that the biologic, nervous substructure is less than normal, the intellectual and mental functioning of the person will be subnormal. Beyond the limitations of a damaged or malformed nervous system he cannot develop in intelligent ways of living. Penrose has attempted a categorization of mental deficiency according to the physiologic level of the patient.[13] He feels that certain signs of physiologic malfunctioning can mark a group with lower intelligence from one that is more intelligent. The two groups are roughly equivalent to an idiot-imbecile group on the one hand and a moron-borderline group on the other; but the distinction between them is not intelligence level per se but physiologic level. For example, the lower group almost always is sterile, but the higher group is capable of reproduction. The determination of such biologic signs serves to distinguish, not only a level of intelligence (with its administrative and treatment implications), but also certain etiologic clues. Those of lower intelligence are the result of rare but easily discriminated causes—isolated genes and gross prenatal, natal, and early postnatal effects of disease and injury. The more intelligent group seems less easily discriminated; they fall into a nonclinical residual category.

The practical implications that may be drawn from this biologic approach to the grouping of mental defectives lie, for the most part, in the fact that demonstrable physiologic processes are of primary importance in the mental-defective complex in only a relatively small number of the total mental-defective group. Thus, we again arrive at the matter of the 55 per cent unclassified defectives, whose etiology remains undiscovered by the biologic definition of mental deficiency. The great difficulty with the physiologic approach to mental deficiency is that there are no discernible organic differences from the normal in most mental defectives. Their physiologic equipment will show the same amount of variation as might be found in any ordinary sample of normally intelligent people. The limitations of the physiologic approach may, to a certain extent, be laid to the state of knowledge about human genetics and human biology. Certainly the problems of cerebral lesions in birth injury await better means of detection. The perfection of instruments and techniques of biochemical and other organic investiga-

---

[13] Lionel Penrose (1949). Clemens Benda (1952) also has attempted a categorization on the basis of physiology, but this is medical and pathologic rather than generally physiologic. He underscores the important need for a developmental approach to organic deficiency, which Penrose seems to ignore.

tion into human life (with particular reference to the central nervous system) may make possible the acquisition of much more knowledge about mental functioning in general. Thus, the physiologic components or aspects of human ideation, problem-solving, and so on may be laid bare by further development of our tools for research. Such developments would be helpful to the study of mental deficiency from the standpoint of its definition as physiologic failure. Indeed, such basic discoveries about the biologic organism would benefit all of the mental health disciplines by casting light on the physiology of mental activity. But just as psychology and psychiatry in general move on, notwithstanding, as separate disciplines, so the study of mental deficiency need not await the discovery of basic neurophysiologic structure and functioning. Indeed, it seems that in many cases narrowly conceived human biology is of less importance in the complex of mental defect than interpersonal and socio-cultural processes. . . .

## Mental Deficiency as Inherited Defect

The aspect of deficiency that I will treat in this section is probably the most controversial way of looking at feeblemindedness. The inheritance of mental defect—the genetic determination of mental defect—is established conclusively for certain varieties of deficiency that make up perhaps less than 1 or 2 per cent of the total amount of deficiency (Neuer, 1947). Within the category of definitely established genetic deficiency are phenylpyruvic oligophrenia, amaurotic familial idiocy, and Huntington's chorea.[14] Each of these conditions is the result of an individual genetic factor. Each of the factors leads to a particular organic condition that in turn limits the behavior that the person may manifest. And the behavior limits set by these pathologic organic conditions are seen in the intelligence scores and other criteria of what we call mental deficiency.

The fact that such behavior mediated by a pathologic structure can be confused with the type of behavior that is derived from social experience and mediated by a presumably normal structure has led some writers to suggest a criterion for distinction (Anastasi and Foley, 1948). That is, if the behavior is to be considered genetically determined, the peculiar limit-setting structure must be demonstrated. Such a distinction would, of course, cast doubt on the genetics of much mental deficiency that is considered to be inherited, but that does not exhibit any abnormal organic structure. This distinction seems useful but not unequivocally valid.

[14] Huntington's chorea actually does not manifest itself until a long time after birth and, quite frequently, not until adulthood, so that some authorities would not consider this condition under the rubric of mental deficiency. However, it is common English practice to do so (Penrose, 1949). The phenylpyruvic syndrome is considered a recessive characteristic, but some instances would fit a dominant hypothesis better. Thus, the mechanism of genetic transmission is in doubt here (Jervis, 1952).

The basis for questioning this narrow criterion of inheritance lies in the following. First, certain demonstrable anomalies, such as those related to the presence or absence of the palmaris longus muscle, are still as far from hereditary explanations as schizophrenic reactions are. Moreover, there are changes in physiologic structure that are no different from those known to be inherited, but that are produced by environmental manipulation and even may be produced in animals experimentally. Thus, demonstration of structural differences from the normal does not provide the necessary evidence for a genetic explanation. Second, certain behavior patterns, such as that linked to periodic familial paralysis, have been seen to conform to, for instance, easily applied Mendelian laws long before the physiologic or biochemical basis for these conditions and behavior patterns was discovered. These considerations indicate that a criterion of demonstrable organicity cannot be applied indiscriminately.

The crucial conflict in this matter relates to those conditions for which multiple interacting genes are suggested as etiologic bases for certain behavior patterns, where such hypotheses rest on inconclusive genetic evidence. Thus, the claims of some students that 70 or even 90 per cent of deficiency is inherited defect must be discounted as, at present, not founded on any of the elements of genetic science. Whereas, the hypotheses of the etiology of mental deficiency in complex gene combinations remain inconclusive, there is nevertheless a great deal of indirect evidence that indicates multiple genetic influence on the appearance of the behavior pattern of deficiency. What these factors are, how they operate, and what degree of influence they have are, of course, the kinds of questions that must be asked. So far we do not have answers for many of these questions. It may be a good idea to indicate here some of the reasons why we do not have reliable answers and to summarize some of the information that we do have.

The reasons why we know so little about the general inheritance of mental defect fall into two categories, one relating to the nature of deficiency and the other relating to the techniques of genetic science in regard to human inheritance (Snyder, 1946). Deficiency itself presents problems to genetic (as well as other) investigation because of the diagnostic difficulties in the determination of deficiency. Not only is it difficult for the examiner to establish a diagnosis of deficiency that he can use in a genetic study, but to get sufficient cases he often must rely on records of patients whom he is unable to see himself. These difficulties, in themselves, are not insurmountable, but they pose definite limitations on using diagnoses made several or even many years ago in order to reconstruct family histories.

Moreover, deficiency is of several varieties and thus cannot be considered as a homogeneous whole for genetic investigation; it is necessary to single out some distinguishable type of deficiency to study genetically. Environmental influences are known to affect the appearance of a mental-deficiency pattern of behavior, and it is extremely difficult to isolate such extraneous influences. Finally, deficiency per se does not segregate from normality but blends into it; thus, no single genetic factor may be hypothesized. A hypothesis of multiple and interacting genetic factors that is, therefore, required in such cases of deficiency is extremely difficult to handle and to validate at the present state of genetic science.

The second category of difficulties besetting the genetic investigation of mental deficiency results from the techniques of genetics itself. That is, the standard techniques require experimental breeding and other manipulations that are impossible to achieve with human populations. Thus, other and less satisfactory techniques have had to be developed for studying human inheritance. For example, statistical methods may be used. Certain statistical treatments of an acceptable sample of human family histories would be conclusive when there is random mating. But, as has been often pointed out, human beings do not mate randomly but assortatively, which throws a degree of doubt on concordance of some kinds of data (such as on intelligence) with a statistical ideal (Penrose, 1949).

Some of these difficulties that limit the reliance that can be placed on genetic studies of deficiency are overcome to a certain extent in the instances of deficiency with a well-established organic syndrome owing to a single gene that shows up in family-history inspection; and strong evidence is thus presented for which no other hypothesis is as tenable. On the other hand, those cases where environment is more likely to be influential and where it is almost impossible to isolate such influences are just those for which genetic methods of studying deficiency phenomena are less effective. Naturally, this situation has led to confusion and contradictory conclusions, and the tendency has been to try to separate the hereditary from the environmental influences in wholly unsuitable and artificial ways so that the picture becomes even more clouded.

In the end, it is the assumptions and predilections of the investigator that determine what interpretations are made of heredity–environment studies such as intrafamilial intelligence correlations or twin studies. The estimates of the relative percentages of hereditary and environmental influences vary considerably. The data from one study have been interpreted to show both 34 per cent environmental influences and 66 per cent hereditary influences (Burks, 1928) and to show 22 per cent environmental and 78 per cent hereditary influences (Loevinger, 1943). Another study shows environment percentages in the 40's (Willoughby, 1928), and still another implies that environmental factors are overridingly important (Schmidt, 1946).

This is not the place to discuss all the ramifications of the differences in the various interpretations and studies (Loevinger, 1943). Nevertheless, "it appears that there are at present no practical applications or accessible consequences of the percentage analysis of the causation of intelligence in terms of which to test the accuracy of the various estimates" (Loevinger,

1943, p. 754). And, indeed, scientists are in general less motivated these days to separate one from the other, at least, from the standpoint of assigning numeric values to the two broad categories. It is true, though, as Penrose says, that

> the more recent [in the lives of the defectives] the occurrence of a disturbance which is responsible for existing cases of defect, the more easily will it be controlled and eliminated as a cause of new cases in the future. The crucial point makes the antithesis between nature and nurture so important practically (Penrose, 1949, p. 63).

· · · ·

There are some practical implications of mental deficiency as inherited defect, and they extend into the social organization of the country. Most outstanding of these is the question of a possible national decline in the intelligence level of the general population. If a country does not do something about the reproduction of mental-defective parents within its population, must it be faced with a general lowering of the intelligence level? This is an important question that we must answer as a result of looking at deficiency as inherited defect. Whatever may be the other influences of deficiency, must we not attend to the general social problem of the hereditary influences that may threaten our national intelligence level?

Although there are many who would answer this question in the affirmative—including the eugenics societies all over the world—there does not seem to be any tangible basis for pessimism (Thomson, 1947). Penrose has discussed the pros and cons of such a position and states that there is nothing to fear in this regard: although it seems as if those of lower intelligence have a greater reproduction rate than the more intelligent parents, the latter must depend not only on "the less scholastically inclined for manual labor but [also] for replenishment of genic material." [15] In other words, those of lesser intelligence probably produce enough intelligent children to offset the low birth rate of families of higher intelligence. Penrose maintains that "so far, no satisfactory direct evidence of declining intelligence in a modern community has been presented" (Penrose, 1949, p. 121). Most geneticists probably would agree to this, though they might not agree that there is no basis for pessimism about possible future developments.[16] The technique for

---

[15] Lionel Penrose (1949, p. 125). That less intelligent parents with different kinds of defects can give birth to normal and higher than normal children has been questioned by Clemens Benda (1952) on the basis of Sidney Halperin's work. Actually, Halperin's studies of defectives and their families do not permit any such conclusion. Not really amenable to any pertinent manipulation in this regard, the data seem to indicate, on the surface, agreement with Penrose's contention. See Sidney Halperin (1945; 1946).
[16] For a discussion of the trends that support a pessimistic view, see Frank Hankins (1942).

conclusively settling questions of this sort is a study of net reproduction rates. In the instance of mental deficiency, such a study would be virtually impossible because of the difficulties in singling out the cacogenic portion of the population—especially those childbearers, not themselves defective, who are likely to produce defective children.

In summary, mental deficiency as inherited defect is in certain cases a sufficient frame of reference for etiologic investigation. This is particularly so in cases where the structural mediation of behavior can be demonstrated. Where this demonstration is impossible, the hypothesis of the inheritance of defect is ordinarily less tenable since the same kinds of behavior may be shown growing out of the social or physical experience of the organism, about which our knowledge is also limited. The etiologic basis of the mental defective behavior in such cases is thus uncertain. And, moreover, we are at a loss to elucidate the integration of genetic predispositions with the influence of social experience in these or other instances.

Up to this point, I have attempted to describe the various means by which one can look at mental defectives from the standpoint of the individual involved. Now I will discuss the mental defective on the level of situation-centered inquiry, which will point up other problems involved in studying and doing something about mental deficiency. A good bridge between the consideration of the defective as an individual and the defective as only part of a larger situation is afforded by the discussion of mental deficiency as a pattern of interpersonal relations.

## Mental Deficiency as a Pattern of Interpersonal Relations

Very little work has been done to elucidate the patterns of interpersonal relations of mentally defective persons. The reason for this probably lies in the fact that the study of these relationships has evolved generally from work done in a psychotherapeutic setting, as most of our knowledge of psychodynamics derives from psychotherapy. But mental defectives have been considered not to require such therapy or even if they have emotional difficulties,[17] they are not amenable to therapy. Even those who contend that defectives can benefit from therapy may feel that more intelligent patients are more worth treating—first, from the standpoint of the patient's possible contribution to society and, second, from the standpoint of reward to the therapist. The mental defective presents a particular problem to the generally verbal procedures of the psychotherapist, for the defective ordinarily finds it difficult to verbalize his feelings and ideas, and his most obvi-

[17] In fact, existing studies seem to show that institutionalized defectives tend to be emotionally disturbed (Beier et al., 1951; Neuer, 1947).

ous deficit will be in this area. So, unless there is a trend toward psychotherapy with defectives,[18] workers are not likely to learn a great deal about the interpersonal processes involved in the mental-defective complex.

Aside from considerations of psychotherapy, there is an important relevance to mental deficiency in the study of interpersonal relations. First of all, a clearer picture of the patterns of interpersonal relations found in mental deficiency would be a definite aid in diagnosis: another aspect of the total situation gives the diagnostician more on which to base his decision. Second, there is the problem of institutional management of the mental-defective population, which could be aided by more information about interpersonal behavior patterns. Of course, the greatest interest in the interpersonal functioning of the mental defective is likely to obtain in the cases of those workers who consider measurable intelligence as a potentially variable product rather than a constant given. To them problems of etiology and treatment of mental deficiency as poor and inappropriate patterns of interpersonal living are very important.

To attempt to delineate a pattern of interpersonal relations for all mental defectives—in other terms, a character structure—may be as useless as trying to outline a general pattern for all psychotics. Since mental deficiency is a condition rather than a clinical entity or syndrome, variations among mental defectives in personality structure are likely to be as great as among any similar sample of the general population of more intelligent persons. The similarities in interpersonal relations that appear to exist—for instance, those referred to in such descriptions as "dull," "unresponsive," "not interested in surroundings," and so on—may have a great deal more to do with the social structure in which the defective is found. A large part of the study of defectives is carried on in resident institutions; thus, instead of delineating the character of a mental defective, such observations may have more relevance to the environment in which the character structure is viewed. For instance, maternal deprivation as a general characteristic of interpersonal relations in the institutional setting may be of importance. Many studies seem to point in this direction; without the degree of relatedness inherent in a maternal-like environment, a child may be seen to deteriorate in the degree of interest in his surroundings, in relating to other people, and in measurable intelligence.[19] . . . Thus, what may seem to be the mental-defective character may be little more than a function of the mental-defective institution.[20] . . .

Looking at mental deficiency as a pattern of interpersonal relations

[18] Recent issues of the *American Journal of Mental Deficiency* appear to be carrying more material on psychotherapy than previously. See a critical review of the literature on interpersonal relations and psychotherapy with defectives by Sara Neham (1951).
[19] John Bowlby has summarized a good deal of this literature and reports work of his own (Bowlby, 1951).
[20] Studies of dominant behavior indicate no particular differences between what is to be expected with normals and with subnormals (Albee and Pascal, 1951; Abel, 1943).

brings one to a consideration of the broader problem of human development and what happens in the serial social maturation of the growing human being. Within the frame of reference of mental deficiency as a pattern of interpersonal processes, intelligence, like other aspects of a person's personality structure, is conceived as varying according to the developmental era through which the person is proceeding. To take specific cognizance of this fact, psychologists weight scores on an intelligence test according to the age of the subject.

This kind of developmental approach to the intelligent behavior of the person is used in a common criterion of mental deficiency. That is, deficiency is to be distinguished from intellectual deficit produced by trauma or disease in a mature or near mature person. The assumption involved is that the deficit will differ in appearance, for the immature person will not have achieved certain of the feedback benefits of mature development that will remain in cases of intellectual deficit occurring at a later age.

The concept of developmental maturation in interpersonal relations suggests that a particular intelligence level during the maturation process may be an indication of previous intelligence levels but does not suggest that the levels may be identical or similar. In other words, the vicissitudes of interpersonal experience will permit dramatic and radical personality changes up to the age of twenty and possibly beyond (Sullivan, 1953). The changes for better or for worse are mitigated or strengthened in later experience. These considerations can help explain the difficulties in the determination of infant intelligence and in the postdiction of previous intelligence levels and the prediction of later ones.

It should be pointed out that these considerations are quite possibly relevant for certain cases only. Thus, gross congenital and prenatal disturbances of the central nervous system producing mental deficiency probably do not permit—from the very beginning of *postpartum* life, social life—the influences of life experience that mark intelligent functioning and its development or deterioration. Similarly, in some cases, the gross experiences of anxiety and similar "noxious states" may preclude this type of reception of influence. In these latter cases, one may be constrained to regard the importance of interpersonal experience in the development of intelligence as quite possibly pre-eminent.

This possibility, though so readily suggested by our present knowledge of child development, has not been sufficiently explored. For example, there is little information that will lead us to understand communalities in the genesis of some presently unclassified mental defectives and childhood schizophrenia, a condition often mistaken for deficiency. Perhaps the experience of anxiety at different developmental periods may have something to do with the similarity of early schizophrenia and some unclassified mental deficiency. That is, the experience of anxiety in one developmental period may be important in the etiology of deficiency and in another period in the etiology of childhood schizophrenia. In both types of cases, some of the underlying processes will be common, the difference lying in the developmental age at which defensive mechanisms are called forth. The common incidence of schizophrenia among young mental defectives gives another lead to such hypotheses.

From another standpoint, the developmental history of the human being as a person—as a focus for a pattern of interpersonal relation—is important for the determination of intelligent functioning. The determination of intelligence in the infant and young child is based on different observable activity from the case of the older child and the adult. In the infant, simple physical and social activity is measured. For example, does the baby follow another person with eye movements? Does he grasp at close objects, at ones farther way, and so forth? In the case of the child, scholastic achievement is the matrix of intelligence measurement—a completely different activity with very different significance, interpersonally, socially, and culturally. And in the adult, intelligence is again a function of adult life that is not necessarily characterized by current interest in or familiarity with materials of a scholastic nature. And, of course, there are cultural differences that obstruct measurement of intelligence. For instance, one tester found that no member of a particular African culture would answer any questions without consultation with the tribal elder. Less dramatic, but of more widespread importance, are the differences in intelligence-test scores between cultures and subcultures within one culture reported by Otto Klineberg (1931), Frank J. Kobler (1943), and many others, that are in part a function of cultural differences.

These difficulties in the definition or determination of intelligence in view of the interpersonal development of the human being are associated intimately with the fact that the growing human being must be seen as a dynamic organism, not only physically, but interpersonally. Specifically, this may mean that, in a case of mental deficiency with unknown etiology, a hypothesis of the existence of the condition at earlier ages is not necessarily tenable without evidence derived from that earlier period. (Such a hypothesis is characteristic, however, of present conceptions of mental deficiency.) The fluctuations of measurable intelligence in a longitudinal study, such as that of Jean Macfarlane,[21] can point up the usefulness of viewing, from the standpoint of etiology as well as description, certain instances of mental deficiency as patterns of interpersonal relations, resulting from past experience with psychologically significant others. Similarly, the work of Samuel A. Kirk (1952) on the influence of preschool education programs for young children may give further insight into the interpersonal aspect of the mental-deficiency complex.

[21] Hers is The Guidance Study, the University of California's twenty-year investigation of physical, mental, and psychologic development from birth to maturity.

### Mental Deficiency as a Socio-cultural Pattern

To talk about the interpersonal aspects of human functioning in mental deficiency requires that one also consider processes that are interdependent with personality systems—social systems and cultural systems. The interdependence of society, culture, and personality is well established in the conceptual framework of the mental-health disciplines. This is perhaps less true in regard to the specific study of mental deficiency, however. If one is to judge from the published material in the field of mental deficiency, very little attention has been paid to cultural and social processes in the mental-defective complex. Yet in the case of measurable intelligence, the relationship between the social and cultural situation and processes with intelligence-test scores is fairly well known and has been the subject of many studies unrelated to mental deficiency.

Otto Klineberg (1931), for example, studied the intelligence of racial and national groups in France, Italy, and Germany. A significant and reliable difference was found between the rural and urban groups as a whole and within each country. The international urban differences were, on the whole, small and unreliable, but the international rural group differences were mainly significant. No significant differences were found either nationally or racially. Some subgroups within one country were closer to subgroups in another country than they were to other groups within their own nation. The differences that were obtained could be explained on the basis of the social and cultural living conditions of the groups studied. That is, the higher the test scores, the more superior were the environments in regard to financial standing, schools, and means of communication.

The same kinds of results from research characterize studies of American intelligence. For instance, Army Alpha tests showed that, in general, American Negroes do not achieve intelligence-test scores in the higher ranges to the same extent as whites. Yet northern Negroes as a group were superior to southern whites. The marginal social, economic, and cultural background in which most members of the Negro race are reared is invoked as a factor in their generally low scores. That is, the impoverished conditions of life that are the lot of a cultural out-group may operate to deny them certain possibilities of intellectual advancement. Despite the fact that Negroes, on the whole, make lower test scores, there has been no reliable evidence of constitutional or biologic insufficiency. One is inclined to believe that the race as a whole has the same intellectual potentialities as the culturally more fortunate Caucasians.

Even within a single city, the mean IQ's of different subcultural groups will differ for the Caucasian category. Thus Frank Kobler (1943) has pointed out the variation between children of foreign-born Germans, Italians, and Irish—as well as of Negro children—in Chicago. Intelligence-test scores varied according to the distance from the center of the city, rising in groups farther out from a mean of 89 to 102. Thus it can be said more generally that all marginal social groups will be depressed intellectually, according to our present measuring instruments. Yet "despite the well-nigh perfect correlation between garden-variety [that is, unclassifiable] deficiency and unfavorable social conditions the consensus among workers in the field is that cultural factors are relatively unimportant" (Sarason, 1953). This consensus, as has been pointed out earlier, is being challenged on the basis of a reassessment of the nature of mental deficiency as a variable product rather than a constant given. Whereas no one today will dispute the depression of intelligence by social and cultural situations, such a lowered intellectual functioning (to the mental-defective level) is not considered by many authorities to be mental deficiency, in that it is not a constitutional unchangeable condition existing since or shortly after birth. The constitutional component, if any, of deficiency resulting from cultural deprivation indeed remains to be demonstrated, but this type of deficiency may, in some instances, be just as unchangeable[22] and of as early appearance as deficiency where early constitutionality is demonstrable. There are two reasons for this. One, at a certain stage in the person's development, what we know about re-education and re-socialization of deprived children will be of no avail; the defective at age fifteen and up could not benefit from milieu changes as a younger defective might. And, two, even for a younger child, it might be difficult if not impossible in certain instances to govern enough of the milieu to effect important improvement; school and other outside activities might be geared to his needs, but the home might remain unstimulating and depriving. Thus, the distinction between a "true" mental-defective complex and one that is a result of a low cultural ceiling cannot be made on the basis of a criterion of irreversibility or early appearance of the condition.

Cultural processes are important in another way to the mental-defective complex: the value systems of a society may help define what deficiency is and how it is to be dealt with. Of course, this has been pointed out already in reference to the concept of intelligence, where one may assume that cultural requirements of American society permitted the acceptance of Binet's technologic contribution, but not the philosophic and conceptual basis of that contribution. Thus, mental deficiency became, for an important segment of professional workers, a particular kind of phenomenon or, perhaps better stated, remained in their understanding the particular kind of phenomenon that I described in the first paragraphs of this analysis. From another point of view, the values attached in a particular society to what a person gets out of the educational practices to which he is expected

[22] The cases of extreme isolation are examples of such relatively irreversible states. Such well-known cases as Kasper Hauser and the Wild Boy of Aveyron generally have been considered from the standpoint of familial deprivation, but of course they also were deprived of the usual cultural experiences.

to submit also will determine the definition of deficiency that is applied in that society. Similarly, the demands that are made in general on the members of a society or subsystem of the society will determine how easily or how poorly its members will compare with their fellows. Thus, a society of simple and few demands tends to submerge the differences between its members, so that most of the less intelligent do not stand out as appreciably below the standard required. These considerations will be taken up in more detail in the next section.

## MENTAL DEFICIENCY AS A PROBLEM

In a manner of speaking, the preceding pages have discussed the mental defective from the viewpoints of the psychometrician, the clinician, the medical scientist, the geneticist, the psychotherapist, and the cultural anthropologist or sociologist. By its particular methods and theories, each of these professions approaches the mental-defective complex from a different starting point and ends by defining mental deficiency in a way peculiar to those methods and theories. There are other definitions of mental deficiency that do not have to do with the techniques or conceptions of a particular discipline, but indeed have to do with them all. In these final pages I should like to take up the definition of mental deficiency as a problem and follow up the indications that such a definition provides.

If mental deficiency is a problem, whose problem is it? In what way and to what extent is it a problem? Three general foci for the answer of these questions suggest themselves: the defective himself, his family, and his society. Let us examine what deficiency may mean from each of these standpoints. First, it should be understood that this section deals with matters on which not very much work has been done. Therefore, much of what will be said here will be speculative, at worst, and, at best, only suggested by incomplete evidence.

### The Problem for the Defective

For the defective himself, the handicap of deficiency is presumed to be important in several ways, yet workers have never taken much time to study whether this is true. As far as his feelings are concerned, the few reports of psychotherapeutic interviews have indicated conflicting testimony from the defective himself, though generally to the effect that the handicap is an emotionally charged one (Sarason, 1953). It is true that intellectually disadvantaged persons can smart under the realization of their handicap to the extent that they are aware of it; yet it is also true that the subnormal person does not feel bad about his handicap if he is not forced into situations where it is constantly or frequently apparent. These are "common sense" conclusions. Yet one wonders whether or not there will be some relationship between the intelligence level of the defective and his awareness of his handicap. Will only the higher-grade defective be aware, to his own discomfiture, of the difference between himself and others more fortunate? If so, then deficiency, so far as the emotional problem is concerned, is important primarily to the higher-grade defectives, and, then, only when they are called on to perform beyond their capacity.

What about the economic liability that mental deficiency is presumed to mean? Certainly lack of intelligence can limit severely the kinds of jobs that are open. But are the jobs that are open sufficient? There is very little information about this. Ruby J. R. Kennedy (1948) and the Connecticut studies seem to show that mental defectives are about as well off as the normal members of their social classes (Baller, 1936; Charles, 1953). This seems to deny that there is a great economic handicap for the higher-grade defective. The economic liability generally may be confined to the lower-grade defective.

It often is said that the defective may be the victim of many impositions by his more normal associates. But this statement is based on impressionistic and anecdotal evidence. Is the sort of imposition to which one is vulnerable a function more of his whole pattern of interpersonal integration than of his degree of intelligence? Again, however, one is forced to believe, on the basis of "common sense," that the lower-grade defective is likely to be very much less able to protect himself from any sort of imposition or injury. But whether this is significantly true of the higher-grade defective is another question.

There are perhaps other ways of considering how the defective may find his subnormal intelligence a real handicap. But what is apparent from the preceding discussion is that almost nothing is known about whether mental deficiency may be a problem to the defective himself, to what extent, and how. It is surely a social and economic liability for the lower-grade defective. Even so, the low-grade defectives comprise only one-quarter of the total defective group. It does not necessarily make sense to project this conclusion on the entire group of defectives.

Since workers have so little idea of exactly how the defective himself is affected by his handicap, it becomes important to explore the possibility that the problem of mental deficiency, as it is commonly appraised, is in reality not the defective's problem but someone else's—that is, the family's, the neighbors', the society's problem. If this is so, then meeting the problem of mental deficiency may require quite a different approach than if it is the defective's problem. To a certain extent, the problem may exist because one feels and acts on that assumption.

### The Problem for the Family

Certainly, for the family the defective may be an economic and social liability to the extent that the family assumes responsibility for his care and treatment. Such an assumption of responsibility for differential care rests, however, on the family's ability to discern a significant difference between themselves and the defective. Otherwise there is no problem of mental deficiency for them. Again, the lower-grade person is easily differentiated, but the higher-grade may not be; indeed, he may be smarter than the other members of his family. The distinction then will rest on the intellectual, cultural, and social level of the family into which the defective is born. If the general level of the family is impoverished on these counts—and it appears that a good deal, if not most, deficiency appears in the lower strata of society— then the family will be less inclined to find its defective member appreciably different from themselves.

This point seems to be borne out in the facts on membership in the parents' organization for the help of retarded children. Most, if not all, of the members of such groups are from the middle and upper classes, who are self-consciously able to distinguish the less capable members of their families from themselves. Another factor that aids this differentiation of the mental defective from his more normal kin in upper and middle-class families is that he is likely to represent some of the obviously pathologic or anomalous conditions that are associated with deficiency—conditions like mongolism or hydrocephaly. For, as has been pointed out, these sorts of pathology and anomaly are distributed almost evenly among all strata of society; whereas the unclassifiable, indistinguishable varieties of mental deficiency occur almost exclusively in the lower strata. Medicine and other outside agencies of assistance that more affluent families can afford also operate to differentiate the mental defective from his family and associates. And, again, the varieties of mental defect accompanied by readily discernible organic defect are likely to be in the lower grades of intelligence, making nonadjustment to the demands of family and society that much more evident.

In lower-class families, the defective is likely to be in the higher grades of intelligence deficit. Therefore, he is that much more likely to escape detection and to meet the fewer demands of his family, associates, and, on a marginal level at least, the legal and economic requirements of society at large. In such cases there is no mental-deficiency problem as far as the defective's family is concerned.

### The Problem for the Community

However, there are three ways in which he may come to the attention of his community as being significantly different and therefore to the family's attention. One is by way of poor school performance. He may be segregated by the school to a special class, if one exists; or he may be excluded from public-school instruction; or he may be pushed along with his regular class; or he may be institutionalized. From this standpoint, the problem of mental deficiency is merely a problem of poor scholastic performance; as such, it is important only if the community demands a certain standard of scholastic performance for its own sake, for scholastic performance need not have any significance for what happens to the person in later life, in terms of his general adjustment to his community. Probably a great deal about this matter of a high value being set on scholastic ability is related to the era of psychologic tests of intelligence, though of course the general social values in our society place a premium on top performance in all social activity. The discrimination resulting from such an artificial criterion of social good is especially important in regard to the mentally defective individual, but he is not alone in this situation. It is quite possible that the dull normal person, poorly provided for—for instance, in terms of special classes—may be more discriminated against in this hierarchy of intelligence. As a matter of fact it appears that the dull group may be more delinquent and maladjusted socially than mental defectives as a group (Baller, 1939). What relationship this may have to the early school experience or to not quite measuring up is another question; but in the case of defectives, clinical opinion seems to give importance to such experiences in the later anti-social behavior of the defective.

Another way in which the defective may be singled out is by legal difficulties. Intellectual deficiency in a delinquent or criminal may become more important to the social agencies of the community than his delinquent or criminal act, for it is assumed that the deficiency has something to do with the transgression of social standards. Actually there do not appear to be any more defectives who are delinquent or criminal than is to be expected in proportion to their absolute numbers in delinquency strata in the society (Tulchin, 1939; Robinson and Pasework, 1951). Nor are crimes of a different nature. Yet it would be safe to say that, in England, of all the high-grade defectives who are in residential institutions, the greatest proportion are there because of some anti-social activity.[23] The more normal miscreant may be given an ordinary sentence, even a suspended sentence, and put on probation; but the defective is headed for a training school, especially if he is a recidivist. And there he may stay for the rest of his life. In other words, mental deficiency becomes a problem when the defective gets into court.

The third way in which defectives are singled out as problems for the community is in regard to the family standard of living and behavior. Thus,

---

[23] *Cf.* Lionel S. Penrose (1949). Whether such a great proportion is thus institutionalized in America is another question. Yet there does appear to be a general similarity of practice in regard to such cases (Tarjan and Benson, 1953).

wards of the community whose families are considered incapable, financially or morally, of raising their children and who, by test or otherwise, are diagnosed as defective are institutionalized as such. The more normal child may have a better chance of adoption, or of paid foster-parent care, or of a life in an orphanage until such a time as he reaches a working age. But the defective child may not have any other opportunity except life in an institution for defectives. Institutional life being what it is—ordinarily an under-stimulating, depriving environment—even normal children will tend to regress, and the defective is further handicapped. With a long-term experience of institutional life, the defective may never have the chance to develop enough to leave the institution. Thus the community can create its own mental-deficiency problem.

From this discussion it can be concluded that mental deficiency in the case of 75 per cent of all defectives—the high-grade defectives—is a problem mainly because it has been so defined by the demands of the community. The actual problems that lead to institutionalization, for instance, may indeed have much or nothing at all to do with mental deficiency per se or with a condition derived from deficiency. Certainly there is little evidence that the young sex offender who is mentally defective is much different in the difficulties he exhibits from the normally intelligent sex offender. As a matter of fact, it is undeniable that some inmates of institutions for defectives are perfectly normal in intelligence by any criterion that can be applied; they are there because of legal, economic, or personality difficulties. Thus, the nets of community attitudes and practices in regard to mental deficiency catch also those who are normally intelligent.

It surely may be questioned whether the handling of legal, economic, personality, and other such problems in the case of normally intelligent persons under the generic term of mental deficiency makes much sense. One wonders, too, whether the same problems experienced by defectives should be handled as the mental-deficiency problem. In other words, we may be ignoring the real problem of mental deficiency in favor of a presumed set of problems. About 150,000 people are confined to institutions for mental defectives. This is approximately one-tenth of the 1 per cent of the total population of the United States who are presumed to be defective by the best (and conservative) estimates—that is, one-tenth of the group of people who are both intellectually and socially incapable of operating on an acceptable level. But of this institutionalized group and of all those in special classes in public and other schools, many are thus singled out not because they are defective but because they are behavior, welfare, delinquent, or other problem children. For these, "mental deficiency" has become a problem because their communities would have it so.

One other conclusion that may be drawn refers again to the distinctions that must be made within the mental-defective category. As not all defectives are alike from the standpoint of symptomatology and etiology, so not all defectives present the same problem to themselves, to their families, and to their communities. There is a certain amount of sense in discriminating between high- and low-grade defectives from the standpoint of the social attention that must be directed onto them. However much the low-grade defective may be a problem because of his deficiency, the mildly deficient cannot be similarly categorized. The problem that each defective presents to himself, his family, and to the community is, again, dependent on the total mental-defective situation—not merely on the deficiency itself.

## CHANGE AND STABILITY IN THE MENTAL-DEFECTIVE SITUATION

Since the problem of mental deficiency turns out to be a number of problems, it is appropriate to discuss in what ways these problems could be met. I do not intend to do this, but rather to indicate how we might look for ways to meet these problems. Although the traditional view of mental deficiency has included a concept of irreversibility or permanence, the material that has been reviewed here indicates that such a conception is misleading. There are, to be sure, many indications of irreversibility, but there also are many indications of reversibility. Therefore it behooves the worker to consider, instead of the question of reversibility per se, the aspects of the various mental-defective situations that tend to prolong, to render stable the mental-defective pattern, and the aspects that tend to induce change in that pattern.

Perhaps the most important reinforcement proclivities in a mental-defective situation are the attitudes, knowledge, and concepts in the situation that are brought to it by others than the mental defective himself. If, for instance, the professional worker continues to act on the assumption that the mental-defective situation is irreversible, to deny the possibilities of intervention or essential improvement, then certainly this will operate to prolong the condition. This is the general handicap under which the study of mental deficiency has proceeded for a long time.[24] Of course, some workers have refused to accept the handicap and have sought to find ways of influencing the situation. On the other hand, medical science indicates, as much by what it knows as by what it does not know, that little can be done to change or to cure some varieties of mental deficiency where there is an associated gross physiologic damage or malformation. Thus, gross injuries by accident or disease, cerebral hemorrhage, and pathologic increases in spinal-meningeal fluid, present at this point in the history of medicine al-

[24] Historically, mental deficiency was considered to be a condition amenable to the techniques of pedagogy, if only the proper variation of such techniques could be discovered. However, in America, this way of looking at deficiency died out by the first decade or so of the twentieth century (Haskell, 1944).

most insuperable obstacles to changes in mental-defective situations charac-terized by such conditions. These important organic disorders tend to pro-long the mental-defective situation indefinitely.

Aside from these problems of knowledge and theoretic concepts that tend to reinforce the mental-defective situation, there are the attitudes of significant others—family members or their substitutes—toward the defec-tive. In a case of functional mental deficiency, a significant prolonging force seems to come out of the way in which the defective is treated according to the attitudes of those with whom he has contact. Nancy Staver's study (1953) of the relationship of mothers to their retarded children is pertinent here. She found that the mothers in many cases encouraged the helplessness of their children. By this means the mother could continue to take care of her child as if he were a baby. The mothers were themselves characterized by strong dependency needs, and these ends seemed to be fulfilled vicari-ously in taking care of their retarded children. David Levy's study (1943) of overprotection has shown that even neurologic signs of poor perform-ance capacity are induced by a practice of doing everything for the child. The inhibition, then, of the child's potentialities for manipulation of his environment can lead to the point where the mental-defective situation is stabilized into irreversibility.

Other forces tending toward the stability of the mental-defective com-plex may derive from the subsystems of the defective person himself. In certain cases of severe brain injury at a late age, abilities that have been lost may be recovered because functions seem to be taken over by undamaged areas. But in early injuries to the central nervous system, the development of the brain as a whole may be insufficient to permit undamaged areas to make the necessary adjustments (Strauss and Lehtinen, 1950; Hebb, 1942). The problem in early injury, even if minor, is that it has occurred at such a time that the limitations seem to feed back to inhibit experimenta-tion and activity that might have been possible if the same degree of injury had occurred in an older and more developed and elaborated organism. This is always, of course, a problem in mental deficiency: every failure that the defective experiences inhibits further attempts, not only in the same immediate area of activity, but in many associated activities (McCandless, 1952). Thus mental-defective situations are reinforced by the lowered intel-lectual and social functioning with each failure and inhibition in exactly the same way as the neurotic situation becomes more pronounced and stable as the symptomatology continues to fulfill its usefulness in avoidance of anxi-ety. In other words, the maintenance of the mental-defective situation de-pends not only on what sorts of processes are introduced—such as those involved in a cerebral injury—but also at which period in the development of the person they occur.

Further examples of stabilizing influences are found in the process of institutionalization of the mental-defective situation—that is, the general mode by which society may handle the mental-defective situation. The functions that the epileptics, hysterics, and possibly some psychotics perform in certain societies as holy men are performed also by mental defectives in certain cultures. Tolstoy in *War and Peace* speaks of the Russian mental defectives who are religious mendicants—*les enfants du bon Dieu*—who were protected and revered as holy. Certainly a person who began in such a role would have difficulty leaving it; so too in the modern society's treatment of the mental defective by isolation in a residential school. Labeled or recognized early and therefore dealt with as mentally defective, the person will live out the later portions of his life having different experiences than he might have had, had he not been dealt with as defective. For instance, living in a residential institution is not only very different from normal experience, but it is pretty well established that it is a grossly handicapping experience in many instances. The deprivation and lack of stimulation that are inherent in most institutional life will tend to stabilize the mental-defective situation. Few, if any, studies have been made of the rather important kinds of social and intellectual experience that are fairly common for the normal person but lost to the mental defective. A study of this aspect of the mental-defective situation might throw light, not only on what happens with the defective, but also on the common patterns of experience undergone by others within the particular society concerned.

One might assume that constructing the respective opposites of the various stabilizing forces of the mental-defective situation would suffice to specify the tendencies toward change in the situation. This is not necessarily so, however. It is not merely the actual activity that means stability or change; it is also the point in time and development of the mental-defective situation at which these processes are occurring. Thus, biochemical therapy is important at one point in the treatment of cretinism, but good results do not occur at a later point in development. Similarly, the chemical balances of the physiologic organism may be retrieved at a certain stage by the introduction of thyroid therapy, but the effect of such therapy at that time in regard to the psychologic processes in the mental-defective complex may be minimal. That is, although the cretin may be treated early enough to stave off critical physiologic changes (so far as we know), the other elements of the mental-defective situation may not have received adequate attention soon enough to reverse the mental-defective situation.

Similarly, in cases where emotional deprivation may be assumed to be the most important etiologic factor, the usefulness of psychotherapy is affected by the point in the child's development at which therapy is introduced. After the defective situation has been stabilized for a long period of time, no psychotherapeutic milieu or individual treatment that workers are presently capable of can be expected to achieve important results in the reversal of the malevolent processes. The purely educational efforts of teachers to raise the scholastic performance of retarded children are similarly limited by the context in time and the child's development at which such efforts are begun.

It is probably because of this general problem of developmental eras and stages that so much controversy has arisen about the beneficent effects of any kind of therapy. Mere attention to chronologic age of the defective as an indication of the developmental stage of the defective situation will not suffice to indicate the point at which therapy may achieve good results. Clemens Benda (1952) and Theodore Ingalls (1952) have implied this important consideration in their discussions of the period at which various organic defect or deficiencies seem to begin. The relevance of the developmental periods is but poorly outlined at the present state of knowledge about the growth and maturation of the human being. Quite likely, workers will continue to stab in the dark, by trial and error, in an attempt to devise therapeutic measures for mental deficiency until their grasp of the course of development, biologic, emotional, and social, is more secure.

In the meantime, probably the most that can be done is to attempt to diagnose the particular mental-defective situation as early as possible and begin treatment immediately as the occasion warrants. Thus, the institution of psychotherapy or milieu therapy, for instance, with very young retarded children with suspected emotional-deprivation etiology of the defective processes can have only equivocal implications even if the child becomes apparently normal in time, or is "cured." This equivocal nature of the results will not be merely because, as has so often been said, diagnosis of such a disorder in younger children is tremendously difficult and thus the "cured" child was not defective in the first place, but because of the fluidity of the early developmental eras and because of our ignorance of the actual manner in which therapy is effective.

At any rate, there is certainly no specific treatment for mental-defective situations, any more than there is a specific treatment for all stomach disorders. Therapy, as the institution or strengthening of whatever forces tend to keep the mental-defective situation fluid or to reverse it, must be governed by the type of deficiency. Except for such easily discernible types as cretinism, there rarely has been much attempt to differentiate treatment according to the variety of deficiency. And at this point, there are no therapies that can claim conclusive positive results.[25]

[25] Such treatments as glutamic acid or revascularization or "developing cerebral dominance" may continue to have support, but other therapies probably will displace these with the same kind of over-enthusiastic support that leads eventually to complete disillusionment. The few psychotherapeutic attempts are, of course, harder to evaluate. Benjamin Mehlman (1953) conducted nondirective group play-therapy, and his careful attempt at evaluation indicated that, in the cases of the familial category of thirty-two patients with whom he worked, this therapy was not successful regarding changes in IQ and only equivocally successful regarding personality change in general. Of course, no possible avenue of treatment can be ignored, but one must feel doubtful of mere empiric trial-and-error techniques.

A final point remains to be reviewed. It pertains to the concept of the extreme stability of the so-called true mental-defective situation as opposed to pseudo-feeblemindedness (Arthur, 1947; Doll, 1947; Kanner, 1948). Most current and past authorities have felt that if the mental-defective situation changes markedly in the direction of improvement so that there is no longer any evidence of deficiency, then to characterize the earlier state as defective is erroneous. In a way it is difficult to object to this concept of the defective state—the usefulness of a construct that is always stable is obvious. On the other hand, the indications for possible marked change in so many of the defective situations and the lack of knowledge about most defective situations and what constitutes them give this concept of unchangeableness little empiric value.

One must be concerned with the possibilities for normal functioning for most, if not all, mental defectives, as a value goal for the realization of which scientific investigation is applied. And to look for the possibilities of change while maintaining that there can be no change does not make sense. Moreover, this concept is incongruent with what else is known about human life. The result of all knowledgeable investigation has been not to establish that there are stable situations that do not change, but to establish that changes do take place according to relatively stable laws. The most basic example is that changes can and do take place in a stable situation that we know as life; these changes sometimes result in another and antithetical situation that we term the absence of life, or death. Certainly, when confronted with such an antithetical change, we do not say that the state of life never existed in that particular instance. Analogously, the antithesis of feeblemindedness, what we call "intelligent functioning," does not preclude the prior existence of deficiency. It would seem to make good sense to look at mental-defective situations, not from the standpoint of answering the question whether this is true or pseudo-feeblemindedness but from the point of view that seeks to elicit what processes are going on that make for stability or change in the situation, and for what sorts of change or stability.

## SUMMARY AND CONCLUSION

This analysis has attempted to point out the main issues and problems that characterize present-day conceptions of mental deficiency and to indicate some of the implications for action that may be deduced. It has emphasized that mental deficiency is a term that includes a large number of very different kinds of conditions, the only really common element of which is a presumed or demonstrated characteristic of subnormal intelligence. Thus, it is necessary to speak of varieties of mental deficiency, just as we talk about varieties of mental illness.

Mental deficiency in its many varieties has been shown to look somewhat different according to the means with which it is investigated. Mental deficiency as subnormal intelligence, as social failure, as organic failure, as inherited defect, as a pattern of interpersonal relations, and as a socio-cultural pattern, has been discussed to indicate that the mental-defective situation complex is made up of several different kinds of processes, requiring as many different methods of investigation.

I have discussed what we call the mental-deficiency problem from the standpoint of the defective himself, his family, and his community, with the result that several problems are abstracted. Viewing mental-deficiency problems broadly in a situation-complex calls for the delineation of the proclivities or forces that influence stability and change in the mental-defective situation. Thus, one can understand the deterioration, stabilization, or remedy of the mental-defective pattern and avoid the meaningless controversy over reversibility or irreversibility of mental deficiency.

It should be apparent to the reader that the most important action implication to be drawn from this discussion is the pressing need for a fundamental reconceptualization of the study of deficiency. The field of study demands that we rethink our ways of looking at mentally defective people and of dealing with them, if we are to progress toward a better understanding of their situation and toward ways of remedying it. Naturally, a better understanding of the mental-defective complex will rest on the common sense, hard thinking, and insights that mark the development of any field of study. These insights and efforts cannot be manufactured, but perhaps they can be facilitated by establishing conditions under which some of the leading specialists can work on them at leisure. . . .

## REFERENCES

THEODORA M. ABEL, "Dominant Behavior of Institutionalized Subnormal Negro Girls," *American Journal of Mental Deficiency,* XLVII (1943), 429–436.

GEORGE W. ALBEE and GERALD R. PASCAL, "A Study of Competitive Behavior in Mental Defectives," *American Journal of Mental Deficiency,* LV (1951), 576–581.

AMERICAN EUGENICS SOCIETY, "Freedom of Choice for Parenthood," *Eugenical News,* XXXVIII (1953), 25–31.

ANNE ANASTASI and JOHN P. FOLEY, JR., "A Proposed Reorientation in the Heredity–Environment Controversy," *Psychological Review,* LV (1948), 239–249.

GRACE ARTHUR, "Pseudo-Feeblemindedness," *American Journal of Mental Deficiency,* LII (1947), 137–142.

W. R. BALLER, "A Study of Behavior Records of Adults Who, When They Were in Elementary Schools, Were Judged to be Dull in Mental Ability," *Journal of Genetic Psychology,* LV (1939), 365–379.

W. R. BALLER, "A Study of the Present Social Status of a Group of Adults

Who, When They Were in Elementary Schools, Were Classified as Mentally Deficient," *Genetic Psychology Monographs*, XVIII (1936), 165–244.

ERNEST G. BEIER, LEON GORLOW, and CHALMERS L. STACY, "The Fantasy Life of the Mental Defective," *American Journal of Mental Deficiency*, LV (1951), 582–589.

CLEMENS A. BENDA, *Developmental Disorders of Mentation and Cerebral Palsies* (New York: Grune and Stratton, 1952).

JOHN BOWLBY, *Maternal Care and Mental Health,* World Health Organization Monograph Series, Number 2 (Geneva: World Health Organization, 1951).

BARBARA S. BURKS, "The Relative Influence of Nature and Nurture upon Mental Development," *The 27th Yearbook of the National Society for the Study of Education*, XXVII (1928), Part I, 219–316.

DON C. CHARLES, "Ability and Accomplishment of Persons Earlier Judged Mentally Deficient," *Genetic Psychology Monographs*, XLVII (1953), 3–71.

KARL W. DEUTSCH, "Community Theory and Social Science," *American Journal of Orthopsychiatry*, XXII (1952), 469–483.

EDGAR A. DOLL, "Is Mental Deficiency Curable?" *American Journal of Mental Deficiency*, LI (1947), 420–428.

EDGAR A. DOLL, "The Essentials of an Inclusive Concept of Mental Deficiency," *American Journal of Mental Deficiency*, XLVI (1941), 214–219.

EDGAR A. DOLL, "The Feeble-Minded Child," in Leonard Carmichael (Ed.), *Manual of Child Psychology* (New York: Wiley, 1946), pp. 845–885.

KURT GOLDSTEIN, "Concerning Rigidity," *Character and Personality* (now *Journal of Personality*), XI (1943), 209–226.

FLORENCE L. GOODENOUGH, "The Measurement of Mental Growth in Childhood," in Leonard Carmichael (Ed.), *Manual of Child Psychology* (New York: Wiley, 1946), pp. 450–475.

SIDNEY L. HALPERIN, "A Clinico-Genetic Study of Mental Defect," *American Journal of Mental Deficiency*, L (1945), 8–26.

SIDNEY L. HALPERIN, "Human Heredity and Mental Deficiency," *American Journal of Mental Deficiency*, LI (1946), 153–163.

FRANK H. HANKINS, "Is Our Innate National Intelligence Declining?" *American Journal of Mental Deficiency*, XLVII (1942), 25–31.

ROBERT H. HASKELL, "Mental Deficiency Over a Hundred Years," *American Journal of Psychiatry*, C (1944), 107–118.

DONALD O. HEBB, "The Effect of Early and Late Brain Injury upon Test Scores, and the Nature of Adult Intelligence," *Proceedings of the American Philosophical Society*, LXXXV (1942), 275–292.

THEODORE H. INGALLS, "Biologic Implications of Mongolism," in Milbank Memorial Fund, *The Biology of Mental Health and Disease* (New York: Hoeber, 1952), pp. 389–401.

GEORGE A. JERVIS, "Mental Deficiency and Aberrant Metabolism," in Milbank Memorial Fund, *The Biology of Mental Health and Disease* (New York: Hoeber, 1952), pp. 422–429.

Leo Kanner, "Feeblemindedness: Absolute, Relative, and Apparent," *The Nervous Child,* VII (1948), 365–397.

Ruby J. R. Kennedy, *The Social Adjustment of Morons in a Connecticut City* (Hartford, Connecticut: Mansfield Southbury Training Schools, Social Service Department, State Office Building, 1948).

Samuel A. Kirk, "Experiments in the Early Training of the Mentally Retarded," *American Journal of Mental Deficiency,* LVI (1952), 692–700.

Otto Klineberg, "A Study of Psychological Differences between 'Racial' and National Groups in Europe," *Archives of Psychology,* XX (1931), 1–58.

Frank J. Kobler, "Cultural Differentials in Intelligence," *Journal of Social Psychology,* XVIII (1943), 279–303.

David M. Levy, *Maternal Overprotection* (New York: Columbia University Press, 1943).

Jane Loevinger, "On the Proportional Contributions of Differences in Nature and Nurture to Differences in Intelligence," *Psychological Bulletin,* XL (1943), 725–756.

Boyd McCandless, "Environment and Intelligence," *American Journal of Mental Deficiency,* LVI (1952), 674–691.

Benjamin Mehlman, "Group Play Therapy with Mentally Retarded Children," *Journal of Abnormal and Social Psychology,* XL (1953), 53–60.

George A. Muench, "A Follow-up of Mental Defectives after Eighteen Years," *Journal of Abnormal and Social Psychology,* XXXIX (1944), 407–418.

Sara Neham, "Psychotherapy in Relation to Mental Deficiency," *American Journal of Mental Deficiency,* LV (1951), 557–572.

Hans Neuer, "The Relationship between Behavior Disorders in Children and the Syndrome of Mental Deficiency," *American Journal of Mental Deficiency,* LII (1947), 143–147.

Lionel S. Penrose, *The Biology of Mental Defect* (New York: Grune and Stratton, 1949).

Richard G. Robinson and Richard Pasewark, "Behavior in Intellectual Deficit," *American Journal of Mental Deficiency,* LV (1951), 598–607.

Seymour B. Sarason, *Psychological Problems in Mental Deficiency* (2nd ed.; New York: Harper, 1953).

Bernadine G. Schmidt, "Changes in Personal, Social, and Intellectual Behavior of Children Originally Classified as Feebleminded," *Psychological Monographs,* LX (1946), 1–144.

Harold M. Skeels and Harold B. Dye, "A Study of the Effects of Differential Stimulation on Mentally Retarded Children," *Proceedings and Addresses of the American Association on Mental Deficiency,* XLIV (1939), 114–136.

Laurence H. Snyder, *The Principles of Heredity* (3rd ed.; Boston: Heath, 1946).

Nancy Staver, "The Child's Learning Difficulty as Related to the Emotional Problem of the Mother," *American Journal of Orthopsychiatry,* XXIII (1953), 131–141.

Alfred A. Strauss and Laura E. Lehtinen, *Psychopathology and Education of the Brain-Injured Child* (New York: Grune and Stratton, 1950).

HARRY STACK SULLIVAN, *The Interpersonal Theory of Psychiatry,* Helen Swick
    Perry and Mary Ladd Gavell (Eds.), (New York: Norton, 1953).

GEORGE TARJAN and FOLEY BENSON, "Report on the Pilot Study at Pacific
    Colony," *American Journal of Mental Deficiency,* LVII (1953), 453–462.

G. H. THOMSON, *The Trend of National Intelligence,* Occasional Papers of Eu-
    genics, Number 3 (London: Hamish Hamilton, 1947).

ALFRED FRENCH TREDGOLD, *A Textbook of Mental Deficiency* (8th ed.; Lon-
    don: Ballière, Tindall, and Cox, 1952).

SIMON H. TULCHIN, *Intelligence and Crime: A Study of Penitentiary and Re-
    formatory Offenders* (Chicago: University of Chicago Press, 1939).

DAVID WECHSLER, *The Range of Human Capacities* (2nd ed.; Baltimore, Mary-
    land: Williams and Wilkins, 1952).

RAYMOND R. WILLOUGHBY, "Family Similarities in Mental Test Abilities," *The
    27th Yearbook of the Society for the Study of Education,* XXVII (1928),
    Part I, 55–59.

About forty workers were contacted personally. It is not possible to note all those
who contributed to this paper in one way or another. However, the following helped
so considerably that they must be gratefully mentioned: Gordon Allen, M.D.; Joseph
M. Bobbitt, Ph.D.; Donald A. Bloch, M.D.; Lewis A. Dexter; Karl E. Heiser, Ph.D.;
Helen Swick Perry; and Harold M. Skeels, Ph.D. Much of the literature consulted will
not be cited, for reasons of brevity. Most uncited references will be found in one or
another of the bibliographies of three works to which the reader is directed: Leo
Kanner (1948), Lionel S. Penrose (1949), and Seymour Sarason (1953). The substance of this paper is condensed from an administrative report prepared for the
National Institute of Mental Health, U. S. Public Health Service, and published
originally in *Psychiatry,* XVII (1954), 45–73. It is reprinted here with some omitted
material indicated by ellipses marking.

# 22

# Changing Concepts for Programs for the Retarded

## DONALD STEDMAN

It is a mistake to undertake a consideration of changing concepts in an area as complex as that of mental retardation without first dealing with underlying issues affecting program development and operations. We have had an unusual opportunity over the past few years to view both stimulation on the national level of a variety of programs and state and local reactions to and attempts at implementation of federal plans. The federal stimulation of programs has met alternately with roadblocks and beds of roses. Some of the roadblocks are inherent in local structures; others are necessary perversions of federal notions to suit local needs. Some of the rosebeds represent readiness to fill gaps with federal support; others are naïve and grandiose receptivity to federal support without planning and preparation for long-term commitment or follow-through. For this reason it is dangerous to try to identify new concepts of lasting value.

Mental retardation has blossomed into a national issue of considerable dimensions. With the advent of federal legislation, including long-term construction funding, it has inherited the political and professional disputes and discontinuities that cloud the issues and can lead to misidentification of sources and destinations of changing concepts. Having thus determined that changing concepts are difficult to identify and are complicated by issue complexity, variations in local readiness and planning, and politico-professional grumbling, we shall describe the positive and negative reactions evident in American communities.

## The Issues

Incidence figures, professional needs, directions for research, and community-agency coordination are local problems. They will be determined by the issues. This is the essence of changing concepts and alteration of professional and lay attitudes toward actual and potential programming in mental retardation. There are at least seven issues directly affecting the rate and quality of program development.

### Biologically Determined Mental Retardation versus Socio-Cultural Factors

Major emphasis in mental-retardation programs has been on the more severely retarded, multiple-handicapped population of children and adults requiring close medical supervision and planning. This group is smaller in absolute number than the group of mildly retarded, nonphysically handicapped of unknown or undetermined etiology. The mildly retarded group now is receiving greater attention as a source of difficulty in areas of education, employment, and economic programming. This change in emphasis has given rise to problems of early identification and habilitation as well as to controversy over the relative importance of biologic and environmental or socio-cultural determinants of subnormal intellectual function. Approximately two-thirds of the retarded population is thought to be "cultural-familial." The bio-behavioral or genetic aspects of this group are not clear. At any rate, this segment of the population needs attention and will require primarily educational and vocational programming and correlated training and placement efforts to meet its needs and to soften the economic and social burden it represents to the community.

### Professional Competition for Programs for the Mentally Retarded: Mental Illness versus Mental Retardation

Following the shift in attention from the more obviously retarded to the mildly retarded, there has been a subtle, and sometimes not so subtle, struggle for the "ownership" of the problem of mental retardation. This is, in a way, a delightful turn of events from the time when nobody wanted it, and may be a result of the existence of professional, as well as lay, stereotypes of what the mentally retarded person is. Perhaps the more biologically oriented have not adequately incorporated the heavy behavioral and psycho-educational implications of diagnostic and treatment programs for the retarded. Perhaps the more behaviorally oriented have too often dismissed the biologic implications of the wide variety of disorders and conditions that can lead to the symptom of mental retardation. These inadequacies and dismissals (together with overly specialized professional training) have led us to a separatist position in which mental illness and mental retardation are considered by many to be separate and discrete processes, requiring similar but separate approaches to planning and programming at the community level.

It would be naïve and dishonest to ignore the presence of this separatist tendency and to discount the effect of the position statements on plans and programs for those whom we call mentally retarded. Age of onset, reversibility potential, and treatment approach tend to be the major criteria for defining differences between the mentally ill and mentally retarded. The last criterion affects our preparations and operations at the community level the most. The two are clearly separate, in terms of administration, at the national or federal level. As programs develop at the regional, state, and community level, they become less well defined and overlap increasingly because of manpower and fiscal deficiencies and reluctance at the local level to duplicate programs and facilities. There is a major difference in management techniques and therefore in programs; but I would be inclined to recognize the realities of life in the city where resources probably never will be sufficient to handle both problems separately with any degree of effectiveness.

We cannot afford professional competition any more than we can afford the luxury of just planning. We must settle differences and develop combined programs to suit the needs of the population as a whole. In an address to the National Industrial Conference Board in February, 1961, President Kennedy saw a need for cooperation by business and government. He said, "We know that your success and ours are intertwined, that you have facts and know-how that we need. Whatever past differences have existed, we seek more than an attitude of truce, more than a treaty; we seek the spirit of a full fledged alliance . . ." (Kennedy, 1962). His plea may be appropriate to our situation.

### "Neurosis Structuris"

In the process of implementing the plan for "National Action to Combat Mental Retardation," a syndrome has developed that has been characteristic of other massive assaults on population problems. We might call it "neurosis structuris." Panels have spawned councils, which have committees, which have advisory groups, which enlist private consultation. The small group of professional people involved in mental retardation before the development of the "plan" are busily traveling throughout the country, assembling for pronouncements of sage advice, and populating the hierarchy of key national councils and facilities, while communities struggle to respond to local problems with fewer consultants than they had before. The one clear need that the federal legislation still has not met is provision of the training and personnel supports required to develop comprehensive community programs. The supply of community resource specialists is critically low. As a result, the comprehensive plans submitted to state councils may not be so intelligent and effective as will be required to effect a change in currently inadequate services for the retarded. Instead, a rigid structure of federal, regional, state, and local chains of command may be set up that could inhibit progress toward good program development. Flexibility is required; premature legislation can be damaging. Coordination and cooperation of existing and of new programs are necessary and they must have clearly defined lines of communication. Overemphasis on structure and tables of organization can reduce our ultimate effectiveness and ability to respond to changing needs in an expanding population.

## "Competition" with Other National and Local Needs

Those who have been in the business of developing community programs for the retarded know the difficulties of competition with other health, education, and welfare issues. Problems center mostly around financial and manpower needs. This friendly competition for visibility has served often to confuse the public and dampen its readiness to respond to and rally around "our cause." Exaggerated incidence figures, overstatements of current capacity to affect the problem, and responses to public information and public-relations pressures sometimes have made subsequent programs appear inadequate when they could not fulfill "campaign promises." In a country in which private and public resources continue to be called on for support, it is important that competition for support does not distort the reality of our needs and our capabilities. Mental retardation has long been neglected, and the needs and promise for fulfillment of those needs, if clearly stated, will attract the support required. There are other great needs, and we must compete for funds, interest, and political support. But we must be careful not to weaken our long-term support potential by not being able to follow through on programs that are unrealistically developed and operated.

## Changing the Consumer: Poverty and Mental Retardation

With the advent of the anti-poverty program, mental-retardation programs have received an additional impetus. The scope of the anti-poverty program will be wide indeed if it succeeds in reaching its identified target population, and a great deal of benefit will accrue to individuals in the mildly retarded range, especially. There is not 100 per cent overlap between the two, but many of the culturally deprived or their offspring could benefit intellectually from the anti-poverty effort. Certainly the health, cultural, and motivational changes that would be brought about by a successful anti-poverty program would contribute a great deal toward reducing the incidence of mental retardation as we now define it.

Anti-poverty and mental-retardation programs have another thing in common. They both attempt to change or modify the consumer, to optimize and raise his level of function. Motivational change is often the most difficult aspect of rehabilitation, and the success of rehabilitation programs hinges on the techniques devised to be used in massive programs—in anti-poverty for the unemployed, in mental retardation for the culturally deprived. In some cases, at least, the techniques appear to be the same, and anti-poverty and mental-retardation programs can proceed together with mutual benefit.

### Research Utilization

Community planners thirst for research results and help to utilize them. This requires personnel and perhaps some of the "neurosis structuris" mentioned earlier. But a circular system must be established whereby successful local programs can be brought to the attention of distant communities and whereby successes and failures of demonstration projects can help to upgrade the many programs springing to life around this country. Such a plan would increase the availability of information to process in research as well as the availability of subjects on which to do research. I believe we will find the retarded to be psychologically different from the stereotype we now hold as a result of our past major emphasis on the institutionalized individual.

### Attracting the Volunteer Groups

Community programs will always depend heavily on free time and talent. Volunteer groups, service clubs, and fraternal organizations must be involved in local programs. Practical problems, such as transportation, medical aid, supervision, fund-raising, and political support, are ever present to the program coordinator. The degree to which groups join in cooperative local efforts will depend on how the program affects the group and what the group will derive from its contribution. Use of volunteer groups is necessary to maintain long-term support of facilities and services even though original bricks and mortar may come from outside help. Otherwise, the program will be seen as an outsider and will suffer from the weakness of relative isolation from the community, except for the special-interest group that helped initiate the program. Never underestimate the need for a continuing education of the community. Sustained support is the most difficult to get,

For this reason, involvement of volunteer and service groups at the service and administrative or board level is essential.

## Changing Concepts

Service programs are shifting from the piecemeal to the long-required full circle of services for the retarded person and his family. These services, in the form of comprehensive, integrated programs, extend along the age continuum required by the extended period of dependency of the retarded child. As the retarded child grows to adulthood, the variety of disciplines required to meet his needs increases. Each in its turn plays a major role during the phases of his physical and adaptive growth and development. Depending on the severity of retardation, medical and educational services identify and begin to plan for him with his parents. And so on through recreational, vocational, psychologic, and employment phases until he emerges into community life in a manner consistent with his ability, his motivational drives, and the receptivity of the community in which he lives. Throughout the continuum, the retarded person and his family require varying degrees of social and welfare support. He does not become the ward of the community. Rather, he remains the child and young adult of his family, bolstered by external supports or social casework where necessary. Only through such a multidimensional program can the environment allow for the highest level of function of the retarded person.

In a hypothetic average American community of 100,000, not less than 3,000 mentally retarded persons of all ages and all degrees of retardation would be found. The services needed by these persons are many and vary greatly, depending on age and the severity of retardation. This hypothetic community would be confronted with large numbers of retarded preschool children, retarded children of school age, young adults, and adult retarded. Because of the demands of school, incidence may be higher than estimated in the school-age range. This will vary most from community to community.

TABLE 22–1. *Degree of Mental Retardation in Various Age Groups in Hypothetic Average American Community*

| DEGREE OF MR | PRESCHOOL UNDER AGE 6 | SCHOOL AGE AGE 6–19 | YOUNG ADULTS AGE 20–25 | ADULTS AGE 26 AND OVER | TOTAL ALL AGES |
|---|---|---|---|---|---|
| mildly | 341 | 596 | 150 | 1,416 | 2,503 |
| moderate | 54 | 95 | 24 | 226 | 399 |
| severe | 13 | 23 | 6 | 56 | 98 |
| all | 408 | 714 | 180 | 1,698 | 3,000 |

The following are a few of the major services that this community must have if it is to combat the problem of mental retardation.

1. Diagnostic and counseling services for all retarded and their families.

2. Welfare, social, and educational services to enrich the learning opportunities of the 341 mildly retarded preschool children, many of whom live in slums or in otherwise depressed circumstances.

3. Public health nursing and homemaker services to assist in caring for the fifty-four moderately and thirteen severely retarded infants and young children.

4. Forty special educational classes for the 596 mildly retarded pupils who will become with specialized training self-sufficient adult citizens.

5. Twelve special educational classes for the ninety-five moderate or trainable retarded who also will become with appropriate training productive workers in protective, supervised settings.

6. A day-care, recreation center for the twenty-three severely retarded children of school age who are unable to profit from formal schooling.

7. Vocational counseling, job training, and placement services for the 150 mildly retarded young adults who can become self-sufficient, independent, working members of the community.

8. Sheltered workshops for the 250 moderately retarded adults of all ages who can contribute to their own and to the community's welfare, if given an opportunity to work in a protected environment.

9. Activity centers for the fifty-six adult severely retarded who may never take their place as workers in the community but who are no less important from the humanitarian and social standpoint.

10. Residential centers to meet the needs of those of the retarded with problems of care and training so complex as to require twenty-four-hour effort.

Professional training programs are being expanded to include the medical, psychologic, educational, social, and vocational aspects of human development peculiar to the life of the retarded child and adult. Whereas the mongoloid child was seen previously as primarily a patient with a cardiac defect or as an automatic candidate for the residential school, the training physician and the community practitioner now are aware of the psychosocial and vocational vistas open to victims of this condition. The more enlightened medical counselor seeks to achieve family acceptance and vocational planning consistent with the trainability of this moderately retarded child in order to make him a more fully participating citizen than was imagined possible before. Whereas the mildly retarded, educable child often was left to drift upward through the elementary school system, only to end in a delinquent or withdrawn life of failure and derision, the educator and psychologist now are identifying and placing him in special educational and vocationally oriented programs suited to his academic and emotional needs.

The planning community must take these changes into account and prepare its systems for special programs of education integrated with clinical and employment supports and potential.

Research and demonstration projects in the community are difficult to organize and finance. Yet the long-term effectiveness of programming will depend on continuous evaluation and innovation. Like the consultant, the program researcher often is considered a fifth wheel and the first to go when the budget needs cutting. This tendency is costly and foolhardy in the long run. Planning requires information, objective self-appraisal, and anticipatory modification to meet the changing community. Only research will accomplish this job. For this reason, today's forward-looking comprehensive plan has a built-in, long-term, self-correcting mechanism in a research person or group charged with the responsibility of modifying the program in accordance with changing populations needs.

Public information has proved to be a key factor in program development. Current programs and plans-in-the-making make sure that, at every step of the way, the community—professional and lay—is fully informed of the scope, intent, and purpose of the program-to-be. The more successful community programs have captured local support prior to active planning and have, in some instances, employed "Madison Avenue" techniques to the great advantage of the retarded and consequently of the community.

Coordination requires a population concept of levels of coordination. When approaching problems of coordination of services, activities, or programs directly relevant to large groups of people, we are accustomed to dividing or otherwise manipulating the population in accordance with established political boundaries. We divide the country into directional segments such as Northeast, Southwest, North Central; states are subdivided in accordance with county borders; cities become fragmented to wards or block groups. Alternately, we may focus on stratified levels of the population based on major variables such as race, age groups, social class, or economic class. Rarely do we account or plan for population mobility or continuity across established political borders except, perhaps, to monitor mass behavior such as that of migrant labor groups, species of rare birds, animals approaching extinction, or criminals on parole. It would seem prudent and potentially fruitful to evaluate problems of coordination of mental-retardation programs, recognizing the mobility and contiguous nonpolitically defined population areas in order to provide maximal coverage and coordination from the national to the local level. We have been thinking of the local, state, regional, and national divisions of popular jurisdiction, but we will operate more profitably if we integrate the mobility and expansion characteristics of the population.

In addition to these four traditional divisions, it must be recognized that metropolitan centers, metropolitan-statistical areas, and contiguous nonpolitical areas represent discretely and qualitatively different sets of situations for planning and coordinating activities within each of them. By recognizing these characteristics that are the result of the mobility and expansion of the population, we will develop a more effective population coverage. Metropolitan centers represent communities exceeding 100,000 in population and demanding more than local, but less than state-level, coordination activities. An example is Rochester, New York, where planning exceeds the limits of the city and Monroe County, but does not involve a large enough area to require a multicounty, regional, or state coordinating body.

Metropolitan-statistical areas represent population areas centering on large cities and having over 650,000 people within their permeable and flexing borders. Such areas require more than metropolitan-center coordination, but less than state-level direction. An example is the Minneapolis–St. Paul area whose population periphery does not cross a state border.

Contiguous nonpolitical areas represent super-urban and city strips such as the Boston, New York, Philadelphia, Washington, D.C., complex or the population "crescent" in North Carolina extending from Raleigh to Durham, Greensboro, Winston-Salem, High Point, and Charlotte. Such areas include millions of people in nonpolitically defined and yet interdependent and interacting areas requiring mental-retardation-program coordination. In addition to super-urban areas or city strips, a contiguous nonpolitical area may constitute a geographic area incorporating cultural factors that require separate or peculiar coordinating activities. Economically depressed areas such as "Appalachia" are examples. If the administrative existence of these three additional population levels is accepted, the hierarchy of population levels in need of coordinating bodies will include the following areas: nation, regions, contiguous nonpolitical areas, states, metropolitan-statistical areas, metropolitan areas, and local areas.

Each of these levels requires its own "fixed point of referral." The individual, staff, or agency that represents the fixed coordinating point must be an aggressive coordinator as well as a point of information and referral to existing programs, services, and facilities. In some cases, this fixed point will be a privately supported office, and in others it will be an individual in a governmental agency office. In still others, it may be a privately supported individual on a governmental staff who is charged with the responsibility of coordinating the circle of services required to meet the needs of the retarded person over his life span.

## OBSTACLES TO CHANGE

Any new community program threatens established patterns. Property, attitudes, ways of life, political boundaries, and even laws often have to be reshaped to admit a new process. In rigid communities, programming is forced into the existing mold and may suffer or be inhibited as a result.

Other communities may change their modes of thought readily and admit, even encourage, new ways of treating their population. In no case can a community be forced to change. It must be re-educated. In today's community, two factors may be major determinants of receptivity to new programs for the retarded: the degree to which the community is sensitive to prerogatives of "home rule," and the entrenchment of the existing program patterns and personnel. A conservatism in certain regions makes approaches to community planning and the rate of planning different from those in more liberal communities. Planning must be geared to the existing political conditions as well as to future needs. Otherwise, long-term support will not be forthcoming and programs will stall and stagnate. Entrenchment, even in the most liberal of communities, can frustrate attempts at innovation and coordination. In either case, a demonstration of fiscal as well as humane advantage must be made to show mental retardation programs to be an integral part of a growing, prospering community.

Still another obstacle to change that can, in a way, present a larger and more difficult problem than either conservatism or entrenchment might be called the community's inability to "let go." There have been, over the years, active groups that have advocated the needs of the mentally retarded who now find themselves in competition with and, in some cases, taking a back seat to newly formed groups representing the retarded. The older and often well-established group finds it difficult to share its work and in many cases considers itself to be in competition with groups who would seek to plan for and minister to the needs of the community's retarded children and adults. Unless the "established" group is willing to take others into its confidence, the degree to which the plan and the developed program will suit the total needs for the retarded in that community will not be optimal.

These are superordinate issues. I cannot prescribe exact methods for each community because of differences in the relative importance of the issues in each case. Programming for the retarded will vary from place to place and succeed or fail in accordance with the manner in which these issues are taken into account.

# 1984

The current incidence of mental retardation in this country is equal to the combined populations of Chicago and Los Angeles. At the current rate of incidence and population growth, we can add Philadelphia and Detroit by 1984. This is not a bright prospect, but one that soon may be with us unless our efforts at prevention through research and maximization of function through rehabilitation are redoubled.

If we do this, then we may look forward in that year to seeing the provision of the full circle of services, along the age continuum, to the retarded. We may observe rapid research utilization and clear channels of communication between community projects and national, state, and university centers. We may observe clinicians and educators who are sophisticated in planning with parents for the future of the retarded child. We may see flexible administrative lines between and within communities with "fixed points of referral" coordinating agencies and reducing the mileage now covered by parents seeking help for their children. We may see little competition between disciplines for service to a condition with multiple causes. We may see a reduction in the number of retarded and alleviation of the impact of retardation on the individual and his family.

This is possible. We may see all these things. But shall we? Community programming must be soundly planned and executed. It must involve, not only relate to, experts in the field. Present planning is good; it is "grassroots"; it is being integrated into state planning. If adequate coordination develops, it will provide the programs we need.

As with the weather, forecasting change is risky business. Where complex organizations such as communities are involved, change may be noted only in retrospect and then only when people themselves are affected. Establishing new programs is often an illusory business, and often only the successful innovation is recalled or claimed. Those changes noted here represent the parts of the iceberg now visible. The pattern of these changes has yet to be felt, for we are still too near to the great revolution that has occurred in mental retardation and in all the areas affected by the increased social consciousness now characteristic of the professional and lay person alike in America. This is perhaps the most fundamental change of all, the increased willingness of those who are "in the know" to become directly involved. It is a change suggested to us by recent events and the example of our best national leadership. The question is whether we are spawning a generation of professionals and laymen who will enhance our efforts, not just at national symposia or presidential commissions, but in the communities throughout our land. It is at this level that all fundamental change of lasting value has taken place since 1769. It is at this level that change is taking place now. The question is whether it will be sufficiently strong to endure and progress to the point where mental retardation will no longer have to command the full attention of the community.

REFERENCE

JOHN FITZGERALD KENNEDY, *To Turn the Tide* (New York: Harper & Bros., 1962), p. 90.

# 23

# The Organization of
# Community Services for
# the Mentally Retarded

## HAROLD D. CHOPE

Civilization has always had the choice of two broad philosophies, that of Sparta which was to destroy the weak, the sick, and the handicapped, and that of Athens which was to heal, to nurture, and to restore. With the outstanding exception of Hitler's Nazism, western civilization has chosen the way of Athens. However, progress in service and research usually has been stimulated when a disease entity or complex enjoyed a champion to dramatize the cause, for example: Helen Keller for the blind, Franklin Delano Roosevelt for the polio patient, Beethoven for the deaf, Edward Livingston Trudeau for the tuberculous, each such championship evolving from a personal tragedy. Not until 1963 did mental retardation have such a champion when, for the first time in the history of the nation, the President of the United States sent a message to Congress dealing with mental illness and mental retardation. He stated,

> I am proposing a new approach—This approach is designed, in a large measure, to use federal resources to stimulate state, local, and private action. When carried out, reliance on the cold mercy of custodial isolation will be supplanted by the open warmth of community concern and capability. Emphasis on prevention, treatment and rehabilitation will be substituted for a desultory interest in confining patients in an institution to wither away. . . . This situation has been tolerated far too long. It has troubled

our national conscience—but only as a problem unpleasant to mention, easy to postpone, and despairing of solution (Kennedy to 88th Congress).

Historically, the care of the mentally retarded has been assumed to be a state responsibility, and the only solution, that of institutionalization or the removal of the retarded person from the local community. National figures indicating that only about 5 per cent of the nation's retarded are institutionalized testify to the obvious failure of this superficial approach to the problem. In California, six institutions for the retarded provide care for 11,825 individuals. However, with the burgeoning population of the state and the development of newer concepts of providing service locally, the present state system is inadequate in size to cope with the demand for service. Institutions are removed from centers of population and from the families of the patients.

Local services for the mentally retarded have been developing in California over the last two decades. In 1947, classes for the educable were authorized, and, in 1951, classes for the severely or the trainable mentally retarded were authorized in the public schools. These two accomplishments were beacons of hope to parent organizations that had been pleading for years for better local services for their handicapped children. But these services, particularly programs for severely retarded children, developed sporadically and unevenly throughout the state. In 1961, President Kennedy appointed the President's Panel on Mental Retardation, which filed a report on October 16, 1962. On June 13, 1963, the Governor of California signed Assembly Bill No. 1193, which created a Study Commission on Mental Retardation. On April 9 through 11, 1964, the American Medical Association held a special conference on the problems of the mentally retarded. The proceedings of the conference are published in the January 18, 1965, edition of the *Journal of the American Medical Association*.

During the legislative hearing of 1961, Dr. Daniel Blain suggested that, rather than spend in the neighborhood of $22,000,000 for the construction of a seventh large state institution, funds be provided for the construction of smaller (250 beds suggested) community centers. A $4,750,000 bond issue was voted for this purpose in the general election of November 1961. Four communities applied for these funds: Los Angeles, Santa Clara, San Francisco, and Contra Costa. To date, only two have been approved, Contra Costa on January 22, 1964, and San Francisco on March 20, 1964.

On October 24, 1963, President Kennedy signed into law the Mills-Ribicoff Act (HR 7544), now known as Public Law 88–156, and the Mental Retardation and Community Health Centers Construction Act (Public Law 88–164), which provide federal funds for construction of mental-health centers and facilities for the mentally retarded. In the 1964 session of the Legislature of California, Assemblyman Waldie introduced legislation (AB 91) that assigned the distribution of these funds to the Hill-Harris mechanism of the Bureau of Hospitals of the State Health Department. A companion bill (AB 92) proposed that the Advisory Committee, which recommends allocation of funds for health facility construction to the state Director of Public Health, be augmented by the appointment of the Director of Mental Health and three additional persons, one from the field of mental health, one with interests in mental retardation, and one from the area of community mental-health services.

In short, a new and vigorous concern for local services for the retarded is developing in this nation and in this state. This should result in improved local services to this group of handicapped citizens. Now is the time for communities to marshal their forces for the intelligent utilization of funds available.

In planning a community program, it is essential that the planners do not fall into the trap of confusing incidence with prevalence, thereby arriving at a much higher estimate of prevalence than actually exists. George Tarjan has described this difficulty clearly:

> It is often stated, on the basis of reasonably hard data, that 3% of the newborn will develop as mentally retarded individuals. It is estimated that (1) once in 1,000 a child is born whose IQ will not exceed 20; (2) the birth frequency of children with IQ's between 20 to 50 is four times higher; and (3) 25 of 1,000 newborns will later in life score between 50 and 70 on intelligence tests. On this basis, it is assumed that 3% of the population is mentally retarded. Such direct transfer of incidence data to prevalence is fraught with pitfalls. The incidence and prevalence rates would be equal only if mental retardation were always identifiable at the same age, for instance at birth, if the condition remained unchanged through life, and if the mortality of the retarded was the same as that of the average population. Facts do not conform to these requirements (Tarjan, 1965, p. 226).

Many communities initiate their community reports using the 3 per cent figure applied to the total population as a "scare headline," and, when it is impossible to locate this number of retarded, the efforts of the study group seem to be discredited.

There is no fixed pattern for local communities to follow in developing services for the retarded. At the outset it should be stated categorically that no rigid pattern should be promulgated by the higher taxing authority for the local communities to follow. The counties of California are too diverse in their population, available professional and financial resources, attitudes of governing bodies, and administrators of public health service agencies to attempt to impose one stereotyped program on every county. So, although no proposed "standard," "minimum adequate," or "ideal" program can be outlined or proposed, some general guidelines can be recommended (Gardner and Nisonger, 1962).

The provision of community services for the retarded is a multi-faceted, multiphasic, and complicated interdisciplinary problem. It is multi-faceted because the degrees of retardation vary, the problems of different age groups vary, other physical and emotional handicaps frequently exist, there is no known single specific etiology, and there is no single effective preventive measure. It is multiphasic because so many variable services are required: (1) education of the community about facts, attitudes, and services available; of the professions about their potential contributions to the solution of the problem; education of the retarded; training of the uneducable; education of management and employers about the potential of the handicapped as employees; (2) research in the fields of genetics, cellular physiology, neurology, clinical medicine, psychiatry, sociology, administration, techniques of learning; (3) provision of services in the fields of diagnosis, consultation, education, sheltered workshops, vocational training, placement services, social services, foster homes, housing for adult retarded, home- or visiting-nurse services, temporary twenty-four-hour care, day-care centers, religious training, guardianship. The services must be interdisciplinary by their nature and may include the following professionals: geneticists, cellular physiologists, obstetricians, pediatricians, psychiatrists, neurologists, psychologists, family physicians, attorneys (guardianship), social workers, public health nurses, specially trained teachers and educational administrators, speech therapists, vocational counselors, executives of voluntary agencies, occupational therapists, and physical therapists.

It is an all too frequent experience on the community level to find that some special-interest group will start a program for some segment of a mental-retardation service without knowing what exists in the community. So, the first need is to take an inventory of what already exists in the community before planning and initiating new services. A meeting to discuss such an inventory could be called by the local health officer, the president of the medical society, the chairman of the pediatrics and mental-health section of the medical society, the director of special education in the school department, the welfare director, the local mental-health director, the presidents of any of the voluntary agencies interested in the problem, one of the parent organizations, or perhaps by the chairman of the board of supervisors, if his interests happen to include such special humanistic aspects of local government. No matter who calls the meeting, care should be taken to involve everyone in the community with an interest in, involvement with, or knowledge of, the retarded. The inventory of services should determine whether any overlapping or duplication of services exists and should delineate any hiatus in the existing services. Second, the aspects of the program that are missing and most needed should be determined and placed on a priority list designed to pinpoint those easily obtainable soon, possibly obtainable with time, and remotely obtainable. Third, some one person from a discipline related to the prevention, diagnosis, treatment, or education of the retarded should be selected to organize the program and work for the selected objectives.

It would seem that one of the most important aspects of any program for the mentally retarded would be provision for early and accurate diagnosis. Much fear, uncertainty, and heartache, as well as unnecessary expense, could be saved parents if such a service could be developed within or made available to every community in the state. Such clinics should be developed on a local basis in any county with over 100,000 population, state-supported clinics being provided for less densely populated areas. A basic diagnostic team includes a pediatrician, psychiatrist, clinical psychologist, psychiatric social worker, public health nurse, and neurologist. Federal funds are available from Maternal Child Health Services by Public Law 88–156 to aid in the development of these services. Moreover, this bill has increased federal subsidies for Crippled Children's Services (*Public Health Programs,* 1964). There is no need to defend the importance of an accurate diagnosis, but it cannot be overemphasized that many children labeled "retarded" are, in fact, suffering from loss of hearing, visual defects, or emotional problems, or a neurologic handicap other than retardation. Such diagnostic clinics could be financed in five ways: (1) directly by state funds, (2) totally by local funds, (3) by use of a Maternal and Child Health Funds grant from the state health department, (4) by the use of the Crippled Children's Services mechanisms, and (5) by state or national mental-health program funds.

A second basic service would be consultation with the parents of diagnosed retarded children. Such a service is a key to the acceptance of the diagnosis by the parents and to realistic planning for the immediate future and the long-term outlook for the child. Consultation in this situation is not a one-shot relationship, but a long, continuous one. The consultant could help the parents understand the diagnosis, assist them to adjust to the problem with reduced feelings of guilt, inform them of available services, and help with sibling acceptance.

A third problem is the long time-lag between diagnosis in early life and out-of-home care at educational facilities. The committee might, therefore, be concerned with the provision of nursery school and recreational activities for retarded children. It would be wise to avoid segregating as much as possible these handicapped children from so-called normal children. Two experimental child-care centers have been established in California, one in Stockton and one in Oakland. Two additional centers are now in operation, one in San Jose and one in Seaside (Monterey County). These are expensive to operate, and experience has indicated that a child-care center for thirty to thirty-five retarded children will cost about $51,000 per year to operate, or $1,400 to $1,700 per child per year.

Fourth, classes for the educable and the trainable are needed in every community. During 1963–1964 there were 48,388 educable children in special classes and 4,207 trainable children in special classes, a total of 52,595. Although these figures are impressive, the California State Department of Education estimates that only 63 per cent of the potential number of educable retarded children are attending special classes. The classes for the trainable are less developed and less well distributed throughout the state than the classes for the educable.

Fifth, some type of day-care center is needed in nearly every community for retarded children or multihandicapped children who do not fit in or are not eligible for any other tax-supported service. Such a service involves skilled people with warmth and tolerance. Thirty to thirty-five of these severely handicapped children may be taken care of at a day center for a cost of about $1,000 per child per year, including transportation. It is surprising to see the improvement, in spite of their handicaps, in certain individuals that results merely from socializing.

Sixth, some long-term plans must be made for the retarded in collaboration with the parents. These include sheltered workshops; vocational training, leading to a method of support or livelihood for the retarded; and job recruitment and placement.

Seventh, one of the great worries revealed by parents of the retarded is what will happen to their handicapped family member when the parents are dead or disabled. In response to this problem, communities should plan for housing, guardianship, foster homes, job supervision, and medical care for the retarded citizen prior to the parents' death or disability.

These seven services and their corollaries can be developed in local communities by voluntary and official agencies with state or federal subsidies. The idea presented here, that counties should develop their own services, will fall far short of satisfying many people long impatient with the lack of any evidence of local official interest or financial responsibility for the care or training of the retarded. Long experience in other fields—such as public health, education, agriculture, and mental health—has demonstrated that the state cannot administer such programs directly. The closer the administration of a service is to the people it serves, the more stable and more productive it proves to be. Those who maintain that the omnipotent state can do the job faster commit a serious disservice to the development of effective local programs for the retarded. Local initiative in the development of community services may well be slower and spotty throughout the state, but it will prove to be more permanent, supported better financially, closer to the people served, and more sensitive to their needs.

These seven essential services for a program for the retarded are suggested for any community with more than 100,000 population. In fact, many could be provided by populations of over 50,000. When a county reaches 500,000 or more, another element should be added to the program —namely, facilities for long-term and short-term residential care. Long-term beds are needed in cases of parental neglect, where the welfare of the child requires removal from the family; medical or behavioral problems of the retarded requiring hospitalization; physical- and mental-health needs of the family; lack of family to care for the retarded person; and unwillingness of the family to care for the child. Short-term beds should be provided as a substitute home for the retarded person on such occasions as illness in the family, death, necessity to leave the community for short periods on business or vacation, or when the needs of the other children in the family require such a respite, or for intensive diagnostic studies.

These facilities will in no way be a complete substitute for the large state hospitals for the retarded. Local communities at the present time cannot be expected to care for the very severely damaged children, such as the hydrocephalics, the microcephalics, and those with multiple severe handicaps. These patients probably always will be charges of the state. Neither would it be anticipated that, even if every county with a population over a half-million could provide short-term and long-term residential care, the state could greatly reduce the number of beds now existing, except to retire those becoming obsolete.

During the public hearings held by the Governor's Commission throughout California during 1964 several communities presented segments of our proposed program for local services to the retarded, but no community presented a program that covered all of the listed facets of a minimum adequate program for counties of California. It was sensed that in some communities disagreements and dissension between official and nonofficial groups had delayed development of good services to the retarded. Also, there appeared to be friction between the pediatrician and the psychiatrist as to which specialty should take prime responsibility for the development of diagnostic centers.

Another field of disagreement is in program administration. At the federal level, neither the Children's Bureau, the National Institute of Mental Health, nor the Public Health Service is favored as the prime administrative mechanism, but rather the Vocational Rehabilitation Service. At the state level, legislation has been introduced to place the responsibility for some segments of the program in the state health department, the state institutions in the state Department of Mental Hygiene, the education aspects in the state Department of Education, and a coordinator in the office of the Administrator of Health, Welfare, and Mental Health. At the local level, also, many government departments may be involved in addition to the voluntary agencies and the parents' groups. These include the department of education, the public health department, the local welfare department, and the mental health services, parks and recreation departments. Probably one of the most logical approaches to the administration of such a complex program with so many disciplines and special interests involved would be to follow the plan now being initiated in Los Angeles County by developing a "Joint Powers Agreement" that will provide the mechanism for a Mental Retardation Services Board.

Many a well-conceived program for the retarded has been vitiated because a segment of the program favored by one department or voluntary agency was not given a high priority. The Los Angeles Plan, although not without its frustrations, would seem to be a desirable approach to a difficult community administrative problem.

Another serious deterrent to progress in the field of service to the retarded is the attitude of the physician toward the problems of mental retardation. At the Chicago Conference of the American Medical Association, the main theme was the responsibility of the "principal physician," that is, the first physician to suspect an abnormality, be he specialist or general practitioner. Emphasis was placed on his responsibility to follow through with the family, to know of community resources, to realize that the solution of the problem includes many disciplines with which he must collaborate to maximize his services to the family.

In collaboration with the local health department, the private physician is in an ideal situation to exercise a major role in the prevention of mental retardation through good prenatal care, careful supervision of the mother for hypothyroidism, diabetes mellitus and other metabolic diseases, the prevention of the excessive use of drugs during pregnancy, particularly teratogenic agents, genetic counseling when indicated, prevention of prematurity, careful delivery technique, and early detection of inborn metabolic errors such as phenylketonuria, galactosemia, or maple syrup urine disease. The physician or pediatrician in charge of the baby should not only instruct the mother in good infant care, but check to see that she is providing the infant with sufficient "mothering." Here, the public health nurse may be an important observer for the physician if he does not see the infant in the home.

The physician does not have so much opportunity to prevent cultural deprivation retardation, but he can depend on the social worker or the public health nurse for reports. "A majority of the mildly retarded are children of the more disadvantaged classes of our society, characterized by low income, limited educational opportunity, unskilled occupation and generally impoverished environment" (*Mental Retardation Handbook,* 1965). These are the children who never have a crayon to play with, learn colors, or hear a story read to them; they arrive at kindergarten or first grade unable to compete with other children, soon become frustrated, anxious, and difficult to handle, and are considered retarded.

It would appear prudent for physicians to assess the ancillary services available in their communities, such as social work, classes for the educable and trainable, nursery schools, foster-home placement services, tax-supported consultative and diagnostic clinics. If these basic services are not available in a community, who has a greater responsibility to exert leadership and assume initiative in helping organize such services than the physicians?


REFERENCES

WILLIAM I. GARDNER and HERSCHEL W. NISONGER, "A Manual on Program Development in Mental Retardation," *American Journal of Mental Deficiency* (Monograph Supplement), LXVI (1962), 1–192.

JOHN FITZGERALD KENNEDY, "Message from the President of the United States," *88th Congress, 1st Session,* HR Document Number 58, pp. 2, 4.

*Mental Retardation: A Handbook for the Primary Physician,* Report of the American Medical Association Conference on Mental Retardation, Reprinted from the *Journal of the American Medical Association,* CXCI (1965), 183–232.

*Public Health Programs for the Mentally Retarded* (Sacramento, California: California State Department of Public Health, March 1964).

GEORGE TARJAN, "The Next Decade: Expectations from the Biological Sciences," *Journal of the American Medical Association,* CXCI (1965), 226–229.

WELFARE PLANNING COUNCIL, LOS ANGELES REGION, MENTAL RETARDATION JOINT AGENCIES PROJECT, *Mental Retardation Survey of Los Angeles County: Summary of Findings, Conclusions, and Recommendations* (Los Angeles, California: Mental Retardation Joint Agencies Project, 1965).

# 24

# Legal Aspects of
# Mental Retardation

## ELIZABETH M. BOGGS

### THE CONSTITUTIONAL PRINCIPLE

In 1968 we will be celebrating the centenary of the adoption of the Fourteenth Amendment to the Constitution of the United States, whose first section provides that:

> All persons born or naturalized in the United States, and subject to the jurisdiction thereof, are citizens of the United States and of the State wherein they reside. No State shall make or enforce any law which shall abridge the privileges or immunities of citizens of the United States, nor shall any State deprive any person of life, liberty, or property without due process of law, nor deny to any person within its jurisdiction the equal protection of the laws.

Sir Maurice Amos devoted one of six *Lectures on the American Constitution,* delivered in 1938, to the Fourteenth Amendment, and particularly to the "due process" clause that he considered at that time to be pre-eminent (Amos, 1938, pp. 99–122). This pre-eminence rested on the extent to which "due process" was invoked in the period between 1890 and 1940 and on the power of the interpretations given to it by the Supreme Court. For example, he notes that in a case involving freedom of contract, Justice Rufus Peckham, speaking for the Court, enunciated the principle that the liberty mentioned in the "due process" clause means

> not only the right of the citizen to be free from the mere physical restraint of the person, as by incarceration, but the term is deemed to embrace the

407

right of the citizen to be free in the enjoyment of all his faculties; to be free
to enjoy them in all lawful ways; to work and live where he will; to earn his
livelihood by any lawful calling; to pursue any livelihood or avocation; and
for that purpose to enter into all contracts which may be proper, necessary
and essential to his carrying out to a successful conclusion the purposes
above mentioned (Amos, 1938, pp. 113–114).

H. E. Willis, a contemporary of Sir Maurice, opined that "due process of
law, better than any other Constitutional guarantee, gives the Supreme
Court the opportunity to draw the line which ought to be drawn between
personal liberty and social control" (Amos, 1938, p. 101).

The applicability of the principle of "due process" to laws providing
for involuntary admission (commitment) of the mentally ill has long occupied the attention of state courts and of jurists, administrators, and psychiatrists. Indeed, in New York State a recent report by a special committee to
study commitment procedures was published under the title, *Mental Illness
and Due Process* (Association of the Bar of the City of New York, 1962).
Another measure of the extent to which attention has focused on the "due
process" aspect of management of the mentally ill or mentally retarded is
found in the recent massive study by the American Bar Foundation, *The
Mentally Disabled and the Law* (Lindman and McIntyre, 1961), approximately half of whose 400-odd pages are devoted to the procedures for and
legal implications of admission and retention in mental institutions. Debate
continues and it still is not agreed, for example, that notice and a hearing
are essential parts of "due process" when liberty is curtailed through involuntary commitment.

Since 1950 the emphasis in appeals to the United States Supreme
Court that invoke the Fourteenth Amendment has shifted from "due
process" to "equal protection." The best-known case is, of course, school
desegregation, but there are others, such as the Gideon case, in which it was
held that "equal protection" means equal opportunity to be represented by
counsel in a trial for a felony, and that an accused who cannot afford an
attorney must be supplied with one by the court. This new focus has not,
however, been applied with the same zeal to the rights of the mentally disabled, especially those with long-term disability.

For the vast majority of the retarded the issue of "institutionalization," for example, is merely an instance of the more fundamental question
of choice of treatment and choice of residence and the locus of legal authority to make such choices. The preoccupation with "due process" in relation
to physical restraint, such as incarceration, has been at the expense of attention to the right of the mentally retarded person "to be free in the enjoyment of his faculties, . . . free to use them in all lawful ways" and to
receive the kind of protection that maximizes this freedom. It is time that,
as is already being done in other fields, we examine more closely the impli-

cations of the principle of "equal protection" in our legal dealings with the mentally retarded.

The Constitution of the United States has validity and vitality today largely because it contains statements of principles that are recognized as having wide applicability and credence in today's world. The general concept of "equal protection" is readily accepted—the concept that the law itself must not distinguish arbitrarily between one man and another and that its administration and application must be equally impartial; this concept is also expressly incorporated in the California Constitution.

It has been said that the constitutional mandate of equal protection requires that "all persons . . . shall be treated alike, under like circumstances and conditions, both in the privileges conferred and in the liabilities imposed" (Smith, 1955, pp. 105–106). It is easy to see that circumstances and conditions are never precisely the same and, indeed, the major body of case law revolves around an analysis of what is "essentially" alike or comparable in two manifestly different situations. Moreover, even in comparable situations, the principle of "equality before the law" is, in practice, meaningless unless the persons to whom it is applied are themselves substantially equal in their ability to discharge duties imposed and to utilize rights accorded by the law in question. As the *Report of the Task Force on the Law* of the President's Panel on Mental Retardation notes,

> Usually the law takes for granted a minimum "normal" set of personal characteristics in the population. But it must have means for recognizing when and where that assumption is invalid. It must also say what is to be done in a case where the departure from the norm is very great. It is in these areas that mental disability presents its greatest difficulty for the law (President's Panel, 1963, p. 1).

There is, of course, nothing novel in the idea that all persons are not, in fact, equal in ability to comply with the law or to take advantage of the rights it gives. What is new (or undergoing renewal) is the determination to find and use social instrumentalities to achieve a better balance. How good must such a balance be and how much effort is justified to achieve it? An attorney with many years of experience in private practice and public affairs has said,

> . . . in areas where law has undertaken, traditionally, and necessarily under the Constitution, to deal with people on an objectively equal basis it has achieved this goal through the age old science of classification . . . . To classify in the strict sense, you start by identifying certain criteria as the basis for your determinations. These criteria must bear a rational and logical relation to the primary objective of the law or program. Then as you proceed to apply these criteria in individual cases, you will identify, in terms of these criteria, a group whose treatment under the law or program

will faithfully carry out the authorized objective. The crux of this method lies in comparing the criteria of exclusion or inclusion with the actual objectives of the law or program (Smith, 1955, pp. 110–111).

This leads us to the concept of a *legally significant difference*. A legally significant difference must be relevant to the objectives of the law in question, substantial, and defined by means of objective criteria. It is clear that we cannot have objectivity, let alone a practical system for administering justice, if every gradation of difference must be considered legally significant. Thus, any practical system of classification tends to make a continuum into a step-wise system. The question is how big may the steps be, how much latitude may be allowed between the objective criterion used and the actual characteristic that is relevant to the purpose of the law in question.

## THE PRACTICAL ISSUES — EQUALITY VERSUS INDIVIDUAL DIFFERENCES

Age, a convenient objective index because it generally is verifiable without expert testimony or detailed individual examination, is a common criterion for classification. It is, for example, usually used as a rough measure of the equality of individuals and hence their equal right to perform certain specific functions. It is accepted that there are differences between a seven-year-old and a twenty-seven-year-old that are relevant to such issues as the right to drive a car, to marry, to make contracts, to decide whether or not he will submit himself to instruction, and so on. It is also recognized that the difference between a given seventeen-year-old and a given eighteen-year-old may not be significant; but since the legal discrimination is temporary and not usually far-reaching in its serious effects, precision in classification is permitted to yield to convenience. Classification by age is widely accepted, not only with respect to minority, but also with respect to "senior citizen" status, involving eligibility for social security and special welfare benefits.

The health field offers many parallels to these legal approximations. Only some of the Americans who travel abroad are not immune to smallpox, yet the Public Health Service requires that all be vaccinated within three years prior to re-entry. The risks of over-vaccination are considered negligible and the price in vaccine and time is judged insubstantial relative to the alternative of determining by other means who is and who is not immune. On the other hand, where the possible consequences are serious, more elaborate discriminatory procedures are justified and, indeed, required. Many states have adopted procedures for the mass screening of newborn infants for abnormally high blood-phenylalanine levels. However, before a baby found "positive" by the screening method is placed on a low phenylalanine diet, more elaborate individual diagnostic procedures are employed. This is justified because of the substantial consequences (medical and financial) of placing a baby without phenylketonuria on the diet.

In the legal field, as in the medical, it is desirable to have simple and easily administered criteria that do not require the intervention of experts. Yet, the approximation or substitution of criteria (such as age for maturity or mental age for social competence) can be predicated on false assumptions and can lead to error and injustice. Where much is at stake in a critical decision, the chance of error must be narrowed to the minimum, even at some cost. In our society, which continues to respect the individual, such costs must be incurred even where the consequences of error are serious only to a single human being. It may be said that the court hearing or trial is the legal equivalent of the full and detailed diagnostic work-up that the physician undertakes only when the consequences of an incorrect judgment are great enough to warrant it. Some forms of mental retardation do have socio-legal consequences that are so serious for the affected individual as to justify this kind of scrutiny.

There is no law for whose objectives the differential classification of "mentally retarded" per se is significant. Contrary to popular opinion, there is no legal need for a universal statutory definition of mental retardation. On the other hand, there are a number of subgroups among the "mentally retarded," as clinically defined, whose differences from the general population are substantial, relevant to specific legal objectives, and capable of being established by reasonably objective criteria. Such groups should be defined in the statutes in terms specific to the purposes of a particular law. For example, the California education code defines "mentally retarded" to mean "all minors who because of retarded intellectual development, as determined by individual psychological examination, are incapable of being educated efficiently and profitably through ordinary classroom instruction" (California Education Code, Section 6901). This definition establishes a legally significant difference.

Many other legal provisions should and do differentially affect particular subclassifications of the mentally retarded, such as retarded adults incapable of productive work, or retarded children up for adoption. In 1964, the California Study Commission on Mental Retardation commissioned a survey of such laws in California (California Study Commission on Mental Retardation, 1964). Nineteen separate state codes were searched and more than twenty major topics covered. Some relate to programs; some to rights of the individual in relation to marriage, voting rights, insurance, sterilization, and defense against criminal charges. It would take a book to cover these topics adequately; therefore the remainder of this chapter will concentrate on one area, the general continuing protection and maintenance of an adult incapacitated by mental retardation.

Under this heading, three subtopics will be considered: incompetence, guardianship, and maintenance. These are of fundamental importance to any retarded adult whose condition is such as to impair seriously his ability to make constructive use of the power of choice, and to command for himself the "equal protection" that the Constitution guarantees to "all persons born or naturalized in the United States."

## Provisions Relating to Guardianship and Incompetence in California Law

In California, as in most other states, guardianship is a legal relationship between a competent adult and a minor child, or between a competent adult and another adult who has been adjudicated incompetent. Under the California Probate Code, the term "incompetent" applies to any person who is unable, for any reason, to manage properly and take care of himself or his property unassisted, and by reason thereof is likely to be deceived (California Probate Code, Section 1460). A minor is anyone under age twenty-one. It follows that a mentally retarded child is protected formally by general laws, and one need not prove mental retardation or incompetence in order to secure for him the protection of guardianship. Section 1440 of the Probate Code permits the court to appoint a guardian for the person and/or estate of a minor "whenever it appears necessary or convenient," on petition of a relative or other person. The advantage of using such a provision for a retarded child when the natural guardianship of parents fails during childhood is that it avoids a premature determination of incompetence.

The Welfare and Institutions Code defines a mentally deficient person as one

> who is not psychotic but who is so mentally retarded from infancy or before reaching maturity that he is incapable of managing himself or his affairs independently, with ordinary prudence, or being taught to do so, and who requires supervision, control, and care for his own welfare or for the welfare of others, or for the welfare of the community (California Welfare and Institutions Code, Section 5250).

When applied to an adult, this definition is a good working description of incompetence arising from mental retardation; it suggests the need for guardianship. It does not necessarily imply need for hospitalization. It is significant, however, that its location in the code indicates that it was drafted to delineate those who may be admitted (or committed) to California institutions for the retarded. In the past, institutionalization has been the poor man's guardianship. And where lifetime supervision and maintenance are needed, 95 per cent of us are poor men.

The concept of the institution as the primary resource for care and protection of the dependent retarded individual is reinforced by Sections 227 a and b of the Civil Code. These provide that when adoptive parents seek and secure vacation of an adoption proceeding on the grounds that the child they adopted had a pre-existing condition of "feeblemindedness," then the court *shall direct* the district attorney to have the child committed to a state institution for the mentally deficient. No provision is inclined for the appointment of a personal guardian to replace the parents whom such a child has twice lost or to secure means for community placement other than through the machinery of the institution. In theory, personal guardianship of such a child is not precluded by law, but the language of the Probate Code (Sections 1440, 1461, also 1402–1403) suggests that this is unlikely to happen for this or any other child without an estate unless someone who wants to be guardian will petition the court to act. Parents who wish to assure that any minor child will have a guardian in the event of their death will be well advised to so provide in their wills.

California's laws pertaining to general private guardianship of the incompetent adult already cover certain essential formal provisions not necessarily in use in all states. These include (in addition to the protections of "due process") the option to separate guardianship of the person from guardianship of the estate, with corporations, such as banks, being eligible only for the latter (California Probate Code, Section 480). Thus, an incompetent may have one guardian performing either or both functions or two guardians, each performing one function in complementary fashion. There is an express provision for restoration to competency at any point at which the ward develops ability to act for himself. Testamentary guardianship, through which a parent or prior guardian designates by will or deed that person preferred to succeed in the role of guardian, is recognized in California with respect to incompetents as well as children (California Probate Code, Sections 1462, 1402). It weighs heavily with but is not binding on the court. (Such an appointment, when made on behalf of an adult, must have been preceded at some time by an adjudication of incompetence.) There is no limitation on the power of any court to appoint a guardian to protect the interests of an incompetent person in a particular court action (California Probate Code, Section 1607). Admission to a mental institution does not constitute an automatic adjudication of incompetence, although, as indicated before, the definition of eligibility for admission to a state institution for the mentally deficient, if scrupulously observed, would certainly limit admission to those who are incompetent in fact, if not in law.

The option of providing only a guardian of property makes available one form of the "limited guardianship" that the Task Force on the Law saw as a desirable part of the legal spectrum (President's Panel, 1963, p. 25). It can be a useful device when a person of marginal ability has financial assets that are beyond his capacity to manage. This occasionally happens to the mentally retarded, although with foresight on the part of parents such substantial resources can be diverted into trust arrangements under which title does not pass directly to the retarded person at any time.

Another form of *de facto* guardianship appears to be formally available in California law under the name of "conservatorship" (California Probate Code, Sections 1701ff, 1957). In most other states where this term is used, it applies only to property; but in California a "conservator" of person and/or property can be appointed by the court for an incompetent person, whether committed to an institution or not, or "for any other person incapable of caring for his person and/or property."

Although many states provide public guardianship for minors left without parents or appropriate private guardians, California is among an apparent minority of states that also provide public guardianship of incompetent adults in certain circumstances. Under a law originating twenty years ago, county governing bodies may establish such salaried positions. The official so designated *may accept* appointment as guardian of the person or estate, or both, of a minor or incompetent adult whose financial assets are small; he *may apply* for appointment as guardian of the person or estate of any county resident who is in a mental institution or is receiving public aid where it appears that guardianship is needed (California Welfare and Institutions Code, Sections 5175ff). I. Weissman *et al.* (1949, p. 57) found the Los Angeles county appointee was indeed managing affairs for and representing incompetent residents in business and legal matters. As pressures have increased, however, the public guardians' clientele has become more restricted (Welfare Planning Council, 1965, p. 29).

When a mental patient has substantial property, the Department of Mental Hygiene is more likely to be appointed as guardian of the estate, in the absence of any other guardian (California Welfare and Institutions Code, Section 6660). A large staff now is engaged within the Department in garnering and conserving the assets of patients. The objective of protecting the patient's interest is joined here with the objective of preserving the state's stake in the patient's liability for the cost of his care. Otherwise it would seem more reasonable to assign management of substantial estates to banks and fiduciary corporations. The members of the recent Mental Retardation Joint Agencies Project in Los Angeles recommended that the interests of less affluent patients also be protected and that the Department "develop procedures for the collection and administration of benefits that may be due patients but which are too small to be handled by the Guardianship Division." Amounts under $500 are reserved for the patient's personal use without attachment for maintenance costs (Welfare Planning Council, 1965, p. 61).

Recently, in California as in other states, there has been increasing uneasiness about the propriety of nonjudicial appointment of "representative payees" to receive social-security benefits or public-assistance payments on behalf of certain aged or disabled beneficiaries where the beneficiary is deemed (administratively) to be incapable of handling these small sums wisely and in his own best interest. In the absence of court review, such action can well be construed as denial of "due process." In California (as in a number of other states), this question has resulted in recent explicit statutory provision that a guardian be appointed for any applicant for, or recipient of, public social services who is incapable of managing his own affairs (California Welfare and Institutions Code, Section 103.9, 1963). This would, in theory, give some protection to the not inconsiderable number of adult retarded who are receiving disability assistance.

The foregoing eclectic description of the formal side of California law as it pertains to guardianship demonstrates that this state, at least, does not lack legislation. Yet it cannot be said to assure that those so identified receive the services required, to say nothing of those who fail to penetrate the barriers to identification. In the words of the state Study Commission:

> Singly or together, however, these sections do not bring about a service which is available to every retarded person who needs it, nor do the statutes provide for coordination of the services needed by each individual. The Study Commission believes that public guardianship service should be available for every retarded person who needs it. . . . For mentally retarded persons, the greatest need on a continuing basis will be for someone equipped to carry out social management (Study Commission on Mental Retardation, 1965, p. 77).

In the closing hours of the 1965 session, the California Legislature enacted one of the alternatives suggested by the Commission when it added a new Section 416 to the Health and Safety Code. This will permit the Director of Public Health to accept testamentary guardianship of a mentally retarded person on the death of the parents or (other) guardian, if the state has assumed responsibility for providing care for the retarded person through one of the proposed new "regional centers." The purpose of this guardianship is to carry out recommendations of the center and to assure "continuity of care." New Jersey also enacted a new law requiring the Commissioner of Institutions and Agencies to provide "guardianship services" to selected mentally deficient adults in the absence of private guardians (New Jersey Commission on Mental Health, 1961, p. 67).

Past history has indicated that adding one more public official to the list already entitled to accept guardianship responsibilities will scarcely go to the heart of the problem unless its true character is better understood and a new and more appropriate approach used. Since the issue of responsibility for continuing protection and supervision of the mentally retarded is common in most states, it may be reviewed in more general terms.

## GUARDIANSHIP OF THE PERSON—
## LEGAL FICTION OR SOCIAL ASSET?

Guardianship is an ancient institution. It was devised originally for the benefit of the mentally deficient and was later extended to all who are incompetent from whatever cause. Because we have entered an era in which recovery from mental illness often is relatively fast, we frequently can avoid the legal implications of the temporary incompetence that may be associated with some forms of mental illness. On the other hand, mental deficiency carries with it a prognosis of continuing incompetence. This is one of several implications of mental deficiency that differentiates it from mental illness. Since guardianship today is becoming, on the whole, less needed for the mentally ill and more widely needed for certain of the retarded, it is time to recast our concept of guardianship with the characteristics of the mentally deficient clearly in mind.

1. The condition of mental deficiency is not one with a rapid onset.

2. Because mental deficiency appears during minority, diagnosis need not be coupled with any legal emergency related to immediate care and control.

3. Predictions about the degree of impairment in ability to handle oneself and one's affairs as an adult frequently are unreliable in a young child, but can be made with greater confidence in late adolescence, especially when there has been a consistent history of retarded mental development and demonstrated social inadequacy.

4. Since the condition originates in childhood, the affected person will have had no experience in discharging adult responsibilities and, in particular, no recollection of the enjoyment of the rights and status of an adult. He is thus more likely to submit to an imposed authority and less likely to protest infringement of his rights.

5. The social inadequacies of the mentally deficient person are likely to be generalized and diffuse in contrast to the more focal irrationalities or delusions characteristic of some forms of mental illness.

6. The mentally deficient are less likely than the mentally ill to own property or have substantial financial resources, since they have no history of well-remunerated employment, seldom marry, and, if their parents are well advised, seldom receive direct gifts or legacies.

7. Because of the early origin and longer duration of his condition, the mentally deficient individual is less likely than other incompetent people to have close relatives (spouse, children, parents) who can continue to be concerned about his welfare as he himself ages.

It is, of course, recognized that certain forms of childhood psychosis give rise to the same conditions.

Less than a third of the children who might be identified for one purpose or another as mentally retarded grow up to be mentally deficient adults. A marginally disabled group is composed of those whose ability (as adults) to handle the ordinary decisions of daily living and the modest sums they may earn appears sufficient to justify leaving these responsibilities in their hands, preferably supported by good counsel from a capable relative or qualified agency. Although retarded, these persons would not be considered mentally deficient.

From the point of view of education and planning ahead, prognostic indicators in childhood and adolescence are important. From a strictly legal point of view, it is usually immaterial whether a child is considered mentally deficient or not, as long as he is a minor, since long-term incapacity to manage one's affairs has legal significance primarily for the adult. The natural guardianship of parents is to be preferred for the minor retarded child, as for the normal child. A judicial substitution of another guardian, public or private, should be made in either case only when circumstances make it necessary to replace parents in this function. Where guardianship of the person of one child rests in two distinct and independent agents—for example, a parent and a public guardian—a basic conflict in authority arises. Such a conflict may remain latent, as was the case in many instances under the Minnesota guardianship program, but should be avoided (Thomson, 1963, p. 176). Those under parental guardianship should have equal access to other services, public and private, including counseling, care outside the home, and continuing evaluation, as do those under judicially created private or public guardianship. The World Health Organization Joint Expert Committee has emphasized this point (World Health Organization, 1954, p. 39).

Since all children enjoy the legal protections of minority, it is fortunately possible, in most instances, to postpone giving judicial recognition to mental disability until late adolescence, when predictions of social viability can be made with greater accuracy. Recent experiments with voluntary admission of retarded children to California institutions rest on this view. However, the legal problems associated with attainment of majority must be understood and anticipated. An adult must be presumed legally capable of directing his own life unless and until adjudicated otherwise. It is sound to approach the years of chronologic maturity with this presumption, but it is unsound not to challenge it in the face of contrary evidence, whether out of delicacy, inertia, or misplaced notions about individual liberty.

It is true that many mentally deficient adults live for years as dependent or semidependent members of their families, without the formal protection of guardianship. Parents frequently assume the functions of guardian of the adult person without any judicial procedure. This omission produces an ambiguous situation and leaves the retarded person vulnerable on two counts. In the first place, there is a hazard in encouraging the assumption by

one adult of an attitude of control over another, except when the justification for this relationship has been impartially reviewed and sanctioned and
when, in fact, the sanctioning authority has considered not only the need for
protection but the qualifications of the protector. Secondly, by postponing
the formal enunciation of the need for such protection, parents leave the
retarded adult exposed at such time as the informal parental supervision is
interrupted. By seeking judicial recognition of the retarded adult's incapacity and securing appointment of himself or another suitable person as
guardian of the person of the adult and establishing a relationship with a
person or agency that can provide at least transitional continuity in an
emergency, the parent can obviate these situations.

Over the years there has been a great reluctance on the part of parents
and others to institute proceedings for the determination of incompetence
and appointment of a guardian for a variety of reasons. Where substantial
property must be managed, the question cannot be evaded, and, partly for
this reason, the property issue has largely obscured the primacy of guardianship of the person as a positive protection. Since the retarded less frequently acquire wealth, guardianship is less frequently sought for those
among them who are indeed mentally deficient. Guardianship of the person,
no less than of the property, requires a commitment of time, thought, and
action (not always conveniently timed) on the part of the guardian. If the
ward lacks property, private guardianship is a labor of love, a fact that
again militates against its use.

Another deterrent arises from the antiquity of the legal concept of
incompetence and accretions of use in many jurisdictions. As the Bar
Foundation study revealed, the prohibitions associated with incompetence
are by no means clearly defined (Lindman and McIntyre, 1961, Chapter
8). Perhaps it was partly to clear the slate and start fresh that California
enacted its conservatorship law alluded to earlier, since the conditions in
which it may be applied appear to be substantially the same as those that
define incompetence, and the conservator's powers are at least as great as a
guardian's. Nevertheless, the Los Angeles study group thought conservatorship was to be preferred as a way of providing supervision and guidance for
the retarded adult, so that he "may lead as normal a life as possible" (Welfare Planning Council, 1965, p. 60). It should be stressed, however, that
the appointment of a conservator may follow only after a judicial determination that the retarded person is in need of such supervision. Thus the
nuisance and embarrassment are not likely to be eliminated by a change of
name.

All these factors tend to hide the positive uses of guardianship for the
individual who does in fact need it. As Smith has observed,

> . . . the stigma attached to the finding of incompetency upon which the
> service of guardianship has been conditioned, and indeed the nature of the

proceeding itself, have all combined to blind us to the role which this legal institution is designed to play. The emphasis has been upon the legal establishment and declaration of incompetency and not upon maintaining legal capacity and providing the individual with the means of expression and protection (through guardianship) (Smith, 1955, p. 137).

Attitudes and "the nature of the proceeding itself" can be considerably improved, but efforts to short cut "due process" by formalizing or eliminating the careful review of the circumstances in each individual case are scarcely the answer. Although incompetence creates a condition analogous to minority, it is not so readily verified. The objective criteria are not simple or easily applied. Moreover, since for the individual in question the consequences of a wrong decision (either way) are serious, it is necessary to give adequate attention, including expert evaluation of social as well as medical factors, to determinations in individual cases. Since a modification in the exercise of liberty is involved, "due process" must be observed.

The dilemma of "due process" in this instance is twofold. It shares in the practical difficulty that arises whenever a significant number of people must be admitted to a legal "class" by criteria that are not easily verified. This situation is additionally complicated by the constitutional requirement that an adult may not be deprived of his right to run his own life or handle his own funds, small or large, except with the sanction of the courts. With the increasing number of aging persons, some proportion of whom do need protective services, the dilemma of providing meaningful court review without unreasonable expense and burden on the courts is receiving more attention, as shown by the provisions on protective payments added to the Social Security Act in 1965 by Public Law 89–97. The issue is equally important for the adult mentally deficient; for although their number is smaller, it is growing; and the period of their dependency, both social and economic, is more prolonged.

Even "due process" does not dispose of the problem of "maintaining legal capacity and providing the individual with the means of expression and protection." An attorney can, of course, represent an individual, including an incompetent one, in legal matters. A good trust company, if appointed as either trustee or guardian of the property of an incompetent usually will discharge its duties faithfully and efficiently. It is through guardianship of the person, however, that the individual achieves at least a substitute means of personal expression. The guardian makes the kinds of personal decisions on behalf of his ward that the ward ordinarily would make for himself, including choice of residence (halfway house, family care. state hospital), choice of physician, and the like. One of the most important responsibilities of a guardian of the person of a mentally deficient individual is to decide how much to consider the ward's apparent wishes and how much to permit him to choose for himself. This same important kind of judgment must be exercised by parents of normal children, especially adolescents.

What is lacking today is the means to assure conscientious and enlightened implementation of this *service of guardianship,* a service that restores meaning, through exercise, to the ward's freedom of choice, a choice made not impartially but by a partisan person, a person sworn to act for the incompetent one. In the words of the Task Force on the Law:

> To give a person liberty to choose between alternatives of which he can have no appreciation is to defeat and mock the concept of liberty. It goes without saying that restitution of a missing capacity in the person himself, through every available form of treatment, should be the primary objective. But for those among the mentally retarded for whom restitution of the capacity to use liberty is not now and not foreseeably possible, justice requires an effort at substitution. Just as a paralyzed limb may be amputated and a prosthetic device which functions with comparable effectiveness substituted, so occasions arise when a vitiated legal right must be excised and some substitution made (President's Panel, 1963, pp. 15–16).

The finding of incompetence in a mentally retarded person is legal surgery, removing certain rights ordinarily accorded the adult, but rights which, for this particular adult, have become useless and, indeed, an impediment. Whether the amputee is then left in a legal bed or helped to get about and maintain contact with his surroundings depends to a considerable extent on how well designed and functional is the legal and social prosthesis that we call guardianship of the person.

One of the real problems in achieving adequate action-oriented discussion of the significance and potentialities of the *service of guardianship* is the limited perception of the situation by the various parties who must cooperate if it is to succeed. These include the legal profession, the helping professions, and the parents of the mentally deficient.

Men of the law still tend to view incompetence proceedings as an adversary action in which the alleged incompetent must be pitted against the avarice of those who would deprive him of something. So long as "due process" appears to be observed, many jurists see little need for change in the approaches to guardianship. Few remark that, in fact, the "process" is seldom initiated unless there is someone who wants to be guardian, or unless a crisis has already arisen that affects the interests of some competent person. This crisis is generally a fiscal one, such as the settling of an estate. Nor does it seem to be a source of concern that, when appointing a guardian, the courts seldom seek out and question those who could tell most about the social functioning of the individual, nor do they in fact exercise their powers of post-appointment supervision and review beyond requiring a financial accounting. Most courts may be compared with the skilled sur-

geon who amputates and fits the prosthesis, but does not assume any responsibility for the patient's rehabilitation following surgery.

The social worker or agency and even the physician working with the
retarded adult and his family may, on the other hand, err in the opposite
direction, applying "rehabilitation" without first taking care of the "surgery." The modern social worker has been trained to shy away from the use
of "authority" and does not always recognize that the assumption of responsibility for managing the life of another adult person without a clear
authority vested in law can be subversive to the structure of a free society.
Moreover, when no one person has been assigned such authority, there can
well be conflict when several informally assume it. "Going to court" is like
"going under the knife"; no one approaches it lightly, but there are times
when it is irresponsible to avoid the issue.

Parents of mentally deficient children, confronted with the question,
"What will happen to my child when I die?" may tend to think of guardianship in more positive terms, but terms that too often revolve around "pie in
the sky." Some want the authority of "guardianship" without judicial intervention or sanction. They want to determine for themselves whether their
adult child should remain a child at law. They may also confuse "guardianship" with income maintenance. Many parents are seeking some sort of
device that will guarantee an adequate lifetime income for their retarded
son or daughter, regardless of inflation or life duration. Their expectations
that such an income can be bought without pain by the parent earning
$15,000 a year or less could be realized only by insurance companies that
are either magicians or philanthropists. Professional people who do not do
the arithmetic often foster these misconceptions about the fiscal realities.

These financial concerns are real and almost universal. It is likely that
less than 5 per cent of families can set up, through insurance or investment
or trust or any other mechanism, a life income for their retarded son or
daughter that confidently can be expected to meet reasonable expenses
without reliance on outside sources. A partial approach to this problem has
been made under the social-security system, but its deficits have to be made
up out of permanent- and total-disability assistance, old-age assistance, or
public-institution appropriations for all but a few who survive immediate
relatives. Burdens so great that no insurance company will underwrite them
cannot be sustained except by public subsidy. One day we may arrive at
ways of recognizing this that are less painful to parents than at present. It
only makes it worse that the anxiety about reasonable maintenance frequently distracts the attention of parents (and their attorneys) from an
even more fundamental issue, even less recognized by society—the basic
issue of guardianship: who is going to make important week-by-week or
year-by-year decisions on behalf of the mentally deficient person?

Parents also sometimes confuse guardianship with trusteeship. Present
laws in most states permit the placing of money in trust to be used for the

benefit of designated beneficiaries (whether retarded or not) under circumstances delineated by the person establishing the trust. Such funds are not subject to the same liens or restrictions in management as might be placed against property that the beneficiary owns in his own name, and for which a guardian of the estate will have to be named. When parents are in a position to place sufficient funds in trust, a bank can be named as trustee with instructions to make available part or all of the proceeds to the guardian of the person, to be used by the guardian to implement his discretionary decisions. This may be well worth doing even when the funds available fall considerably short of assuring full maintenance. However, when funds are small, costs of establishing an individual trust are disproportionately high.

One solution to this problem, a kind of communal trust fund, has been initiated by the Massachusetts Association for Retarded Children. It is called the MARC Retardate Trust. This is a corporate body with a self-perpetuating board of trustees interlocked with the Board of MARC itself. A parent may become a "mutual member" by paying an annual fee of $5.00 or by a lump sum payment of $1,000 or a bequest of $2,000. In return the Trust assumes (on the parent's death) a benevolent interest in the welfare of the retarded person who becomes a "participant." A representative of the Trust will keep track of him, so to speak, visit him, and advise relatives. If the total resources permit, the Trustees may at their discretion make some modest expenditures on the participant's behalf out of the Trust's accrued pooled funds. In addition, they will manage on an individual basis, for the benefit of a named beneficiary, any amount in excess of $10,000. The MARC Retardate Trust does not, however, undertake to act as guardian either of the person or property of a mentally deficient person, although it will offer advice and consultation to private individuals or banks who may be so named. Established in 1960, the MARC Retardate Trust has now accumulated sufficient funds to warrant the part-time employment of a person with social work skills to carry out the responsibilities it has assumed vis-à-vis the retarded sons or daughters of deceased "mutual members." These now number several dozen, both in public institutions and in the community. The California Study Commission on Mental Retardation has recommended that the California Council for Retarded Children organize a similar trust, and the Maryland Association already has done so (Study Commission on Mental Retardation, 1965, p. 77).

It is, of course, legally possible to set up nonprofit, nonpublic continuing corporate bodies or agencies to perform personal guardianship services, apart from or in addition to the legal, moral, and fiscal responsibilities of a trustee or guardian of estate. Questions of stability and continuity arise, however, unless all wards are fully funded. A lesson can be learned from the experience and attitude of voluntary child welfare agencies. Late in the nineteenth century private child protective agencies were developed that were legally empowered to assume responsibility for the guardianship of

children. Today these agencies are still actively exercising short-term protective functions, but shy away from assuming responsibilities for long-term
care and supervision of children, especially legal guardianship, even though
there is definite assurance that the responsibility will terminate in eighteen
to twenty years, or less. It seems, a fortiori, unlikely that private agencies or
organizations can be expected to assume a major role in longer-term guardianship of the mentally deficient.

Precisely because it does not provide guardianship or guarantee maintenance, participation in the MARC Retardate Trust is within the means of
many conscientious parents of the mentally deficient. It does not, of course,
cover the like needs of the mentally deficient whose parents have not the
forethought to invest in it. It leads us once again to an apparent need for
some public participation in this arena. There are two major reasons why
this issue of guardianship of the person and of the public role therein are of
growing concern. First is the expected increase in numbers of adults who
may require it. In the past, mortality among the mentally deficient had been
relatively high, and for those who have reached adulthood, society has
offered one instrumentality of protection—namely the residential institution. A quasi-guardianship role has been played for these people in most
states over the years by the superintendents of institutions, and indeed admission to institutions has often been sought by parents for their adult mentally deficient children in order to assure them this protection. Thus, the
past availability of residential care has cloaked the more fundamental issue
of protection for all the mentally deficient.

At the present time there are between 80,000–100,000 mentally deficient adults in residential institutions and a comparable number of similarly
handicapped people who are not in institutions but who are receiving social-
security benefits as the dependent adult children of persons insured under
the Social Security System who have either died or retired. The discovery of
these seriously retarded people came somewhat as a surprise following the
enactment of the 1957 Social Security Amendments (U.S. Social Security
Administration, 1963). We can only guess, therefore, how many more
mentally deficient adults there may be whose fathers either were not covered under Social Security or have not died or retired. One thing we do
know, however, is that their number will begin to grow in the next few years
at a very rapid rate. The count of youths turning twenty-one each year will
increase about 50 per cent in the next four years. The proportion of those
who should be found to be mentally deficient will certainly not be less and
probably will be considerably more than in the past, because those who will
reach twenty-one in 1967 will represent the vanguard of the generation that
has benefited most from antibiotics and other medical advances. Thus, on a
numerical basis alone, we will be hard put to provide protection for these
adults in the classic pattern—by placing them in full-time segregated residential communities of their own, under expert supervision.

Fortunately, contemporary thought does not favor such an oversimplified approach. Although specialized facilities for the twenty-four-hour-a-day care of mentally retarded children and adults certainly will continue to be needed, and probably in increasing capacity, the future appears to hold a much more flexible array of living, working, and leisure-time arrangements for many of the mentally deficient, as well as for those with a less marked degree of mental retardation. These changes were noted and abetted by the President's Panel. As physical custody and control become less complete, both the legal authority and the social service of guardianship will become increasingly more important.

The exciting thing (and the second reason for renewing attention to guardianship) is that real choices are now more frequently presented for the retarded or mentally deficient adult. It is therefore imperative that the latter be provided with a "legal personality" authorized to make these choices in his best interest. Thus there is today increasing need for the service of guardianship to be available independent of institutionalization. In addition, there is reason to advocate that even when a person is in residential care he should have a guardian who is not part of or subordinate to the apparatus of the care, training, or treatment that he is receiving.

It is not enough, however, simply to designate some public official as "public guardian" by statute. As we have already stressed, guardianship is a personal relationship and depends on some degree of continuity and active partisanship, as well as authority. Such guardianship should, therefore, be exercised and implemented by individuals who have a continuing responsibility for a limited number of specific wards. A person having other direct service responsibilities to the ward should not be deputized as his guardian. Public guardians should be salaried, on a full- or part-time basis, and should have some training and experience related to the social problems of the mentally retarded, but the service should not become over-professionalized. In short, what is called for is a public guardianship program. Such programs are available in some European countries, but in the United States, only Minnesota has demonstrated what it means to provide an active guardianship for mentally deficient persons outside institutions (Minnesota Department of Public Welfare, 1959 and 1965).

Minnesota's fifty-year-old program is now undergoing review and renewal (Levy, 1965; Minnesota Department of Public Welfare, 1959 and 1965). Greater recognition will be given to the guardianship function performed by parents, with less enthusiasm for early commitment to state guardianship of children who have parents active in their behalf. Priority for admission to other state services, both residential and nonresidential, will not be given to persons under state guardianship to the exclusion of other retarded persons. The need for counseling to parents will not in itself be sufficient cause to request authority over the retarded child. Judges, attorneys, and professional workers in mental retardation will seek closer agreement on the extent and kind of impairment of adaptive behavior associated with degrees of subnormality of measured intelligence that justify the "surgery" of commitment to state guardianship. It might be added this will continue for some time to be an art rather than a science.

Despite some healthy criticism, the Minnesota guardianship program remains a remarkably vigorous institution that has brought peace of mind to many parents and helped to maintain as many socially inadequate retarded persons outside public institutions as in them. The essence of its success lies not in its now somewhat antiquated framework of law, or even in its original legislative intent, but in the implementation of the *service of guardianship*. The sense of responsibility that goes with the authority of guardianship was developed with purposefulness through the difficult periods of depression and war as well as in the more optimistic recent decade by the director of the state's Bureau for Mentally Deficient and Epileptic, Miss Mildred Thomson, and her dozens of caseworkers in the offices of the county welfare boards, one of whom succeeded her in 1959 at the close of her thirty-year leadership (Thomson, 1963). If there is one lesson to be learned above all others from the Minnesota experience, it is that state guardianship can be given meaning only by the hard work of a sufficient number of qualified and conscientious people whose careers reflect that continuity of concern that the retarded require.

California will now venture into this intricate field, filled as it is with new needs and new potentials, to be followed, no doubt, by other states. Creative administration of the new legislation can develop it into an instrument of service to individuals that not only will result in better use of our social resources for the care, training, productive activity, and leisure time of the mentally retarded, but also will contribute in some measure to redressing the inequality before the law that mental deficiency inevitably creates and implies.

Equal protection for the unequal will remain a far from attainable ideal for the foreseeable future, especially when, as with mental subnormality, we have an infinite variety of inequality and a basic contradiction between normal modes of "liberty" and the devices available to shore up "equality." Yet, we would be less than true to our traditions as a nation if we did not seek to include within the benefits of our expanding social doctrines those least able to claim their rights for themselves.

## SUMMARY

The twin guarantees of the Fourteenth Amendment, "due process" and "equal protection," apply to mentally retarded citizens as to others. A considerable body of statutory and case law as well as scholarly discussion centers around the meaning of "due process" applied to involuntary admission to and detention in mental institutions and to situations in which a person may be deprived of the control of his property (but not its benefits) because of mental incapacity. The doctrine of equal protection has been less well developed as it affects the mentally disabled, among whom the mentally retarded are in particular need.

"Equal protection of the laws" cannot be confined to the courtroom, but must encompass devices by which the mentally retarded are assisted to enjoy the liberties and opportunities of a democratic society. For those who, as a result of the character and severity of their mental disorder, are unable to exercise with reasonable prudence the freedom of choice that is their birthright, "equal protection" can be more nearly achieved by deputizing a guardian of the person to exercise the right and responsibility to make choices on behalf of the disabled one.

Although all states have some legislation on this subject, few have recognized the necessity of assuring that effective guardianship is available to the quarter-million or more adults who may be expected to need it. For this aim, a program of public guardianship is required to supplement the private sector. In either case, more emphasis must be placed on the service of guardianship, the actual exercise of individual choice on behalf of an individual person who happens to be too retarded to exercise it himself. Social management of the mentally deficient adult in the community or residential facility, using the authority of guardianship constructively and creatively to extend the options made accessible to him and to assure continuity of concern, has been one of the neglected forms of service to the retarded. The development of such services is especially needed now, as new opportunities and especially alternatives to institutional living are expanding, even as the number of adults who are severely and profoundly retarded can be expected to increase rather sharply after 1968. There are real legal, social, and administrative obstacles and dilemmas to be tackled, but they cannot be allowed to prevail against the justice of enabling the retarded to share more fully in the egalitarianism of our times.


NOTE. The long-neglected subject of the mentally retarded and the law is now the subject of much active research. At the National Law Center of George Washington University, Washington, D.C., a detailed empirical study, focused specifically on the mentally retarded, was initiated early in 1965, under the direction of Professors Richard C. Allen and Elyce Zenoff Ferster. It will cover such topics under civil law as marriage, sterilization, contractual relations, and commitment, and under criminal law as validity of confessions, right to trial, capacity to stand trial, disposition of retarded defendants, whether tried or not, as well as other aspects of the problem of securing equal justice for the unequal. Additional studies are under way under other auspices in the District of Columbia and in California. In addition, a number of states have set up "task forces" on the law as part of the current emphasis on comprehensive state planning in mental retardation. All these activities may be expected to extend the literature significantly in the next few years.

## REFERENCES

SIR MAURICE AMOS, *Lectures on the American Constitution* (London and New York: Longmans, Green 1938).

ASSOCIATION OF THE BAR OF THE CITY OF NEW YORK, SPECIAL COMMITTEE TO STUDY COMMITMENT PROCEDURES, *Mental Illness and Due Process* (Ithaca, New York: Cornell University Press, 1962).

MICHAEL J. BEGAB and HARRIET L. GOLDBERG, "Guardianship for the Mentally Retarded," *Children*, IX (1962), 21–25.

CALIFORNIA (State) STUDY COMMISSION ON MENTAL RETARDATION, *Mental Retardation and the Law: A Survey of California Laws Affecting the Mentally Retarded,* Compiled by Kay Werdegar (Sacramento, California: Office of State Printing, 1964).

CALIFORNIA (State) STUDY COMMISSION ON MENTAL RETARDATION, *The Underdeveloped Resource: A Plan for the Mentally Retarded in California,* A Report to the Governor and the Legislature (Sacramento, California: Office of State Printing, 1965).

RICK HEBER (Ed.), "A Manual on Terminology and Classification in Mental Retardation," *American Journal of Mental Deficiency* (Monograph Supplement), LXIV (1959), 3–111.

VAN R. HINKLE, "Legal Rights of the Mentally Retarded," *American Journal of Mental Deficiency,* LXIII (1958), 501–505.

IOWA LAW SCHOOL, "Guardianship—A Symposium," *Iowa Law Review,* LIX (1960), 21.

R. J. LEVY, "Protecting the Mentally Retarded: An Empirical Survey and Evaluation of the Establishment of State Guardianship in Minnesota," *Minnesota Law Review,* XLIX (1965), 821.

FRANK T. LINDMAN and DONALD M. MCINTYRE, JR., *The Mentally Disabled and the Law* (Chicago: University of Chicago Press, 1961).

LEE MARINO and BERNARD GREEN, *How to Provide for Their Future* (New York: National Association for Retarded Children, Inc., 1964).

MASSACHUSETTS ASSOCIATION FOR RETARDED CHILDREN, *The MARC Retardate Trust* (Boston: Massachusetts Association for Retarded Children, 1960).

MINNESOTA DEPARTMENT OF PUBLIC WELFARE, *Manual of the Department of Public Welfare—Mental Deficiency and Epilepsy* (St. Paul, Minnesota, 1959), with supplemental *Memorandum* dated July 26, 1965.

NEW JERSEY COMMISSION ON MENTAL HEALTH, *Towards Better Mental Health in New Jersey* (Trenton, New Jersey: New Jersey Commission on Mental Health, 1961).

PRESIDENT'S PANEL ON MENTAL RETARDATION, *Report of the Task Force on the Law* (Washington, D. C.: U. S. Department of Health, Education, and Welfare, Public Health Service, 1963).

GERHART, SAENGER, *The Adjustment of Severely Retarded Adults in the Community* (Albany, New York: New York State Interdepartmental Health Resources Board, 1957).

ARTHUR DELAFIELD SMITH, *The Right to Life* (Chapel Hill, North Carolina: University of North Carolina Press, 1955).

MILDRED THOMSON, *Prologue: A Minnesota Story of Mental Retardation* (Minneapolis, Minnesota: Gilbert Publishing Company, 1963).

U.S. SOCIAL SECURITY ADMINISTRATION, *The Social Security Disability Insurance Program: Facts and Figures* (Washington, D. C.: Government Printing Office, 1963).

I. WEISSMAN, *Guardianship—A Way of Fulfilling Public Responsibility to Children* (Washington, D. C.: Government Printing Office, 1949).

WELFARE PLANNING COUNCIL, LOS ANGELES REGION, MENTAL RETARDATION JOINT AGENCIES PROJECT, *Mental Retardation Survey of Los Angeles County: Summary of Findings, Conclusions, Recommendations* (Los Angeles, California: Mental Retardation Joint Agencies Project, 1965).

WORLD HEALTH ORGANIZATION, JOINT EXPERT COMMITTEE ON THE MENTALLY SUBNORMAL CHILD, *The Mentally Subnormal Child* (Geneva and New York: World Health Organization, 1954).

# 25

# Mental Retardation: Implications for the Future

## GEORGE TARJAN

### INTRODUCTION

A discussion of expectations for the next decades assures a wide range of topics and gives freedom from the need for factual proof. The practicalities of space and time, both for the reader and the writer, pose the only limitations. One may choose between concentrating on a few items or touching on many briefly. A mid-course appears desirable. My comments will be anchored in the present, but my thoughts will be projected into the years to come. My discussion will be based primarily on medical concepts, but I hope that it will emphasize the important contributions of other professions. I will start with the topics of definition, epidemiology, and diagnosis of mental retardation; continue with prevention and treatment; and close with some thoughts on planning.

### DEFINITION, EPIDEMIOLOGY, AND DIAGNOSIS

The professional market place is oversupplied with definitions of retardation. The conceptual differences that exist among specialty groups are well known. Most workers in the field have a sufficiently clear, though individualized, image of the condition to eliminate the need for a new definition. Such new definition might serve only the purposes of a semantic exercise.

We can agree that mental retardation is a constellation of behavioral manifestations, among which we assign greatest significance to impairments of intelligence and of general adaptation (Heber, 1959). The behavioral deficits may be accompanied by physical signs or laboratory findings. The syndrome can be caused by many factors acting singly or in combination, with the onset prior to the seventeenth year of life (*Mental Retardation Handbook,* 1965; Wright and Tarjan, 1963; Knobloch and Pasamanick, 1962; Group for the Advancement of Psychiatry, 1959). This useful and brief description is not a precise definition. Its lack of specificity hampers epidemiologic research and diagnostic work. As an increasing number of rigorous scientists will concern themselves with retardation, one can expect that definition will become a focal point of debate. Each professional discipline will bring its own frame of reference into the field and insist that its viewpoint be given preference. Medical specialists of various backgrounds will continue to have two basic approaches. Those accustomed to microscopes and test tubes will advocate that the definition of retardation should depend on demonstrable changes in the brain or in other elements of the body. They will emphasize organic etiology. Those who rely to a greater extent on the behavioral sciences will focus on the functional nature of the impairment in adaptation and concentrate on the psychologic and sociocultural components of causation. Some of us will continue to try to bridge the gap.

Both groups probably will subscribe to the principle that retardation is a developmental aberration—a deficit in behavioral performance being the most significant symptom. Within the context of medicine, a resolution of differences might be reached when the relationship between behavior and its biochemical correlates is clarified. When memory, learning, and the sequelae of psychologic, social, and cultural deprivations become explainable in chemical or neurophysiologic terms, we will reach this sophisticated level of basic knowledge. The nature–nurture controversy will no longer trouble medicine. We will be able to express, measure, and correlate human performance in behavioral as well as biomedical terms, and establish the etiologic time sequence of the two types of events.

That day may seem far off, but advances in genetics, chemistry, neurophysiology, and the behavioral sciences hold much promise. One already can assemble several reasonable somatic models that could explain, on an organic basis, even such biomedical enigmas as the cultural-familial type of retardation (Tarjan, 1965a). These models can be based, among other things, on our present knowledge of the inborn errors of metabolism; on concepts about neurons and synaptic transmission; on principles involving additive genes; and on the role of cumulative, mild, diffuse damage to the brain. Progress in the behavioral sciences will soon factor out the causative roles of psychologic traumata, and sensory and cultural deprivation. A combination of somatic and psychologic approaches will result, first, in the separation of the "functional" retarded groups into at least two subtypes. In one, minute organic impairments will be identifiable, and, in the other, their absence will permit focusing on the primary etiologic roles of psycho-social factors. A major breakthrough in the biochemical understanding of behavior will accomplish the final step in conceptional unification. Until we reach this point, however, medicine must retain a broad view concerning the definition of mental retardation. A prematurely rigid definition would hamper research and deny needed services to large groups of patients because of their diagnostic exclusion from the category of the mentally retarded.

Clarification of conceptual differences between somatic and psychologic medicine will not resolve all the problems of definition because retardation transcends medicine. The retarded are children and adults who are part of our total social existence. They attend schools, seek jobs, succeed, or, usually, fail in almost every aspect of human performance. The most elegant medical conceptualization might not satisfy the requirements of the classroom, the job market, or social and economic life. Better understanding of the basic medical aspects of retardation should help in the clarification of concepts in other contexts, but we also must encourage educators, vocational counselors, lawyers, and many others to seek, in collaboration with us or independently, to define mental retardation from the viewpoint of their professions.

Problems in definition lead to problems in epidemiology. Today, when planning of services is in the limelight, there is particular need for data on prevalence and incidence. We have only limited information on institutionalized patients and even less on retardation in communities (Tarjan, 1963). If we are to avoid planning inadequately or excessively, we must fill the gaps in our knowledge. In the meanwhile, we must use the best available estimates, with insight into their limitations.

Epidemiologic studies are hampered by the lack of clear definition and a diagnostic test that can separate precisely the retarded from the rest of the population. In clinical practice, the diagnosis depends on the concurrent presence of significant impairments in intelligence and in adaptation (Tarjan, 1962). Intelligence can be quantified with reasonable accuracy, but the measurement of general adaptation is in its infancy. No test—somatic, behavioral, or a combination of the two—has been devised that effectively takes into account these two criteria.

Intelligence tests in use today assign an IQ rating of less than 70, the usual cut-off point, to approximately 3 per cent of the population (Dingman and Tarjan, 1960). But test performance does not establish a diagnosis of mental retardation. Many individuals with an IQ lower than 70 do not show significant impairment in general adaptation. Intelligence quotients are good predictors of success only during the school years. When case-finding starts with the identification of those who have IQ's below the cut-off point, a large proportion of the subjects do not qualify for a diagnosis of retardation on further screening for adaptation. An approach measuring adaptation first and intelligence later would have similar results. Additional criteria would lower further the numbers found (Mercer, Butler, and Dingman, 1964; Jastak, MacPhee, and Whiteman, 1963).

We are acquiring data on the incidence of specific types of retardation, particularly those that can be diagnosed on the basis of somatic or laboratory signs. As actuarial information increases, prevalence rates also will become available for these conditions. For retardation in general, it is reasonable to state that once in a thousand births a child is born whose IQ will not exceed 20, and that four times as frequently children will have IQ's between 20 and 50 (Masland, Sarason, and Gladwin, 1958). Most of these individuals will be recognized as retarded throughout their lives. Approximately twenty-five out of 1,000 newborns will score during adolescence between 50 and 70 on IQ tests. In this last group, however, there are many individuals whose retardation by present definition is symptomatic only during school age.

On the basis of these figures, it can be stated that 3 per cent of the newborn will manifest mental retardation. It is misleading, however, to say that 3 per cent of the population is retarded. Direct transfer of incidence data to prevalence is justified only when the condition is identifiable at the same age in each afflicted individual, when the condition remains unchanged, and when mortality rates are not affected by it.

Evidence about retardation points to the contrary. Individuals diagnosed as retarded during adolescence disappear from the labeled groups on reaching adulthood and are absorbed into the general population. It is unlikely that an increase in intellectual performance alone accounts for this, though many such instances are encountered in practice. Acceptable or, usually, marginal social adaptation is a more likely cause of this phenomenon. It disqualifies the individuals as retarded by our current criteria. Mortality also affects prevalence (Tarjan *et al.,* 1958; Tarjan *et al.,* 1959; Sabagh *et al.,* 1959). In spite of advances in lifesaving methods, mortality among the retarded exceeds that in the general population. The mortality rate is at least twice the average for the profoundly retarded and approaches the normal rate only in the mildest group. As a result, "visible" retardation in the general population is probably closer to 1 per cent than to 3 per cent. Prevalence varies with age, and distribution of IQ's differs among the various chronologic age groups of the retarded.

Significant epidemiologic consequences result. In a community of 100,000, 1,000 rather than 3,000 mentally retarded individuals would be found. The total number of those with IQ's below 20 would be fifty rather than 100, and those with IQ's between 20 and 50 would be 150 rather than 400. There would be only 700 visible mildly retarded instead of 2,500. The total number of diagnosed retarded children under six years of age would be seventy-five rather than 360, with corresponding figures for those above age twenty being less than 250 instead of nearly 2,000. The most striking differences would be noted in certain age and IQ categories. Instead of 300 mildly retarded children under the age of six, only fifteen would be found, and instead of 1,400 mildly retarded adults over twenty-four, there would be only sixty-five. The 3 per cent prevalence would apply to only one group —the mildly retarded of school age.

Epidemiologic studies cannot await the development of a fully agreed on definition and an ideal test (Mercer, Dingman, and Tarjan, 1964). In the meanwhile it might be advantageous to approach prevalence studies from new points of view. A variety of observers, including parents, physicians, teachers, youth workers, and vocational and social counselors, may suspect the presence of mental retardation (Mercer, 1965). Some of these groups only nominate candidates, others also label them for special or general purposes. It would be desirable to learn in what ways mentally retarded individuals diagnosed by the various professional groups differ from one another and how these labelings affect their future adjustment. Meaningful prevalence studies also could be conducted with a new specificity of the type of retardation being enumerated. For some purposes, retardation could be defined as including only those individuals who "obtain" retardation services or those who "seek" them. Differences between these two rates could be used to estimate deficiencies in programs. In another context, one may seek information about those individuals who pose social, behavioral, or other adaptational problems that, on diagnosis, are found to be related primarily to retardation; this group could be designated as those "in need" of services. Finally, one might enumerate all individuals whose intellectual test scores are below a specified cut-off point and whose social adaptation could be improved through supportive programs. Such a group could be labeled as the mentally retarded who could "benefit" from services. The prevalence of this last group may be around 3 per cent today, with the rate subject to change by modifications in child-rearing practices or by the impacts of automation, and anti-poverty and new education programs.

Individual diagnosis is established at different age levels, depending on the severity of the condition, the presence or absence of concomitant signs, and the acuity of the observer. Some conditions, for instance mongolism or phenylketonuria, can be diagnosed very early on the basis of physical or laboratory findings. In general, however, diagnosis depends on the observable difference between the child's performance and age specific norms. When the deficit is of a major degree, the condition is noted early; when it is of lesser severity, years might elapse before diagnosis is made. This interferes particularly with the early diagnosis of mild retardation. Sociologic and medical information can identify the groups at high risk, but diagnostic technology cannot as yet ascertain which infants or very young children will later be labeled mildly retarded.

In the coming years, great emphasis will be placed on early and comprehensive diagnosis. Early diagnosis will become increasingly important in light of new biomedical and behavioral-science discoveries about preventable conditions. As soon as mental retardation is suspected, an array of diagnostic resources will have to be mobilized. Some caution is in order, however. The diagnosis of retardation has a major impact on parents and others in the environment. The child's growth and development are highly sensitive to parental emotions, attitudes, and actions (Group for the Advancement of Psychiatry, 1963). Denial, projection, guilt feelings, expectations of magical solutions, overprotection, and rejection are common reactions. To minimize the negative effects of these psychologic forces, counseling of parents will have to be incorporated into the diagnostic process.

In the future comprehensive diagnosis will include broad areas of study. In addition to the ascertainment of the degree and type of retardation, emphasis will be placed on causation and its implications for counseling. Assessment of the patient will include reviews from the somatic, psychologic, social, educational, and vocational viewpoints. Secondary handicaps will be determined. Since the diagnosis will remain at times difficult to establish on one examination, accurate recording of observations also will gain importance. The diagnostic findings will be organized for utilization in immediate and long-term planning. This type of diagnostic work will require complex and expensive settings with genuine collaboration between several medical specialties and other professional disciplines. There is no assurance, however, that the attitude of parents toward the diagnosis will soon change. Diagnostic work-ups, even in the best of places, still may result in parental dissatisfaction and in visits to a series of offices, scientific or opportunistic, in pursuit of negative findings.

New diagnostic techniques will be developed. Measured intelligence will remain a basic dimension in our diagnosis, but the tests will change. The global IQ will be replaced by a "profile," measuring factors of intelligence and aptitude (Meyers *et al.,* 1962; Meyers *et al.,* 1964). It will emphasize assets as well as liabilities and therefore will be more meaningful for planning of treatment. There will be greater emphasis on neuromotor and sensory tests, on measurements of thought processes, and on diagnostic learning experiments.

## PREVENTION AND TREATMENT

Prevention is our ultimate goal (Tarjan, 1961a and b). To avoid the need to discuss the relationship between treatment and some aspects of prevention, I will combine the two subjects. The aim of a preventive program in retardation is to assure every child of a healthy central nervous system and of a set of early experiences supportive of intellectual and social growth (Tarjan, 1964b). No child, however, can escape all somatic and psychologic traumata. Therefore, we must strive to increase his chances for having a brain with minimal genetic and developmental defects that is maximally protected from noxious agents. We must provide the child also with an environment of warm interpersonal relationships and adequate intellectual stimulation, and protect him from psychologically oppressive influences.

We have made significant advances in these respects. General application of present knowledge would enable us significantly to decrease the frequency of retardation. Factors in a program could include

1. The protection of the population from agents detrimental to germinal tissues.

2. The education of prospective and new parents on the importance of somatic and psychologic factors supportive of or detrimental to healthy growth and development of children.

3. The physical and emotional preparation of women of childbearing age to assure ideal health for each period of pregnancy.

4. Counseling toward proper spacing of children.

5. Identification of carriers of genetically transmittable diseases, and effective counseling.

6. Early diagnosis of pregnancy with prompt and continued prenatal care.

7. The protection of the fetus from detrimental infections through immunization of the mother and through her intensive treatment when infections occur.

8. Protection of the fetus from unnecessary medications and teratogenic agents.

9. Judicious use of medical intervention in threatened abortions.

10. Clear delineation of indications for therapeutic abortions.

11. Physical and psychologic preparation of the mother for labor.

12. Prevention of prematurity and special provisions for the care of prematures.

13. Monitoring of the fetus before and during labor and the avoidance of unnecessary anesthetics and instrumentation.

14. Prenatal or early diagnosis of conditions that might require special treatment shortly after birth and the availability of proper facilities when such labor occurs.

15. Avoidance of drugs for the mother and newborn that are potentially harmful to the infant.

16. Careful examination of the newborn for congenital anomalies and their correction when possible.

17. Sufficient recording of pre-, peri-, and postnatal events, including social and economic data necessary for the establishment of a risk register.

18. Testing for detectable inborn errors of metabolism and prompt treatment when available.

19. Adequate nutrition, proper immunization, careful intermittent health review, and early treatment of illnesses for the infant and child.

20. Prevention of seizures, particularly during febrile and toxic periods.

21. Prevention of accidents and poisonings.

22. Sequential developmental assessment of infants and young children, including search for sensory defects and emotional problems.

23. Intensive diagnostic studies at the time of first suspicion of retardation.

24. Corrective measures, including early treatment of emotional and behavioral maladjustments.

25. Counseling or treatment of parents for the conflicts surrounding the diagnosis of and the adjustment to retardation in their child.

26. The provision of early psychologic and social enrichment programs for the culturally deprived infant and child.

27. Specialized schooling and training.

I expect that during the next decades many, if not all, aspects of such a program will be implemented. Research will add further to our armamentarium for prevention. New types of inborn errors of metabolism and additional dietary treatments will be discovered. Screening of newborns will acquire major proportions, and it will become necessary and possible to search for groups of metabolic errors rather than for individual conditions. Techniques for the identification of heterozygous carriers will put genetic counseling on a much firmer ground. Following present examples with phenylketonuria (Mabry *et al.,* 1963), we will find that mothers afflicted with errors in metabolism, if untreated during pregnancy, can damage the fetus without the latter being homozygous for the condition. Screening of women of childbearing age or during early pregnancy will be important therefore. New preventive treatments will replace the cumbersome dietary ones. Compounds will be developed that will block the action of toxic metabolites or interfere with their production. The critical enzymes will be isolated, stabilized, and synthesized in suitable form for oral or parenteral administration. Chemical miniaturization will produce filters that can be implanted in the blood stream to purify the circulation of toxic substances.

Cytogeneticists already have clarified the causation of several types of retardation. In the future there will be greater emphasis on the role of carriers in chromosomal aberrations. Current techniques probably have reached their research limits. Emphasis will move toward the development of new approaches that will enable us to study more minute aberrations in the genic material than the numerical or gross structural abnormalities of chromosomes that occupy our interest today. The mapping of genes will gain momentum. The processes of meiosis and mitosis will be better understood, and we will learn to control the forces that produce improper separation and recombination of the chromosomes.

These developments will open new vistas and raise new issues in genetics. Today, most of the afflicted do not reproduce. In the future many will grow to adulthood with relatively normal mentality. Social and dietary habits will produce a trend toward their intermarriage. For a time, improvements in the identification of the carrier state will offset the negative contributions of the reproduction of the afflicted, but soon there will be increasing concern, professional and lay, with voluntary or mandatory sterilization and with artificial insemination. Research efforts will be directed increasingly toward altering the genotype in a positive direction.

With our present knowledge we could almost eliminate several types of retardation, for instance, those due to certain infections, inborn errors of metabolism, and blood-group incompatibilities. New discoveries will extend our potential. In general, however, skills for protecting the brain from damage have not kept pace with success in lifesaving. An emphasis on the former must therefore gain in importance.

New methods of treatment will be developed and traditional ones improved. There will be increasing recognition of the significance of emotional pathology in mental retardation. Psychotherapy used with the retarded will be modified. Techniques similar to play therapy will be emphasized, with a diminished reliance on verbal communication. The outlook concerning the potential of moderately to profoundly retarded individuals will improve. As they come under systematic observation (MacAndrew and Edgerton, 1964a, b, and c), it will be noted that they show marked variability in behavior and that their behavior can be influenced by training techniques based on the principles of operant conditioning.

Clinical experience and research findings will give us a firm base for recommending modifications in child-rearing practices. The changes will improve the chances for maximal maturation of retarded children. They also will serve as preventive measures in the high-risk social and economic groups through systematic intellectual stimulation at home and in day nurseries (Project Head Start, 1965).

Educational approaches will undergo major changes. Enrichment of the curriculum, particularly in kindergarten and in early grades, will replace the current trend of downward scaling. Specialized classes in adult education will be developed in public schools. Vocational rehabilitation, too, will shift its focus (Tarjan, 1964a). Industrial engineering will succeed in modifying production procedures, giving the retarded greater opportunities for vocational contributions. New job training techniques will enable many of them to compete effectively along several occupational lines. A series of sheltered work opportunity centers will be established in addition to the traditional workshops. In such protected environments many of the moderately retarded will be able to work for prolonged periods of time.

## PLANNING

Scientific advances will rapidly improve the therapeutic outlook for retarded individuals. It is more doubtful, however, that the organizational aspects of services will keep pace with the progress in clinical knowledge. Defects in arrangement of services could, unfortunately, deprive many retarded persons of benefits. Adequate planning, therefore, will become a critical need (President's Panel, 1962; Gardner and Nisonger, 1962). Improvements in clinical practice depend primarily on scientific success (Tarjan, 1965b), but often planning is influenced by political and economic considerations. Not being an expert in these latter fields, I will try to restrict my comments to those based on my professional experience.

Ten or fifteen years ago only the most optimistic people would have predicted the current surge of professional and public interest in retardation (Tarjan and Wright, 1953; Tarjan, 1956). Medical specialties and other disciplines vied in showing the greatest indifference toward the subject. Public institutions were overcrowded, underbudgeted, and understaffed. Though they were the major resource of care, they could not cope with their long waiting lists for admission (Tarjan and Forbes, 1955). Their attempts to establish closer ties with the community usually met with disinterest and resistance. Public schools often shunned the establishment of special classes. Several health and welfare programs excluded the retarded. Professionals, including research people, considered interest in retardation a sign of mediocrity. Those who sought progress were without financial and other resources.

The scene has changed completely. State and federal departments, professional classes, and specialty groups compete for the new "Cinderella." Included in the ranks of new champions are persons who but a short time ago could only be drafted into the service. Many individuals and groups are involved in planning today. Opinions are diverse, with few agreements and many differences. Most planners are well-intentioned people; few, if any, seek self-aggrandizement. But the popular notion that planning must be bold produces an exaggerated search for entirely new ideas that often result in the unjust criticism of traditional approaches without too much thought for constructive substitutes. Logical or magical, evolutionary or revolutionary solutions are suggested with equal frequency. At times judgment is passed first, and confirmatory professional advice sought later. I am confident, however, that when all is done, history will show that the constructive concepts will be the ones most generally implemented.

There is substantial agreement on several principles (President's Panel, 1962; Gardner and Nisonger, 1962). Services needed by the retarded and available to others should not be denied because of the diagnosis. Generic programs are preferable to specialized ones. The latter should be restricted to those situations where their use is demanded by unique needs or by the shortage of specialized personnel. An array of coordinated services, close to home, with guaranteed continuity of care should be developed. The disagreements start at the point of practical implementation. Some people advocate direct program management by government, others champion the roles of private sectors. Some favor local administration, others prefer to rely on state and federal agencies. There are demands to concentrate all programs for the retarded under a single management, but most people advocate the utilization of the special skills of several existing departments. Financing through subsidies is contrasted with direct appropriations.

Much time will be spent in deliberations and debates. I hope some wise decisions will result. There will be genuine and pseudo-experimentation in programming, with considerable competition between professionals and entrepreneurs. Final implementation frequently will require legislation, and humanitarianism often will be modified by political and fiscal considerations. In this complex process, it must be remembered that retardation is a chronic, handicapping condition that makes strong emotional demands on family members. Parents, particularly of moderately to profoundly retarded children, will continue to demand, with much justification, stability in programming and in financing. Their concerns are becoming increasingly noticeable in their resistance to extramural programs for their currently institutionalized children.

Major solutions will call for substantial financial outlays. Today the major economic resources for the long-term care of the retarded include local and state funds for education, direct appropriations and fees in support of institutions, welfare funds, and payments by such agencies as Social Security and the Veterans' Administration. In addition, short-term benefits are available through programs for crippled children, vocational rehabilitation and, to a limited extent, through voluntary health insurance. Training of personnel and research are underwritten by a variety of sources, from private foundations to the federal government. This picture emphasizes that today the major costs are borne by taxation and that it will necessarily take years before private insurance systems can assume much of the burden for this catastrophic condition.

The high cost of medical care stresses the need for separating welfare problems from health problems. An overgeneralized public-aid approach, however, could result in new problems. It is relatively simple to assume that all the retarded need public assistance, but implementation demands an adequate diagnostic system, the establishing of which is much more complicated. Who will make the diagnosis that will determine public-aid eligibility? Physicians usually establish their diagnosis with a specific treatment in mind. In this context their system functions adequately. It might not operate equally effectively for global welfare purposes. Undue broadening of long-term aid programs might also foster long-term dependency. If the diagnosis of retardation becomes a direct avenue to financial assistance, much of the present motivation to shed the label after school age may disappear.

Progress will be gradual, if for no other reason than that further advances in service as well as in research and professional training will depend on the availability of adequate manpower. The shortage still is marked, but we can no longer complain of a complete lack of this resource. Schools of higher learning soon will have an opportunity to incorporate retardation into their teaching efforts. I hope that these new facilities will train all members of the relevant professional groups in the problems of retardation and not restrict their efforts to those specializing in the field. Only under such a plan can retardation services be incorporated into generic programs.

In these new centers, it is essential also that mental retardation be viewed as a multidisciplinary problem. Improvement of interdisciplinary communication must become an important aspect of training. Lack of adequate communication could seriously hamper research and deprive the retarded of clinical benefits that can best be provided through the harmonious collaboration of a variety of physicians and other professionals. Medical specialists can be used as an example of communication problems among disciplines. Physicians are involved increasingly with colleagues in various scientific fields. Some relate primarily to psychologists and sociologists, others to chemists and physicists. These desirable affiliations, however, can impair communication among specialists. As members of a specialty group acquire greater fluency in language with a basic science group, they are in danger of losing the ease with which they can speak to physicians across specialty lines.

The traditional state hospitals and residential institutions represent a particularly complex problem in planning. They are still a main component of our system of care, yet they are endlessly criticized and rarely defended. Some of the criticism is justified, but it often is forgotten that most of the inadequacies result from insufficient financial support and that often those responsible for providing the support are the most vocal critics. There are among today's planners several persons who hope that the traditional state institutions will somehow magically disappear. It is unlikely that this will happen until at least equally good alternative programs are developed in the communities. The existing waiting lists clearly demonstrate that no substitute program has yet been established. The development of community programs can be at best gradual. Mental-retardation and mental-health centers represent the most important step in this direction to date.

During the next decades, reason calls not for the abolishment of the state institutions, but for strong re-enforcement and broadening of their programs. I expect, as a consequence, major changes in their role. The institutions will become increasingly medically oriented with more flexible admission and release policies. New types of service will be developed by them, and they will become the testing laboratories for new modalities of treatment. They will serve population groups within a reasonable traveling distance and will be closely linked to neighboring communities, universities, and medical schools. They will gain in stature as training and research resources, and they will specialize in the care of the most difficult patients, those with superimposed physical or emotional problems.

## SUMMARY

We have made much progress during the past ten years. Many forces have contributed, and some were clearly outstanding. The parents of the retarded have organized and brought to public attention the serious plight of their children. Federal agencies, among them the National Institutes of Mental Health and of Neurological Diseases and Blindness, and The Children's Bureau, assumed early leadership. Several state departments responsible for institutional programs succeeded in obtaining more adequate budgets. The American Association on Mental Deficiency acquired a new vitality. Major breakthroughs in research encouraged the interests of scientists. The Joseph P. Kennedy, Jr., Foundation, through its awards and grants, brought respectability to the field and started the new motivation of medical schools and universities toward greater involvement. The American Medical Association and several specialty organizations increased their activities in the service of the retarded.

The leadership of President Kennedy gave the field the most important momentum for advance. The report of the President's Panel and the legislation that followed opened avenues toward a very bright future. The memory of his tragic death calls for a dedication on our part. We must commit ourselves to lasting interest, to the abandonment of chauvinistic attitudes, and to hard and collaborative efforts. On such determination rests the fulfillment of the great promises of the next decades and the hope of all the retarded.

## REFERENCES

HARVEY F. DINGMAN and GEORGE TARJAN, "Mental Retardation and the Normal Distribution Curve," *American Journal of Mental Deficiency,* LXIV (1960), 991–992.

WILLIAM I. GARDNER and HERSCHEL W. NISONGER, "A Manual on Program Development in Mental Retardation," *American Journal of Mental Deficiency* (Monograph Supplement), LXVI (1962), 1–192.

GROUP FOR THE ADVANCEMENT OF PSYCHIATRY, *Basic Considerations in Mental Retardation: A Preliminary Report,* Report Number 43 (New York: Group for the Advancement of Psychiatry, 1959).

GROUP FOR THE ADVANCEMENT OF PSYCHIATRY, *Mental Retardation: A Family Crisis—The Role of the Physician,* Report Number 56 (New York: Group for the Advancement of Psychiatry, 1963).

RICK HEBER (Ed.), "A Manual on Terminology and Classification in Mental Retardation," *American Journal of Mental Deficiency* (Monograph Supplement), LXIV (1959), 3–111.

JOSEPH F. JASTAK, HALSEY M. MacPHEE, and MARTIN WHITEMAN, *Mental Retardation: Its Nature and Incidence* (Newark, Delaware: University of Delaware Press, 1963), p. 184.

HILDA KNOBLOCH and BENJAMIN PASAMANICK, "Mental Subnormality," *New England Journal of Medicine,* CCLXVI (1962), 1045–1051, 1092–1097, 1155–1161.

CHARLTON W. MABRY, JOSEPH C. DENNISTON, THOMAS L. NELSON, and CHOON D. SON, "Maternal Phenylketonuria, A Cause of Mental Retardation in Children without the Metabolic Defect," *New England Journal of Medicine,* CCLXIX (1963), 1404–1408.

CRAIG MacANDREW and ROBERT EDGERTON, "A Procedure for Interrogating Non-professional Ward Employees," *American Journal of Mental Deficiency,* LXIX (1964a), 347–353.

CRAIG MacANDREW and ROBERT EDGERTON, "IQ and the Social Competence of the Profoundly Retarded," *American Journal of Mental Deficiency,* LXIX (1964b), 385–390.

CRAIG MacANDREW and ROBERT EDGERTON, "The Everyday Life of Institutionalized 'Idiots,' " *Human Organization,* XXIII (1964c), 312–318.

RICHARD L. MASLAND, SEYMOUR B. SARASON, and THOMAS GLADWIN, *Mental Subnormality, Biological, Psychological, and Cultural Factors* (New York: Basic Books, 1958).

*Mental Retardation: A Handbook for the Primary Physician,* Report of the American Medical Association Conference on Mental Retardation, Reprinted from the *Journal of the American Medical Association,* CXCI (1965), 183–232.

JANE R. MERCER, "Key Conceptualizations in the Sociology of Mental Retardation," in *Proceedings of the 16th Annual Conference of the California Association of School Psychologists and Psychometrists* (1965), in press.

JANE R. MERCER, EDGAR W. BUTLER, and HARVEY F. DINGMAN, "The Relationship between Social Developmental Performance and Mental Ability," *American Journal of Mental Deficiency,* LXIX (1964), 195–203.

JANE R. MERCER, HARVEY F. DINGMAN, and GEORGE TARJAN, "Involvement, Feedback, and Mutuality: Principles for Conducting Mental Health Research in the Community," *American Journal of Psychiatry,* CXXI (1964), 228–237.

C. E. MEYERS, R. E. ORPET, A. A. ATTWELL, and HARVEY F. DINGMAN, "Primary Abilities at Mental Age 6," *Monographs of the Society for Research in Child Development,* XXVII (1962), 3–40.

C. E. MEYERS, HARVEY F. DINGMAN, R. E. ORPET, E. G. SITKEI, and C. A. WATTS, "Four Ability-Factor Hypotheses at Three Preliterate Levels in Normal and Retarded Children," *Monographs of the Society for Research in Child Development,* XXIX (1964), 5.

PRESIDENT'S PANEL ON MENTAL RETARDATION, *A Proposed Program for National Action to Combat Mental Retardation* (Washington, D. C.: Government Printing Office, 1962).

*Project Head Start: Community Action Program* (Washington, D. C.: Office of Economic Opportunity, 1965).

GEORGES SABAGH, HARVEY F. DINGMAN, CURTIS MILLER, and GEORGE TARJAN, *Differential Mortality in a Hospital for the Mentally Retarded* (Vienna: International Population Conference, 1959), pp. 460–468.

GEORGE TARJAN, *Objectives of the President's Panel on Mental Retardation: Program Development and the Need for Data,* Public Health Service Publication Number 1126 (Washington, D. C.: Government Printing Office, 1963), pp. 45–50.

GEORGE TARJAN, "Prevention, A Program Goal in Mental Deficiency," in J. H. Rothstein (Ed.), *Mental Retardation: Readings and Resources* (New York: Holt, Rinehart, and Winston, 1961a), pp. 125–235.

GEORGE TARJAN, "Rehabilitation of the Mentally Retarded," *Journal of the American Medical Association,* CLXXXVII (1964a), 867–870.

GEORGE TARJAN, "Research and Clinical Advances in Mental Retardation," *Journal of the American Medical Association,* CLXXXII (1962), 617–621.

GEORGE TARJAN, "Somatic Etiologic Factors in the Prevention of Childhood Mental Disorders," in D. A. Van Krevelen (Ed.), *Child Psychiatry and Prevention* (Switzerland: Hans Huber, 1964b), pp. 93–107.

GEORGE TARJAN, "Studies of Organic Etiologic Factors," in Gerald Caplan (Ed.), *Prevention of Mental Disorders in Children* (New York: Basic Books, 1961b), pp. 31–51.

GEORGE TARJAN, "The Next Challenge to the Association Presented by Its New Opportunity," *American Journal of Mental Deficiency,* LXI (1956), 302–308.

GEORGE TARJAN, "The Next Decade: Expectations from the Biological Sciences," *Journal of the American Medical Association,* CXCI (1965a), 226–229.

GEORGE TARJAN, "The Role of the Primary Physician in Mental Retardation," *California Medicine,* CIIC (1965b), 419–425.

GEORGE TARJAN, HARVEY F. DINGMAN, and CURTIS R. MILLER, "Statistical Expectations of Selected Handicaps in the Mentally Retarded," *American Journal of Mental Deficiency,* LXV (1960), 335–341.

GEORGE TARJAN and LORNA M. FORBES, "A Preadmission and Diagnostic Service for the Mentally Deficient; A Report on 2000 Cases," *American Journal of Mental Deficiency,* LXI (1955), 340–345.

GEORGE TARJAN and STANLEY W. WRIGHT, "Mental Deficiency—A Challenge to Medicine," *American Journal of Mental Deficiency,* LVIII (1953), 316–322.

GEORGE TARJAN, STANLEY W. WRIGHT, HARVEY F. DINGMAN, and RICHARD K. EYMAN, "Natural History of Mental Deficiency in a State Hospital: III. Selected Characteristics of First Admissions and Their Environment," *American Journal of Diseases of Children,* CI (1961), 195–205.

GEORGE TARJAN, STANLEY W. WRIGHT, F. DINGMAN, and GEORGES SABAGH, "The Natural History of Mental Deficiency in a State Hospital: II. Mentally Deficient Children Admitted to a State Hospital Prior to Their Sixth Birthday," *American Journal of Diseases of Children,* XCVIII (1959), 370–378.

GEORGE TARJAN, STANLEY W. WRIGHT, MORTON KRAMER, PHILIP H. PERSON, JR., and RICHARD MORGAN, "The Natural History of Mental Deficiency in a State Hospital: I. Probabilities of Release and Death by Age, Intelligence Quotient, and Diagnosis," *American Journal of Diseases of Children,* XCVI (1958), 64–70.

STANLEY W. WRIGHT and GEORGE TARJAN, "Mental Retardation: A Review for Pediatricians," *American Journal of Diseases of Children,* CV (1963), 511–526.

Appreciation is expressed to the staff of Pacific State Hospital, particularly to Stanley W. Wright, M.D. (Chief of Research, Pacific State Hospital, and Professor of Pediatrics, School of Medicine, University of California at Los Angeles), and Harvey F. Dingman, Ph.D. (Director of NIMH Grant MH-08667 "Socio-Behavioral Study Center for Mental Retardation," Pacific State Hospital).

# Index

ability, sex differences in parent-child correlations in, 100–105
ABO blood groups, 183–184
abortion(s), 126; spontaneous, 128, 190; therapeutic, 435; threatened, 26, 435
*abruptio placenta,* 56
abstractions, capacity to deal with, 19, 63
academic failure, 41
academic retardation, 63, 64
achievement tests, 63, 67, 118, 119, 121
adaptive social behavior, 116; Negro–white studies on, 113
adenoma sebaceum, 47
adoption, 75, 86, 155, 228, 377, 413
adult myxedema, 8
adult retarded, counseling for parents of, 325; definitions of, 309–310; parental problems associated with, 78, 80–82, 325, 327–328, 402
adult-retarded community programs, 216–217, 304–305, 308–331; case-finding and, 329–330; comprehensive evaluation of retarded for, 318–319; comprehensive planning for, 317–318; considerations in development of, 308–309, 313–317; long-term supervision and guidance, 327–328; physiologic and psychologic needs as factor in, 310–312, 331; professional training for, 329; recreation services, 326–327, 330–331; supportive services for, 328–329; vocational rehabilitation services, 319–321, 331; *see also* community programs
affectional deprivation, 126, 138
age changes, in nature of intelligence, 107; in relation to socio-economic status, 89–90; in relations between mother-child behavior, 91–93
agenesis, cerebral, 26, 115

aggressive behavior, 77, 117, 120–121, 279, 282, 283, 285
Aid to the Totally Disabled, 217
alcoholism, 11, 224, 350
Allen, Gregory B., 249
Allen, Richard C., 426
Alvord, Ellsworth C., 31
Alzheimer's disease, 29
amaurotic familial idiocy, 363
amentia, 62
American Association on Mental Deficiency, 263, 309, 317–318, 328, 342, 344, 441
American Bar Foundation, 408, 418
American Eugenics Society, 358
American Medical Association, 16, 399, 405, 441
American Psychiatric Association, 226
amino acid abnormalities, 46, 134, 202–205; in blood, 27, 36, 202, 203; in urine, 27, 36, 47, 48, 134–136, 202, 204
Amos, Sir Maurice, 407–408
amphetamines, 214
Amsterdam Dwarf, 46
Anastasi, Anne, 363
anatomists, 126
Anderson, V. Elving, 177
anemia, prematurity and, 56, 128
anencephaly, 39
angiokeratoma, 38, 39
anoxia, 26; animal experiments on, 129–130, 210; neonatal, 45, 129–130, 210; perinatal, 201
anticonvulsants, 214
anti-poverty program, 83, 164, 295, 301, 314–315, 390–391
anxiety, 369–370
Apert's disease, 55
Apgar, Virginia, 211